D1557251

COLLECTED
NOVELS AND PLAYS

J M

James

COLLECTED

NOVELS AND PLAYS

---

edited by

J. D. McClatchy and Stephen Yenser

Merrill

Alfred A. Knopf • New York • 2002

This Is a Borzoi Book
Published by Alfred A. Knopf

Copyright © 2002 by The Literary Estate of James Merrill at
Washington University

www.aaknopf.com

Knopf, Borzoi Books, and the colophon are registered trademarks of
Random House Inc., New York.

The editors are grateful to Renée and Theodore Weiss for their generous
permission to reprint The Bait, *which was originally published in*
The Quarterly Review of Literature.

Library of Congress Cataloging-in-Publication Data
Merrill, James Ingram.
[Selections. 2002]
Collected novels and plays of James Merrill / edited by J. D. McClatchy
and Stephen Yenser.
p. cm.
Includes index.
ISBN 0-375-41137-2
I. McClatchy, J. D., 1945– II. Yenser, Stephen. III. Title.
PS3525.E6645 A6 2002
818'.5408—dc21   *2002020953*

Front matter (and cover) photograph: © Foto Vasari Roma
The Birthday (p. 425): Courtesy of Amherst College Archives and Special
Collections. By Permission of the Trustees of Amherst College.
The Bait (p. 453): Walt Silver
The Immortal Husband (p. 493): Alix Jeffrey.
Courtesy of Special Collections, Olin Library, Washington University

Manufactured in the United States of America
First Edition

EDITORS' NOTE

This volume collects James Merrill's novels and plays. Other fiction—short stories and translations—appears in *Collected Prose*, and his short play *The Image Maker*, because it was originally included in a book of his poems, *The Inner Room*, can be found in his *Collected Poems*. When, decades after their original appearances, his two novels were reprinted, Merrill added a preface to the new edition of *The Seraglio* and an afterword to *The (Diblos) Notebook*. They can be found here in the Appendix. We include in this volume a previously unpublished early play in blank verse, *The Birthday*, not least because it anticipates many of the concerns the poet took up much later in *The Changing Light at Sandover*. For a new production in 1988 of his play *The Bait*, he undertook revisions that are extensive enough (he even changed the sex of a character) to merit printing this short play twice, in each of its versions. The revised version may also be found in the Appendix.

As throughout this series of books, misprints in the original editions have been silently corrected and spelling or punctuation very occasionally changed for consistency's sake.

JDMcC and SY

CONTENTS

THE NOVELS
The Seraglio (1957)   3
The (Diblos) Notebook (1965)   305

THE PLAYS
The Birthday (1947)   425
The Bait (1953)   453
The Immortal Husband (1955)   493

Appendix
   Preface to *The Seraglio*   629
   Afterword to *The (Diblos) Notebook*   633
   The Bait (1988)   635
Notes   671
Biographical Note   675

THE NOVELS

The Seraglio

(1957)

For my nephews and nieces

PART ONE

---

1. Exactly a year later Francis learned the truth about the slashed portrait—by then, of course, restored with expert care. The gash running from the outer corner of his sister's eye to her Adam's apple had been patched, sewn, smoothed, painted over, until he really had to hunt for the scar. Enid was posed against a cultivated landscape. Her face, formal above velvet, discouraged even Francis from filling in the details of the crime. No doubt he could have. The intervening year had left him with a key to such matters. Besides, he knew the scene by heart. It was not, despite lawns, flowerbeds, terraces, the scene in the painting. Over the dunes a whitish haze trembled, thinning upwards, to the thunder of waves. Windows facing the sea were usually frosted by the salt air. All this could give you a feeling of loneliness, of being the one real person in a ghostly world. He guessed how the scene must have worked upon the little murderess; its effect upon his own first ten summers, if it came to that—but here again the portrait stopped him. As with Enid herself,

where appearances so handsomely denied offense, it no longer seemed fair to probe.

The facts, however, were these:

Enid's children had moved out to Long Island with their nurse. From her window, Lily, the oldest, caught a familiar sparkling. The entire summer awaited her, tomorrow was her tenth birthday, and she had been misbehaving all morning. Nobody knew what had come over her. Worse yet, her mother and Alice and the cook reacted as if the little girl—Lily kept telling herself, "I'm still only a little girl"—was disobedient out of choice, as if she had enjoyed torturing the twins, or screaming in the kitchen till a bowl of icing slipped from the cook's lap. Far from it. Her unhappiness mounted with every naughtiness. Finally she had been sent up to her room.

She leaned now on the windowsill, deliberately letting the last of her lunch slide off its plate into the boxwood below. Somewhere nearby Lily's pet snail would still be lying, stunned from having been flung there by her mother, who had seen it early that morning, slithering blandly—unbearably—across the drowsing child's naked stomach. Oh *please,* sweetie! a dirty old snail!—and as in a dream both it and Mummy disappeared, one out the window, one down the stairs, a loose robe of blue chiffon trailing behind. A new baby was coming—from the Stork, said her parents; from God the Father, said Irish Alice. Lily had sat then until the feelings of crossness and loneliness grew keener, and the tears began.

The morning of her punishment passed. She had listened to her mother on the steps with Alice, describing in a soft sweet voice the day ahead: the hairdresser's, the hospital, the Cottage . . . Had Michele gone over there already? He mustn't forget to meet Mr. Buchanan's train. As for the twins, why didn't Alice take them to the beach after their nap? Be good now! And the door slammed, the car started, with not a word of reprieve for Lily, and nothing of the little girl's usual privilege—to be shown which dress her mother had on, which hat and gloves, which jewels. Lily had stood back against the wall while the car drove off, so that anybody who hoped she would run to the window to see would be disappointed. But her dull satisfaction did not last. She had had to pity herself in the mirror till Alice came up with her tray.

She poured a half-glass of milk into the shrubbery. It landed with the sound of cloth ripping. The rest of it she drank. She then set her tray in the hall. The twins put to bed, Alice and the cook would be eating now. Lily locked her door and, pocketing the key, went downstairs on tiptoe.

The cool fragrant rooms, rose and green, glimmered off on either side of the entrance hall. Their house wasn't (her father had once explained) a showplace like the Cottage. "Money's not the question," he had said, cracking his kuckles. "We have as much to spend each year as Grandpa does, considering what we save on taxes and alimony. But your mother and I want our home to be simple and comfortable, with a few nice things. Now your grandfather's house, though not much larger, is on a different scale entirely." A different scale . . . The words, coming upon Lily's two years of piano lessons, called up a Cottage augmented, chromatic, a far cry from the plain triad of their own house—whose "simplicity," on the other hand, was news to the little girl. Next to her friends' houses it seemed embarrassingly splendid. Much of the furniture had been brought back from her parents' tours. Lily could have led you about, reciting: "These white-and-green chairs are from Venice; the chandelier, too. The tiles on the floor are Spanish. Where they're scuffed shows how antique they are. That painting's a Renoir. They bought it in New York, but it's French really. We're getting new drapes next month, yellow with tiny purple and white daisies. Here's Mummy's collection of Battersea boxes—that one's new." But the more polite way, her mother said, was just to let people notice things. With each addition a less perfect piece would be turned over to the Rummage Sale or crowded into the attic, where on wet days Lily and a friend climbed up on tables that didn't totter or chip, then flopped onto great rectangular sofas, rebounding high into the dusty air. Now *that* was simplicity and comfort! Downstairs she copied her mother's decorum, even today in full revolt against it. The hall mirrors made much of silver bowls filled with roses. Tiptoeing out, Lily crept from tree to shrub until she came to the road.

Not quite a half-mile separated the Buchanans' house from the Cottage, which Lily approached by way of the beach. Promptly the grotesque brick chimneys swung into view then the roof, whose steep angle recalled roofs in fairy-tales. She reached the bulkhead at last, and leaned against it, panting.

A sign nailed there read: *Trespassers will be Prosecuted*. It brought to mind first the Lord's Prayer, then, for she personally imagined the prayer addressed to an old man with white hair, her grandfather. Some years ago, as a *very* little girl, she had heard him call Uncle Francis his only begotten son, and upon her asking that night, "Is Grandpa God?" her mother had laughed and laughed and told the story to everybody, even to Grandpa himself. Lily was beyond all that now. Alice had given her a long shocked sermon, also a little silvery medal of Mary, to be kissed those nights her mother wasn't home to tuck her in. Today sand had drifted high enough to let Lily scale the bulkhead without using the wooden steps.

The door opened easily into the ocean room, huge and high—the Cottage had no upstairs. All the furniture had been massed together under stone-colored canvas, making the room look like a drained lake. Through the far windows workmen could be seen eating lunch, and beyond, on the sunken lawn, the rose-arbor in bloom. The whole house smelled of fresh paint and wax. All the paper had been ripped from Fern's bedroom walls. Grandpa used to call them his two flowers, once even trying to put Lily into his buttonhole. How she had shrieked! Now Fern and Grandpa were divorced. On the threshold she found a note in her mother's handwriting: "Walls, pale green or blue, something *restful*. Twin beds. A pretty chintz?" Lily moved on, feeling lonely.

In Grandpa's room, face down on the bureau, were photographs in leather or silver frames. She turned them over, one by one: Mummy; the twins; Uncle Francis when *he* was ten, grinning and holding a big black snake—not poisonous, Grandpa had assured her, and blind anyhow; finally some individual likenesses of smiling ladies. She recognized among them Cousin Irene Cheek, in appearance certainly not the tramp she was said to be. But no picture of Fern, or of her real grandmother. And no picture of Lily! Only bottles of medicine in the top drawer, a few handkerchiefs, a silver paper-knife. This last she picked up, and aimed at her breast. "Farewell, cruel world!" Lily sighed, then crumpled to the floor. She performed the act a second time before catching sight of the painting.

It was set face to the wall next to Grandpa's oxygen tank. Turning it around, she exclaimed in what she felt must be the voice of a particularly nice little girl, "Oh, I'd forgotten this was here!" It showed her mother wearing a blue velvet gown with bare shoulders, and diamonds in her hair. She was smiling the gently bewildered smile of somebody soon to be scolded or punished. Poor Mummy, thought Lily. All her resentment melted. With the tip of the silver knife she caressed, as with a wand, her mother's features, traced the curve of the lips, the eyebrows and cheek. The faint grating gave her gooseflesh. Resting the point against the surface at a certain angle, she saw how the blade reflected the whole face dully, in miniature distortion. She moved it this way and that; her mother vanished, reappeared. Before long a puzzlement came over her, to see that a speck of paint, no bigger than a gnat's wing, had chipped away, leaving a tiny patch of paler color beneath. How? When? Just at the corner of her mother's eye, in which a streak of white created an uncanny liveliness. Lily's heart began to pound. She wouldn't have dreamed this face could be so fragile. Experimentally she touched the point of the knife to the same spot; a second, larger flake of paint fell off, exposing the dead white canvas. She had now a sense of fatigue. It was becoming such a slow, complicated process, not like the shattering of an ornament. And beyond repair. That fragment of a face could no more be put back than could the daisy petal pulled to see whether you were loved or not. The child knelt spellbound at her task.

A door slammed. The knife with a will of its own pierced the canvas and tore briskly downwards five or six inches before she succeeded in letting go. She closed her eyes. She knew that she was going to die.

A burst of Italian song came from down the hall—Michele, her parents' gardener. His footsteps grew louder, stopped with the song, then evenly faded. Another door slammed. Ten minutes later Lily was back in her room.

Alice hadn't even taken the tray downstairs.

She lay on her bed exhausted. "You don't understand," she said aloud once, "I loved you."

Then Lily fell asleep, and it was nearly six when Alice came in and told her, in a pleasant everyday voice, that her mother had said to go downstairs now.

They were talking about it.

"I don't know what got into me. I just sat down and began to cry. Honestly, I couldn't stop. I kept thinking, this is so silly!"

"It's not one damn bit silly!"

"Michele and the painters thought *I'd* been hurt—can you imagine? 'No, no, my little friends,' I had to say, 'it's only the picture!'"

"It's a damn lot more than only the picture, Enid."

"Well, it wasn't the moment—oh sweetie!" she cried as Lily appeared, steeling herself in the doorway. "Forgive your witless old lady! I meant for you to come down right after lunch. Go and kiss Daddy!"

"Your mother's just had a miserable experience, Lily," he said, looking flushed and furious. "That portrait over at the Cottage, the one we gave Grandpa, remember? Well, someone took a knife today and slashed your Mummy's face to ribbons!"

"Let's not get carried away! Only one little slash, if you please!"

"Oh Mummy!"

"We're sitting around just so relieved that whoever it was got the old portrait instead of poor little me," she went on in lilting tones, patting the sofa. Lily sat down automatically. Her mother could transform the most disagreeable event into a kind of fairy-tale. Neither her voice nor her face had ever betrayed anything but sweetness, gaiety, at worst the soft disappointment with which she had sent Lily upstairs that morning—no, one other thing her face did express; she had terrible headaches the specialists couldn't seem to help. But how little showed! Only, as now, a dimple would quiver above one eye. Her light-brown hair shone from brushing, her lipstick and powder were freshly applied. A scent of lilac started tears in the little girl's wide eyes.

"I think we're lucky to have such a sweet sympathetic daughter," said Lily's father as if he meant it. "Look at her face, she's so pale, it might've happened to her. She's thinking how you feel."

"And that, my pearl," said her mother with a squeeze and a smile, "is why people like to have babies. Because they grow up into such lovely dependable friends."

Lily stared back flabbergasted. They didn't know!

"What about Fern?" her father asked. "Did she have a key to the Cottage."

"She wouldn't have needed one. The doors were wide open."

"And the workmen saw nobody?"

"Mummy," Lily put in, "I thought Fern and Grandpa were—"

"Divorced." Her father glared. He was very high-strung.

"But Fern has rented a house for the summer," explained her mother. "She hasn't moved out yet, Larry. It's too early in the season. I saw her on the street last weekend, but I heard she'd gone back to New York Monday."

"That's something we'll want to find out. Did she speak to you?"

"On the street? Goodness, no!" She actually giggled.

"Mummy, will we see Fern?"

"God forbid!" said her father.

"Then why has she rented a house?"

"She has lots of little friends, sweetie, who come here every summer."

"She's doing it out of spite, Lily. She hates your grandfather, she

hates your mother, she hates me. She's renting a house for the sole pur-
pose of making everybody uncomfortable." He lit a cigar. Almost an inch
was missing from his little finger.

"She doesn't hate me," corrected Lily.

"That's true, Larry. Fern was always very sweet to Lily."

"You see how remarkable your mother is. If ever there's a good word
to say for anybody, she says it. People who don't even know her call her
an angel. No," he went on, rapid clouds of smoke pouring from his
mouth, "Fern's good and bitter. She'd be capable of a thing like this."

Her mother gave a tinkling laugh. "Mercy me! I'm married to Mr.
Scotland Yard!"

"What about fingerprints?" asked Lily tonelessly.

Her mother laughed all the more. "My dear, if you could have *seen*
the weapon, after five souls had examined it!"

"It's not an incident we'd care to publicize, Lily," said her father.
"No matter who did it, it doesn't reflect very nicely on any of the family.
Enid, a drink?"

"Daddy means," she explained in reply to Lily's blank look, "that
Grandpa's been the subject of enough gossip as it is."

Now Lily understood. They had shown her a clipping at school:
NO LOVE, ASSERTS TYCOON; MATE ASKS 500 GRAND. Wasn't that Lily
Buchanan's grandfather? Oh yes! she had proudly admitted to an envi-
ous circle.

"You see," her father was saying as he poured Campari into one
glass, then whisky into another, "your grandfather's an important man.
Original. Successful. Thanks to him, you'll be a wealthy young lady one
of these days. Now let's talk about something else."

Lily tucked one leg beneath her, trying not to look conscious of her
good fortune. It tickled her to suppose that her father had changed the
subject because she was too young for it. She watched him drink. His
high coloring and the brilliant shades he liked in his shirts and ties—
broad stripes of orange and olive against pink, or deep yellow checkered
with black, brick reds, purples, apple greens—overpowered the pale set-

tings contrived for them. In much the same way he acted upon Lily's affections, making her feel agreeably small and innocent next to him. How fiercely, for example, his cigar glowed now! He had risen again at the end of a long moment's silence, to say in a paralyzing voice: "God damn it, if you don't know who did it, I do!"

Both Lily and her mother managed to avoid his meaning.

"The portrait, Enid," he said crossly. "Hasn't it occurred to you?"

"That some particular person——?"

"Of course!"

She hummed a high soft note by way of showing reluctance. "No," she said, "no, it hasn't occurred to me."

Already he was rubbing his hands together. "Are we thinking of the same person? Are we?"

But she made a funny, final movement, and set down her untasted glass.

He stared, then cried, "And now you've got a headache!"

"I've had a teensy one since being at the Cottage. Sweetie," she turned to Lily, "see if there's some hot coffee in the kitchen. It's the first in weeks," she added apologetically.

"God damn it!" he shouted, striding about. "The smallness! The spitefulness!"

Lily was holding her breath outside the door.

"If you don't know who did it, I do!" her father repeated at the top of his lungs. "Irene Cheek did it!"

Cousin Irene! The tramp! Lily ran to fetch the coffee.

Throughout supper she let the twins chatter. They were only six; poor little girls, their time was coming. Soberly she got into her pajamas, attended to teeth and prayers, let Alice put the medal under her pillow. Out went the light, but Lily lay, for hours perhaps, intensely wondering. Was Cousin Irene a misfit? Could portraits be slashed by grown-ups?— those stately eccentrics, cordial yet vacant, who wore bathing-suits but didn't swim, who were always thirsty but never for water. Lily took for granted this coincidence of dullness and daring in their behavior, also its complete remoteness from her own. However, if something *she* had done could be blamed on Cousin Irene, either Cousin Irene wasn't a real grown-up at all, or she, Lily, a little girl swept towards a whirlpool visible only to herself, had started turning into one. Her father's having called Cousin Irene a tramp tended to support the former view. But her own common sense confirmed the latter.

For instance: "What dress are you wearing to your party?" her mother had asked the other day.

"My blue one?"

"Sweetie, you're getting too *big* for that. What's wrong with your pretty new yellow one?"

In the dark, Lily shook her head over the futility of it.

She was forever being reminded, "You're the oldest, Lily, we expect more of you." Or, "My, what a big girl! This can't be Lily!" As for dresses, who could put into words that sense of how they were constantly outgrown? Of how the wearer's whole person had altered and elongated during the six weeks since last, in gray taffeta or blue, with velvet hair-ribbon and slippers of patent-leather, it had curtsied in dancing class or played Sinding while Mrs. Clement Younger and all her pupils' parents nodded approval? No, change kept happening. Alice had stated that childhood ought to be the happiest part of your entire life, and here was Lily's draining away like a lovely warm bath while she scrambled to replace the plug. With that, she sprang out of bed.

A faint light shone under her parents' door. Receiving no answer to her knock, she ventured in. The large room was done in tones of cream and sugar. On bright days, with only the dotted-swiss curtains drawn, it seemed the inside of a pearl. Lily's advance through its present gloom could not be heard above her father's distant thrashing in his tub. And her mother lay with shut eyes, her long hair loose, her profile, like that on a medal, rising in low relief against the pillow. Lily stifled a little sob.

"Sweetie? Aren't you asleep yet?"

"Does it still hurt?"

"It's better lying down. I took my pill."

Lily touched the damp cheek unwillingly. "Is this where?"

"No. Way inside."

"I'm sorry."

"I think I'll survive."

"For today, I mean."

Her mother's eyes opened, though Lily could see that the effort hurt her. "I am too." She smiled. "Go to sleep now. Dream about tomorrow. You're having a magician, did you know?"

"Don't try to talk," said Lily consolingly; clearly *she* wasn't going to be consoled.

From the bathroom came a blurred, guttural sound—her father's throat being cleared. "Oh," her mother said, as if just then reminded of the fact, "we spoke to Grandpa in the West Indies. He'll be up here the end of this month, for the summer."

"Did you tell him about the portrait?"

"Yes. He took it very well." Whatever that meant. Unexpectedly, her whole face quivered.

Lily took her hand. Once Enid had been somebody's little girl. Indeed, she seemed, just now again, to have gone all hurt and helpless, with great fringed eyes that shut like a doll's. She hadn't even power to send Lily back to bed, but lay, her wrist surrendered to a gentle stroking, and neither, at that particular moment, certain which was mother and which child.

2.

Francis Tanning received Enid's letter in Rome.

Before collecting their mail he and Jane had just "discovered" San Giovanni Decollato, and were full of the crazy frescoes in the refectory. Fancy watching a decapitation while you ate! They planned to have everybody go see *that*, and so bring about an unwilling recognition, by the cross-eyed monk who kept the gate, of an *attrazione turistica* within his precincts.

They sat now on the rim of the Piazza di Spagna fountain, their bare legs hanging in dazzling water, and as he glanced through Enid's thin blue pages, "Oh melodrama!" exclaimed Francis. "No thank you! Not if that's the sort of thing I'm going back for! *You* go back, Jane, you marry your young man! I'm glad I listened to the tiny voice that said not to book passage!"

Jane blinked. *"Non riesco a capire—"*

So he showed her the letter, rereading it over her shoulder and from time to time—for she never kept it straight—distinguishing among his father's wives: Enid's mother, *then* his own, finally Fern. "Or rather *not* finally, it now appears," he said, rolling back his frayed shorts, actually trousers he'd trimmed himself, to get more sun.

Enid dwelt mostly upon Mr. Tanning's response in the matter of the portrait. He hadn't taken it well at all. Reading between her cautious lines, Francis marveled at the old man's egoism. He had assumed from the first that the blow was aimed not at Enid but at himself. And by Fern. It hurt him to admit that a person with whom he'd lived intimately for so many years was capable of this cruel spiteful act. When Larry, having already ascertained from three sources that Fern was indeed in New York, had grabbed the phone and tried to express his own suspicions, Mr. Tanning had blown up. Irene Cheek was a fine straightforward woman. Nobody's on God's earth liked to be snubbed and talked about as if she were dirt under the Buchanans' spotless feet. Then to pretend that Irene—! The wires to Jamaica had crackled and buzzed as he ranted. What about the dinner party Larry and Enid, deaf to his entreaties, had declined to give in honor of the Cheeks, the previous summer? What about the Cheeks having taken *him* into their bungalow in Jamaica, the previous winter, at great inconvenience to themselves, but knowing he wasn't physically up to the season at Hobe Sound with Fern? What about the transformation Irene had wrought in Cousin Charlie, who had been the town drunk before she married him? On and on. "Now there are rumors," Enid's letter said, "of Daddy's wanting to marry Irene."

"There you are!" cried Francis, gesticulating cynically in the warm light. "Why can't Larry and Enid be nice to Irene, instead of *driving* her to Reno? Wait and see—she'll *be* the fourth wife if they don't take care!"

"Think of wives outnumbering children," said Jane.

"Think of each wife lasting thirteen years."

She did, and called it creepy. As an art-historian Jane appreciated these formal touches, but her inner life—or whatever went on beneath her healthy sunburned face and black curls straining against combs—was a chaos. Or so Francis assumed. They spent hours together every day.

Nevertheless each had warned the other that, back in America, they would most likely not be friends at all. Francis would settle in New York, Jane would marry her childhood sweetheart, now a graduate student at Harvard, and since neither of them really enjoyed traveling, that would be that. The great topic between them was less their love of monuments than their dislike of Italy, of Italians, of the Americans who pretended to feel at home there. They agreed vigorously as to the unreality of any given Italian. "Nothing but gesture and vanity," Francis would say, "like a trip through a progressive school. Italians have never understood the difference between expression and self-expression. They have no feelings because they're forever showing them off. Such people *are* unreal. No wonder they produced Pirandello."

"The men think of nothing but sex," said Jane.

"And they're utter failures in bed."

"You don't say!"

"So Xenia tells me," he hastened to add.

"*Speriamo!*" She often lapsed into Italian, not so much from ostentation as to poke fun at those who spoke nothing else.

Alessandro Allori kept Jane in Italy. She had dutifully covered half the country in search of his work, and Francis once or twice, having nothing better to do, went along. Whenever you passed a chapel without bothering to look at the dull dark unstarred painting above the altar, you were like as not neglecting an Allori. Francis had watched his friend, during a Sunday Mass in Pesaro, interrupt the Elevation by crossing in front of it—bareheaded in dirndl and sandals, her arms full of notebooks—on the heels of a corrupt sacristan whose genuflection she dared not imitate, only to find herself examining something truly awful, worse than Allori, a *scuola d'Ignoto*. Allori was awful enough, but what could she do? All the interesting painters had been snapped up by her colleagues. Still, when the Caravaggio wave was over, people would look about for new figures to rediscover. Jane took the view that Allori's very unlikeliness gave him a certain advantage.

What kept Francis in Italy? A hunch that he would be asked this question on his return had helped him dawdle there all through the winter and spring.

Jane handed back the letter. "But who is Irene, really?"

Cousin Irene? Stretching in the sun, he felt hungry and wondered if he could do justice to Mrs. Cheek. After what Enid had written, could anyone? She looked, he began, like a lady golfer, tanned, with small eyes. She was actually a cousin of the Tannings—at least her husband was—but the connection, and for that matter the Cheeks themselves, had played no part in Francis's consciousness until the winter before he came to Europe. They turned up, as if from nowhere, in Hobe Sound—Irene and Charlie and two beagles, these last going directly into a kennel because Fern wouldn't have them in the house. Francis understood that; the house was new, all marble with oyster-white carpeting—very Fern. Even the grass outside felt like paper and rustled dryly underfoot. To go on, Irene had brought her hostess a kind of Guatemalan fiesta dress, purple and orange, one that couldn't have been worn as a joke—not at any rate by Fern, although Irene turned up for dinner that night in flesh-colored slacks and a silk T-shirt on which one of the beagles had been *painted* with a slipper in its mouth. Mr. Tanning did his best to make up for Fern's remoteness, Fern herself grew wild with jealousy, one thing led to another. "Mind you," Francis finished, "I like Fern. She's extremely fond of me. For that matter, she was extremely fond of him."

"Then why—?"

"He divorced *her*. None of the wives ever dreamed of divorcing *him*. One thing, of course, that's accomplished by divorcing them is," he paused, unable for an instant to recall the point he wanted made, "well, that before long they're on such splendid terms. They start having lunches alone with him, sometimes even dinners, laughing and crying over old times, burying the hatchet. Naturally none of them ever remarries. They get cases of champagne at Christmas and on birthdays more or less undemanding pieces of jewelry. The poor man can't bear to fail with people."

Reading in Jane's expression that his tone was baffling, he searched her dark glasses for a clue. There was this about Francis: he had little sense of how he sounded or looked. Years went by before he accepted that his voice had changed. And, while a good head taller than his father, taller even than Larry Buchanan by a few inches, he invariably saw himself as littler than anyone else—children and dwarfs aside. He squinted now, but the green lens gave back only a tiny greenish handsomeness with teeth that, straightened in childhood, had reverted to some glinting disorder of their own. It did no good to know that in Jane's eyes he was handsome. He had to ask outright what her smile meant.

"Nothing," she said. "Just that you can be so patronizing."

"Towards whom? Towards Irene?"

"Forget it."

He would be glad to. Such matters weren't for Jane to judge; he felt it in all kindness. Despite her modest emancipation, despite Allori and sandals and a medical student named Bruno, she came from a plain Midwestern household in which no painting had ever been hung, let alone mutilated, and divorce, a thing unknown, could blacken cousins two states removed. The world of the Tannings, Jane's parents would have

agreed, was a dungheap. And it did no good to know that in her eyes
Francis had grown up out of it like a rose, until her world, by contrast,
seemed as dull and artless as her way of talking. (She said "mere" for
mirror, "Yurp" for Europe, "broke" for baroque—or "barrack," as he
himself sounded it.) It did no good to guess that she adored him. He
preferred to pass for a celibate, to tell his tale with an air of dry com-
edy. They were sitting after all like cut flowers, up to their calves in the
purest water.

He had a polite afterthought. "Did *you* get anything interesting?"

"A postcard from Roger. He's going to meet the ship."

"A postcard only!" Francis took it from her. On one side was a sepia
photograph of an empty restaurant. A motto read: *Escape into the Real-
ity of Fine Food.* The other side bore a few scrawled lines. "I never
believe things written on postcards," said Francis.

"Neither do I."

"You'd think he'd have more to say."

"That was our understanding about this year."

Francis shrugged. He found incomprehensible that Jane should risk
her marriage for a trip abroad. She hadn't needed to accept the grant
from the Foundation. As for her "understanding" with Roger, it left both
free to do as they wished, form what attachments they chose. Jane didn't
even carry his snapshot. "I guess I'm old-fashioned," he sighed. "Will
you really get married?"

"Why not?" she returned, out of her brown study.

He handed back the postcard. "Shall we have lunch, then?"

Outside the *trattoria* they came upon Xenia Grosz in the act of dis-
missing, with a yawn and a nod of her golden head, a ferociously hand-
some young man. She watched him mount his motor-scooter and bounce
away over the cobblestones. "*Hopelessly* in love," she laughed. "Come,
I'm starving. I see you've taken my advice and eat here now. It's the best
food in Rome, and the cheapest."

Francis and Jane had eaten there—in fact they had *met* there—long before Xenia's appearance on the scene. But this was Xenia's way, and for that matter Xenia's scene, there being no corner of the Old World in which she hadn't abundantly lived, as a tiny child, a girl, a young woman, as whatever she might now be in respect to age. It was simpler to forget that she had any.

They followed her to a central table, close to the cool splashing of water. Xenia took one swift glance upward to make sure the light, filtering through vine-leaves, was flattering to her, then another about the crowded garden in search of friends. "Ah!" she exclaimed, "Mr. Durdee is eating here with his wife. He's a very rich American, but quite intelligent, who has just ordered one of my pieces—the abstract torso, only *big*, to go by his pool. And in pink granite instead of marble." She caught his eye and waved. "I told him if he wanted real Italian food to come here. *Cameriere!* Today you're my guests. We'll celebrate."

As they downed their first liter of Frascati, a half-dozen people stopped at the table to kiss Xenia's hand, slap her bare brown shoulder, exchange a joke in French or Italian. They were all artists, all more or less political: a communist sculptor and his wife, who wove; a film-director who could not return to France—the figures blurred after a bit. Francis knew that Xenia, because she liked him, took for granted that he, too, was "creative." He had soon given up trying to contradict her. "You Americans," she would laugh, "with your modesty and your guilt!" So he ended by letting her see him as a liberal, a writer (though he scarcely now wrote letters) struggling, young, living the *vie de Bohème* in a high bare frugal room. He *had* such a room, but not from necessity. He had wanted the cold tile floors and the smelly stove. The bareness appealed to him, like that of the straight razor he affected; it made *him* seem more real. Accordingly he found Xenia's view of him far more soothing than that held by Jane, to whom he had confided the worst.

Still, he couldn't shake the sense of his own imposture. There had been evenings out under the stars with Xenia and her friends, drinking the cheap white wine for which each had so scrupulously put down his pittance, when Francis could only sit—while they joked and waved their arms and criticized America—smiling but silent, lest a false move betray him. The truth, Francis had come to suspect, was that they didn't care one way or the other; he wouldn't be sitting there if he hadn't wanted to, and as long as he claimed no attention they would pay him none. All but Xenia. "You're so mysterious," she would chuckle, licking her lips, "I like that!"—never guessing his secret, although she kept a studio in New York and had dealt, by her own confession, with the rich.

Their food was slow in coming. *"Subito, signora,"* the waiter chanted, and brought more wine. Jane had promised to take some cousins of Roger's, virtual strangers passing through for two nights and a day, on a quick tour of the splendors. It was now half past one, and she had begun to fidget. Francis watched her a full tolerant minute before she looked up, blushed, and blurted out, as if anything that came to mind would do, "Then you *aren't* going back to America next month?"

He ran a hand through his cropped hair. "Why? Did I say so?"

"I thought you had, after reading your sister's letter."

"What!" cried Xenia. "Aren't we all planning to go back together? I booked my passage last month. For two weeks from today, out of Naples."

"So did I, but Francis didn't."

"I'm afraid to go back," he laughed apologetically.

"Well, I wish you had told me," said Xenia, glaring briefly at Jane. "Now it's too late to make other plans. We're in July already. It seemed like such a good idea, our cozy little group, absorbing the shock together."

Francis winced. But he hated not to oblige. "I'll see about it this afternoon. You're both in," he faltered, *"second* class?"

"Good heavens, no!" said Xenia, thinking to put his mind at rest. "Do you think we're millionaires? Besides, on the Italian line, there's no difference between second and third."

He saw Jane smile. He had had to confess to her his taste for first-class carriages. Francis had few extravagances, had indeed picked, on their trips, hotels not even amusingly squalid—but let them board a train! "*Do you mind?*" he would ask, sinking with an embarrassed grin into red plush, as he paid the difference on both tickets, "so as not to have to talk to people . . . !"

"Write it down, Francis," she said firmly, offering him her pen. Jane repeated for him the name of the ship, the date of sailing, and when at length he looked up with the distant fixity of a child who has incriminated himself at a schoolroom blackboard, she was on her feet. He guessed that she dared not linger, after taking such conscious advantage of him.

Meanwhile, the waiter appeared with their food, a look of horror crossing his face. The Signorina leaving? Impossible! His dismay, Francis knew, was no more genuine than the long reprimand from Xenia that met it. Both were behaving as the Americans wanted them to. Only at the end of their duet did they risk beaming at one another, or rather at Jane, their victim, who had torn open a roll and was gingerly stuffing it with *saltimbocca*. Before she could finish, the Durdees, he sallow and blue-eyed, she pink and white with blue-tinted glasses, had made their way over to the little group.

"I'm enchanted to see you," said Xenia suavely, extending her hand at an angle prescribed by old books of etiquette, so as to give Mr. Durdee the choice of kissing or of shaking it. Without hesitation he shook it. "I told you to come here, remember? Did they give you something good? May I present my friends? Miss Westlake and Mr. Tanning—Mr. Durdee."

"And this is Mrs. Durdee. Bertha, Miss Grosz is the sculptress."

"I've been hoping to meet you in my studio, Mrs. Durdee. Won't you sit down with us?"

"I really must go," Jane put in, following the newcomer's eye to her sandwich. She picked it up, smiled bravely, and was gone.

"They do seem to cook everything in oil," said Mrs. Durdee, gazing vaguely after her.

Her husband turned to Francis. "You're Benjamin Tanning's son, I suppose. I've done business with your Dad. Known him forty years."

Francis colored. "No," he brought out in his most strangled voice, "as a matter of fact, there's no relation." If his father's business associate had read Proust, Francis tried to reason, he would conceivably interpret this show of embarrassment as that of a young man who would suffer his life long from *not* being Benjamin Tanning's son. But as it was, Mr. Durdee had glimpsed the truth.

"Excuse me," he said coldly. "I'd heard somewhere that the Tanning boy was in Italy."

Francis felt his hand trembling. He steadied it on the table. "Isn't it curious?" he stammered. "I met him, last week, actually. He was on his way, I believe, to Munich. We met him together, Xenia," he appealed, feeling her gaze upon him, "or was it with Jane?"

"Oh, the fat young man with ulcers!" cried Xenia, referring to one indeed bound for Munich, but whose name she had forgotten. And, lulled by the authority in her tone, Mr. Durdee let the subject drop.

Francis shut his eyes.

Any given Italian, however unreal, took on a comforting plausibility next to the Durdees. They came by the thousand in search of their kind. With camera and medicines they overran a continent so barbarous that the fellow-countryman rumored to live there was tracked down, taken to dinner, spared no detail of hardship or humiliation. For discomfort itself was what they traveled towards, their goal, their vice. Mrs. Durdee's voice assumed a lyric warmth as she spoke of thieving porters, lost luggage, food poisoning, vermin on buses. "They made us swallow our lunch whole, in order to be ready by one. At *two-thirty* the tour began. Well, after ten minutes in those gardens my feet were soaking wet. I said to Warren, 'You do what you like, I'm going back to the bus.' By evening there were little red marks all over—well, just look!"

In Francis's mind, wealth accounted for the phoniness of Mrs. Durdee. He could see her months hence, telling the same story to friends, their mouths voluptuously ajar, who wouldn't laugh it off as Xenia did, as he himself did to show there was no sympathy from *his* quarter. He had his own catalogue of European discomforts, which straightway, by including Bertha Durdee, rendered hers comical, colorless. Here his incognito really worked. It allowed Francis to make light of those whom, judging by his recent confusion, he took with full seriousness.

Among friends, however, a time came to play the card of truth. Alone, facing Xenia, he drew a deep breath and confessed. Benjamin Tanning *was* his father. He hoped she would forgive the lie her innocence had confirmed; then wondered, with a toss of his head, if she could honestly blame him for it, considering the Durdees.

His manner gave her pause. "But why," she finally asked, "does it upset you so? Why all this bravado?"

"It doesn't upset me. It bores me."

Xenia treated him to a lofty gleam. "Ah, but everyone knows that boredom is guilt. Now I," she went on sententiously, "am never bored."

He was openmouthed. "What do you mean, boredom is guilt? My whole family bores me!"

"Voilà!" cried Xenia. Then she took pains to shrug: it was all a matter of degree. "I've done the same thing myself a hundred times. People like the Durdees ask nothing better than to wear you out, especially if you have work to do. With me, it's different. They're customers. If he'd been a publisher," she made her meaning clear, "then *you'd* have had to be nice to them."

Francis grew more agitated. She hadn't understood. "You see, it's not so much that——" But he broke off and poured a glass of wine.

"You don't like your father, perhaps?" suggested Xenia with an experienced laugh. "Dear Francis, I begin to understand you!"

"Do you know my father?"

"Not at all. You never speak of your parents. I assumed they were dead. What I meant, though, was that it's what the whole world goes through. Some day I will tell you the anguish my mother and father caused me as a child. Enough to keep me in analysis for eight years!" A forkful of spaghetti hovered before her mouth. "Such traumas!"

"The point is that my father," Francis murmured, "is very rich."

On this their eyes met. Now she will scorn me, he thought, almost relieved. But Xenia munched placidly, quite as though waiting for him to continue. When he did not, she moistened her napkin, wiped her lips, and looked at him with a new intensity. "I see. And he gives you nothing."

"On the contrary," groaned the young man, "he gives me everything! I don't even ask for it! It's been mine since childhood, set up in a trust fund—in twenty trust funds, for all I know! I try to live it down, but I can't! The Durdees show up and give it all away!"

Xenia put down her fork and shouted with laughter. Francis gaped and blinked. In a moment they were both laughing, uncontrollably, tears in their eyes.

"But tell me then—"

And so he did. He told her about the divorces, about the Cheeks, about his own picture in the paper at the age of twelve—PAWN IN PARENTS' FIGHT. He told her at length about the Buchanans, whom he confessed he didn't envy. Oh, Larry couldn't complain. He was very high up in the firm. But since Mr. Tanning's retirement, after his second heart attack seven years ago, his son-in-law *had* rather been taken advantage of.

It startled Francis, who was touching on most of these topics for the first time in months, to hear how easily he adopted Larry's view of the old man. Had he himself no view? With alarm he felt the perfect blankness of his mind, like a limb gone numb. Not wanting this to show in front of Xenia, he improvised amusingly and at length on songs the Buchanans had sung to him.

At home, at Larry's office, every other day brought cables or telephone calls from Mr. Tanning's latest retreat; this year, Jamaica—in darkest Irene. *Why* (these communiqués said) had the monthly report not reached him? *Why* hadn't he been informed of a partner's wife's mother's illness? *Where* were the figures he had requested on Bishop

Petroleum? Along with these came letters to Enid, once even a *copy* of a letter written to Francis, full of bewilderment and self-pity. Files would be ransacked, subordinates humiliated; Enid would lie flattened by a headache, she took it so to heart—while nine times out of ten the figures, the monthly report, the memo about Mrs. X, would be lying unopened on Mr. Tanning's desk, under a great stack of correspondence. It was now two years since he had fired his traveling secretary in a fit of economy! Economy! Poor Mrs. McBride, the nurse who had stuck it out, was forever on the verge of doing so no longer, because of the demands he made upon her.

So that Larry, as the only member of the family who was also a partner in the firm, bore the brunt of it. He worked like a horse. On the side he handled the affairs of both Enid and Francis, administered their trust funds, invested their profits. What thanks he had from their father seemed at times so tinged with mockery—with the implication that, if Larry was treated as a clod and a convenience, he had only to look at himself to see the reason why: hard-working, humorless, happy with wife and children, all that the imaginative, polygamous Mr. Tanning had never been—"that at odd times," Francis wound up, "I can feel Larry wishing he were in my shoes. For him, you know, I'm the classic image—the young man sowing his wild oats on the continent."

"Your father sounds very disagreeable," observed Xenia.

"But he's not!" cried Francis in surprise. Had he given her that impression? He cast about for images to dispel it.

Money and business, he pursued, these weren't the main issues. No, what upset the Buchanans was rather Mr. Tanning's love life. He gave out an air of sexual wakefulness almost indecent, considering his age and general state of health. Fern at least had discouraged *that* side of it—perhaps too emphatically, for her coldness had made headlines in Hearst papers—but now, in Mr. Tanning's fourth and, God willing, final bachelorhood, what mightn't go on at the Cottage! A nice example for Lily and the twins! There would be women all summer, dropping in, running out, women in towels, women in tears. Fern had kept them at a distance—all, apparently, but Cousin Irene. Francis silently reviewed three or four, each well preserved if not downright pretty, who would be sure to figure.

Then without warning his mind cleared. "What I've forgotten to stress," he laughed, speaking now for himself, "what makes Larry and Enid's point of view so unnecessary," and he took a long swallow of wine to celebrate the fact—"is how *sick* the old man has been!" For Xenia's benefit he sketched in his father's illness, how Mr. Tanning had lain with his limping heart, unable to read or see people, turning his eyes slowly, timorously upon his own life. "Instead of dying," said Francis, "he was given time. He made wonderful use of it. He would lie awake nights remembering all the hurts, real or imaginary, he had inflicted on people, on his mother, on *my* mother. He would find out the whereabouts of women he'd loved as a young man, and send them gifts, or money, something to show how much he remembered and cared."

Xenia wiped cobwebs from her brow. "You say he *isn't* dead?"

"No, of course he isn't dead. Why?"

"You spoke as if he were, just then."

"Well," he smiled, "all that was several years ago. He's much better now."

The sculptress put her elbows on the table. "What a splendid head you have, Francis! I hadn't realized. You must sit for me one day."

Francis blushed.

She let him off easily, asking, "And does your father still send presents to women?"

"Oh yes! More than ever. You'll meet him," Francis was inspired to add, "and then he'll send *you* presents!" It had struck him that Xenia belonged more in Mr. Tanning's circle than in his own.

"Do you think so? What a matchmaker you are! You do it in just the style of my great-aunt. *'Eugénie,'*" she mimicked, "*'il faut que tu sois très gentille envers ce jeune homme. C'est un parti, je t'assure!'*"

"You know," Francis went on, "in a way I do think of him as dead. He's been so ill, he's still so weak. He's more like one's grandfather."

Xenia frowned. He wondered if he was boring her.

"No, really," he almost begged, "he's a very sweet old man!"

"Why, he sounds perfectly charming!" she cried, beginning to laugh again. "I knew there was a mystery about you, Francis! Here we all thought you were one of us, a poor young writer trying to make ends meet on Via Margutta! If it weren't so funny, I'd honestly be annoyed! I'm glad to see you blushing! How dare you allow me to pay my share all the times we've gone out!"

He shook his head wistfully. "I loved it, I loved it. I felt it was *me* you liked. . . ."

"Ah, now you're being silly," said Xenia, summoning the waiter. "Of course it's you I like." Francis detected on her face a faint irrepressible smile of self-congratulation, as when, in a fairy-tale, the maiden who has been kind to the toad is rewarded by its transformation into a prince. "No, no!" Xenia whisked the check beyond his reach. "I invited *you* to lunch."

"You're dreadful!" he moaned.

"Don't wring your hands. Are you busy tomorrow evening?"

"No . . ."

She rose. "Then you may call for me at eight o'clock, and take me in a carriage to the Orso, which is the only *cuisine soignée* in Rome. I've been eating far too much *pasta* in places like this." Xenia glanced about with distance, as if for the first time, at flies, chipped plaster, the dirty fingernails of waiters, cats. "We shall have some good French wine and I'll be wearing a fantastic Paris dress. You see, there are things I've had to hide from *you*, thinking you were poor! Agreed? Mind you phone ahead for a table. And put on some long pants. Where do you go now?"

"To the travel agent, I suppose."

"Ah! Well, the thing to do there," Xenia needn't have said but did, "is get yourself a cabin in first class. Then you can invite Jane and me for dinner every night! Isn't that a splendid solution?"

Hilarious, they parted on the street.

He knew now that he couldn't sail with Xenia. In whatever way he had thought, by letting her know the worst about him, to check the wildfire progress of their intimacy, he saw how miserably he had failed. She liked him more than ever. Not that Francis objected to intimacy with Xenia as a thing in itself; she was clever, wise, easygoing—but here he stopped, feeling abruptly weakened and worn and used. He did object. "I am not up to it," he said aloud to his reflection in a shop-window, a dim transparency of a young man. He watched a woman's hand reach through curtains to remove from the display an oddly shaped bit of coral; it had been glowing up through his glassed image like an enthusiasm, and now it was gone. No, life was too difficult.

It was far simpler, upon hearing that a first-class cabin could be had on a ship sailing the following evening, to take it; to spend the interim feverishly packing, telephoning a dozen people, letting Xenia and Jane believe, if they so wished, that no other passage was available for the next four weeks; finally to catch the afternoon train for Naples and glide, exhausted, out into the gleaming wastes. Francis made his arrangements with the ease of a sleepwalker.

In twenty-four hours he had nothing left to do. With luggage already at the station, his landlady pacified, flowers sent to Xenia, a final *grappa* with a silent Jane—all this behind him—he strolled through the shuttered city, fingering his passport and ticket and rather too much Italian money. Had he done the wrong thing? Mightn't he turn round, go back to the Piazza del Popolo, find Jane still at the table where he had left her, chin in hand? The sky was so blue, the buildings so astonishingly solid, all shades of orange and brown, stones beautifully streaked from their long embrace of weather—what possible meaning could his departure hold? He wasn't leaving, he had never arrived. He had nothing to show for it, nothing of Rome had rubbed off on him.

It made him nervous. He decided to buy something, some small token to take home, a testimonial, a scar. At such moments Francis had the knack of vanishing into the spending of money as into his own room, where none might follow. Across the square a metal shutter went up. He hastened toward the shop, only an hour left before his train.

It was a shop filled with antiquities, which he and Jane had often visited together. They would squint at intaglios, coins, terra-cotta oil-lamps, fragments of pots and statuary, and at length, no purchase made, smile wistfully into the dim corner where the fat old proprietor sat, conveying to him that his things were very fine but, alas, very costly. They were rarely either, to Francis's mind. But the game amused him.

He played it, however, in a different spirit this afternoon. After greeting the old man and reassuring him that no harm had come to the Signorina, Francis bent over glass cases, peered up at shelves, in an almost fearful excitement. The objects seemed to have come alive, to be trembling with the possibility of his possessing them. By the end of a half-hour in which he had smoked three cigarettes, he asked if there was anything he hadn't seen.

The old man made a show of thought, then rose with a wheeze to open a cupboard behind him. Francis watched, elated. He felt in his bones that a treasure would appear.

A big box was placed on the counter. "Since today you are alone," said the old man craftily, and opened it. *"Ecco, signore!"*

Inside, carelessly thrown together, were perhaps a hundred phalluses, of clay, of marble, some primitive—the old man chose one of these and held it high, croaking, "Etruscan! Votive!"—others ("Roman! Artistic!") monumental and detailed, evidently chipped from sculpture under whichever Pope had been responsible for fig-leaves. Was it Urban? or Innocent? Francis stared into the box, his mind blank. Then, coming to himself, "Ah no," he said. *"Questo non è interessante."*

The shopkeeper courteously ignored this remark. What he had in mind, Francis explained in his clumsy Italian, was something small, precious, something that he might offer as a gift, yes, to the Signorina.

Had the old man understood? What gift more precious? he might have been musing, as with a quizzical smile he made a third selection, this one winged and erect. *"Porta fortuna!"* he nodded, and Francis lost his temper.

How exasperating, how Italian, the old man was! *Porta fortuna,*

indeed!—the phrase served up in connection with any miserable acci-
dent. You had only to stumble and fall upon slimy cobblestones, or break
a glass and have to pay for it, and up would come a crone or a smiling
waiter to observe that the misfortune was sure to bring you good luck.
Why, your own grandmother might die, or yourself, a little black bug
of a priest shutting your eyes—from nowhere the dry voice would be
heard: *porta fortuna!*

"That ring, for instance," Francis icily pointed it out, "please show it
to me," and shut his eyes until he felt it resting in his palm. It looked
Greek, of soft gold, with an owl in relief, and very small, a child's ring,
found in the grave of a dead child. It barely fitted over the first joint of
his third finger, and would not be dislodged, causing his hand to suggest
a detail from some Renaissance portrait. "How much does it cost?"

Being gold, and of the fourth century, it could be had—the old man
calculated, dissembling his stupefaction, the sale by now certain—for no
less than fifty thousand lire.

"Here is forty thousand. *Va bene?*"

"Ma, signore mio—!" A wheedling note, a rolling back of eyes.

"Very well!" cried Francis, who loathed haggling but felt called upon
to do it in Europe. He caught with pleasure the old man's look of frus-
tration, that of an actor whose finest scene has been struck from the
script. Throwing down the five implausible bills, rose and umber with
protraits of Dante, Francis added, "I am leaving at once for America!"

What had passed in the shop seemed to have removed any alterna-
tive. He hurried out into the dazzling square.

And in the taxi, and on the train to Naples, his back to fountain and
cypress; throughout the nightmare of customs, squabble and tip; and
before falling at last asleep in his gently rocking cabin, he found that it
soothed him to study the ring. The hand that wore it lay relaxed all night
under the coarse pillow, gathering up each dream of touching or reject-
ing that Francis, awake, tried not to entertain.

3.

"Run into the next room, dearest, and bring me a little cushion. Oh my, there I go! You couldn't have been more than six, the day you said to me, 'Mummy, running's not so easy as you make it sound.' Thank you, I'll fix it. It goes in the small of my back. Oh, and while you're up, if you wouldn't mind emptying your ashtray—that's a good boy.

"But I didn't *want* you to know that I'd been ill. It was too pathetic in the first place, catching measles at my age. I still haven't thought how it happened. I hadn't been anywhere, I hadn't kissed any children. No, if I felt you'd come back to New York on my account, well, I'd never have forgiven myself. I didn't need you. And luckily you were so occupied with your own affairs that you thought nothing of those weeks in which I wasn't up to writing more than a line. I know that sounds full of self-pity but it's not meant that way. I'm honestly and truly glad that you weren't worried. It's a sign that we have a normal friendly relationship. Didn't I write you, when you first went to Europe, the things Annette Woodruff said to me? 'I just don't understand,' she said, '*how* you can let Francis go away like this. He's all you have!' Now there's a woman with four children, all of them married, with families. She spends at least two months out of the year with each child. I've never wanted to be that kind of mother and I hope you'll let me know the day you catch me at it. I said that to Annette. I said, 'Francis is a grown man now, old enough to do as he thinks best. I will never interfere with his life. The only reward I want is the gratitude and respect I get from him, for knowing how to leave him absolutely alone.'

"There's a nice letter from Annette on the dresser. You can read it and tear it up before you go. I've answered it.

"It's perfectly true, at one time I did need you. I needed all the help I could get. And you helped me, way beyond your twelve years—I want you to believe that. You'll remember also, I never kept you from visiting your father whenever you wished. It was your own sweetness, Son, that decided you to spend so much time with me. I did my best to make it easy for you. Did you once see me shed a tear, that whole time? And I know now that I was right, seeing how close you and your father have grown. He's a very sick and a very unhappy man, Francis. He needs all the love you can give him. *I* forgave him long ago.

"That life was never for me. People still stay, 'Oh Vinnie, *how* can you bear living in this little hole, all alone, after those years in that beautiful house full of servants and friends?' For the longest time nobody'd believe that I liked it. 'At least move back to Savannah,' they'd say, 'where your friends are.' And always wanting me to meet some charming new man. No thank you! If the finest man in the world proposed to me, I'd turn him down. I can read as late as I like, get up when I'm good and ready. There's that little hot-plate in the pantry where I can cook rice or grits or an egg. You may not believe it, but I've found peace of mind more precious than riches. I feel sorry for Ben now, from the bottom of my heart.

"You'd better prepare yourself for a great shock tomorrow, when you go out to the Cottage. He didn't stop in town last month, on his way through, but I wrote you about the evening we had in the fall. Of course we went to Pavillon, and I doubt that he ate three mouthfuls. Oh, he got a little tight and started in on how he'd always love me. You know, the old story. I just smiled and squeezed his hand. You could see he was at the end of his strength. *How* he survived the winter I don't know. He told Larry Buchanan years ago that he literally couldn't bear up under the strain of a divorce from Fern. And now, just when you'd think he'd really settle down, want to live quietly and simply—suddenly there's Irene Cheek and Natalie Bigelow and this new Englishwoman who latched onto him in Jamaica, all fussing over him, giving him that false flattery he thrives on! I thank God *you're* not susceptible to it, Son. You're one of the most level-headed people I know.

"Why can't people learn to face the truth? I didn't *have* to let these gray streaks show. But believe me, if I began touching them up, I'm the one who'd be fooled. Those other women are so pathetic!

"Run along now, you have a lot to do. Give Daddy my love and have a nice long visit with him. Do get a haircut, as a favor to me, will you? And don't worry. I'll be on my feet in a day or two. I *love* my presents. And it's," she kissed him, "*so* wonderful to have you back. Wait! I put some lipstick on your chin. Bend down, I've a Kleenex right here."

These were a few of the things Francis's mother said to him on the occasion of their first meeting in over two years. Glancing back from her bedroom door, he saw that she had already put on her glasses and reopened her book, squaring her shoulders as she began to read. It was a gesture he had forgotten, and it touched him as much as any she had made all afternoon.

Not that he had been touched, to speak of. He lingered still in the daze of having arrived, of taxis, telephones, the enchanting summer city, the sickening costly hotel. Houses were being demolished. Women on street-corners were describing to one another their first experiences in Italian restaurants. Beyond all this, his customary response to his mother—and Francis marveled only at how soon he had felt it operate, once settled in the little needlepoint chair beside her chaise longue—was a silence no less marked than her own talkativeness. Both silence and talk, further-more, hinted at states of mind not easily enlarged upon. Forbearance? disillusion?—the words flickered and went out. And yet, on first sight of her, kissing her at the dim door, hadn't he felt like talking? And hadn't she listened? Her eyes followed him about the small room, her laugh met his own. Admiringly she caressed the scarves and gloves he had brought her. Francis had a pleasant sense of being too *big* for her bedroom, of orna-ments rattling as he tramped about; and not till now, strolling down Madison Avenue, was he able even to put the question of how thirty months of enviable experience could have, in as many minutes, evapo-rated. It wasn't right. There all at once he sat, as countless times before, bored, smoking, defacing the motto in her French ashtray— "*Qui se mari pour l'amour A bonnes nuits et mauvais jours*"—while Mrs. Tanning talked.

Her soft Southern voice, even if she had been speaking gibberish, would have declared, "I am the voice of a companionable, sensible, well-bred woman of fifty-one, without affectations or illusions. I have never been raised in anger or stilled by passion." Despite traces of illness (she'd been "delicate" since Francis's birth) her face confirmed these words, a face both sweet and ascetic, but wanting in subtlety. In her circle of friends, which had contracted over the years, she passed for the most knowing, the most fastidious, as well as the one with a degree of moral fortitude that sustained her through readings of "strong" novels in the modern manner, military memoirs, terse transatlantic reviews of current affairs. This same fortitude had allowed her, at dinners during the last war, darkly to predict a struggle of fifteen or twenty years, while every other woman at the table, to whom *The White Cliffs of Dover* stood for literature and Ernie Pyle for the unvarnished truth, could only murmur, saucer-eyed at Mrs. Tanning's tough-mindedness, "Oh but surely, Vinnie, it *can't* go on like this!" At which she would turn, faintly shrugging, to what might have been—and in those days of sacrifice frequently *was*—a smoking dish of entrails.

Upon Xenia's remark that he never spoke of his parents Francis had first felt a guilty twinge, then obliged her with several thousand words concerning his father. Concerning Vinnie, however, what *was* there for him to say? It didn't help to remember that she had once been a beautiful young woman, giving herself up, with something more humorous than her present resignation, to the wearing of Paris dresses and oblong jewels. The dresses had long since been cut down for goddaughters; the jewels waited in a vault for Francis's bride. This was but a bit of the baggage Mrs. Tanning had cast off, as on some lonely trek into high clear wastes. She hadn't even wanted alimony. The major part of it accumulated unspent.

In the eyes of others her life had been sown with sand, and Benjamin Tanning would at once have agreed repentantly that he had done it single-handed. But such a view took no account of Vinnie's own will, which, in this or any matter, rose cool and tall from the insufficient ground. It was thus she could touch Francis, even with envy. Squaring her shoulders, opening her book, she had affected him as living on where life itself had ceased—or been so lived, so used, that nothing was left but the past and the vantage from which she saw it, perfect, remote, hers. Would a time ever come when he could mount his own tall pillar, subsist on honey and locusts, with not a pang of regret? The sky burned above him, he moved under rustling trees set in the pavement. Oh, to have lived!

Such thoughts weren't meant to be put into words. But what else to say about her? Well of course, she *did* leave him alone, and he *was* grateful. There was that much to say. Probably she loved him, too—would she otherwise show all that concern for his appearance, his untrimmed hair, the stain on his cuff, each little conscious irregularity? "You see!"— entering the barber-shop, he flung out his hand to an imaginary Xenia— "I don't speak of her because I can't! I begin talking like a child, I stop making sense!"

4. The train was a scandal, its cars sooty and comfortless, no water in the toilets. It stopped repeatedly in full country for minutes at a time. Nobody knew why. Francis pictured the engine's aged metal face turned aside in order to be sick along the tracks.

At last he descended, perspiring, stickers fluttering showily from his suitcases onto the humble platform. A high sweet voice called his name, and there was Enid. How lovely of her to come to the station, thought Francis and said so, kissing her. But he hadn't foreseen the touch of gray in her hair—how old was she? thirty-four? thirty-six? Her face looked tired, too, for all its rose and tan against lavender linen. Well, she was pregnant; that explained a lot.

"I couldn't miss my baby brother's homecoming!" she declared. "How well you look! Lily, would you have known your uncle?"

"This can't be Lily!" he thought of saying, having heard it often enough himself.

The child gave him a stricken smile.

"How well *you* look, Enid!"

"Me? I'm an old bag!" Her laugh ran up and down a tiny scale. "Now, my pearl," she continued, "that we've got the credit for meeting you, I must break the grim news."

"There's Daddy!" cried Lily, and ran towards him.

Had Larry been on the train? Was that Enid's grim news? "I wish I'd known," said Francis, genuinely dismayed. He had had something important to talk over with his brother-in-law. Still wondering, and with his mouth open to ask who, since Enid was meeting Larry, had come to meet *him*, Francis caught sight of his father's colored valet, Louis Leroy. The latter, bald, beaming, cap in hand—Louis Quinze, Leroy Soleil, such names did justice to his exquisite good humor—trotted up with words of welcome. Then Lily returned, followed by Larry laughing, "Well I'll be damned! When you weren't in the Pullman I assumed you'd missed the train!"

Had there been a Pullman? "You see," Francis told them, bravely grinning, "I've got so used to traveling third class. It's the one way to know a country."

He waited for them to laugh, but Enid only reached for Lily's hand—protectively? "What are we going to do about your uncle?" she marveled. "He's just too Bohemian for words!"

"And you know *this* country," Lily reminded him.

"That's all right, Francis, you do what you want. I always say, though," said Larry, not quite accurately—it was Mr. Tanning who often said it—"there's no such thing as a bargain. Not when you're traveling, or eating, or buying clothes."

Louis Leroy said nothing. However, taking up Francis's suitcases, he started a movement towards "his" pearl-gray limousine.

Francis's remark had been so much his kind of joke that the Buchanans' responses perplexed him. It occurred to him that, just as in Europe he had more and more taken for granted their kinship with him, *they* might have developed a real uncertainty as to his place in any world of theirs. Well, there was always the bond of blood. But as he squirmed a bit under their tactful scrutiny, he felt a hesitation about even the bond of blood. He hoped he wouldn't have to test it too soon; he didn't want it snapping in his face like old string.

From the car window he asked when he would see them again.

"Whenever you like," said Enid promptly. "*We* have no special plans. Tonight you'll be having dinner with Daddy, won't you? Tomorrow, let me see—you go to the Cheeks for cocktails. . . ."

"Perhaps I'll see you there?"

"Don't count on it," said Larry.

"No," Enid added, "the little Buchannibals have turned into home-bodies. Give me a ring in the morning, sweetie, and let me know when *you're* free."

"All right . . ."

He must have looked mystified. "Oh, you have a lot of surprises in store for you, Francis my lad!" shouted Larry as the huge engine started. All three Buchanans were left behind, waving.

"What does he mean?" asked Francis. But Louis Leroy, though visibly tickled by any word addressed to him, didn't lend himself to soundings of this sort. The effect was less of discretion than of simple deference; Louis had never learned, or had modestly forgotten, how to make his own view of things noteworthy. He shifted the talk to the weather, to Francis's health. He sped past many a landmark, supposing rightly—if he supposed at all—that his passenger's curiosity would be caught up by them, old familiar sights, the Common, the cannon, the plaque com-memorating three centuries of peaceful village life. Further on, the mon-strous shingled houses began, and the glorious trees. The car slowed down, passed between two columns capped with beasts bearing shields, and at the end of a winding gravel drive stopped. Francis let himself be helped out, the wiser for Louis's illustration of how things were done in his father's house.

There it stood.

The Cottage, so-called because of its mere dozen rooms, its shaggy swollen look, as of thatch copied in teak and slate, formed the fourth side of a vast unshadowed lawn. This had, to be sure, a rose-arbor in the center of it, and shrubbery—boxwood, hydrangea, laurel—that in time would mask the brick walls that enclosed it; even so, it couldn't be thought of as a garden. Nobody used it. Nothing about it invited people in the house to stroll out beyond an elevated terrace that extended from the north porch. Indeed, no steps led down from this terrace to the lawn. The two levels were connected by a ha-ha—you had either to jump or, re-entering the house, come out another door. The lawn seemed therefore so much sheer space, watered clipped magnificent space, against which any person approaching the Cottage on foot would give the illusion of tarrying, of fumbling, pitched forward as if walking into a fierce wind. But once indoors he would understand, puzzled by an air of intimacy out of all proportion to the giant scale of the rooms, that the lawn *had* been used, that if the fruit were sour it could no longer be tasted as such after biting through the bitter green husk.

The sea glittered on the far side of the house. Also out of sight, down a narrow drive, four smaller buildings faced one another like card-players, over a square of gravel—a garage, a greenhouse, a cottage for servants, and one for the overflow of guests. Here Francis was to stay. He had just been staring up dazedly at the big house when a voice from inside called, "Mr. Francis goes to the guest-house, Louis, not here!"

A little apartment had been contrived. Louis Leroy ushered him proudly in, opening doors: bedroom and bathroom, a kitchen with beer on ice and the makings of snacks. For the present, Francis was to be the one occupant of the house.

The rooms smelled of fresh paint, the bed felt very soft, there were flowers everywhere. None of it was to Francis's taste, really, but all that thought and effort absurdly touched him. He couldn't help it. As a child he had wept to read a recipe for apple pie, a dish he hated. "What is it? what is it?" his nurse had cried when he came to her sobbing with the cookbook. And he couldn't explain, nor could he now. It had something to do with the very idea of patiently choosing "small tart apples," dotting them with butter, baking "till tender"—how could they resist such loving care? How could *he*, each time they were set, small, tender, full of love, before him, continue to gag at the first mouthful? Surely the rejection of love was wicked, even if it turned your stomach.

Still, wondered Francis looking straight into the eyes of a Royal Doulton fruit vendor, to what purpose had he developed a taste of his own, if not to tell that bit of rosy-cheeked porcelain how much he didn't like her? But he couldn't do it, he turned away. Something in him had grown mild and melting. The unpalatable means vanished into his sense of the motive behind them. He was wanted here.

He washed quickly, left Louis to unpack, and walked over to the Cottage. Up from the basement came the voices of maids. Entering, Francis caught what could have been the scent, lingering, transmuted, of all his younger entrances there.

Although the ocean room had been done over by Fern, and altered, he noticed, in the general reaction against her, what hadn't altered were the clues to Mr. Tanning's presence. They were three: illness, wealth, women. It had always been so.

A piece of knitting ornate but dreary, the work surely of a trained nurse, lay on the coffee-table next to a hypodermic, gauze-tipped, ready for use. This brought back from long ago the nights Mr. Tanning, then perfectly healthy, would elect to spend in the hospital, a patient subject to all regulations, for the luxury of an alcohol rub, a tranquil sleep, the cool voice of a nurse waking him early. He had mastered the mannerism of illness, like a prodigy too young to learn the brilliant lesson of the sonata he performs, though it will be at his fingertips when the time is ripe. We play with fire, his son thought.

For evidence of wealth he had just to look about, and for evidence of women as well, the two being here curiously intermingled. Not the small careful pile of bills and change, prominent against the pale leather of the desk—this stood for wealth on the same low rung as the nurse's knitting, the raw symbol, the mere gender—but the room itself told, and in a high hushed voice, how it had been furnished by women, for women, would be in a little while (if Francis cared to sit and wait) positively furnished *with* women. What it had been furnished without, it all but blushed to confess, was any visible regard for expense. Bland satins, fruitwood and lacquer, massive peonies, English paintings of Childhood in its most handsome and least credible aspect, these things at once murmured their testimony, then, as it were, half-closed their lovely eyes and drummed their dainty fingers.

If Europe had taught Francis to dislike a Royal Doulton apple woman, it had taught him also the extreme fineness of all that confronted him here. He recognized the little oil sketch, a view of a floating child, by an artist whose clownish name had struck him at the age of six. Of course, he ruefully smiled, it would have to have been Tiepolo.

Turning, he made out, through a window oily with the salt air, a figure sitting on the south terrace, which overlooked the sea. At this moment the nurse came in.

"Oh," she exclaimed, "you must be Francis! We're certainly glad to see you! I'm Mrs. McBride." They shook hands. Gray-haired, motherly, if not downright grandmotherly, she wore a little starched cap. He felt at once her willingness to talk throughout the better part of a sleepless night. "I must say I'd have known you anywhere. You're so like your father. Besides, he's shown me photographs. That one of you wrestling with the snake, remember? He talks about you all the time. I said to him this morning, 'I'm afraid to meet your son, Mr. Tanning. If he's as intelligent as you say, he's going to think me an awful dumbbell.'"

"How is he?"

"Oh, we have our ups and downs. Last night," she lowered her voice, "he didn't sleep too well, so I've let him nap longer this afternoon. I was going now to wake him and give him his shot."

"This is the pace that kills, all right," said Francis, immediately flushing as his own words reached him. He had hoped to have outgrown the way, in his father's house, his speech became awkward and corrupt, like that of the Italian seeking to ingratiate himself through a command of American idiom.

Mrs. McBride, however, smiled with delight. "I've said the very same words to him a hundred times. Oh, I can see you're on my side. He'll listen to you. Do you know," she said, picking up the hypodermic, "he gave me all the stamps from your letters, for Mary Ann; that's my seventeen-year-old daughter"—a bit too old, thought Francis, to be collecting stamps—"and what a pity, she was here last week for a little visit with me. How she'd have loved hearing about your trip! She studies French in school, it's her favorite subject. Remind me," she finished with a special smile, her thought now painfully clear, "to show you her photo."

"I will. Who's that on the terrace?"

"Probably Mrs. Bigelow. No, she went into the village."

"I'd heard she was here."

"Yes, poor soul."

"Poor soul?"

"Well, she can hardly see. She has cataracts. Lady Good took her shopping, she can't go anywhere by herself. Oh, that would be Mrs. Cheek on the terrace. She likes to wash her hair in that fancy shower your father has. Come with me, I'm going to wake him now."

He followed her into the hall, a bit dazed by the amount she had managed to convey, unsolicited. She led him on tiptoe through Mr. Tanning's study and quietly opened the bedroom door. "He's still asleep," she whispered.

Francis looked over her shoulder. In the full light of afternoon his father lay, a black mask shielding his eyes, one hand on his heart. The big fourposter had been replaced years ago by a narrow hospital bed whose cranks and hinges kept the old man in a half-sitting position, like invalids in opera. The bedclothes seemed undisturbed, he slept so gently. His lips were parted. He wore a stocking on his head.

As they watched, Mr. Tanning cleared his throat. "The show must go on," he mumbled to his audience.

"Well, it looks like we've had a nice sleep," said Mrs. McBride, advancing. "Are you ready for a pleasant surprise?"

"Yes, my love." He pursed his lips to indicate, with fine economy of movement, what sort of surprise would be acceptable. Francis laughed aloud, delighted.

"Is that my stalwart son? Welcome to the seraglio." Francis bent to kiss him but Mr. Tanning shifted slightly. His son's lips touched the mask instead of the brown wrinkled cheek. "I haven't been too well, Francis," he went on. "I had another mild stroke last month, which seems to have affected my eyes. They're sensitive to sudden changes of light."

"They're clearing up very nicely," said Mrs. McBride, swabbing his arm with alcohol.

"I tried to play a rubber of bridge yesterday. I couldn't see the damn cards." The needle went in. "Ouch! Mrs. McBride—"

"Now that's a new needle, Mr. Tanning!"

"I don't give a good God damn what it is. There's no reason on earth for me to feel such pain. I told you to throw out all those needles and get new ones. It makes me so mad I don't know what to do."

"There, there," she sang. "Now we'll get the oil."

"I must inherit it from you," said Francis. "I can't stand sharp things in me." He wished to be obliging. Actually, he had never minded hypodermics.

The nurse fetched a flask of warm scented oil from the bathroom and, folding back a corner of the covers, poured into her palm a few drops with which she began to massage Mr. Tanning's feet. Swollen and darkened by a complicated tracery of tiny blood-vessels, they looked deprived of any life but the one stroked into them by her gleaming hands. "My circulation is no good, Francis," the old man explained drowsily.

"It takes him a while to wake up," murmured Mrs. McBride. Presently she anointed her patient's hands.

Francis looked on spellbound. There was an atmosphere of helpless old age in the room, of impotent wrath, slumbers, tears, things he had never so vividly before connected with his father. He had of course known him old and sick, but not to this degree. Perhaps the "mild stroke" hadn't been mild at all—yet wouldn't the old man, in that event, have been removed to a hospital? Was it simply a matter of his having aged three years since Francis's last sight of him? What other changes were there? A new nurse, the riddance of Fern—surely *that* was all to the good. . . . He scanned the photographs on the bureau, a question slowly forming in his mind, when the floor creaked and there on the threshold, older and more haggard than the glamorous likeness from which Francis turned to see her, stood Irene Cheek.

"Why, look who's here!" exclaimed Mrs. McBride with brisk emphasis. Francis got up to greet the visitor. But a gesture imposed silence. Her lips compressed, her eyes aglitter, she stole towards the bed and bestowed a lingering kiss upon its drowsing occupant.

Francis wound his watch.

"'I arise from sweet dreams of thee,'" Mr. Tanning tried to say. The words were muffled by her mouth.

"The shower's all ready, Mrs. Cheek."

She straightened herself. "Thanks, Bridie, I'll go right in. You sleep well, Lover-cousin?" Her voice was soft and slurred.

"Yes, thank you." Mr. Tanning removed his eyeshade. "Irene, you know my boy, Francis."

"Sure I do. Hello, Francis." She showed him that she not only had, as he'd told Jane, small eyes, but small teeth as well. Worn down, he supposed, by use. Her dress was Kelly green. A gold tennis racket, with rubies set in the handle and a pearl ball, hung round her neck. "Are you here for long?"

"For a couple of weeks at least."

"Good! Then we'll see you tomorrow. You'll bring him, won't you, Benji?"

"Yes, Irene."

He sounded tired and cross. Mrs. Cheek glanced appealingly at the others. "Everything O.K.?"

"No," said Mr. Tanning.

"Oh I know what's bothering *you!*" she cried, her face clearing. "Your bridge winnings! Right? Well, I left the money right on the desk in the ocean room. Twenty-two dollars and fifty cents. Your father's a real whiz at bridge. Said he couldn't see the cards, but he piled up the score."

"I'd be very happy, Irene, if you used that money towards something *you* wanted. I mean that. I've got everything *I* want."

She shot her friend a provocative smile. "Everything?" And when he didn't respond she continued gaily, "The money's on the desk, in any case. You come early tomorrow? Bishop said *he* would."

"For God's sake, Irene, go in the damn shower and let me get up!"

"Temper, temper!" she laughed. "He's got the finest shower on the East Coast, Francis." Whereupon she vanished into the bathroom and began to sing above the roar of water.

"Next time," said Mr. Tanning, "I promise to obey orders."

Mrs. McBride chuckled and went out.

"What do you mean?" asked Francis.

"Mrs. McBride said, 'Look who's here!' She said it in words of one syllable. And I didn't look. If I was punished it was my own fault."

"It didn't seem to me you were being punished," observed Francis. "Or had you expected someone else?"

For the first time that afternoon Mr. Tanning smiled, broadly, enigmatically. "My own kind understanding son," he drawled.

Getting out of bed, ringing for Louis to help him dress, pouring and downing a shot of whisky from a decanter on the bureau, he slowly dispelled, or at least complicated, Francis's early impression. Helpless old age, by countless small touches, was transformed into something approaching a parody of itself. The slumped shoulder, the wisp of white hair disarrayed had to be reconciled to the roguish rolling of eyes, a stagger and groan that smacked of the footlights, as he leaned on his valet's arm. Mr. Tanning had furthermore a face that would have made the fortune of any actor. Frank, earnest, noble in repose, it was kept from plain tiresome fineness by being always on the verge of some unlikely humor, mischief or doltishness or greed; and would fall at times into a subjectivity so stricken, so elegiac, that you thought of a schoolboy deep in a *Life of Chatterton* and wondered, as before each new aspect, if you hadn't finally hit upon the man's real face.

Next to such mobility whatever likeness Mrs. McBride had found between Francis's rather stiff face and his father's disappeared. Probably it could only have been seen in a photograph.

Mr. Tanning said quietly, "I've missed you more than I can say."

Francis trembled. How much he needed to learn!

The years in which to acquire from his father an image of mature behavior had passed Francis by, taking this opportunity with them. He had spent them under his mother's roof. The long trousers, his first pair cut from the cloth of superior poise, had been tried on, as it were, with no mirror handy. *She* thought he looked well enough; he was forever made to feel his responsibilities as "man of the house." He emptied ashtrays and mixed drinks. He sat at the head of her table while she told of conflicts in which he took no part. As it happened, he never did take part in them. After a month in the army Francis caught cold, was discovered to have chronic low blood-pressure. They sent him home. Once again he sat in the needlepoint chair until he simply couldn't bear it another day. His "condition" left him as mysteriously as it had come; he went back to college. Vinnie moved into an even smaller apartment; he fled to Europe. He had begun to see more and more of his father, but by then Mr. Tanning was already an invalid.

Well, something could be learned even now. Picking a name at random, Francis asked, "Who is this Bishop Irene spoke of?"

"He's the President of Bishop Petroleum," said Mr. Tanning.

So long a pause followed this remark that Francis was casting about for another topic when his father, who had stopped to watch Louis Leroy tie his shoelaces, continued. "He's one of the finest men I've ever met, decent and honest. He's a Mormon. Bishop's his title as well as his name. He's also a very clever businessman."

"A special friend of Irene's?"

"So *she* says." But Mr. Tanning wasn't to be coaxed out on a tangent. "Tanning, Burr financed about sixty per cent of the company. That's my own foresight, Francis. Nobody else had much faith in the deal. The way things look now, we can't possibly make less than ten million dollars over the next year and a half." Another pause, then: "Last year I asked Larry Buchanan to fly out to Alberta and submit a report on the place to me. His report—*when* he got round to it—was very thorough and very luke-warm. You can't run a business from a distance, Francis. It just burns me up to be treated like an old poop. The next thing I hear is that *Mister* Buchanan has bought, for the account of his loving wife, twenty-four thousand shares at sixty cents. Plus ten thousand for your account. By the time the good word got passed to me the stock was selling at a dollar and twelve cents. Every God-damn member of the family was in on the deal except me."

"But you said you financed the company," Francis ventured.

"The *firm* financed the company. The firm's profit goes . . ." He proceeded to explain where it went, but Francis, while knowing the meaning of nearly every word his father used, could make no sense out of them. This didn't annoy him. High finance was by nature dull and inscrutable. As for politics—! Here Francis actually smiled. Mr. Tanning, in years gone by, had been a great one for unfolding the *Herald Tribune,* gasping, turning purple, striking the arm of his chair over some bill that, though it had reached the Senate, was destined, in the fullness of time, not to be passed.

"I'm not complaining," he finished, misunderstanding Francis's smile. "I guess we all like to feel sorry for ourselves, don't we? I've managed to overlook the fact that Bishop Petroleum closed last night at three and seven-eighths."

Francis let his eyes widen. He reluctantly calculated his own profit, saw the money swelling like a mushroom in a nightmare. The old man frowned and swallowed a very small white pill.

"What is that?"

"Nitroglycerine."

"Won't you explode?"

"It stops the pain in my chest." A minute passed, then his face relaxed. "The important thing's to check that first spasm of pain, before a chain reaction sets in. I don't have any resistance, Francis." He rose and slipped one thin leg into his trousers, leaning heavily on Louis Leroy.

Mrs. Cheek came out of the bathroom in her slip, glowing. "God, that felt good! Aha, Benji! Caught you with your pants down! Who's going to dress *me?*"

Louis enacted a brief but expert scene, the recollection of some distant chore. As he withdrew, Mr. Tanning said, "We must try not to offend the pure in heart."

"Oh Francis isn't shocked, are you, Francis?" Irene wriggled and smirked.

"Certainly not," he replied. "I've often helped my mother get dressed."

Mr. Tanning broke into silent laughter.

"What's the joke, Benji?" But she was never to know. Far off a door slammed; the sound of women's voices reached them from the hall. Mrs. Cheek enjoyed a fleeting smile before exclaiming with concern, "Bad news! Guess Irene's got to make herself decent!"

She began a prolonged struggle with the green dress, during which the study door was heard to open. "Benjamin, we've had such a lovely afternoon! May I intrude?" The tones, ripe and British, were of a cultivation Francis had given up hope to hear at the Cottage. This then would be—what was her unlikely name?—Lady Good. When she appeared in the doorway, tall, gray-haired, gray-eyed, with her proud pleasant fifty-year-old face, Francis could judge how much it *hadn't* been Irene's kiss his father had expected on waking.

"Prudence," Mr. Tanning began.

Her eyes had come to rest on Francis. "It's only when *he* says that that I ask myself whether I'm being admonished or merely called by name." She held out her hand. "I'm Prudence Good. I'm very pleased to meet you, Francis. Your being here will make all the difference for your father."

"I hope not," said Mr. Tanning.

Lady Good laughed uneasily. "Well, *some* of the difference, shall we say?"

"Hello there, Prudy!" Irene called over her shoulder, finishing with a zipper. "How are you? I'm sick about not having seen you till now."

"I'm very well, Mrs. Cheek, thank you."

"Charlie and I were sunk when you didn't come over yesterday."

"That was most kind of you, but as I don't play cards I'd just have been in the way."

"Well, we missed you. How's Jamaica? How's Sir Edward?"

"Why, he's having the time of his life, isn't he, Benjamin?"

Irene sighed. "You're so smart, Prudy, to leave him alone for a spell. Any man wants a little vacation now and then."

"Ah well, I daresay you're much wiser in these matters. Yet I don't know, or rather I *do* know, that I, poor silly creature, should never think of leaving *my* husband."

"Don't tell me you're *both* here!" gasped Mrs. Cheek, comically peering behind her.

The rhythm of onlookers at a tennis match had been imposed upon father and son. This was a nice try of Irene's, but her lob fell short of the net.

"Yes, Benjamin very sweetly asked us." Lady Good fingered a sea-green cushion. Addressing no one in particular, she slipped into a vague rapid babble, some British substitute for silent thinking. "As a matter of fact we left Kingston exactly a week ago today, didn't we? Ned had a lovely holiday here, and set out this morning for two weeks in Washington. He has all kinds of men to talk to. Naturally he hated to go but he couldn't possibly have afforded a pleasure trip. Poor Ned, one feels the entire welfare of the island rests on his shoulders." Suddenly she looked up. "Francis, *are* you coming to Jamaica this winter? We *long* to have you with us!"

Whatever her motive, he felt at once that she meant it; it made him like her then and there.

Her words had a further effect. "It's nearly six!" Mrs. Cheek exclaimed. "I can't stay a moment longer!" She did, though, as if not knowing how to get away. The question in all four minds seemed to be whether or not she would kiss Mr. Tanning. Evidently she couldn't risk it—yet how was she otherwise to leave? Would she just hang her head and slink out? Francis found her predicament strangely touching. How little her Benji had told her, and how much she had to feel her way! Seeing her then as no menace to anybody's peace of mind, he'd stretched out a hand before he knew what he was up to.

"Thank you for asking me tomorrow, Irene. I'm looking forward to it."

Not expecting help from this quarter, Mrs. Cheek stared at him out of a still deeper daze. Francis might have been a figure dashing from the sidelines to return the last impossible ball; he spoiled the game but he covered her defeat. For a moment it seemed that she would even kiss *him*. "Splendid, Francis," she said, "see you then"—adding in a confidential undertone, "Try to get your father to come early."

"Goodbye," said Mr. Tanning jovially.

And out she went.

Nobody gloated. Mr. Tanning poured himself another drink.

"I had *such* a lovely afternoon," said Lady Good at length. "Natalie and I did the shops. My, they have lovely things. I saw one dress I'd die for, except that I'd never have an occasion to wear it. Then I drove her to the Yacht Club for tea. Did you have a nice nap, Benjamin dear?"

There came over Francis a beautiful sense of leisure and spaciousness. Above all, he felt he'd had a hand in bringing it to pass. Slowly revolving the small gold ring on his finger, he smiled to remember (and smiled to think how this had slipped his mind at the time) Vinnie's reaction to it. She had, on seeing the ring, let out a little groan of distaste. How *could* he? It looked so eccentric, a *child's* ring, the way he wore it, couldn't he have it made larger? and *please* would he not wear it to his father's house, for *her* sake? Yes, and precisely then his feeling of stifling boredom had arisen. "You were wrong," he wanted absurdly to tell her, "it doesn't matter here, one way or the other, we are all eccentrics here, it's what keeps us likable." Outside a light wind ruffled the dune-grass, the sea beyond had turned rose and silver. He felt at peace for the first time since his return to America.

The best was yet to come. "Well, I shall leave you two alone," said Lady Good. "Francis musn't think you have a lot of silly women in your hair. Natalie and I have received instructions, Francis, to dine elsewhere this evening. I shall get my first taste of the Inn."

"I don't envy you," said Mr. Tanning. "Where's your new dress?"

"What new dress? The one I saw in the village? I presume it's still in the shop-window."

"And why, pray?"

"Well, as I said, Benjamin, I'd have no occasion to wear it. Besides, it was probably *much* too dear."

"Oh I see." The old man winked at Francis. "She's already forgotten what color it was."

"It was a mass of blue and gray and white chiffon," Lady Good rapturously began, "cut rather low in back with a—oh, you're making fun of me, Benjamin! What sort of woman will Francis take me for?" She had at last understood that Mr. Tanning was about to offer to buy her the dress. "I know what's in your mind and I'll not have it! Just because, whilst you were napping, I innocently amused myself on Main Street, I will not be put in this position. My answer is a pleasant but firm 'No thank you!'" She finished with a toss of her head, looking highly pleased.

"Sit down," said Mr. Tanning. She did so. "Would you mind telling me what you're talking about?"

Realizing then that he hadn't after all made the offer, Lady Good blushed and stammered. Her confusion, which knew no bounds, was so direct a result of the threat to her pride that Francis, no less than his father, found her irresistible.

"Never fear, my love," Mr. Tanning grinned. "Heaven will protect the working girl."

"Oh Francis," she sighed, "what are we to do? I fear we *have* to get along, in order to please your father. But now that you've seen the hopeless creature I am, I can't blame you for thinking what you will of me. Shall we even be able to talk about books, I wonder? You look like the sort of person who prefers Eliot to Christopher Fry."

"I do," said Francis. "So that I imagine," he nodded towards his father, "we'll have to talk about *him*. That ought to please everybody concerned."

This was the happiest stroke. It set Benjamin to beaming. Lady Good got up and kissed them both, awkwardly, tenderly. All three appeared to feel a bit flattered and safe.

5.

"What am I supposed to do with this?" inquired Mr. Tanning. A silver pillbox had been set beside his coffee-cup.

Louis Leroy broke into a little shuffling dance. "Miss McBride, she gave them to me. May be she wants you to swallow them?" He showed surprise when this answer proved acceptable, and reluctantly left them alone in the dim curtained dining room, with sea sounds in their ears.

"I wonder what Louis thinks of us," said Francis.

Mr. Tanning swallowed two red pills before telling an illustrative story. His answers to many questions took the form of parables. The young man saw himself as a neophyte listening to some expert ancient.

Two winters before, Mr. Tanning and his valet had arrived in Jamaica to find no room for Louis in the Cheeks' bungalow. Irene's butler recommended a small hotel in Kingston, from which to commute by bus. Later, a rooming-house down the road from the Cheeks advertised a vacancy, but Louis had by then learned to enjoy town living. Mr. Tanning laughed and shook his head. "The hotel wasn't a hotel at all. At least Mr. Leroy had been such a distinguished guest that the proprietress hadn't even been charging him for his room."

"So he didn't move?"

"Oh yes, he moved."

Francis lit a cigarette from the candle in front of him. Was there a point to the story?

Finally Mr. Tanning went on. "A month passed and I moved, too. I moved because the Cheeks' house wasn't big enough. But I told Irene that Louis Leroy had set me an example I was ashamed not to follow. By God, I didn't think she'd ever forgive me!"

Francis thought it was very funny, and said so.

"I thought it was funny, too," Mr. Tanning said, "but the Buchanans didn't. They're highly sensitive. They don't want their daughters to grow up believing Grandpa was a Casanova."

It seemed to Francis, who had been thinking how nice that the old man could talk as if still capable of amorous exploits, nicer yet of Enid and Larry to take them seriously. Not for a moment did he suppose they were really to be taken so; Francis's idea of physical love was a violent one, a matter of anguish, lies, recriminations.

The idea needed to be distinguished from that of mere sex, which was after all what Mr. Tanning talked about, at merry length. He seldom talked about his wives. These, presumably, he *had* loved, deeply but cheerlessly, while turning, banal as it sounded, to other women for companionship and fun. To Natalie Bigelow, for instance, whose presence before dinner, curled on the sofa between Francis and Lady Good, spoke louder than any word of her host's. Longer than anybody she had been younger than anybody. Even now just the faintest puckering of her wonderful unimpaired face, the contours stippled rather than etched, her over-intricate hair and its unlikely tint, the small searching movements of her head and hands, hinted that of her threescore years and ten, sixty would not come again. She lived like a churchmouse in a closet on Lexington Avenue. It was too divine, she whispered, to be back at the Cottage; she wouldn't leave till Ben threw her out. She asked so little and it meant so much—breakfast on a tray, a cocktail before dinner, the blessed certainty of dinner itself. What Ben asked, it appeared, was simply that she be there, lovely and going blind, to acknowledge his own long easy loyalty to the good times they'd had. Natalie had outlasted Vinnie and Fern. Had she known Benjamin that early in life, she would have outlasted Harriet, too. From this a lot could be deduced about her, even more about the wives.

Mr. Tanning sipped his coffee and began yet another story. "Harriet was in New Jersey one summer with Enid. I'd spend the week in town with Howie Burr at an apartment he shared with one Warren Durdee."

"That's the man I met in Rome!" Francis interrupted. "He said he was a friend of yours."

"I'm surprised to hear it. We couldn't stand the sight of each other. He was younger than Howie or me *and* the biggest stuffed shirt on Wall Street. Whenever we'd bring a couple of girls up to the apartment half the fun was to lay them on Warren's bed. Howie and I developed this system. We'd get home from the office and sleep five hours or so, then shave, put on dinner-jackets, and go out on the town. By that hour every pretty girl in New York had had all she could eat or drink, and was bored to hell with her escort—some rich old poop who could hardly keep his eyes open. Like your loving father *now*. We'd go to the bar and lay bets on the ones we could make. Howie lost a lot of money both ways, on the ones *I* made and the ones *he* didn't. God damn," Mr. Tanning shook with laughter, "one night Paul Whittaker (who became President of Southwestern Stores) drove Howie and me and these three girls out to somebody's vacant cottage in Rye. Along about the fourth bottle of champagne Howie's girl said she was going to bed. Alone. There were just two bedrooms in the house. She took one, Paul and his girl took the other, so I——"

Louis had reappeared. Mrs. Buchanan had driven over, wanting to know could she see them.

"Tell her we'll be right there." Mr. Tanning's mood had broken. He stared now into the candle-flame wooed by a reeling moth; his eyes filled with tears. "Francis," he said, "the first time I was unfaithful to your mother I went home and cried all night long."

"Don't tell me things like that!" Francis spoke before he knew what he was saying. These *were* things he wanted to know. "I mean," he added quickly, "unless it helps you to say them, or . . ."

"It doesn't help me to say them."

"I've come, I mean, so much to feel that *she* must have been a difficult person, even then." Francis, blowing out both candles, faltered in the gloom. "That, having thought always of *you* as the one at fault . . ." But his words still moved in advance of his thinking; he couldn't go on.

They gazed in bewilderment at one another.

Once years before, at dinner with his father, Francis had tasted mangoes for the first time. "What delicious mangoes!" he recalled exclaiming affectedly. And Mr. Tanning had replied with a smile, "How would you know?" It seemed to apply now. "Tell me, tell me then!" the young man might have cried, wondering at the same time, miserably, what he needed to hear. Some word of reassurance, yes, some sign from the one who had lived so much, to show that life was no prerogative of his own—that it might equally be the road he, Francis, traveled. Just at this point, however, behind every clear look and guileless anecdote, he felt his father saying, "Show me your life, first, the way I show you mine. How else can I give you my view of it?" Ah, but what life to show? He had chattered about Jane and Allori, impressions of landscape, comic mishaps, fatigues. Was this all he could produce, the poor furniture of his two dozen years? No piece of it had met with an acknowledgment of value. Mr. Tanning's vacant pauses seemed rather to overflow with misgivings as to what could be said in the face of such poverty.

". . . I begin to see, I mean," Francis tried to find his way, "the part *she* must have played, the part she may still be playing. Does that make sense? Did you ever feel something of that in her, a remoteness?" He rose from his chair. "A self-sufficiency?"

Mr. Tanning had waited for him to finish. "It's a mistake to simplify," he said.

Francis took it as a clue. "The first time, then, it wasn't with Natalie?"

"No, it wasn't. I don't know why it wasn't, except that your mother had always suspected Natalie in particular. I was very fond of Natalie, she'd had a hard time. One day Vinnie found a letter from her, a perfectly innocent, lovely letter. Women can be really cruel when they have an easy victim."

"I'm glad she's here with you," said Francis, his fingers on the table, looking deep into its smooth dark. "Shall we go to Enid?"

Mr. Tanning smiled gently. "Don't you think it's strange that you and I should be so lonely? I've been lonely all my life, and I think you will be, Sonny. I guess we're just made that way."

"It's a mistake to simplify," said Francis, hoping that his father would laugh. He didn't.

Enid was waiting in the ocean room.

Her call would have been the most ordinary thing in the world, except that from the outset she created, in spite of herself, a complex impression. She rose with her lilting laugh to kiss them, then at once returned to her chair in innocent confusion, as if remembering how carefully she was dressed, how scented and combed, a pink tourmaline at her throat, and wanting them suddenly *not* to notice. She threw round her

shoulders a light "daytime" sweater, she pulled knitting out of a bag—
some tiny garment all rose and white—but the easy effect failed, proved
merely the lengths she would go in order to play it simple. "I don't feel I
need to be so formal," Enid began, after explaining that Larry was dead
tired from his week at the office. "If I've peeked in at the wrong moment,
just say the word."

Mr. Tanning cleared his throat. "I'd rather see you than anybody I
know, Enid. You ought to have learned that by now."

"Mercy me!" she cried, her eyes shining. "Such complimentary
remarks! Actually," she went on, "we'd hoped to coax everybody over
tomorrow afternoon, but when I talked to Natalie this morning she said
you were already engaged."

"It's no mystery," said her father. "We've been asked to the Cheeks'
tomorrow afternoon."

"Yes, Natalie told me." Enid was very gay about it. She chatted on
and on, mostly to Francis, never dropping a stitch. What had been his
favorite restaurant in Rome and did he know of a good tailor there (she
and Larry were thinking of a trip next Easter) and weren't the Italian
people cheerful attractive little souls? Outside it had begun to rain.
Wasn't it cozy, the three of them sitting together? And what did Francis
think of the changes she'd made at the Cottage? Why, it looked lovely,
he said—and was startled to see her blush with pleasure. So he went on,
beyond plain sociability, to praise as much as he could, the grouping of
chairs, the texture of fabrics. He felt himself going too far, but Enid
drank it in, nodding agreement, pointing out things he might have
missed. The ocean room, she confessed, still needed thought. Well, he
was sweet to say so, but it did. And she was thinking, yes indeed, she had
schemes up her sleeve! Francis had the oddest notion of being appealed
to, all unconsciously on her part—Enid had never in her life entertained
an ulterior motive. From time to time, however, she interrupted herself
to ask Mr. Tanning if she'd remembered to tell him how many thousands
of dollars her committee had raised for the Hospital, or whom she'd run

into on the street the other day, or what progress Lily had made with her tennis lessons. Until at last Francis guessed what the matter was.

"You sound," he said ingenuously, "as though you hadn't seen one another for a very long time."

"Well, we haven't!" exclaimed Enid, her eyes squeezed shut with amusement. "It's been a whole week! We might as well not be living in the same country!"

"I asked you to lunch the day before yesterday," her father reminded her.

"But you called up at eleven o'clock! We were leaving for the beach with a picnic, the twins and Lily and I." Once again she seemed to appeal to Francis. "You just don't disappoint little people that way, do you?"

"If you remember," said Mr. Tanning, "I suggested you bring the picnic over here. Grandpa has a beach in front of *his* house, too."

"I'm sorry," said Enid, "I felt you had enough on your hands as it was, without the additional strain of three wild Indians."

"Oh I see." Mr. Tanning swallowed a nitroglycerine pill. "You'll soon come to realize," he told Francis, "that your loving father sets an unsavory example for his grandchildren. We can only pray that they manage to live it down."

"You *know* that isn't true, Daddy," she said, her voice quieter and sadder now that she was indignant. Francis had a movement of tenderness. Enid, after all, lived far more than himself in the world of the Cottage; she played the game of kinship in a way that Francis, who tended to make up the rules as he went along, simply didn't. Mostly he was touched by her having come to make peace alone, without Larry, trusting her brother—virtual stranger that he was—to see her through. "Sunday," she was earnestly saying, "when you had us to meet the Goods, I told you I had a busy week ahead. Monday I went into town with Larry for the night. Tuesday—"

"Say no more." Mr. Tanning smiled wearily. "All is forgiven."

Enid gave a helpless laugh. "By the way," she said after a bit, "I took the portrait to be restored. The little man thought it would take about three months. I said to him, 'What is this, the *season* for slashed portraits?'"

"Have you found out who did it?" asked Francis.

"Oh dear," their father sighed, rising.

Did he have a pain? They were both alarmed. But no, he wanted only to wash his teeth. He tottered showily out of the room.

Francis repeated his question. Had they found out who slashed the portrait?

"Alas," Enid giggled, "the culprit is still at large."

For no reason that he could tell she lowered her eyes. "It's such a wild thing to have done," he said encouragingly. "Who on earth would want to hurt you that much?"

"Daddy's theory," she observed, avoiding her own, "is that somebody wanted to hurt *him*. He was very fond of the portrait."

"Does he still think Fern did it?"

"She couldn't have done it," Enid flew to her defense, "unless she hired an assassin! She wasn't in town. It happened on a Friday, the next day was Lily's birthday. Not that *that* interesting fact," she quickly added, her manner growing more and more social, "has anything to do with the case, but it's one way I'm able to remember. Don't you find you have funny little ways of remembering things?"

By way of reply he swung round in his chair. Knowing that Enid suspected her, he had remembered the money Irene Cheek had left for Mr. Tanning. It was, of course, no longer on the desk. He felt sure that his father hadn't picked it up.

"You have the answer after all, I think," he said. "There's nothing a certain person wouldn't do."

For the second time Enid refused to meet his eyes. Could she be hiding something? "Oh well," she murmured, "the milk is spilled. We'll never find out."

"*I* will!" Enid blinked. Francis chuckled at the idea of cross-questioning every woman who came to the Cottage. "I'm serious, though. I'll find out, you wait and see!"

But she didn't enter into it. "Sweetie, it wouldn't do any good, even if you were able . . ."

"Nonsense! The scene of the crime is overrun with suspects!"

"I mean, I don't believe Daddy really wants to know. It would upset him so. He'd lie awake—"

"Don't *you*?"

She looked puzzled. "With my headaches?"

"No—don't you want to know who did it?"

"Oh, naturally I'm curious," began Enid lightly. Then with a gentle, almost apologetic smile: "It's funny, but no, I don't really want to know."

It was his turn to lower his eyes. For a long time Francis had dreamed of doing her some important service, of a day when, no longer able to sustain the rare buoyancy with which she went her way—revolving as it were on one toe—Enid would reach out for him to support her full weight. The moment seemed very close. The gravities she withstood, whatever form they took—headaches, committees, another child to bear, the nameless enemy near at hand—he had felt these things more than once during the past half hour threaten her balance. Francis went so far as to hold his breath. Would it be *now* that she broke down, her eyes brimming over, her head on his knee? He could imagine the very words stammered out: "I cannot bear my life . . . I've never let myself think . . . he doesn't love me . . . so much depends on me. . . ." And he would be stroking her hair, whispering, "Let it go, let it go. . . ." He needed to know that Enid suffered, for proof that his own world was real. Still she gave no sign.

"Did Daddy tell you he was going to Boston next month?" she presently asked.

"What for?"

"He's found a wonderful doctor there, who treats his kind of heart ailment very successfully. If it works it's meant to leave you entirely free from pain."

"How weird," said Francis.

"Daddy's terribly excited over it. So am I. When you think of the years he's suffered, with no hope at all . . ."

"But would it really be wise?" Francis wondered after a moment. "I mean, doesn't pain serve to warn him when he goes too far, physically or otherwise? You saw him take that pill just now, and then leave the room. I don't think it was to wash his teeth at all, so much as to escape from a painful conversation." He waited to make sure that Enid knew what he meant. "And don't we all do that," he pursued, "to greater or lesser degrees? We needn't be as sensitive as he, but doesn't pain teach *us* what we must avoid?"

He saw it as applying marvelously to his sister. But Enid had a wider experience of the subject. "I'm afraid that it"—she wouldn't in her modesty say "pain"—"teaches us what we *can't* avoid." And Francis knew she was right.

"In a way, yes," he said. "We can't at least help *others* avoid it. We're none of us magicians with ointments or heroes with lances. Look at him. He suffers in his mind from not being strong enough to do—what? To do the things he would suffer ten times as much from the physical strain of *doing*, now."

Enid hummed a single high note.

"No, I think it's fascinating," Francis went on. "He knows what hurts him, but does knowing save him?" His eyes brightened to glimpse the purpler reaches of his thought. "Mightn't the answer be that *everything* hurts him? Pretend he's a bad example for Lily, call him a Casanova," he lingered ironically over the word, "and presto! you've offended him. Admit that he's no such thing, and you've made matters even worse. What do you do at his age? Whatever it is, it injures him! One sees what the Hindus were getting at when they said that all action was immoral. It is. It hurts me to talk as I do, it hurts you to listen!"

He was by now very far afield, and as puzzled as Enid by the passion in his voice. What had happened to him? He felt all elated and nervous.

She, however, knitted and nodded. Francis had a glimpse of the advantages that went with playing by the rules.

So he let her off, fell silent; and yet a lie had been given not just to Enid but to the room they sat in, so rich with her ideas. He felt he had seen through her ceremony of blandness and taste; it wasn't a ceremony because it concealed nothing, composed nothing, cost nothing. He decided then and there that she had no other way of being. If she had, dear gentle creature, she might have given it a try. Her poise, as she smiled understandingly at Francis, became the wistful poise of a child, her mother's hat drooping over her eyes, her feet lost in her mother's shoes, pouring out colored water and making conversation. Equally with the ocean room, where each piece was so harmonious and so fine. It no longer appeared to Francis an emblem of the truly adult so much as a naïve aspiration towards that state.

Ah but in a certain light, how the room sustained Enid! How it sustained, against his will, himself! Even a *real* child entering there would have had to sit as Francis did, its little legs crossed, talking of the weather, refusing a second chocolate, charmed into forgetting the friends outside who waited to play leap-frog or "games" in a garage attic.

Wouldn't it help, he brooded, to leap up, cry out, smash something? But the room met his eye so trustingly; it was easier to do violence to himself. As if casually he brought his knuckle down upon his knee, once, twice, again and again, feeling the pain that made at last the beautiful room unreal, Enid unreal, and gave Mr. Tanning, when he paused frowning on the threshold, an air of patiently putting up with a good deal of nonsense. "There's not one really comfortable chair in the whole damn house," he had remarked during dinner. "They're all either too narrow or too low."

Francis hoped his father would never say this to Enid. She was so easily upset.

For a time the old man stood behind her, stroking her hair. The rhythm recalled words: Let it go, let it go. . . . "In April, 1929," Mr. Tanning began, "I convinced Howie Burr to send out a circular I'd written myself, warning all the firm's customers, here and abroad, that in *our* opinion the stock market was in a most precarious state. Things were sky high. None of our competitors could understand why in hell we were prepared to lose so much business. But it made sense to the President of the United States; he wrote me a personal letter. I'll get you a copy of it for your scrapbook, Francis, if you like. The recommendations we made were very simple. . . ."

Francis swallowed a yawn.

At eleven o'clock Mrs. Bigelow and Lady Good joined them.

"Benjamin, I wished for you!" the latter exclaimed. "We've seen such a lovely film, all about the friendship between a crippled boy and an English sheepdog. It brought tears to my eyes." She took it upon herself—while Natalie conveyed in pantomime that it was no good taking *her* to the movies, she couldn't see a thing—to tell the whole plot, like a bedtime story.

"Oh, Lily would like that," said Enid at one point. "She's been badgering me for a turtle."

The others said nothing at all. Mr. Tanning's eyes never left the speaker's face until, with a slight drop of his head, he fell asleep.

They smiled at one another and at him. "Poor little fellow," said Natalie. "All tuckered out."

"Has it stopped raining?" Enid wondered. Nobody could be sure.

"How one hears the sound of the sea," Lady Good breathed.

In silence they let it speak to them, not knowing what else to do. Natalie drew her finger along the leg of the coffee-table, and held it up pensively; they saw it was black with dust.

Francis got to his feet and stole out. He paused by the hall mirror, whispering, "I'm tired, too." When he returned with Mrs. McBride the women looked up gratefully.

"Gracious!" said the nurse. "Do you know what time it is? I've let him stay up a whole half-hour later than usual, because tonight was an occasion." Mr. Tanning stirred and woke. "I want you to be good now and come along with me. We know what happened last night. That's why you've been so tired today."

"Yes, my love," he groaned. Did he always say that, on waking? It was amusing enough, but soon the old man, worn out, rose to do as he'd been told. He kissed each of them goodnight, solemnly. "I leave," he told Francis, "the seraglio in your hands."

"What's the keeper of a seraglio called?" mused Natalie aloud.

"A unique," said Francis. This met with laughter.

"Benjamin," said Lady Good, "you don't mean *me* to go to Irene's tomorrow?"

"Why not come to us?"

"That's very dear of you, Enid. I'd infinitely rather."

"I like the way you call her Irene," said Francis, "after taking such pains *not* to, this afternoon."

"Ah well," Lady Good said, memorably, "I daresay she'd love being called Irene to her face and Mrs. Cheek behind her back. But there are those with whom one tends to reverse normal procedure."

"Miaow!" put in Mr. Tanning from the door.

"I'm sorry, Benjamin, but I'm used to speaking out."

"Prudence, you can do as you like about tomorrow," he said. "I'd be happier if you were along, but I'm just selfish."

Lady Good pursed her lips. "Very well, I shall go to Ire—pardon me, to Mrs. *Cheek's*. But only because you wish it."

"We all wish it," said Francis.

"Oh dear," Mr. Tanning mumbled, taking his nurse's arm. "Off to the Casbah." Francis had to smile to think that, after so much innuendo, it was with plain old Mrs. McBride that Casanova retired. But he found it funnier yet, the way she, before leading him off, cast a backward glance, all starch and common sense, to reassure them of her own propriety. He might *talk* of casbahs, she conveyed, but they needn't worry, that was as far as it would go.

The evening had ended. Before dispersing, Enid to her car, Lady Good and Natalie to their rooms, each in turn told Francis how glad she was that he'd come home. "Everything's all right *now*," Lady Good even said, quite as if still talking of a sheepdog.

He followed Enid out into the drive, asking, "Do you think *now* that Irene means anything to him?"

"I don't know what I think," she said cheerfully, no longer visible in the gusty dark.

"But you *had* been alarmed. Your last letter said that Irene—or hadn't you known then about Lady Good?"

"I'd never heard her name until last week. Things are too mysterious for words."

"You understand of course that it's she who will save him from Irene." Enid was silent. "And don't start wondering who's going to save him from Lady Good. I can tell that's in your mind."

She gave her little gasp of a laugh. "You'll do that? Oh my goodness!"

Francis had meant simply that Lady Good was someone from whom nobody needed to be saved. Enid drove off, nevertheless, leaving him to reflect upon the increasingly lucid part he had been given to play at the Cottage.

6. In the community, that is among the people you knew, there were various assumptions about places. The most widespread was that whoever summered here kept a second, in some cases a third, residence elsewhere. It went without saying that one of these would be very large and handsome; a place in town sugared the pill of a too modest place in

the country, and so forth. Some few conformed excessively. The Buchanans, for instance, moved between *two* large handsome places. They kept a house here and a triplex in New York, both of which—unlike the structurally so blatant Cottage—were perfection. This got said by somebody once a week at least: "Enid's place is perfection." But you had to be the right sort to get away with it—just as in another set of assumptions, those by which husbands and wives took mistresses and lovers as naturally as they moved from one house to the next, there would always be a few couples (again, like the Buchanans) whose faithfulness to one another either refreshed or exasperated. The Buchanans' refreshed, for they were not only rich but *attractive*. This was the key word. It allowed them, by and large, to do as they pleased.

Irene and Charlie Cheek, however, were not the right sort. *He* had been known to drink both too much and, of late, too little to be attractive. Still, you had known his family (if indeed you weren't part of it), and he did love to sail. Irene's position was graver. Before and after her marriage she had been on the jolliest terms with a number of rich older men (whom you knew and liked)—friendships that, like others of their kind, would have been shrugged off, but for one damning circumstance. The Cheeks themselves weren't rich. They had, to be sure, their two places, one here, one in Jamaica. But Irene made the mistake of pretending, in whichever of the two she found herself, that *this* was their simple summer (or winter) lodging, while the other house was, oh, quite a different matter, grand, serious, well staffed. It cut ice for a time. Then certain friends with whom she no longer put on certain airs, like Mr. Tanning or the Governor-General of the Island, having visited the other house, praised in all innocence, but to her enemies, its unpretentiousness. Overnight her stock went down. She was seen wearing the same dress too often. When she appeared in a new one you wanted to know who had given it to her, and why. You took for granted that her interest in Mr. Tanning was of the most mercenary order. It had even been whispered that her husband was party to the plot, that if Irene succeeded in marrying Mr. Tanning, Cousin Charlie would have only to wait till the old man died, then take her back and live at the Cottage happily every after. "Poor Ben," people said, "when will he see that it's not *him* she cares for?"—which was the purest slander. Irene didn't much care for *anybody*, rich or poor. Either security or imagination was needed in order to care for others; Irene lacked both.

This didn't keep you from going to her parties.

"Stay with me, Francis," Lady Good begged, taking his arm to walk the weedy path. Already some fifteen cars were parked on what passed for a lawn, and the small house, buzzing with talk, had swallowed up Mr. Tanning and Natalie under their very eyes.

Francis, as it happened, had stayed with her the better part of the day, since her coming upon him early in a fine sunny haze beside the sea. All but ignoring his greeting, Lady Good had embarked on what he later saw to be a single inexhaustible conversation. Little had he reckoned, with his graceful naming of Mr. Tanning as their likeliest topic, the reaches of *her* interest.

She had wanted first to make her position clear. Francis was not to infer, from her presence at the Cottage, any resemblance between herself and the other women there. Her marriage to Sir Edward had been, still was, full of comfort and mutual esteem. If Benjamin had brought—she threw up her hands at the word—"*romance* into my drab life, who am I not to enjoy it like a schoolgirl? I'm very sentimental, Francis. Ned isn't, not one bit. He's far too busy for that, although I've sometimes asked myself what he'd do, the poor man, were I not there." Had she really? wondered Francis to himself. It put her friendship with his father on a more complicated footing. Oh, Mr. Tanning loved her—Mr. Tanning loved everybody; but here was an inkling of the possible depth of Lady Good's own feeling.

Throughout their talk she remained highly dignified. No one could have doubted that the affair was platonic.

Leading Francis back down the beach, she had gone on to describe her first meeting with Mr. Tanning, through mutual friends in Jamaica. It took place after he had moved away from the Cheeks' and into the beautiful old plantation house, Weathersome, which he had bought a few months later—such a truly beautiful house, she sighed, high on a hill, surrounded by trees, eucalyptus, palm, manchineel, and such flowers! Inside, wonderful gleaming floors, chandeliers, decorations in plaster that were the work of *genius!* She hadn't wanted to go, that first time. Mr. Tanning was American and well-to-do; it followed that he would be insufferable. Lady Good hadn't, moreover, been invited, and it simply didn't amuse her to barge in on strangers. How little a stranger she found him, after a brief hour in his company, was still a source of amazement. "Not that it should be," she told Francis, "for of all the charming men in the world Benjamin's surely the most charming, and the sweetest, and the saddest. Why, he needs affection the way a child does!"

Affection, the capacity for feeling and showing it, led her finally to speak of Irene. In fact she was still speaking of Irene now, as they entered her house. Lady Good felt very sorry for Irene. "One has to face it, Francis, she simply isn't your father's intellectual equal."

By then Francis had begun to feel very sorry for Lady Good. Though equipped with a few intellectual advantages of his own, he'd never found them useful in his father's circle. And though Vinnie Tanning was still proud of her last withering retort—"Kindly tell me what you and Fern are going to *talk* about!"—the *mot* hadn't kept Benjamin from marrying dear mindless Fern. Nor would Lady Good's *intellect* save him from Irene.

Oddly enough they collided with Irene in the hall. "A drink just spilled on Natalie," she said, extending a dripping hand to each. "Go on in. I'm scurrying for a towel."

They obeyed. Mr. Tanning was already seated across the room, talking to a florid man with wavy white hair—Mr. Bishop, evidently. In a corner, unnoticed by them, Natalie, vigorously shaking her head, rejected napkins and handkerchiefs. Small aimless groups stood by. From under a table two beagles peered expectantly. Francis could see Irene having spoiled Natalie's dress on purpose, hoping to draw everyone together by means of some lively incident.

Cut-glass bowls had been piled with potato chips or nuts enough for a hundred people. It promised to be just the kind of formless party Mr. Tanning hated.

A dapper, fattish little man, black-browed, gray-templed—the face of one who has never worked in his life—hurried up to Lady Good and seized her hand. Francis recognized him a moment later: Charlie Cheek. He had aged ten years during the past three. He asked what they wanted to drink.

"What are you drinking?" asked Francis thoughtlessly.

"Oh I'm on the wagon," his host replied. "Haven't touched a drop for six whole years. This is ginger-ale." He hadn't, at least, said wormwood; in fact Mr. Cheek appeared to enjoy the role of an alleged cuckold. While pouring her sherry he kept beaming at Lady Good with clear brown doglike eyes. How nice to see her, how was Sir Edward? Yes, yes. In Washington? Well, well. Probably Charlie knew better than anyone how his wife could behave, and was trying to make up for it.

Irene, reappearing, fussed over Natalie with a towel.

"Don't bother about me, pet," Natalie said. "Introduce Francis to some of those pretty gals."

So he gulped half his cocktail and let himself be led away, under the reproachful eye of Lady Good—though, as he told her later, he would have preferred to stay at her side.

Francis had known most of the pretty gals before. They had been his playmates at the Beach Club, at afternoon birthday parties, at dancing school. They had thrown sand into his eyes and he had put gum in their hair. One of them (now "little" Mrs. Drinkwater, twice divorced) had followed him behind a hedge, to watch him urinate. He had thought it funny to wet the front of her dress, but she ran screaming to her nurse and Francis was taken home and spanked. Ginny Neale, yes, that had been her name. She seemed, today, to have forgotten the episode. She had very sleek red hair and wore gold bracelets on her lightly freckled arms. "I'm dead to go back to France," she said through her nose, "but I'm stuck with my heaven child." Another girl, "big" Matilda Gresham, had given away all *her* dolls on her tenth birthday. She drank beer and gruffly told Francis about working last winter for a theater group in the Village. "Tilda's always been a daredevil," her mother joined them long enough to explain. "She can't abide League work. I beg her just to try Palm Beach *one* more season, but do you think she listens to me? People wonder what she does—I tell them I don't know." Mrs. Gresham (Boopsie) gave a bright drunken smile. Years back, during a great luncheon at the Cottage, she had grasped Francis's wrist and asked a passionate question: "Do you now, looking straight into my eyes, *dare* to deny the ethos of the Anglo-Saxon race?"

She lingered to speak of his mother. This showed that Mrs. Gresham, like Matilda, was no slave to fashion. She had her loyalties, however rarely she exercised them—"I haven't laid eyes on Vinnie for years but I've always loved her. I don't care who hears me say it."

"She's very fond of *you*, Boopsie," Francis improvised.

"Really, Boopsie," said her daughter crossly, "is your mind utterly gone? We had a long talk with Mrs. Tanning two days ago, in front of the five-and-ten. She told us Francis was back."

"That will have been Fern," he said. "My mother is Vinnie."

It turned out to have been Harriet. She had driven over from Sag Harbor to have lunch with Enid and buy something for the people she was staying with. Place mats, Mrs. Gresham believed.

Matilda snorted. "You think my friends on Christopher Street have mixed-up lives."

"Darling, I want you and Francis to see each other this winter. Remember what fun you had when you were little!"

Matilda remembered having pushed Francis, fully clothed, into the pool. He remembered having entreated her to do so.

"Call that fun?" said Ginny Drinkwater.

Mrs. Gresham's eyes misted over. "I never had fun till I was fifteen," she sighed.

"Are you going to work for your father, Francis?" a dark girl asked.

"No, I think actually . . ." But they were all gazing at him with pretty interest, and he had no further ideas.

"Now why not, Francis?" demanded Mrs. Gresham. "It would please him so."

"Well, doesn't his own example," said Francis flippantly, "show us that we must first of all please ourselves?"

Did he imagine the exchange of glances provoked by this? "Please ourselves, Boopsie?" the young women appeared to wonder. "We do it constantly, but do we ever *say* so?" And Mrs. Gresham, mistress of herself, flashed wordlessly back, "That is right." Once she had been something of an arbiter in the community; even now her presence did much for the tone of any gathering. Irene was smart to have made a friend of her.

"Isn't it good to see Benjamin looking so well?" said a blue-haired lady with her arm in a sling. "Irene told me he was coming, so I'm carrying the bag he sent me last Christmas. Isn't it swanky, Boopsie? It's from Tiffany's."

"I know," said Mrs. Gresham. "I got one, too. Mine's suede."

The ladies smiled guardedly—were they rivals or accomplices? From far off, Mr. Tanning, his head bent, a handkerchief to his mouth, had the air of a Parsifal caught by the scent and twitter of aging doxies. As Francis himself was.

"Tell me," whispered the newcomer, "is *that* the Englishwoman, talking to Charlie Cheek?"

"Lady Good?" Mrs. Gresham gave an apologetic laugh for Francis's benefit. "I can't say I've really met her. . . ."

"You could say you haven't," Matilda put in.

"True, darling. But," her mother suavely pursued, "Irene's been singing her praises—"

"Has she really? Why, I thought——"

"*Singing* her praises, Nell." Then, while the blue-haired lady's face slowly emptied itself of malice: "You like her very much, too, don't you, Francis?"

"Oh, this is Francis!" drawled the other, understanding her mistake. "I'd never have known you! How naughty of Boopsie!" She revealed herself as the Mrs. Sturdevant who had run off with her brother-in-law and never been asked anywhere till after his death, when Mrs. Gresham, deciding that she had suffered long enough, championed her at a quiet dinner.

It was that kind of party. Irene had summoned all her allies. You felt even Mr. Bishop had been used, to procure Benji's attendance at the spectacle of her popularity.

An extra man of many summers' standing was admiring her jeweled tennis racket. "You never seen that?" she laughed, tossing her hair. "Why, it's from my favorite fella! Charlie Cheek gave it to me on our tenth anniversary." Though Francis didn't doubt her word—the thing was too ugly to be a gift from anyone but her husband—an unlucky falseness in her tone caused some to glance, involuntarily, at Mr. Tanning.

Francis gritted his teeth. "Irene," he said, "*Did* you leave Daddy's bridge winnings in the ocean room? Because they weren't there when he looked, and one hates to accuse a servant——"

"Oh dear!" she cried with a look of loathing. "I understood I was to keep the money! How embarrassing! I'll speak to him now!"

He had gone too far. "There's no hurry, is there?" Smiling casually, Francis tried to lead her out of earshot. "The poor man forgets so much. He just didn't remember—though *I* do, of course—that part of it. It was all so vague, perhaps he *would* remember now."

"Well," she glared, "it's something we ought to clear up, Francis, don't you agree?" Irene was really forcing his hand. He saw her ready to carry her grievance to Mr. Tanning, and get for herself some public commitment from the old man.

"By all means. I know as well as you," his confidential manner deepened, "how trivial the issue is"—a loud burst of laughter from her husband prevented Irene's taking exception to this—"but so *many* little details strike me as wrong at the Cottage. One gets a sense of things going to seed. Is it the servants? Mysterious accidents happen. Take that business of Enid's portrait." His eyes sociably met her own, but she brazened it out. Cousin Irene wasn't to be trapped that easily. His hope now lay, Francis divined, in making her see him no longer as an enemy by letting her see him, more vividly yet, as a fool. "I've already noticed," he went on, "how disgraceful the food is! Haven't you? Why, the meal last night . . ."

He realized gratefully that he could speak the truth. The food *was* bad. Cooked for false teeth, served without wine, of an almost studied pallor (jellied broth, fish in a bland sauce, boiled potatoes, big yellowish beans), and cooled by its journey up from the kitchen in the basement, their dinner had had a quality of disinvolvement, like dishes served on the stage. An illusion of food. At the end had come a custard, pale, frightened, a virtual Mélisande of a custard, proving to Francis that Mrs. McBride must have planned the meal. Or worse, that nobody had planned it, that it represented some languid daydream of Loretta's, fat and black, over her sunless ovens. It wasn't a meal, he told Irene, that Fern would have let pass. But Mr. Tanning had eaten it; no food tasted right to him, he said.

". . . and not only the food, Irene," Francis was warming to his subject, "but you know perfectly well it's the kind of house that *must* be kept up. Last night I didn't notice, but in daylight"—this also was true—"I saw cobwebs! The piano keys are filthy! The next we know there'll be chewing-gum on the underside of tables! Now that Fern's gone," he bravely drained his glass, "well, more than anything, he needs a woman in the house! I'm serious!"

That did it. "*A* woman!" Irene stared at him as if he were mad. "Excuse me," she said mechanically, "I must get back to my guests."

They had wandered into a neighboring room which by now was

beginning to receive some of the overflow. Francis made his way back through the crowd. "I deserve another drink," he said under his breath.

What tickled him first was to have put these things to Irene, beside whose house the Cottage fairly glistened. Everywhere at the Cheeks' were signs of squalor and neglect. Francis had noticed, even during the early stages of the party, filled ashtrays, fallen petals, surfaces streaked with dust. His impression now, after a second drink, was of some allegorical dwelling of Sloth. Irene must have reasoned that only the first ten or twelve guests would blame her for the filth; whoever got there after would hold those early arrivals responsible.

But the need for a woman at the Cottage—*that* had been the delicious touch! All by himself Francis began to laugh. And when Lady Good put her hand, still gloved, upon his arm, he led her into a corner and made much of the whole conversation. "I mean," he finished, "what we now see at the Cottage is the result of a relatively short spell of celibacy. Unless, of course, it's to be felt as the first trace of Irene's influence— *'She comes, she comes! the sable Throne behold Of Night primeval and of Chaos old!'* Just think what the years will bring?" He treated her to a comic vision of Mr. Tanning left to the mercy of servants well-intentioned but forgetful, every month or so, of yet another minor chore, until a time when the sight of mop or dustcloth should arouse in them, like an object in a dream, only some puzzled inkling of its original purpose.

"When you come to Jamaica," Lady Good said mildly, handing him her empty sherry glass, "you will see—put that down somewhere, will you, dear?—that we live in quite a shabby old house, Ned and I."

Francis turned red. "At least now you know," he flung out a hand, "what becomes of me among these people! I take their tone, I'm not myself! As if I cared about cleanliness, or houses, or who sleeps with whom!"

"Don't you, Francis?" asked Lady Good, interested.

"No I don't!" he retorted. "It bores me. In Rome I lived for a year in a big bare cheap room with no heat, and I loved it. I had mice, what's more." He could have gone on arrogantly to admit that he hadn't, either, slept with anybody while in Rome—but here he checked himself. He didn't want to appear *too* eccentric in Lady Good's eyes.

"Ah Francis," she breathed, "you're very young. The way one lives, externally, doesn't matter . . ."

His eyebrows went up; had he said otherwise?

". . . though, to be sure, in Benjamin's circle—oh *why*," she broke off, "am I at this silly party? Benjamin's talking business, he has *no* need of me! Neither do you, so run away, leave me! Talk to that pretty red-haired girl."

It was as though she had been chilled by the thing Francis hadn't said, a moment before. She gazed wearily over the crush. The sun, fallen behind trees, no longer did its best for colors and shapes; these blurred into something like the dusk of sensibility itself.

Just then, however, she brightened. "I meant to say, I had such a jolly talk with Charlie Cheek! I'd never credited the man with that much charm. Look at him now, will you—laughing, chattering away!"

"Perhaps *we* must start drinking ginger-ale."

Lady Good considered his empty glass. "*I* think that Charlie Cheek is grateful to me," she said a bit smugly, "for taking up Benjamin's time. I've sent Irene back to her own hearth."

"Except that for that to be the case," smiled Francis, "Charlie'd have to be fond of Irene. Is he? Now, I can see him fond of *you* and grateful to *her* for not standing in his way." In Francis's mind this kind of perception, facile but forced, often passed for a subtle view of things. It didn't impress his companion.

"Don't talk nonsense." She raised her voice above the incessant din. "Unless I'm greatly mistaken Charlie worships Irene. Why shouldn't he? She's most attractive."

"You see," he cried, shaking his head, "already they've corrupted you! Must you call her 'attractive'?"

"Well, she's far more so than I, to a certain type of man." Missing his point, Lady Good grew more and more distant. "It's true *I* don't see her beauty, but then I expect I'm not a certain type of man. . . ." She trailed off inaudibly before getting a grip on herself. "As for a woman at the Cottage," she then declared, "it seems to me, Francis, that the Cottage *crawls* with women. Besides, there are a dozen right in this room who'd do anything to keep house for him. I met a Mrs. Sturdevant—"

"Precisely! Something between a vampire and a meringue—"

"I thought her rather pathetic and sweet—"

"—the last kind of person he wants! Believe me, Prudence—may I call you Prudence?—he needs a woman—"

"Goodbye, Francis," said Ginny Drinkwater as she edged past them. "Divine seeing you. Call me."

"—with some reality, some nature of her own!"

Lady Good grew cheerful. "Well, what about Natalie? I asked Benjamin the other day why he didn't marry her. Natalie'd be ideal for him."

"What did he say to it?"

"I can't remember now," said Lady Good, and turned pink.

Francis stated his objections to Natalie. The main one was that Mr. Tanning didn't want her. Oh, she was amazing; art had kept no less inviting what time had rendered no more satisfying. But their friendship dated from too long ago; he had had with it, presumably, a too close knowledge of her pretty face and her pretty ways. Natalie would always have *that* advantage over Irene and Nell and Boopsie and the rest. Benjamin had loved her at a time when they were both strong, lively, able to enjoy completely. Some such intelligence lay behind the twinkling with which their eyes met twenty years later. Nothing conceivable was left them to ask of one another.

Lady Good nodded. "Well, *I'm* not available for the job, if that's in your mind."

"What job? Really, Francis," Irene, vexed afresh, interrupted them, "I invite that charming gal just for you, and you haven't a word to say to her! Don't look around for her now, she's left!"

Ginny? Had she? His bewilderment was sincere. And on his account?

"Don't be silly," laughed Irene, "I'm just teasing you." Whereupon she slipped across the room, lit a lamp above Mr. Tanning, and effaced herself.

"I wonder if Benjamin's ready to go," said Lady Good.

Hard to believe, Mr. Tanning had been sitting in one place for two hours, talking. Whenever Francis looked he had seen the old man's head bent, all earnest concentration, towards his associate. There was no limit to the pains he would take where business was the issue. Even at a party, thought Francis impatiently, forgetting that his father, whose health varied from day to day now, had no choice but to seize opportunities as they arose. Also, Mr. Bishop was returning, Monday, to Alberta.

In comparative seclusion they sat, nodding, frowning. Mr. Bishop made notes. Technology, Management, Capital Expenditures, Venezuelan Interests, the Consumer—these were a few of the topics that filtered past a silken but purposeful cordon of adventuresses to lose themselves in the general hubbub. You didn't need to watch very long to question whether they were being protected, the two men, or frankly imprisoned. With what casual sign from Boopsie or Nell, Cissy or Thelma, bound for the peanuts or the powder room, did Irene each time appear, ready to stand guard and smiling the very smile of Management itself? She knew better than to interrupt her captive; it was enough to take credit for the privacy he enjoyed. "See," she and her cohorts conveyed, "see how we care for our splendid sick old lion! Without us he'd be at the mercy of you others!"—thus accounting for the presence of about thirty people, nonentities whose names you intuitively failed to catch on first hearing. They had been invited, some still naïvely thought, in order to meet Mr. Tanning? No. In order to experience directly the clear-eyed scorn with which Irene kept them from that. She didn't mind being called rude if it would make the right people call her discriminating.

Nor did Mr. Tanning appear to mind. He was like a Moses who, white-haired and wise, had nonetheless never shaken off some early magic, half memory, half myth, of women glimmering down upon the gently rocking raft of reeds; and whose happiest moments, all his life long, were those in which he relived a part of that bliss. "Ah yes," Francis repeated under his breath, "he needs a woman in the house. But not you, or you, or you . . ."

Who then? Wasn't it one of the poor man's—that is, the rich man's—peculiar troubles, the unlikeliness of his meeting agreeable strangers? How many years had Mr. Tanning *not* frequented those places where, often enough, friendships begin?—in galleries, at concerts, alone at neighboring tables in modest restaurants such as the one in Rome where Jane and—

Xenia!

Xenia as his father's chatelaine! What it would do for both of them!

Francis wouldn't risk taking even Lady Good into his confidence. He poured a drink and lit a cigarette. He frowned in mock disapproval of Matilda Gresham, who, sprawled underfoot, was still fighting the battle of *Hernani*—"It speaks to our time!" He did his honest best to hesitate, to reflect, but the vision was too demanding. Before long he had settled himself, with a bright blank smile, on a little stool at Mr. Tanning's knee.

"Orson, this is one of your stockholders," his father said.

Bishop Bishop was cordial, but cold sober.

"I haven't wanted to interrupt," began Francis.

"Go right ahead, young man. I'd say that Mr. Tanning and I have got through just about all—"

"I merely thought the time had come," Francis told his father, "to describe what I found for you in Europe."

"Now this sounds interesting," said Mr. Biship civilly.

"It is!" Francis rewarded him with a look. "The trouble, of course, is that he's the most hopeless person to give presents to. He has everything! Or *will* have," he counted it out on his fingers, "ten days or so from now."

"I see. You didn't bring the—ah—gift with you?"

"No. But she sails from Naples, the day after tomorrow, for New York."

"God damn," Mr. Tanning laughed, shaking his head, "you young rascal!"

From then on Francis had only to paint Xenia as a woman of the world, charming, handsome, who happened also to be a gifted artist. *Was she gifted?* It didn't matter, he stressed the point anyhow; it was ostensibly in the role of sculptor that he meant to bring her on the scene. All *she* had to do was accept his commission for a head of his father. The rest would follow naturally.

"God damn," Mr. Tanning kept chuckling. It seemed to appeal from all points of view, not least that of the brazen image itself, moving through posterity with perhaps something sly and humorous about the mouth, as if an attractive woman were still being looked at, coming and going in a room filled with the noise of the sea.

"How about it?" Francis wound up. "I could send a cable to the ship, then meet her in New York. There'd surely be room for her in the guest cottage, with me."

"Ah, *now* we understand!" grinned Mr. Tanning with a nudge and a wink that Mr. Bishop let pass.

"That's not at all the point!" exclaimed Francis, flustered. Irene drew near; evidently the business talk was over. "I'd just been saying to Irene," he appealed to her, "that you needed a woman in the house!"

"What's all this about?" she asked.

Mr. Tanning had started to laugh afresh.

Irene turned lightly to Mr. Bishop. "What's the joke, Orson?"

"Yes, what's amusing Benjamin so?" inquired Mrs. Sturdevant. "Did you catch it, Boopsie?"

Francis said it was just a family joke.

"Well, while we're at it," Irene began, deciding that it had been at her expense, "let's clear up this matter of my bridge debt. Didn't I understand you, Benji," she raised her voice to make sure the others heard, "to have called it off, yesterday after your nap?" A meaning, not implicit in her words, shimmered upon them like a film of oil.

Mr. Tanning wiped his eyes. "I don't remember, Irene. If you say so—"

"Well, fine! It's just Francis," she added musically, "who thought you were upset over the twenty-two dollars."

"To tell the God's truth, Irene," said Mr. Tanning, "I don't remember and I don't give a damn. Maybe I was upset. I'm not now. You're perfectly welcome to the twenty-two dollars."

"Thanks, Benji, but listen, I wouldn't accept it," their hostess chattered on, "if it weren't for the old business of those yard men of ours, down in Jamaica. I paid their wages the four days they helped put your garden in shape. After that freak storm, remember? We never settled that."

"You never spoke of it before this minute."

"Oh I did, Benji! You just don't remember."

"I happen to remember very well," said Mr. Tanning in a muffled voice. "I took it as a generous gesture on your part—"

"Well, we're quits now. It was about that time," Irene told the others, "my favorite fella came down with jaundice. I had to cart him back to the States, to nurse him."

"Oh dear," Mr. Tanning sighed. He rose laboriously out of a swamp of chintz.

Francis, who blamed himself for the whole scene, exhaled.

Lady Good had said that morning, "It's idiotic of Irene to be so possessive. Benjamin can't stand it when she tries to claim him. She's ruining her chances—doesn't she see that she is?" Shrewd and just as these observations were, Francis had a further sense, watching his father shuffle to the door, of the queerest failure of spontaneity. Irene, of course, had already vented her first annoyance; what Mr. Tanning encountered was its pale reconstruction. How much I'm able to spare him, thought Francis, pleased. The queerness, though, lay more in the old man's indifference. He seemed not to care what was said; the ground, his tone implied, had been covered many times. It was the simple pretense of intimacy that mattered.

Francis could see easily why it mattered to Irene. Scorned as she was for being poor, so long as people supposed she could wrap Cousin Benji round her little finger, her credit, socially speaking—economically too, no doubt—was established. (You didn't have to reckon with the decreasing minority that would have known Mrs. Cheek under no circumstances whatever, not even if she had revealed herself editor of the *Social Register*.) Yet Francis was convinced that Irene meant nothing to his father. Why then did he lend himself to her plot, tolerate her scenes to the point of taking public part in them? "Why does he put up with her?" The question was to be echoed the following morning by Lady Good. "How should I know, Francis dear? I expect he's left so guilty each time he gets angry with her that, for his own peace of mind, he has to make amends. Besides, he has no resistance."

It was possible, after all, that Irene would have her way.

But Francis plumped for Xenia. "How about it?" he asked again, walking his father down the little path towards the car. Lady Good and Natalie had gone ahead, vague in the dusk, while from the porch, unnoticed, Irene and her cronies waved and called. "How about Xenia?"

Mr. Tanning laughed and took his son's arm. "I think it's a fine idea," he said gruffly. "Bring her on!" At that moment he was feeling particularly well.

Somebody else was feeling even better.

With a bellowing cry of "So long, Ben! So long, Lady Good!"—at which they turned round obediently—Charlie Cheek lunged out of the house, a beagle underfoot, and went toppling down four ramshackle steps to lie at last in the overgrown path, flat on his face and dead drunk.

7.

Twelve days later, a Thursday, Francis took the early train to New York. In the noon heat he made his way on foot from the station to the river. He had assumed that Xenia's ship, being Italian, wouldn't dock on time—with the result that, strolling onto the cavernous pier and (thanks to a card secured in advance by his father's office) past a fenced-in crowd of welcomers, he found the inspection of baggage already under way. He caught sight of Xenia at once. Flanked by two friends, she stood clucking over boxes and suitcases. Her voice reached him from far off: "You'll find only lotions in that one!"—with eyes raised to heaven when the inspector decided to see for himself. She was brown and buoyant and bursting out of a pink beach dress. According to the cable Francis had had in answer to his own, he'd saved Xenia's life, and, "You have saved my life!" she promptly cried on seeing him, then threw her arms about him where he stood grinning like a fool. Up and down the stifling customs shed her same gesture was being resorted to, but with no such bravura.

Xenia then turned to her friends. "This is Francis, who has saved my life, as I just finished telling you." She put an adoring hand on his shoulder. "I was coming back with *no* prospects, *no* place to stay, *no* money in the bank. Those Durdees, insufferable pair! canceled their order for the big abstract torso. I had to telephone three times to Paris. I'm not used to being treated that way. I'm an artist, not a *fournisseur de tapis*. It was the wife of course—she hated me from the first minute we met. *Une femme jalouse et tout à fait* neurotic. So you can imagine how blue I was feeling that first day out, before your cable came. *Then* I bought champagne for everybody at my table. I tell you, it was a Godsend!"

Even the customs inspector looked impressed. Xenia's two friends peered at Francis as at some studded dish, which might be used for cigarettes, in a pinch. One was a woman, Adrienne de Something, plump, orange-haired, talking with Xenia alternately in Russian and French. At her side, apparently belonging to her, towered a good-looking inarticulate young man from Milwaukee, a composer of genius. "Just you wait," Xenia told Francis, "Tommy's opera is getting produced in the spring. We'll have a box for the *première*." Adrienne, she whispered a moment later, turning aside to unlock another suitcase, had once been the mistress of R——, the celebrated impresario.

They were giving Xenia a party the following evening, to which it went without saying Francis was invited—"but from Saturday morning, or whenever you were planning to take me to your father, I'm at your disposal. My baggage stays at Adrienne's—you'll tell me what clothes to pack. Oh," elated, she patted his cheek, "how I was going to scold you for running off, leaving Jane and me to console ourselves ten days *en pleine mer!* But if *this* is what you've accomplished for me—!"

Francis had almost forgotten Jane. Had they made out well together?

"Ah, she's sweet, poor thing . . ." Xenia crooned, disturbingly, before going on to explain. Jane had written her fiancé a letter from Rome. She hoped he would want to get married right away, set up housekeeping wherever it was—in Boston, yes—and live happily ever after. She even had the ship's doctor give her a blood-test.

"Why such haste?" wondered Francis.

"Between ourselves, it was a pure case of pique."

"Over what?"

"Over you!—But listen!" Nothing, continued Xenia, stood in the way of the poor thing's bliss, except a stretch of brilliant ocean and—her receiving no further word from Roger. Every day Jane looked for a cable, "growing," as Xenia put it, "more insecure by leaps and bounds. 'Have I scared him off?' she kept saying. Can you imagine? Any man who treated *me* that way—! No," she addressed the inspector, "*I'll* unwrap that."

Francis could have wept. He wanted to see Jane.

Xenia understood. She gave him Adrienne's address—"Bring Jane if you like, tomorrow night"—kissed him once more, then waved him off into the swarming distance.

Leaving her, Francis realized that he had counted on spiriting Xenia back to the Cottage that very afternoon. Now he would have to call his mother. And buy a summer suit, a shirt, a toothbrush. And stay in a hotel. Luckily he had pocketed his straight razor at the last moment, just in case.

"She can't have meant that Jane was seriously in love with me," Francis muttered once, to hear how it sounded, while keeping a sharp eye out. He tried not to recall or understand her silences, that final hour in Rome. The thought of Jane's really getting married, after so much talk, changed her for him; all at once she was grown-up, dependable, poised—qualities that till then he'd never have looked for in her. Roger's defection, on the other hand, helped Francis imagine a tear-stained Jane, a Jane at loose ends, turning perhaps to *him* for support. Either way, it wouldn't be his love she principally needed. His face wore the glazed smile of a child as he strained to see her.

It happened that Jane saw him first, and called. His heart quickened. She *did* look like a poor thing, drooping tanned and tense beneath the huge initial W which stood—whoever let her head rest briefly against his shoulder could believe it—for Waiting and Wondering and Woman's Woes. Nobody'd met her. Roger hadn't cabled. A suitcase was still missing. On lighting a cigarette (here Jane fell into a kind of laughter) she had been reprimanded—*was* this America?—by a person in uniform. What had she done with her life? Oh Francis! Could he guess how much it meant, that he should have come to meet her?

"I know you came to meet Xenia," she said in a more sensible tone, "but just let me pretend a little while longer." He squeezed her hand. Jane had a real talent for gratitude; she'd never made him ashamed of not having given more.

"Nonsense. Xenia's got other friends here. I've already said goodbye to her. She wants us at a party tomorrow night, unless—Oh, isn't it," Francis broke in on himself, "a relief to be back where one's *wanted!* One knows absolutely where one stands!"

"I don't know." Jane sank wearily onto a suitcase. "Do you like my new shoes?"

"Very much," he said to cheer her, although they were of red lizard.

She fixed him with big eyes. She *was* at loose ends. "Should I think about trains to Council Bluffs? No, I don't want to go home. I can't afford it anyhow. Thank God," she kept on in her funny flat voice, "I never wrote the family I was getting married."

"Is Roger in Boston?"

"Don't ask me. I haven't heard from him all month. Not since that postcard."

"In which he said he'd be meeting you."

"I know." Jane looked away. She wasn't going to tell Francis about the letter she'd written meanwhile.

"Perhaps Roger and your parents are planning a surprise wedding in Council Bluffs," he offered after a solemn pause.

"Ah me," she broke into giggles, "I do love you."

"I love you too." They felt at home in the lightness of it. Soon he was asking her again, "Isn't it a relief, seriously, to be back where you belong?" But again she hesitated, as if without Roger she hadn't much to belong *to*. Francis pursed his lips; he would tell her, later on, what he thought of Roger. He'd never liked irresponsible people. Picturing Roger at the age of fourteen, he saw him as a bully and a cheat with a heavy sneering look that wouldn't yet have left his face. Francis quite understood why Jane carried no photograph of Roger, just as he would never understand why she was engaged to him. Probably there was some perverse physical attraction—in which case, however, she *would* have carried a photograph. More likely, she had seen in Roger her only chance.

Along with his resentment of a perfect stranger Francis experienced a growing compassion for Jane. *"Elle l'a voulu,"* he tried to think, but it made no difference. Deserted, unwanted, wondering (while bravely painting her lips) what was to become of her, she showed at her very best—bereft but trustworthy. Francis admired women who didn't weep and men who openly, like his father, did. Six months ago, perhaps, Jane *would* have wept. She was changing now, as if learning the rules of an intricate game.

They played it by asking each other a hundred questions. He told her, in part, the story behind his little Greek ring, which she had pounced on and called a treasure. She described Xenia's adventures during the crossing—one unbroken adventure, rather, of drowsing all day on deck and carousing all night on the first-class dance floor. Jane still didn't really like Xenia, but supposed Mr. Tanning would. Oh, and Mrs. Cheek, how was she? Francis sketched in the developments, watching her grow more lively by the minute. "I really don't care any more," she said—it struck him as her most expert move thus far—"if Roger comes or not. You don't believe me? All right, just wait—look what I have!" She plunged her hand into a crammed purse and brought out a flask half full of something colorless. "You may think it's holy water," Jane told him, "but taste it!" It was *grappa*. Without further ado they polished it off.

"Why marry Roger?" said Francis. "Why not marry *me?*"

"You're not an art historian. We take vows not to marry outside the Field. Now where," Jane turned from his amusement, "could that suitcase be?"

"At least," Francis pursued, "we can spend today together. You have nowhere to go immediately, have you?" He went on in great good humor. There were sights in the city that he *had* to show her—churches, ruins, the vast rectangular voids of sunlight and noise and dust which marked wherever you looked the disappearence of yet another landmark fifty years old. Why, he proposed gaily, he'd even take her to see his mother; she was *over* fifty and still standing, sound as a bell.

Jane bit her lip. "I have no friends in New York, no place to stay."

"Neither do I." This was true. Vinnie certainly had no room; he wouldn't have stayed there if she had. And the three or four friends who did have couches—friends to whom Francis had announced his return by casual postcards from the Cottage—presented other problems. They had written him, during the past year, a kind of letter he hadn't known how to answer. He was half in earnest when he blamed them for it—for lectures on laziness and not facing things. "So I'll go to a hotel," he shrugged, having pretended to Jane that he had already called his friends and failed to catch them at home.

"It's only Thursday," she said. "Wouldn't they be at work?"

"At what?"

"Don't they have jobs?" Jane wondered. "All *my* friends do."

Francis looked uneasily away. "Well, most of mine don't. And not," he added, wishing to be scrupulous, "because they're in my position. No, they paint, or write. . . . They live in lofts. . . ."

"Oh," said Jane, who had planned, with or without Roger, to have found at least a part-time job by mid-August. "And are you very fond of them?"

"No, I can't say that I am." Upon which they stared with interest at one another. Things began to happen. Sprightly music sounded in the distance. Jane's missing suitcase was delivered. The sticker had come unstuck, an old man in overalls explained; he had had to read the writing on the tag. They thanked him. Jane ran off and returned with a customs inspector, who cast hardly a glance at her luggage. She was free to go. Francis whistled for a porter. "But really, though," he resumed, "can't we please spend this lovely day together? We'll get rooms in a hotel. It'll be like Italy. We'll go out and look around. I must buy clothes and a toothbrush. Would that amuse you? Are you listening?"

"I'm listening," said Jane, gazing backwards. They had started to follow their porter the length of the dim resounding pier.

"It's so strange, so good to see you. I feel—"

"No, Francis!" she broke in sharply; he saw a face no longer familiar—"this isn't Rome, let's not pretend! Here you have people who put claims on you. I want to say that you don't need to be nice to me. Our friendship is too important, it mustn't become a burden to you."

"Burden?" Francis smiled in amazement. She seemed to be struggling so, just when *he* had never felt more confident. "You're wrong." He stopped in his tracks, discovering the truth as he spoke it. "I feel I can talk to you, I feel really at ease. I think I'm tired of grown-ups. I've been with them so much, I understand them so little. I seem to have to protect them from one another. Don't ask me why. Anyhow, a day like this comes as a blessing."

Jane blinked and blushed and brightened. She took his arm and, whispering, "Thank you," put herself gently in his care. The oddest part of their walking, then, down the long pier *into* their day, kept on being the way Francis, who felt as never before that he didn't know where he was, that he had no point of reference, felt also as never before a calm, a sureness about—well, about whatever he might be up to. It was as if Innocence and Experience had each, slyly, sweetly, put on the other's clothes. By sundown he would have fallen in love with Jane, just like that.

But she gave a cry, there on the very threshold of the city.

Roger. She had seen, among the faces behind the barrier, Roger. "Oh Francis," she gasped, "tell me what to do!"

"Are you crazy?" he laughed. "Your problems are solved! Now don't feel that *you* need to be nice to *me!*" He was pleased to have thought of echoing her own words. It made the game end in something closer to a draw.

Jane faced him, but for no more than an instant before rushing onward into her young man's arms. Taking his time over joining them, Francis observed with a certain amusement that Roger Massey had a pleasant intelligent face, neither brutal nor stupid. Jane was sure to be very happy with him.

She had done well to have her blood-test on the ship. For now they could be married the next day, at City Hall. Roger, it emerged, had formed a plan to fit any set of circumstances.

They would leave immediately after the ceremony, for Cambridge, where he had a lead on an apartment. Time was short. He had this job teaching summer school near Hartford—a friend was taking his classes today and tomorrow. No, there wasn't room for Jane at the school, but weekends were better than nothing, and think how rich they'd be by September! He kissed her happily on the brow. To Francis he was extremely cordial. "You'll be our witness tomorrow, I hope?" Francis said he would be delighted. There was no evidence, and indeed no feeling, of rivalry on either side.

Jane could not stop crying. Francis understood the shock of it for her; however, in respect to the tears that streamed down her pink cheeks, whether they were of joy or of some private dismay, he refused for the time being to consider. Nor did he ask himself what might have happened if Roger hadn't shown up. After all, it was on Roger's shoulder that she wept, while Francis, hailing a taxi, tipping the porter, lapsed with relief into common helpfulness.

8. From his hotel that afternoon, exhausted by shopping, Francis telephoned Larry Buchanan. They made an appointment for the next day, down at the office. He wanted to discuss an idea that had begun to tantalize him, one to which the formal setting of walnut and leather, fifty floors above the street, would be wholly appropriate.

He then called his mother and accepted her invitation to share a "pickup" supper. When, in the course of this, Francis outlined the day ahead of him, Mrs. Tanning guessed he'd already heard the splendid news about Larry.

"I don't think so. What news?"

"How do you expect to keep up with things," she sighed, "if you won't read the paper?" Not asking whether he wanted it, she transferred her untasted sandwich to Francis's plate, plugged in the electric coffeepot, and read the article aloud.

It announced that Tanning, Burr, "the largest and most progressive, if not the only firm of its kind in the world," would henceforth be known as Tanning, Burr and Buchanan, in recognition of Larry's accomplishments. Simultaneously, two more offices were being opened, one in Oregon, one in Rangoon. "All that expansion is Larry's doing," Vinnie added approvingly.

"I know," said Francis. "I take it as the worst possible sign. Everything nowadays is doomed to depersonalization. The bigger you get, the more inevitable it is."

"You've never been fond of Larry."

"That's not fair. I like Larry very much as a person. I can't get excited over what he stands for."

By "Larry as a person" Francis meant the following anecdote.

Larry had spent the last eight months of the war in a small Japanese prison camp in China. As senior officer among the prisoners, he felt responsible for the morale of perhaps a thousand men. They put up with the predictable amount of bad food, cruelty, cold, illness, death; but as the spring advanced, their rations, far from improving, shrank to a diet of spoiled rice or maggots in weak broth. More men were dying than ever during the winter. Once a month a General inspected the camp. On one occasion, as the General was passing within earshot, a certain professor of Oriental languages, the fellow-prisoner closest to Larry's age, had called out a petition for food and medical care. By way of answer the man spent two days with no nourishment at all. Afterwards, talking to Larry, he recalled from his studies a more drastic way of presenting a petition. It was a custom centuries old; he couldn't vouch for its success now. But before the General's next visit Larry had memorized the simplest words for hunger and sickness.

It happened in a clearing on a hillside, where the General had come upon a group of them gathering and chopping kindling. Four guards accompanied him, a delicate pear-shaped man past middle age. The pale sun yellowed his face and uniform. "We are hungry! We are sick!" cried Larry in Japanese. The General spoke to a guard, who started up the slope. Larry ran for an ax, so small as to be useless for anything else, and placing his hand on a stump deftly chopped off the tip of his little finger. Blood spurted onto his quilted sleeve. Crying the words again, he ran a few steps forward. Then he flung what he had amputated into the General's face. The General stared, burst into tears, and embraced Larry like a brother. From that time till the end of the war the prisoners lived comparatively well.

Whenever Francis remembered his brother-in-law's hand he felt a shudder of admiration for this strange poetic gesture.

"What Larry stood for" was a different matter.

One of Benjamin Tanning's staunchest beliefs, as well as the basis for the firm's most successful advertising campaigns, was in the need to do business with the man in the street, the small investor, the small independent manufacturer, Mr. and Mrs. Potential American (or South American or Indonesian) Purchaser of anything from an aspirin to a shipload of anthracite. Every day hundreds of thousands learned from newspapers all over the globe that, however modest their means or projects, they would find courteous prompt attention at any of Tanning, Burr's ninety-nine world-wide offices.

Well, now there were a hundred and one. Francis shook his head sadly, ironically. He acknowledged, under pressure from his mother, that the firm would have expanded with or without Larry Buchanan. Try and stop it! Banking, chemicals, shipping, underwriting—what didn't it do? What didn't it *over*do? The whole trend was towards the disproportionate, the inhuman, the unreal. No firm founded in 1912 with a capital of six thousand dollars—

"*Eight* thousand." Mrs. Tanning respected facts.

—and presently taking in six hundred million a year—

"That's *gross* you're talking about now." She had often viewed with apprehension Francis's grasp of these matters. He could remember figures, now and then, but never their significance.

No firm, he had had to raise his voice, with a hundred and one offices and seventy-two living partners could expect its entire personnel to abide by principles set down, years and years ago, for an organization totally different in scope and influence. "Do you think the Constitution has anything to do with America's government today?" he threw out cynically, having once heard the phrase on Xenia's lips. The firm was in the same position. Francis saw what his father meant by saying it burned him up to be treated like an old poop. Not Larry, if Vinnie cared, but a score of "aggressive younger men" toadied and picked up the check, patted his back, and, once it was turned, consulted their own ambitions. The Boy Scout virtues would still be inscribed on the escutcheon of Mr. Tanning's firm; nevertheless, for some of the second generation, these had become meaningless luxuries.

Many a meaningful one, the next morning, confronted Francis as he stepped out of the elevator.

There were, as foreseen, walnut and leather; also soft carpets and mammoth free-form glass receptacles for something grander than his own extinguished cigarette. Spread over one wall of the vast foyer, a mural depicted in restful colors an idealized Main Street quite taken up by every chain store that Tanning, Burr had helped to finance. From a wharf at the end of the street two company ships, laden with tractors, belched smoke of an unearthly purity. The mural had been added since Francis's last visit to the office. So had an oil painting of Mr. Tanning, done from a photograph but bearing little resemblance to him. In one corner a World War II Honor Roll rested on an easel. A breezy booklet, entitled *Bread on the Waters* and published by the firm, caught his eye; it was his for the taking.

A note more telling yet was struck, there where the foyer joined the hall, by a parade of men and women connected with the firm. Back and forth they went, young people in shirtsleeves, in summer dresses and ballet slippers, tanned executives, one or two youthful old ladies with haircuts, a single sheet of paper in hand. This, to be sure, was the Partners' Floor, a glassy maze of air-cooled suites and breathtaking harbor views.

Here conferences were held, statements issued to the press, clients large and small made welcome by two attractive hostesses in uniform. Few needed or cared to travel, by private elevator, the forty-odd stories down to what Mr. Tanning humorously called the Sweatshop. It covered three whole floors: mail room, cable room, printing press, first-aid station, a mile of metal brains keeping track of not merely their own operators but also workers in neighboring cells—the sales-by-telephone team, insurance or tax experts, research men, advertising men *and* their secretaries, all no doubt stooping and wan, ill-nourished, temperamental. Somebody had to be, Francis argued; for the denizens of the Partners' Floor were nothing of the sort. Each might have been picked for that look of healthy good nature, of clear-eyed dedication likely to be seen on faces in Utopia.

They made Francis glad he'd come. It was time some meek stand be taken against the system. With over an hour before meeting Jane and Roger at City Hall, he gave his name to a dazzled young woman.

At first Larry was all graciousness. He himself ushered Francis into his office. Framed upon the gleaming desk Enid, the children, and Mr. Tanning smiled. The closing of doors set up a rich hush. Francis refused a cigar and naïvely began to speak his mind.

He sensed within three minutes that Larry assumed he had come to ask for a job. The older man nodded encouragingly; sooner or later, he seemed to say, we all discover the wisdom of settling down, toeing the line; and while, frankly, he still had qualms about the Tanning heir, the name counted more, in any long view, than the personality. . . .

Reflections which presently gave way to cold disbelief.

Did Francis *know* what he was talking about?

The young man had managed to explain, with a faint stammer, that he wished to consult Larry in his capacity of trustee of the Tanning children's accounts. He wished to know if it would be possible to get rid of his money.

"What money?" Larry had asked, uncertain, lighting his cigar and glancing at the time.

"My own—what I have. My share of things—"

For some reason Larry remained very patient. Francis, who had half-expected him to lean across the desk and slap his face, took heart. Earlier he had tried to rehearse a few of the points to be made—that it was a considered decision, that none of the family should take it as an affront, but that he simply couldn't bear any longer the burdens of fortune. Now, once Francis had begun to mouth these platitudes, he understood just how false they rang. For a frightful moment he nearly broke down. "I don't know why I'm here," he all but said, "I have no reason for asking what I ask," until, to his own surprise, his way shown perhaps by the pale dawn of irritation in his listener, a crackle of leather or flash of gold at the cuff, Francis found words to convey some part of his feeling: "What I mean is, I don't want the power that goes with money. It's a crippling power; whoever uses it is at the mercy of it. No freedom goes with it. One's forever being watched and plotted against, or else protected from the very things that *don't* do harm! One's never in a position to find out what's real and what isn't—with the result that *nothing*'s real, nothing in the whole world is real!" He was remembering his father at Irene's, hemmed in by calculating women. The poor old man had been rich too long. Wherever he went, something in his appearance would distinguish him, would cause the woman who put her arms about him to do so, in spite of herself, first because of the fineness of his linen, the fragrance of his cologne, the meal they had enjoyed—and only to a lesser degree, if at all, because he was handsome and amusing, or lonely and in need of her. To Francis it seemed a monstrous wrong. Better to form no friendships whatsoever. "I've wanted," he said, "to be free, to really have a chance at life."

Larry cleared his throat. "Well, haven't you? It certainly looked to us at home as if you were doing what you liked. Believe me, many's the time I envied you. I like Europe, too."

"There's another misunderstanding!" cried Francis. "Europe wasn't the point. I was there in order not to be *here!* I hated Europe—it solved nothing. So here I am, back, trying to get at my life in another way. At least," he said with conviction, "I've found what keeps me from solving things."

"Now, come on, Francis," Larry gave a cajoling smile, "where's your sense of humor? Show me one thing you can't solve, and I'll show you three that I can't!"

"Larry, I'm asking you a straight question," said Francis grimly. "We needn't go into my reasons." But without pausing he proceeded to do just that. "What I hate is—I'll say it again—the *power* I have, of walking in and out of situations. When I'm fed up with one place I can travel wherever I please. Instead of enduring and suffering the way other people do, I need only write a check." Once more he thought of his father, the marriages, the loves stepped out of casually, like clothes. "One has to *work* for one's life—" Francis broke off; he'd let himself in for it this time.

Larry reminded him that any job, within reason, he cared to hold down at Tanning, Burr—

"No, no, I was talking metaphorically," Francis brushed it aside. "You should know I'd do anything before working *here*. That is," he floundered, wanting to repair a possible tactlessness, "being the son of—" and then recalling, too late, that Larry himself was a member of the family. "To work *anywhere*, for me, wouldn't be real. I shouldn't need to do it, I'd be inventing a life—don't you see, Larry?"

He looked unconvinced and rather annoyed. "When you say," he began in a metallic voice, "that you hate walking out of situations, what do you think you're trying to do right now? That's what *I'd* call running away from a problem."

It startled Francis. He saw at once the justice of the observation.

"I don't know and I don't want to know," continued Larry, profiting by his silence, "who put this notion in your head, but if you imagine for one moment that you can break the trusts established by your father, and from which your income and Enid's derives, you're greatly mistaken.

Now, if all you want is to have your monthly check stopped, I can arrange that in no time flat." He reached for one of four telephones on his desk.

"No," said Francis, "I meant stopping it at the source."

"Yes. Well, it's legally impossible, the way the trusts are set up. The principal goes to Enid's children and to your own, after your death. I hope that answers your question."

They stared narrowly at one another.

"Thank you." Francis stood up. "It does." He paused, then asked, "Are you taking the train out this afternoon?" turning aside, for his cheeks burned as if he had received a mortal insult. "I'll be going out sometime tomorrow, along with a very charming person, a sculptress. . . ." He felt a hand on his shoulder.

"Sit down," said Larry gently. "Forgive me if I lost my temper."

"It means I'm doomed," Francis kept repeating, "I'm doomed never to be real."

Larry was able to say a great deal, uninterrupted.

He started by praising money, to whose honorable uses there was no end. Did Francis realize that, each year since coming into his fortune, he had drawn the merest fraction of the funds at his disposal? Why, he could do so much for himself, for others! He could build a house, a theater, start a magazine, encourage artists, musicians, scholars; he could collect things, paintings or furniture, subsidize scientific research, feed the hungry, clothe the naked—Benjamin Tanning's children being, year after year, in a virtually unique position to bring comfort and happiness to thousands of people. And at a minimal cost to themselves, thanks to the tax set-up. There was also, Larry went on, letting his cigar go out, one's own family. Francis would understand better, once he married and had children, the joy of making a home, of giving them every possible advantage, the pride he, Larry, would take in showing Lily Europe next year at Easter. He said it all in a husky down-to-earth voice. Had he been using colors for words Larry would have produced a naturalistic portrait of himself smiling over a checkbook, surrounded by family and pets.

"Just think," he urged Francis, "what your father did for you! Education, security—"

It was true, thought Francis miserably, all true.

"—freedom to travel, *power*. Think of the love and pride he felt. The money your father gave you represents years of work and daily decisions made. It's been his life and his genius, Francis." At this point Larry dropped his second unexpected remark of the morning. "If Ben had heard the things you've said to me here and now, I honestly think it would have broken his heart."

Francis sat up and uncovered his eyes. He couldn't tell how far Larry saw, but it was further than he had seen himself. As for Mr. Tanning, his photograph gazed straight at the Statue of Liberty.

Was that why Francis had come?—for he was suddenly beyond constructing a more likely motive—to break the sick old man's heart? Less to strip himself of power than to prove how powerful he could be? He found that he was staring fixedly at Larry's mutilated hand. What did he know of violence, he, Francis? Nothing—yet it was possible, all the same, that he had resorted to it.

Frightened now, he rose. "All right, Larry. Thanks for letting me bother you." He didn't want to be late for the wedding.

"Now listen," Larry said, looking relieved. "Not one boy in ten has your brains and ability. Did I say ten? A hundred would be nearer the truth. Naturally if you were a stupid slob you'd be unfit to manage your own affairs. Nobody's asking you to do that in the first place; that's *my* job. But you're a damned bright guy—I know, I've seen your college record—and I want to say before you go that if you ever have any pet project you want my advice on, I'll be not only delighted but truly flattered to do everything I can."

With which Larry relighted his cigar and guided Francis through the outer office, towards the elevators. He took, Francis felt in a kind of anguish, unnecessary pains to introduce him to every humming young woman or prosperous oldster encountered on their way. All were impressed, wanted to know was Francis going to work for the firm. Some remembered him from long ago and sent regards to his mother; one of these wept. At last he was down on the street. The whole idea had been hopeless, he would know better next time. Next time?

Next time what? he was still asking himself twenty minutes later, while watching, in a sickly pink room full of artificial sunlight and the sound of an unctuous voice, the marriage of Roger (whom he saw as a perfect stranger) to Jane (whom perhaps he knew too well); then wondered, as they kissed, how long it would be before they decided to have a child, and whether the child would grow up to be happy and strong or lonely and sickly, or whether indeed the child would live at all.

9. The party for Xenia took place on upper Fifth Avenue in a penthouse paid for by a wealthy lover of Adrienne's. Only a few days each month did this person spend in town—days on which Tommy Utter would withdraw to a cold-water flat ten miles distant, in the shadow of Brooklyn Bridge. When the lover left, back he moved. He worked at an ancient concert grand from six in the morning until two in the afternoon, the hour his mistress left her bed and began to think about lunch.

"Let's hope the lover never finds out," said Francis.

"But he knows!" cried Xenia. "Of course he knows! Adrienne would never dream of hiding it from the sweet old man. She hasn't told Tommy that he knows, however."

"Why not?"

"Ah, he'd be furious, he wouldn't understand. But Max thinks it's wonderful for her to have a young lover. He says, '*J'en aurais un moi-même, si j'étais pédéraste!*'"

"Is he French?" was all Francis found to say.

"No, he's a Pole."

"Oh dear, everything's so easy for you Europeans!"

"What do you mean?" his companion laughed. But he saw that she knew. Xenia was by far the most striking woman present, as well as being, curiously enough, the youngest. There had been, furthermore, a moment in which Francis, glancing about at the male guests, felt himself positively the *oldest* of these. He wasn't; three or four gentlemen who looked like gigolos and turned out to be Counts—one, even, a Prince—were much in evidence with their powerful tanned profiles and gray curls thick above their ears, kissing hands and refusing drinks. The rest, however, were very young men, as young, that is, as the women who outnumbered them were ripe. You had a sense of several "Judgments of Paris" being simultaneously acted out. Also unlike the women, most of the young men were American, Tommy's friends.

Adrienne's salon, though elegantly proportioned, had the bare unfurnished look of a makeshift dwelling soon to be boarded up. On entering, Francis had admired an Empire mirror shaped like a lyre. "How odd you should pick that out!" his hostess marveled. "I've been keeping it for a dear friend who wishes, I *think*, to part with it."

Red wine flowed. Later, Tommy played gems from his opera.

It made a difference, Tommy's opera. Knowing it was to be produced kept the group around him from being dismissed, too casually, as trivial or corrupt. Whatever he was, the gangling gauche handsome young musician, he wasn't an amateur. Neither, as yet, had he been ruined by his charm. Francis took to him at once. He attributed to Tommy a childlike unconcern for whatever other people did or felt. The idea of wearing, to an evening party, corduroys and a gray unraveling sweater! I could never carry it that far, admitted Francis with a sigh. How long, indeed, could Tommy get away with it? Already in his music Francis thought he detected an ease that hadn't been earned. "France will appreciate that," nodded Xenia at the end of a strangely lifeless passage.

"D'ailleurs, c'est tout ce qu'il y a de plus français!" This gave Francis a clue to Tommy's difficulty.

"He ought to be left alone and allowed to be American," he told her, deliberately sententious.

"Chauvinist!"

They were sitting in a window-seat at the far end of the room, over-looking lights in the Park, sparse and romantic, below.

"What do you mean, 'being American'?" Xenia presently asked.

It had to do, he tried to say, with not taking the easy way out, with not being glib, well mannered, probably depraved—casting about, his eyes met the sinister gaze of a Count. Xenia had begun throatily to laugh.

"I never dreamed you were such a Puritan, Francis—you who have lived there! Oh the neuroses of Americans! Of course there's depravity in Europe, there's depravity all over the world. But," pointedly, "those who are shocked by it are the ones I suspect of being drawn to it."

"I am not shocked by it," Francis declared, blushing, in the tone of a prim old man.

"Besides," resumed Xenia after a pause during which the piano had become very suave indeed, "of what does this 'depravity' consist? The student with his *petite amie?* The *femme de trente ans* with her lover? The whore who goes to Mass? *Voyons!* Everywhere there is discretion and nowhere is there guilt. A woman hates her husband? *Bon!* She kills him with a kitchen-knife and the judge sympathizes. No, it's *here* that sex is really messy. Just look at your American man—brutal, stupid, completely inexperienced; you get him in bed (God forbid!) and all he thinks is to *sfogarsi* as quickly as possible—*e basta!* Well, that's thanks to your famous American mothers. In France, now," she shrugged, "a mother says to one of her intimate friends, 'Look, *ma chère*, Jean-Pierre has turned fifteen, he's getting a bit restless, I was wondering if it interested you to . . .' Nine times out of ten the friend is *enchanted* to be of service and there are no more problems! While *here*—I'm sorry to say it, but I've reached the conclusion that the single exception among American men is the homosexual, who at least knows how to *enjoy* himself in bed. But my God! The effort to get him there!" She gestured widely about the room, her eyelids agleam. "You can see for yourself!"

Although he didn't dare think what she meant, Francis was determined not to bat an eye. He gave Xenia his blandest smile.

"What have I done," she went on, inscrutable, "to deserve such a fate?"

His silence had to be broken. "It seems to me," Francis reminded her, pleased to have thought of something, "that you were complaining of the same thing in Italy."

"Oh, Italians are the worst lovers in the world!"

"But then who does satisfy you?"

"Nobody!" she cried promptly, incorrigibly, and burst again into laughter. "See how easily you've found me out? I have nothing to hide— nobody has *ever* been able to satisfy me!"

These words removed Francis's last trace of nervousness with Xenia. She was extravagant, grotesque, of a reality far beyond the mere plausible surfaces arrived at by others. He felt he could tell her anything.

A shout of delight announced the arrival of Greta Stempel-Ross, the contralto. "Now *there* is a vampire," whispered Xenia before rising to greet her. The singer was a big woman, simple and friendly. Bits of Tommy's opera had been written specially for her. *"Buona sera! Wie geht's?"* she said, and shook hands all around.

Francis's major reservation about Xenia and his father had been the sittings themselves, whether they mightn't exhaust the old man. But she had quickly set his mind at rest: there was no need for a sitter to "sit" in any strict sense; he could walk about, smoke, talk—she needed to see the head in many moods. As for the number of sittings, an hour or so each day for two weeks would bring the head to a point where she could work on it alone. If necessary, a few finishing touches, that fall in New York— Xenia made it sound very easy, very expert. More and more she struck Francis as the perfect companion for his father. "I feel I know exactly how to behave with him," she had said; "I shall be as I am by nature, open and sincere." "And rather soft and womanly," suggested Francis. "Oh that, of course!" she chortled. This much had been agreed on earlier, along with what train to take the next day. Then, from his hotel room late that afternoon, Francis called his father. The old man, his voice mild and dull with distance, said he would be glad to see them. He was glad also that the sittings weren't to be strenuous, because he had passed a whole night of pain. Mrs. McBride had phoned and phoned to get the oxygen tank refilled; it was plain luck that he hadn't choked to death. "I don't understand that," Francis had said, unsure, really, of what he meant. "Neither do I," his father replied. After an intolerable pause, "Well then," said Francis, "we'll—" but breaking off politely because Mr. Tanning was trying to say something, "excuse me? I didn't hear . . ." "Nothing, Sonny, I'll see you tomorrow," and his father hung up, leaving Francis alone in the senseless colorless room. His clothes were strewn here and there. A new French novel lay face-down on a stool next to the tepid bath he had drawn.

It was odd. He liked French novels, and said so to Adrienne when she caught him examining her little shelf of books; he liked anything French except—abruptly laughing, he saw no reason to spare *her* feelings— French people. Ah, but did he then like people at all? she countered fairly enough, her face taking on a lively interest to show that bluntness pleased her. "Besides," Adrienne confessed before long, "I'm not very fond of them myself. I'm three-quarters Russian, you know." One finger with a red jewel swept back an orange lock from her brow. "Now talk to me about yourself."

This made for a most agreeable hour.

Later, trying to rationalize it, he saw to what degree his elation stemmed from the failure that morning, at Larry's office. Such a failure seemed final. Francis had done all he could; henceforth he would have to face his doom philosophically. Fully aware that he *was* doomed—he'd said so first to Larry—it nevertheless kept coming over him while he talked, while Adrienne nodded, replied, beckoned within earshot this one or that, how much he deserved their attention. How natural, suddenly, to talk, since she had asked, about himself—to draw his own conclusions and to take, above all, his own sweet time! He felt he *knew* more than his listeners, more about books and music, more even about Europe. In the heat of a sentence he wondered if he weren't illustrating his earlier point. "Being American" meant, along with what he had told Xenia, having grown up assuming Vincent Youmans to be better than Ravel, but so unquestioningly that to assume the opposite never implied any simple evolution of taste; rather, a stand taken against dark forces. It made a real difference. Just as Mr. Tanning's nearness to death conferred an urgency upon his pettiest anecdotes, so Francis's exhilaration over the stand *he* had taken, regardless of failure, made everything he said sound right. He caught confirmatory glances. He didn't forget that he was doomed; so was his father, so were they all. And he smiled the more broadly for the amusing, the delightful sensation of being doomed and not minding, doomed and, well, truly exuberant, doomed and unable to think why or to what.

After midnight people sat about in a sociable daze while Mme Stempel-Ross sang Serbian folk songs, unaccompanied. Presently Xenia tiptoed to Francis's side and led him back to their window seat.

"I can't begin to tell you what a success you've made!" she hissed, flushed with some success of her own. "Adrienne has fallen in love with you, literally. I've been watching, so has Tommy. He's madly jealous."

"You're exaggerating!" protested Francis. He had never learned how to receive compliments.

"Only the tiniest bit!"

"Then all I can say is that it's perfect nonsense." He felt duty-bound to appear safe and dependable, a guest who will not violate the rules of hospitality. It was often as though he disliked being liked—which, however, wasn't the case.

"Ah, you're too modest! Adrienne's a darling." Xenia let out a con-spiratorial chuckle. "Anyhow, I've been consoling *him*. There's something *très fin* in Tommy. He said at once that he would like to have you for a friend. So you see, you have only to choose!"

"Between Tommy and Adrienne?" he laughed.

"Or whoever you like!" It was all part of the joke. "After all, I know nothing about you, Francis. Women, boys? What *do* you like?"

He saw in it, after his initial wave of stupefaction, but one more sign of the grotesque intimacy possible between them. A second later, he could even appreciate how nice she was, not to have conjectured behind his back. Her curiosity was so forthright, so—yes, so *tender,* that almost resignedly he heard himself telling Xenia what had never before crossed his lips. "I don't like anybody. I mean," foolishly smiling, "I don't go to bed with anybody. I never have."

"But how extraordinary!" she gasped, biting her lip more, Francis imagined, to flatter him than because she really thought it so. Xenia had already shown that nothing surprised her. A light from below gleamed in her eye. "Not even with little friends in boarding-school?"

"No." He felt rather apologetic about it.

"And never with a woman?"

"Well, with a—woman I had to pay . . . once, long ago."

"I see."

Francis was touched by something that had come into her face. "Don't feel sorry for me," he said. "*I* don't mind!" "Being American" meant, finally, the ring of truth in your voice at times when the truth could not be spoken.

"Sorry, indeed!" Her lashes fluttered. The moment recovered its exquisite comedy. "I have the pride of my sex to consider. If it's true, what you tell me, then I'm under an obligation to seduce you, that's all!"

He fought back a horrid misgiving. "You're not serious!"

"But I am!" cried Xenia. The lashes kept fluttering, though, and Francis knew better. Besides, his upbringing told him that sex could only be joked about, in conversation. His father's stories bore out this impression.

European dance music on the phonograph had somewhat brought

the party to life. Adrienne came gaily towards them—"Francis dear!" re-
moving her earrings, "dance with me!" He looked up, helpless, while
Xenia, one hand raised, the other resting on his arm, pleaded the earnest-
ness of their talk. As a matter of fact Francis was eager to pursue it. He
wanted a chance to tell her that she hadn't understood, that he was
doomed—but would he be able to say it with a straight face?

"You see, I'm profoundly intuitive by nature," she went on as soon as
Adrienne had left them alone, "but here are *two* things you've told me
that I'd never have believed about you."

"Oh? What was the first thing?"

"Why, in Rome—that you had money."

Quite so, thought Francis, twisting his ring: money, and *that* was why
he was doomed.

He did his best to call up the usual easy rhetoric of hurt and indigna-
tion. He squared his jaw, he clenched his fist. Foremost in every mind,
there at the party, must have been his identification as the son of wealthy
Benjamin Tanning—in every mind but his own. *He* had behaved, idiot,
as if he hadn't failed that morning in Larry's office; as if, all evening, it
was at *him*—fatherless, empty-handed, real—instead of at the golden
image towering behind him, that Xenia's friends had been smiling. He
wanted badly to be angry with her for having represented him to them as
a patron, for letting Tommy and Adrienne, from that first meeting in the
customs shed—but he could carry it no further. He hadn't managed to
feel any of this.

What Francis did feel was relief at having told Xenia his secret, both
his secrets. He felt all unburdened. She seemed to understand him com-
pletely. Nothing was as difficult as he had fancied. Who could tell? Per-
haps positive joys were involved with the having of money! Upon his
finger, "Who can tell?" the little gold owl might have echoed, sagely. He
thought of sending flowers to Adrienne, or to his mother. He looked for-
ward to showing Xenia the Cottage. In the dark glass her profile shone.
Briefly now, it could be seen as a pity that she didn't seriously mean to

seduce him; and yet how much wiser and nicer, Francis reflected, to keep such a person forever as a trusted friend, rather than to spoil everything the other way!

Full of trust, he stood up. "Come, let's dance. Only I warn you, I'm a terrible dancer."

"You're absolutely right," she said after two minutes on the floor. "Terrible." Leaning on his arm, Xenia hobbled to a chair, made room for him at her feet, and began asking one of the Counts about rejuvenation.

Francis closed his eyes, smiling. Now that he had confessed to Xenia both his wealth and his sexual inexperience, he saw her morally bound never to take advantage of either.

10. Xenia was installed in the guest house, down the hall from Francis.

"I think you'll be safe there," Mr. Tanning told her dryly, at the end of her first evening among them.

"I hope not!" she tossed over her shoulder, causing him to shake with laughter. God damn, there was a woman!

Actually, no alternative to the guest-house could be found, short of putting her up at the Inn. During Francis's two nights in New York the Cottage had seen drastic changes. "It just goes to show," he sighed, deadpan, to Enid, "a constant watch must be kept. I shan't risk running off again." Sir Edward Good had returned from Washington. Mr. Tanning's new doctor, Samuels by name, had flown down from Boston for an indefinite stay. Then Mrs. McBride had to move in with Natalie, to the discomfort of each, because the only remaining bedroom had been turned over to one Miss Tagliaferro. She was the last straw: a tall angelic blonde freelance writer whom Irene Cheek had hired—with or without Mr. Tanning's consent, nobody could say—to write his biography.

"I can't bear to think," Francis imagined Irene saying, "of all those wonderful, wonderful stories lost to the world. Besides, Lover-cousin, you're a pretty important fella!"

Brother and sister wrung their hands over it for a full hour.

"I do believe," Enid declared from the depths of a fringed hammock, "there's no limit to Daddy's vanity. It's kind of pathetic."

"I have the funniest feeling," said Francis, "of competing with Irene. As though we were each backing a candidate. This is a clever stroke of Irene's. It flatters him, as you say, but more important, by throwing him together with a gorgeous number, it shows him that Irene hasn't a jealous bone in her body."

"Miss Tagliaferro's no slouch," Enid agreed.

Francis raised a finger. "True. But neither is she a match for Xenia. Younger perhaps; prettier perhaps—but not a match. It's Irene who's pathetic," he smiled. "She fails every time; she simply can't recognize *quality*. Oh, Miss Tagliaferro's not bad, but Xenia's so much better, don't you think?"

"Artistically?"

"Well, that too. Miss Tagliaferro's a hack. She'll tire him out talking and there'll be nothing to show for it but an unreadable book, as bad as that portrait at the office. Whereas if Xenia wears him out, not that she will, the result—"

"—will be something worth the effort!" Enid knew just what he meant. Across the lawn they saw Lily ambling towards them, consulting a daisy as to whether she was loved. Enid gave her half brother a funny half-apologetic laugh. "I think Xenia's a very entertaining person," she went on enthusiastically. "So does Lily, don't you, sweetie?"

"Oh definitely," said Lily. "So does Grandpa."

"Hmmm," said Enid.

"I suspect," Francis told them, "that Grandpa plans to commission a head of Lily."

Lily exchanged a surprised look with her mother. A slow smile of vanity—inherited from Mr. Tanning?—overcame the child's truly quite lovely face. "Mercy me," Enid blinked, "the little Buchannibals are the last to hear . . ." but Francis could see how the news pleased her. She took it as a sign from her father that Lily was being correctly brought up.

Francis, himself pleased, had taken it as a compliment to Xenia. "And then she should do one of you, Enid!" he laughed, playing with the fringes that partly hid her now that he was on his feet. "You'd find it so much more *durable* than a painting! We know what happens to paintings, don't we, Lily?"

But when he tried to put his arm about her the little girl ducked out of his reach.

Sure enough, within a week's time, there were *two* heads in progress at the Cottage. Xenia had made her studio out of a small but skylit pantry, up to which food was sent by dumbwaiter from the kitchen. Doors were shut while she worked, and the heads shrouded, at other times, in moist cloths which, however, she was always cheerfully undoing in order to get opinions of her work. "It's not to be believed," she said to Francis, "how that flatters people!" And it did. Louis Leroy and the maids moaned softly, rolled their eyes. Even Mrs. Cheek, once appealed to as a connoisseur—"*You* can tell me," Xenia had whispered, "if I'm catching the spirit"—stood back, squinting, and approved.

Xenia had made an undoubtedly favorable first impression.

The evening of her arrival, at a dinner table paralyzed as usual by the general wish to be selfless and gay for Mr. Tanning's sake, *she* had dared to speak of politics and art (she had studied with the great Zyozcy, now in exile); also to whisper so long in Dr. Samuels's ear that Mr. Tanning had had to interrupt them, humorously: "What's going on down there?" They were talking about *him*, replied Xenia, and was straightway forgiven. She looked her best, handsomely erect, smacking her lips and crossing her knife and fork upon her plate. At her breast something glittered, starlike but false. It was wonderful how, having discovered that

Natalie and Miss Tagliaferro were the least significant guests, she took pains to treat them with particular courtesy. Xenia, that is, was doing as thousands of continental women had done at dinners since girlhood. But at the Cottage it all seemed very refreshing.

"What do you think of her?" Francis soon found occasion to ask his father.

"I like her, Francis," he said, dabbing his eye. "She's so simple and straightforward." Upon which Francis looked sharply at the old man. Xenia simple? Xenia straightforward? Well, perhaps so; certainly Mr. Tanning meant it without irony. After all, only her air of *reveling* in straightforwardness had made Francis question her.

She had another admirer in Sir Edward Good.

"I can't think when I've seen Ned *talk* to a woman," his wife marveled. "He thinks the average female most frightfully silly, as I daresay she is; yet he seems quite under the spell of your friend Zinnia."

If Lady Good's husband surprised her, he surprised Francis even more. During their mornings on the beach Prudence had given him such an earful about her "duty to Ned," her "obligations as a wife," had said so much about respect and so little about love, that Francis, on finally seeing Sir Edward, taller than she had implied, also fairer and younger and more affable, couldn't help wondering at her standards. For Sir Edward was the kind of man Francis, growing up, would have liked for a father. Correct and well informed, given neither to wrath nor to self-pity, companionable, safe. He had read Auden but preferred Bridges. You could not imagine him deliberately placing a burden upon another person. "Yes, that's so," Lady Good nodded thoughtfully. "And I ask myself if you don't remind me of him, Francis, at times."

"Thank you!"

"Because, I mean," she drained her coffee-cup, "you take it all upon yourself."

"And you think one shouldn't?"

"Oh, I don't go that far," she murmured, looking towards Sir Edward.

"If one must, one must. Good heavens, he's laughing now. Miss Grosz is a real tonic. Benjamin's going to enjoy his sittings."

"That's the idea," said Francis merrily. "We must keep him out of trouble."

Lady Good's smile went bleak. Was she the jealous type? Francis had his first glimpse of disagreeable possibilities.

Nevertheless, alone with Xenia, on their starlit way to the guest-house, he reassured her. All of them had liked her.

"Even your father?"

He told her what Mr. Tanning had said.

Her relief was considerable. "Ah, what a dear sweet man that is!" she exclaimed tenderly, almost sadly. "He has the soul of a child, but also," brightening, "a real *tête de lion* which I assure you is going to be fantastically difficult. His expression changes every second! Already I wonder how I can finish in two weeks."

"Take as long as you like." Francis profited by the dark to make a magnanimous gesture. "Your being here is the best thing in the world for *me*."

"You don't know what you've done for me," she said and, as they were parting for the night, kissed him roundly on both cheeks.

Oh yes, he trusted her completely.

By the following week, of course, when the head of Lily—"A Renaissance page! A jewel of a head!"—had been spoken for, there was no further talk about the length of Xenia's stay.

Her success with men could be understood. Among the women at the Cottage Lady Good's hesitation might have prevailed, had not each of them discovered that Xenia *brought* something to the life there. Lady Good herself, starved for intellectual nourishment; and Miss Tagliaferro, rereading her notes in the sun, feeling unwanted; Natalie with her fancy dark glasses, terrified of collisions; Mrs. McBride, too, whom no one else had patience to hear rattle on about her daughter; even the servants, of whose families Xenia had informed herself during the first days—each was left a bit warmed and embraced by her passing greeting. And when the occasion permitted there would be intimate hours, mid-afternoon or late at night, in the course of which thoughts that had probably never been uttered at the Cottage, secrets amorous or biological or both, were exchanged between her and some member of the seraglio. She had a remedy for everything. There stretched behind her the vast Middle European tradition of a loyalty to her sex that was no mere matter of beauty-parlor gossip or any collective prideful sense of superiority to men; indeed, it rested squarely on an acceptance of woman's secondary place in society, and had to do with the subtlest campaigns, deceptions, philters. Xenia never minded being personal. Also, she was interested in life.

She never minded being *impersonal*, either, and this, more than the rest, explained her novelty. Enid's description of her as "a very entertaining person" carried with it a melancholy irony. Life at the Cottage, whatever its other attractions, was seldom entertaining. You weren't expected to be serious or witty or to have formed a friendship or to have read a book. All that was for a rainy day that never came. Meanwhile the Queen Anne shelves, packed with beautiful sets and trash thirty years old, faced glassily out to sea, mute reminders of the worst that could befall you. Lady Good's moments at the piano caused embarrassment, for she played well; only when it emerged that she wasn't hurt if you talked during it was her music applauded. You had no recourse to formal or abstract conversation. It wasn't enough to speak of yesterday's electrical storm; it had to have provoked dreams of skyscrapers, whirlpools—symbols barely disguised but mulled over and over ("Now *what* could that possibly mean?") by the company at large. The talk was confined for the most part to events of the previous twenty-four hours: a dress seen in a shop window, Benjamin's good appetite at lunch, any hopeful international event. You frequently pretended to have "just got round to seeing" one of last winter's movies or plays in order to be able to discuss it. But Xenia *entertained*. Enid had chosen the word carefully; she would never have called Xenia attractive.

Mr. Tanning, accordingly, hung upon the everyday chatter like the slow-witted student for whose sake the whole class is held back, and didn't value Xenia's efforts to raise the tone. One evening, when Miss Tagliaferro's eyes were shining over Paris before the war, over many an elbow Xenia had rubbed with artists and statesmen, Mr. Tanning let out a low groan.

"Are you feeling poorly, Benjamin dear?" Lady Good asked.

"No," he said. "But I'm bored."

After a silence Sir Edward proposed a rubber of bridge.

And yet *he* would talk about the past for hours on end, thought Francis angrily. A day later, hearing Xenia tell the old man the story of her mother in German prisons during the war, and seeing tears in his eyes, he understood the difference. Mr. Tanning had worshipped his own mother; therefore Xenia's words moved him easily. As usual, the subjective was his only touchstone.

Although Xenia had hated and feared *her* mother, she knew how to tell a story. In this she resembled Mr. Tanning, many of whose boyhood exploits—the burning bridge, the cave, the time at bat with bases loaded—had haunting literary overtones. Miss Tagliaferro jotted them down doubtfully, but Xenia called them exquisite—"no, I'm serious, it's Americana, *c'est du vrai folklore!*" Thus, with a trace of the charlatan on both sides, they got along famously.

Even if Lady Good hadn't liked Xenia, she would have had to approve. Dr. Samuels had said that the best of all medicines was for Mr. Tanning to enjoy himself—any way he pleased.

She had an involuntary start. "Any way?"

"*Any* way," declared the wise little doctor with a look that made her blush. Francis had laughed aloud—poor Prudence, couldn't she see that her leg was being pulled? *He* knew what his father was capable of. Why would a doctor *be* at the Cottage if Mr. Tanning had nothing wrong with him?

But Lady Good had gazed out to sea. "I'm very glad," she breathed, "for Benjamin's sake." And on another occasion, to Francis, as they passed the shut pantry door: "He needs all the affection he can get."

So that what went on in the pantry lent an air of purpose and accomplishment to the entire household. Where once you had had a sensation of drifting at loose ends, of each day's being, if anything, rather less meaningful than the previous one, *now* you had tangible proof to the contrary. The head of elephant-colored clay underwent daily a cautious process of refinement. Bit by bit it grew into some ideal definition of the master of the house, consequently of the house itself and of the life contained therein. It was an image around which clustered unending reveries.

"Appearances are nothing," said Xenia. "I must show what he is really like, inside." Larry and Enid nodded, uneasily, but Lily couldn't be torn away. Still as a mouse she sat till nearly suppertime, watching Xenia work.

Before long the head had acquired a character. It wore a surprisingly lyric expression, almost elegiac. Much as the donor of an altarpiece used to be painted kneeling within sight of the Cross, perpetually devout— though in the flesh drowsing, sinning, dying—so the old man's nostalgia for the past, for powers and loves lost, became abstracted, fixed in the worked clay to a point where (it seemed to Francis) his living face had been left that much freer to shine with goatish humor. Or did it just shame Mr. Tanning to have been seen so poetically? For like a little boy he did his utmost to dispel the impression.

Each morning at eleven he would show up at the pantry door, leaning heavily on Louis Leroy's arm. Xenia, who began work two hours earlier, would look up and chortle over some truly absurd piece of clothing the old man would have on—a French sailor's hat, or a tailcoat worn with plaid flannel shorts, or a hand-painted necktie on which, clad in three sequins, a naked redhead pranced. Eyes popping from his head, mouth foolishly ajar, he next would shuffle nearer and nearer until his nose was but a few inches from Xenia's bosom. At this he would gape as if hypnotized; then, shaking his head in parody of one who wakes on the brink of a precipice, stagger, paw the air, reel backwards calling upon onlookers to marvel at his narrow escape. "Out! Out!" Xenia would cry to Francis and Louis. And the sitting would begin.

At half past twelve Mr. Tanning would emerge, looking tired. He found the sessions harder than he'd bargained for. Xenia did make him sit in a chair, a high chair at that; she did ask him to hold still, and once when he complained she had him feel the water on her knee, warm and wobbly, telling him not to be a baby—if she could stand it so could he. "It's the only way to deal with him," she told Francis. "He likes people who talk straight out. I'm doing him a world of good!" Certainly, for several nights in a row, Mr. Tanning had slept like a child.

After lunch Francis and Xenia would seek each other out, to compare notes.

"I wonder if you know," she said earnestly on one of the first days, "how he loves you, how he thinks about you. All morning he talked—"

"*Why?*" Francis interrupted. "Why, when I do nothing whatever to please him?"

"Exactly! That's the child no parent can resist!"

He let this pass. "The son he really'd have liked is Larry Buchanan. He works for the firm, he gives him grandchildren—"

"Yes, yes," said Xenia, bored with having to explain the obvious, "every old man wants someone to carry on for him. But he's already told me about Larry Buchanan. The man works himself like a lunatic; he wants to die of heart trouble just like Ben. Your father's worried sick about Enid and her headaches. And he's right—why shouldn't she have them? while her husband's busy modeling himself upon his father-in-law!"

"He sees all that?" Francis marveled.

"Ben? Of course! Do you think he's blind? It's true," Xenia mused, "Enid was raised a Catholic. That explains a lot."

He could only stare openmouthed.

"Yes! Harriet's Catholic—didn't you know? Your sister was a Protestant convert at fifteen. She didn't like the questions the priest asked her!" And Xenia roared with laughter while Francis's amazement underwent a set of modulations towards melancholy.

Xenia then said, "Ben's worried about you, too. He asked me if there was anything he could do."

"About me?"

She nodded.

Francis couldn't have explained the sadness that had come over him. "Why can't he say these things to *me?*" he finally brought out.

"Ah," explained Xenia, justly, "think a moment: what do you ever say to him?"

The next day she took up Mr. Tanning's entrance into the pantry, the shuffling and the ogling. "What interests me is that, so far as I've seen, he treats every woman alike. Even *l'Anglaise* with whom he's meant to be so much in love."

"That's just his dirty mind," said Francis.

"Ah no!" Xenia shook her head vehemently. "Ben does not have a dirty mind! Of course he thinks *constantly* about sex, like every good American. But he thinks about it," she melted, grew wistful, "in such a sweet pure way, like a boy! *Il ne connait qu'une seule position, je vous assure.* Between ourselves, he's scared to death of sex."

"Precisely!" Francis was jubilant. "And he dresses up like a clown so that nobody will make a mistake and take him seriously!"

"What else can he do at his age?" said Xenia with a shrug. "All he needs is for me to unbutton my smock, crying, 'Take me! I'm yours!'— and he'd be frightened out of his wits, *le pauvre!*"

This struck Francis as wildly funny.

But a day later Xenia said, "No. We're wrong about him. I've been prejudiced by *your* view, and you're not altogether right. He's neither as old nor as sick as people like to think." Her eyes were sparkling.

What had happened was that Mr. Tanning had naughtily refused to pose that morning, until Xenia let him kiss her on the mouth. "But, *mon Dieu!*" she exclaimed to Francis. "I tell you, he must have been a fantastic lover in his day! A kiss so passionate—!" Clearly, nothing had so pleased her in a long while.

It also pleased Francis. "You see? You may turn into my next stepmother, after all!"

Seeing that he meant it, Xenia drew herself up. "Ah no. That, my dear, is *out* of the question."

"But why?"

He looked so puzzled that she laughed—"I see now," coquettishly, "it's all along as a mother that you've wanted me!" And as he gazed mutely down the beach, "*Voyons*, Francis," she cried, "contradict me! *Il faut avoir de l'esprit!* That's the trouble with all of you. Ben's a sweet dear good man, and what's more, he's a *real* man, but—married to him? Giving up my freedom to lead *this* life? Why, I should die of boredom!"

"You once told me you were never bored," said Francis reproachfully.

"I must have meant," Xenia replied, throwing her cigarette into the sea, "that I hadn't yet lived at the Cottage."

Up to then, Francis had tried to discount his own boredom as purely subjective. But if Xenia felt it too, if life at the Cottage was *really* dull—why, dull was what it stopped being, then and there. Backed by her authority, finding himself on the right track, he gave in and confessed that he was fascinated.

More and more he saw things through Xenia's eyes.

She explained his father to him—supplied him, rather, with attitudes. "*Laugh* when he tells you his adventures with women!" or, "Be *interested* when he talks business. The figures aren't important, but ah! the way his mind works, that's what *you* can appreciate!" Another day she said, "He calls me now the female Casanova. That's why we get on so beautifully. We talk man to man about our conquests." This was true; Mr. Tanning had already told Francis how Xenia had wanted to know which women, of them all, had given him the keenest satisfaction. The old man willingly described a certain affair he had had forty years ago. "And what was her specialty in bed?" pursued Xenia, all healthy curiosity; then: "Oh yes? What a small world! That's *my* specialty, too!" So they had roared with laughter like two bachelors.

On the subject of Lily Xenia had plenty to say. "What a tragic little girl! Her parents expect her to be perfect, but no matter how she tries nothing she does is good enough. She told me these things, very gravely, while making a little statue of her mother. Now, *that's* the child who needs the confessional! She has nowhere to go for forgiveness. Already there's something neurotic in Lily, something cold that craves warmth. . . ." On and on, with light defining touches, as deft as any worked in clay, she revealed to Francis the figures he lived among.

How much *everyone* seemed to have told her! Natalie's menopause, Sir Edward's impotence, Miss Tagliaferro's abortion—Xenia knew about each in detail and passed it on casually to Francis, who was flabbergasted. These new insights floated beneath his eyelids like dazzling afterimages decked with which the person concerned became grotesquely vivid and alive. "Yes, yes, of course, it's what *had* to be," he would murmur after the first shock. "How fascinating, Xenia! To think that Sir Edward, so strong, so civilized—yes, I *see* it now!" Perspiration, like some thought made visible, glistened faintly on his brow. Oh, the experience of others! Francis had come to picture it wound within them like reels of film, a moving X-ray, various, serious, never episodic, plumbing the flux wherein *he* floundered, down to the shelf of rock below. In short, something inaccessible. With the result that what Xenia told him no more influenced Francis's daily behavior towards his father or Enid or Sir Edward than his knowledge of the swarming life contained in a drop of water kept him from thinking pure the glassfuls he drank when thirsty.

At last I am beginning to live, thought Francis nevertheless, content at his oracle's feet.

Ignorant of women, he could grow vastly sentimental over them. He read into Enid's little history proof of an intense inner life, and divined the vestiges of Rome in her recourse to ceremonial forms. Xenia, it went without saying, drank from purer springs, deeper sources than his own. She had found the emerald in the fire and the water in the emerald. She was intimate, as befitted the *Ewig-Weibliche*, with river, tree, the night, the underworld. She read minds, she consulted the stars; she was both promise and key, and it might have been the secret vaults of nature she would unlock for him, so dumbly did Francis listen and assent.

Even when she discussed her own love life (she had long been attracted *follement* to Tommy Utter; were it not for her friendship with Adrienne, etc., etc.) he felt he was witnessing as never before the *workings* of a human soul. Lemons and prunes, such were the other women Francis had listened to; Xenia was his first mango. "I learn from you!" he told her with shining eyes.

And on one terrible morning, bitterly, "I've learned enough, thank you."

It was a questionable statement, but for the rest of that day he would neither speak to her nor meet her eye, except inadvertently—you might say, out of habit.

11.

He woke that morning in Xenia's bed.

It was the Wednesday of her third week at the Cottage. Mr. Tanning had begun to wonder how much longer the sittings would go on. He wanted to leave for Boston by the following Monday, and had understood that both Lily's head and his own would be finished before then. But Xenia had been dropping remarks about what a restless sitter the old man was, and how Enid only let Lily pose for an hour a day. "I work slowly," she complained. "You can't ask an artist to meet a deadline."

"Then why did you say it would be done in two weeks?" said Francis. "Or that he wouldn't have to sit still? You assured me he could smoke, move about—"

"Ah," Xenia answered jauntily, "if I'd made it sound too difficult, he'd never have agreed to pose. Then where would I be? It's not a hobby for me, Francis, it's my career!"

At the time he had laughed and seen her point. But their conversation came back to him on the particular terrible day, and left him trembling with anger. How must he, how must all the Tannings have appeared to her! As great soft stupid things, from whom you had only to reach out and take? Who parted wordlessly with their wealth, their time, their very *selves?* If this had been her view, thought Francis, his eyes narrowed to slits, then she had made a bad mistake. Those were possessions to be fiercely guarded. Xenia, of course, had been accepted at first. In the community you accepted everybody at first. People were so hemmed in by their own sort that a stranger couldn't get close to them, who hadn't been passed on by at least one trusted friend. And naturally, Francis argued, no one at the Cottage would have suspected the visitor *he* introduced. How *dare* she have used him! Not that alone, but to have talked as if his father were a strong man, able to pose as rigorously as she desired . . . His thoughts raced on unchecked.

A large dinner had been planned. Four or five of Mr. Tanning's partners and their wives were driving out from the city. There were to be thirty guests at small tables on the south terrace overlooking the sea. Since early morning maids had hurried back and forth through the ocean room, carrying dresses to be ironed. A huge box for Lady Good lay unclaimed in the entrance hall. Loretta the cook had three assistants. Sir Edward was off playing golf with Dr. Samuels. Natalie Bigelow, rising at eight for the first time in as many years, had revised the menu, approved the selection of china and linen, helped arrange centerpieces, and by eleven, exhausted, telephoned for a cab to take her to the hairdresser. She promised she would eat a sandwich there, but didn't.

Rooms had been reserved at the Inn for the oncoming guests. Among them was a couple named Underwood whom Mr. Tanning felt he had treated coldly of late. He had these periodic spells of remorse whereby some forgotten friend was summoned, made much of, his wife flirted with—given, in fine, what Vinnie Tanning still liked to call the works. For in the years that followed his first heart attack the old man had seen less and less of people like the Underwoods. Possibly they were quieter and nicer than most of his business friends, and had hesitated, knowing him unwell, to press themselves upon him uninvited. Possibly, too, they had lives of their own, which couldn't really be said of the Maxons, the Feuermans, or Wally Link, each time a crowd of them showed up seldom expected and never fed.

At half past eleven Mr. Tanning, dressed in a flannel robe with his hair in a stocking, peered round the pantry door. Where was Xenia?

"She's on her way over," said Francis. "Did you sleep well?" He himself was still haggard from the scene he had just had with her.

"No, I didn't. Dr. Samuels had to get up in the middle of the night. I'm not going to pose today, anyhow. I want to save my strength for this God-damn dinner. Now where in hell is Louis Leroy?"

"Right here, Mr. Tanning, Sir," said a cheerful voice.

"Louis," he continued on a single expressionless note, "Mrs. McBride will sleep on the couch in my study tonight. Have someone pack a suit-case for Mrs. Bigelow. She'll be staying over at the Inn. I want Mr. and Mrs. Underwood to have that room."

The valet bowed and started off.

"Wait," said Mr. Tanning. "Kindly tell me what this is doing here." It was the package for Lady Good. It might have been the coffin of a friend, he studied it so mournfully. Then he turned his back, swallowed a nitro-glycerine pill, and headed for the ocean room. Francis, not quite exchanging an apologetic smile with Louis, followed.

Seated at the desk, Lady Good looked up from her letter. "Good morning, Benjamin darling. Did you have a lovely sleep? Good morning, Francis dear."

She was wearing shorts. The old man stared at her inscrutably.

"Why, what's the matter?" she asked, but in such a way that Francis knew that she knew.

Mr. Tanning resorted to a fake British accent. "There is a parcel for Her Ladyship in the vestibule."

"Yes, I saw it," Lady Good smiled, "but there must be some mistake, Benjamin. I've ordered nothing from that shop."

"Oh dear," he moaned, rolling a mournful eye to heaven, "I never met a girl with so little curiosity."

"What *is* he talking about, Francis?" She returned to her letter long enough to underline a phrase. "Why I should open a box that doesn't belong to me I can't for a moment understand. Doubtless some other poor woman is waiting *most* impatiently for it, whilst it just sits there. I'd best ring up the shop." On which she rose.

Francis was appalled. Had she behaved like this from the start, and had *he* learned from Xenia how to see through such displays? Why, Prudence was no better than Irene!

The box contained, of course, the evening gown she had admired some weeks before. Mr. Tanning had bought it in connivance with Natalie—a matter of measurements surreptitiously taken, even a pair of Lady Good's shoes stolen in order to have matching slippers made. To all of this she had lent herself, if you could believe her, in absolute innocence. Francis did believe her; he liked her too much not to. But watching her blink and protest and finally gasp, scarlet with pleasure, over the open box, he had a glimmering of the truth. Luxury was at work upon her. Softened by days in the sun, nights on smooth clean sheets in a bed she hadn't had to make herself, growing used to roasts and chops and, above all, used to the devotion of their provider, Prudence found less and less occasion to recall her life in Jamaica. Moreover, along with the routine of that life, she relaxed her grasp of the ethical system that had kept it useful and noble rather than flatly exhausting.

Well, she was only human. Even as high-minded a woman as Vinnie Tanning had eaten and drunk and dressed in keeping with the opulence of the Cottage. Still, Francis wished Lady Good had shown more fortitude.

He wondered if she wasn't, in her heart of hearts, sickeningly conscious of the change at work. She might have been reproaching *him* for having deserted her in favor of Xenia. She hadn't bothered lately to invite him on walks along the beach. Those mornings Francis had accompanied her he found her listless, distracted. He suspected now that Prudence had responded to a distraction of his own, had seen that he was in no state to help her. The sobs of an hour before rose in his throat. Why was it to *him* that everyone turned?

At the tarnishing mirror Lady Good twisted and preened, the dress held up in front of her. "I think I shall go right now and try it on," she said, but couldn't tear herself from her image.

"Yes, yes," sighed Mr. Tanning, "you'll be surprised how many opportunities come to put it on."

"Oh dearest, it's so lovely!"

"*Or,* I might add, take it off . . ."

"*Benjamin!*"

Just then, however, hearing a step in the hall, Lady Good sped to her room.

It was Xenia, in hairnet and smock, ready to begin work. She gave Benjamin a good-morning kiss. Francis strolled to the far end of the room, pleased that his father, today of all days, had chosen not to pose.

"Ah," she coaxed, "not even a very short session? There's a tiny place at the corner of the mouth that I wanted—"

"I said," Mr. Tanning broke in with an authority that seemed to impress even himself, "that I just don't feel up to it. Can't anyone in this God-damn house give me some plain consideration?" And out he went, reappearing instantly in the doorway long enough to add, "Don't mind Grandpa. He's feeling sorry for himself."

A frightened look had come over Xenia's face. "Oh God, what's the matter?" she breathed.

Francis could have told her. Who wouldn't be worn and vexed, forever pampered as the old man was, sought after, *drained* by people he cared nothing about? His son felt unusually close to him that morning. Before long the Maxons, the Feuermans, and Wally Link would be setting out gleefully from New York, with tanks full and tops down and no doubt whatever of Benjamin's eagerness to see them. As it happened, Benjamin was eager to see nobody except Prudence Good. Damn friendships, damn contacts, Francis could imagine his father thinking, and above all—at a moment when even Sir Edward had had the tact to remove himself—damn Xenia and *her* demands!

Sir Edward was a different story. "I'd feel a hundred percent better," Mr. Tanning had brooded only a day ago, "if Prudence's husband were less of a nice guy and more of a son of a bitch." Whatever that meant. Didn't the old man *know* about Sir Edward? wondered Francis at the time, and now thanked heaven he hadn't repeated the remark to Xenia. A similar one having been made about Charlie Cheek, "There you are!" she had cried, "here's proof Irene's your father's mistress!" That was nonsense enough—couldn't she see how sick and old Mr. Tanning was?—but if she were further to imply that Prudence—! Although Xenia had done no such thing, Nonsense! thought Francis in a fury, nonsense and damn her! She couldn't be expected to understand so fine a person as Lady Good.

"I haven't the vaguest notion," he said distantly in answer to her question. "I doubt that anything's the matter unless he wishes not to be bothered for a little while. I'm surprised you can't make an effort to respect that."

Tears sprang into Xenia's eyes. "Have the human kindness, Francis," she whispered, "to remember I'm a guest in this house. More than a guest, a friend—yes, in spite of what you think—a friend whose life, whose whole career is at stake!"

"Xenia, for pity's sake!"

"I can turn only to you! If you turn from me, if Ben does——"

So that explained her distress! Xenia believed he had just been telling his father what had taken place the night before. In a calmer hour Francis might have smiled to see that *she* was as conscience-stricken over the whole miserable business as he himself. Instead, "*How* can you think such a preposterous thought?" he shouted. "*What* do you imagine I'm capable of? Answer me!"

Xenia stared at him, her face streaming and white. "You are capable, Francis, of anything," she said quietly, and turned to go.

By then he, too, had begun to weep. Fumbling with the screen door, he escaped towards the sunken garden, away from the sea, whispering to himself, "I must go, I must go. . . ." And when Lady Good reappeared in her finery to strike a not altogether humorous attitude on the threshold, she found the ocean room deserted.

It was one of those days for tears. The next to succumb was Natalie Bigelow.

At four o'clock, back from the village, a picture with hair now sleek and golden as a greengage plum, she had literally stumbled over her packed suitcase. No maid answered her ring. Xenia and Lily were in the pantry. Mrs. McBride had gone to rub her patient's feet. Still thinking nothing bad, Natalie groped her way back to the ocean room, where Prudence was playing patience. Did *she* know why a suitcase had been packed?

"How very peculiar, Natalie dear!"

"Well, *I* think so," laughed the victim. "I guess I've outstayed my welcome, after all."

"Now you're being silly. Besides," Lady Good grew complacent, "Benjamin said nothing about it to *me*."

"Pardon me," Francis interposed from a distant sofa, "he told Louis

Leroy that he wanted the Underwoods to have Natalie's room, and that she'd be sleeping at the Inn tonight. I assumed," he couldn't resist adding, "it had all been settled between them."

There was a brief silence. "That," said Natalie gaily, "answers my question, doesn't it?" But as she started out her shoulders began to tremble. Before Lady Good had time to rise and embrace her she was heartbrokenly sobbing.

It caught Francis off guard. He had always thought of Natalie as a good sport who, having got what she wanted from life years ago, no longer cared much how people treated her.

Nerves, he decided at first—accustomed to that view of his father whereby the old man brought nothing to pass, good, bad, or indifferent, and couldn't therefore be credited or blamed for what went on. Still feeling *he* was needed, Francis got up and approached the women.

"Darling," Lady Good was saying, "you shall sleep in *my* room tonight. We'll send Ned to the Inn."

"We'll do nothing of the sort!" cried Natalie, coloring, swallowing. "He wants me out, I'm getting out. I'm definitely not a gal who has to be told twice!"

"Natalie, dear, think! He can't have meant—"

"Prudence, my pet," through clenched teeth, "I've known him twenty-five years."

"Francis, *did* Benjamin—?"

"I'm afraid so."

"Certainly he did!" Her wonderful half-blind eyes flashed. "But would he have the guts to tell me to my face? I should say not!" Whereupon Natalie broke away. By the time she returned, struggling with her suitcase, it was to confront a circle swelled by Xenia, Lily, Mrs. McBride, and Louis Leroy whom, in a dulcet whisper, she requested to call a cab.

"Natalie," begged Xenia, "take *my* room!"

"Don't do it!" exclaimed Francis. He gave Xenia a look to show he knew what had prompted her offer, then hurried to intercept Louis. "*I'm driving Mrs. Bigelow to the Inn.*"

"Thank you, my sweet."

"And *I'm* going to speak to Benjamin," Lady Good announced, decisively pivoting.

"If you do," said Natalie on a note that froze her in her tracks, "I'll never forgive you."

Lily simpered. Francis picked up the suitcase.

"But the dinner party," said Mrs. McBride.

"Don't worry." Natalie smiled over her shoulder. "I'll be here for that. I'm a gal who fulfills *her* obligations to the letter."

Francis relaxed only when the Cottage began to writhe in the rear-vision mirror. In silence he headed for the Inn. He felt a gradual dancing clarity. Natalie's nerves, indeed! No, Benjamin was at fault, Benjamin—his lips kept forming the words—was thoughtlessly, stupidly at fault.

For Benjamin had to have his own way. He no more considered Natalie's feelings, in packing her off to the Inn, than Lady Good's, in forcing on her an embarrassingly lavish gift. Benjamin consulted nobody. Whatever he decided to serve—whether caviar or humble pie—the victim was meant to choke it down and be grateful. Nobody had ever had a chance to refuse the brutal bounty. Here the car just missed crashing into a tree.

I must be terribly mixed-up, thought Francis, remembering how often he'd represented his father to Xenia and others as sick, old, irresponsible. Not since childhood had he felt such direct antagonism towards Benjamin—but all at once an odd, elated antagonism, more like an acknowledgment of Benjamin's reality; as if what had happened the previous night—and for the moment Francis didn't mind despising himself for it—as if what had happened in Xenia's bed had actually *given* him a kind of strength. He smiled, but it was so. Strength enough, at least, to admit that Benjamin was strong. Father and son seemed now to drop a charade kept pointless by fear, on the part of each, that the other could bear no intenser relationship. Something caved in. They might have been living adversaries, laughing now across a chasm. Yes, Benjamin was strong, thought Francis with a glance at Natalie's swollen eyes. He had learned, however, a way of opposing Benjamin.

Or thought he had.

They were at the Inn. Stopping the car, full of tenderness, Francis reached for Natalie's hand, as he had reached twelve years before for his mother's when *they* had driven away from the Cottage together. But his gesture, while signifying nothing darker than "Never mind, *I* shall be loyal and loving," was met by such poor mechanical gratitude, the squeeze, the sniffle, the reach for Kleenex and rouge in order to hide her misery from whom it didn't concern, that Francis withdrew as if he had touched ice. Staring once again at the world through glass, he heard the dim chime of that earlier lesson: one couldn't hope to triumph where Benjamin had already done so.

During dinner an accordion player, hired by Enid, went from table to table.

This man, swarthy and balding, had been seen at parties thereabouts for close to a quarter century. Off and on, that night, he accompanied Wally Link (who loved to fit old songs with exhaustive lyrics all about life at the Cottage—a bard of yore, Mrs. Gresham called him); but most of the time the musician spent gazing with meaningless impudence down the bodice of whoever had requested "Some Enchanted Evening," which he sang as if she alone, all summer, had flattered him by naming a little-known number they both loved. By the meal's end, with nobody asking for it, he sang this song to some who hadn't glanced in his direction.

Whenever his gaze lit on Lady Good she turned pink. Her gown was an astonishment, dewdrop and gossamer, but it might have been cut from the very tissue of sin, she wore it so cheerlessly. A cable had come, while she was dressing, from Jamaica; Sir Edward was needed. He had read it quickly, shrugged and told her to do as she wished—*his* duty was clear. Prudence then fled to Benjamin, who, tying his tie, had shrugged and told her he couldn't advise her in such a matter. Did nobody care whether she stayed or went? Finally, just before dinner, it hadn't helped to discover that the only other "important" gown at the party was being worn by Irene Cheek, who under the stress of compliments had given way to baby-talk. "I'n't it pwetty?" she gurgled. "'s Iwene's birthday pwesent fum Cousin Benji!"

"When was your birthday?" Francis thought to ask.

"Week before last," she replied, snapping her fingers for Louis to bring her a cocktail. Francis and Lady Good exchanged a bleak look. Evidently Mr. Tanning had decided, all by himself, that evening gowns made highly acceptable gifts.

And so Lady Good was the next to weep.

She feared that everyone was making fun of her. "If, as he swears, he's grown tired of Irene," she was murmuring by the end of dinner, "why is he afraid to tell her so? It's fair neither to her nor to me. How do I know that he *has* tired of her?" It truly hurt Francis to see her caring so deeply. Why, Irene wasn't worth the smallest tear fallen into her ice cream. "If I were that silly doll-faced Mrs. Maxon pirouetting in a frock of natural chamois—in this weather!—I should know the line to take. I'd wiggle my hips and paint my eyes. As it is—oh, *make* that man stop!"

"Thank you," Francis said to the accordion player. "We're trying to talk."

"He's getting to behave more and more like Benjamin as the years go by," tittered Mrs. Sturdevant across the table.

"Do you mean me?" inquired Francis, startled.

"Oh dear me, no," she put his mind at rest, "not you, no, no—the *accordionist!* The way he flirts with all the old women—tell me, Lady Good," the blue-haired smiler pursued naïvely, but at the top of her lungs, "I'm crushed over Sir Edward's having to leave, but *you* won't rush back with him, will you?"

"I've not yet made up my mind," said Lady Good, instantly regaining her poise in the face of an overt challenge. "It may be that I shall accompany Benjamin to Boston next week."

Francis raised his eyebrows. He had been invited to Boston himself. And Mrs. McBride, of course. The Cottage would be abandoned, a sinking ship.

"You mean, to the hospital," said Mrs. Sturdevant, looking wise.

And so it went.

Wally Link had seen a flying saucer. But he was such a prankster that nobody believed him. The more shrill and red-faced he grew, the more Mrs. Gresham and Natalie and Charlie Cheek pounded the table, howling with laughter. Only Miss Tagliaferro nodded, paled, lowered her eyes—there *was* a higher form of life; the earth *was* being watched by Venus. When the accordionist struck up a waltz, Francis asked her to dance.

"Careful now, Cutie-Pie!" Charlie Cheek called after them. "That boy Francis is up to no good!"

The poor man no longer even pretended to be on the wagon.

"Do you know the Cheeks well?" said Francis. Xenia had told him to be nice to Miss Tagliaferro.

But it emerged that she was only a freelance writer whose name somebody had given Irene. As if this weren't interesting enough, she added, "I was fired a few hours ago."

"Really?" Heads were falling right and left, thought Francis, remembering Natalie. "Fired, you mean," he went on, "by Mrs. Cheek?"

"No." Miss Tagliaferro shook her silken mane. "By Mr. Tanning. He didn't think we were getting anywhere."

"With the biography?"

He was just keeping the ball rolling, yet she gave him an odd arch look. "With the biography," she smiled.

"Well, were you? Getting anywhere, I mean. With the biography."

"Not really. There's so much material, what with all the claims on his time . . ." She seemed to be taking it in her stride.

"Fancy, Enid," said Francis, pausing on his jerky progress past her table, "Miss Tagliaferro's lost her job."

Enid was genuinely sympathetic. Nevertheless, brown and beautiful in a full Chinese robe, she exchanged a significant flicker with her brother. "Poor Cousin Irene must be very disappointed," she said. "It's a pity when little plans don't materialize."

"I've got a feeling Mr. Tanning hasn't told her yet," said Miss Tagliaferro.

Indeed? All three looked involuntarily towards the old man, who was in the act of kissing Mrs. Underwood's wrinkled cheek, while her husband grinned. "But gee, don't feel sorry for me," continued Miss Tagliaferro with an angel's smile. "Your father gave me a beautiful big check and a few inside tips on the market. I can't help it, I love him, that's all."

"Ah, so do I!" said a familiar voice behind them, as Xenia swept by in the arms of Sir Edward Good.

At last, with a din of spoons striking crystal, the speeches began.

Dr. Samuels rose first. Mr. Tanning had asked him to explain briefly a treatment his patient was to undergo next week in Boston. It was one with which the doctor had been experimenting for a number of years. He wanted to say at once that it involved serious risks. But after much observation and many tests right here at the Cottage—he hadn't been playing golf the *whole* three weeks—he felt reasonably sure that Mr. Tanning would respond to it.

His listeners composed themselves into an earnestness. It was right that *they* had been chosen to hear the worst.

As simply as possible: one fine morning Mr. Tanning would swallow perhaps a shot glass full of some colorless liquid, faintly flavored with iodine. This treat was to be served in a leaden casket, sipped through a leaden straw, in a room equipped with a special toilet that didn't empty into the city sewer. For two days no visitor could be admitted. Benjamin, in a word, was going to be radioactive.

"What? No mushroom cloud?" laughed Charlie Cheek tactlessly. The others sat sobered.

Only a fraction of the atomic cocktail, Dr. Samuels went on, is retained by the system, and of this all but an infinitesimal amount is absorbed by the thyroid gland. The gland, alas, is destroyed. The patient's throat swells up and he can go through some painful hours. But within six or eight weeks the miracle happens: he no longer suffers any heart pain whatsoever.

That was all. A few guests looked troubled, as though it meant Benjamin was going to live forever. Then Wally Link had them sing "For He's a Jolly Good Fellow" in honor of Dr. Samuels.

"I know," said Larry Buchanan, rising, "that the prayers and good wishes of all of us here will follow the grandest guy I ever hope—" and so forth, fluently, for five minutes at the end of which Harold Feuerman rephrased it, adding a sentiment or two of his own, these last deftly echoed, when her turn came, by Mimsey Maxon. "I cannot understand," whispered Lady Good through clenched teeth, "how Benjamin endures such fatuity."

For he was listening soberly, hanging on their words, and when at length, with a creak and a groan and a tardy flourish from the accordion, he stood up to thank them, a telltale brilliance trembled in his old blue eyes. Number five, said Francis to himself. But Mr. Tanning was always crying. Xenia had said it proved he was still potent, emotionally.

"An old man is always saddened," he began, "when those dear to him take their leave. No matter how long they stay away he wants them to feel present and cherished in his heart. We see too little of our loved ones, unless we make an effort. I'd never have known my own father if I hadn't made an effort. He was a country doctor. Some mornings he'd hitch his buggy and not come home till midnight. The days I went along, it meant giving up a swim or a baseball game. But I never regretted making the sacrifice."

Here the speaker choked on a swallow of champagne. He took his time coughing. The floor was his, nobody would interrupt.

"I only hope," he said, then spat very noisily into an immaculate handkerchief, "that *my* children never regret not taking the many opportunities I've given them to know *me*."

A queer silence ensued. Mrs. Cheek looked enigmatic. Francis had his hands squeezed by Lady Good. "Remember that he's sick, my dear," she breathed. Enid, across the terrace, bowed her head and was the sixth to weep. But Mr. Tanning simply refused to be at fault in front of so large a crowd. Peering about innocently, he went on with his speech.

"The first departing friend I should like to pay my compliments to is that gentleman planter, manufacturer of molasses, Minister and Right Hand to his Excellency the Governor-General of Jamaica, *and* the luckiest man in the whole world"—this with a comic leer in Prudence's direction, while adopting the tone of a barker introducing a freak. "Ladies and gentlemen, I give you: Sir Edward Good!"

Applause. Lady Good caught her breath, "Honestly, the *impudence* of Benjamin!" but laughed a bit in spite of herself. He hadn't, at least, brought up *her* departure.

"Ned is what I call a truly good sport," continued Mr. Tanning, a fresh frog in his throat. "Let's drink to him."

He spoke as if he had just won Lady Good from her husband in some friendly tournament. Glances were exchanged over the champagne. But she seemed not to mind. That she didn't was further proof, to Francis, of her moral decline. Ten days earlier she would have left her place and swept proudly to her room.

"And now," Benjamin was saying, "my most affectionate blessings on a fair and charming friend whose stay is over. I've enjoyed every minute spent in her company, and trust she will forgive and forget all but the sunlit hours at the Cottage."

"Is he referring to poor Natalie?" gasped Lady Good. "I do feel that's rather rubbing it in!"

"Wait and see," Francis told her, amused. He noticed, however, that Natalie herself wore a look of grim attention. Had no one else heard about Miss Tagliaferro?

"But the old poop's not what he used to be." Mr. Tanning shook his head. "Paresis is slowly settling in."

"You'll have to prove it to us!" Mrs. Gresham heckled.

"My one regret," he said, ignoring her, "is that this departing guest and I have been unable to complete the ambitious project outlined before either of us had had the chance—in my case I should say the privilege— of knowing the other."

As it sank in, "Oh, so *Zinnia's* leaving!" marveled Lady Good.

"Why no, of course not," Francis laughed, forgetting that he would have welcomed this piece of news. But gazes had begun to converge upon Xenia from the many who shared Lady Good's misapprehension. Xenia herself, during a vivid instant, half rose from her chair, one hand at her throat, pale with the imagined humiliation she had received.

Once again, the little drama his words caused played itself out unnoticed by Mr. Tanning. And of course, after all the fuss, it was only a question of poor Miss Tagliaferro. She stood up now, tried to convey that the privilege had been hers. By then who cared? The speeches were over in a sudden flurry of drinking, though Mr. Tanning had the puzzled air of one with much left to say. "I could have gone on talking all night," he told Francis later, in Boston. "There I was headed for the Valley of the Shadow of Death, and not a damn soul wanted to hear about it. Oh dear," he sighed comically, "I hope you'll always be able to laugh at yourself, Sonny."

The dinner was a great success. Even Irene withheld her venom. Miss Tagliaferro's dismissal seemed a trivial matter next to the retreat of the Goods. *That* was the victory over which, all evening, Irene glittered and gloated, not having heard yet what in her narrow-mindedness she wouldn't have believed—that Prudence expected to stay on. Not return to Jamaica when your husband had been summoned by the Governor-General? Fat chance! Why, the Governor-General was a far bigger catch than Benji Tanning!

Xenia, when Francis looked again, was ruddy and laughing, her glass raised. But he was longest to see her in her hunted aspect of a moment before. Granted she did nothing that wasn't theater, her fear, though another might have shown it less fluently and more convincingly, had been real. In a flash she had known herself shamed, her career threatened, her status as an alien—who knew?—remarked upon to some personage both able and eager to order her out of the country. As a citizen Francis couldn't imagine how *careful* foreigners had to be. "Our phones are tapped," she would nod over his protests, "our letters read. In any crisis we call each other up and say, 'Isn't it a lovely day? Let's take a walk in the Park!'"

This was ridiculous. "*Become* a citizen, if you feel that way," he had said. Really, Kafka had done untold harm.

"No thank you!" Xenia replied, sunny and prompt as when speaking of marrying Mr. Tanning. "I value my freedom!"

The deeper assumption behind her panic, Francis saw with a movement of impatience that sent him up from his chair, away from the popping corks and down to the loud dark beach, the deeper assumption was that he and Benjamin were capable of dismissing her from the Cottage, coldly, without warning. "How can she be so stupid?" he said aloud to the powerful wind that nearly always rose at night, down by the shore. "She knows us, knows that we're not monsters. Why must she act as if we were? It's ridiculous—we're so gentle, really, so full of trust and readiness to love. . . ."

At which point he remembered Natalie, and how *she* had been dismissed from the Cottage—coldly, yes, and without warning—that very day. He gave a little helpless laugh. Could he turn nowhere without stumbling upon the power to harm? And was it Benjamin's power or his own? Just then Francis couldn't see that it made much difference.

He faced full into the wind that came now mixed with light rain or spray, as if power were learning how to weep over itself. The sand was damp and firm; wherever he stepped a meager zodiac of phosphorescence glimmered about his shoe. The harder he trod, the brighter it spread, greenish, before fading. Tiny creatures, Francis thought, waiting for the blow to fall, in order to shine.

The terrace, distant under festive awnings, might have been a stage viewed from the last row of a huge dark theater. Could it be raining back there, also?

Calmer than he had felt all day, Francis tried to look back on his awakening with Xenia.

He could not have said, at first, that he *was* awake. A brilliance lay upon his closed eyes like a mask, as if it was very early in the day, or as if, already, fall had come. More clearly than he had ever seen them he imagined leaves scarlet and gold whirling across lawns, across beaches into the pearly churning of an autumn surf.

The noise of the sea had first suggested that he wasn't in his own room. Which room faced the sea? Benjamin's room? Well and good, he all but murmured, then he would play at being Benjamin, and rolled over. At once against his shoulder was a softness, something that, if touched at all, would scarcely have been felt, so far did the concept of Shape lie beneath vaguer notions, warmth, fragrance, tint, thrown like veils over the sleeping figure. Against his shoulder and now against his cheek. He would not open his eyes. I'm *not* Benjamin, he tried to think; but the body remained beside him, veiled in its warmth.

Whereupon Francis woke fully.

He understood that he was in Xenia's room and in Xenia's bed and that he had drunkenly made love to her during the night. Horrified, he recalled her mouth against his neck and chest, her fingernails along his thighs, things she had uttered in a number of languages. What he couldn't bear was the suspicion that it had been, for both of them, an hour more gratifying than not. This suspicion, easily enough quelled, nevertheless lent violence to his ensuing thoughts.

He suffered then two rapid hallucinations. Frozen outside the shut pantry door, he heard Xenia's laughter, followed by his father's mocking chuckle: "Well, I'll be damned!" Next it seemed to Francis that he was gazing into his mother's eyes as into a couple of spun-sugar Easter eggs. Deep within the pupils a flowery scene of forgiveness was acted out. Growing tinier and tinier, "What did I do?" he piped, and let go of the needle. "Whatever you do, I shall love you," she replied, blood welling from her forefinger and staining her embroidery.

Worst of all, that sense of commitment! Francis pictured the years ahead as a succession of intimate French meals ordered by Xenia and served beneath pink lanterns. While he listened in silence, she would make one interesting energetic remark after another. He felt drained by a fierce languor. Only then did he count the dangers—blood, pleasure, peril in the dark, an endless falling. His lips formed words: the vampire, the *vampire*.

Opening his eyes he met her own, the somewhat blurred eyes of middle age, whites tinged with ivory, a milky blue fleck upon one iris. A golden braid lay uncoiled; but its roots were somber. The more I see, he told himself, the less I shall have to feel. However his glance wavered perilously. Nothing had foretold that she would still be naked.

"*Eh bien*, darling," said Xenia on a friendly note, "do you hate me now?"

"What do you mean?" he mumbled, wishing to be polite, but slipping nervously out of bed before he had time to wonder whether or not he was supposed to kiss her. "Excuse me, I must go to the . . ."

"Turn around," she said.

Again not thinking, he obeyed.

"*Tu es très beau*," whispered Xenia after a pause. "Come back when you're through."

In the bathroom he stared despairingly at his reflection, looking for *clues*. Why couldn't he hide in the little damp room forever? He had not the least desire to make water but, feeling that this was expected of him, wasted over a minute in a vain attempt. Finally, on a table littered with tubes, jellies, implements Francis had never dreamed existed—certain of which, however, showed signs of all too recent use—he noticed a plain rubber syringe. This he filled from the faucet, then squirted the contents gingerly into the toilet bowl. He gave a sigh of relief; it was an adequate *trompe l'oreille*. When he had replaced the syringe and washed his hands he looked about for something to wear. "Just so she won't get ideas," he said softly. But every last towel lay wet and trampled underfoot, thus limiting his choice to a frilled white nylon negligee. It was on the tight side, surprisingly—how monumental Xenia seemed without it!—but he kept it on. Anything was preferable to nakedness.

His own clothes lay here and there on the floor. Before long he would be free to change into them. But the negligee gave him, during the interview that followed, a comforting sense of not being quite real.

"So," said Xenia roguishly, pulling the sheet up over her breasts, "it's going to be *that* kind of affair!"

Not to appear a prude, Francis sat on the edge of the bed. "What kind?"

"The *Rosenkavalier* kind, of dressing up in your mistress's boudoir. Once in a while it can be very amusing."

Francis turned pale. Was she his mistress? Was it going to be an affair? She sounded so authoritative, he dared not doubt her. "Do I look funny?" he managed to croak.

Now Xenia had begun to understand, but only barely. A silence grew and grew. "My dear," she said at the end of it, "I've spent far too many years in analysis to think that you look funny."

"You think then that I'm sick," he concluded, trying to sound indifferent, but his heart pounding.

"You sound," she laughed, "like a guilty child with his mother"—in a tone that indeed was very *like* his mother's. "Please realize I'm your friend, Francis. If last night was a mistake, or if this morning you think it was, then no harm's done, is there?" She kept up her sickroom gaiety to the end. "We can still have a normal friendly relationship, can't we?"

The phrase was not fortunate. He had to strain to speak. "Can we?" he said, adding an apologetic grin that showed, for all his power to withstand her, he was only a little boy.

The first look of real distress crossed Xenia's face. "How old are you, Francis?" She raised herself and lit a cigarette. "Twenty-five?"

"Not yet," he protested, "not till October."

"But why be so helpless?" she broke out. "Do you imagine you're not a good lover? *Voyons!* It *worked* between us, you know!"

He knew. "If only you wouldn't talk about it," he said slowly through his teeth.

By now the room was brimming with sunlight. Xenia held out her hand, which he took, ever wishing to oblige, and drew Francis into a kiss—dry, reassuring, maternal. He endured it awkwardly. "Do you want to go to your room?" she sighed at length, releasing him. "Is that it?"

He began to tremble then like a child being sent from the dinner-table, as much afraid to leave as to stay.

"Tell me!" She grasped his wrist. "Can you give no thought to any-one but yourself? Was it such a terrible experience, Francis?"

The justice of the reproach together with its overtone of weary irony—which, had he been less frightened, might have persuaded Francis that he was but one in a series of disappointments—stung him into sobs.

His fear was of what she might do to him, now that he'd shown him-self unable to give what she asked. "You have no right, no right at all!" he kept saying as he shuddered on the edge of the bed, in his white gown, like a bride.

In time the *degree* of his emotion became his principal source of fear. Why didn't it end? Although the drop was slight, and he could glimpse calm waters beyond, still he clung and clung to the brink, letting the unguessed power break over him.

He heard Xenia say, "Get dressed now, why don't you?" and felt the mattress shift as she got out of bed. It annoyed him to picture her wash-ing her face, smoothing away with lotions the wrinkles *he* had caused, finally bestowing upon the mirror a long wry shrug, a roll of the eyes to heaven while painting her lips. What did Xenia, what did any foreigner care for innocence or its corruption?

The slow minutes passed. Much as Francis hated to admit it, the worst was over. He sat, however, eyes shut, perplexed as to how one decently retreats from shows of intense feeling. Sunlight fell hot upon his bare feet, the robe hung sweet and cool against his ribs. Mortified, he knew himself utterly without thought, and on the verge of sleep.

At the sound of a brisk cough his eyes opened. There was Xenia seated across from him, fully dressed, a little black book in her lap. Ignoring his weak smile, she began at top speed:

"This has been a profound shock to *me*, Francis, I hope you realize. I doubt that another woman could *ever* compose herself sufficiently to say what I am about to say now. I blame myself for the entire situation. I ought to have understood, from observing your father's *milieu* and your own mixed responses to it, what your sexual problem would consist of. I didn't mean to say sexual, for it seems to me that you have no *sexual* problem to speak of; rather the barriers, the emotional walls that have grown up within you. No wonder, with all the open talk about sex in this house, and all the nonsense that surrounds any attempt to live it out, no wonder—"

Francis had raised his hand helplessly, unable to take in more than the fact of Xenia's agitation—for which, in the bargain, he saw no reason.

At once she was on her knees beside him. "Listen!" she cried, fixing him with wet and anguished eyes. "I know you'll never hear it from me! You're set against whatever I say now. But let me help you, I beg you! You've saved my life, Francis! You helped me to work, you brought me these commissions when I had nobody to turn to! Relieve my conscience—read this little book! You're intelligent, you'll understand that it has nothing to do with religion." She pressed it into his hand, *Modern Man's Quest for a Mother* by Mother Ann Veronica of the Buffalo Ursulines. "And one thing more—*go* to an analyst! Talk it over, find out what he thinks!"

She had made up her mind that Francis was feeling certain things. He studied her with pity, spitefully pleased to prove her wrong. For just then he felt nothing—nothing, that is, but that he was stronger than Xenia. He would never again learn about life from *her*.

Off and on during the whole long day he attained these reaches of mindless calm, only to discover that a hairsbreadth divided his emptiest smiles from a need to weep uncontrollably. Now, stumbling late along the beach towards the Cottage, Francis was truly tired. The spray and wind had sent people into the ocean room. By her dress he recognized Xenia and somebody else pausing at one window with a man who might or might not have been Benjamin. It didn't matter. Francis had resolved well in advance not to join them. He felt like a ghost, haunting his father's house. But it was *all* unreal. The whole crowd wavered like ghosts through the beautiful trusting room.

12.

The next several days Francis spent in bed with what Mrs. McBride called a bug. Only when he saw that she and Benjamin and Lady Good would be off to Boston without him did he pull himself together in time to take his place, though still not well, in the car. Louis Leroy circled the gravel drive, waving regally to Loretta and the maids—a wave his master copied for the bleak remainder of *his* seraglio, Enid, Lily, Xenia, where they stood in the doorway. Mrs. Cheek had made a point of telephoning to say she wouldn't be on hand. "That's your tough luck, baby!" the old man told her jovially.

What joy to be away! At last they could be *natural* with one another. To prove as much, they ate hard-boiled eggs and cookies on the ferry across the Sound. Prudence had brought a scarf for her hair, Benjamin wore dark glasses, Francis unbuttoned his cuffs. They were clearly taking their cue from any of a dozen little family groups—father, mother, child—sitting or romping about the deck, younger in years but not in spirit. And they tossed their crumpled wax paper overboard with the best.

With their arrival in Boston, the vacation seemed really to have begun. They gawked at a gilded dome. Nobody spoke in sentences. "Those *trees*," wondered Mrs. McBride as though she had spent her life in a slum, "so green!" "Benjamin! Swans!" cried Lady Good, clapping her hands. He nodded happily. At the hotel a pink-and-gold suite awaited them. They ordered highballs. The young waiter switched on the television set without even being asked. For a blissful spell they stared at the screen, lively but dimmed by daylight. Every so often they turned for sustenance to the great green Common that all but sang up to them, "Come on down! You're nice simple folks like the rest of us! Everybody's welcome here!"

Gone were the responsibilities, the rivalries, the riddles of life at the Cottage. They tottered down to dinner in a daze of freedom. With no pressure upon them to talk, how beautifully they did without it! Once Mr. Tanning said, "Please explain to me how a freshly grilled lamb chop can be served stone cold." But he was addressing the headwaiter, it couldn't fairly be called conversation. The rest of the time they conveyed their extreme self-satisfaction in dumb show, sighing and smiling and smacking their lips. The warmth that made Francis's skin tingle, was it fever or family feeling?

After dinner he and Lady Good escorted the old man to the hospital. He would sleep there, take more tests on the morrow, and join them for, as he put it, a last supper. Francis bit his lip; he had already arranged to dine with Jane Westlake. "Bring her along, Sonny," his father smiled ever so sweetly, "I'd love to meet her." "Francis and I have a date to look at pictures tomorrow," Lady Good murmured. Once again all three exchanged adoring glances.

She added mildly, as Louis headed back to the hotel, "This is my last week in America, you know."

"No, I didn't know," said Francis.

"Well, it is. So hush, there's nothing more to say."

Her mildness was that of some remembered childhood, *Paul et Vir-*

ginie or a Song of Innocence. It brimmed with a romance that excited no scruple. Lady Good might have been painted by Burne-Jones in color-of-thought robes, holding out to her lover a grail of forbearance and otherworldly comfort. Straightway Francis perceived that she had stayed on for the sole purpose of this gentler renunciation, before following her husband. It wasn't she who had been corrupted by the Cottage, so much as Francis himself by Xenia's Mediterranean view of things. In his heart he confessed to Prudence that he had doubted her, and begged her pardon. If only all women loved as wisely as she!

They drank Mrs. McBride's hot milk, then parted for the night. "I'll be right in this middle bedroom," said the nurse, "so just call if you need me. I wonder if you still haven't a touch of fever," she added, feeling Francis's cheek.

"I think it's just that I'm already asleep," he smiled.

Morning found him hot and exhausted by dreams. But he had swallowed aspirin and guided Lady Good dutifully among the old masters. Planning to see the remaining galleries after lunch, they groped their way now out of the blinding noon into some dim ice-cold restaurant, Italian as it soon appeared, sank into a booth and ordered tall glasses of ale. "Would ravioli be light?" she wondered, resolving in the same breath to try eggplant. Then, with foam on her lip and elbows on the table, she started in. Last night there may have been nothing more to say. Today there was plenty.

Francis saw that she wouldn't be dissuaded. "What's so moving about Poussin," he had begun hopefully, "is the way he never *insists* on things." Lady Good was far from taking the hint. "I might as well admit that I'm at my wits' end," was all the response he got.

"I frankly don't understand him," she went on. "I fail to see what he gives or what he gets. Had we not come away yesterday, my private opinion is that he would have *collapsed*. All those people, not one of whom he can abide! And yet he welcomes them, listens to them, lets them sap his strength—why?"

"He likes people. He forgets that he doesn't like *those* people," said Francis, covering a yawn.

"Is that it?" she wondered.

"The firm still means a lot to him. Most of those men were partners."

Lady Good sneered. "Partners! Why," speaking with renewed force, "*why* has Charlie Cheek taken to drink? I'd always thought it *fatal* for a reformed alcoholic to touch even a drop of liquor."

"Probably Irene put him up to it. Let's see, what would her plot be? Oh of course," Francis brightened to think how plausible it sounded, "she means to have him die of drink. Then she can marry her favorite fella."

"She could as easily get a divorce. More easily, I daresay."

"All right. Then she means him *not* to die, but to turn back into a hopeless lush. He'll be her Cross. Benji will think: That girl has guts. The old flame will burst from the ashes."

Lady Good looked dubious.

"Don't you agree?"

"Finish this for me, like a dear." She pushed her glass of ale towards him, seeing that his own was empty. "I'd forgot it makes me sick. No, I think it's because Charlie loves her."

"Perfect!" Francis clapped his hands. "He loves her enough to start drinking for the sake of her plot, at the risk of his health, his life!"

"No, Francis." She covered her eyes for a second. "Charlie loves Irene and her conduct makes him unhappy. When you love somebody—" She broke off.

A remarkable hour followed. Francis began to see what he would never before have suspected—that Lady Good was mistress of many moods, that in her blunt Anglo-Saxon way she could play the Serpent of old Nile as well as Xenia. Better than Xenia, he soon decided, because less artfully. She rambled on, now earnest, now resigned, now positively incoherent. Her subject, often at two or three removes, seemed to be Benjamin's bewildering attachments to other women—or was it his neglect of Prudence herself? What could she do but return to Jamaica?

She refused to be made a laughingstock—not that she cared in the slightest what a bunch of silly women thought. A moment later she revealed that Benjamin's feeling had no bearing on the *main* issue, that of her duty to Sir Edward. She waxed sententious. Marriage brought with it distinct obligations. For over twenty-five years the Goods had shared a life rich in intellectual exchange and mutual respect. Ned had his molasses factory, she had her books. The life had taught her—as the kind of book she cared for hadn't—that marriage was no solution. The majority of her married friends would have gone much further, as human beings, without it. One wasn't meant to live shut up with a member of the opposite sex. Among the London fogs Lady Good would have thrown herself into the packed career of a bluestocking. But among breadfruit and sugar cane, those passionate climes, the only white woman for ten miles, with moreover nothing but contempt for the other colonial wives, it seemed natural that she had cultivated, alone at her piano, a longing for variety and romance. Hence Benjamin. The rub was that she hadn't been the only one so honored. Complaining? No. What right had she to complain, considering how little he had had in return for all his—here Prudence threw down her napkin. She wasn't Irene, wasn't going to endanger that quarter century of companionable esteem, not on your life, no! and *that* was why she had made up her mind to go home. That was *exactly* why, she concluded with a look of pleased surprise, as when a game of patience comes out unexpectedly. Had Francis done eating? Lady Good drained her coffee cup, feeling up to anything, even a second look at the Boston Museum.

His first reaction was to be entertained. Later, though still entertained, Francis found himself growing more and more depressed. What's wrong with me? he kept wondering. The complexities of his father's world and his father's women had absorbed him in the past. They seemed now, however, on the point of no longer doing so. Together with something close to fear, Francis felt a real resentment of the way his companion summoned him back, step by step, from the simplifying half-lights in which she had shown herself the day before. He had loved that dim ikon of her, wisely renouncing. He had loved even more Benjamin's air of acquiescence to it, of final willingness to admit that the last love of a long life was soon to take leave of him. But today brought to light nothing renunciatory about Lady Good. Like all the others, she gazed at Francis from the very heart of her dilemma. "You have played the child long enough," she might have been saying. "Please to remember you are a grown man, one who must reasonably be expected to witness without flinching the moral crisis of a grown woman." He scowled at the ruins of his gorgonzola. If such were the thrills and chills of maturity—! Signaling to their waiter, he tried to reason with himself. She *wasn't* like the others. She was kinder, finer—Francis reached for the essential point to be made but it kept eluding him. They were on their feet, weaving through tables in the cold gloom they had so swiftly grown used to, before it came to him. She was unlike the others because nothing sexual entered into her feelings for Benjamin. Yes; that made sense. Reassured, he smiled, although a bit mechanically. Outside the sun broke on them like a wave.

For Lady Good had waited for the brilliant racket of the street to deflect what he knew to be her most pointed words.

"A thing I wish *you'd* decide for me," she said in the tone of one who must choose between crumpets and cake, "is whether or not I should go to bed with Benjamin."

Francis gave a little start, more like a twitch, the relic of some old disorder. He put a hand to his hot cheek. Quite so, he tried to think, one mustn't neglect that side of it. But hadn't he always known the truth? Wasn't it—going to bed with Benjamin—for all of them, *the* side? What else explained cocktails, silk dresses, flowers in the ocean room? Here now was Lady Good impeccably giving him the clue to *her* charade. He might have known. Still, he wanted to be polite, and caught her eye with a glare of nervous interest.

"Oh, it's not a matter of satisfying him physically," she sang out as they paused on a curb. "I'm certain I could do that. But there's so much else to consider."

Francis thought of his father's body, so feeble, so veined and scarred. "I'd always imagined he wasn't well enough."

"It appears now that he is. Didn't Dr. Samuels say he was? And if Irene—" but she stopped herself. "I've wondered, too," she smiled, "if I mightn't simply be afraid of *that*, of his no longer caring for me, Benjamin I mean, were I once to let it reach that stage. Is it really what *he* wants? I can't think that it is. But then, I'm not a man, I don't know."

Had she appealed to his own experience? "Perhaps," said Francis, "he's afraid not to want it."

Lady Good stiffened. "If he didn't, you mean, his life would be over? Is that his criterion—potency? Is it yours?"

"Isn't it everybody's?" Francis ventured, though surely her question had been rhetorical. She kept right on talking, at any rate.

"Then there's the whole thing of what I owe to Ned. Would it be fair to him? He's been so wonderfully understanding up to now. Dear Francis," breaking in on herself, "I seem to be caught in a squirrel run. What a trial for you! You must think me very silly. But I'm not like those other women, I can't treat things lightly."

"Oh look!" he exclaimed in spite of himself, squinting at a yellow poster. "A revival of *Intolerance*." But it had taken place the previous month.

"You're right, of course," Lady Good sighed, "it's not *your* decision. You can't help me."

Francis blushed. He wished she hadn't found this out.

"I think you're wrong about his not caring for you," he said. "Whatever happens, he's tremendously loyal. Just look at all the others, the women at the Cottage, the *wives!* He's loved them and he's loyal. They may be the death of him, but he's loyal."

"Then I am selfish," said Lady Good, "in not wanting to be the death of him."

"He's even loyal to Irene!"

"Precisely." Her voice reached him over water. Francis looked at her, impressed. Then, without warning, she laughed. "You've helped me make my decision after all."

"What do you mean?" he asked with excitement. "Your mind's made up?"

Whereupon she laughed again, and took his arm.

It was amazing. He had never admired her more. Throughout the dreadful avowal she had kept a truly breathtaking dignity. If Prudence had been the heroine of a novel he would have fallen in love with her on the spot. As it was, however, Francis had already begun to distinguish between her perfect form and what she had managed to convey with it. From then on, he knew, they would have less and less to say to one another. The knowledge left him melancholy, as though *he* was the renouncing figure. Then, after a bit, he felt in his heart that he was bored with her.

"Of course, I believe in a hopeless passion," he threw out as he led her up the steps of the Museum.

But this was going too far. She gave him a stern gray twinkle. "I wish I thought you did, Francis."

Back inside, they started through the Persian and Indian rooms. These being empty, Lady Good, soon baffled by the calligraphy on a blue tile, took up her topic afresh.

"I honestly *don't* see what Irene gets out of it."

"Nothing at present," he murmured distantly.

"I beg your pardon, dear?"

"Nothing at present, I said."

"I know one thing, *I* should never be so insensitive. At the first sign of any loss of interest in *me*, I should hastily withdraw." It was then, at last, that Lady Good must have felt something of the sort in her listener, for she said no more.

So they walked, neither together nor as yet very far apart, and did not speak, unless to remark upon the glaze of a pot, the curl of a lip suggesting at once laughter and tears, the great gods of porous stone, seated or dancing, their flesh like folds of lava. There was a distance between these figures and Francis which did not shrink as he approached them.

It wasn't, he knew, the shimmering glass—wherein Lady Good's movements were reflected from the far side of the room—that kept him from a nicer apprehension of the picture beneath. Something in the picture itself, a perfection that it had, or an understanding of its subject that he didn't, put him off.

He had stopped to examine a miniature of Krishna among the milkmaids. They smiled up at the slate blue god, eight or ten damsels. Behind a wall palms rose; behind these, princely terraces. A yellow-and-black sun with a man's face looked down on it all.

Were they dancing? What did it mean? Francis felt that his brow was burning. I have caught some terrible disease, he thought.

13.

What odd ideas people had of how to act when first married! Jane's was to pretend it hadn't happened, that she had hardly reached the age of fraternity pins and high-school yearbooks. She skipped off the elevator, shrieked, kissed Francis smartly as if still vague about the possible meaning of kisses, then peered up and down the carpeted hall with the wariness of one fresh from the farm, who'd heard what went on in hotels. He had to admit she looked the part in her pale lilac dress, virginal, high-throated, puff-sleeved, a matching ribbon wound in her black curls. She wore less lipstick than before, and no nail polish. It was well he had asked her up for a drink in their sitting room—she'd get little more than lemonade in the bar downstairs. As against her battered appearance on the pier in New York, the effect today was of a really extraordinary youngness. It wasn't only an effect, either; she *was* young, younger than Francis had ever known her.

What with an hour's nap, more aspirin, the knowledge of a cocktail already poured, he was feeling better when Jane arrived. A moment before he had carried two brimming glasses to where his father and Lady Good sat on the loveseat, holding hands. The day at the hospital had worn Mr. Tanning out—not so much the tests as the waiting, the sense of being ignored for long minutes at a time. That he was old and ill had been put to him strongly enough by his mere presence there, seated on a table, wrapped in a starched smock. At such times a great deal of attention was needed to ward off the foretaste of pain and death. And there hadn't been, Benjamin told them ruefully, a single sexy nurse.

"Well, Francis's friend is bound to be most attractive," said Lady Good, her glass dribbling.

"Then there was this smart aleck of a young doctor," Benjamin went on. "Do you know what he wanted to do? He has a theory about deadening the nerve that connects the heart and the brain. He uses a needle six inches long, inserted just over the collarbone. I tried to ask him how he could be sure of hitting the nerve. 'Oh Mr. Tanning,' he said, 'don't worry about that—that's *my* business!' 'The hell it is,' I said. I just didn't like the sound of it, Francis. The old poop's been deadened enough in his day."

The telephone rang, announcing their guest.

Of course, when Francis brought her in, he couldn't think of her married name. Jane herself took a few seconds to produce it. Both of them seemed to have forgotten not only Roger Massey but the whole nature of his connection with Jane.

"What's this?" cried Mr. Tanning. "Married? Do my old ears deceive me?"

"Four weeks Friday," confessed Jane. "Isn't it crazy?"

Crazy or not, the old man said, her husband would be a pretty lucky fellow. Where was he, by the way? In Connecticut? Teaching? While

Jane catalogued etchings at Harvard? "Oh I see," he drawled with a comic look of *not* seeing that sent her into enchanted giggles. "And are you going to invite me up to look at the etchings?" he pursued. "Or is that what all the boys say?"

"No," Jane said demurely. "You're the very first."

"Oh I am?" The old man peered round at Francis. "What's wrong with *you*, my stalwart son?"

Lady Good sent Francis a secret smile, to find Benjamin so full of fun. But for Francis the fun soon took on a darker aspect. "Here I understood I was going to meet my future daughter-in-law," Mr. Tanning was telling Jane almost petulantly, "and who shows up but an old married woman like you!"

"Is it that you have an exclusive claim over old married women?" said Lady Good.

"Oh dear . . ." He shook his head and wiped his eye with exaggerated self-pity. His shaky hand held out an empty glass. Jane was laughing away, a bit uncontrollably. Francis tried to do the same, but his mouth hurt from the effort. Clearly enough Mr. Tanning's day at the hospital had set him, bored and with sterile odors in his nostrils, to thinking about grandchildren, not Lily and the twins, rather a child who should bear his own name, Francis's child. He filled his father's glass in a kind of anguish, guessing more and more. Because he trusted no one else to tell him the truth, he shrank from meeting Benjamin's eye. He feared reading then and there the old man's knowledge that such a child would never be—a knowledge that might have come upon him at any time during the past years or the past minutes, watching Francis and Jane together. It wasn't just that Jane was married. No, what Benjamin would be wanting was to see his son behave as men *did* behave with a pretty woman—whether she was married, or one's mother, or one's daughter. This Francis knew he had never learned to do. So that his fate was clear . . . was it? he wondered; there would be no child? The thought affected him in the strangest possible way. Not for months did Francis recall that instant, or begin to understand his emotion. Right then, he needed something to hold on to. He reached for his glass. Mr. Tanning raised his own, still thinking of the morrow. "Let it not be said," he sighed, "that the condemned man met his destiny uncheered."

They went on to dinner. More cocktails were ordered, along with wine and the richest food. "If Mrs. McBride can go out on a heavy date," said Benjamin, "so can I." The poor nurse, who as of tomorrow would be on duty at the hospital, was spending the evening with a cousin's widow.

An hour later Mr. Tanning had ordered *crêpes suzette*. Beneath so many half-empty plates and glasses the tablecloth couldn't be seen. "And clear away this mess, please," he told the waiter. Then, turning to Francis, "Do me a favor, Sonny," he said dully. "Put in a call to Xenia tomorrow morning and ask her, as politely as you can, to limit her visit to another ten days. I never dreamed the sittings would be such a strain on my system. I'd understood they were to last only a week or so, also that I'd be able to move about, talk or write letters. Instead, I'm put in a baby's high chair and told to keep perfectly still. I like your friend, Francis. You know that. She's a fine woman. But it's like eating goose or venison; after a while you just can't take any more. Tell her whatever you like, that I promised her room to another guest—I don't give a damn what you say. I expect to be back there in a week's time. Tell her she can have two more sittings, but that's the limit. O.K.?"

These words, uttered slowly and wearily while the women looked elsewhere, appalled Francis. It was true, he wanted never to see Xenia again; but, once away from her, he had easily persuaded himself that by seducing him *she* had suffered wrong at *his* hands. The pity was that he couldn't recognize the classic remorse of a young man brought up to believe in—if necessary, to invent—some kind of surpassing purity within even the unlikeliest woman. Experience had taught Francis—at least Vinnie's experience had, his own amounted to so little—that "the man" was invariably to blame in these matters. He saw no way of complying with his father's request.

"What about the bust of Lily?" he objected feebly.

"That's between Lily and Xenia," said Benjamin.

"You commissioned it, though."

"Francis, I'm sick and tired of the whole question."

"Can you see how it's rather embarrassing for *me?*"

"Don't let it be. Blame it all on the Monster," Benjamin grinned, alluding to Fern's name for him since the divorce. People who saw Fern brought back word that she was still very bitter, to the point of forbidding you to speak of the Monster in her hearing. An enormous basket of snapdragons and smilax, accompanied by a letter in the old man's round careful hand, had gone unacknowledged. At times you wondered, or Francis did, if he'd done anything in life but give offense to women.

He looked helplessly at his father. He wanted to say, "Please! *I* can't be the one to send her away! She'll think it's my doing—*I'll* be the monster!" But he held his tongue, flattered by the novelty of a direct request from Benjamin. He would have to find some way of his own not to carry it out.

It was late when they parted on the street. Lady Good said, "I'll escort Benjamin to the hospital, Francis, whilst you and Jane go dancing, or whatever young people do. That fearsome ordeal lies ahead of him in the morning, and look at him, he's worn out!" Benjamin gave them all a crumpled smile. He shuffled forward to kiss Jane, then Francis, on the cheek, contriving to slip a bill into his son's hand. "Go on now," he whispered, "paint the town red!" Francis checked a movement of protest. He was shocked not so much by a gift of money, which just then he lacked wit to refuse, as by the implication that he was caught up with Jane in the kind of romance that fed on dance bands and expensive corner tables. Paint the town red! Hadn't Benjamin understood that Jane was married? Indeed he had. From the car window he waved and Prudence blew a kiss. And then she tenderly kissed the old man, before their very eyes. The last thing Francis saw his father do, as Louis Leroy drove away, was wink at them over his companion's shoulder. That was how you behaved (the wink said) with married women.

"What a dear old man." Jane spoke in a dreamer's voice.

"He wanted you for a daughter-in-law."

"Yes, that was sweet."

"How is Roger?"

"You'll see him Friday. He thinks they're going to draft him."

"Into the army?" cried Francis. "But he's married!"

After thinking it over, she said indulgently, "There are lots of things being married doesn't prevent."

He stopped and stared. "Aren't you happy?"

"Oh, of course!"

"Of course?"

"I mean, I've known Roger all my life," said Jane, a shadow of impatience crossing her face. "Whether or not he makes me happy isn't the point."

"But you make *him* happy?"

"Oh, of course!" she said a second time.

"I see. Have I said that I like Roger? I do."

"I'm glad you do. He's a wonderful person. Francis? Are you all right?" He had stumbled, somewhat.

"I've had a slight fever these days. . . ."

"We oughtn't to be standing here. . . ."

"Would a taxi be wise?" He watched Jane hail one, seeing her, for all their drinking, a bit embarrassed now by what she had conveyed. Francis hadn't cared to hear about her marriage, had in fact come close to falling flat on his face, he so much hadn't cared to hear about it. Both of them leaned back against the creaking leather, frowning. He gave the driver her address. Unaccountably Jane's mood changed to one of atonement.

"When I think what a *pig* I made of myself!" she groaned. "Letting your father order that second bottle of champagne! Eek! Why didn't you stop me?"

"*Cálmati, cálmati.*"

"Oh dear, you still remember!"

"What?"

"Your Italian. I've forgotten all of mine. They just *stare* at me in the fruit store!" In this way Jane recovered her girlishness of before dinner. But Francis had had his glimpse of what dark machinery kept the merry-go-round revolving. While they sped across the river he studied her profile dim against ten dozen watery lights. She was once in love with me, he reflected, letting his eyes glaze as over some ancient irrelevant bit of gossip.

She ushered him into the apartment. He saw a room spacious but bare; a bed, two chairs, bookshelves partly built, unpacked boxes—all lit by a kerosene lamp in the middle of the floor. The building, it seemed, was being rewired. Sheets had been tacked for privacy across the lower halves of windows. It made Francis think of a setting in which children played at keeping house. Here and there he recognized, perhaps by their look of having been promised a better home, objects acquired by Jane in Europe—art books, a stylish umbrella, the worm-drilled Negro king from a Neapolitan crèche and, slumped in the lamplight, a straw doll with a felt bean pod for its head. There were three faces in this pod. The first looked out on the world and smiled; above it a smaller one slept, eyes closed, as though waiting its turn; the topmost bean had as yet no features of any description. Francis shivered in spite of himself. The thing gave out an uncanny air of clairvoyance. If he had had such a doll as a child, he would have told secrets to the little faceless head at the top, then let them filter slowly down into the head that smiled.

"Here." Jane handed him a tumbler. "Tell me if you like it. It's apricot brandy." He noticed that her hand was trembling. "What do you *think* about it all?" she added vaguely.

He had been wondering at her nervousness. He wasn't going to touch her. Still—thanks to Xenia—the idea had crossed his mind, angering him. "I think we are drunk," he said.

"Be serious! I mean, tell me what colors I should use."

"Violet. Violet on this wall. Perhaps a gamboge pouf below."

Her brow puckered.

"And at the windows something blue and gauzy, so people outside may know that the room is filling up with tears."

"Oh, Francis . . ."

"What's wrong?"

"Aren't *you* happy?"

The question caught him off guard. He'd fancied her on the verge of some further confidence. "Of course!" he replied quickly, but missed the natural note she had sounded with the same words.

Jane didn't miss it, evidently. She gave him a strange calm smile and brought out for the occasion her flattest idiom. "I'm glad," she said. "Because you deserve to be."

It provoked Francis to say more. He couldn't bear to have *her* take him at face value.

"You ask if I'm happy," he declaimed, "when you've given yourself to another man!" Whereupon he grasped her by the shoulders and shook her, insolently, the way he'd seen it done in the movies. Even then Jane didn't understand it as a joke. For a moment her puzzled face wobbled back and forth, eyes seeking his own until, puzzled now himself, he had to turn miserably away. "I'm too conscious to be happy," he began, addressing the bean-pod doll. "If I were to fall nobody would catch me. I have to keep dodging people on the street. They never look where they're going. They could walk right into me and knock me down. It's always *my* consciousness. He sits in that house like a Pasha in his harem, while I run to and fro delivering messages, making peace, like a—like a . . . I'm sorry," Francis lowered his voice and sipped the sweet liquor, "I mustn't talk about myself." But Jane was gazing at him with parted lips.

"I should like," he pursued therefore, "to do something at cross-purposes, something *against* my consciousness. I should like to feel, no matter what I thought I was up to, that the real meaning of my action was hidden from me. I want—"

"Please!" Jane held up a hand. "This isn't *you* talking."

"Isn't it? So much the better!"

"You're so wise and sure of yourself," she almost pleaded. "When other people are with you they feel that what they do makes sense. Roger said this, though you'd hardly—"

"I'm not talking about other people," said Francis. "They have their lives. I want mine to be like the ship that seems to sail for a certain mark, but instead gets sucked miles and miles out of its course by an unseen current."

"You wouldn't enjoy that," said Jane unhappily. "It sounds too much like what I go through every day."

"*I'd* enjoy it. Other people would have to watch out for me, for a change. No," Francis managed a dark gleam, "better yet: someone who resembles me as I am now would have to watch out for me."

They were sitting on the floor by now. "Besides," Jane presently said, "I'd never describe you as *specially* conscious of things." Francis looked up amazed. Why, she was arguing with him!

"Of what things, pray?" he snapped.

Not answering, Jane bent sideways, towards the chimney of the lamp, to light her cigarette from its invisible uppouring of heat. She was asking to be let off, but the damage had been done. It remained for Francis to show her something about his consciousness.

"If you're trying to say I never noticed," he said, pleased by his own cunning, "how close you came—how close *we* came, in Rome, to . . . to loving each other . . ." He stammered to a halt, however, in the gentlest, mournfullest of voices. Each sat silent with surprise. These might have been the first intimate words ever to be spoken between them. For Francis, who felt he'd given himself away, the moment held an unbearable anxiety. It was easier for Jane, he supposed; that is, she could fall back upon her new role of matron, "lady of the house": she would rise now offended, show him firmly to the door, quite as any woman in his mother's world, confident that he would obey out of his regard for Forms. But to Francis's astonishment, to his despair—he took it as the clearest sign yet of the power he had over her—Jane did no such thing.

Far from stiffening with outrage, she seemed to have gone weak, acquiescent, sadly nodding over what he had said. She actually untied the ribbon in her hair. The black curls, shaken, fell below her shoulders.

"Yes, I know," she sighed, "your ship put off its course—that's what I go through every day. Maybe it doesn't happen to men, that drifting feeling, day after day being beside the point." She wrung her hands in the lamplight, not absurdly. "Of course I loved you in Rome. I love you still—"

Had he ever heard these words from anyone? He all but fainted with apprehension.

"—though not in the same way—"

His eyes closed with relief. Jane haltingly completed her thought: "—yet life's so strange. A year from now I'll be an army wife, maybe. I'm already so far from where I once imagined being, I wait for it to start making sense. . . ."

"That's it!" he breathed. "You're afloat!" She *was*. Little Jane, he mused, grown up now, married, in midstream suddenly, on her way to the fulfillment of her own mysterious nature—some green and growing island arrived at over deep waters, or so he pictured it from where he loitered on the mainland, risking at most the lukewarm shallows. "I think it's glorious," he said; "it makes you so tremendously real." Though Francis couldn't have explained his meaning—was reality that which floated further and further from his reach?—it appeared to please Jane. She blinked, looked away, might have turned pink in a stronger light. He had a vision of how enjoyable it could be, this business of giving pleasure to women. How easy, simply, to *give!* Provided the woman didn't, like Xenia, begin by *taking*, why, there was nothing to it!

He felt a real gratitude towards Jane, which he mistook for love long enough to wonder why he'd never loved her before. In Italy they'd spent whole days together, without his feeling the first tremor, the first ache started in him by the sight of her, now that he could never possess her. *That* made the difference: it was too late, it was wonderfully, blessedly too late! It might as well have been love he felt, after all. The dark side of love, the whole degrading panicky sexual side, was what she would never endure from him and what he'd never dream of asking her to endure. How joyously he intended to protect her marriage! The naked sword dangled no longer over their heads; it had fallen, cutting him free, and would lie henceforth between them. He saw himself throughout a long life giving her comfort, an angel helping her to bear no matter what earthly union. This was something Francis knew how to ask of women; he remembered Enid, he remembered Lady Good. He held out his hand, which Jane took gently, chastely. A spot of color in her cheek made him think: carnation. They needed one another, he knew then, in exactly the same way.

After a while she whispered, "Put your head in my lap," and there he lay, mindlessly, for how long he couldn't tell, her fingers stroking his hot brow. A thousand infant impulses toward food and sleep drifted over him like snow. "It's been so long," he mumbled incoherently.

Then on the very edge of sleep—just as in nightmares, when he had frantically barricaded himself from the approach of footsteps, and, panting, back to the door of his retreat, thought, "At last, at last!" only then to catch sight of the insane face of his pursuer filling up the open and forgotten window—his whole body, like a tuning fork or crystal goblet flicked, began to tingle with lust. It was horrible. He had never felt desire so urgent.

Without pausing to see whether there mightn't have been something of the sort on her side, Francis scrambled to his feet, trying clumsily to hide from Jane what had already betrayed him to himself. He made a stab at excuses, that it was late, that his head ached, that he'd hope to see her the next day. If he didn't leave at once all would be spoiled. All *was* spoiled, her silence told him, by his haste and confusion. Still he dawdled, stammering, lying, until he perceived that she was in no way detaining him. Her eyes were fixed upon the glowing chimney of the lamp. A minute later Francis found himself outdoors, walking, then running through the pools of brilliance shed at intervals by streetlamps, and, in between, the wells of darkness rustling under the tall trees.

14.

At the end of an avenue he came to a subway station. "Will this take me anywhere near the Common?" he asked the old man behind bars in the change booth, who wearily named the appropriate train and stop. Francis paced the platform, past thought; he felt each internal organ, turned to iron, grind dully against its neighbor. The train arrived, its green gothic cars unexpectedly crowded with old and young, white, yellow and black, some evidently married and accompanied, Francis noticed frowning, by children so young they were hardly able to walk. The only vacant seat was next to the mother of such a one, a tiny boy with skin like quartz, clinging to her flowered skirts. He sat down. The whole group struck him as wrong. Each face wore the dazed look of a person in a state of shock, limp and unresponsive. A young girl moaned as the train got under way. Each might have recently died, Francis among them, heading now for his predestined place in hell. But this suspicion no sooner crossed his mind than the train swung upward into the starry night. The air blew warm and fresh, the river glistened beneath them— there would be no easy way out of life. Far from any real world his companions had abandoned, it had been (a chance word from the young mother to her husband explained) the world of a late movie that had released its patrons to joggle listlessly home. The train clattered and shrieked, causing the woman to stroke her child's colorless hair. The child itself showed no sign of hearing or feeling. Too young to talk, too small to think, it lurched back and forth in the alert stupor of infancy. When the train slowed down for a stop the little thing lost balance briefly, recovering itself by resting a hand not much larger than a postage stamp on Francis's knee.

He glared at the child, at its brainless faith in the world as a kindly place, where upon reaching out one was steadied by powers gigantic but benign. It hadn't yet learned that one wasn't welcome to lean on others. Perhaps, thought Francis, the crashing down of a fist onto those fragile fingers would bring home the lesson, which could never be learned too early in life—still there remained the sickening vulnerability of the child to contend with. It tottered and clung, its tiny translucent hand flexing in an almost celestial incapacity on the giant knee. It lacked even strength to plead for its life; all simply it trusted the knee would be merciful. Francis stood up in a rage. Even so, the child neither fell nor—idiot!—felt any part of Francis's ill will, though its mother's gasp of reproach sent him striding down the car and out onto the ramshackle platform. This wasn't the right stop. No matter, he would walk the rest of the way; and down the stairs he went, shuddering with anger at everything he knew.

The streets were empty, and were not. Footsteps kept drawing closer. In the vitrine of a pharmacy knives and scissors wavered towards him through flawed panes. Rounding a corner, Francis made out far ahead the dim treetops of the Common and headed for them. Now human figures began to detach themselves from doorways; others came walking, bearing down on him. He fought a desire to peer into their faces. When they had passed he heard them stop, humming softly or whistling, turning like tops. Once he saw a tall shadow revolve against a building and set slowly out in his direction. His heart pounded. Before long he couldn't distinguish desire from terror. In the dark turnings of the Public Garden a woman called to him. Within a thicket a boy lit a match and smiled. Farther on, leaning over a railing, a figure considered its image in water. Somebody at least was looking elsewhere—but how could one see for the lapping of the little waves?—and then the figure turned, an old man with his clothes open, beckoning. Francis hurried past. He understood what had gone on in the hearts of those who now and then were found dead in parks at dawn, grass-stained, anonymous.

Back in the hotel he found a light burning in the foyer of their suite. Lady Good's door was shut, but not Mrs. McBride's. Was it so early she hadn't yet come in? His watch read five minutes to twelve. It could have been three in the morning. How was he ever going to sleep? Francis undressed and went into his bathroom, locking the door.

While the tub filled he watched his body in the mirror that backed the door. He couldn't feel that it was his. It belonged to Xenia, to Jane, to a whore whose name he had never known; it belonged, no less, to Vinnie and Benjamin, of whose love it was the only living reminder— disturbingly marked with the two flat rose-brown eyes set in the chest, the navel, the patch of hair, the thing, a desolate pallor of skin encircling, dividing. Unlike the face, which did belong to him, hanging white and worried above it, his body had no meaning. Like a hieroglyph, a sun or a ship, it signified something quite apart from what it represented. It felt warm to his touch, full of life, while his face and the hands that obeyed his face were cold, passive, drifting with the body's currents of desire, anger, and fear.

His bath was full. He sprinkled it with a handful of pine-scented salts. Before dipping a foot in the water he unlocked the door—it had never been his wish to die—and looked about one last time. There was the mirror, the razor, the towel. He took from his finger the little gold ring with the owl, kissed it and set it upon the basin. Presently he heard—but from where?—the voice of an old man whispering *Ecco, Signore!* and the razor was placed in Francis's hand. Paint the town red! Up to his neck in warm water now, almost afloat, he used his last defense against the flesh. The blade was very sharp; something began easily to separate, then to resist, tougher than a thong of leather. The water, so dazzling clear when he began cutting, turned red instantly. *Porta fortuna!* He could no longer see what he was doing, or tell, when the severe pain overcame him, whether or not he had succeeded. He cried out once, and lost consciousness.

15.

House after house came into view, each very like the next. It shocked her to see how much building had been done. On the cramped lawns, barely shaded by saplings, children were playing with pets. So much activity, so many lives!—she shook her head, a bit puzzled and sickened by the sight. Didn't people know better than to put up houses, bear children, let kittens live? Hadn't they *learned*, during the how many years since Vinnie'd last left New York? Now especially, when it was crucial for Defense that people not live in tight communities, why, the whole country had turned into one endless suburb!

Outside a high wind blew, she deduced from the dance of laundry on lines. As the train sped by, house after house wheeled slowly, rank upon rank, to follow its passage wide-eyed. Knowing no motion or singleness of their own, they were staring directly at Vinnie, the solitary, the city dweller hurrying now between cities in a gray "off-the-rack" dress with cotton roses, yellow, at her throat. And as they stared they slowly backed away.

Her imagination peopled every house with a mother and child. Time and again, under green roofs with aerials or red roofs with gingerbread, a scene evolved between them. The mother would be standing at the head of a dinky little stair that led perhaps to the cellar, calling down to the child who had disobeyed her, or shortly would. Was there something damaged at his feet? Had she herself lived through such a moment? The scene asked of her some really exact feeling, but her mind kept wandering, toppling over dully, or playing like lightning on a deserted house, too brightly and too briefly for any sense to be made out of it.

Nevertheless she faced the scene, straining until her mind's eye hurt. Vinnie had always faced things, with a kind of beautiful fatality. You had never seen her turn away. No matter what gale life thrust her into, she bore it, a sister to those weathered mermaids on the prows of whalers. In between had come spells of tense and watchful calm—the eight years between her father's death and Ben's first proven infidelity; the thirteen years between their divorce and the ringing of her ivory-white telephone today, at seven in the morning. Disaster brought her to life. She had had, that day years ago, only to see the familiar script, smell the scent with which Natalie Bigelow had drenched her disgusting letter; she had only to hear, today, the strange British voice repeating, "Mrs. Tanning? Mrs. Tanning? This is Prudence Good speaking. You may not know who I am . . ."—although of course she did know, and knew at once, as on that other morning looking down into Ben's handkerchief drawer, knew with a sense of canvas being hoisted and yardarms creaking that more would follow. The houses dwindled in her wake, the depths raced beneath her. It was another voyage, and what would be left of her at its end, already worn silver here and there with age?

"Is this what I was created for?" cried Vinnie, silent and apprehensive among the fleeing vistas. "Tell me," she went on, addressing no one, "because I've got to know. The very last thing I want is to be dependent on others. I have my own room, my own habits—if that's not little enough to ask! Just tell me this is my duty and I'll *do* it. Don't be afraid! *I'm* not, I can face it. Just tell me! I've got to know!"

What troubled her was that something lagged behind. Something refused to be dislodged from her familiar gray room, from between the pages of *Time* ("I don't trust it but it puts me to sleep") or from the needlepoint garlands she'd stitched to cover her little provincial chair. Here and now, ridiculous as it sounded. Vinnie missed the assurance that anything belonged to her. This wasn't her chair she rode in; it wasn't her view, her window, her world. Her mind had outstripped her feelings. Miles from port, the wooden mermaid kept glancing back with misgivings, for the ship seemed not yet to be under way.

It was exhausting not to feel, not to know what you felt. Three hours later, in Boston, Vinnie stepped off an elevator. Somebody led her into a sunny parlor full of plants and empty chairs, asked her to wait, and left. Before she could decide where to sit, a tall, badly dressed woman strode through the open glass doors, crying, "Dear Mrs. Tanning, how do you do? His condition's still serious. But we think the tide has turned."

The woman put an arm round her shoulder. "No," Vinnie said distractedly. "Tell me right out, don't be afraid."

"He's been given a second transfusion. The doctor will talk to you presently. Now, what have you had to eat?"

She had had nothing, wanted nothing, but Lady Good rang for broth and toast, and only allowed their talk to continue in earnest after the traveler had lowered the cup from her lips. "First of all," she said then, "I love Francis. Almost as much as I love Benjamin. You won't be offended by my saying that?"

"Not at all. You mustn't spare *my* feelings," replied Vinnie in a dry whisper, as if Lady Good had confessed to an impropriety.

The Englishwoman bowed her head. "I can't help it, I feel I'm partly to blame. He wasn't himself yesterday, but I had no inkling. I kept talking throughout lunch like—"

"You mustn't!" exclaimed Vinnie, her eyes filling with tears at last, her mouth working.

"—like the silly woman that I am—while he—"

"Hush!" Vinnie leaned forward. The vision of another person's emotion had roused and defined her own. The situation lost its dreadful strangeness. "You mustn't think that way! Francis has told me all about you, how much you mean to Ben, so please! Please!" Her words, for all the good will they conveyed, carried a certain implied reproof. Francis was *her* son. If anyone blamed herself it would be Vinnie who did so, without flinching—not Lady Good. "Look!" She blinked back tears and blew her nose, then, gently taking the other woman's wet chin in her hand, raised it until their eyes met. "*I* can bear it. Can't you do the same, for my sake?"

"Ah, you're braver than I!"

The little shrug with which Vinnie disclaimed this insight only illustrated the truth of it. "Tell me what you can," she said. She fixed her gaze on Lady Good's flat, creased lips.

"Well, of course," she heard as they began to move, "the person we have most to thank is Mrs. McBride. Without her he would surely have bled to death. She'd been to a late film with her cousin, you see, and had no sooner come in than she heard a moan from his lavatory. The ambulance was there in a matter of minutes."

Vinnie held up her hand, struggling to speak. She recalled now that Lady Good had said "transfusion," but it hadn't registered yet. Hearing on the telephone no more than that Francis had made an attempt upon his life, Vinnie had assumed him to have swallowed an overdose of sleeping pills. In this one way she had often imagined her own suicide. "Bled . . . ?" she finally brought out.

"Dear Mrs. Tanning, how thoughtless of me! Of course you'd not have known, would you? I somehow took for granted—"

"It's not your fault," whispered Vinnie. "Give me a moment, though, before you go on."

Within her range of vision stood a plant that had stalks covered with pink bristles, and big triangular leaves, greeny brown, each of which seemed to have split open to reveal a jagged form, membranous and pink. It wasn't a plant she would have chosen for display in a hospital. Now I'll be sick, she thought. The idea of cutting had always appalled her. She had never doubted that the prick of a needle could put the princess to sleep for a hundred years. If Francis as a child ran to her with the slightest rose-thorn-scratch on his hand, something would rise in Vinnie's throat; she grasped her own hand in a panic of empathy. Oh God, she thought—for there would be scars as well, at his wrists no doubt where cuffs might easily slip back to reveal them, perhaps even at his throat—and her hand flew to her own throat and its thornless roses. Until now Vinnie hadn't thought to ask, how could he do this to *me?*

"All right," she nodded nevertheless. "Mrs. McBride found him. She's Ben's nurse?"

"Yes."

"Did she say—?" Here Vinnie checked herself. "You were there, too!" she exclaimed, confronting Lady Good with the fact.

"Yes, I was there."

Vinnie's curiosity left her. She refused to profit by another's advantage. "Has Ben been told?" she asked instead.

"No. He's here in the hospital, on the floor above, as a matter of fact." Lady Good proceeded to tell all she knew about the radioactive medicine. "At nine o'clock this morning," she finished, "I peeked in his door—only the nurses are allowed to go into the room—and waved and chatted, naturally, as if I were just there to say hello. I'm sure he could tell nothing from my face. Dr. Samuels said it would be most foolish to upset him at such a time."

Well then, Vinnie would bear the full consciousness by herself. She touched Lady Good's arm. "Do me a favor, Prudence, dear—may I? I think of you as Prudence—and get some rest. You've had none all night."

"I have, though—from two o'clock till just before calling you, at seven. The doctor gave me something." Lady Good looked helpless. "He said there was nothing for me to do."

"Well, you've been wonderful, believe me." Too late Vinnie caught the note of dismissal in her words. "Or is there," she added, embarrassed, "something else I should know?" It crossed her mind to question Lady Good about recent circumstances that might have driven Francis to will his own destruction. That she didn't came in part from her conviction that it was nobody's business but hers—neither Prudence's, nor the doctor's, nor even poor sick Ben's. Her upbringing had taught Vinnie to be humiliated by violence of any description. You couldn't discriminate. It was wicked to murder, but no less so to *be* murdered; it gave rise to speculation, it hinted that the victim had knowingly roused an immoderate passion. If some ugly motive lay behind Francis's deed, she prayed he hadn't been so foolish as to betray it in front of outsiders. It would be a painful enough thing for her to live alone with.

But Francis, she knew and thanked God for the knowledge, didn't go around shooting off his mouth. He was blessed with tact and judgment far in advance of his years. Often, indeed, Vinnie would have preferred him to be more open about himself, to tell her what he was doing, what his friends were like. She recalled in particular one afternoon when, just back from abroad, he'd fallen from a real animation into a silence, a sullenness. A cold hand closed upon her heart. She had let herself forget, till then, how he could injure her. Still, as Francis no longer confided in her, she assumed he confided in no one. Useless, for instance, to ask Lady Good where he had spent the previous evening, and with whom.

Jane's name, however, was already jotted down in a little notebook Dr. Samuels carried. This cheerful person came upon them now, just as Lady Good was agonizing over whether to tell Mrs. Tanning what she hadn't yet heard. He solved her problem by shooing her blithely away, begging her not to start a jealous scene; all he wanted was a private word with her companion. "Are you sure it's Mrs. Tanning?" he went on, taking Vinnie's hand to show he was joking. "Why, she looks more like that young man's sister! And stop worrying your pretty head over *him*. He's coming along elegantly!"

Alone with Vinnie, his tone changed. "Don't be alarmed," he smiled. "I'm not a comedian at heart."

She couldn't hide how much this put her at ease. The rough humorous attentions of certain men filled her with disgust.

"I'm a doctor of the old school," he continued, sociably reminiscing. "At my age I can't be anything else. Oh, I use up-to-date methods. What I'm doing for Ben might be called revolutionary in a modest way. But I'm old-fashioned in that I never really got the hang of the so-called psychiatric approach. I'm not proud of that one bit. I'm just admitting it to you because you look to me like a perfectly lovely and intelligent woman who never got the hang of it, either." He grinned and slapped his knee. Vinnie smiled in spite of herself, thus proving Dr. Samuels equipped—if only accidentally—to deal with a disturbed mind. "Now," he said, "with a patient like your former husband we have the plain human problem of persuading a man who's been spoiled all his life by getting his own way—" "Spoiled rotten," Vinnie put in with a sensible but weary shake of the head—"persuading him that, while he'll never be as well as he once was, he's not nearly so ill as he'd like to think."

"He's always lived by charm," sighed Vinnie. "Now he's begun to see that charm isn't all, and he's like a little boy, he doesn't know what to do. I honestly think Francis is more grown up than his father will ever be."

"I wish I knew your son better," the doctor resumed after a thoughtful pause. "I had no clear picture of him (that's how psychiatrists talk) during my stay at the Cottage. I was saying, Ben's state of mind is an easy one for an old fuddy-duddy like me to handle. Most states of mind are. Then one comes up, like your boy's here, where I have to admit right off the bat that I'm beyond my depth. I just don't trust myself to see into the motives."

"Neither do I," declared Vinnie gratefully. "He's always been way beyond me. I guess you and I are both in the same boat." With a sweet smile of complicity she let one hand rest on his starched white sleeve.

It didn't surprise her that, whatever there was to find out about Francis, the doctor, so far, hadn't succeeded. In fact it rather pleased her, as though her son had made a vital scientific discovery or written a book nobody could understand. It didn't mean that *she*, once in the room with Francis, wouldn't know—mothers always did know. But outsiders lacked such sharp eyes. Behind her pleasure, if it was pleasure that Dr. Samuels had been so hard put to produce in her, lay the fear of his prying out something—she couldn't think what; it waited, vague and awful, a skeleton in her closet, something bare, grinning, of which any medical man had been trained to recognize the littlest finger-bone. She resorted now to a tried and true social blackmail, one that worked not only in Savannah but up North, in the following way. Meeting for the first time—especially under painful circumstances—a lawyer, a college professor, a traffic cop, Vinnie would start to practice a democracy unorthodox in its purity. She would look, say, a minister straight in the eye and speak to the human cipher she saw there, sweetly but firmly ignoring whatever a lifetime in the Church might have bestowed upon such a man, some understanding of good and evil, possibly, or gift for comforting the bereaved—to say nothing of his investment with divine authority. Soon the minister would be feeling, with her, that his most casual allusion to Scripture was a blow below the belt. Vinnie held the unspoken opinion not that you should modestly hide your light under a bushel, but that you should have no light to hide; and much as this attitude infuriated her in her friends—"They don't read, they don't think, they sit all day at the card-table!"—she found it indispensable in any crisis involving a professional man. Right now, like a kind of Circe, she had set about transforming the all-seeing doctor into the *man*—the decent blind insignificant man, belonging to her world and to no other. But Dr. Samuels hadn't lost his sprig of moly—given him by the god whose caduceus was the very emblem of practiced medicine— and it was with a sinking dismay that Vinnie took in his next words.

"So, I've called in a younger man, who's had all the training I lack in these cases, for his opinion. I want *you* to talk to him, too—oh, not today," he chuckled, seeing her stricken face, "but tomorrow, the day after, as soon as you feel stronger. By then, Dr. Sullivan will have had time to interview Francis."

"Am *I* to see Francis?" asked Vinnie feebly.

"By all means. I'm taking you to him now. He's conscious, but we're keeping him under morphine. You stay with him as long as you like." The doctor slapped his knee to show that he was a busy man. "I'm sure Ben would be pleased to see you, by the way."

"Ben? Wouldn't he—?" she began, horrified.

"Wouldn't he what?"

"Suspect, from my being here . . . ?"

"Then lie to him!" laughed the doctor, his bald brown head agleam. "Tell him you're passing through town on your way to visit friends."

Vinnie stiffened. "I'm afraid I'm not very good at that."

"Suit yourself. Ben values your friendship, he's told me how much. It'd do him good to see you. In two or three days, of course, we'll have to tell him the whole story."

Vinnie closed her eyes. "I'd give anything to spare him this ghastly, ghastly shock. Does he *have* to know?" She knew he did. If nothing else, he'd see Francis's scarred wrists. "I know, I know . . ." she said, and started wearily out ahead of Dr. Samuels.

"One moment, Mrs. Tanning." When she turned he was shaking his finger at her. "My dear lady, we don't help those we love by hiding disagreeable things from them, any more than we help ourselves by refusing to face these things."

What haven't *I* faced? thought Vinnie, squaring her shoulders.

The doctor kept right on. "I honestly don't know why Ben *isn't* as sick as he thinks, living in an atmosphere where people spare him, coddle him, treat him like the senile invalid he's sure to become if this nonsense doesn't stop. Believe you me, he's strong enough in mind and body to cope with a far greater shock than this. I don't know that it won't do him good to cope with something real for a change. It might just lead him nearer to life."

These were ideas that Vinnie herself tried scrupulously to live by. But they left her uncheered, skeptical, even, of their relevance to the moment at hand. Something *real!* she thought wryly—real as a nightmare! She looked Dr. Samuels straight in the eye, as though she had found him out. He said no more, but beckoned her down two lengths of shining linoleum. Pausing in front of a door ajar, he expressed a final doubt. "Lady Good did tell you precisely what happened to your son?"

"Yes, oh, yes!" said Vinnie, rapidly nodding.

The doctor made the gesture of washing his hands. "It's unlikely, I'm afraid, that he'll be able to lead a normal life, in the fullest sense."

"Naturally, naturally!" she brought out with a sound like laughter. What on earth was he trying to say?

"We'll do all we can for him, though, Dr. Sullivan and I." And with this the little doctor, to whose solicitude there were limits, bowed her into Francis's room and went his way down the corridor.

The room, dim and green, had an effect of underwater. A nurse floated up from her chair. In pantomime Vinnie asked her to resume her seat, indicating that she preferred a straight chair nearer the bed. Once sitting, she whispered, "Mrs. McBride?"

"No," the nurse smiled. "I'm Mrs. Fletcher."

Thus Vinnie had no alternative but to turn and look at her son.

Her forehead puckered. Something wasn't as she expected. Francis lay flat, facing away from her; his arms, bare from the elbows down, rested on the unnatural whiteness of the sheet. This was raised, a kind of tent beginning at his chest and obscuring the contours of his body. He seemed puzzled himself. Now and then he moaned or shook his head in a faint, disbelieving gesture. Vinnie wanted to take his hand, full of love, to tell him she was there and loved him, but whatever kept striking her as wrong prevented her. She gave the nurse a helpless look of inquiry: what *was* it? what *was* it? Mrs. Fletcher beamed back, advancing nevertheless in case something had gone amiss. Delicately she took Francis's pulse. The tanned wrist drooped from her fingers. Where were the bandages? Vinnie nearly cried out. Instead she shut her eyes. Oh please! if he had slit his wrists, why weren't they bandaged?

Hearing the nurse say, "Fine and dandy," and the squeak of her shoes as she resumed her seat, Vinnie felt sick again. A sweet sterile smell was more powerful here than in the corridor. Too proud to ask, she let the question sound and sound: what had he done? what had he done?

A memory of the last scene of *Lucia di Lammermoor* allowed her presently to visualize the deed. A dagger had been held high during an exquisite burst of song, then plunged into the tenor's breast. Earlier, the heroine had gone altogether out of her mind.

Something real for a change—those were the doctor's words.

Having for so many years cultivated an impersonal, an international idea of disaster, Vinnie had to rediscover private grief. Storms were brewing the world over. One day the bomb would be dropped and that would be the end of everything. Meanwhile, the mermaid walked on knives.

A minute before, Francis had been *her* flesh and blood. It hurt now to know that the life he'd tried to take was his own, no more hers than his way of going about it. The flesh injured and the blood shed were *his*. The mystery of his act profoundly shook her.

Later, she did stop by Ben's room.

Seeing her coming, Lady Good rose from an armchair placed in the doorway and drew her out of earshot. "Where are you staying tonight, my dear?" Vinnie hadn't thought. "Then do take Mrs. McBride's room at the hotel! She was saying, it's a crime for it to go begging. And I'd be there, should you want company."

Vinnie was touched. "Thank you," she whispered. "I'll need somebody."

Then Lady Good, after announcing the visitor, withdrew.

"What a nice surprise!" warbled Mrs. McBride, to whom it was no surprise at all. "Why, I'd know you anywhere, Mrs. Tanning—Francis has your eyes. Sit down! Aren't we pleased!"

There Vinnie was, her legs crossed, talking gaily from the threshold to a Ben indistinguishable in the shade of the room.

"Of course Francis had told me you'd be in Boston, but I hadn't remembered the exact date. Then when Annette Woodruff (she always asks after you) wrote me to join her for a week on the Cape where she's visiting young Dan and his wife, I had a few hours between trains and on a hunch caught Francis at the Ritz. He told me the name of the hospital, which I'd just been scatterbrained enough to forget." Lie upon lie dropped like snakes and toads from her lips; Vinnie was past caring.

"Prudence said Francis was sick today," Ben croaked.

"Our throat's beginning to hurt a little," said Mrs. McBride.

"Then hush! Don't talk. Yes," Vinnie went on, "I stopped in to see him. He caught a freak summer cold, and you're not to worry. I declare, I hate to see you lying in bed. That *was* Lady Good who left when I came in? She's really very striking, with such a sweet face. You know, I haven't *always* approved your taste in women!" She laughed and paused for breath. "Oh, Francis keeps me informed about the goings-on at the Cottage. I hope it's not as lively as it sounds!"

"Well, I call it the pace that kills!" said Mrs. McBride, to whom Vinnie had appealed.

"Francis is a fine boy, Vinnie," Ben struggled to say, "but he's not happy, is he?"

"Oh, now!" exclaimed the nurse on a scolding note.

"Isn't he?" Vinnie wondered, all lightness, but recalling how Ben, thirteen years before, in his efforts to obtain custody of Francis, had declared her, in print, unfit to raise the child—a purely legal maneuver, yet it had rankled and still did. She considered her possible belated thrust. "No," she could say, "except that Francis spends all his time at the Cottage. Mightn't that have some bearing, Ben, on his unhappiness?" Ah, but the time for recriminations was over. Years, also, had passed since the summers she would pack Francis off for a week with his father, saying, "Now remember, dearest, to be on your best behavior. Your every gesture and word reflects on me." Vinnie felt so tired suddenly. "All I know," she said aloud, "is that he loves being with you, and that makes *me* happy, Ben, honestly it does." They peered through the dim air seeking each other's eyes. She began to make out Ben's face now; it was puffy, old, not a face she knew. By then she had fallen silent. She could hear the sick man fighting for his breath.

Back at Francis's bedside, Vinnie stared and stared at his bare throat, his smooth wrists. Mercifully, the wound wouldn't be visible, wherever it was. Her gaze shifted. She froze.

He had turned towards her a face whose open eyes, though unseeing, expressed wonder and joy. It came over Vinnie that *he* knew, that nothing short of realizing what he had done could have produced the look on Francis's face.

PART TWO

---

16. Autumn made slight difference to the Island. If rain fell, it fell for a mere hour after midnight, so that each day dawned upon a landscape fresh and springing, of pliant hilltops, palm-crested, of pale-green fields of young sugar cane around which gray roads cut to the sea. Every few miles, even inland where the hills gave way to cliffs and gorges, you might happen on a ruined wall, its plaster, whose washes of pink or ivory had long ago vanished, broken off in places to reveal dry, rounded stones. Nearer, on roads and in fields, the Negroes would be dressed in pale colors, grays, whites, bleached yellows and blues. It was always a shock for the newcomer to see how often their faces, hands and feet seemed the only really dark tones in an entire perspective. The Island was that ethereal. At twilight, along the beaches, following the famous Green Flash perceptible for the split second in which the sun disappears, a haunting grisaille might translate the scene. You noticed the long pine-needles against a sky less lemon-tinted, by now, than wholly without color. Beyond a few feet of beach, traversed perhaps by a black dog or a woman with a cloth about her head—but both of a blackness so powerfully textured as to recall an episode in some early film, made before anybody had learned to control the intensity of an image—the water stretched, smooth, opalescent. Three or four sailboats might be lying at anchor, their masts at three or four different angles, rocking quietly in silhouette. Occasionally in the early evening a formal garden annexed to one of the more imposing plantation houses was floodlit, for an hour of almost violent artifice. The sky would still retain some greenish natural light, but below, the reds alone, the scarlets and purples that colored nearly every flower that didn't grow wild, were gaudy enough to withstand those great shafts of light, passing through palm leaves like X-rays. The lamps were fastened to the ends of a flimsily built gallery which you counted on being blown off by a hurricane. As the guests moved indoors a servant would be picking up a tipped-over highball glass from beside the lily pond. The lights had served their purpose. At night you could see nothing. There seemed never to be light near by. Only from the crevices of great trees—eucalyptus, breadfruit, the manchineel that in a rainstorm was known to drip a painful irritant onto the skin of a person, white or black, taking refuge beneath it—came the chirp and squeak of small creatures. The Island at these moments struck you as having taken in more darkness than it could possibly endure. Which was perhaps why, by mid-morning, it had an air of having exhaled every last trace of it. Even the Negroes' skins would be shining then with a moisture which reflected the surrounding pallors.

Ah, and how easily you went to pot in the tropics!

This thought entered the minds of at least two white women, one fair November morning.

Mrs. McBride phrased it without reservations, flinging herself into a rattan rocker and flipping the pages of her log. Twelve miles from Weathersome, towards Savanna-la-Mar, it made up Irene Cheek's first waking reflection; but she put it to herself with an ambiguous smile, as if not at all sure it was a bad thing, to go easily to pot. Her little eyes blinked at alternating stripes of darkness and gold across her body. "Charlie," she growled, "I'm a tiger." But she might have known he'd have been up and out hours ago, sailing.

In hundreds of small neat spaces Mrs. McBride had registered, four times a day, her patient's temperature and pulse. Every seven pages came a set of graphs to which she had painstakingly transferred these findings and others. She looked with pride at one that showed the drop in Mr. Tanning's nitroglycerine consumption over the last month and a half, from as many as forty grains a day to only three grains in two weeks. Yes, he had been Restored to Health. And it wasn't a miracle, the way all his friends claimed, so much as the result of Good and Devoted Care. Which, however, he would get no Benefit from so long as he insisted on abusing his Reprieve from Pain. Down the right-hand margin of every other page ran a column headed, "Remarks." Mrs. McBride checked a dry laugh. An entirely blank notebook wouldn't hold the remarks she felt like making about *this* case. Nearly three years of her life—she reckoned them with an uneasy glance upward, a direction from which spiders were apt to drop—had passed in an environment foreign to what she could no longer even think of as her tastes, they'd been so seldom consulted. Now of late her Professional Status was being ignored. She wondered if Mr. Tanning had any conception of the responsibility placed on her shoulders. Couldn't he have seen that her duty was to forbid him—in the pleasantest way she knew, with an arch laugh and a wag of her finger—to drink the Martini Louis Leroy brought? Before noon, what was more. There'd been no call for him to come back at her, sipping it, with : "Mrs. McBride, have you stopped to think that you annoy the hell out of me?" It had sent her upstairs, smarting. In the log she wrote, "Most irritable and Disobedient. Insisted on Cocktail before lunch." Oh, it had been quite a different story in the Hospital, those first two days, with his throat puffed out like a bullfrog's. All he'd wanted then was to have his feet rubbed and his hand held. His eyes had followed her about the room, just like a sick little boy who Needs his Mother. Whereas now—Mrs. McBride compressed her lips. She rose, peered anxiously down onto the lawn. Two red birds were screaming at a metallic black one. His chair was empty, the glass on its side in a flowerbed. She exhaled sharply and started back downstairs.

Irene couldn't figure out how somebody who drank as much as Charlie Cheek woke up morning after morning so bright and chipper. It contributed to her picture of him as an easygoing meathead. One thing for sure—he lacked whatever inside *her* skull unremittingly ached and throbbed. It took brains to be sensitive, she guessed. Catching sight of something green and yellow trailing off a chair, Irene slapped a hand across her eyes; she had conjured up the image of herself wearing it the night before, a short polka-dot dress with the motto *Live it up! Live it up! Live it up!* embroidered all the way around the hips. What had caused her to laugh so wildly, there on the terrace? A second later the steel band struck up another calypso:

> *When I see belly meat*
> *I don' want nothing more to eat. . . .*

"Oh, it's the 'Belly Lick!'" she remembered exclaiming. "That's my favorite!" As the Lord Regaler, whose band it was, well knew. She had thrown him her widest smile. Somebody had taken her in his arms then, and around she'd spun, skimming the uneven flagstones, head fallen far, far back in order to see, upside down, the rows of black figures watching from behind the barbed wire where her property ended. There must have been two hundred of them, keeping soft time with the music, letting escape an occasional laugh, muffled, brief, yet always controlled so as to send a ghostly black finger up and down the inside of her thighs. A dim feature of Irene's moral landscape had come to be this emotion of twirling, one of two or three dozen white women watched by those hundreds that wholly blotted out the sea's shining. They lived in revolting shacks along the coast. By day she could observe them through the jalousies, or from behind *Look* under the manchineels. Their torsos, emerging from the milky-blue water, were often of a grace and color that left her mouth dry. Those nights she had the Lord Regaler—and he cost so absurdly little!—the shoe was on the other foot. *They* were invisible, their eyes fixed on *her,* a white woman behaving as only a white woman can, a bit drunk in evening clothes, insolent and, in manner, approachable to a degree no proud man (she fancied) could tolerate; it didn't matter what side of the barbed wire he was on. "Oh Christ!" she muttered, remembering now what had come next. The letter. She'd run to fetch it in her room—yes, the bureau drawer was still open—then returned to the party, waving it over her head. The gesture, though florid, seemed right. It was as if Irene, bored with performing merely for blacks, had been inspired to display, in a circle of her own race, her mastery of a conduct utterly devoid of the ethical fiber prized, to hear some of them talk, even above their color. "Oh Christ!" she said again, beginning to laugh. "Well, you devil, you've done it this time!" she scolded, but couldn't keep a straight face. Irene had always considered herself so lovable that she failed to see how anybody might hold a grudge against her, now or ever.

"Marlborough," said Mrs. McBride, entering the pantry, "where is Mr. Tanning?"

"I surely don't know, ma'am. I never did see him."

"He was right on that lawn five minutes ago. Where's Louis?"

"Mr. Leroy? He's surely to be around somewhere," said Marlborough and shifted his weight. He was a slender smiling man, no blacker than her thoughts about him just then. Mr. Tanning had called him Louis Leroy's aide-de-camp.

"What car just stopped at the back door?"

"Man brought a telegram, I think, ma'am."

"A telegram? For whom?"

"I surely don't know."

From elsewhere a singsong of faint voices reached her:

". . . feeling poorly."

"Two shillings a week to support his child."

". . . brand-new dress . . ."

"Never you mind. How do he know it's his?"

"I said, 'Man, you better take me someplace I can wear that gown!'"

". . . injection . . ."

"What?"

Following them, Mrs. McBride darted into the kitchen, where, by a window giving on a wealth of glowing leafage, she found Louis Leroy settled down for a few moments' banter with his own—what word did Mr. Tanning use?—seraglio. Around him were grouped, languorously, Marlborough's sister Vanessa, his cousins, two shiftless girls bursting out of their clothes, the cook Roxane and her daughter Mary Ann—a far cry, Mrs. McBride thought each time she saw the minx, from *her* daughter Mary Ann. A cloud of smoke wavered above the group. The five women were facing Louis Leroy expectantly for an observation never to be uttered, the nurse's face having driven it from his mind.

"Louis, have you seen Mr. Tanning?"

"Oh yes, Miss McBride!" he said, rising and expertly concealing his cigarette somewhere in his clothing. "I took the telegram to him. He's out on the lawn." Louis Leroy was always glad to supply this kind of simple empirical fact.

"No, no . . ." sighed the nurse, turning away and motioning him to save his breath. She took an irresolute step towards the door into the yard, and was trying not to notice six flying-fish on a drainboard, when far down the winding drive, so small as to have seemed at first a flower, she glimpsed a red beret. "There he is! Look!" Without caring whether they looked or not, she lunged into the sunlight. The ill-paved drive was crisscrossed with lizards that paled and froze at her approach. Walking, Mrs. McBride went on talking. "He can't be let out of sight for One Minute. Why, if I hadn't seen him he'd have gone right out onto the road! All by himself, too! He's getting far too rambunctious to suit my taste!" By then she was close enough to see that the old man had a square of blue-and-white paper in his hand.

Irene padded about in a wrapper from Hawaii. She found the kitchen empty and swore this time not to let it pass. Last night's glasses were still in the sink. A roach hesitated before backing away from her bare foot. Ah, what did she care? Balancing a cup of cool coffee, she went out into the patio. A freakish wind, which hardly ever blew from that direction, wafted about her the sweet black stench of Sir Edward Good's molasses factory, two miles inland. Irene sank onto one of a circle of white wooden chairs, then saw that it faced squarely the one from which she'd read aloud the letter.

"Mrs. Cheek," Lady Parrott had implored, casting rapid shocked glances at the others, "*do* not read us these letters!"

"There's no harm in it!" Irene recalled having laughed. "This one is dated last June twenty-fifth. Listen: 'My dearest, it is already midnight here. Whilst you are winging your way to New York, I cannot sleep without sending you these few lines that do scant justice to the gratitude and tenderness I feel.' Get that?" Irene chortled. "Here's a dame who knows how to express herself!"

On that Lady Parrott had abruptly quitted the circle. The others— among them Mrs. Widman, Coco Rappaport and old Aubrey Savage— had, if anything, drawn closer.

"'How could I have hesitated to say yes to your so flattering invitation for the summer? I still feel qualms'—whatever *they* are," Irene shrugged—"'when I realize the three of us will be together under one

roof. But I know now that I am less concerned for myself or for dear
Ned, than for your own peace of mind, Benjamin dear. I should never
forgive myself were I to threaten it.'"

"Perhaps you'd better not go on, Irene," Coco had put in with her
nervous titter.

"Wait! Listen to what she says down here: 'Now, back from the air-
port, I have spoken to him. The idea seemed to please him. He likes you,
you know, and admires you tremendously. So, we *shall* come, if you still
will have us. Ah, I may be selfish, do you think I am? Yet my life is so
empty without you!' Can you bear it!" Irene shrieked. "Why, I'd no more
lower myself to write a letter like that than live in one of those native
shacks along the beach!"

"*Can* you write, Irene?" old Aubrey had murmured at that point.

"I had thought," Mrs. Widman said coldly, "you were such great
friends with Mr. Tanning."

"Oh, I *am!*" she had cried, perceiving how little they understood her
motives. Why, they imagined she was trying to hurt *him* by reading the
letter! "You've got me completely wrong," she went on, striking her
breast. "I don't know anybody I love more than Benji Tanning. He's not
only my cousin by marriage and a charming man, but terribly generous,
what's more. I'm sure Prudy Good really means it about her gratitude.
Not that *I* ever accepted anything from him, nuh-uh! my favorite fella
wouldn't go for that. . . ."

Irene had taken care not to mention the small trust fund that Mr. Tan-
ning had set up in her name, unknown to Charlie.

". . . But I've had some first-rate tips on the market from him and
Orson Bishop. I guess I realized about twenty-five grand last year on
their oil wells in Canada. So, what I mean, Benji's my f*wiend!* It's just that
Good woman—ha-ha, get the joke?—who needs putting in her place.
He's not strong enough to hold her off. Now *I*, if I do say so, have con-
sideration for Benji. It'd never cross my mind to ask him to a brawl like
this—he wouldn't come if I did." It happened that Irene *had* invited Mr.
Tanning, who had declined. "A guy like that's at his best in a cozy inti-

mate atmosphere. Many's the hour I've spent just sitting and *talking* with him," she finished on a serious, intent note, as if the truth, now that she was speaking it, was too bizarre for her hearers readily to believe.

Mrs. Widman showed her upper teeth. "Tell me, Mrs. Cheek, how did you come by these letters?"

After a brief stare over the rim of her glass—the naïveté of the woman!—Irene had broken into incredulous laughter. "Why, how do you think? I found them in his desk one day last summer, and took them home to read. I've every intention of returning them, if that's what's eating you—though personally I say they ought to be *burned!*" Her voice had been so easy and gay, her affection for Benji so clear to anyone who really listened, her whole figure so appealing—a woman expressing her deepest convictions—that Irene just couldn't figure out what had made them keep on taking it amiss.

"Not going already!" Charlie Cheek had boomed jovially, weaving up to Aubrey Savage and Mrs. Widman in time to receive the brunt of their dry adieux. Was it, Irene wondered now, because they were all *British* and felt some kind of funny loyalty in the matter? "I just bet that's it!" she whispered, nodding, narrow-eyed, as she reached for a cigarette. A flake of soft coal dust settled on her wrist. Wouldn't it be just like that troublemaker Mrs. Widman to hustle over to Weathersome today, in one of her dowdy sharkskin suits, not even a scatter pin on the lapel, with the whole story?

She had dismissed the premonition when the butler called her to the telephone. "Uh-oh," she said under her breath.

It was Bridie. "Mrs. Cheek? Mrs. Cheek?" she kept screaming, the connection frightful as usual. "Hold the line—here's Mr. Tanning."

"Hel-lo!" came the extra-cheerful voice that meant trouble.

"Hi, Lover, how's the kid?" replied Irene, blowing smoke at her face in the mirror. She'd decided to brazen it out. "Missed you last night."

"I'll bet you did." She held her tongue. "I didn't mean to say that, Irene," he said then. "You know how I am about those big parties. Last time I went to one of yours the flying-fish pie poisoned me."

"That was nearly a year ago."

"My, my!" Now he came to the point. "I've heard something I can't understand, Irene, and wondered if you had any explanation for it."

She made the face of a burning witch. "What's that, Benji?"

"I just had a cable from Larry Buchanan. Orson Bishop has resigned as President of Bishop Petroleum."

"Huh?" For an instant Irene found nothing else to say. At length she let out a whoop of delight that must surely have baffled her listener. "Oh, is that all? No, Benji, I haven't the slightest idea. How funny! Why'd he want to do a thing like that?" She babbled on giddily, then, inspired: "Just a minute! He's a Mormon, isn't he? They're said to be very straitlaced."

"Now what in hell do you mean by that, Irene?"

"Temper, temper! I only wondered if something mightn't have reached him."

"Such as what?"

"Oh, some gossip or something—don't ask me!"

"One thing I know about Mormons," replied Mr. Tanning, made cynical by rage, "is that they don't give a damn who sleeps with whom or with how many. Besides, Orson's your friend as well as mine, and too nice a fellow—"

What did that have to do with the price of beans? Irene was nice, too, yet it had never kept her from gossiping about friends.

"—to pay attention to rumors about you and me."

"I don't mean you and *me*, Lover-cousin. Don't you know who I mean? P.G.—that ring a bell? And I must say," Irene couldn't resist adding, convinced that he would never hear about the letter if he hadn't by now, "I must say I've heard a certain amount of talk, myself."

"Ouch!" exclaimed Mr. Tanning. "That's the size needle they give penicillin with!"

"I beg your pardon?"

"Forget it. Whether you know it or not," he wound up, "it's very serious news from my point of view. From yours also, as a stockholder, I might add."

"Is it? Oh, Benji, then I'm certainly very upset—"

But he had hung up.

Mrs. McBride watched him from over her knitting. His face was round and tanned, his silver hair freshly washed. He groomed himself more beautifully than any man or woman she had known. Each morning a slow solemn ritual took place. Louis Leroy worshipfully selected shoes, ties, the shirt, the suit, one of twenty very light sweaters in different shades—at which Mr. Tanning would hardly cast an eye, sitting like an old Cardinal who lets a sprightlier priest perform the service his presence dignifies. "Look at you now," she told him silently, "dressed so fine!" But she didn't like the way his mouth kept crumpling up over whatever he was thinking. Dr. Samuels had said for him by all means to take an interest in his firm. If you asked her, however, it was a grave mistake. He oughtn't to have a care in the world. Mrs. McBride found it in her heart to curse Mr. Buchanan for sending that cable; just as in Boston she had felt real, though passing, revulsion towards Francis for having caused the good kind man all that suffering. His Reserves of Strength were her chief concern. Let them become depleted and he'd have another stroke, sure as she was sitting there.

Louis Leroy tiptoed in from the gallery. He carried a bottle of pills on a salver.

"Now what do I have to do?"

"That's your new thyroid dosage, Mr. Tanning," said the nurse. "It came yesterday from Boston, by air mail."

"Oh I see."

Louis took heart. "Lunch is served," he said.

"Ask Roxane to boil me two four-minute eggs," said Mr. Tanning in a gravelly voice. "I'll have them out here with a piece of toast."

"Yes, Sir." The valet turned to go.

"*And* a double shot of bourbon on the rocks."

"Now what's this!" cried Mrs. McBride, pursing her lips. "I think I ought to have some say in this matter!"

"Kindly go to hell," said the old man. Then, as she fumed, he broke into his enchanting grin. "But first go and eat your lunch."

An hour later she found him still at his desk, pencil in hand, the eggs tasted, the toast half eaten, the drink drained. "Go away," he told her without looking up.

At three o'clock he sent for her. She was shocked by his face. He said, "I don't know what's wrong with me. I've spent two and a half hours phrasing these cables. I could have done them in ten minutes before my first attack."

"Will you go lie down now?" asked Mrs. McBride, her finger on his pulse. It was very slow.

He nodded consent. "Send these two cables first, if you please."

"I'll send them when you're lying down."

"I asked you please to send them first. I don't have the strength to shout at you. I can lie down without your help."

She watched him shuffle across the hall into his bedroom. The white door floated shut at a nudge of his elbow. While dialing the cable office Mrs. McBride heard a voice below her, singing:

> *"All the boys love Mary Ann.*
> *Why do the boys love Mary Ann?*
> *'Cause she can cook like no one can—"*

"Hush!" she hissed, having first caught the gardener's attention by rapping on the windowpane. Though knowing the song was aimed at Roxane's daughter, Mrs. McBride took it as a personal affront to hers. A decent, obedient girl. "I'm telephoning," she mouthed. "Can't you be quiet?" The handsome black man grinned.

Mr. Tanning's first cable was for Mr. Buchanan in New York:

WHEN WILL YOU LEARN NEVER TO WIRE ME NEWS OF SUCH
VITAL IMPORTANCE WITHOUT GIVING FULL PARTICULARS
REPEAT FULL PARTICULARS STOP BY TOMORROW NOON I
EXPECT TO BE IN POSSESSION OF ALL THE FACTS

THE MONSTER

The second went to that Mr. Bishop in Alberta:

DEAR ORSON I AM PROFOUNDLY DISTRESSED BY NEWS FROM
BUCHANAN STOP I PRAY THAT YOU WILL IN THE LIGHT OF OUR
GRAVE JOINT RESPONSIBILITIES TO SHAREHOLDERS CONTINUE
TO SERVE THE COMPANY IN SOME CAPACITY EITHER DIRECTOR
OR CHAIRMAN OF BOARD LEST WE FIND OURSELVES OPERAT-
ING A YOUNG COMPANY IN YOUR COUNTRY WITHOUT THE
NAME OF SO RESPECTED A CANADIAN AS YOURSELF TO REAS-
SURE BOTH THE PUBLIC AND YOUR ADMIRING FRIEND

BENJAMIN TANNING

It took some time to relay these messages. When at last Mrs. McBride put
down the receiver and tiptoed into her patient's room, she found him
stretched on the bed, dressed but for shoes and jacket. His breathing was
calm, his pulse regular. She covered his legs with a thin white blanket,
then left him to sleep. Care, tempered by her own sense of when to let
well enough alone, had Averted the Crisis.

He needed now, she was thinking at half past four, some distraction
from the whole business. At the Cottage you reeled beneath a steady
onslaught of guests; it could be equally depressing, here on the Island,
to have several days go by without more than a telephone call. Lady
Good lived twenty miles to the south; even if a car were sent she couldn't
come every day. Not that she cared—fine upright woman!—what people
thought, but the distance was too great, she had her house to run. She and
Sir Edward had dined at Weathersome last night; she was expected,
alone, for lunch tomorrow. Mrs. McBride, nevertheless, had nearly

resolved to call up Lady Good, tell her a bit of what had happened, and ask if she couldn't run over casually for a cup of tea, when she heard the distant honk of a horn. Soon a small gray old-fashioned car swung into the drive. It looked familiar, but the nurse couldn't call to mind its owner's name. She saw her clearly in her imagination, an older woman gray and decorous as the car she drove. Mr. Tanning was fond of her, but in the right way for a change. Smiling, Mrs. McBride headed downstairs. This visitor, though paying her first call of the year, wouldn't stand on ceremony, could be led right up to Mr. Tanning's bedroom. She was trustworthy, safe; she would sit by his bed and tell him all the Island gossip. Now, what was her name? Not till she threw open the front door did the nurse find it on her lips. "Why, Mrs. Widman, this is a treat! Come right on up! It's past time he was awake!"

Irene had a secret terror of water. She could sit watching it for hours, and did, loud in praise of its beauties, but in swimming would never venture beyond her depth. This was curious, because she swam well; but she had always insisted upon *seeing* as far as she could into the sparkling element that upheld her. She refused to swim where the bottom was invisible, or near rocks behind which creatures might be lurking. Even now, leaning over the side of the sailboat, she peered anxiously at threads of darkness, of light, plunging downward and backward as they moved, her head and shoulders the merest transparency overlaid upon the purplish depths. Her fear was of what might rise up from them and devour her. She had known herself to panic even in swimming pools, to race for the steps kicking, thrashing, while a huge imaginary mouth opened to swallow her up. Certain representations of sea creatures had so terrified her as a child that Irene would never again open the *Book of Knowledge,* lest she choose the wrong volume and happen on them. In later life this fear didn't keep her from lying lazy and insolent and gold-brown on a white-hot beach or immersed in pale shallows, or from joining her husband for a sail when she had nothing better to do.

They had met and married during the war. An uncle of Charlie's, a one-star General and Mr. Tanning's first cousin, had been having a friendship with Irene, at the time a truly pretty woman. She was so pretty, in fact, that the friendship passed for platonic. You didn't want anyone to possess those clear tints and delicate ovals—not if you were Charlie Cheek, at least. Transferred to Washington, he had been asked to a large dinner at which his uncle (like himself, well on the road to alcoholism) had repeated a number of stories so obscene as to have been out of place in an officers' barracks. In the course of these excruciating moments a gentle blush spread over Irene's face and throat—a blush that Charlie, already charmed by her good looks, quite failed to interpret. He saw her offended by the turn the conversation had taken, when in truth Irene's embarrassment came from having herself told the General a couple of the stories, and her fear that someone would read this fact in her eyes. But Charlie Cheek had been hooked by the gentle blush whose meaning he never fathomed and which, even if he'd been right, would have remained the only proof he was ever to receive of Irene's refinement. You imagined how easily he had been driven, through the years, into a blind devotion—the blindness simulated whether the devotion was or not. He had actually stopped drinking for a time, in hopes of pleasing her. As for Irene, she lost all interest in her husband upon learning that he was poor, unambitious and (when sober) a bore—in each respect a far cry from his uncle. By the time he took to the bottle again, Irene couldn't have cared less. She had long before resumed the only life for which she was fitted. Their marriage, as displayed to the world, was rooted in mendacity and ignorance of one another's real nature. Furthermore, left to themselves, the Cheeks showed no mastery of the artifice that made life bearable for many unhappy couples. Charlie, for instance, had never learned to approach a point circuitously. "Irene," he said when a brisk swelling of the sail caused their eyes to meet, "what was all that to-do last night, about some letter?"

She let her face make leisurely transitions from blackness to bewilderment, bewilderment to recollection, recollection to wan amusement. "Oh," she finally said, "that was just foolishness."

A minute or two went by. Charlie waved to a white man in the stern of a fishing-boat that passed them, quietly sputtering. The man waved back. He was strapped into his chair and held a giant rod. "But what was it all about?" repeated Charlie.

"I've told you—nothing," she answered without petulance, thus closing the incident until a few days later when it became clear that, contrary to Irene's calculations, Mr. Tanning knew everything. On this future occasion out came her explanations and her petulance, both.

An instant later Irene caught her breath. Not a hundred yards away a dolphin broke water, a large one, brilliantly colored. She had time to see that it was green, mostly, with yellow markings, and to be vaguely disturbed by the combination. Cries of excitement from the fishing-boat made her understand that this handsome fish had been hooked by the white man in the stern. Now his line was ripping through the water as the dolphin headed, or so it seemed to Irene, straight for her. For protection?—she drew back. She kept sight of it, shining, elongated, inches beneath the surface, but only a soft whistle from Charlie warned her of what came next. A dark fin had almost lazily approached; there followed an abrupt assault, then stillness; a wreath of red foam dispersed. Presently the man in the fishing-boat could be seen holding up the dolphin's head, still hooked to his line, and mouthing words they couldn't catch.

"That's one of the fastest fish in the sea," said Charlie. "Shark couldn't ever have got it if it hadn't been hooked."

"Oh God," Irene whispered, terrified. "Let's go in, huh? I mean it! What if we turned over out here?"

She saw him begin to laugh, protectively, his manhood renewed. You poor fish! thought Irene and smiled in spite of herself.

Shortly before dark a delirium of leaves and pineapples glistened along each post of Mr. Tanning's bed. Re-entering the room after accompanying the local doctor downstairs, Mrs. McBride stood gazing at the old man. He was out of pain but restive. The luminol hadn't taken effect yet. "Think to yourself," she told him in a lulling voice, "that your toes are going to sleep, then your feet, your ankles. Think that your calves and your knees and your thighs are relaxing and going to sleep. Say that your stomach is going to sleep, and your lungs and your heart. Get each part of your body to relax, and before you know it you'll be fast, fast asleep."

He tried it. She watched his lips form the words: "My toes are going to sleep, my feet—" Then he opened his eyes and started once more, as earlier, before the pains began, to show what was really bothering him. "Ring for Louis," Mr. Tanning gasped. "I'm getting dressed. Has Mrs. Widman left? How long ago? Tell Marlborough to bring the car around. I'm going to Canecrest. I have to talk something over with Sir Edward. It can't wait."

"Yes, yes, we'll do that in a little while," said Mrs. McBride soothingly. She wished the doctor were still at Weathersome, although his blue-black face, tilted in lamplight, had filled her with apprehension. "Think of pleasant things," she continued, "like your lunch with Lady Good tomorrow. You'll be having a new grandchild before long, think about that. Think about Francis's visit. He'll be here within a month. Say to yourself, 'My toes are going to sleep, my feet and my ankles . . .'" She had been told not to give him morphine except in an emergency.

"My toes . . ." he began, but whimpered. Mrs. McBride saw his whole face tighten against a spasm of pain. In no time the blue and white stripes of the mattress were showing through the sheet his weak tears dampened. "It's not the pain," he tried to say. By then the needle glittered in her hand.

"Mrs. McBride—"

"Don't tire yourself so!" she begged, near weeping herself. The worst was not to understand what had upset him. The new pills? Composing those cables? Mrs. Widman's call?

"Mrs. McBride, don't give me morphine!" he cried as she withdrew the needle and dabbed his arm with alcohol. "Tell Marlborough to get the car ready."

"Yes, yes," she hummed. "You'll sleep a little now."

"I'll be damned if I go to sleep. I've got something to talk over with Ned Good. I'd no more hurt either of them . . . Call Marlborough. . . ." Mrs. McBride kept crooning and stroking his hands until he stopped talking. Take Their Minds Off It, she had learned from a textbook on Grief. She rose at last and, as it was quite dark, pulled down the windowshades.

"What did you do?" he asked drowsy.

"Just pulled down the shades. Don't worry." He said no more. She tiptoed into the hall and dialed Mrs. Widman's number. Mrs. Widman was out for dinner—well, that could wait. The nurse next called Lady Good, but in the middle of their conversation heard a cry from her patient. Saying, "I'll phone you back," Mrs. McBride hung up and hurried to his side. He was staring about, roused from a kind of waking nightmare which, over her protests, he insisted on recounting.

He had been gazing (Mr. Tanning said) so intently at the window-shade that it presently seemed a field through which he was walking, a field or valley—the valley of the Shade. Looking down at his body, he had found it clothed in the uniform that, along with certain distant regular explosions, brought back the war in which he and his comrades took part. What comrades? He was walking alone, entirely so, through a field of golden flowers, daisies perhaps, or daffodils, flowers that grew only here. Stooping to examine one of them—and at the same time sensing the approach from far off of somebody else—he observed its slow and magical change into a golden butterfly. He held his breath, kneeling enchanted there, knowing every flower, as far around as he could see, transformed, fluttering. This, he was aware, had been foretold in a poem his mother had read and explained to him as a little boy. The poem told how caterpillars became butterflies, and butterflies in turn were changed into the flowers they loved best.

Nervously he looked over his shoulder. There *was* an approaching figure, but still so distant that he turned back to study the wonderful opening and shutting of wings before his eyes. A fearful notion now began to work on him—it was all backwards! The flower had changed into a butterfly, not, as his mother had promised, the other way around! How horrible if then—! and he might have been overheard, for the wings stopped moving, fell ever so slowly to earth, while what was left fattened and started crawling down the stripped stem. He got to his feet in a panic. The same change was taking place throughout the valley—countless thousands of caterpillars in the place of butterflies. All life had become a process of uncreation. One flower only, between his leggings, hadn't changed. It was like his own child, or his own life, a small five-petaled golden blossom, slightly crushed. Save my life, he prayed. Drenched with the task ahead, he looked once more at the approaching figure.

It was that of an old woman dragging behind her a huge oxygen tent. This was to save him. Sunlight fell on her upturned face, she shouted words he couldn't hear. Looking down, he saw with horror a fat gray caterpillar at the base of his flower and, forgetting that it must on no condition be uprooted, seized the blossom, held it tightly. The stem had snapped. Now the oxygen tent was very near. In the instant before it parted to receive him, he thought he recognized the old woman. Mother? he whispered timidly. Inside he found violence, churning, a stifling blackness. The flower's petals, luminous through his fist, began slowly to separate. "It's no good!" he tried to tell his mother. "Stop! It's not doing any good!"—as something cold, fat and soft, a worm finally, fastened onto his wrist.

It had only been Mrs. McBride's finger, counting his pulse. When he was able to speak he tried to tell her about it.

"You mustn't tire yourself," she kept saying. "I've just talked to Lady Good. She says you're not to worry. She'll be up to see you in the morning. Now you go to sleep. Say to yourself, 'My feet are going to sleep, my legs and thighs are going to sleep. . . .'" She paused until his lips began to move, dutifully. "'My stomach is going to sleep, then my heart, my shoulders and arms. My fingers, my neck, my tongue. My eyes and my brain are fast asleep.'"

Mr. Tanning's eyes flew open. "Marlborough," he said. "The car. Ned . . ."

"Now hush!" said Mrs. McBride, remembering only then what Lady Good had told her. "There's no use fretting about going to see Sir Edward—he hasn't even come home for supper, that's what Lady Good said five minutes ago on the phone. She's had no words from him, she's waiting supper for him—a nice baked fish drying out. So there! Even if you went you wouldn't find him!"

Before she had finished he was asleep. Her heart went out to his white hair in need of brushing, his wide gentle mouth ajar. Mrs. McBride thanked heaven for having recollected that bit about Sir Edward. Nothing remained now to bother the old man. The voices of nocturnal creatures entered the room, bringing her to herself. She straightened her cap in the bureau mirror. "And *you*," she scolded, catching her own eye, "*you* haven't had anything to eat, either! That's a fine way to Keep up our Strength! I've got enough on my hands without having to watch over *you!*"

17.

Up North—"back home where things happened," as Mrs. McBride, overlooking many a drama on the Island, would say in letters to her daughter—winter came early. The first snow fell in mid-November. By Christmas most people suffered an odd delusion of the holidays' having already slipped by. An atmosphere prevailed of hasty, shamefaced preparation. Wreaths are hung, which surely had been taken down just a few weeks before; at the last minute you wrapped your own belongings as presents, for lack of others; invitations went out to a holiday eggnog that seemed already to have occurred.

Xenia, the morning before Christmas, was a complacent exception. Upon the big worktable under her skylight, half-empty cups, spilled sugar, ashes, all bespoke leisure. She sat licking her lip over the last of three dozen letters to friends, each to be accompanied by a single white rose and explaining that, *hélas!* she could afford to send only this, a rose, but that it carried thoughts and prayers more numerous than its petals. The violet ink streamed from her pen like tears of happiness. When the last of three dozen envelopes had been addressed in her pointed heartfelt hand, she gathered them up, cried, "I'm going round the block! Do you want anything?"—waited a moment for an answer that didn't come, then cautiously descended the steep stairs to the street.

In one direction Lexington Avenue still claimed a certain wan gentility; clients from Park and Fifth, she had reasoned, wouldn't mind crossing it. In the other lay a Third Avenue frankly Bohemian. Here were shops crammed with blackamoors, Tiffany glass, papier-mâché chairs, wicker beds; here were disreputable bars into whose windows bewildered old Irishmen (their patrons for forty years) peered at youths in fishnet pullovers, velvet gondoliers' slippers from Venice—supposed to have been given as gifts, slightly used, by their original wearers, rather than paid for in the shop behind the Danieli—summer suits of mattress-ticking, winter suits of homespun. In such a neighborhood Xenia had found a studio. It saved her life. She was no longer welcome at Adrienne's.

On aching feet she rounded the block. The day was lifeless, damp, her beaver coat weighed on her shoulders, but she was so happy! She flirted with the young Greek who managed the corner flower shop until he had to be coaxed into accepting money for his thirty-six roses. Oh, Xenia had rapidly become, in her own words, the favorite of these good simple people. From whom, by the way, to hide anything was impossible. Only yesterday the *patronne* of her little bakery had asked, "How goes the cold of Monsieur? Better?"

She bought cottage cheese from a Pole and small gummed stars, gold and silver, from a Virginian. Before long she was back upstairs, braids agleam, cheeks aglow, calling, *"C'est moi!"*

A narrow staircase led to sleeping quarters from which somebody could look down or not, depending on whether curtains or sailcloth, the length of the balcony, were parted or drawn. The big room had style, with its skylight and lanterns, its ferns, basil, avocado seeds splitting and sprouting; sculpture, too—some finished pieces (a watchful shape in gray marble, a spiraling shape like a root in brass); others in plaster, shrouded or uncomfortably prone on the tile floor; also a shelf of tentative forms in clay, most of which she knew would never outgrow the meager, expressionless gestures of dolls. On a plaster-encrusted stand the head of Lily Buchanan gleamed dully in brown wax. The little girl was coming after lunch to have one last look taken at her, before Xenia sent her head to the foundry. Mr. Tanning's head, already cast in bronze, lay on the sofa, gazing upward.

Two objects in particular drew smiles from her. The first was an old-fashioned dressmaker's form, an undulating torso covered in black muslin. Xenia had lugged it up from the street, brushed it off and set it on a low pedestal in the center of the room, which it could now be said to dominate. In the tubular wire cage beneath the upholstered thighs she had hung Christmas ornaments. These revolved on threads of varying length, a gay cosmography, bringing to mind as well those circles filled with text and connected by lines to points on an anatomical drawing of, say, the glandular system. (Xenia had had a lover from Danzig who thought of nothing but glands. "Marry a woman," he would harangue, "who is not a virgin, preferably a woman who has had a child—so that her whole endocrine system you have seen in action once!") The dressmaker's form, with its imaginary glands, was Xenia's Christmas tree. She had to step over a number of packages, gifts to her, to get to it, chuckling to herself as she pasted her little stars in extravagant clusters across the black breasts and belly. Already from the neck's neatly sewn stump a jet of plumes and baubles rose, as if in memory of some guillotined courtesan. All this Xenia deftly associated—thanks to eight years in analysis—with what she'd begun to speak of as her *old* life.

The second object she smiled at was an upright piano.

Her affair with Tommy Utter had started hard upon her exile from the Cottage. *"Figures-toi,"* Xenia told anyone who would listen at that time, "I thought I was in their house as a guest, as an internationally known artist, and here I am kicked out, sent from the door like a *fournisseur de tapis!* I have no studio, no place to go, no money and no prospect of getting it because *le fils* Tanning, who commissioned the head of his father, is in the hospital at death's door. I am ruined!" She had to humiliate herself by a trip—a subway trip, she was so poor—down to the offices of Tanning, Burr and Buchanan. "I was received," she said afterwards, "like dirt, like shit, by *le gendre* Buchanan. I put the whole case before him, that Francis (whose affairs he handles) owed me this money. He said, 'Has the head been delivered?' 'How can the head be delivered,' I said very politely, 'when I have no studio in which to put on the finishing touches, thanks to having been invited to leave the Cottage?' 'Well, if the head hasn't been delivered—' he kept repeating, exactly like Salome—*der Kopf, der Kopf, der Kopf des Jochanaans!*" Here Xenia, transported, would mimic the snarl and hiss of Strauss's heroine, eyes ablaze with indignation over the snub from Larry.

Adrienne and Tommy, and of course Max, had taken her in. They were friends whose like you didn't often see. Tommy had just received a thousand dollars from the foundation that commissioned his opera, the *première* of which was scheduled now for late March. Half of this money he put at Xenia's disposal on her return in a taxi, speechless with fury, from Larry Buchanan's office. She burst into tears and fell in love with Tommy. From then on, as her astrologist had predicted, good fortune came her way.

Once her conscience had been relieved by a few terrible scenes with

Adrienne, Xenia realized that she was wildly happy. Forgotten were the Tannings, the Buchanans. A check came from Francis. Within the same week she found her studio and discovered that she was pregnant.

By her *new* life she meant this. She never dreamed of keeping it secret. When she had told everyone else she telephoned Adrienne—who was reaching for the receiver in order to call *her*, having had the news that moment from a mutual friend. In twenty minutes they were in each other's arms, laughing like schoolgirls. Xenia's friend hadn't found a new lover. "But, my God!" she cried, "how agreeable it is to live alone! Now, when Max is away, I read, I get asked to dinners, I've even gone dancing! I'm having the time of my life, and it's all your doing! And Max—he'll be so amused, so pleased!" He was. One of Xenia's first presents was a case of champagne from Max with a note accepting her invitation to a party on Christmas Eve, wishing her and Utter a happy holiday, and thanking her (if he hadn't already) for having arranged that, at his age, he should once again have a mistress whose favors he wasn't asked to share with a younger man. Exquisite Max! His thumb and forefinger were orange with nicotine. One day at lunch a lower tooth, small and brown as a grain of rice, slid out of his mouth onto the plate. "Regard," he sighed, holding it up; "is it not sinister to outlive one's body?" It was decided he and Adrienne would be the child's godparents.

The only people Xenia hadn't told were the Tannings and the Buchanans. They had mysteriously dropped her, vanished from her life. Why, it hadn't been a week ago that she received a card from Francis, a bare greeting but with a city address to which she promptly sent off an invitation to her party, and *would* send a rose. The same day came a call from Enid. "I'd been wondering," she said in her tiniest, gayest voice, "if we were going to have Lily's head for Christmas. That was Daddy's idea. I think he'll be disappointed if his present's not under our tree." Xenia was stunned. "Enid, I've called you time and time again," she began passionately, truthfully also, "left message after message to say I needed another sitting with Lily, and that *you* should come and see the head before it was cast—" "Oh well, I've had my hands full," said Enid, "with our new little friend born December first." "Ah! what joy for you!" Xenia cried, relaxing all her defenses at the thought of motherhood. "Tell me, is it a boy or a girl?" It was a boy at last, named Tanning Burr after the firm. "So I guess," Enid went on in the silence that greeted the latter detail, "it's nobody's fault about the sittings." Xenia let it pass. An hour was found that conflicted with neither Lily's piano lesson, nor her dancing-school, nor her ice-skating. "Actually," Enid admitted, "I don't see how she could have fitted it in before the holidays. She had her part to learn for her school's Christmas play. They did *Macbeth* this year, it was really quite convincing." An eerie giggle escaped her. Enid promised to call for Lily after the sitting, so that she could write to Jamaica about the finished head. *"A rivederci!"* she signed off in the sweet singsong she used for no matter what language.

Lily arrived on time, left at the door by her nursemaid.

"Come in, both of you!" cried Xenia.

"Thank you, Miss," said the apple-cheeked Alice, "but there's a special service at St. Patrick's I'm hoping not to be late for."

"Ah, then say a prayer for me," Xenia smiled, waved her down the stairs. "Come in, Lily."

The child put out a hand. "It's nice to see you, Xenia." Graciously she let herself be helped off with her "things," a pale gray coat, fur-trimmed, with matching gloves and earmuffs of fur. She wore gray wool stockings with little red and white pom-poms at the top. "Lily, how you've grown!" Xenia couldn't help exclaiming, finding her on the threshold less of puberty than of a precocious womanhood. "Would I have known you? You're a big girl!"

"Isn't it ridiculous?" replied Lily, pleased. "Actually, I won't be eleven till next summer." This came out with a deprecating wrinkle of her nose, borrowed from Enid. It showed that, while discussion of your age wasn't especially well bred, she didn't mind confiding in Xenia. The dressmaker's form caught her eye; she had a good laugh over it. "I think your studio's very attractive," she declared. "May I look upstairs?"

"No."

"Why not?"

Xenia kept firm and cheerful. "Because I keep my secrets there," she said. "I like this studio, too. It's a kind of room one often finds in Europe."

"I know. We're going to Europe this Easter. To Rome."

"Rome!" sighed Xenia, slipping into her old blue smock. She added absently, "Why? You're not Catholics, are you?"

"Catholics!" her visitor gasped. "I should say not!"

"All right, sit here." She patted the high-chair beneath the skylight. "We have an hour of good light, so you keep still as a mouse." Cautiously she wheeled the stand into position. Lily's waxen head teetered.

The real Lily made a face. "That isn't *me?*"

So she was turning into that sort of little girl. Xenia shrugged, feeling no less good-humored because of it. "You haven't changed so much, really," she laughed, knowing presently as she began to squint at the two heads, the one alive, the other triumphantly *not*, that Lily had been right; she wasn't the same person. A look was missing—the Tanning look. Enid had it, so did Francis, Benjamin too, at times: a look of being roused against one's will. Xenia had seen it on her lover's face also, a slackening of the lips, not a smile, as he nuzzled closer to her fragrant pillow. Lily, however, was wide awake.

"What did you mean," she wanted to know, "about being a Catholic?"

Xenia explained that Rome held a unique interest for Catholics. Lily would surely see the crowds in front of St. Peter's, the saint's toes worn away, the Pope on his balcony.

The child looked skeptical. "Alice never told me that."

"Didn't your mother?"

"Mummy? What would she know about it?"

"She used to be a Catholic when she was your age."

"That's not true!" cried Lily, on guard against novelty. "How do you know?"

"Your grandfather told me," Xenia said pleasantly.

For the next several minutes Lily sat as still as could be wished. "Daddy says," she finally brought out, "that Rome's the best place to have clothes made."

Putting down her little curved stick with which she had been half-heartedly skimming the waxen mouth, Xenia said to herself, "No." She saw no point in going on. Lily had turned into her mother's image. The child's head was finished.

They sat over tea—Xenia putting rum in hers—while Lily told about her baby brother. She made him sound like a yardstick to measure how far she herself had come. "He has eyelashes and teensy little finger-nails—his whole hand isn't as big as my thumb! Of course he can't smile yet, he's too little, but he knows me. Mummy says he's going to look like me. Yesterday I held him while he had his bottle!"

Xenia's eyebrows went up. "But a little baby should be fed by its mother," she said in real concern, "not out of a bottle."

"Oh no," Lily corrected her. "Mother's milk doesn't supply *half* the nourishment a formula does."

"Have another cookie," said Xenia. "All this business of formulas has been disproved. Nothing takes the place of breast-feeding. I sound as if I knew all about it, but the fact is—" she gave an idiotic laugh; it was the irresistible topic—"I'm having a baby myself, and have had to read a hundred books." A wave of her hand dismissed them all. "Each says something different, but what they *do* agree upon is that one must trust one's natural instincts." The hand came to rest on her bosom.

"You're going to have a baby?"

"Isn't it wonderful?"

"But you're too old to have a baby!" the little girl pursued indig-nantly, seeking foothold on the glassy slopes of another's behavior.

This had been Xenia's own thought, that change of life was upon her; after all, she'd expected it for a number of years. Nevertheless she laughed, "How old do you think I am, Lily?"

"Forty?" guessed Lily, looking away.

"Enchanting angel!" cried Xenia. "I shall be forty-six next birthday—there! That's not so old to have a child. Your mother must be close to forty, no?"

Lily turned crimson. "I don't know. Besides," she went on, freely displaying the narrowness of her upbringing, "you're not married! People can't *have* babies without being married!"

They heard a muffled sneeze from the balcony.

"Somebody's up there!"

"Only the Pope," said Xenia in a gay loud voice.

The doorbell rang.

"You see, it's somebody at the door." She rose gratefully. "The acoustics are very strange in this room. I've had that happen before. It'll be Enid, come to admire your head." And Xenia threw the door wide open.

"Hello, hello!" cried the newcomer, shedding packages and enfolding her in a kiss. "Am I too late? Has Lily left?"

It was Francis.

"I realize I wasn't asked until nine o'clock," he said as he flopped into a chair, "but I've been around the corner at Natalie's—you knew she was your neighbor?—and I'm on my way to Fern's, after which I must drink with some people, *thence* to a solitary dinner with my poor mother—we always open our presents Christmas Eve, it keeps the Day free for debauchery. Anyhow it occurred to me I might give Lily her present now, as the shops are delivering the rest of her family's things. At least they said they were. The only reliable messenger boy is, of course, oneself. Enid on the phone let fall that I'd find her here, so," Francis got up and produced a small, carelessly wrapped box from the pocket of his Lodenmantel, "with love to my favorite niece—don't spend it all at once!" Lily smiled shyly and held the box to her ear.

Only now he removed his coat. He was wearing evening clothes, though it was not yet three. "I've found an apartment in the Village," he told them, "miles from here. So I said to myself, 'What's the point of dashing home to change? I'll just wear my dinner jacket all day!'" He laughed into their very eyes. Xenia waited in vain for any sign of illness. Francis was deeply tanned, with hair bleached by sun, so that he suggested a photographic negative of his old self. Perhaps he had gained weight. He spoke, too, in a new way, at once more mannered and more assured, never pausing for a word unless purposely, as a means of holding his listener. His waistcoat was of black brocade shot through with purple violets. The pump dangling from his toe sported a lining of scarlet. For studs he had two black pearls, and he wore the wing collar that hadn't been in vogue since before the war.

"So tell me, tell me!" he said. "I feel I've been away forever. Tell me what's new." Then, while Xenia and Lily smiled helplessly at one another: "All right, don't tell me. I know what you'd be saying, anyhow."

"I'm not so sure of that," replied Xenia, and winked at Lily. "I don't think your uncle has any idea of *my* news."

"Come off it, Mona Lisa," said Francis blandly. "How naïve can you get? There are no secrets in New York." He fixed her with a slow appraising stare. "True, with that smock on, it's rather hard to tell."

Xenia threw up her hands. He knew! "But who could have told you?" she demanded, almost cross.

"And Lily's news is: she has a baby brother, she's going to Rome for Easter, and she's fresh from a frantic success as Lady Macbeth."

"I wasn't Lady Macbeth! Who told you that?"

"Don't be modest, child, it's an extraordinary part. Actresses go through lives without a chance to play it." Francis leapt to his feet and declaimed:

> *"Come, you spirits*
> *That tend on mortal thoughts, unsex me here!"*

He spun about in a way neither understood, as if to catch a certain expression on their faces. "Or that bit about dashing out the brains of the babe at her breast—it's all so wild and up-to-date." He sat down, this time on the sofa next to his father's upturned bronze face. "Good heavens!" he cried, recognizing it.

It was wrong for him to happen on it like that. Xenia had planned to have it on a pedestal, with proper lighting, so that Francis's first view would be of a serious, imposing piece. But there he sat, his hand brushing back and forth across the features, the way you tousle a child's head or a dog's. "Bring the head over here, Francis," she told him. "You'll see it in a better light."

He obeyed, lifting it easily from the cushion where it lay, cradling it in the crook of his arm. *"Attention!"* warned Xenia, and only breathed when she saw the old man's head placed where she had indicated. It stood now somewhat taller than Benjamin himself, while Francis continued his recitation:

> *"Had he not resembled*
> *My father as he slept, I had not done it!"*

"I *had* done it," Lily interrupted. "You've got it wrong."

Francis paused, suddenly perplexed. "Are you sure?"

"Yes—the King looks like her father and so she *doesn't* do it, she makes Macbeth do it."

"Of course," said Francis. "Oh, it's a fantastic scene, whichever way you look at it. *Give me the daggers!*" he cried, advancing upon Lily,

> *"the sleeping and the dead*
> *Are but as pictures; 'tis the eye of childhood*
> *That fears a painted devil. If he do bleed,*
> *I'll gild the faces of the grooms withal,*
> *For it must seem their guilt.*

And *then,* scaring the audience out of its wits—the knocking!"

The doorbell rang.

Francis reacted with a stage shudder—"You see!"

"That's only Mummy," Lily said. She had watched his performance distrustfully. "I wasn't Lady Macbeth either, I was only Fleance. I'm not old enough for one of the big parts."

Up to then Xenia would never have thought it possible to be soothed by the presence of Enid Buchanan. "Hello, my pearls!" she sang out on the threshold, and it was like a cool hand upon her hostess's brow. "Why, look who's here! How are you, sweetie?" She kissed her brother on both cheeks. "Don't you look well! How was the *tripolino?* Listen to me!" she giggled apologetically, letting Xenia take her coat. "All the Buchannibals are learning Italian like things possessed!"

Enid looked lovely, svelte, pink, chic. She had almost a boy's figure. She gave no evidence of having borne a child within the month. Bottle-feeding had its advantages. Whereas *I,* thought Xenia but with more pride than envy, will look like a pig for a year!

"I did," Francis was saying, "but my poor mother came down with something local and had to fly home after a week."

Enid clicked her tongue. "So I heard."

"It was purely psychosomatic. I'd persuaded her to go on to Jamaica with me and in less than six hours she had a fever. She's just not *ready* for a full life. I stayed right on. I lay in the sun and stared at the sea and read Shakespeare all day, as Lily can vouch. I've never felt better in my life. You must go there. The natives are so beautiful as not to be believed."

"Where, Francis?" Xenia asked out of habit, forgetting that she was getting her fill of beauty right there in New York.

"Haiti, where I've been," he replied, as though she ought to have known. "Wait till you hear my new French accent."

"Don't forget," she let a hurt note sound in her voice, "I've had no word from you these many months."

"Neither have I!" Enid sent Xenia a twinkle of sympathy. "And no word from Daddy—not even an acknowledgment of his first grand-son—since the cable about Sir Edward. Poor Lady Good! Did you get to Jamaica, then?"

"Sir Edward?" Xenia tried to ask, but the talk swept by her.

"Did I not!" cried Francis. "My new English accent ought to have told you *that*."

Enid hummed her high note. "I see we must have a *chattino* soon."

A look of curiosity settled on her face like a mask. It showed how desperately Enid wanted to hear, yet how resolutely she would let the chance go by—would indeed force it to go by—should Francis start bringing them up to date on Mr. Tanning's love life. What nonsense, thought Xenia; she'd hear all the dirt from Francis later, why not now? Enid's way of turning aside, of murmuring to Lily, "And how's my tiny pearl?" brought back things both Francis and his father had said. The Buchanans were prudes. They lived in terror lest their offspring be corrupted by the old man's sexual excess—by anyone's, for that matter. Xenia wondered briefly whether Enid would thank her for having discussed her pregnancy with Lily. She had already seen Enid's eye rest on the dressmaker's form with the same look she might have cast a nude photograph of Xenia (there were in fact several upstairs) had one been set out on the mantel. The artist tossed her head. These absurd Americans, what did she care? She simply couldn't take them seriously.

They had gathered about Mr. Tanning's head. It shone dimly in the weakening light, the patina at once rose and brown. How she had toiled over that! At Xenia's insistence the old Italian at the foundry kept swabbing the raw bronze with acids, igniting them, quenching them, beginning again until the right effect had been secured. She took pains to tell these things to Enid and Francis; she wouldn't have troubled herself for the ordinary client, *le cochon de payant* who'd have been just as pleased, more so perhaps, by a surface of the brightest vulgarest green. Xenia knew as she spoke that she was falsifying her motives, that plain pride in her work, rather than love for the Tannings, was responsible for the fineness of the results. But the rich needed flattery even more than artists. Unhappily she gave them, at times such as this, so little credit for intelligence that she failed altogether to connect what she said that afternoon with the way Enid was henceforth to let it be known among her friends that Xenia had a wee touch of the sycophant about her and, in the last analysis, lacked professional pride.

As it was, Xenia waited in vain for any understanding of her effort to show on their faces. They made, after a bit, the agreeable, easy remarks characteristic of the pig who paid. Daddy looked young; Daddy looked spiritual; Grandpa looked tired. It was hopeless. They hadn't felt the features shaping beneath their fingers, hadn't seen flames dart—blue, amber, green—from the whole head, or heard the awful hiss as it was doused with water. These experiences might have helped them distinguish the particular human face from the face made by art.

"Where will you put the head?" she asked Francis. "In your apartment?"

"Oh, heavens no," he replied. "I'm giving it to *him*, so where it goes is his problem."

Xenia drew herself up. "The only *problem*," she said, "is that it be properly displayed."

"Ah, you can trust him to do that," grinned Francis.

Lily's head was no more successfully received. One drawback, Xenia tried to explain, lay in the color and texture of the wax, a glossy brown that, annihilating highlights and shadows alike, made the whole impossible to see except in profile. Besides, Lily had changed so, hadn't she? Enid nodded, lips pursed. She then turned her lovely smile upon Xenia. "I'm at a loss for words," she said. "It will be a lifelong joy."

Xenia knew perfectly that Enid meant no word of this. How could she? The head did look dreadful in wax. It was mortifying to be so patronized. By tomorrow, of course, Xenia's own self-deceptions would have done their work. She would be boasting over the telephone: "Ah! La Buchanan adored the head! She said it would be a lifelong joy. No, naturally she can't appreciate the workmanship, still it's good to have such a heartfelt response." For the present Xenia went behind a screen and swallowed a shot of rum. All her annoyance with the Buchanans and their ways returned. She had expected, also, *some* support from Francis. Wiping her mouth, she peered out. "Who would like a drink? Enid? Francis?"

Enid refused. She and Lily would have to toddle along.

"I'll have one," said Francis from beside the dressmaker's form, whose stump he was idly caressing. "Aren't you going to open your present, Lily?"

"Now?"

"Of course. We always open our presents on Christmas Eve. It leaves the Day free—" he stopped himself.

When Xenia brought his drink they were bent over Lily's gift.

"Goodness me!" cried Enid. "Somebody has a very nice uncle!"

"See if it fits," Francis whispered.

"Oh, Uncle Francis!" breathed Lily, her eyes ashine. "I've never *had* a ring."

Xenia saw that it was his little ring, with the gold owl.

"I wore it for a while myself," said Francis as if none of them had seen him do so. "It's really a thing of great beauty. I fancied I'd lost it, but my poor mother turned out to have been keeping it for me, ever since Boston." A faint smile preceded the last word, allowing Xenia to identify it as a synonym for his mysterious illness.

Lily turned and turned the ring upon her finger. "Look," she exclaimed all at once, "it bends!" and held it up for them to see. The ring did bend.

"Be careful," Francis warned her.

"Pure gold will always bend," said Xenia.

"Pure gold is very soft and fragile," Enid added.

"I'd better not wear it," the child murmured delicately, decisively.

"Oh, it must be *worn*," said Francis with a yawn. "Things must be used. If they break, it can't be helped. I'm bored by so many beautiful things under glass." Lily looked unconvinced, but put the ring on, to please him. She struck Xenia as having lost most of her pleasure in it, upon learning how easily it could be damaged. Francis seemed, accordingly, to have lost interest in his niece, now that she had picked out the flaw in his gift. "*I* must start looking about for things," he continued, sipping his drink. "There are too many bare walls and floors in my apartment, and naked bulbs on cords. I've noticed some crazy antique shops down the street. The other night, looking in a window, I saw what could only have been a tortoise-shell baby carriage. The trouble with something like that is, how to use it?"

Was Francis spending his evenings down the street? In those bars? Xenia gave him a roguish look which he met blankly at first, then misinterpreted, adding, "Unless *you*'d like it for Christmas!" Already Enid was gathering up her purse and gloves.

But Lily let out a squeal of recollection. "Mummy, you haven't heard! Xenia's going to have a baby!"

It must have perplexed Enid to find herself, rather than Xenia, the sudden object of scrutiny. More likely, she didn't even notice. In her innocence she let sound the cries of amazement and joy with which she never failed to greet such announcements. She took Xenia's hands, she beamed into Xenia's eyes. Xenia had her first, her only sense of the promptness and beauty of Enid's warmth. It couldn't last. "I have cobwebs in the old head," she marveled, shaking it, "I honestly don't think I ever knew you were married!"

"That's what I said," said Lily.

Xenia held her head high. "You're right, I'm not," she suavely declared. "Not *yet*, that is."

A soft sound escaped from Enid. She searched her compact mirror for something other than her face.

"But I've had a recent proposal of marriage," pursued Xenia, "which I'm almost ready to accept."

Her "almost" had its effect. All three leaned forward. The compact shut with a snap.

"I mean," she finished, "it's so crucially important for a child, here in America."

"I couldn't agree more!" Enid's head fell to one side, nodding reflectively. She rose and chanted, *"Mais je pense qu'il n'est pas bon de mention-ner ces choses devant les petites personnes,"* ending with a mild apologetic smile, or grimace, that showed she couldn't help being old-fashioned and straitlaced. "One feels so well, though, so alive!" she kept on, feeling behind her for her coat. "I hardly had a single headache the whole time I was sitting on the *nestino*. Your system manufactures ACTH, which doctors are using now to treat headaches. I think that's interesting, don't you? I just can't go along with the little people who say babies are headaches—mine still haven't come back!"

Enid's manner was so perfect, so like the sway and tinkle of a delicate timepiece, enameled, gilded, surmounted by some goddess in whose lap children played, that Xenia had already imagined the moment carried off with a minimum of embarrassment when Francis intervened. He took his sister's elbow and guided her with comic solicitude to the door. He kissed her cheek, he pinched her chin. *"É mia colpa, sorellina,"* he said gravely. "But we mustn't work too hard, must we? The Lily of the field will give us lessons in sophistication."

And Lily, who a half-hour before hadn't believed that children could be born out of wedlock, now peered up at them precociously. "Don't ask me!" she exclaimed. "I don't even know what you're talking about!"

"You see?" Francis laughed.

Xenia's face started to tingle. In just such dulcet syllables as Enid used to say goodbye, clocks struck an end to the Age of Reason. Francis might have spared her that.

Each, nevertheless, cried, "Merry Christmas!" twice, with handshakes or kisses, whereupon Enid and Lily would have left, had not a thick voice echoed, "Merry Christmas!" from high behind them. Through the sailcloth curtains Tommy Utter's head appeared, handsome, flushed, and disheveled. He was really thirty-two, but looked nineteen just then. "Oh," he said stupidly. "I've been asleep. Who's that? Francis? Hello, Francis."

Francis raised his empty glass in greeting.

"My fiancé, Mr. Utter," said Xenia with Russian ballet gestures. "Mrs. Buchanan and her daughter, Lily."

"We've been hearing such intriguing news," said Enid, her voice all silvery. "I gather congratulations are in order!"

"Oh . . . it was nothing!" grinned the young man, ducking his head. Everyone's eyes wavered a bit. Then the door closed upon the visitors.

Xenia leaned heavily against it. "Are you feeling better?" she asked Tommy.

"I don't know, Pussy. Not too good, I guess."

"Go back to sleep, then."

"All right." He waved and withdrew his head.

To be exposed to such a scene, on Christmas Eve—*ouf!* Xenia fell onto the sofa. "Francis, Francis," she sighed, handing him her glass to fill, "I never thought, the day I got your cable on the ship, that I'd be put through so much. Thank God I'm strong!" She broke into a great jolly laugh, because it was all preposterous as well as shameful. "Oh, these people! What do they think art is? What do they think human life is? On the one hand they treat me like a rug merchant, on the other like a whore!"

"I thought Enid did all right, considering," Francis shrugged.

"I'm proud to be an artist, I'm proud to be bearing Tommy's child. But when I went by subway to ask Larry Buchanan for money, do you know how I was received? Like dirt, like shit! I couldn't believe my ears."

Francis raised his hand. "Please," he said. "I do sympathize, but I can't be responsible for your difficulties with my family."

"Difficulties! I've never—"

"Something's changed in me," he continued. "I *will* no longer endure an atmosphere of quarrels and conflicts. I've forgotten what the different political parties stand for—not that I ever knew. I refuse to wear myself out trying to meet other people's terms. Life's too short. It's time for people to start meeting mine, for a change."

Xenia's eyes narrowed. The light had dimmed; it conferred upon things a kind of glowing Flemish gentleness, in which colors reached beyond their given limits. Against a mustard-gold cushion she watched her friend's foot swing back and forth in its sheer black sock and gleaming slipper. It was odious to make allowances for those one loved. But Francis had been ill, she couldn't now doubt that. She had trusted, despite the strain under which she'd last seen him, that their earlier, their *real* relationship might be preserved. However, if something else was in the stars—*bon!* Her mind performed the first of several melancholy revisions that would in time cause her to treat him as a virtually new person. In this altering light she perceived that he, like Lily, had lost the Tanning look, the look—how had she defined it?—of being roused against his will. Indeed, gazing at him, Xenia found it easy to wonder if he would ever again do anything against his will. He was smiling through the smoke of a cigarette, pleased to see his first warning taken. How was she not to have taken it? Her path had been strewn with sagging boards and wobbly railings; nowadays a glance told her where it was no longer safe to apply pressure.

"Your mother's been ill?" she asked politely, exhaling some smoke of her own.

"Vinnie's always ill," he said. "I broke the machine when I was born."

She obliged herself not to respond. "Then tell me, how did you find Ben?" she went on in the same pleasant tone.

Francis rolled his eyes upward. "The madness that goes on in that house! I couldn't take it, I left after four days."

"Didn't the atomic cocktail work?"

"Work! He's a new man! Nobody gets a minute's peace. He did have one bad spell—weeks before I got there—since which time he's *bloomed.* One wakes to the music of idling motors. He's forever leaping into cars and careening through canefields. I went with him once and, I must say, didn't feel specially wanted. It's all glands and drugs, of course—not the real *him* at all."

"It sounds marvelous," said Xenia, wondering what drugs her companion took.

"Oh, there are drawbacks," Francis pursued, somewhat nasally. "It's true he's out of pain, but his *mind's* not as clear as it used to be. If I were Dr. Samuels I'd be a wee bit embarrassed. Yet it doesn't seem to bother anyone else."

"Does he go to see Irene?"

"Not often. I suspect not at all."

"And *l'affaire* Good?"

Francis stared. "You haven't heard? No, I suppose you wouldn't have. Sir Edward's dead."

"Sir Edward! No!" Xenia felt her throat contract. So that had been what Enid meant. She tried to say something. The charming, cultivated man with whom she had talked, even danced—"How is it possible?" she babbled. "He wasn't old."

"Fifty-four," said Francis. "It happened a number of weeks ago. A cart jammed with Negroes turned into the road. It was twilight. He headed his car into a deep ditch. His neck was broken, or something."

"Good God!" There were tears in Xenia's eyes. She couldn't say which more unnerved her, the news or Francis's way of telling it. "I shall write Prudence," she whispered, "if you leave her address." The vision of a fine florid man, face down in mud, rose before her. And of course, no children. "Poor woman, she'll be all alone."

"On the contrary," smiled Francis, who had taken out his pen and was balancing a strip of paper upon his wallet. "Benjamin has all but moved in with her. I wouldn't know, myself, whether to write a letter of condolence or one of congratulation."

Xenia struck the sofa with her hand. An indignant dust swirled and glinted in the dim air. "No more, Francis, if you please! I won't hear you talk so about those poor lonely people. I can't stand callousness in any form!"

Various expressions crossed his face. He set Lady Good's address on the arm of his chair, and seemed on the point of rising to go. Instead, he looked about the studio, never once at Xenia, and, drawing from his wallet another strip of paper, began to write upon it. He presently held it out to her, saying tonelessly, "I don't know what you need for Christmas. Please take this, and don't be cross with me." The check was for two hundred dollars.

She wanted to refuse it. But wouldn't he then, in the state he was in, get up and go for good? Really, Francis had developed a genius for the disconcerting. Xenia made her second mental reservation and decided to accept the check. One had to be strong to know when to be weak. "I thought for a moment I was being bribed," she laughed, after thanking him, "but I now feel it comes in friendship." Besides, she explained, until after the *première* of Tommy's opera, they had to live on a shoestring. They couldn't even afford to get married.

"You're honestly getting married!" marveled Francis. "I don't *see* you married, somehow."

Everybody said this. How little they understood. "It's what we all need, Francis," she beamed, her lashes fluttering. "You should have saved your little gold ring for a pretty *jeune fille*."

Half of his mouth smiled. "No," he said, "I wanted Lily to have it. It's a child's ring. *I* certainly have no further need of it. My brainpicker— whom *entre nous* I don't need either, but the family feels better about me—says I no longer see myself as a child. And I daresay he's right."

"Your what?" Xenia had understood hardly a word of his speech.

"My brainpicker. My analyst."

"You're in analysis! Ah, I'm so relieved!" The news momentarily explained all his oddities. Xenia knew how patients behaved during the first months of treatment. "Tell me what else he says," she begged, leaning forward and licking her lips. It was a topic she adored.

Francis made a face. "Oh, crazy things like: 'Go ahead and wear women's clothes if you want!' or: 'There's absolutely nothing you can't do!' I keep saying, 'Come off it, Sigmund—there's plenty I can't do!'"

"He's not a Freudian?" said Xenia in alarm.

"*I* don't know," he replied, all at once weary. "Good Lord, I must be off. It's nearly four."

"Where do you go?"

"To Fern's. She leaves for Hobe Sound next week. My onetime step-mother," he added, seeing Xenia's blank face. He stood up.

"You still see her?"

"Oh," Francis grinned, "I sometimes think I see everybody."

They stood in the open doorway, holding hands. "This Christmas I am so poor," said Xenia, "I cannot give presents. But I have sent you a rose, Francis, with a note that says what I think you must know."

"A rose?" he echoed, his voice suddenly very high and soft. "Really, a *rose?* Why, Xenia, how sweet, how—!" He shuddered once almost imperceptibly, from head to toe.

She squeezed his hand. "We still have things to say to one another, don't we?"

Francis looked away. "One thing," he blurted out, "I want so much to know, that's so important to me now—" Again he broke off, waiting, it seemed; then, "You know what it is."

"No. Tell me what it is."

His lips quivered. "About the child," he began, staring now into her eyes, "you're quite sure—you *were* quite sure when you said—it's Tommy's child?"

Amused, vexed, touched, she hesitated, his concern at last clear, try-ing to make out what he wanted to be told. A minute earlier, Xenia would have been tempted to pay him back in his own coin, to reply, "My dear Francis, do you suppose children are conceived on nights like that? One needs love, something you have not learned to feel; and trust, which you have not yet learned to inspire." But now she felt so sorry for him. Peo-ple would always have to *think* how to act in his presence. He had grown, moreover, before her very eyes, so tender, so defenseless, the way she remembered him from Rome and the early days at the Cottage. The spark of love hadn't been put out, it waited for someone's breath. Perhaps all he needed was to believe that he had fathered a child. Yes, thought Xenia, exactly that. She reached out and let her hand rest against his cheek.

"Cher ami," she said, choosing her words slowly, "you must never worry about that, now promise me."

His eyes glistened wide. Lifting her other hand, he softly kissed it.

"I'll see you this evening?" asked Xenia, and patted his cheek to ease him on his way.

"Of course!" Halfway downstairs he turned around to wave.

She closed the door. What an afternoon. Somebody had brushed a star from her black torso. Xenia picked it up and pasted it back, whispering, *"Voilà, ma belle."* In a month or so, when Francis was more himself, she would confess her deception and they would laugh over it.

Passing the head of Lily Buchanan, she stuck out her tongue.

Then she climbed the narrow creaking stair. Before lying next to him, she sat on Tommy's side of the bed, and stroked his damp dark hair. Without waking he snuggled closer. His mouth worked, but if there were words he wanted to speak, Xenia didn't hear them.

On learning she was pregnant she had gone into the nearest church and given thanks. Automatically she conferred upon her lover a godlike sweetness and power. He was the first to get her with child. When he proposed marriage she accepted without thinking. Under the crown! as the old woman said in Russia. More recently she had wondered if marriage would be quite the bliss she'd imagined. *Bah!* she would laugh, dismissing the thought—she was turning into an old woman herself!

She had just forgotten what it was to live with somebody. Each day Tommy would leap out of bed, flailing his arms against the cold, turn on the electric heater, stumble downstairs, and start a pot of oatmeal. While this cooked he went to the piano. Five out of seven mornings the oatmeal boiled over. It took a half-hour to clean the stove. In two short months Xenia had come to listen with apprehension for the noise of saw and hammer—"I want to build things for you, Pussy," he would say—and the vision it called up of fragile objects all through the studio moving, at every blow, a jerky centimeter closer to ruin on the tile floor. One afternoon he had repaired the radio. Xenia came and went, destroyed an old sculpture, began a new one, made a spaghetti sauce and left it simmering for dinner, wrote a letter or two—while Tommy crouched over the dismembered parts. On his face she recognized the squinty drugged look with which, on the streets, American youth gazed at the insides of automobiles, that long sexual reverie, fiddling with wires and plugs to find out "what makes her go." The evenings were charming, he invented waltzes for her, they drank wine. Artists came by, whose talk recaptured cafés. By day, alas! she heard herself more and more adopt a tone long-suffering, without illusions. What was wrong with these American men? why didn't they grow up? She had already one child within her, did she need another for her husband? At first mortified by such thoughts, Xenia came to take them as signs of fatigue.

She was so sleepy now, for instance, with strength only to disengage her hand from his, to stagger round the bed. She kicked off her mules and lay down, pulling a crazy quilt up to her chin. Domesticity. Domesticity was turning her into an old, old woman. And because she didn't believe a word of it, she sent a ravishing secret smile up to the ceiling, dim and narrow—the whole balcony being not much wider than the bed itself.

Before the party she managed to write a letter of sympathy to Lady Good.

18.

Alone among the canefields, Sir Edward's widow was far from easy to woo. In vain Benjamin pointed out how docile a listener she had been before the tragedy. "Please," she would reply, "I value your friendship. I should hate to lose it. I have so little, now." Whereupon, like as not, she would sit down at the piano.

If nothing else, Prudence was giving him a musical education. That he was tone-deaf, that he failed to identify even the catchiest tunes, mattered to neither. She played, he listened—or maybe only watched from the far side of her parlor with its parched ferns and wastes of dark wood, its cabinets of sorry ornaments. She wouldn't stir from the house. Before long Benjamin was responding to her music; he had, poor man, little else to do at Canecrest. Haydn rattled him, Chopin left him tearful, Grieg sent him out of the room. One day he recognized in the andante of a Beethoven sonata his college anthem:

> "Yet, Mother, may thy sons e'er hail
> The crimson and the gray!"

He sang in his throaty lifeless voice, only with the wildest modulations. Prudence had had to turn her head to keep him from supposing the song had made her smile.

She didn't coyly shield herself with music. It had become the one really noble alternative to speech. It lifted her—it lifted both of them, she fancied—to a vantage from which, schooled by truth and beauty, and forgoing all discussion, the heart saw how effortlessly it could give up a great number of things. Benjamin himself, for instance—she wouldn't have him, she wouldn't under any circumstances marry him. This was the message entrusted to, as it were, the highest whitest keys. "I have thought and thought," she told him gently, for once putting it into words. To tell the truth, Prudence had thought hardly at all.

Her style of playing suffered. She was no longer out to please but to persuade. Breaks in rhythm, tentative runs and clumsy trills now marked her performance, like that of the gifted talker who, in order to prove his sincerity, begins to stammer, to search for words; fearing that what is fluent cannot be heartfelt, his lips are dry, he runs a hand through his hair. On one occasion Prudence had frozen on a dissonance, turned, risen exclaiming, "What's in your mind, please, when you look at me that way?"

"Which way?" Benjamin had asked, not taking his eyes from her.

"That way. With that smug smile. As if you knew something."

"I don't know anything, Prudence," he sighed, all humbleness. She had said no more, had even checked an arch look lest he read into it meanings not intended. She understood for the twentieth time that her position was intolerable, yet could find neither will nor way to do anything about it.

Irene Cheek, who had indirectly put her in this position, unwittingly got her out of it.

Prudence was sitting, one brilliant afternoon in early January, deep in a Song without Words. She played with or without Benjamin, he being not the only one her music had to persuade. It was long past the hour of his usual visit—a good sign, by and large; either he had found something better to do, or the drive from Weathersome hadn't seemed worth the trouble. In any case, he didn't *need* her, and wasn't self-sufficiency the first step towards a normal friendship? How exasperating he had been, during Francis's brief stay, by coming nevertheless to sit with her, daily!—until for once she had broken her resolution and gone over to eat with them both, out of sheer annoyance. Thank Heaven he was learning at last!

The cook came to ask if six o'clock would be too early for dinner. Prudence shrugged; she was never hungry. Besides, the girl no doubt wanted to meet an admirer. Her mistress's fingers had discovered a forgotten phrase, five descending notes, like the most tender leavetaking—

had Benjamin only been there to hear it—when, as in a passage from *Carmen* where an incitement to guilty pleasure is thwarted by the far-off bugle sounding retreat, she heard the familiar horn of Mr. Tanning's Triumph. It sent her hurrying to receive him, still smoothing her hair in the doorway, and wondering why she felt so little disappointment at the sight of him.

He looked spruce as ever, with a gay tie, a daisy in his lapel. But something was troubling him. He downed the better part of a drink—from the bottle she permitted him to keep there, as if Canecrest were a sort of private club. The creak of his rocking chair defined a silence. Elsewhere Marlborough could be heard striking up a conversation with the cook. It had the momentary effect of setting an example for Mr. Tanning. "Everyone hates to admit he's been a damn fool," he began by way of a stab at sociability. But he couldn't sustain it, he fell silent again.

At last he sees! thought Prudence.

She nowadays was letting conscience determine nearly all behavior, not just her own. Thus there had been a *guilty* look on the cook's face when she'd asked about dinner, a look that, more than any certain knowledge, required that a lover be waiting for her under the dark boughs of Prudence's fixed idea. As for the look on Benjamin's face, it came to her in a flash—the poor man had fallen out of love and was embarrassed over how to break it to her! Wishing to make it easy for him, she smiled warmly, "It took a long time, didn't it?" and could feel, like sun on her shoulders, Ned's downward, approving gaze.

"I just can't believe it," said Benjamin.

"It's all for the best," she assured him. "You'll see." That Prudence took most particular pains not to gloat over her success was something of a pity, considering what followed. Never again did she enjoy such an opportunity for gloating.

She let the subject drop, knowing Benjamin would return to it soon enough. All their conversation tended to be episodic. He had become no more capable of prolonged attention to one topic than a dog of sustaining his master's gaze. Unfinished business haunted their talk—questions he'd never answered, bits of information or messages she hadn't remembered to give him, "Oh, and in Zinnia's letter," she said now, going back some ten days, "she asked me please to inquire what you wanted done with the bust."

"What bust?"

"Yours. The one Zinnia did of you. The *sculpture*." Prudence watched him uneasily. He might have been hearing of it for the first time.

"Those sittings took a lot out of me," he finally remarked.

"Well, the bust is finished now. It's cast and she says everyone thinks it lovely, but where do you want it delivered?"

"What am I going to do with it?" Benjamin grumbled. "I thought Francis wanted it."

"He commissioned it, but he meant you to have it."

"Oh I see."

The discussion ended there. A week later, were Prudence to bring it up, he would most likely claim that he had explicitly directed her to have the bust sent out to the Cottage.

Remembered from the eve of their trip to Boston, the not-quite-finished clay head had given out the *essence* of Benjamin. She wondered, though, how much resemblance would show now, since the change in him. This in itself was no fixed thing. Every few weeks, depending on the pills he took, his face would shrink or bloat up, a weary blankness settling there, his speech blurring or brightening. Then, following a transfusion, would come days of absolute gaiety. Prudence couldn't any longer be sure of the *real* Benjamin—he had disappeared into a dozen illusory effects, like a maze of mirrors. If only she could ask somebody about it, a doctor or a minister. She had tried once to question Benjamin himself, choosing, however, one of his most exuberant days. He had asked what in the hell she was talking about.

At times he, too, would speak of the change, but in terms so variable as not to enlighten her at all. He did so now, starting with a dull baffled sigh. "Prudence, I don't have any more heart pain. I've had just three bad nights since I left the States. That's wonderful, don't you think?"

"I do indeed!" she declared, not for the first time. "Dr. Samuels is a most brilliant man."

"Isn't he!" agreed Benjamin. "Think of being free from pain, after ten solid years of suffering. He cares how I feel, too. By God, I think he's the finest doctor I've ever known." He looked up. "My father was a doctor. Did you know that?"

"You've told me about him. He must have been a splendid man."

"He was. I used to ride in his buggy. The roads weren't paved in those days—little country roads. My last attack was two months ago, Prudence. Do you remember?"

Her throat contracted. It had been the day of Ned's accident.

Lifting his hand like a blind man, Benjamin let it softly explore his features, the forehead, the eyes, the puffy cheeks. "I don't get the same fun out of life," he produced at length.

Prudence clasped her hands. "Ah, my dear—" she might risk calling him that, since henceforth they were to be *friends;* the phrase, furthermore, came so naturally—"my dear, we can't expect fun every day of the week." Her face tingled innocently with the pleasure of speaking from bitter recent experience.

"Vinnie used to make remarks like that," said Benjamin, "and for all I know, still does."

"Yes, she's not the ordinary silly woman."

He seemed not to hear. "If I hadn't been taking thyroid extract," he informed her, "I'd have turned into a cretin. Did you know that? My mind would have stopped working, I'd probably not be much"—here he startled her by winking—"of a Casanova. See how puffy my face is? That means the dose needs adjusting. It's no fun being dependent on pills and nurses. Nobody cares. I wish you'd known my mother. I just hate people to treat me like a damn fool."

There he was back, almost, where he had started on his arrival. Prudence leaned forward, with much to praise in his acceptance of her greater wisdom. "I can't tell you how this eases my mind, Benjamin dear. How could I ever treat you as a fool?"

He stared at her. "You couldn't. That's one reason I love you, Prudence." The old man drained his glass, belched, and explained. "I've just come from Irene's."

"Oh!" said Prudence, mortified. So their relationship hadn't even been bothering him! She sank back, close to tears, and let him tell his story.

He hadn't met Irene face to face since the matter of the letters. They had talked on the telephone, Prudence knew, at least twice: first when Benjamin called to ask, politely, how soon she intended to give the letters back. Oh, she had protested, she meant to give them back at once, but there'd been an inconvenience, the rumor of a prowler in her neighborhood, so that all her *valuables* had been taken from the house and put in safekeeping. Where? In Kingston, at a certain bank. Their second conversation took place after Benjamin's discovery, through a simple question put in the right quarter, that Irene had lied—she had nothing in that bank, not even money. So he called again. She was pleasant and cool, enough to make Prudence's face burn, hearing about it. Benjamin felt he was expected to make a cash offer for the letters.

This stunned him. For weeks he did nothing more about it. If he spoke of that second conversation it was in a tone of disbelief: could he have heard aright? Was it possible for such malice to lie behind all that tenderness? Prudence tried not to wonder precisely what tenderness of Irene's he had in mind. Something kept her from pressing him for details. Not once did Benjamin see a connection between Irene's vindictiveness and that of certain other women he had discarded.

"I was greeted by the lady of the house," he now began—and, depressed as he was, he couldn't let "house" go by without a weary leer—"dressed in a big red beach towel and nothing else. She *said* her masseur had just left. I said that's what she could tell her husband, but

Irene didn't laugh. She escorted me—oh, very formally—past a dinner-table set for at least twenty people. I'll be damned if I know what fun she gets out of those big dinners. They knock me for a loop. The garden was looking like hell, too. She's had freak winds all winter long, blowing soot from Ned's molasses factory. It's all over the chairs. We couldn't sit down till the butler came with towels, buttoning up his uniform, I happened to notice." Benjamin winked for what it was worth. "It sticks to the leaves. Irene said some days they can't even swim, the soot lies so thick on the water. By damn!" he exclaimed, breaking into a great grin, "I wouldn't put it past your sainted husband to have a hand in the whole business, would you?"

Ned plaguing the Cheeks with soot? To her own dismay Prudence laughed, before glaring sadly off.

"I won't bore you with the whole story. I asked her for the letters. She said she didn't have them. I told her she was lying. Do you know what she did? She looked me straight in the eye and said, 'You always did have brains, Benji.' It made me so mad I wanted to cry. I said something mean then. I reminded her of a trust-fund I'd set up in her name two years ago. I said it was still possible to revoke that. It wasn't like me to do something like that, was it? I don't know what I'm like any more, to tell the truth. My appetite's no good. I feel sluggish and stupid. I don't know . . ." He followed his tangent a step further. "All my heart pain has stopped. . . ."

"*Did* you set up a trust-fund for Irene?"

He gave her an unashamed look. "Yes, Prudence. And she's still welcome to it. I don't want the money. Charlie and Irene were very kind to me in the past. I can't forget that."

Prudence lowered her eyes. How fine he was, how honorable! Did she truly expect to resist him? She made a motion towards the piano.

"Before I left, Charlie came home. Irene had to dress, but asked why we didn't sit there, the two of us, under the machineels with the soot floating down. Maybe she was being funny. She said we ought to wait for the Green Flash, when the sun goes down. It's famous. You can only see it in the Caribbean, she said."

"Also in the Indian Ocean," Prudence added.

"Oh, you've heard about it? Well, I didn't know what she was trying to say. It made me mad. I was absolutely sure Charlie Cheek didn't know the first God-damn thing about those letters. His father and I grew up together, went to Officers' Training School together. And right then Irene made a long face and told him I'd come to ask for the letters back. Her own husband! He gave me the nicest smile you've ever seen, called me Cousin Ben, and said he hoped our 'little misunderstanding' would be settled soon. Can you beat that? A woman with so little pride she could tell her husband a thing like that!" He gazed out the darkening window. "Enid always suspected Irene of mutilating her portrait. By God, I'll just bet she did!"

"Benjamin, dear——"

"What's *in* a woman like that? I wish you'd tell me if you know."

And yet, Prudence marveled, he wanted Irene to keep the trust-fund. How he must have blamed himself for the failure of their friendship!

"Another thing," said Benjamin. "She told me Orson Bishop had advised her to sell her shares of Bishop Petroleum. Now, I *know* that's a damn lie. His own company! Furthermore, I gave her those securities. You'd expect her to have asked my advice, wouldn't you? I don't know what that kind of behavior means. It's like cutting off your nose to spite your face."

Prudence, eyes downcast, frowned at his idiom. The moment, surely, had passed in which to look for returns from his philanthropy. While if what couldn't be understood about Irene was no more than her giving up of a useful connection——! But an odd noise came from Benjamin. She looked up to see him stare about once, blankly. As if those last words had touched a spring, his puffed face appeared somehow to deflate. He brushed the drooping flower from his buttonhole. "It's no good," she thought she heard him mumble. Was he crying? Rather than have her watching, he made an effort and stood up.

She rose herself, divining that he had put himself in mind of Francis. Francis! "Oh, Benjamin," she said.

Why hadn't she seen? If he blamed himself for *that*, how she knew now what was in his heart!—and how blameless he was!

Prudence drew herself erect. *Her* guilt was a different story. One day, a letter had been made public; the next day, Ned . . . Incapable of seriously viewing these two events as cause and effect—for Ned had known what Benjamin meant to her—Prudence all the same censured the friends who took the liberty of viewing them otherwise.

To be at fault sustained her. She became an expert on innuendo. Xenia's letter, though touching, carried impertinent overtones. The way Ned was spoken of, the hope expressed that the New Year would bring "all the happiness she deserved," convicted Xenia of recommending the easy way out. Prudence had shrugged. It amounted, basically, to a defect of sensibility. She had seen it before among continental women— continental but themselves incontinent. Nevertheless, she slept badly.

Waking one night, she had found her bedroom ablaze with—was it moonlight? No; the sugar cane was burning in a neighborhood field that had once belonged to the house. They hadn't been offered a fair price, and so had ordered the crop destroyed. For a while at her window she had watched little figures, black against the conflagration, run back and forth, shouting, controlling it. When she turned it was to see her own room in a light so strange, so devastating, that everything, a mosquito asleep on a black dangling cord, chintz coming untacked from the wobbly vanity, the iron bedsteads painted pale blue, came at her as never before, neither beautiful nor ugly, common nor rare, but *there*. Fantastically, the whole room quivered under the nearby glare.

Now, seeing her life, the way she spent these empty days, in the light of Benjamin's unhappiness, she was left with an uneasy feeling. There were so many lights in which to look at things, sunlight, moonlight, Francis, Ned, Irene, tolerance, fear. . . . It was unthinkable that they should all flatter. Even more, that they should all condemn.

"Oh, Benjamin!" she said again. He turned obediently.

Grief was one thing, guilt another. She set out to prove to him that he wasn't to blame for what Francis had done. How little it helped, at first! How little it helped *her*, in the weeks that followed, to practice what she'd made up her mind to preach! For a while it seemed to mean the death of her moral self; Prudence wasn't ready for the lesson of her own innocence. But for Benjamin's sake a beginning had to be made.

She didn't accept him the next time he proposed marriage. The time after that, however, in April, she did.

19.
On the first day of spring many thermometers approached zero. Though Jane had walked only from the corner she felt chilled to the bone. A buzzer let her in; she hurried for the door she supposed was his, but voices from behind it made her hesitate. It opened, however, without her knocking. "Come in, come in, how are you?" said Francis, kissing her numb cheek. "What's this, ball gown and toothbrush? Put it down anywhere. Take off your coat. Well then," he resumed in a bored voice, "I'll expect a call from you before six-fifteen. *Va bene?*"

"Are you talking to *me?*" squeaked Jane, whose eyes were still streaming from the cold outside. A watery cluster of crystal baubles lit the dim entrance. Presently she made out a fine old mirror doubling a profusion of magnolia leaves. She reached to stroke one; it grated dryly against her hand. Francis hadn't perhaps caught her question. Where was he? His voice reached her:

"Then it's settled. You have your ticket. We'll meet in the box. I particularly hope you won't be late. And if by any chance you should get away in time to join us for dinner, don't hesitate to call. Why not say you'll call in any case? Hmm?"

Someone replied with a brief murmur.

"Oh, wait!" cried Francis, reappearing. "You said you had no black tie. Take one of mine!" He paused long enough to wink at Jane and gesture for her to have patience. "Marcello, come meet Jane!" he called over his shoulder as he vanished down a corridor she hadn't noticed before. Turning, she saw in the mirror the reflection of a slender, lowering young man who an instant later rounded a corner to stand before her.

"Hello, I'm Jane Massey." She put out a hand. To her surprise he expertly kissed it, whispering a surname of which she could identify only the melody. *"Ma Lei è italiano!"* she concluded brightly.

"I speak, however, English by preference." His accent was good, but he'd looked taller in the mirror.

"Have you been in America long?"

"A few months only. I'm staying with friends uptown. I'm due there now," and Marcello consulted a gold wristwatch, frowning to show it had been recently acquired. His pale gray suit, also, was not cut in the Italian style. "You seem cold," he went on, intercepting Jane's glance, his voice now tinged with irony. "You must let Francis brew you a cup of hot tea. His tea is extraordinary. It is bought in one special shop. How is your tea-shop called, Francis?" But Francis, who had joined them, was unsmiling.

"Keep this." He handed his friend a black bow-tie. "I have two others."

"Thank you, I shall be able to afford one of my own," replied Marcello. "I borrow yours only because the day is too cold for shopping."

Francis winked at Jane a second time. "He's trying to make an impression on you, my sweet. Ah well," he sighed, his hand on the doorknob. "And you'll phone about dinner?"

Marcello kept silent.

"The opera starts at eight-thirty, sharp. We'll see you there in any event."

Jane, looking anywhere but at them, caught in the mirror a gleam from the Italian. Intended for her? He bowed to Francis, *"Senz' altro, mio signore*,"—mimicking the servile phrase and intonation of a headwaiter. Until he'd left she didn't trust herself to turn.

"Marcello's from Parma," Francis said. He ushered her around the corner and up two steps. "Come into my parlor, do you like it? Downstairs," he indicated a spiral stair across the wide room, "is the library—where you'll be sleeping—also the kitchen, the dining-room, and a minute garden in ruins. If you ever run across an old weatherbeaten sphinx, wire me, won't you? Like those in the Villa Sciarra. Well," he said in the tone of one reverting to his main topic, "it appears *the* thing nowadays, to have an Italian friend. I said to myself, 'Who are you not to follow suit?' Let's hope the others are less difficult than Marcello. Oh but Jane, something so unbelievable has come from this! Don't let me tell you now, don't let me spill it out. We'll sit you down, we'll give you a cup of very good China tea. The kettle's singing already, with its breast against a thorn. *Then*, once you're fortified, I'll tell you all!" As he started down the stair Francis followed her gaze to a low lacquer table. "That's a clue to the mystery," he called, vanishing—"ever tried it?"

What Jane saw wasn't, as she might have supposed from his words, a rack of opium pipes, but a smooth wooden board on which had been printed the alphabet, the Arabic numerals, and the words YES and NO. At the top was the likeness of a female face, Oriental in spirit, lit from beneath: she peered down into a crystal ball wherein misty letters had materialized. They spelled OUIJA. So that was the secret, Jane smiled, put in mind of a widowed aunt who'd lifted tables, consulted mediums, and the like. Jane had never before seen a Ouija board.

Scattered about, on the table, on the floor, as well as on the *retour d'Égypte* couch where Francis had motioned her to sit, lay pages of foolscap covered with childish characters. Of two chairs drawn up one was occupied by a mirror in the shape of a lyre. It sat, much like a person, erect and gleaming, surveying the high dim room.

The room!—how on earth to take it in? Looking aloft for guidance, Jane saw a great brass chandelier, eighteen-branched, whose candles had burned to their last inch; a bit later, stroking the satin bolster, her hand encountered a congealed dribble of wax. Behind her, on the wall, hung a Flemish tapestry, all but the crimsons and greens faded to a dusty buff. It depicted one of those big senseless scenes, the Marriage of Fame and Chastity, or whatever—since *her* marriage Jane had grown awfully vague about allegory. A harpsichord stood below, across whose painted case, cutting in half a settecento landscape, a length of peacock-blue brocade had been thrown. Upon this lay a tattered roll of music, an ivory flute, and some five or six lemons whose fragrance Jane captured by thinking hard about it. Many white petals, edged with brown, had drifted among these objects. The bare rose stalk leaned from a goblet; discolorations within the glass showed how full of water it once had been. The room astonished her—it aimed so high and had lapsed into such a negligence. She didn't mean the witty disorder copied from Dutch painting; she meant the stains, the squashed, dusty cushions, the hearth strewn with cigarette butts and fragments of glass and china. Austrian blinds hanging the length of the tall windows let in a weak light, a . . . *sorrowful* light—Jane smiled to think how the word would sound in her next letter to Roger, and felt grateful all at once that he wasn't there. She could hear him now, remarking on things, beginning to laugh as he felt more at ease. Worse, he would have started *her* laughing, when to Jane's mind the room evoked feelings almost inexpressible. But Roger had no taste for the ambiguous.

"As you see, it's been days since the woman came to clean. I'd phone her if I knew her name," said Francis, returning from below with the tea tray. A soiled white cat followed him. "My, what a treat to have you here! I hope you don't take cream. So tell me, tell me," he genially added as he handed her a blue-and-gold cup marked with a crown surmounting the letter M.

"Would that be for Massey?" asked Jane, admiring it.

"No, who—ah, tell me about Roger. He's a soldier? An officer?"

She hesitated. She knew her letter hadn't gone astray, for he had telephoned at once, as though reminded of her for the first time in years. "You're really alone in that wicked town? Look, you must come down here Saturday without fail, there's to be a gala at the opera." Then, when she objected that she couldn't afford it: "Nonsense, I've plenty of room for you!" and the next day Jane received a check for her train fare. It brought back with a sweet pang their Italian travels. She stopped minding having had only a card or two from him since the dreadful night in August. He was her dear unpredictable Francis and she wanted to see him. Now, face to face with him, she tried to rephrase her letter, making it sound spontaneous and offhand. No, Roger's training had barely begun. Friends had been pulling strings in hopes of getting him deferred, but had wangled no more than a few months' delay. No one could say why he'd been called up now, married, his thesis near completion—it was the Army's way. At present he would probably be up to his waist in mud, somewhere in Louisiana.

"Are you planning to join him?" asked Francis absently.

"In the mud?" Jane giggled. No, not till he had some permanent assignment. Who knew, with his languages he might be sent to Europe? In the meantime she was making all the money she could. She'd even begun taking in typing, to fill up her evenings.

"But then you're very lonely!" he exclaimed in surprise.

How strange he was! "Of course I'm lonely!"

"Apart from that, though," said Francis, "all's well with you?"

"Apart from that," Jane permitted herself a note of sarcasm, "I couldn't be happier." She wrinkled her nose over the teacup.

Francis didn't notice. One reason their talk hadn't brought them closer was the fleeting look of disinterest, of having been interrupted, that kept crossing his face. As she watched he leaned forward, lifted a sheet of paper from the floor and held it loosely upside down, not to appear to be reading it. He was, however; Jane could see his eyes move under almost closed lids. He felt her glance, looked up. "Oh Jane, forgive me," he said in real dismay. "But what's happened has changed my whole life, and now——" Francis broke off, shaking his head and smiling in a new odd way that affected only half of his face. The cat, who had also been watching him closely, leaped into his lap. He drained his cup and began to tell her about it.

"You understand," he said, "I've never had the slightest interest in any of this rot. Whether the word comes from a medium or from the Mormon Temple or from the Pope himself, I've never in my life supposed that death brings anything but total annihilation. It's always made me the least bit nervous to hear people talk about the 'other world' or the 'life of the soul'——as if such phrases really had meaning. Once or twice before, I'd amused myself with this," he nodded at the Ouija board, "but nothing came of it. It depends so much, you know, on who your partner is. Oh, I did once speak to a young German engineer, drowned in the Indian Ocean sixty years ago; and once, briefly, to someone who *said* he was Beau Brummell, but wouldn't answer a single question. 'Tut, tut, young man!' was the most I could get from him. That class of spirit is so petulant, full of warnings and obscure directives, or given to repeating childish syllables until you want to throw the tea-cup across the room. In the light of what Meno has told me, those are the voices that merely echo one's own subconscious preoccupations." At the sound of a faint ringing Francis stiffened. "It's nothing," he said presently, "just the phone in the next apartment."

Jane was beginning to feel gooseflesh. "Go on," she whispered. "Who is Meno?"

"Our familiar——the spirit who first communicated with us, oh, some three weeks ago. We'd sat down casually one evening and were being bored to tears by a cretin named Patrick, a G.I. who'd recently burned to a crisp in a warehouse, when all at once the cup began to move so firmly, so swiftly——"

"Without your touching it?"

"No, no, of course one has to touch it. . . ." He floundered for an instant, having lost contact with his own excitement. "And out came these messages. We could hardly get them on paper——long, splendidly formed sentences. Well, judge for yourself!" Francis reached past Jane to draw from under the papers that littered the couch a notebook bound in limp red leather. "I've transcribed it all here, along with our questions," he said, flipping through what she estimated to be some fifty pages of fine script. How much time it must have taken him! "Here, for instance, Meno sketches in his family background: *My father,*" Francis read aloud, "*was a highly educated slave from Rhodes, whom Tiberius took to Judea, there accidentally exposing him to the teachings of a 12-year-old child.* Who was that? we asked. *Christ. But for him I should have had a brother. He drove my father from my mother's bed.* Christ did? *Yes.* How old were you then? *An infant.* When did you die? *In 38 according to your calendar. I was put to death by Caligula for having loved his sister Drusilla.* Did she love you? *O yes. We were secretly married. We met often in an underwater cave, luminous and blue.* You mean the Blue Grotto? *Of course.* It wasn't till then," said Francis, looking up, "that I remembered Tiberius kept his court on Capri. Then Meno asked: *That island we were prisoners on, is it still beautiful?* We told him it was, mentioned the scenery, the tourists. He kept saying *Ah!* as if terribly pleased. Well, I shan't read the whole record, but he goes on and on. Oh, it's very charming right here," Francis said, stopping at a later page, "about Drusilla: *I was given her as a slave. We swam together in that blue water. I showed her shells and she looked at them. This was the first lesson in love.* Her first lesson? *Hers and mine.* Was she younger? *5 years. Poor sweet ruined Drusilla.* Why ruined? *Caligula made love to her. It was not his fault. His mother had done the same to him, giving him Spanish powder before her ladies. She said, 'What the Emperor enjoys, so shall I.'* Meaning Tiberius? *Of course. Some say this caused Caligula's epilepsy.*"

"Mercy!" breathed Jane, thinking what Council Bluffs would say to such a story. On sitting down with Francis she had been startled by certain changes in his appearance—his heaviness, the faint weblike lines at the corners of his eyes. These now seemed trifling next to the changes implied by his new preoccupation. Did he mean her to *believe* all that?

"And, my dear, the orgies that went on—six or seven people of any age or sex in a bath of warm perfumed oil, followed by one of cold white wine! Marcello couldn't hear enough about *those*."

"Marcello does this with you?"

"Yes, of course." Francis stared at her as though it were something she ought to have understood from the beginning.

"Well," Jane asked after a moment, "have you checked what he tells you? Is it historically true?"

"I haven't checked, no. I'd say offhand, if there *were* any discrepancy, it would be on the part of history."

Jane gulped. Was he serious?

"Meno has hinted that history's very shaky. What's more," Francis lowered his voice confidentially, "he gets a little put out if we try to test him. Once I asked, was there any way of seeing him? The answer came in one word: *Die*. But then he said if each of us would sit back to back holding mirrors he'd be able to see *us*. So there we were, Marcello with the big hall mirror in his lap, I with this one." Francis smiled into the lyre-shaped mirror across from them. "At first we were laughing like idiots, then something went wrong. I felt seasick from so many reflections rocking back and forth. Marcello thought he saw a third figure in the room. Later Meno told us he'd seen *himself* for the first time in nearly two centuries. *Then* it had been in the mirrors at Versailles. He was the rage there for several seasons. What do you look like?" read Francis, finding the place. "*As I did at 22. A beautiful youth.* What color are your eyes? *Gold brown. A poem to me began*—no, you have no Latin. I will supply a French translation:

> 'Chat d'or,
> Tigre que j'adore,
> Imprisonné au cœur impérial . . .'

The rest is really too risqué. Still, we draw up a mirror for Meno whenever we can. He loves that. He saw me drinking milk once, and called me a peasant. But *cálmati*," he said, for Jane had glanced apprehensively towards the mirror, "it's only when *both* Marcello and I are in view that he's able to watch. Heavens, what time is it?"

"Not quite five."

"Does this interest you?"

By then Jane wasn't sure, and said so. "I don't see," she tried to explain, "how it helps those of us who're still living."

"My God!" cried Francis. "It does everything! Listen: there is another world. Each of us here on earth is looked after, cared for by an individual spirit, a patron as Meno calls it. Think how much this changes! Our lives are not ends but means! The soul begins as an insect, an animal, pig, dog, cat. The cat sees in the dark, sits on the wall, waiting to become human. The soul does become human at last, is helped through one incarnation after another until found worthy of the first of the other world's nine stages. Once that happens, the patron moves to a higher stage, and *you* become a patron!" He was standing up now, the cat displaced, clasping and unclasping his hands. "Far below on earth a tiny savage soul is born, in Naples or the Brazilian jungle. It is yours to care for and lead towards wisdom. Meno has told me all this. He's told me about everybody, who their patrons are, how many lives they've had. Your patron, for instance, is Pilar Mendoza, dead in Granada in 1706. You were first born, I seem to recall, in 1838, and have had some forty incarnations since then—usually dying in infancy because, your patrons tells Meno, you do not take to life. But there's hope. One or two more lives may release you from earth. My father has many lives ahead of him. Vinnie's patron complains that she has stubbornly refused to advance herself for the last three hundred years. Xenia, on the other hand—"

"What about you?" interposed Jane. "Is Meno your patron?"

"Not at all. Meno is Patrick's patron," he said with decision.

"Patrick?"

"Don't you remember? The boy we first talked to, who was burned to death?" Francis reached for his notebook and read: "*He is of a weak if not animal mentality which will not soon be allowed release.* Did you know, by the way," Francis broke off, "that Xenia's having a baby?"

"Why no!" cried Jane, flabbergasted.

"Well, she is, sometime in June." But he didn't enlarge upon the topic, reverting instead to her earlier question. "My patron is a Hindu mystic with an unpronounceable name. My present incarnation is my twelfth and last." With these words an involuntary half-smile flickered across Francis's face. It occurred to her that the spirits had made a snob of him.

"Your last?" she echoed.

"Yes. I shall be going to Stage One." He walked away.

"And you believe that?"

Francis struck a note on the harpsichord. A tone, dry and vital, sang through the air, surprising Jane, who hadn't supposed so elegant an instrument to be in working order. When he turned back, the smile embraced many things. "I believe all of it," he replied. "I've even given up my analyst. I tell you, this other world is *real!*"

She couldn't doubt it; his face shone, his voice rang clear and full of life. Gone were its mute stranglings and cold monotone whereby, in proportion to the seriousness of his talk, Francis had often struck Jane as disclaiming responsibility for anything he might happen to say. Now, clearly, he had dumped the whole burden in Meno's lap. It left him free to snap his fingers blithely at history, at human reason. "Things that once upset me dreadfully," he was telling her, "simply don't concern me any more. Furniture, for instance. Look at this room. I've spent *thousands* of dollars. There was to have been something magical in fine old things, that would have helped me *be*. Now, I could give them all away, and probably shall. You never had a wedding present from me, did you? Pick out whatever you like—I mean it." He took her hand. "I feel warmly towards people for the first time in my life. I need no defenses. I'm like a philosopher in his bath; all the hatred, all the fear has been let out of me, as by an opened vein, painlessly. Sometimes," Francis laughed, letting go her hand, "I don't even know what I'm saying, I who used to weigh every word! Remember our talk? It's happened, Jane, I'm afloat! I can't imagine fearing death. I can't imagine wanting anything—what I've been given's enough. Listen!"

The telephone was ringing; he rushed into the hall. "Oh, Xenia—" Jane heard him say, his voice suddenly listless.

She set about powdering her nose, using her own small mirror in preference to the one in front of her. It embarrassed her not to be sharing his excitement. What had he meant by their talk in Cambridge? Who had been afloat—himself? herself?—and what did being afloat mean? She felt dull, confused, open to the perils of talking or thinking metaphorically. For relief she got to her feet, wandered out of the mirror's range, his voice only a murmur from the hall. At the window Jane held aside the blind and gazed down into his garden: dead ivy and dirty snow the unseasonable cold wouldn't let melt. Francis, Francis, she sighed. She *had* loved him, loved him still, but hadn't foreseen his garden bringing tears to her eyes. Tears? Not quite; a sting, a tiny smart. That would have to do for the present. Already, from the hall, Jane could hear Francis shift into the mode of farewells. He would come back in; there would be more talk, drinks, changing of clothes, dinner, a taxi. . . . If honest-to-goodness-weeping lay in store for her, and Jane couldn't at all be certain that it did, the long evening had first to be lived through. Poor me, she thought, marveling at a world—had it once been her own?—where the heart had time for its troubles and joys, where importunate feelings were cradled to sleep like children; you could look down on them sweetly breathing, with tears or smiles upon their faces.

Francis returned depressed, the cat in his arms.

"That was Xenia. I'd called her earlier, you see, when there was still a question—" Breaking off enigmatically, he suggested they have drinks. When he had brought them he started in on Meno again, but in a tired, matter-of-fact voice. "You see, he told us last night that Patrick is ready to be reborn. What happens at that point is that Meno, as patron, looks about for a mother five to seven months along. To his ears she makes the sound of a cow mooing, then he knows she's ripe. He slips the little soul into her womb, and *ecco!* there's your reincarnation. Well, it was late, we were worn out. I didn't think of Xenia till this afternoon. It seemed so right! Not that, at her age, she mightn't be a vile mother, but I mean, *I'd* always be around to keep an eye on the child. Now doesn't that sound logical to you?"

Jane widened her eyes and wrinkled her brow. Was she being dense? Ought she to know who had fathered the child? Not, surely, Mr. Tanning! But the old man on the subject of Xenia spoke in her memory— "like eating goose or venison," had been his phrase. This interesting suspicion kept Jane from making more of her curiosity.

"Well, whether it does or not," said Francis, pouting, "it did to me. But Marcello was furious. I had to beg him particularly to come. He'd planned something else after lunch. You see how it is. He's been in New York long enough to pick and choose. All of a sudden he has scores of 'charming friends.' Don't ask me where he meets them. I could count on one hand the number of charming people *I* know. And I'm yet to meet any of his—but enough of that!" Francis began to laugh, "I daresay he's ashamed of them, they're probably not charming in the least! How would he know?" Francis shook with the amusement of it—how like his father he *was*—then, controlling himself: "Marcello adores Xenia, that's the point. He says I'm arranging for her to bear a weak-minded child—when it's obvious, if once Patrick's born into a decent environment, he won't *be* weak-minded. But Marcello says it's all a stupid joke and he's sick of it. What can I do? Being Italian and Catholic, he doesn't *think*. You saw the face he was making. I'd been reasoning with him for an hour."

Jane cast about for something soothing. "Perhaps he'll come round," she said.

"Perhaps. But it struck me just now—what if he *doesn't* come round, what if I'm never able to get through to Meno again?"

Twilight had fallen. The cat stirred in his lap. "Darling Pussy," he said, staring intently into its face, "soon you're going to turn into a person. You're going to bear the burden of abstract thought!" The cat looked away in alarm, squirmed, escaped his grasp and scuttled into the hall. Francis lit a few candles, his eyes glittering.

"What if Xenia's child already has a soul?" said Jane.

Well then, of course, he replied tonelessly, it wouldn't matter. They sipped their drinks in silence. Somewhere a clock coughed and struck six. "Jane," he said, "we'll dress in a minute, and I promise not to say another word on the subject. But would you try it with me? For a little while only? Perhaps it would work between us, so that it wouldn't have to be always with Marcello. I need to find that out, so if . . ." His voice trailed off. He was looking at her so shyly, as if honestly expecting her to refuse. Why, he was a *child!*

They composed themselves now in an ambiguous light, partly that of the candles, partly the last cold glow of the March afternoon. Francis with a napkin wiped Jane's teacup dry and placed it upside down on the board. "These are my last two cups," he told her without regret. "Meno has broken the others." Jane recognized their fragments on the hearth; it seemed that nothing was too good for Meno. Following Francis's instructions, she rested three fingers gingerly on the bottom of the cup. She watched him send one slow look into the mirror, as though gazing once about a room before switching off the light; he then closed his eyes.

"First I call his number," Francis whispered. "Eight-five-seven, eight-five-seven . . . Meno, are you there? We want to speak to you, Jane and I . . . are you there?" The cup quivered once. "Yes, yes!" he exclaimed. "Go on! Meno, was that you?" Jane feared, but didn't say so, that she alone had made the cup move. Already the unfamiliar position of her arm, balanced limply forward, the wrist lax, in the manner (she supposed) of some great keyboard artist, had started a dull ache in her shoulder. She wanted to change hands, but shrank from asking Francis if she might, he'd grown so eloquent. "Meno, Meno," he was begging, "we are here, we are waiting, come to us! . . . Can you see us? can you hear us? . . . It is of the greatest importance that you give some sign. We may otherwise never again communicate! . . . Meno, there's so much you haven't told me, so many ways you can help me. . . . Come, speak! if not for my sake, for Patrick's . . . Can you hear? Listen, I can help you, I've thought of a mother for Patrick! . . ." In this way Francis talked on, a suppliant. He gave Xenia's name, he even apologized for her age. He promised extravagantly to look after the child. The cup remained motionless. "It's no good," he finally shrugged, letting his hand fall into his lap. "There's nobody there."

Jane massaged her shoulder. She felt a kind of choking sadness, as though her whole neighborhood had migrated to Mars, leaving her behind to prowl the empty streets and abandoned rooms. Love, faith, truth—the words hung in curling tatters like so much wallpaper, wherever life had been lived. She looked wistfully at Francis, his face flushed but remote, a planet swimming through veils of haze; she was hard put to imagine the life that would go on there.

"Let's try one last time," he said calmly enough, "and then we'll dress. If Meno cannot reach us, another spirit possibly can, who would convey my message to him." Each placed a hand on the cup. "Is anybody there?" asked Francis. "We want so much to make contact with anybody. . . . Please! . . . Is anybody there?"

Presently, to Jane's amazement, the cup began a tentative circling of the board. Could Francis be moving it? For a split second she let her fingers slip off the cool china; it stopped dead. He looked up, startled. Then, her touch restored, the cup started to move as before. "Who is there?" whispered Francis. His pencil hovered above a blank sheet of paper.

The cup wavered towards the letter A.

"A," he nodded encouragingly, jotting it down. "Go on, A, what else? Tell us your name. . . ."

An abrupt swerve left the cup-handle pointing to M.

"A, M, very good . . . That spells *am* . . . Who *am* you?" he joked gaily with an upward roll of his eyes. "Amos? Amazon? American?" He had come alive, like a coal breathed upon. How easily the spirits might have taken pity on him!

Instead, the cup returned to A, then to M, initiating a languorous motion back and forth between the two letters. *Amamamamamama*, the unknown visitor mused, leaving some doubt, in Jane's mind at least, as to whether it was asserting its identity or crying for its mother. Francis stood up in disgust.

"This happens now and then," he said. "You get a meaningless syllable repeated over and over, you can only suppose by an infant or an idiot. There's no point in going on. We seem unable to set the right waves in motion." As he blew out the candles gouts of wax spattered onto the board, the papers, the lacquer table; Jane thought of scalding tears. In the gloom he asked if it was after six. It was? "Come then, I'll lead you downstairs. Do you feel like another drink to help you change?"

"No, I don't, somehow, thank you."

"Nor do I, if one's to hear the music. Wait!" Francis switched on a light, smiled guiltily and darted into the hall. She heard him dial a number. When after a minute's silence he returned, his face was without expression. Jane couldn't look at it. He was carrying her suitcase. She followed him down the winding iron stair.

20.

They dined within walking distance of the opera, in a miserable Italian restaurant, all sawdust and photographs. With the result that, having eaten little and talked less, they were among the first arrivals to pause, shivering, under the brilliant marquee. *Première*, the signs announced in red letters, and: ORPHEUS, *a new opera by Thomas*

Utter. "Do you know him?" asked Jane when her teeth stopped chattering. Francis sniffed by way of reply, his glance moving about the lobby. They mounted the red stair in silence, to where a gray-haired maid unlocked the door of their box. Francis bowed for Jane to go in first. She thought she had never felt such cold, such desolation. The door behind them swung gently shut.

Taking a front chair, she pretended that he hadn't entered with her, that she had been left alone while Francis hurried off into the recesses of his life. Would it now begin, as in the past, the spell of strangeness initiated by his vanishings?—while she just sat and watched, from a café in the Piazza del Popolo, from a sheeted window in Cambridge, at noon or at midnight; the place and time never mattered. His footsteps would ring loud on stone. She would be shivering, she would want to cry. As for the shock with which the strangeness came to an end, if indeed it ever did, it wouldn't be for Jane to question it: the shock not so much of Roger at the pier as of her own tear-filled eyes, her willingness to marry him then and there, the shock of a positive indifference to Francis; the shock, as well, of the doctor's voice, that later day, over the office phone, "Mrs. Massey ... a very tragic thing ... if you could shed light ..." until of course, under her questioning, out came the whole story of what Francis had done. She had kept cool. Walking home beneath the fiery green leaves of Cambridge, she had held her head high, meeting the eye of bird and squirrel and passer-by with gentle wonder. "Something had died inside of me," she kept saying to soothe herself. In an hour beyond her control she even said it to Roger. He had taken her in his arms then, murmuring, "Are you sure? Mightn't something have come to life, instead?" She remembered the smile on his face—that of his own relaxed possessiveness, a reflex of ease now that he had no rival. How primitive he was! she had thought with an interest that shocked and angered her. She had known Roger so many years, she hated to admit his power to mystify her.

Slowly the house filled with people. Back from Mars. It warmed Jane, the sight and sound of them. She undid her black coat, let it slip from her shoulders, forgetting how sallow she'd grown during a sunless winter, forgetting also the wrinkles in the dress she had stupidly not hung up at Francis's. It was a strange yellow dress from a thrift shop, made over, with shoes covered in what had been its train. To get away with it called for more animation than Jane had felt up to now. But the dry stale air was working on her like smelling-salts. From the pit a clarinet let out a wonderful high laugh. Soon the orchestra rocked with scales and trumpet-calls. She let her hand rest on the worn plush, her eyes glazing over. In her imagination she turned gradually beautiful. She looked around to see what Francis would say.

He was not in the box.

Well then, she was thinking, let it begin, the strangeness—when the door opened. He was back, his coat over one arm. "I'm going downstairs to wait. I must speak to Marcello as soon as he arrives." He looked away. "Jane, I—" She instantly put out a hand. "Lest you suppose me utterly out of my mind," continued Francis, grasping it, "I must tell you that I am the father of Xenia's child. Does that explain a few of my concerns? She'll join you here—Xenia—after the curtain goes up. Tell her you know. It's been kept secret, by and large, for reasons she'll make clear enough. Bear with me, my dear, and forgive me." He left the box, not before placing in Jane's hair a kiss, upon which lights throughout the theater dwindled to amber simmerings. The gold curtain swelled, the conductor acknowledged some sparse applause.

The opera began.

From the first, suffering was taken for granted. A suave overture brought to mind less the enormity of Orpheus's loss than the miracle of his charm by which all things—even, it would shortly appear, the impassive dead—were drawn to him. Whatever his mourning for Eurydice, by the time the curtain swung apart, it had given way to the lively prospect of his search for her. The tenor sat at his desk in dungarees and shirt-sleeves, first alone for a brief aria, then with the angel, a buxom aviatrix, peering over her shoulder. She (Mme Stempel-Ross) unrolled maps, consulted weather bulletins, and made of her findings a florid, Handelian report. From this she went on, above the burden of his gratitude, to equip him for his travels. She summoned dancing sprites out of the wings; they bore snowshoes, a pith helmet, a life preserver, a coil of rope. Finally, offering him a small package, she explained that here were extra strings for his instrument:

> *For who can tell*
> *Whether your lyre*
> *Withstands the fire*
> *Of Hell?*

She sang the melody five times, but it had been so skillfully varied for each gift that the effect was enchanting, her voice no less so. Her song at an end, the applause doubled as Mme Stempel-Ross approached the footlights and, with a movement too gauche not to have been rehearsed, curtsied in her jodhpurs.

Jane was finding it all pointless. In ten minutes, she promised herself, she would have a glass of cognac in the café.

But ten minutes later, on the point of rising to go, she admitted to being curiously touched, if not by the performance, then by the vast theater itself, whose dark, not quite scented, audible air she breathed. Far off, the stage might have been seen at the end of a tunnel or from deep within a skull. It placed no claim on her. It left her glance free to wander down the rows of pallid faces turned like heliotrope upon the ringing spectacle, from box to box at this early hour occupied, if at all, by old people whispering or one ecstatic child, her hair in a black velvet ribbon; from these to the dingy gilt of the proscenium, its cherubs and nymphs, despite their loftiness, scarred with white where they lacked noses or fingers—Jane looked everywhere, in short, except at the stage. When at last she did turn to watch the opera, which all the while had been glowing softly along the cheek, she found what she saw meaningful.

Against a moving panorama of trees and flowers Orpheus walked, singing his insipid, irresistible song. Animals drew near with gifts of leaves and fruit, adding to his human voice the deprived idiom of growls, hisses, and twitterings. He stroked them all, let them fawn at his feet, peck from his hand, dance after him as he walked singing. The changing backdrop of orchard, stream, and rock rippled and swayed. No matter what creature approached, lion, rabbit, tortoise, finch, the trivial tune had its way with each, and who was Jane not to nod, tap her finger upon the red plush railing, while the song penetrated her?—until with a shattering effort she stilled her finger and the tiny movement of her head. Her face showed nothing, but the trap had shut.

Hitherto, even before what happened in Boston, she hadn't really believed Francis capable of love for a woman. With her new knowledge came another. She wanted it to have been not Xenia but herself through whom he had tasted this love.

From then on Jane gave little or not thought to Francis. She was remembering, instead, Bruno, a medical student in Rome, small, courteous, threadbare. She had known him the summer before she met Francis. One night, walking her to her door, "You know," he told her, "we are alike, you and I. We fall in love with those who will never love us in return." Jane blushed to remember it. How could he have said that, knowing how she needed him? Other specters rose up, whose names in some cases she'd actually forgotten, faces she had loved, innocently or ignorantly, and thought to put from mind. But she hadn't forgotten them; worse yet, she hadn't forgiven them. A cold began to churn inside her, that of a winter pond with many frozen lives. How crazy to care so violently for what might never be revived! At such a moment only an exercise of will could hold the mind together. Not only the mind—her whole body stiffened as if in order not to come apart, the limbs separating like petals of a shaken stem—white petals, she had seen them somewhere. Help me, let me go! she cried out to Bruno and the others. I don't hate you, I just want to give you up! But how to give up what has never been had? As at the sound of a sane voice, Jane cocked her head. She understood what for some reason nobody had ever told her—the cause of Eurydice's death.

Now the tenor paused in front of a smoking aperture. Jane rose; she had had enough. But the door behind her opened. Without turning she readmitted Francis to her mind, coldly, a simple phenomenon like anything else.

It was not he. "Jane, how are you? Hush!" And with a commanding smile Xenia sent her back onto her chair.

During the song of Cerberus, a lugubrious trio, she grew calmer. For the first time in eight months her eyes met Xenia's. Wrapped though she was in a flame-colored sari shot with gold—a gift from Francis, she hissed in reply to Jane's few mild admiring gestures—the older woman looked both fat and shrunken. The child, evidently. At Xenia's age it was a risky business to create life, rather than the images of life. At any age, Jane supposed.

"What's to be done with Francis?" his mistress went on. "He won't leave the bar. Perhaps you can get him to come in for Act Two. Otherwise Tommy will be really hurt, that I know."

Jane murmured she would try; she saw no reason for Xenia to be specially concerned over Tommy's feelings, whoever Tommy was. "Has Marcello come?" she asked a moment later.

Xenia, a finger to her lips, imposed silence. The flute was reiterating some minor complaint in which strings gradually joined. "Genius!" she breathed. "Now the song of the honeycakes. No," she said as soon as it had begun, "why should he dance attendance? He's not the *best* sort of Italian, but a sweet honest boy. Why should he put up with Francis's behavior? Though if you've met Marcello, you've seen what a flirt he is!" Xenia lapsed into laughter, recollecting escapades, but noiselessly, like an old woman. "Between ourselves, he couldn't be more my type."

"According to Francis, he likes you too," Jane remarked.

"*Voilà!*" Xenia threw up her hands. "I can't abide by these restrictions! I haven't the temperament of a *fiancée!*"

Such real irritation flickered up through Xenia's words, it seemed safer to let them pass. Indeed, the act ended before their sense registered upon Jane. Much later, looking back on that quarter hour, she was to wonder at her own inaccessibility to experience; it might have been a strong drink of which abruptly she had had her fill, leaving her a bit stupid and sick. Things were neither reasonable nor startling. That Xenia was pregnant in no way explained her intention to marry, any more than it provided the name of her future husband. That Xenia looked old—well, people *grew* old; that couldn't be helped. Jane saw now, in the stronger light, how little it could be helped. Throughout the theater people were rising, calling to each other, wanting to smoke and stare. But the two women in the box sat on, in their almost drunken calm. Xenia had thrown back her head to counterbalance the live weight of her body. Expressionism, was all Jane could think.

"As you see," Xenia finally said, "I'm worn out. These months have been in-cred-i-ble. I'm not myself. My feet have given out, I can't work. I spend my days telephoning, from my couch, for Tommy. Without me there'd have been no performance, he would have had to give back the money. I've kept behind him every minute, pushing."

Jane decided it was safe to assume that "Tommy" and the composer were one person. "Why isn't he here?" she ventured.

"He's backstage going insane. I say to him, 'Listen,'" continued Xenia, "'I've got one child here,'" patting her belly, "'which is all I can handle for the present. If you can't manage your own affairs, how are you going to support Junior here—tell me that!'" She leaned forward now with tragic, painted eyes. "I've all but decided not to marry him. I'll keep my freedom and I'll love him more than ever, you'll see! I've purposely not talked about it to him, because of the pressures of these months, but now—!" She chuckled as though her minute of reflection had settled the matter for good. "That's just what I'll do. I'll persuade him to use the money for the honeymoon, to go into analysis. Ouf! what a relief!" Xenia fanned herself vigorously with her program.

A quiet tremor went up and down Jane's back, a sign that something temporarily out of order was now working—enough at least to let her perceive that Xenia's was a painful and complicated state of mind. Even so, she paused in rich uncertainty before reminding Xenia that her predicament had its brighter side. "About supporting the child," she brought out, "won't Francis help with that?"

"Why should he?" inquired Xenia defensively.

Jane blushed. She had never before discussed what Council Bluffs would have called a "needless offense to right-thinking people" with the offender in question. At a loss, she studied Xenia's face and so bore witness to an almost comic sequence of expressions. It was clear that some mistake had been made, some miscalculation. Xenia opened and shut her mouth, then her eyes. "Francis said to you . . . ?" she began, stopping to shake her head very rapidly while pinching the bridge of her nose with thumb and forefinger. "You understood from him . . . ?" she hazarded next. Jane just blinked. Mercifully the door of the box swung open.

It was Marcello, still in his pale gray suit. "I see I am very late," he began in a hard, guilty voice. He looked prepared for some disagreeable reception. Finding only the ladies, his defiance crumbled. By the time he had fully explained his delay, the dozen civilities preventing his earlier withdrawal from—he faltered slightly—the home of an uncle's business associate, his mouth had turned full and childish, his lashes were fluttering; Jane wanted to ask his age. "You see," he cried, thinking to prove his good faith, "I did not take time to change into evening clothes! I hurried here, in a taxi—though now I see that I ought to have changed. You are both so elegant, I feel out of place." However, an easy movement of his eyes back and forth among the neighboring boxes showed whom he considered the fairest occupant of their own. They didn't detain him. Jane even caught an urgency in the directions Xenia gave him for finding Francis. Oh, she laughed and glittered, *her* lashes fluttered—there was your Europe for you, Jane told herself—but when he had left Xenia turned back at once. She actually pinched the bridge of her nose again, unnecessarily, for her question now came without hesitation:

"Francis told you the child was his, didn't he, Jane?"

She nodded.

"Well, it's not true. The child is Tommy's, of course."

"I see." Jane stupidly smiled, as if a trivial typing error had been rectified. "I haven't met Tommy."

"Let me assure you, I've done a very peculiar thing," Xenia went on with growing animation. "In the bar Francis said he'd told you 'everything,' but notice what I did!" She held up one finger. "Instead of stopping to remember what *he* thinks the truth is, I've been taking for granted, talking to you, that he knew the *real* truth! It's many a year since I caught myself in such a classic mental block. The subconscious never fails, though, does it?" She was all hearty laughter, as over the latest prank of an incorrigible child.

Other details followed, to do with the various anguishes—emotional, economic, biological—that had kept Xenia from sitting down with Francis and making a clean breast of it. The deception had begun so innocently! "Believe me, it was what he needed to hear at the time. He wasn't himself. He put the words in my mouth, I couldn't tell him no. He'd been through some illness, some breakdown—you perhaps know more about it than I; he never speaks of it to me. What am I to do, Jane? Can I let one white lie, told months ago out of pure kindness, poison my life? If Tommy were to find out! I'd be on the streets! Shall I tell you what it means, my interesting slip of a moment ago? It's a voice from inside," Xenia pointed to her heart, "telling me that Francis must face the truth. I'll speak to him tonight, at the party—no, better tomorrow, next week at the latest. . . ." Xenia had more to say but Jane couldn't hear it.

She had begun to feel again. The sweet relief of it helped her judge what violence she had done herself. All at once she relaxed, slumping a little, lips parting, fist unclenching like an opened flower. Now that it was over, what? Jane looked around as country people did, emerging from cellars after cyclones. Things cautiously reassumed their meanings. Wherever her mind's eye rested she saw damage, but she felt warmth.

"Must you?" she said quietly, the next time Xenia paused. "If there's any way of not telling him, couldn't you—"

"What!" cried Xenia, staring.

"—let him think the child is his? It helps him, he needs to believe it. Don't tell him."

Objections rose easily to Xenia's lips. If Tommy found out? If Francis made claims? What to tell the child itself? Had Jane been skilled in argument she might have hit upon answers to these questions. But to give reasons paralyzed her; she momentarily forgot what the reasons *were*. "Don't tell him," was the best she could do, "let him believe what he likes." Until Xenia, who often argued merely for the intellectual fun and fierceness of it, finding so little, let herself be swayed.

"This may not be the right moment," she agreed, casting an ironic eye at two bald heads in the next box. She continued as if to herself: "Who knows what the stars hold? *Zut!* I'm not ready to marry. For one thing, Tommy doesn't satisfy me physically. On the other hand, I'm no spring chicken. Suppose I drop dead in a restaurant? Then who takes care of the child?"

"But you don't understand!" Jane leaned forward, thinking herself inspired. "Francis would take care of the child! He wants to! And all you have to do," she sounded her refrain one last time, "is never tell him!"

Xenia appeared to shake herself awake. "Ah, but that's utterly out of the question, utterly!" she explained, finality in her voice. "Let's not talk about it any more"—leaving Jane to contemplate her own tactlessness in a silence which much peculiarly good-natured chatter from Xenia did nothing to dispel. "There's Max! He's waving to us! Come here, come here!" she mouthed without uttering a sound. "He's a dear, you'll adore him." Or: "See that distinguished man in the third box down, with the mustache? He's flirting with me. Now *that* is my type!"

Years passed before Jane ever suspected Xenia of asking, that whole evening, nothing better than that her secret be kept forever from their friend. What she gave, during the interval before the others joined them, was hard to recognize as satisfaction, it had been so frosted over by sacrifice. "It would be for his good, you really think so? In that case, there's nothing I wouldn't do for Francis, within reason . . . ah Max, *te voilà! et toi, ma belle!*"—this last to the old man, his face an embroidery of wrinkles and capillaries, and the red-haired woman, very powdered, whose name Jane was never to hear. They had just encountered Tommy in the vestibule; he was heading for the box, but in a black mood—let Xenia beware! "All day, every day," the latter groaned. "I shall go mad, wait and see." She addressed Max's companion: "If ever you want to go back to the *status quo* you've only to say the word." This sent the couple into shrieks of laughter, the old man showing a smattering of discolored teeth set here and there with gold, like primitive jewelry.

When Tommy joined them he tumbled noisily onto the floor, there being no vacant chair. Francis, in his wake, paused before stepping over him to waver in their cramped midst.

"Here you are, aren't you ashamed?" said Xenia to one or both of them.

Francis had taken hold of the powdered woman's hand. He pressed it, played with it, let that take the place of speech while gazing from one to the other pleasantly. Even when he bent to whisper in Jane's ear he kept his hold upon that white hand, less now to be cordial than to be upheld. Beyond him, framed by the entrance to the box, Marcello stood, their coats over his arm.

"Listen," began Francis; his breath was strong and damp against Jane's cheek. "I'm going now, going home. I feel awful. You understand, I have to go. Here are extra keys." He dropped them in her lap. "Big one's to outside door, brass one opens apartment. I'll see you in the morning, all right? You don't need money? You're sure?" He fished for a bill, dangled it before her; Jane had to thrust his hand away. Francis straightened up. "Xenia," he said, "you'll take Jane to the party afterwards, won't you? Mamoushka, won't you?"

Marcello was watching Jane. Once their eyes had met she couldn't think how or where to look, except into that familiar gaze—familiar to whoever knew Italy—of sexual provocation. "Command me," his eyes said as clearly as any recitative, "command me, O fair one!" His lips parted, he began to smile—horribly. Jane's fist tightened upon the keys. How did he dare, when it was Francis who suffered, who needed him?

"You're not leaving!" cried Xenia, piecing it together at last. "When the best part's coming!"

"Let him go, Pussy," a voice from the floor said. "I'd just as soon go myself. It stinks."

"What stinks? We've sat here enraptured, Jane and I!"

"Yes," Jane managed to say, "we have."

The young man lifted his head. "Are you Jane?"

"Forgive me," said Xenia. "I've forgotten your married name."

"What *is* it?" mused Francis. "I had it on the tip of my tongue."

Jane could give them no help in the matter.

"Well, you're very pretty," Tommy said. "Are you leaving, too? Let me flirt with you and see how jealous my Pussy gets."

"Max," put in the red-haired woman quietly.

Looking away, Jane once more met Marcello's eyes. The lights had begun to dim. At least she was living up to the yellow dress. Was this what other women called "success with men"?

"Now, *you* can't leave us!" Xenia called, only then noticing Marcello.

"But, my dear," the old man, Max, sought to reason with her, "we have seats downstairs. If we don't leave now we shall be late."

Tommy scrambled to his feet. "That's true," he said gaily. "Everybody's leaving. I'm leaving, too." He turned to Jane. "Want to come?" Xenia seized his wrist.

"I cannot *bear* this," she announced in a savage whisper. "There are people tonight you must meet. They are watching you. Look!" Indeed, many glances had converged upon their box, piercing the gloom. A few people even hissed for silence. Xenia rose. "Francis, you reason with him! Oh you *children! Tant pis!* We'll go outside!"

They left the box, all six of them. Jane could hear their voices in the vestibule. In no time Xenia was back.

"You have control over Francis," she begged. "Why is he in this state? He could help. Tommy really values his taste. Go out, please, talk to him, Jane. See what you can do!"

"I can't!"

"You can't!" scoffed Xenia. "Why can't you?"

"That boy, Marcello," Jane brought out nervously, "I don't like him, I don't want to be near him."

"But that's nonsense, that's childish—" Xenia broke off and shot the girl a look of triumphant perspicacity. "You're still in love with Francis, then!"

No, thought Jane. The remark needed only to be made for her to see its irrelevance. Oh, she could shrug and look down in a hurt helpless way that soon got Xenia out of the box, satisfied; but when Jane looked up she was smiling. What she now felt for Francis was something ineffably sweet and sad; remote, too, as if his life had become the closing chapter of a novel in which the characters keep on talking and behaving, quite unaware of a reader already planning what to do, once finished with their fictive lives. What had Jane to do—go to a party? write Roger? Not that she felt, yet, any great resurgence of interest in *him*. He was, however, part of a world she recognized. Naïvely, she wondered if she would ever see Francis again.

Another person entered the box. It was Marcello.

"They're quarreling outside," he said. "May I sit here, if I'm not in the way? Oh, *scusi!*" For he had let his knuckle graze her bare arm.

She stared outraged into his eyes, into Xenia's eyes, into the eyes of all who took for granted that love—*their* kind of love—mattered more than anything else. Then Francis's voice sounded from the door: "Marcello, I'm going now."

"I'm not ready to go, Francis," he said, not looking round.

"Oh I see," said Francis sarcastically. "Excuse me!"

Jane took a deep breath. "Go!" she told them in hushed fury. "Go this minute, I command you!"

The word "command" undid all three. Francis gave a little helpless croak. Even Marcello backed away. The door shut behind them. Jane smiled wildly into the dark. How Roger would have laughed, had he been there! A hush overcame the audience.

It ended almost at once, as if something unforeseen had interrupted the performance. Vague voices filled the theater, laughs and coughs. The two bald old men in the next box glared about, failing to realize, like many others, that with these rude noises the second act had begun. As the curtain parted a slow warm gasp of amusement greeted the scene. The old men, bent over their programs, whispered and winked. So this was Hell!

Before them, beyond the glowing apron of the stage, could be distinguished the lights and boxes of a theater so like their own that a vast mirror might have been set up inside the proscenium. The view being from the vantage of the stage itself, hence unfamiliar to most, heightened the illusion. Gilt and puce, cherub and luster, all had been copied. Somewhere infernal musicians tuned their instruments. The ranks of the damned chattered, called to one another, ruffled their libretti or wielded great plumed fans, wiped steam from monocles—there was a sense of extreme heat—until at a nod from a horned demon in white tie, a bit elevated above the unseen players, the music began.

First came an overture solemn but shallow in the early-nineteenth-century style. A French horn disgraced itself before seeking shelter in a thumping *tutti*. Everything had to be heard twice. At last, after prolonged chords, Orpheus stepped into a pool of light directly facing the prompter's box.

This was the treat they'd been waiting for. While Orpheus bowed, smirking in scuffed black tights and gold-laced doublet, a ridiculous hat under one arm, the damned souls hailed him with such fervor as a living audience would have reserved for the latest Italian tenor, possessed of a continental or cinematic reputation, to appear before them in the mustiest Italian opera, the oldest chestnut of all. Then, silence; upon every ear fell the famous *pianissimo* that opened his lament, the gem each would have sat till dawn to hear. He unwound it like a spool of gold. Tears from his throat, that sobbing petition in six-eight time (save for those highest, softest notes—how did he sustain them?) rang beyond the comprehension of the decorous awe-struck orchestra. Eurydice, Eurydice had been taken from him, was lost forever—*ristorate il mio amore,* and not just the melody but the language of romantic loss was his, *viver' non voglio più,* in all its rich incoherence. His notes began to flutter now within a net of runs and turns. *Non dirmi che sia perduta, sento gelar il cuore!* When he had done, the damned souls (in certain of whom there had been leisure to discover, by reference to the location of their boxes or the eccentricity of their dress, suspicious likenesses to their worldly counterparts, those jeweled and decrepit patrons known to all) rose from their seats, weeping. Flower and glove rained down upon the singer. Fans, themselves enthralled, trembled ignored on the rims of boxes. *Encore! Bis!* the listeners cried. *Bravo! Bis!* And he began again.

But Eurydice, where was she? In rapture they heard his plea, her cruel chaperons, yet not one stirred to summon her. Orpheus himself could be seen to scan the boxes, alive with singers who in soft harmony began now to remark upon the bliss they suffered. Could it be that she alone hadn't come to hear him? He sang more fervently, one hand to his heart, the other high in the air for guidance, begging again and again, *dunque, bell' alma, vieni!*—nor was it possible to tell at which point in his song a high unearthly voice mingled with his own.

It seemed to have come from nowhere, clear and cold as a stream, reaching at once an indifference of volume and passion from which it was not to depart. As instructed by the angel, Orpheus turned his back on the theater of Hell and on its central box which, hitherto in darkness, was now suffused with a weak violet light. One could just make out, against cloths and shadows, the sparkle of a diamond, a white hand limp on the plush rim and, within, the aigrette rising like an idea from the seated woman's brow. The voice, frigid and clear as ever, belonged to her.

Little remained but for Orpheus to hear the song that, with his own and the chorus that reconciled them, wove so mysterious a braid; to hear in her music how she was perpetually unmoved, how alone (or was there a figure behind her, tall, shadowy?) in her box, narrower it seemed than the others, she sat beyond the reach of his wooing. At last he would know that he had placed her there himself, for at her death he had enshrined in his song not Eurydice but her loss, her absence that, growing bearable through his art, had as well grown irrevocable. With sickening force his knowledge was to break upon him by the end of the ensemble. Then, as foretold, he would turn incredulously to read it in her eyes—only to see her fade, a second and last time, past his reaching voice. His song at an end, again the damned souls would weep, applaud, hurl flowers, cry for encores. There would be no denying them.

PART THREE

21.
The Buchanans learned of Mr. Tanning's impending marriage on their fourth day in Rome.

They stood together outside the Hotel Eden. The cable still fluttered in Larry's good hand. A doorman splendidly outfitted—all he lacked was a flaming sword—signaled for a taxi.

"It could have been much worse," said Larry. "You know who it could have been. *La trampessa.*"

"We must be on the lookout for a nice present," said Enid.

Lily asked, "Would you call Lady Good attractive?"

"Oh, definitely!"

"We like her very much, Lily," her father said.

"It's intelligent of Prudence," added her mother, "to have the wedding in New York."

"Will we go to it?"

"If we're invited, sweetie."

"Another thing," said Larry. "I won't have you killing yourself to get the Cottage ready by," he glanced at the cable, "May fifteenth."

"I was thinking," Enid mused, "she may not *want* red in the ocean room."

The doorman asked where they were going.

Enid had started for the taxi, but stepped back. Where *were* they going?

"Mummy," Lily whispered in her ear, "can we go do what you said?"

"What did I say, my pearl?"

"That if I wanted you'd ask Daddy if I could sell it."

"Now what's the trouble?" he demanded.

Enid was flustered. The ring, the gold ring Francis gave Lily for Christmas. She had thought of taking it to a shop and asking—

"I'm sick and tired of shops," said Larry. "We've done nothing but spend money for four days. Why don't we try to see something?"

"Villa-Borghese-Vatican-Museum-San-Pietro-Foro-Romano-Roman-Forum," recited the doorman encouragingly.

The taxi-driver shot for the moon. "Tivoli! Villa d'Este! Villa of Hadrian!" he wheedled. "*Molto bella giornata, Signori. Spendere poco!*"

No. Tivoli was too far. Besides, half the fun of Tivoli was a soufflé, and that evening they'd be going back to Alfredo's for rum omelets. It didn't do to overdo. As for the Vatican, they would see it tomorrow. A business connection had arranged a Special Audience with the Pope, not the easiest feat during Easter Week. Lily and her mother had already bought black gauze veils, lace-trimmed, and rehearsed obeisances in their suite at the Eden. "What would Alice say!" Lily kept exclaiming. As yet, neither Enid nor Larry guessed the extent of Alice's influence.

Wasn't there, Enid was asking, something of Michelangelo's they could go see? "You're interested in sculpture, sweetie," she reminded Lily. The famous Moses—where was that?

"San Pietro in Vincoli!" cried doorman and driver in unison. Soon the Buchanans were rattling over cobblestones towards it.

Larry did his best. "Isn't this great?" he said, rubbing his hands. "Look at those palm trees. You'd never think we were on the same latitude as Trenton, New Jersey." But a vein ticked angrily at his temple. "What about Francis and some ring?" he growled.

"It's the little antique gold ring Francis gave Lily for Christmas," said Enid cheerfully.

"This one." Lily spoke as if she had numberless rings. She removed her new white glove and showed it.

"That was a damn nice present," Larry declared, "say what you like about Francis."

Enid agreed. "It was. Lily just thinks she's a little grown-up for it now. I can understand that, Larry, can't you? After all, a ring with an *owl*, like her baby plate and mug . . ." Her mother's reasonable voice made light of Lily's real feelings about the ring, its dangerous fragility. The gold was too soft, she could bend it without thinking. Once it snapped, she would have damaged a precious thing, impossible to repair. Also, the owl's eyes unnerved her, round and knowing, like Francis's own. If ever she left the ring on her dresser, it gazed after her so reproachfully! ". . . I told her she might sell it to buy something she really wants," Enid wound up.

"Such as what, Lily? What do you want?"

She looked away. Did she have to want something? "I don't know yet," she said.

"I'm not butting in." Larry wiped his brow. "The ring belongs to you. But why don't you think it over?"

"She has, Larry."

"I have, Daddy."

"*Eccovi, Signori!*" said the driver, stopping the taxi. "Lovely day. Good luck."

"They won't let you practice your Italian," Enid pouted.

"We'll talk about the ring later," said Larry firmly.

Inside, they made for the monument. It was barely visible behind a breathing shroud of tourists, passengers of four CIT buses the Buchanans had remarked, pretending bravely not to, in the piazza.

"God damn it!" Larry hissed. "Don't tell *me* these baboons know what they're seeing!"

Lily hoped he would be forgiven. Her new straw hat sat squarely on her head. Alice had described to her the torments in store for bare-headed women.

When the crowd pivoted and marched away, the Buchanans moved forward to where a gray-haired couple remained in conversation with the English-speaking guide. From behind bars Moses stared furiously over their heads. The marble had an oily unwashed look. Horns grew from his brow. One huge hand clutched not only the tablets of the Law but a few thick coils of his unnaturally long beard.

"Moses was very wise," said Enid. "That's why his beard's so long."

Oddly enough, Moses' beard was the subject of the tourists' debate.

"I do *not* see it," said the woman. "I'm not sure I *want* to see it."

"There, below his lip, and a little to the left." Her husband pointed. "That's her head. About six inches on down, the waist begins, then the curve of the buttock. Right?" he appealed to the guide.

"Do I understand?" asked the latter, a civil young man. "You have seen a nude figure in the beard of Moses?"

"There's her breast. There's her knee. See her now? She's partly wrapped up in the beard."

"Don't listen to him, he's crazy," the woman told the guide, who forthwith, as if at last perceiving how to deal with this type of crank, broke into a smile of illumination.

"Ah!" he exclaimed. "Quite so. There in the beard."

"See?" said the man.

"No, I do not see," said his wife, putting on one-way-mirror dark glasses.

"Thank you, Sir," continued the guide. "Wisdom and woman. I shall mention it next time. It is very interesting."

When they left, Enid giggled: "Grandpa would have been amused by that, don't you think?" Larry glowered. This oblique remark was one of the few Lily heard either make, throughout their stay in Rome, that could be taken to bear on her grandfather's marriage. The omission didn't bother her. Stranger things had been occupying her thoughts, much of that winter.

It had begun with Xenia's telling Lily that her mother had been raised in the Roman Church. Since then, the child had developed a curious susceptibility to incense, to droned Latin and red flickerings. Alice furthermore—it was Alice who now and then exposed her to these novelties—had flatly stated that nobody was ever converted *from* the Church. An amazing suspicion then dawned on Lily; her mother *hadn't* left the Church, but chose, for reasons of her own, to either neglect or dissemble her faith. At once the little girl felt engaged in some dark communion with her mother, too strange and sweet ever to be hinted at. Strolling down a side aisle, Lily would be overcome by a guilty warmth, a dizziness nearly. The give-and-take shocked her most. The fonts of holy water, the poor boxes, old women in black waiting to be paid for the candle you lit, above all the confessionals—to what did they add up, if not the weird notion of bringing out into the open what you felt; the notion, weirder yet, of confessing to *any*one what you had done? That should be between you and God. But Alice disagreed and more than once, after vanishing into the carved recess with its whispering and perhaps the fold of a black skirt visible, had emerged smiling, rosary in hand. It had worked.

It worked in Rome on a scale for which even Alice couldn't have prepared her. Lent had turned the city into a vast humming clay-colored baroque greenhouse for the conscience. In every church a pleasurable moaning from behind the little grilles told of sins sprouting like bulbs, soon to grow tall and fragrant for the Mother whose image, sometimes lofty and unapproachable, sometimes sadly smiling with hands outstretched, met Lily on all sides. She made now for a freestanding statue.

Maria! Santa Vergine! sighed the women pressing forward, black shawls slipping off their heads, to fondle her garment, kiss her hand. A sudden gap in the worshippers made Lily gasp. She had never seen *that* before. The Virgin wore a cluster of knives at her breast, but casually, like a big brooch. Her hand, moreover, had been entirely worn away by love. These glimpses both excited and alarmed Lily. She wanted to know whether the women were to be punished for what they'd done.

Her alarm extended, as she toured the church, to include a number of paintings, large and small, draped with black veils. She didn't care to think what had happened to them. Still, before she could check herself Lily had pictured a tiny monkey of an Italian child leaping up in a passion to plunge a knife into the canvas. Shrouded like corpses—or as she and her mother would be, tomorrow at the Pope's—she counted a dozen such in this church alone. No wonder the confessionals were full.

To tell a *priest* what you had done was easy. To tell your own mother—! Sick at heart, Lily swore, not for the first time, that she would do this before Easter.

Or if not—for she'd put off her confession so often as to have grown a bit cynical about it—if not, she would know what to buy with the money from the ring. A lovely present. A present to show her mother how she felt.

Lily had had, the past two days—they spent the first day being measured for suits and dresses; the second day, Sunday, shops were closed—her first concentrated vision of *how much* money could buy. Shopping in the States was a tame ritual, involving perhaps two shops in an afternoon; each purchase would be charged and sent. But in Rome Enid's great bulb-shaped leather bag kept opening. The beautiful money, pink, gold, green, blue, unfolded like blossoms, to be spent like perfume in one shop after another. All but the biggest items were carried off in triumph. People turned on the street to point out the rich Americans. Back at the hotel you could hardly sit down. Packages open or sealed contained: baby clothes for little Tanning, wardrobes for the twins; luncheon sets, dinner sets, breakfast-tray sets; leather boxes, pocketbooks, wallets;

Roman scarves; eighty meters of red damask for the ocean room; ceramic roosters; two pairs of Venetian glass candlesticks in the shape of blackamoors, tubular, flecked with gold; ties and gloves and pullovers; compacts, two of silver, three of amber; a pile of fruit in bisque; dolls dressed as little Dutch girls, as Spanish dancers, as peasants from Sicily—where Michele, the Buchanans' gardener, had been born; dolls with carrots or peapods for heads; a grasshopper of colored felt, an octopus of the same; a guaranteed Canaletto, on approval for a week; a pair of electrified baroque cupids; and six alabaster dishes, rims marked by alternating indentations for cigarettes and white doves bending, no doubt, to sip the ashes. Bulkier purchases—antique chests, chandeliers, a carpet, etc.—were being shipped home.

The end of a day's shopping left Lily feverish, ecstatic. That first dinner at Alfredo's had seemed a foretaste of Paradise. With lights switched off and special music playing, the mustachio'd old proprietor waltzed towards them, an omelet flaming blue in one hand, a solid-gold fork and spoon in the other. The surrounding diners, saintlike, their chins resting on white napkins, craned and cheered.

The second dinner, that night, ended in disappointment. "Why, all the people here are Americans!" complained Lily, late in the meal.

"I know, sweetie," said her mother.

"But you made us promise to bring you back here, Lily," her father reminded her. "Which we're very happy to do. Your mother and I, by ourselves, prefer a more authentic atmosphere—you know, candlelight and perhaps just one singer strolling from table to table with a guitar, instead of these fancy bands." He sipped his wine. The musicians, not hearing him, began to play. "But it's a pleasant occasion all the same, and if it helps teach our little girl the difference between average and top-notch, it won't be wasted."

"The food's still delicious," said Enid, because Lily often needed to have what her father said interpreted. "We just think the restaurant has grown the least bit commercial over the years."

"That ring of Lily's, for instance," he went on, "may not have cost a thousand dollars (though Francis could damn well have afforded it if it had). It may not even have cost ten dollars. The point is, it's old and interesting and probably the only one of its kind in the whole world. Some things can't be measured by everyday standards."

"We mustn't always think of the price," put in Enid.

"Hear what your mother says? Now, if you've made up your mind to sell the ring, we won't stop you. Bear in mind, though, once it's gone you'll never be able to replace it." He paused significantly, as if talking about something quite different, a carefree childhood or a first love. "All *we* ask, your mother and I, is that you spend the money intelligently. It's never too early to develop taste. Learn the value of things. You might consider buying a few shares of a good, inexpensive stock. The money that gets thrown away in this family makes me see red."

Lily didn't need her mother to interpret that remark. The day Xenia delivered her head, bronze set on a base of black marble, their murmurs of delight and wonder hadn't outlasted the closing of elevator doors upon the sculptress. Then, silence in the living room, already dense with objects. "I don't like it," her father said, "not one bit, do you, Enid?" "It's *starker* than I expected. . . ." "It's the face of a sly scheming child, not Lily at all. Look, you can't even see where her hair begins. I wouldn't put it past that woman to have done this on purpose, to get back at us." "Get back at us for what, Larry?" "For not being taken in by her continental charm. For not paying her in advance for the head of your father that Francis commissioned. Never deal with artists, Lily. They're all spongers and ne'er-do-wells." He paused, remembering, "But you *saw* the finished head!" "We did, didn't we, sweetie? But it had been cast, and the light was bad. Besides, I told you, Francis was there. I don't think we'd have noticed anything. Did you, my pearl?" "No," said Lily. At such times, the way they kept appealing to her, Lily would feel like a hollow tree, one in which messages were left. "Well," her father summed it up, "that's another five thousand dollars down the drain. It makes me good and mad, doesn't it you? What'll we say to your father? By God, he ought to be told when he's been taken for a sucker!" "He hasn't been, Larry. Some people think very highly of Xenia's work." "Your mother's always so sweet and open-minded, isn't she, Lily? Next to her, I'm the bull in the china shop." "Goodness me!" They decided to write Grandpa that his gift went so well in their apartment, they wanted to keep it there rather than in the country. This wasn't entirely a lie. The head "went" into the hall closet. Lily would unwrap it now and then to see whether she was growing to resemble it. That, Xenia once told her, was what great art made you do.

Ice tinkled in Enid's glass. "Francis may see Lily without the ring," she said.

"I could tell him I lost it," suggested Lily.

"Tell him the truth," said her father. "Francis doesn't spare *our* feelings."

"All the more reason to spare his." Lily and her mother exchanged smiles. Poor Uncle Francis had to be protected.

"*Cameriere!*" Larry snapped his fingers. "*Aspettiamo dieci minuti per le nostre* rum omelets."

"Here they come, Sir!" cried the waiter, and the lights went out and the music played. Gasps of wonder rose from the diners. "We should have ordered that," somebody said enviously in the dark.

Lily felt duty-bound to clean her plate. She didn't see the omelet again till nearly midnight, when Enid had her stick a toothbrush down her throat.

The next morning they went to the Vatican.

Soberly attired, gloved and veiled, they presented their invitation to one stately functionary after another. Each waved them—down a corridor, up a stair, through a packed antechamber—a degree nearer to His Holiness. The Pope was very nice, Enid had been saying in the taxi, to want to give them a Special Audience. "Oh well," Larry had replied, "where would the Catholic Church be in Italy without American dollars to fight Communism?" Lily understood her mother's gentle smile. They had speculated next upon the length of the interview, whether they wouldn't be received in the Pope's *den,* over a glass of unsanctified wine. Their high spirits, as the Buchanans left the taxi, made even the Swiss Guard smile.

They had reached the end of their quest. "You will please wait in this room," said a handsome, grizzled man in morning clothes.

"I'm so thrilled I can't stand it!" whispered Enid. "And to think we don't even believe it!"

Again, Lily knew better.

Larry looked about. "Does everyone in here get the Special Audience?" he asked a passing official.

"That is correct."

"Then what's an ordinary audience?"

"In the first room you entered," the man explained, "five hundred people are waiting for a regular audience."

"Oh I see," said Larry in a voice his father-in-law often used.

The Buchanans spent a half-hour studying the room—whose walls, Lily observed, were only painted to look like marble—and a group that might have illustrated one of her United Nations storybooks: little children, hand in hand, Swedish, Chinese, Liberian, every color and creed. They lined the room, sixty all told, no longer children, to be sure, nor—except for one sari and three tailored suits of tweed, worn with low heels—in native costume. The range of feature and complexion made up for this. There were a Siamese nun and a Samoan priest, the latter weighted down with medals and rosaries. "Why is that?" Lily inquired.

Enid didn't know. "Why does that little priest have all those rosaries?" she asked her neighbor.

"Why, to be blessed!" said the woman, Irish like Alice. "Everything you're wearing or carrying gets blessed by the Holy Father."

"Oh my goodness!" breathed Enid involuntarily.

At that moment the Pope made his entrance. The crowd knelt, then at a signal rose.

Among the first in line, the Buchanans could scarcely get to their feet before having to kneel again, as instructed, and kiss the Pope's huge ring. Lily watched her father do this, half-expecting *his* conversion then and there. When her own turn came she grasped the Pope's fingers, squeezed her eyes tight shut, and aimed for the ring with her lips. Unaccountably, she missed. She felt it graze her chin—too late! Her pursed mouth had already made contact with the Pope's dry cool flesh. Mortified, she stood up and faced him, a white old man with glasses.

He spoke. "A lit-tle girl going to school?"

Lily just stared.

The Pope repeated his question in a mild automatic voice.

"Oh," she finally answered, "to school? Yes." She could see that he knew everything about her. He knew about the ring, *her* ring, burning beneath her glove. Dared she sell it after his blessing? He raised two fingers. Lily steeled herself.

"A special blessing on you and all your dear ones," the Pope murmured with a look of complicity. The child's jaw dropped. He hadn't mentioned what she was *wearing!* Then he moved on to Enid.

A major-domo lost no time in ushering out those whose audiences were over. Below in the Piazza, Enid complained that she hadn't had a good look at the Pope. "Boopsie Gresham met him," she recalled, "when he was still a Cardinal. He used to go to East Hampton for weekends. People said he was terribly attractive."

"Well, we've done it and I'm glad," Larry said, first clearing his throat. "The times we've been in Rome and never seen the Pope. You'll remember today all your life, Lily."

"I know." Lily had been feeling the papal blessing at work, much like her mother's wonder drugs, upon all her sins. Deceits and disobediences, soon she'd be cured of them, incapable of them!

By that afternoon, in fact, her motives had grown so pure that Lily went ahead and sold the ring.

Enid took her first to a fancy jeweler. Lily gaped at diamonds and emeralds, coveting them not for herself—the Pope had stopped all that—but for her loveliest of mothers. Meanwhile, a polite clerk was expressing regret; they did not buy old gold. A second shop directed them to a dealer in antiquities, right in the Piazza di Spagna.

Inside, a fat old man wheezed. It wasn't a shop in which you'd have thought to buy anything. It seemed to specialize in the old, the dusty, the unbeautiful. Lily looked around and saw nothing *whole:* a head of veined marble with a nose missing; a shelf of terra-cotta fragments, here a foot, there a face. The old shopkeeper encouraged his clients with a toothless grin. Their own faces expressed both disgust and assurance. They had come to the right place.

Lily watched her mother produce the ring, watched the dreadful old man's eyebrows go up and down, once only. "*Beh!*" he said finally. "*Facciamo dieci mille lire.*" Enid turned.

"What he'll give us comes to about fifteen dollars, sweetie. I really do think that's too little." She then told the shopkeeper as much, in a language closer to birdsong than to speech. It wasn't her ring, but the ring of the little girl, the *figluola,* the *ragazzina*—who all the while listened spellbound to her mother bartering with the terrible old man.

He threw out his hands. He was poor! There was no market for old jewelry. "*Sono vecchio,*" he croaked, "*vecchio, Signora!*" He would be dead, in his grave, before a customer came along for such a ring.

Enid thanked him, wrapped it in Kleenex, and turned to go. They would find another shop, she said cheerfully, seeing Lily's bewilderment. When the shopkeeper called her back, she winked once slyly, as though she had known he was going to.

Out of pure curiosity—what price did the Signora have in mind?

The Signora pursed her lips. Oh, she hadn't really thought—forty, fifty thousand lire seemed reasonable. Lily had to hide a giggle; she was learning how in Italy you named a price much higher than you expected to get, but the funny part was to see her mother do it as coolly as any native.

It even amused the shopkeeper. He clapped his hands and laughed a fine dry laugh. He made the gesture of wiping his eyes, then begged her pardon. "*Scusi, Signora,*" but he couldn't help it, it was to laugh, that a ring so small should sell itself for a price so big. However—he held up two fingers, like the Pope—seeing that the ring belonged to the Signorina, he would make a special price—fifteen thousand!

"Take it, take it!" Lily wanted to say, chilled by the old man's smile and fear lest the sale never be completed. But Enid had already picked up the ring, pleasantly shaking her head. "Special prices are as bad as Special Audiences," she said out of the corner of her mouth.

What then did the Signora want! Money?—impossible! The shopkeeper's rolling eyes took in silk, fur, fine leather, a ruby-and-pearl brooch. A sweep of his arm showed how poor, by contrast, his own treasures were. On the floor near the counter Lily saw a cardboard box full of fragments, marble, clay, some still caked with dirt, fingers and things broken from old statues. How funny! What would anyone want with them? Then, recalling her father's missing finger, she decently averted her eyes from the box.

"Sweetie, he's offering you twenty thousand. I think that's fair, don't you?" Lily looked up. The old man was holding out two big bills, pink and gold, one clean, the other filthy—standing for that half of the price he would pay only under pressure. The ring had already disappeared.

"*Va bene, Signorina?*"

Lily nodded.

"Take the money, sweetie. What do you say to the nice man?"

"*Grazie . . . ?*"

"*Grazie a Lei, Signorina!*" the shopkeeper returned, wheezing and bowing. They had reached the door when he called them back. "*Un momento!*" He lifted from a cabinet, with reverent flutterings of his hand, an intaglio mounted in pale gold, blood-red as he held it to the light. It showed the profile of a fattish young man. "*Bello, eh?*"

They considered it briefly, out of politeness, then, thanking him once more, left the shop.

"He must have thought we were either blind or cuckoo," said Enid. "I don't call something *bello* when it's cracked clean through. Without that silver band it would have fallen apart!"

Lily led her mother across the Piazza, made her promise to wait at the corner, and started down a street towards a shop she remembered. That morning, waking, it had come to her, what to buy with the money. It was the perfect thing.

It was still the perfect thing twenty minutes later when, back at the Eden, flushed and happy, Lily found a cleared surface on which to set it down. The box was three feet long, and heavy. "I simply cannot bear this excitement!" said Enid, bug-eyed.

"Then open it!" cried Lily.

"Don't you want to wait till Daddy's awake from his siesta?"

"No, it's for you!"

"For me?" Enid had been about to take off her hat, but stopped. "Oh, my goodness!"

"So open it!"

It seemed to Lily that her mother took an exaggerated time to undo the string, the shiny white paper, finally to lift the lid, beginning to coo as she folded aside layer after layer of tissue. At the end, however, she stepped back, as genuinely surprised as Lily could have hoped.

"Why, Lily! Of all the . . . *oh!*"

Not trusting herself to say more, Enid lifted it from the box and stood it upright facing the window. The late sun did wonders for the figure, richened the whites and pinks, the powder blues, woke all kinds of sparklings within the glass jewel of the crown. Though not the largest, it had been to Lily's mind the loveliest Virgin in the shop. She'd chosen it from a rainbow thicket of plaster images. Significantly, no knives protruded from its breast. *All that,* its soft forgiving smile conveyed, was over and done with.

"Mummy, Mummy, didn't you guess? Where will you put it? In your bedroom?"

Enid found her tongue. "I can't decide now, sweetie, I'll have to think. . . ."

Maybe in time they could build a chapel around it!

The little girl easily imagined, in her mother's heart, the sweet relief of having brought to light something that had been overlooked or hidden for so many years. Often all you needed was a *way* of doing this. And she had thought of it, she alone! Also, the Virgin was *whole,* not cracked across or chipped. Lily remembered her father's lecture in the restaurant. I'm developing taste, she thought radiantly, I'm learning the value of things!

Enid meanwhile had removed her hat. "Tell me," she begged, "how you ever dreamed up such an original present."

Original? "But I *know!*" said Lily. "You never told me, but I found out. Couldn't I be a Catholic, too? I already have a little medal at home, that Alice gave me. . . . I wanted to be like you, that's all—it's the truth, Mummy!"

For at the mention of Alice an indecipherable look had crossed her mother's face. Then the explanations began. From that moment on, Lily's happiness in her deed shrank and soured.

The following afternoon, Thursday, when her parents carried the Virgin back to the shop, Lily was blushing for her babyishness. Fortunately they seemed to understand this. At least the matter was never brought up again. When they took her to spend the refunded money, neither her father nor her mother made a single suggestion. All by herself Lily chose what she wanted, a stunning leather purse with a shoulder strap and ornamental brass clasp, a Roman scarf, and the most exquisite doll—a Spanish Señorita wearing a mantilla of real lace. By then, of course, everything had changed. Lily had even begun to rehearse a conversation with Francis, years hence. "Yes, I sold the ring," she would say, crossing her legs in some wonderful way she'd have learned, "I sold the ring, but only after the Pope had blessed it." She practiced the remark aloud, with different inflections, getting it to sound very clever and wise.

The three Buchanans had decided Wednesday before dinner that the Virgin was to be returned—"even if they won't give back the money," said Larry. In the course of a long adult hour—she supposed it was adult because they allowed her a splash of Campari with water and ice—Lily quite forgot why she had picked out the statue, the real reason, not just what she'd told her mother. The room was too thick with other revelations. Listening, awed, to "what we believe," to "what *our* faith says about Mary," and "our Episcopalian attitude towards confession," Lily forgot Alice. She even forgot that she'd heard it all before in Sunday School, till they reminded her. She peered down unsuspected vistas. Her mother had been right to leave the Catholic Church. Confession *was* a private matter. And here were Lily's own parents sharing the secret substance of their lives with her, as if at last finding her worthy.

"We think you're one of the most attractive people we know," said Enid. "We like being with you."

"We have a real companionship, don't we?" Larry cracked his knuckles. "We can talk things over with you—"

"—in a friendly, natural way—"

"Not like most parents. Love's an investment, Lily, which your mother and I feel has been repaid, in your case, a thousand percent."

Lily's head was reeling. The Virgin gazed sweetly from the table, forgiving them all. But Lily found that she cared not very much for Jesus' mother, and immeasurably for her own. Nothing made of plaster was adequate to patch up a real difference between people. The Virgin's blue robe, aglitter with the hilts of no knives, didn't keep Lily from hearing the rip of canvas, her own breathing, her mother's hurt voice afterwards.

She had no choice. It was dreadful, only the exact truth would help.

"Mummy," she said hours later into Enid's ear, when she came to tuck her in, "I was the one who did that to your portrait." There! Lily fell back on her pillow, weak with the effort it had cost her.

She'd had two glasses of white wine at Ranieri's, a place full of atmosphere. She'd kissed her father goodnight, screaming as he pinched a fold of innocent fat through her seersucker pajamas—"Goodnight, my little oyster!"—and giggling at his admonition not to dream of the Pope. Then to bed, waiting, listening, their talk muffled by the thin wall. "Alice . . . church . . . fuss . . ." her mother murmured. "Rot . . . God's name . . . money . . ." he replied. Lily tried to hear more, but the room had begun to hum, to quiver like a compartment in a train hurrying you towards a place you'd never seen. A light widened on the wall, then narrowed and went out with a click. Her mother had entered, closed the door behind her, maybe knowing all along what had to happen.

The words uttered, Lily's responsibility came to an end. She fell back on the pillow. Whatever followed wouldn't be *her* doing. In a dull curiosity she watched Enid sink to her knees beside the bed. "Oh sweetie!" she cried, and made a soft crooning noise, while over the child's skin sleepiness crept, strange, slow, a tide of honey. It turned out that her mother did know, had known from the very day.

"I know, I've known from the day it happened," she breathed, stroking Lily's forehead and cheek. "I found out, I couldn't help it— Michele had seen you leaving the Cottage. . . ."

"Then you lied," murmured Lily wearily, unable to cope with the tenderness in her mother's voice, speaking *her* words of a few hours before. She felt part of herself tremble, break into tears, but the rest of her, from some vast distance, watched, caught in that paralyzing sweetness.

"Yes, I lied. Baby, don't cry! Nobody else knows! Michele didn't suspect—don't! I'm crying too!" she laughed, her voice high and squeaky with love. "Think of your old lady's predicament! *She* didn't want to say anything about it until *you* did!"

Lily's eyes closed. She needed to be told whether it was bliss or pain she felt. What did her mother feel, laughing and crying both at once? Whatever its name, the feeling was strong enough to put you to sleep.

An hour seemed to pass. The high soothing whisper continued:

"You see, my pearl, your Mummy really loves you. She hasn't felt close to you this last year. It's no fun when two little friends can't tell each other their little problems, is it?"

Lily had stopped crying. Her mother's dress, where she had hid her face a while before, was still damp with tears.

"And nobody your Mummy knows is as sweet and attractive as her oldest daughter!"

"Not even Daddy?" asked Lily, opening her eyes.

Enid put a finger to her lips. "I thought this was *our* secret," she said, misunderstanding the question. Later, when Lily lifted a hand out of her trance to smooth back a wisp from her brow, her mother winced.

"What's the matter?"

"Nothing. Well, nothing really . . ." She touched the top of her head experimentally.

Lily yawned in spite of herself. She knew the signs, but she was so tired. "It's the first since the baby came? Will they start again now?"

Enid looked at her fingers, as if expecting to find them smeared with blood. "Yes," she said, her voice gay and young, a giggle almost. "I guess I'll have to have another, won't I? Our little friends seem to be the only cure for the old headaches!"

Lily gave in, let her eyes close again. She couldn't help it, she was exhausted. Once, startled, she felt Enid's kiss, then heard the quiet opening and shutting of the door. The little girl lay for hours, waking, sleeping, the receding din of Rome in her ears. Like the sun and the moon, feelings of love and fear rose shining above her, faded, set, returned. Nothing seemed right or even reasonable. All night Lily had vivid, bewildering dreams. They rose up like flowers out of her closed eyes. For days she hesitated to admit how happy she really was.

22.

And Francis was happy, too. Skidding sharply on a curve, he saw his mother bite her lip, and knew that he had frightened her. It made him want to laugh—*he* was never alarmed by other people's driving, why should she be? As the road straightened, wind buffeted his head from all directions. Trees flew past, not yet burdened by the stifling green of midsummer. His lopsided smile of the past months had mended; even his teeth seemed straighter. He was taking Vinnie to the Cottage.

Earlier that day, over lunch, he had been talking with Matilda Gresham about their *revolts*. It was a stimulating hour. The Stage Door Grill echoed with their mutual admiration. "You've carried it so much further than I," he'd told her. "Why, you go months at a time without even seeing Boopsie."

"Yes," said Matilda, "but that's such a negative way out. I mean, I could never hug the bear the way you do."

Hugging the bear! He felt warmly towards the big clumsy girl in dungarees, who had seen him as a hero. He wanted to have given her more than beer and chow mein on Eighth Street. But she was caught up in a Clyde Fitch festival, her time wasn't her own; things fell apart backstage without Matilda. She expected a week off in August. "I'll go out *there*," she said, crunching Francis's hand. "It'll help if you're still around."

He had formally moved to the Cottage the previous week, for the summer. His old room was filled with roses. On the dresser he arranged photographs of Xenia, of Jane, of his mother. Natalie was already installed at the main house. But something was missing. No sooner was Francis settled than he returned inspired to town, where he kept after Vinnie until she agreed to drive out with him, in his new convertible, for the christening of—well, whatever Enid's child was to her. An ex-step-grandson? The relation, if any, didn't call for Vinnie's presence at the ceremony. She had made this objection, and many another, which Francis met with laughter. "Nonsense!" he urged. "Where's the harm? Prudence loves you, Enid loves you! You needn't meet Harriet and you won't see Fern. You'll stay at the Inn and I'll drive you back Monday. So come along! Be a sport!" Prevailing at last, he had hugged her out of happiness.

Francis had begun to feel a new tentativeness in his mother, a puzzled, passive air, an air, indeed, of asking to be taken advantage of. It only added to his high spirits. She had followed the doorman out to the curb, her face stark, unpainted. One look at the low open car and she covered her hair with a scarf of gray and brown chiffon, tightening it under her chin. Francis kissed her, and away they went. Grime from the river settled upon Vinnie's white face; her hands, however, did not leave her lap. Once or twice, seeing that they were clenched, he smiled to calculate the satisfactions in store for her.

One winter day she had said, "I wait for you to tell me things." So, as they headed over the bridge, he mentioned having seen Matilda.

"Is that Boopsie's child? What's she doing?"

He told her; or rather, invented a Matilda twenty pounds lighter, wearing a fresh denim dress, with clean hair—like one of the daughters of Vinnie's Savannah friends, up North for a "year" in a woman's hotel, an interesting job, the shops and the shows. Francis talked fluently until his mother had relaxed enough to risk a more personal question:

"Will someone be in your apartment this summer?"

"No."

"I just hope you take care of your lovely things."

He reassured her.

"Who's keeping your cat?"

"It died."

She made no comment, having always loathed cats. But he felt her shift somewhat toward him in her seat. Everything would be all right. Even when the car skidded, and she bit her lip, Francis only smiled, hugely relishing his role.

By then they were in full country, under an egg-white sky he remembered from every summer of his growing up. In another hour the first windmills would begin, and the potato fields stretching, so flat as to appear concave, towards the far-off sparkle of pond or ocean. There would be time for a swim that afternoon. Ah, the summer was really under way! People he knew were already in Europe, among them Jane and Roger, who, by a great stroke of luck, had been stationed in Germany; Marcello, also, bound for Greece—or so Francis gathered from certain friends, their own friendship having cooled. His blessing followed each traveler. For himself, he was content to stay behind, hugging the bear.

As for Vinnie's nervousness, he had to smile at it. She might have been a child headed for her first summer at camp, white-faced and tense. "I don't *want* to go out there, Francis," she had insisted. "I have nothing to say to those people. I have no part in that life." Of course she didn't! Why should she, after fourteen years? But let her wait a bit, give the place time to work on her. Meanwhile, Francis trusted his own happiness would put her at ease. Impulsively he squeezed her elbow, but Vinnie withdrew.

"I'd keep both hands on the wheel," she said in a dry whisper.

He felt some fleeting impatience now—as if accidents happened in their world! Then he understood; she saw herself at his mercy. Vinnie would never have feared a stranger at the wheel. But to Francis her imagination had granted the power of destroying her. Slowing down indulgently—he *had* been going over seventy—he smiled at her with tenderness and love. "Has the cat got your tongue?" he said presently, as a joke. The Cottage drew nearer and nearer.

Francis found it empty; at least there were no other cars out front. He had left his mother at the Inn to rest and change, had changed quickly himself, passing through the house on his way to the beach. The murmur of maids reached him from the basement. In the little pantry where Xenia had worked, stacks of china stood in readiness for tomorrow's christening luncheon, which had been planned to precede Lily's birthday party.

"Hello?" he called once, softly. "I'm back!" He expected no answer, but took pleasure in announcing the fact.

Again and again, since returning to the Cottage, Francis had been stirred by a sense of arrival, to which the place itself just wasn't adequate. Even with the ocean room newly covered and curtained in Enid's red damask from Rome (like Christmas at St. Peter's) it couldn't absorb all that he felt for it. This welled up, overflowed, till Francis came to wonder if he hadn't arrived in quite a different place, one that the visible house, with its lacquers and lawns, gave no clue to. What is this place really? he wondered as he ambled, where am I? And he peeked through a door ajar as if to catch himself there beyond it, in his father's study.

To his surprise he saw Lily on the window-seat, gazing out to sea.

Francis hesitated, nearly retreated, expecting to hear Benjamin's voice take up some lecture or reminiscence, so vividly the child's posture brought back the submissiveness with which *he* had listened, at ten. But no voice spoke. Little Lily, he thought with an uprush of tender affection, alone on the eve of her birthday, dreaming about the world and time. In a queer revulsion—for he had caught himself too often of late smiling over inanities, winking back tears like a grandmother—he crossed the threshold.

"Hello, child. Is Grandpa here?"

She started. "Oh! No, Grandpa's over at Fern's."

"Ah, to be sure." Francis grinned. He had been working on Fern all spring, and finally she had asked the Monster over for a drink. He guessed now that she couldn't have done this earlier, in the New York house which was part of her settlement. Another part, the place in Hobe Sound, Fern had decided to sell. It was so out of the way.

"Why do *you* call Grandpa Grandpa?" asked Lily.

"Because that's what he is." Francis perched on the edge of the desk, still grinning. He toyed with a silver paper-knife. His niece looked sad and he thought he knew why. "We grow up too quickly, Lily, don't you agree?"

"No, I don't."

"Well, I did." Francis laughed. "Are you so very happy?"

"No."

"Why not?"

She had to think. "I'm too little to have a permanent. Mummy says wait till I'm twelve."

"Then you'll be happy?"

"Then I'll be very happy. I'm happy enough now."

"So am I," he hastened to agree. "My point was simply that time goes so fast." His eye had fallen upon a photograph of himself holding a blacksnake at a certain distance. Vinnie had snapped it, how many years ago? He retained an impression of the snake's squirming body, its blind blue eyes. "A year ago today," Francis went on, "I was in Rome, not even thinking of coming home." Then, in order not to keep talking about himself: "What were *you* doing a year ago today?"

"I don't remember. Nothing special."

"Oh come!" he coaxed. "The day before your birthday? One always remembers that."

The child gave a little stage yawn. "Well, *I* don't," she said, casting in spite of herself a rapid glance elsewhere, as if for reassurance. So that Francis, instead of shrugging and letting the matter drop, looked up with her to see the portrait of Enid above the mantel. Restored, refinished, beautiful, it showed no trace of the damage done to it. *That* lay in Enid's mind, and in the mind of whoever had struck the blow. His own mind, then, sustained an idea that astonished him. The paper-knife fell from his hands. Words uttered long ago sounded in his ear: "The next day was Lily's birthday. . . ." Also: *'Tis the eye of childhood That fears a painted devil. . . .*

Her face gave it all away.

"No, wait, Lily," began Francis, rising to block her way out. He felt unbearable concern for the little girl caught in the toils of her guilt, to what degree he could well imagine! He saw her paralyzed by her deed, as by a constrictor. Lily, Lily! She was staring at the carpet, a panicked smile on her face as she waited, he knew, for nothing less than the blacking out of consciousness.

What *he* had to do was somehow to set her free—but lightly, deftly, harming not a hair of her head. Francis saw himself uniquely fitted to accomplish this, a Perseus hovering before the maiden.

"Oh Lily, how well I know what's in your heart," he began, "but I also know how much more terrible it seems to *you* than it actually is. People are constantly making that mistake. The truth is, nobody's hurt but oneself. Look! you can see no harm's been done! The picture's back in its place, lovelier than ever. That's one reason we keep pictures, isn't it?"— Francis was quoting his erstwhile analyst—"in order to use up feelings of love or of anger that we'd never dare show to the person's face. Look! see how easy it is!" Inspired, Francis took up the photograph of himself grappling with the snake and, removing it from its frame, tore it lovingly into little pieces. The child's lips parted. "You see?" he finished. "The picture's gone, but I'm still here, *I* haven't been hurt by what I did, and," his mouth had grown very dry, "you mustn't be either, dear Lily. It doesn't *matter*. Please believe me!"

Lily was speechless, but no longer tense. It had worked.

"Now," he assured her, "I'll never speak of this again. To anyone. There's no reason for anyone to know, is there?"

Her eyes met his in innocent perplexity, as if it were now his turn to be left off gently. "That's what Mummy said," she ventured at last.

Francis stared. "What do you mean, Mummy said? To whom? When?"

"To me, when I told her."

"You told her?" he echoed. "But everyone thinks—"

"—that Cousin Irene did it?" offered Lily. "I know, but Mummy said, just like you, that it was all over, it didn't matter. She'd known all the time." The child hesitated. "I don't think she wanted Daddy or Grandpa to find out."

Francis sat down. "Or for that matter *me*, I daresay."

"I thought you knew," said Lily sympathetically. "You kept making remarks." She gave a smile that might have been seen, in the movies, to accompany her next words. "You were smart to guess it, Uncle Francis."

The lesson was plain. "And stupid to speak of it, no?"

Lily balanced herself on one leg. She could afford to.

"Are we still friends?"

"Oh my goodness, yes!" she exclaimed.

Seeing in whose world she belonged, he rose and kissed her lightly on the cheek.

She had her own questions, however. "Won't Grandpa be upset when he finds out what you did? Are you going to tell him?"

"Grandpa knows what I did, Lily."

"I mean, about the photograph."

"Oh." Francis turned red. Her tone took for granted innumerable shocking things in his past. "Yes, one of these days."

Lily snickered. "I didn't have the nerve to tell Mummy. I waited almost a year."

"A year is a long time."

"Yes, but it goes faster as you grow older."

They exchanged a loaded look, partners no longer in crime but in expiation. "In that case," said Francis, opening the door, "I shall wait for the year 2000 before telling Grandpa about the photograph. Bye now."

But she followed him onto the beach, the smallest in a family of babbling golden-haired Eumenides, eager now to cement their new complicity. "What's the worst thing *you* ever did? I had to finish supper in my room last night because I wouldn't eat my string-beans—so guess what! I flushed them down the toilet! Did you ever do that, Uncle Francis? Did you ever kill a kitten? Did you ever eat a doll?"—lapsing, while he absently replied, back into childhood with a virtuosity that bordered on reproach. He had to throw himself into the icy surf before she let him be.

Reborn, nearly dry, padding back through the house, he heard a phone ring, then silence. An amber light filled up the ocean room. "Oh Natalie!" called Prudence from somewhere else. "Mrs. McBride! Has anyone see Francis?"

"Here I am!"

"It's the telephone, dear! Take it in the hall closet if you like! How was New York!"

"The absolute end!" Francis called back, then switched on the light in a crowded, irregularly shaped coat-closet near the front door. "Yes?" he said into the receiver.

It was Xenia. He winced with remorse.

"I hope I'm not disturbing you," she said. "I haven't heard from you all week."

"Oh my, has a week passed?"

"It's so hot in town. What have you been doing out there?"

"Reading. Nothing. You know."

"How is Ben? And Prudence?"

"Fine. My mother's here."

"What a bore."

"On the contrary. How's the little stranger?"

"Sucking me to bits like an old lecher. He has big blue eyes like you. The doctor's very pleased."

Francis had brown eyes, but let it pass.

"He wants to say hello to you," she continued. "*Viens, mon trésor, dis gentiment bonjour.*"

A tiny noise, half cry, half gurgle, reached Francis. "*Allô, bébé,*" he answered softly. He had let the closet door swing to, shutting him inside among the odds and ends.

"Have you told your father yet?"

He had, but said he hadn't, wondering why.

"You don't want to wait for the Buchanans to tell him." Xenia saw herself eternally under discussion at the Cottage.

"Look," said Francis, "if it's so hot why don't you get an air-conditioner? Just send me the bill."

"You're an angel! That's exactly—what? One moment." He heard some muffled speech. "Hello," said Xenia. "Tommy's written a folk song he says you must hear. When are you coming to town?"

"One of these days. Are you married?"

"God forbid!" she laughed. It had come to be a joke between them. "Oh, and I wanted to ask," she went on, "did you mean what you said about getting us all a cottage for August?"

"Of course."

"Because Adrienne knows of a place on the Cape, very cheap. It sounds perfect. Five bedrooms for four hundred dollars."

"I'll send you a check."

"You'll come up and stay, won't you?"

"If there's room."

"Dear Francis," said Xenia, "there'll always be room for *you*."

Sliding down onto a low wicker stool, he hugged his knees. Above him hung all his father's coats, most of them too big now for the old man, never worn but kept hanging there like flags in an attic. As he put down the receiver, Francis lifted his face into the folds of one. It felt cool and opulent and smelled of mothballs. He had no thought of leaving the closet. "I'm here!" he whispered. On the floor, golf-shoes, probably older than himself, bade fair to outlast Benjamin. "I'm here!" Something gleamed back at him from the shadow of the furthest corner. Bending double, Francis identified his father's head, in bronze, face to the wall.

He smiled from ear to ear. Really, what good was art, or being a patron? It boiled down to this—all representation failed. If he hadn't just heard differently from Lily, he could have imagined Enid's portrait stabbing itself, desperate over such a truth.

Meno, too, had talked of patrons—spirits wise and loving, now beyond all reach. Francis supposed it was for the best. Here on earth it hadn't been wisdom that guided Lily in her emblematic gesture, instead of the other kind, the kind whose meaning couldn't be undone. Francis himself had only lately arrived at this comprehension. As for love, here on earth it was a different kettle of fish.

He suspected frankly that he hadn't fathered Xenia's child. True, nine months and a week after his night with her, a son had been born, a frail, purple-faced thing, weighing not quite four pounds. Tommy Utter wouldn't leave the hospital. The infant spent its first days between life and death. It occurred to Francis, though nobody volunteered the fact, that the child had been prematurely born. If so, it could easily have been conceived during the early weeks of Xenia's affair with the young musician. Francis amazed himself by the skill with which he didn't draw conclusions. Never bothering to express his doubts, he planned to do everything he could for the child. The other day, when he told Benjamin, the old man had seemed very pleased. He spoke of putting money in the baby's name (Alexey, after Xenia's father). Francis didn't know when, if ever, he would tell Vinnie.

And yet, and yet—it was exhausting never to know the truth. Hearing a car-door slam, and then his father's voice outside, Francis smiled. How good to be away from Xenia, mirrors, cities, words that a teacup spelled out, pale allusions, equivalents to the actual. Summer had come and he had arrived at a place in which for a while he couldn't be plagued by images for things. Nobody knew what to do with them here. They were relegated to stuffy closets, left facing into corners, gathering dust. He was having trouble breathing, himself. Flinging open the closet door, he met Benjamin in the hall.

"Hello, Grandpa," he said.

"Hello, Francis," said the old man, and kissed him. "I'm glad you're back." He was wearing a fez, which he handed to his son, calling, "Prudence!"

"One moment." With the corner of his towel Francis rubbed his father's neck. "Fern left some lipstick," he said, deadpan.

Benjamin laughed and shook his head. "God damn," he said, starting for his wife's room and calling her name as he went.

23.

The next morning, clear and rare, things were humming throughout the Cottage. Before leaving to pick up Vinnie at the Inn, Francis strolled over for a short tour of inspection. Starting with the basement, he watched Loretta mix icing for three enormous cakes. On the counter behind her, thirty-six chicken breasts—capons, really— waited to be dredged with flour and fried in fat already heating on the stove. A drop of perspiration fell from her chin into the icing, to which she then added drops of red coloring. "Pink, that's for young men," she explained, and gave way to a fit of laugher. Upstairs in the pantry, he found Prudence, looking hectic. She had never seen so many roses, she was telling Louis Leroy and a maid. Yes, they would need the silver vases. Where were the shears? She turned one of the vases round and said in the pleasantest possible way that they'd have to be polished more carefully. And at once, please. It wouldn't do for even a fragment of tarnish to show. Which reminded her, the piano keys looked very grubby. They wanted to be gone over with a clean rag dipped in benzine, then carefully wiped. She took a handkerchief to her throat, by way of illustration. Oh, and had Mrs. Bigelow's things been moved yet to the guest-cottage?

Francis laughed. Was Natalie being thrown out again?

"It's Benjamin's notion." Prudence turned, her eyes rolling upward. She kissed him distractedly. "Some people are coming, whom he insists take that room. A name I've never heard, and don't want to think about—A Mr. Dirty and his wife. Wally Link's coming too. And the Feuermans. And the Maxons. And Mrs. McBride's daughter. And twenty children after lunch. I'm thinking only of the strain on Benjamin. Louis, go ask Mrs. McBride for one of her headache pills. Thank you. You see, Francis, this luncheon is my first *test*—do you think I shall pass it?" She counted the roses she had trimmed, found one stem snapped almost at the blossom, and gave it to him for his buttonhole. "What a jolly evening we had, just the four of us. You mother *is* so attractive. Of course, I've know so few Southern women, it's not easy to get their quality on a first meeting."

"You'd met her before, though, in Boston."

"Absolutely! Now where is Louis? I may just not go to church."

Francis sauntered out. Tables were being laid on the terrace overlooking the sea. No whitecaps broke that suave blue surface. From time to time a slow undulation would sparkle shorewards, perform a somersault, and quietly, without shattering, overtake a stretch of dry beach. For any clue to the power of that water you had to have felt the undertow sucking at your calves. Francis looked down upon it. He had put on a new white suit, a shirt of yellow muslin, and a blood-red bow tie.

"Is that the way you ordinarily dress out here?" asked Vinnie as he helped her into the car.

"When I do dress."

She didn't laugh. "*Don't* wear that rose. Will you do me that *one* favor, Son?"

Francis removed it from his buttonhole, sniffed it, and handed it to her. She tossed it into the road. Her tone had changed little since their parting talk the night before. The evening itself, as Prudence said, had been jolly. It was distinctly a family affair, with Natalie neither seen nor mentioned. Mrs. McBride, whom Vinnie kissed on entering, ate off a tray in her room. Before dinner the Buchanans looked in for a bit of drinking and hand-holding. Enid had a Roman scarf to give the visitor. For Francis it was an evening full of mysterious pleasure and significance; indeed, he had spent the better part of it in silence, watching his parents and foolishly smiling. The pleasure was not to be rationalized. He thought of great works of painting, and wondered if his emotion couldn't be compared to the artist's who sees his labor justified, his vision realized—in this case by some rich candlelit interior, with gifts, flashing looks and feasting, a subject almost Biblical: *The Prodigal Mother*—what else? She, the central figure, chatted easily of this and that. Her hand, still with its engagement and wedding rings, rested for emphasis now on Prudence's arm, now on Benjamin's. Once or twice Francis could have wished for a less natural flow of talk, a phrase broken off, a hesitation as to the point of an anecdote, something by which to measure the depth of her feeling, back in that house, at that gleaming table, smiled on by servant and master alike. For a moment, after dinner, she came close. "This room," began Vinnie, then sipped her coffee while Francis felt the ocean room come alive with meaning for her, "this room has never looked smarter. It's big enough to *take* red." "Oh dear," said Prudence, "you must save your compliment for Enid. I can't tell chintz from cheesecloth." "You'd better learn damn quick," Benjamin told her, "if you want to keep your job. My own opinion," he went on after a spell of heckling from his wives, "is that the damn room was *never* pleasant to be in. It's too pretentious. I like a simple room." Vinnie said then, "Just think, my dear, how few of us get what we *like* out of life." And she nodded shrewdly.

Her remark, though banal, had been just. Like many rich men Benjamin tended to look back on his life and grow wistful over how poor he had been, in the same way that shabby-genteel families recalled a vanished wealth. It was Vinnie's air of knowing better that troubled Francis. He saw no reason for her to play the philosopher in the barrel, one withered hand upturned in deprecation of a monarch's power. All was forgiven, forgotten; she'd been saying so for years now. Then why couldn't she give in to the charm of the reunion?

As they entered the church a bald vestryman came up, remembered Vinnie, chatted awhile, and led them to a pew. It was a modest building, Victorian, drab, which had gathered chic over the years. People had had to stand in the aisles during Enid's wedding. Vinnie knelt at once, her hands clasped, her lips moving. She was wearing a dress Francis recognized, gray, but with cherries at the throat where there had once been roses. Slowly the church filled up. Boopsie Gresham took a seat not far in front of them. When she saw who Francis had with him she gasped, waved, blew kisses. Vinnie smiled pleasantly in return. Oh, she was a hard nut to crack!

Last night, stopping at the entrance of the Inn, he had been about to help her from the car when she said, "Wait." Her eyes were wide and tragic. "Why are you putting me through this?"

His heart sank. "Through what?"

"Through this experience. Do you imagine, Son, that there's any place for me here? Don't pin your hopes on that, Francis, it's utterly out of the question."

Her vehemence surprised him. Pure nerves, he decided, a sign of healing like the itching of a wound. Still, she had put her finger on something he'd never bothered to think out.

"I'm here because you asked me to come. I'm not a sport and I've no interest in being one. I'm doing this for you." Her voice went mild and uncertain. "It seemed like little enough."

"Oh God, oh God," Francis murmured. All round him he felt a conspiracy of solicitous women. His idea had been to do something for *her*.

"Now don't *you* start," she said, squeezing his hand. He gathered that Vinnie supposed him about to cry, which he saw no need for. His mistake amounted to having assumed that a single exposure to the scene would do the trick. "Don't worry about tomorrow," she finished bravely. "I'll face them all, I won't let you down."

As the organ swelled, she rose, facing them all. Francis held the hymnal under her eyes, but the words—"Rock of Ages"—were written in her heart. A hard nut to crack; he wouldn't give up, though, he simply wouldn't. After all, Fern had come round. Women, as Benjamin said, could never resist attention—or was it Benjamin himself they couldn't resist? Another summer, if not this one, would find Vinnie installed nearby, in a rented cottage, what the society columns called "a familiar sight at the Beach Club." That winter they might give the West Indies another try. Francis would see to it she didn't get sick before reaching Jamaica. A sidelong glance at her, earnestly singing, filled him with happiness. No, despite her efforts, Vinnie was coming alive. She couldn't hold out much longer.

Halfway through the service she whispered, "Who is that stout pink-faced woman next to Ben?"

"Don't you know? That's Harriet. The first Mrs. Tanning."

"Oh."

Later, while the church emptied, the christening party moved into the front pews. The organ's mind wandered. "No," said Vinnie, "let's just stay put. Or you move up if you want." But Mrs. Gresham turned round and beckoned with such authority, they ended by joining her. The two old friends kissed. "Vinnie, Vinnie, Vinnie!" she exulted. "Did I ever dream I'd see you here! It's been a long time, darling, much *too* long! You out for the summer? No? Now why not? Where else is there to go? All the *resorts* are ruined. Look at Southampton. I say we're in Heaven's back yard, by comparison. You remember Nell Sturdevant. It's Vinnie Tanning, Nell!"

"Vinnie, angel! Hi there, Francis! You're getting fat!"

"So are you, Nell—isn't it fun!"

"Hi, Nelly!" said a familiar voice directly over Francis's head. He twisted and saw a jeweled tennis racket dangling at eye level. Automatically he started to rise, then realized that Irene was gazing coolly past him and had no intention of speaking. Charlie lingered in the aisle, a certain distance behind her. Now there was somebody who'd *really* gotten fat.

"How are you, Irene?" said Mrs. Sturdevant without smiling, ostentatiously loyal to Benjamin.

But Boopsie, who was loyal to everybody, had her reputation to protect. "You cute thing!" she cried. Francis and his mother leaned forward to let her hold Irene's hand. "When'd you get back? You look divine! Come see me!"

His head bowed, Francis considered Irene's foot. A blue vein throbbed against the cutting braid of straw that fastened her sandal. It was a distinctly human foot, he thought, a mortal foot, neglected, down-to-earth, one painted toenail peeling. It told a simple story of scars and calluses, one he would never have been able to read in Irene's face. Francis felt wiser and warmer for his glimpse of it.

Tied to the church door, her beagles whined in anticipation.

"You're not leaving!" Boopsie was saying. "Stay for the christening! It's Enid's child!"

"I know," said Irene in a voice that carried. "That's why we're running along. Charlie Cheek and I've stood about all we can from the Tanning family." Francis looked up in time to see her small eyes, narrowed, range from pew to pew. She dared anybody to say she didn't belong there. Benjamin, catching sight of her, nodded gravely, mischievously. It had been wise of Prudence to stay at home. "This is so pathetic, so familiar," sighed Vinnie. But by then Irene had pivoted and, with a toss of her head that impressed no one, was marching Charlie Cheek up the aisle, as if marrying the poor man all over again.

The ceremony got under way. Grouped round the font, Enid, Larry, the godparents (Lily among them), and the baby itself were reminded that the soul cannot die. "Dost thou, therefore, in the name of this Child," asked the rector, a fine amateur athlete, "renounce the devil and all his works, the vain pomp and glory of the world . . . ?"

Smiling, they did so. The baby shook its fists in delight or protest.

Outside the church, professional photographers snapped pictures. Vinnie didn't want to be in any of the groups, but Francis overrode her objections. After all, little Tanning Burr was the center of every shot. Now in Enid's arms, now in Lily's, now in the arms of the new nurse, Alice's successor, the baby smiled beautifully, trustingly. A far cry, Francis thought, from Xenia's little monkey, who any day now would have to start living by his wits, while his mother lived by hers. A picture taken just then caught Francis with a comic, dazed expression on his face. He had been thinking that, when all was said and done, a real advantage went with being born where there was security and love. Although he had been told so all his life, it had never before struck him without irony.

People came up to Vinnie, whom Francis held firmly by the arm. He felt her stiffen under Wally Link's kiss. Once, unaccountably, they met head-on Enid and *her* mother. Introductions were sketched in. Both Mrs. Tannings laughed airily without saying very much. The moment passed.

To Francis's surprise Vinnie kept on smiling. "At least somebody else is in the same boat," she whispered.

"Not one bit," he replied sternly, tightening his hold on her. "Why, Harriet's here, off and on, *all* summer."

The worst was Natalie. As they strolled through the churchyard Francis caught sight of her standing nearby, alone. She was looking about, a dazzling smile on her face, but seeing little more than blurred forms, colors, light and shade. He remembered an afternoon in her bed-sitting-room in town, its blind drawn upon a sooty court. "What would I do with a view, my pet?" she had laughed. Having missed her yesterday, he impulsively detached himself from Vinnie, went over to kiss her, tell her he was back and, without thinking, escort her across the short stretch of grass that separated them from his mother. "Look who's here!" he gaily announced.

Vinnie checked a backward movement. "Well, Natalie," she managed to say in a gentle voice.

"Is that Vinnie?" the other asked, squinting in vain. "Oh good heavens," she added under her breath.

Both turned on Francis in exasperation. Only then he recalled that, for his mother, Natalie was the Other Woman, the first of several, equaled in malignity only by Fern. He grinned idiotically, imagining all the things Vinnie would say, once alone with him. That moment was postponed by Benjamin's coming up to them, leading Mr. and Mrs. Durdee, whom he presented ceremoniously. Francis gave no sign of recognition. Even after Mr. Durdee's "Well, how are *you?*" with its note of hearty reproach, he replied merely that he was very well, thank you, and risked a bewildered shrug not lost on his father; the old man seemed already at a loss to know why in God's name he had invited Warren Durdee in the first place. They had gone thirty years without meeting, a fact that ought to have warned Benjamin. Responding to his silent appeal, Vinnie set about being nice. She'd heard Ben speak of Warren Durdee for years, she felt she'd known him all her life. Father and son watched her tenderly. Natalie meanwhile had drawn out Mrs. Durdee on the subject of names. "I hate mine," she was saying, "always have. Bertha—Birdie Durdee. Could you *invent* a duller name?" "I think it's a perfectly lovely name," said Benjamin, and leaned over to plant a kiss on her veiled cheek. "I wouldn't put it past Warren," he added, "to have spent the last thirty years keeping us apart." "Listen to him!" cried Bertha and Natalie together. "Hey now," Mr. Durdee said feebly, no doubt reliving the months he had shared his quarters with Benjamin and Howie Burr.

At a light kick from his mother, Francis took her arm. "Oh, should we be going?" she asked. "I'll see you all at lunch, then."

As the car started so did she. How could Francis have exposed her, deliberately, to that hideous meeting? What had he thought he was doing? What did he think she was made of. Francis shot quick looks at her face, stricken, white, from which the mild voice proceeded, that even now could not sound other than controlled and reasonable. "Why, that woman lived in my house, ate at my table! I know what I'm talking about, Son. I found letters from Natalie in your father's handkerchief drawer!" Francis sighed, hating to acknowledge the reality of her suffering.

"Well, you handled it beautifully," he risked.

"What else could I do?" Vinnie lapsed into a dry silence. Presently she had him stop the car while she powdered her nose and arranged her hair, which was decidedly gray now. He felt a vast relief. The camel's back hadn't been broken. In time even the obstacle of Natalie might be surmounted. For that matter, Francis had already witnessed an instant he was long to treasure. It had come when the two women, recovering from their initial stupefaction, turned towards one another and partook of a certain wry amusement that could only have been at his expense. They checked it promptly. But he had had time to read, in both Natalie's face and his mother's, how young you had to be, how hopelessly inexperienced, to have contrived a situation in such wild bad taste. Francis's eyes shone. He guessed that he had hit upon a most valuable tactic. Not until seeing Benjamin draw near with the Durdees did he relax the stupid grin that had provoked that spark of sisterhood.

The main stumbling block, of course, *was* Benjamin; he saw this now. To the degree that Vinnie had loved him and been hurt by him, she would continue to resist any prolonged immersion in his element. Well, Benjamin wouldn't last forever. Francis had his first glimmering of a scene: the Cottage with himself as master; the summers to be spent there with Vinnie, with a whole little crowd—Prudence, Natalie, Jane, Xenia, Adrienne. For it would all be his one day.

Towards the end of lunch Mr. Tanning stood up, but not to make a speech. "Too much excitement for Grandpa," he mumbled and, draining his glass of champagne, made his way into the house. A few guests looked up, half-rose, their faces puckering in inverse proportion to the concern they felt. Beyond, the blue sea sulked and smoked. The air had lost part of its early morning clarity. You were not invited to scan the distances. When the cakes were brought everybody agreed it was a crime to cut them. They had been decorated with beautiful white sugar roses, the name *Tanning Burr Buchanan*, and, best of all, a border of babies—oval candies not an inch long, to each of which had been applied, in sugar, a tiny pink face, three dots for buttons, the frill of a bonnet.

You would have thought they were real, to hear the women talk. "These are the cutest things I've ever seen!" declared Mrs. Gresham. "Whose idea! Enid, it was *yours!*"

From the neighboring table Enid shook her head, mouth full of cake.

"Then Francis! With his cute sense of humor!"

"Not I," he assured her.

"I'll bet it was Prudence," said Mrs. Sturdevant. "Wasn't it, pet?" She looked slyly round to her hostess's chair, but found it empty.

Boopsie was vexed. "Louis Leroy," she called, "where did these babies come from?"

"Somebody *please* tell Boopsie the facts of life!" a distant male voice put in.

"At least she asked the right man!" cried Natalie.

The accordionist struck up "Some Enchanted Evening." Everyone was uncontrollably laughing.

"Shut up!" shouted Boopsie, laughing herself. "I want to know!"

Louis Leroy smiled and shifted. "Loretta, she brought them from the village, Miss Gresham."

"Well, you tell her for me, Louis," she said, speaking very distinctly lest he forget or garble her message, "that *I* think they're perfectly adorable. Can you remember that?"

"Yes, ma'am," he replied, all agleam.

Mrs. Durdee turned back to Francis. "I don't know when I've had so much fun," she sighed. They had been talking about spiritualism. Francis, describing his own experiences, found that Meno served brilliantly as a conversation piece. His companion had laughed till she cried. She wondered if she mightn't make a good medium. Once in Marseille she'd been another person for an entire evening—"Don't ask me who. All I know is, I wasn't myself." Her slice of cake had two babies on it. "Here," she said, scraping one onto his plate, "you don't have any."

She *was* psychic. "I hope you stay longer than the weekend," said Francis.

"We'd love to, but Warren has to get back to his office."

Better yet, he thought. "Then why don't *you* stay?"

"For one thing, I haven't been asked."

"Don't imagine you won't be!" he chuckled, resolving to suggest it to Benjamin.

Mrs. Durdee smiled at him. "We've met before, Francis, only you've forgotten."

"Have we really? Where?"

"Last year in Rome. Through that sculptress, Xenia Grosz."

"Xenia? How funny! Yes, she's a dear friend. She was out here last summer, did you know? But we were never in Rome at the same time. You have me confused with one of her other young men. I sometimes wonder how *she* keeps them all straight," he finished with a malicious smile. What he meant to deny was not the fact of his earlier meeting with Mrs. Durdee, which Francis remembered vividly, so much as his impression of her, ill and querulous in that "authentic" restaurant. It embarrassed him to have taken the easy view of her, the Italian view. Falling through vine leaves, the light of Rome had splotched her face with greens and yellows, like camouflage. He hadn't once questioned the evidence of splashing water whose lovely voice made hers sound brittle and unmusical. He saw how the skins of eggplants, of apricots and cherries, to say nothing of the other diners', brown, olive, red-mouthed, lustrous—he saw how he had let all that, itself illusory, make the American woman unreal. And here she was today, perfectly nice, delightful really. Seeing her where she belonged, against a whitening sky and flat sea, Francis found in her exactly the kind of cool artificial prettiness he most liked. She was rather in the style of Fern. He imagined her having a very tonic effect on Benjamin. For Prudence, wonderful as she was, could be the least bit tiresome and self-righteous. As now, for instance, leaving her guests to their own devices.

A cry of distaste rose from the ladies at the far end of their table. Mrs. Gresham had just decided to eat her candy baby.

"Don't *do* it, Boopsie!" laughed Vinnie in spite of herself.

"Too late!" she said, and bit it in two. A ruddy syrup ran down her chin. The others screamed. "Ummm!" She smacked her lips. "They're full of liquor!"

"What are you *doing* over there?" Enid called.

"Mummy, Mrs. Gresham ate her baby!" squealed Lily, jumping up and down in ecstasy.

"Oh my goodness!"

"I'm going to get mine," Francis told Bertha Durdee. "Are you going to eat yours?"

"Absolutely!" She popped it into her mouth.

The idea was catching on. "I like sweets," he heard his mother say, "but they don't like me."

"Play something!" Mrs. Gresham commanded the accordionist.

"Play 'Baby, It's Warm Inside!'" said Wally Link.

"I don't mind sucking mine," Mrs. Sturdevant was explaining to Vinnie, pointing to the bulge in her cheek, "but I could never have *bit into* it like Boopsie."

The music began and didn't stop, though all but drowned out by shrieks and laughter, until every baby in sight had been consumed. Those too squeamish to eat their own saw them gobbled up by their neighbors. The first arrivals at Lily's birthday party, two neat little boys accompanied by a nanny, looked at one another with misgivings.

Lunch was over. Rising from his seat, Francis entered the ocean room, where card tables had already been set up. On the north terrace, which faced the sunken lawn, children were gathering. Shyly they offered Lily their gifts. Francis sighed to think he had nothing for her. Outside his father's door he met Mrs. McBride, her hands full of knitting. A startling green-eyed young girl stood next to her; Francis waited to be introduced. "Go on in," the nurse said, "You'll find a nice quiet *family* party." He watched them move away, neither looking back, then put his head into the dim room.

Benjamin lay flat on the bed with a thin white blanket over his legs. On one side, holding his hand, sat Prudence. They seemed in a trance of contentment, beyond speech. "Is everything all right?" asked Francis.

His father's eyes opened. "Everything's under control," he said.

"Everything's just wonderful, Francis," came from the gloom behind the door, where he had failed to notice Larry Buchanan sitting peacefully. Francis tiptoed across the room and took a chair. Ornate curls of smoke rose from his brother-in-law's cigar, like the clouds surrounding a representation of some powerful spirit, in Chinese painting. His face was purplish red in the suppressed light, his tie cobalt and cream. The stump of his little finger pointed up. Dreamily he repeated for Francis the good news he had been telling the elder Tannings. Benjamin's pet project, Bishop Petroleum, had closed at 18½ Friday afternoon. That meant a

500-percent profit since a year ago—a profit in which both Enid and Francis shared, and for which they could thank their father.

The latter cleared his throat. "Don't be modest, Larry."

"Me modest?" He grinned. "I'm a private in your ranks, Ben. You give the orders, I try to carry them out. How about it, Francis? Want another ten thousand shares in your account?"

"Go right ahead," said Francis pleasantly but flippantly. "I love money."

"Don't let your father fool you," Larry went on. "Look how he handled the mess last winter, when the President of the company resigned. We all stood to lose plenty that day."

Benjamin remarked, "Orson Bishop's a fine man," and yawned.

"A high-minded man, a man with ideals. We know now," Larry addressed Francis, "why that crisis occurred. Irene Cheek had been poisoning his mind against your father, writing him a lot of nonsense about your father's immorality."

The old man leered. "Every word of it true, what's more."

"But why?"

"Because she was jealous of *me,* Francis," said Prudence. She touched her hair, causing a star sapphire he hadn't seen before to twinkle victoriously.

"Anyhow," Larry said, "that's all settled now."

"Grandpa's decently married," groaned Benjamin. "Lily Buchannibal can come to the Cottage without being corrupted by the old poop. He's harmless as a baby and hairless as a French whore."

"Benjamin, I've *begged* you . . ."

"Was that Mrs. McBride's daughter just now?" asked Francis.

"Yes, Mary Ann. She's sweet, isn't she?"

"She has phenomenal eyes," was the best he could do.

"My goodness!" exclaimed Enid from the doorway. "Aren't we the shining examples of hospitality!" She perched, nevertheless, on the edge of the bed and took Benjamin's other hand.

"We've been talking about Irene," said Larry.

"Irene mutilated your portrait, Enid," her father said. "It wasn't Fern. I'm sure of that now."

"Enid and I have always been sure of it."

Francis watched his sister smooth out the folds of her dress, pale blue with little yellow suns, and say nothing. They all fell silent for a bit, following her example, as if that world in which violent deeds were done revolved far beneath their own concerns.

"Why don't you tell us how pleased you are with your grandson?" asked Prudence.

Benjamin gave her an enigmatic look and said, "Which one?"

She snorted. "Are we to suppose that you have grandchildren in all corners of the earth?"

Each one smiled wisely out of an imperfect knowledge of the others that amounted to a real community of feeling. How much they had kept and would keep secret all their lives! Indeed, thought Francis, their equilibrium as a family seemed to depend upon separate orbits, a law preserving them from collision or eclipse. He took pleasure in reflecting that he knew more than the rest, that in a sense, if they smiled, it was largely because *he* hadn't yet told Larry about Lily, Prudence about Fern, Benjamin about the true fatherhood of Xenia's child. He held in his hands their peace of mind. As for secrets they might be keeping from *him*—for not doubt it worked both ways—he felt at once incurious and complacent. Of course he was being spared something, *some* joke had to be on him—well and good. Like a tired child on the eve of his birthday, glimpsing gifts but too drowsy to speculate upon them, Francis chose to leave it at that.

He couldn't leave *them*, however, without a trifling test of his power. As he got to his feet he produced Bertha Durdee's name. She was an attractive woman, wasn't she?

"Oh, very!" said Enid.

"Terribly," said Prudence.

"Who is Bertha Durdee?" Larry asked.

"Warren Durdee's wife."

Benjamin spoke. "Warren Durdee hasn't changed. He's still the biggest stuffed shirt on Wall Street."

"Two incarnations ago," said Francis, "he was a white dog."

"He's not the most alert little soul," Enid admitted.

Francis came to the point. "I wondered, Daddy, if you mightn't like Bertha to stay on for a few days, after he leaves. I have a feeling she'd enjoy a holiday from her husband."

"Do you really think so?"

"Yes, I do," said Francis; a note of interest in his father's voice had made him smile.

The old man studied him quizzically. "Very well, my loving son, bring her on! If you prefer we can move her into *your* little house."

"You'd have to move Natalie back first," said Francis, before understanding that he was being made fun of. He added without inflection, "In any case, it's for you to decide."

Benjamin thanked him. "Have *you* issued the invitation?"

"Of course not."

"Then may I suggest you let *me* be the judge—" But in mid-sentence his tone changed. "Don't mind me, Francis. I'd be glad to have Mrs. Durdee stay on if you think she'd like to."

"Really," said Francis, "it was only an idea."

"It's just that new people tax Benjamin so," Prudence explained. "I'd selfishly been hoping for a quiet week, after today's celebrations."

"Come to town with me tomorrow," said Larry. "It'll be quiet enough there, I promise you." He grinned and cracked his knuckles. Enid let out her lilting laugh, as if Larry's solitary week was a joke they shared.

"It's for Benjamin that I want quiet," insisted Prudence, "not for myself."

Francis sighed, reading into her concern the anxiety of any reigning favorite, caught in a web of watchers and whisperers. More telling yet was to find her eyes on him. "It appears that nothing," she all but said aloud, "helps the poor woman who marries Benjamin. She must pass her test alone. Even *you* are no longer my ally." Granting the justice of her reproach, Francis still couldn't expect Prudence to understand how much his position demanded a firm line taken towards favorites. They, by definition, had passed their test, stopped needing help, unlike others he knew of. The recent talk, for instance, had started him brooding over Irene. He didn't like her, but she *had* been falsely accused in the matter of Enid's portrait—perhaps in the Bishop affair as well—and the injustice of it caused Francis a real pang. He thought of her in that cheerless house, alone with Charlie Cheek. Would she receive him if he drove out there one day next week? Why, she'd have to—they were relatives! And it might do something to help ease the tension.

The reconciliation he envisaged never got very far. That following winter, Charlie Cheek's sailboat capsized in a heavy sea. Both he and Irene were washed up onto the beach days later, badly mutilated by sharks. The news was to leave Francis with an odd feeling, not quite annoyance, not quite frustration. "The emptiness, the pity of it," he wrote his father at the time, remembering his high hopes, the day of the christening.

"I'm off," Francis said. "We needn't decide about Mrs. Durdee now." As nobody contradicted him, he started for the door. Larry and Enid rose at the same time.

Benjamin's eyes followed them. "I'm glad you're taking an interest in your own affairs, Sonny," he said drowsily.

"What do you mean?"

No answer came.

"What does he mean?"

Prudence smiled and put a finger to her lips. The old man had pulled a black mask over his eyes. So that Francis, going out with the Buchanans, had to content himself with Larry's explanation. Mr. Tanning had meant the interest shown by Francis on hearing about Bishop Petroleum.

"Oh come now!" he protested. "I wasn't serious, I was being ironic!"

"I know, I know," said Larry, patting him on the shoulder so amiably as to leave uncertain which of them had the greater command of irony, in the last analysis.

All three paused in the shade of the north terrace, watching children play hide-and-seek on the lawn down beyond the ha-ha.

"They're learning fast," said Francis.

Enid nodded vaguely. "They'll have their supper at five-thirty."

"A cake with parents on it . . ."

"Let's go in," said Larry, "and do our duty."

Francis thought he would stay outdoors. His brother-in-law took a step or two away, then returned. "Your father and Prudence and I," he said in a low voice, "were talking before you came in. Did you know that the Cottage would be yours one day?"

Francis nodded dreamily.

Larry gave him an annoyed look. "Well, it was news to me," he said, and went into the house, leaving a funny doubt in Francis's mind. How *had* he known?

Between games he caught Lily's eye and beckoned to her. She took a long time to reach his side. "I have no present for you, Lily," he said when she did; "will this do?"—offering her a five-dollar bill.

"Oh, Uncle Francis!"

The twins had followed her. He produced coins for them. Their real pleasure brought back his own childhood, and the subsequent painful process of learning to hide his love for money.

"What are you playing?"

"Hide-and-seek. Would you like to play?"

"Good heavens, child—well, why not?"

He let her lead him out onto the sunny grass. Coming to the brink of the small artificial precipice—the ha-ha—they jumped, hand in hand, down to the sunken lawn. Presently Francis was in the midst of children, their faces flushed and grave as if he were going to wrench some vital secret from them. Lily alone couldn't stop giggling as she rehearsed the rules he had obeyed at her age, in the same walled garden.

"Uncle Francis is It," she announced proudly at last. "If he wants to play he has to be It."

So Francis obligingly buried his face in a hydrangea bush, hearing the muffled running of children seeking to elude him in far corners of the garden. As he slowly counted to one hundred, his mind wandered from the simple rules of the game—he, she, or It—to the shrubbery, the rose arbor, the wicker chairs on the terrace; he relished in advance the found child's shriek of excitement. A vast silence now defined itself, in which he distinctly heard the opening and shutting of a screen door. That was odd. Somebody must have come out of the house to watch him, beneath the egg-white sky, his face deep in foliage, take part in a children's game. He responded to the quiet attentiveness of that person, whoever it was, advancing to the edge of the ha-ha. The green eyes of Mrs. McBride's daughter shone unbidden in his memory—would it be she? It would be somebody, at any rate, to whom Francis had never been a child, though seen as one among so many other greennesses; to whom indeed, rising from the growing discomfort of his position, he might turn with a smile, idly begin to talk. One by one he would shed, in favor of others more pressing, his obligations to the game. He would join his watcher, they would stroll together back into the house. The children, sensing the sudden drop in tension, the way a string goes limp when snapped, would come out of hiding and, accepting his withdrawal as they had his appearance, reshift the delicate balances of their play.

"Ready or not!" he shouted, more to his observer than to the twenty little hearts pounding out of sight. Then he raised his head, looked round to the ha-ha.

There was nobody in sight.

Well then, thought Francis, managing an empty smile, what else but to play the game? *Their* eyes, at least, were on him, peering through leaves, peeking through wicker. With exaggerated stealth and flashing stern glances into the greenery he started across the lawn. Something winked in the rose-arbor, he darted forward—a bird. Something rustled out from the bushes behind him; crying "Aha!" he pivoted—a rabbit froze on the hushed lawn. Where *were* they? No sound of smothered laughter came to ease his confusion. It took Francis another few minutes to connect the sound of the screen door with the children making their escape. He was alone in the garden.

The game had broken like a bubble—or had not, had rather, by ending on terms so incongruous, left him still inside it, sustaining it all by himself. He thought of some old stage uncle, living on in a boarding-house, friendless, wedded to the mannerism of a once famous role. He felt ridiculously lonely.

At last he started back towards the house, regaining first the higher level of green, then the shady terrace. The cardplayers, intent on *their* game, scarcely looked up as Francis slipped into the great, red, scented room. He paused behind his mother while she fingered a face card. "Do you know what I'd love?" she murmured, feeling his presence. "A glass of cold, cold water."

"So would I, Francis," said Mrs. Gresham.

"Make it three," whispered Bertha Durdee, and played a heart.

Francis hurried to the pantry, positively afraid lest now, too late, he should hear from somewhere a chorus of mocking voices sing out the start of a fresh game, in which he, once again, would be It.

On his return Natalie Bigelow asked for water. The grown-ups did not otherwise detain him.

But only after coming upon the children building castles at the sea's edge, oblivious to him, did Francis stare out over the lulled water and understand. He *was* It. He tentatively said so the first time, then once more with an exquisite tremor of conviction: "I am It."

The words carried with them wondrous notions of selflessness, of permanence. His father coughed behind him in the house. The children trembled against the sea. He knew the expression on his own face. The entire world was real.

THE (DIBLOS)
NOTEBOOK

(1965)

Isidore a menti, je ne méprise personne
et ne hais point mes parents.

Ayoub Sinano, *Artagal*

~~Orestes~~

The islands of Greece

Across vivid water the islands of Greece lie. They have been cut out of cardboard and set on bases of

at subtle odds with one another, upon bases of pale haze. Their colors are mauve, exhausted blue, tanned rose, here & there crinkled to catch the light. They do not seem

It is inconceivable that they are of one substance with the warm red rock underfoot

rock of one's own vantage point (?)

One early evening

(Name) had grown used to this contradiction. She

Late one ~~spring~~ afternoon a woman no longer ~~puzzled~~ troubled by this illusion left her house, the largest on the island of (Name), and set out on foot in the direction of town.

At the top of a hill she met Orestes. He

Her body was strong and graceful, her features first darkened, then silvered by the dry summer. White strands in her iron-colored hair shot backward into an elaborate plaited bun. Her ~~large, Byzantine~~ eyes, immense & shining, though set in webs of age, attended without curiosity to the path which rose and fell never far from the water's edge. She wore sandals, a gray skirt, not embroidered, & a night-blue shawl

and had wound a thin night-blue shawl around the upper part of her body, to produce an impression of deliberate, coquettish antiquity. Drawstring looped over her wrist, an old-fashioned beaded purse sparkled mustily as she walked, making light of the mission she did not have. She had told them she was going to the pharmacy. They had

She had said she was going to the pharmacy, not that there was anything to do, now, but wait. The others had appeared to understand.

So did the few people she passed; they greeted her courteously, without lingering.

On a small promontory she met Orestes. He was walking away from the town. It stretched on either side of him like a robe, its hues of white & stone hanging down into the still harbor.

"Pardon me," he said. "Do you live here? I am looking for the Sleeping Woman."

His Greek, fluent but incorrect, made her examine him carefully.

"Ah," she said at length, "but the best view is from the town. Did no one point it out? You must turn back."

Whereupon they fell into step together and Orestes set about

O., who found all his own traits extraordinary, set about marveling at his ~~stupidity~~ imperception. Did she mean those slopes directly facing the port? *Their* silhouette made up the Sleeping Woman? He laughed out loud, swinging his zippered notebook from his little finger.

At this juncture, I think, no serious evocation of landscape. What else will serve?

Let me see. Orestes can give her ice cream at the café. (It must be Summer. O.'s sabbatical year will just have begun.) A mild dusk. The awnings that close me in won't be needed. It will divert her to sit in full view of the populace—the grande dame of the island, already on such jolly terms with the newcomer.

He will talk.

"I was born 35 years ago in Asia Minor of Greek parents. My father, a goatherd, fell in love with a beautiful etc. Dead of cancer. Poverty. New York. Mother remarried, lives in Texas. A stepfather, a half-brother

No. Avoid plunging stupidly into exposition. Let him be felt a bit. Let *her* be felt.

(Orson—Orestes. Now another name for Dora.)

And let *me* not be part of it. It's hard enough being O.'s brother in life, without sentencing myself to it in a book.

Maria
Psyche
Fifi (Serafina)
Kiki (Pulcheria)
Artemis

Orestes

Little stream, have you petered out so soon?

This is my first prolonged exposure to the *town* of Diblos (1800 souls). It has, I can report so far, a hotel & a café. In the hotel are 12 rooms, 2 baths, a manager in pyjamas morning and night, an energetic Italian-speaking maid named Chryssoula whose children—Yannis, Theodoros, Aphrodite, six all told—run errands & whose big black cat does not. Here at the café, the canvas, still rolled down, is flapping furiously. An umber heat pulses through it. My table lurches from side to side as I write, at one with the incomprehensible voices, rattle of beads,

311

the click & screech of crockery. It is 4:00 of my 2nd day here, and of my 7th in Greece for as many years. I'd thought one of the first things to do would be to walk out to the House, but I haven't. Nor have I wanted in any way to "use" my previous visit, or my connection with O. & Dora. The natives have shown, up to now, no glimmer of recognition.

5:30. The boat from Athens has come & gone. The awnings are rolled up. Nobody in sight. I could be giving thought to

5:45. The American girl, Lucy, from the N.'s lunch last week, was on the boat. I hadn't noticed her getting off. She seemed ominously glad to see a familiar face. Then: "But you're *working*, excuse me!"—leaving me with the choice of being amused by her view of the Writer as finer & nobler than the rest of us or being undone by the whole sorry banality of writing so much as a postcard in a public place. Anyhow, she couldn't join me. A luggage-bearing child led her off to a room taken, sight unseen. Will she be here long? I didn't ask. I am so cold to people. And keep forgetting that it's that, the coldness, the remoteness, that attracts them. If I were warmer, talked more, showed more interest, *felt* more interest—

To fit in somewhere:

(Dora) was constantly polite and respected, but Orestes had *time* for people, time to talk and show interest, to make his listeners feel that their minds were rare & flexible, time to welcome a stranger into the circle with some deft bit of nonsense from the speaker's well of inexhaustible friendliness. This kind of conversation finds its happiest expression in the dialogues of Plato, where for all Socrates' avowed humility it is certainly he who does the talking & remains the center of attention. The system worked like a charm at the waterfront café where a half dozen idle citizens would be held spellbound, hours on end, while (Dora) knitted. "How do you do it?" she asked one day.

"What do you mean? I like doing it," he said.

"How can you?" was on the tip of her tongue. Instead she returned to her ~~knitting~~ handiwork, head bowed in acknowledgment of her friend's superior humanity.

(The Greek restaurant in New York: a contrasting scene.)

17.vi.61

From the post-office (no letters yet) a strange view of the Sleeping Woman, seen only by afternoon light until today. Barely recognizable, a collapsing tent of whitish bluffs & uncertain distances; let Orestes see her that way just before (after?) the confrontation on the terrace.

Seen from the café, now, the Woman is more distinct: knee, belly, ribcage, breast (a shallow hemisphere) slung backwards to the long throat; a firm jutting chin, nose ditto; mouth shut, refusal of a kiss.

She gives the landscape an intense dreamlike quality. In the foreground, set low, an Italianate composition of peeling villa, cypress, palm, lemon trees, all green-black between the sky-colored water & the hills pale as clouds.

Even the narrow channel between island and mainland struck Orestes as emblematic. He thought of the "tight straits" of his early life.

18.vi.61

Along the quai are moored the little water taxis, each shaded by a canopy of white cloth. This, on Dora's more stylish boat, had a border of scarlet fringe.

She sent the boat for Orestes the following afternoon. The young boatman

313

"Well, this has been very nice," said (Dora)—they were now speaking English. She gave him her hand, adding as if it meant nothing, "You wouldn't be a bridge fan?

He stared at her, thinking of ~~Hart Crane~~ water to be spanned.

"Or any card game. It helps to pass the time."

"Oh you know," cried Orestes joyously, understanding & savoring his conquest, "I have no talent for such things. I would play a diamond instead of a heart—is that what the suits are called?" He ended by noticing her smile. "Would you like me to play cards with you?" he said meekly.

She sent the boat for him the following afternoon. The young boatman, Kosta, knew him by sight. In those days before the tourists discovered (Diblos) every stranger was known, through someone's hospitable interrogation, within an hour of arrival.

(It's moving too quickly.)

(That same night) Orestes strolled the length of the waterfront to a taverna above the beach—from afar, a diamond blaze, a faint blare of song; once there, 8 tables, a central rectangle of earth, unshaded bulbs strung on wires. A whitewashed cube, windowless, in whose forehead burned the strongest bulb, completed the setting. Two couples sat at one table, two sailors at another. ~~Orestes~~ The music had stopped. O. nodded about politely, seated himself and ordered wine & cheese from the child who came stumbling out over an apron that covered him from chest to ankles.

Ah wait. Insert:

At a 3rd table sat a small, plump infant of a man, dashingly dressed, an Athenian on holiday, O. supposed in the moment it took to nod about & choose a table removed from the outsider. He seated himself, etc. ¶A rhythmical grating, ominous & blurred, the needle in its groove, heralded the next selection. From the loudspeaker issued a splatter of twanging sounds, a melody any fragment of which seemed feverish but whose final effect was one of tragic lassitude. A voice put words to it:

"In Trikala where two alleys meet
They murdered Sahavlià . . ."

(Or find other words. Love & Betrayal. Make them up?)

One of the sailors rose to dance. He snapped fingers, leapt, dipped, never looked up. Above him, counterwise to his movements, a lightbulb slowly revolved. When the dance ended, the small plump man, who had come unnoticed to Orestes' table, asked permission to sit down.

The Enfant Chic.

He is forever pursing his pale mouth and rolling his pale eyes. A silken swag of hair, a lightly pitted face like the moon's. The rest of him vanishes into his new clothes; the white collar stands out from his ears, only his knuckles show below the pink cuffs. In talking, he spreads out his hands & the two middle fingers stay glued together as on fashion dummies. He would be, oh, 40. One thinks at first he is a photographer; he leers at one, mimes the snapping of a picture. Is he mad? His manner changes. He asks if one knows an Athens shop called l'Enfant Chic. No, no, no, he does not own it. No, no, he doesn't buy his clothes there, hahaha. The outspread hand flattens upon his heart. Ze suis, moi, l'Enfant Seek. Actually his name is Yannis, as whose isn't, and he runs a shop of his own here called Tout pour le Sport.

That's not going to work. There's no place for the Enfant Chic in this story. Yet he lives here. ~~Orson~~ Orestes could have to reckon with him, & for O. he'd be a rather different person, able to speak his own language, dispense with those airs of complicity, of knowing more than he tells, put on by his utter ignorance—of me, of English, even of French—like one more piece of smart clothing.

I touched one glass too many with other revellers, & cannot account for a big blue bruise below my hip.

What one *can* use is the poetry of the night, the lights running across black water toward us from the mainland, the music dwarfed, though at top volume, by the immense starry silences around it. To swim then: one's limbs, stippled with phosphorescence, bringing to mind—to my mind—ectoplasm, the genie conjured up out of oneself, floating & sporting, performing all that's asked of it before it merges at last into the dark chilled bulk of its master's body stumbling over stones to sleep.

19.vi.61

"Come in here." She opened the door. Orestes followed her into a sunny library. Lamplight revealed

Near the bright window, but lamplit as if for a faint increase of warmth, a shrunken old man lay on a chaise longue. A blanket covered him to the waist. "Tasso," she said, "we have a guest."

A second figure replaced a book in shelves near the door and turned. He was a handsome, heavy man of about thirty, dressed in a sheer white shirt & white trousers. "This is my son Byron," said (Dora). And in another voice, "There is my husband."

Orestes gazed at her with admiration. He had talked so much about himself the previous day, and only now realized that she, too, must have a life worth hearing about.

The old man, holding O.'s hand, stared up at him from over a full white and yellow beard. "Siate voi il poeta?" he breathed reverently.

"Oui," said Orestes. "You must forgive me I do not speak French."

Byron ~~on whose face a look of petulance~~ walked over, looking amused. "My father paints, you know. He terribly enjoys meeting a fellow intellectual. We get few visitors of any sort nowadays."

"Solitude is the price the artist pays," said Orestes, mechanically rhyming.

"I would prefer to pay it in Paris," said Byron.

"And I in ~~Rapallo~~ Fiesole," said the old man. "For 32 years I have not left Greece. But small countries make delightful prisons." Although he still had hold of Orestes' hand, he seemed to have mastered his initial emotion.

We should have had a glimpse of Orestes before this—at the café?

He was a slight, graceful

a spare, nimble man in sandals, white trousers, & a white drip-dry shirt through which his undershirt and lean darkening shoulders could be seen. Already balding, his square brow gleamed like beeswax above ~~brown deepset animated heavylidded~~ triangular brown eyes. He rarely wore the sunglasses in his pocket. On his left wrist, a bracelet of paler skin; he had left his watch off, for the sake of an even tan. Below the moustache of a "sharpie," his lips, thin & curveless, tinged with purple, appeared unexpressive in repose. He was at his best when talking. Presently, looking up from his book, he

20.vi.61

Something too odd has happened. The Enfant Chic knows me. He has a photograph of me.

The coincidence tells me I must face up to the "reality"—actual events & people—behind my story. How much to conceal, how much to invent? The name Orson, which still, to my ear, sounds *truer* than Orestes, has had to go already. But who he is (Orson/Orestes)—and by the same token, who I am—ah, that I keep on evading.

At least I understand the E. C.'s picture-snapping pantomime at the taverna. He had recognized me, he knew I was Orson's brother. ("Couldn't the Tourist Police have given him your name?" asked Lucine later, missing the point: we had different names, were only *half*-brothers—she found it strangely difficult to grasp.) Anyhow, today, when I looked in on the Enfant's lair of fishnet, handwoven skirts, san-

dals, postcards & shells, he was ready for me. He had the snapshot to
show.

He asked eagerly where Orson was & wouldn't believe I couldn't tell
him. He had known O., then? Yes, yes. He had known him. Z'étais
grande ami de maison. Próto—avant. Après, pas.

The E. C. can   Tu comprends? I understood mainly how Orson
be present at   would have loathed him on sight. Small wonder I
Orestes' 1st   was never taken to call. The E. C. admits that he
visit to the   doesn't remember me from 7 years ago, but at that
House?   time he had had no shop, he hadn't (adusting imag-
inary furs) needed to work.

But how did he get the snapshot?

Oh yes, & as I am leaving, in a tone of benevolent confidence: Tell
your brother to stay away from Diblos—ne pas revenir, O. K.?

I guess I was right. The Enfant Chic has a place in the story.

Leaving the shop, they shook hands. Orestes was revolted to feel
revolted but not surprised to feel his palm tickled by the proprietor's
moist, long-nailed finger.

On the street I met Lucy, or Lucine as she turns out to be called (name
misheard at the N.'s). Still in state of mild shock, suggested swim. She
considered at length, then said yes with air of an earnest, headstrong 10
year old. Marvelous water, marvelous air. She doesn't know the N.'s any
better than I do. Thought her mother had gone to school with Mrs N. She
seems independent. (Parents think she's traveling with chums.) She must
paint—funny little hands stained orange & blue, nails bitten.

A more formal opening: O.'s arrival in Athens.

No sooner had Orestes

. . .

The snapshot seemed at first to show Orestes & his brother, in pro-
file, face to face. But a closer look revealed that Orestes was there only in
plaster effigy, as if transformed by something in the young, inexperi-
enced

the barely formed, mindless features of the other.

22.vi.61

Dusk of another day. Café awnings rolled up. Ouzo ordered.

Earlier, thinking I'd walk out to the House, I passed the beach. Lucine
sketching, oblivious to the 4 young men not far off who grind their
bellies into the sand & fix her with burning eyes. The Enfant Chic oiling
his plump limbs in the center of a huge blue & white towel—the Greek
flag? He has a few young men of his own. "Bon zour, où vous allez
madenant?"—and when I don't stop, makes elaborate gestures 1st in
my direction, then towards the distant, invisible House. His friends,
too, waved & smiled—ah, they know me from that night at the taverna.
Angry, I did a childish thing: branched off the path—the House would
keep—and struck out up a wooded slope in the direction of, well,
nowhere at all. Fields, olive groves, *lots* of burs. And were the E. C. and
his friends deceived? Ha! Not likely.

To reconsider:

1) Orestes has come to (Diblos) for a week. Meets (Dora). The card
game, etc.

2) Back in Athens, he runs into (Byron) on the street & hears that his
father has died.

3) In reply to his letter of sympathy Dora, now left alone—Byron
works in Athens—impulsively offers Orestes the cottage on her prop-
erty.

Yes. So we see him in residence by early fall. They can have all winter to reach the point at which O.'s brother finds them when he comes in April.

But must the brother really be in the story? If he is, a terrific lot of back history will have to be put in. The Greek father, the American father, even the old godfather, Arthur Orson (who might be useful, though, in New York—someone for Dora to turn to). How much I'd rather there weren't this complexity! I wanted a tale light as air, lightly breathed out, 2 or 3 figures only, in clear, unexpected colors. And now look.

They needn't *be* brothers! Wouldn't that solve everything?

24.vi.61

A Monday. Father's seasonal letter. When was I returning, money not grown on trees, enclosed check the last. "Mother joins in love to you & Orson." Let them think we are together. I need time here, now; the book is starting to take hold.

Yesterday noon, on the bus to the monastery where a festival (panegyri) was being held, Lucine rambled on in her soft sleepwalking away. The Greek boys, she didn't know if she liked them, they followed her about so. She must be almost as young as she looks to expect one to care for her trivial plight. Nobody, that is, has done her wrong. Still, I spent most of the day at her side, pretending a protectiveness not too surprisingly felt by early evening when, full of wine, we reeled the 6 kilometers downhill into the moonrise.

"Have you shown your paintings anywhere?"

"No. Have you had anything published?"

"A few things."

"That's too bad. I think everyone should be unknown."

It may have been then that I kissed her.

. . .

Orestes: I have had more experience than you.
(Name): Must it follow that """ leads to wisdom?

26.vi.61

I want to say something about loneliness and distance. Already I'm not lonely enough. There is L., there is the Enfant Chic, there is a body named Giorgios who asked me for a cigarette on the beach and said "You good man," as he went off with two. In the hotel, there is Chryssoula. However slightly they know me, I find I must avoid them if I am to accomplish anything.

This morning I wrote letters in my room's airless, viewless heat. Chryssoula exclaimed with dismay, seeing me emerge; she had thought I was on the beach, otherwise she would have kept me company! Now, this afternoon, I have picked my way along what can't be called a path, out beyond the edge of town (direction opposite from that of the House). Here it is wild & stony, there are goats high up behind me, some savage green flies. I've had to cross a gulley blackened with human excrement. It may be where the fisherman come to swim, though the water looks unclean & choppy, and nobody is in sight.

Naturally one would prefer the sweep & style of the port, to have a place among the tiny foreground figures (netmenders, women with jars, checkerplayers, coffeedrinkers) beyond whom the lagoon, its silk-pale perspective, leads to the symbolic sleeper—one would prefer that to the awful spot I'm in now. Yet here, in spite of flies, smells, nowhere comfortable to sit, I am somehow able to dwell on that other scene as never before. The region the Sleeping Woman dominates is Troezen—l'aimable Trézène, Phaedra's last home—

not that (Dora) is Orestes' stepmother, but he himself can wax articulate over the ambiguous emotions each rouses in the other.

A sudden attack of diarrhea took me to the water's edge. Instead of climbing back to my rock, or heading back to town for medicine, I went on to the next cove where the channel is narrowest & the water roughest. Here was standing some kind of absurd house, or shed, half built *into* the water, a mess of rotting boards & plaster. A truly hideous smell came from it. I thought I was dreaming: the steps, the doorless threshold, the nearby rocks, were all spattered & stained with blood. One felt it dripping from within, into the current—some of it fresh enough to have been this morning's. I gathered finally that I had found the slaughter-house. I'd never thought of islands' having slaughterhouses! There was a dog, even, yellow, filthy, cringing among remnants of God knows what. A 2nd attack of cramps kept me there, unable to move. Like blood my own excrement ran glittering down the rocks into the sea which feinted & struck back, hissing. Further out—there are meant to be no sharks in these waters—I'm sure I saw fins.

Now, back in the hotel. It is evening, a soft, sweet breeze fills my room. Chryssoula sent out for pills. They are working. But I remain grateful for what I have seen. I have been shown something that my story needs.

Years ago, in his lecture on Darwin & the Poetry of Science, Orestes made much of the chemical affinities of blood and seawater. If he, with his passion for dialectic, ever takes that walk, will he find in the slaughter-house an antithesis to the serene harbor view, or a synthesis of that view & its beholder?

Something to be concealed *by* the story, by the writing—as in *Phèdre* where the overlay of prismatic verse deflects a brutal, horrible action.

30.vi.61

The dream continues. Days have passed. I am sitting on the deck of the N.'s caïque which swooped down upon Diblos Friday like a Machine, gathered us up (L. & me) and swept us off to Epidauros where we have now sat through 2 nights of Drama with nothing but foam rubber between ourselves & antiquity. On our return to Diblos this afternoon we shall find Mrs N.'s telegrams warning us of the evacuation.

It was dazzling. The child, L.'s landlady's grandson, discovered us first, on the beach at noon. Within minutes he'd been joined by 2 of Chryssoula's children from the hotel. In unison they delivered the big news—our friends from Athens had arrived, were looking for us!—before a rapidly forming chorus of beach-boys wearing, like identical costumes, an obligation to share the news at once with their Leader. We ourselves scarcely registered what was up, before some of them were sprinting toward his shop.

We slung our clothes into towels and followed, conscious of the town's impatience. On the waterfront, Lucine stopped: we were still in bikinis, she'd been scolded once already by the Tourist Police for wearing an immodest garment off the beach. Precious moments elapsed while Adam & Eve covered their nakedness before entering His presence who had brought them together in the 1st place.

Mr N. was pacing the quai. The blue & white caïque with its linen awnings and mahogany gangplank lay creaking in its sleep beside him. He is about 60, bronzed, black-browed, silver-fringed; he had on a very elegant pale gray suit, white moccasins, a foulard at his throat. "Here you are, splendid," he hailed us. "But aren't you ready? weren't you expecting us?" Explanations; amazement; the telegraph service deplored. "No matter. My wife says we're ahead of time. Run along, put some things together & meet us at your convenience. Here or at the café—or in one of those shops"—for we had just glimpsed Mrs N. waving from the Enfant Chic's doorway. Her husband motioned her to stay where she was, incidentally sparing her L.'s fingernails & my unshaven face. We made bright signals back, then followed Mr N.'s instructions.

At the hotel (L.'s room is 5 minutes up the hill) we hesitated. It was a moment for consultation. To what end? Had we been sleeping together, we would have had to agree on how to act for the next 48 hours, to which of the numberless halftones between frankness & artifice we should try

323

to tune ourselves. How charming such moments can be! As it was, I merely said I wasn't sure I felt like going on an excursion, & did she? The question baffled her, she knitted her brows at the sky. Now that the N.'s were here, had we any choice? So it was decided. I mentioned her nails. Within the hour we had left our sparse baggage aboard & were pushing our way through the onlookers that clogged the Enfant Chic's doorway.

He had sent out for coffee. Mrs N. (sleeveless lilac dress, sandals) had drunk hers & was wielding an honest-to-goodness fan of stiff silver paper. She rose, greeted Lucine with a kiss and me with a peculiar ironic gaze that trilled above her easy manners like an oboe above a string quartet. I understood it better later. At the time, it seemed, once again, that we *ought* to have been lovers, L. & I, in order further to feel that with charming, civilized people like the N.'s no pretense to the contrary would be called for. The Enfant gave me his left hand. Our coffees were cool, we drank them on our feet. A merry rapid conversation in Greek was pursued onto the blinding whitewashed steps. Our exit causing the teenage chorus to withdraw somewhat, the E. C. had to raise his voice to show how well he knew his smart guests from Athens. One final sally from Mrs N. made him turn & cover his face with a dimpled hand. The audience broke into laughter. "Really!" Mr N. murmured, taking his wife's arm as we walked away.

Lucine: What was the joke?

Mrs N. (smiling): Nothing. Pure nonsense.

Mr N.: Nonsense indeed. My impossible wife said it had been a pleasure, an honor, to visit that gentleman's boutique, and that she fully intended to come back & spend thousands of drachmas there—only she would have to come alone, without any *men* to distract him from making a sale.

Mrs N. (with profound conviction): But you saw, he was thrilled! It made his day!

On the caïque—which is quite grand inside: fox-fur rugs on the divans, & French pictures, & a crew of 5—we changed into bathing-suits and ate lobster salad on deck. We had gotten under way.

The meaning of the look Mrs N. had given me was duly, ever so diffidently & amusedly, explained. They'd just learned from the Enfant Chic that I was Orson's brother, and were astonished. So was I. I couldn't believe that they hadn't known, that Dora's letter asking them to be nice to me had described me simply as a "young friend" of hers. Well, the kaleidoscope has turned with a vengeance.

They were now slightly on guard. I was made to feel that I should have found a way to enlighten them upon our first meeting—despite there having been other guests at lunch and the N.'s not having opened the subject.

However, here I was. Perhaps something could be learned from me.

"You see," said Mrs N. uncrossing her smooth brown legs to hand me coffee, "while we're old friends of Dora's—Akis especially, I am younger" (as if one hadn't noticed)—"we left, a week after her husband's death, for 2 years in London & Paris. I am French by birth, and Akis was an adviser to the X. Y. Z. You can imagine our amazement when letters from Athens began to pour in, telling us that she had gone to America with this man, with your brother who I'm sure must be perfectly charming (I've seen the film he worked on twice, and he was also a great friend of some people we know intimately). All I mean," very apologetically, "is that, absurd as it must sound to an American, Dora had a position here in society. Her father was an ambassador, her aunts were ladies-in-waiting to the old Queen. Her husband belonged to one of our best provincial families. Also, Dora had reached a certain age. One wouldn't have cast her in the role of Anna Karenina."

"You exaggerate," said Mr N. with a smile. "Remember, she was free to do as she liked." Then, turning to me, severely: "She worked as a governess for over a year. Did you know that?"

I nodded. He went on, speaking in a legato tenor voice lovely to hear. Things were different in America. Married women worked, enjoyed independence unheard of in Greece where no husband would permit, etc.

Mrs N. (interrupting): But you're talking as if we knew for certain that Dora had married this man. The rumor may be totally unfounded.

Mr N.: You're hopeless, Nicole. Of course they are married. She has been how long in America? Six years? Without a passport she'd have been deported after 6 months.

Mrs N.: Is it true? I'll have to marry an American if I'm to have my last wish in life?

I: What's that?

Mrs N.: My last wish is to die while playing canasta in Atlanta, Georgia, the home of Scarlett O'Hara.

Mr N.: It's too much, one can discuss nothing with you.

A pause. Mrs. N. (animated): No! I want to say that I can understand Dora. Heavens! Who doesn't want to be American today? Look what dollars are doing for this country. Suddenly we have roads, hotels—ça fait impression, vous savez.

Here Lucine, curled up with her chin in a cushion, made a remark (her own?) to the effect that, yes, America was buying Europe, country by country. The next victim was clearly Greece. L. felt lucky to have come here in time.

We discussed it a while, skimming the sapphire depths of the immense subject. The N.'s wouldn't exactly admit that Greece was being spoiled—"How can you spoil *this*?" with a sweep of the hand that took in sea & sun & the approaching heights of Mycenae—but did grant that a certain quaint charm was being sacrificed. For this we could thank the Greek Americans. They (or a faction that poured money into Greece and so had influence in high places) were responsible for the virtual disappearance of tavernas in Athens. It gave them, the G. A.'s, a bad name when other Americans saw a pair of men get up & dance together. They'd even tried to keep the bouzoukia music—to which such dances are done—off the radio, etc. Mr N. was the first to recall that Orson fitted into the category of Greek Americans, as for that matter did I, despite my appearance. "You understand, I don't speak of intellectuals," he said, as if there were other Greek-American intellectuals besides O. Well, there may be; nothing's impossible.

It strikes me as I write that this national theme could be most expressively illuminated by the story of Orestes & (Dora)—the one coming to Greece athirst for his past, unaware of how it is his coming, and that of others like him, that will in the end obliterate what he has come for; the other asking nothing better than to be changed, to take on the fancied independence & glamor of the American Woman. *Remember this.*

Mr N. said unexpectedly, "I knew your brother. In fact it was I who introduced him to Dora."

His wife stared in consternation. "Akis, it's true? You never told me so!"

Mr N. (winking at L. & me): If you say I never told you, then you must be right, because you are always right. However, you'll recall my going to Diblos overnight not long before Tasso's death. He wanted some slight changes in his will. As the boat wasn't crowded, I sat on deck. Your brother was sitting nearby, reading *Antony & Cleopatra*. I took him for a student. We talked for 2 hours. He had all kinds of lively &, to me, original ideas. Tasso, I thought, would be diverted by him. So I asked him to the house for lunch the next day. In fact I left him there when I went to catch the afternoon boat. That's all.

Mrs N.: That's all! But you're mad! Invited him to lunch? Someone Dora had never met!

Mr N.: What do you mean? I bring strangers home to lunch all the time.

Mrs N.: Watch out, from now on, that I don't marry one of them!

She brought her large blue eyes to bear, humorously, upon me. I had been wondering in what previous life I'd encountered the N.'s— or where they had found themselves. It was in the pages of Proust. Addressing each other, they shared with the Duke & Duchess of Guermantes that same ironic consciousness of an audience.

Mr N. (patiently): Do I have to explain that there was no question, during lunch, of Dora's marrying our friend's brother? They need never have seen him again.

Mrs N.: And you, did you see him again? It's fascinating, this glimpse into one's husband's life!

Mr N.: I did not see him again. Nor did I see Tasso again until 6 weeks later when we went to his funeral.

Mrs N.: I remember! He was barefoot in his coffin. There was an asphodèle in his lapel.

Mr N.: I beg your pardon, it was in his hand.

Mrs N.: I beg yours. In one hand he held his edition of Dante. The other hand was empty.

Mr N.: You see, she's always right.

I still prefer my version of Orestes' & (Dora)'s meeting. Can I use the N.'s in my book? As Lucine said when they'd gone below to take naps, "They're funny."

L. is funny enough, if less useful. I've sat beside her both nights at Epidauros. She watched the plays with a concentration I'd have thought impossible to muster out of doors. The more glorious the natural setting, the less I care for the human figure. At Epidauros it was like a ballet of fleas on a round, lamplit table. When the gods finally came, I wanted them to be 40 feet tall.

What were they doing but the *Oresteia!* A weird neo-Wagnerian prelude, tubas & strings, offstage. The actors unmasked. The watchman cries φῶs! into the afterglow (the first & virtually last intelligible word) and soon the stage is flooded with artificial dawn.

The *Agamemnon* was familiar; the two plays that followed, not. I've been reading them in a translation bought yesterday. They are very strange. For instance:

Agamemnon—a Chorus made up of old men, comically powerless. They wring hands, complain, sympathize, disapprove. Nothing more.

The Libation Bearers—a Chorus of young women. They have considerably more influence. Not that they *do* anything, yet they are able to persuade the Nurse to have Aegisthus arrive unarmed, thus ensuring his death.

The Eumenides—Chorus of Furies (Kindly Ones) which totally dominates stage & action. Orestes enters holding, instead of a sword, a leafy branch—his mind no longer adamant but diffuse, perishable, rustling in a wind none of the others can feel. The furies *possess* him. Only at the end, with the intervention of Divine Wisdom (Athena) do they become civil & courteous, marching off with their judges. Each casts two shadows, one orange, one green. Verdict: O. shall go free; the Kindly Ones shall be given shrines.

This resolution moved me. The gods alone can change turmoil to peace, hatred to love.

Orestes might reply: I refuse to believe that. The tensions within man's soul, within society, must effect the miracle.

How wrong he will be to think so!

Throughout, buzzing of insects, buzzing of time exposures. Hushed explications from the N.'s.

Lucine's attentiveness. The unfolding story must have come as a surprise. When she gathered that Orestes was going to kill his mother, she gave a short gasp, her eyes were sparkling with tears. She impressed me as belonging there, her short curls & clenched hands, uncreasable white dress knotted at the shoulder, there under the rising moon. She was in a sense far more Greek than the N.'s.

I may not see her after tonight.

A car drove us from the theatre to Nauplion where the caïque was already moored. Town jammed. 100's of torches streaming along jetties & up hillsides in honor of the drama festival. We sat at an outdoor taverna. Mr N. thought of going into the kitchen to order our food. L. accompanied him.

Mrs N. began by saying she had gone to a Swiss school with L.'s mother, that they were an "excellent" California family—"Remind me another time to ask you what that means!" They had hoped she would look out for the child this summer, which she was glad to do.

I said that Lucine's having money explained her air of poverty.

"Oh, they have money. That doesn't prejudice me against them, does it you? Who knows, our daughter may go to America one day. Stranger things have happened."

Where was her daughter now?

"With her grandmother in France. She's charming if I do say so myself. Just 16. A pity you can't meet her."

Her tone, pure Guermantes, told me she meant precisely the opposite. Having decided long ago that Orson was an adventurer bent on marrying a rich wife, but never having had occasion to wither him by saying so to his face, Mrs N. was finding it appropriate & economical— 2 birds, 1 stone—to act as if he and I were the same person.

I could have told her then that my father had money, too, even if O. preferred to be proud & poor. Instead, I wanted to know if Lucine had written to the N.'s about me.

"Tell *me* something," Mrs N. countered, giving her marvelous imitation of devouring curiosity. "How old are you?" Then: "I thought so. Along with having a nice face, you're clever for your age. If you're as young as you say, you'll remember what it was like to be still younger— to be *her* age. The age at which whoever one meets makes an impression. Her character is still being formed. It's a temptation, I admit, to add some little touch of one's own. You've added yours, in any case, from the first day."

Several things needed to be said right off. But Mr N. & Lucine were back, a waiter following with glasses & wine.

I wanted to explain about Orson—that there were differences between us, which had gone so far as to be dramatized by our present ~~coolness~~ estrangement. But Mrs N. had given me to feel that he & I stood or fell together. In her eyes at least, *he* had taken advantage of Dora's age, *I* was taking advantage of L.'s youth. Was there no age that couldn't be taken advantage of? Well, there was Mrs N.'s who would, for another 5 years if not for the rest of her life, turn everything to her own profit.

Both her implications, actually, were unjust. I would have liked to correct them.

We began talking about the plays. I said tentatively—the words were Orson's, not mine—that the Greek myths had become more & more literary, that indeed, if it hadn't been for Freud, we should have no key to their shocking power.

Mr N. observed that in Europe Freud was passé, Europe had gone beyond Freud.

"Where has it gone?" asked L., really wanting to know.

Mrs N. (breaking bread): Don't ask him that, I *think* he could tell you! I *think* it has been written down in 500 books of varying thickness which Akis will lend you, or I will—on condition that you mislay them one by one.

Her tone was infectious. Having set out to defend Orson, I made gentle fun of him instead. It was fascinating (I said) how deeply O., as both a Greek & a "modern man," longed to enter that world of myth. For instance, it had never been enough just to be on plain bad terms with his stepfather (my father). Orson wasn't happy until he could see him as Aegisthus & Mother as Clytemnestra, instead of an ordinary well-off Texas oil man (Mrs N. take note) and his Greek-born wife. By the same token Orson, in loving Dora, may have loved particularly the idea of her being "old enough to be his mother." He had been analyzed (met the Sphinx); here he was in Europe. Between the Dowager Queens of Thebes and Diblos there wasn't much to choose.

I still had hoped to show Mrs N. how little of a fortune-hunter Orson was. Her face told me I had succeeded too well; she would think of him henceforth as seriously unbalanced.

L.'s face showed something else. She's taken not my words so much as my tone of voice. Later, under the full moon, she asked what had been wrong, why I'd talked that way. "You sounded like the N.'s, making fun of everything, you know? Are you like them?" Meaning, O God, what? that I was false & superficial, that my heart was withered in my breast? No, I was not like them, I told her, & closed that fearful little mouth with a kiss.

Still at table, L. asked where Orson was now. I'd begun to think no one would, & drained my wineglass before speaking.

"I'm not sure. In New York, the last I heard."

"No," said Mr. N., "your brother is in Athens. He telephoned my office last week."

Sensation.

Mr N.: It has its pathetic side. He's under the impression that he has a claim upon Dora's property, specifically upon a small cottage behind the house, which he says she gave him. There was no legal agreement, I assure you. The cottage was never Dora's to give. Under Tasso's will, the entire property goes to Byron after her death. Your brother is asking us, nevertheless, to write to Dora, and to Byron, how shall I say? Sounding them out—

Lucine (rich girl, identifying): Even though they're married, he wouldn't be able—

Mrs N.: They are married? Still!

Mr N.: Yes of course. But we have no Code Napoléon in Greece, whereby a man is entitled to his wife's estate.

Mrs N.: It's true? You married me for love, Akis?

Mr N. (pressing her hand): You see through me like clear glass.

I: But then you've seen Orson?

Mr N.: As a friend of Dora's I thought it tactfuller to let a younger man in our office handle the case.

Mrs N.: He's not going to court!

Mr N.: Ah no. He's asking where he stands, that's all.

L. (to me): You didn't know he was in Greece? Don't you write each other?

I begged her not to worry, O. & I would find each other soon enough.

That was the time to bring up the famous letter of last year in N. Y. —I'd broken faith, was no longer the person I had been, I had "sided against him." The N.'s I don't think would have believed me, or if so, would have been further prejudiced against Orson. One doesn't *write* letters like that! One certainly doesn't try to answer them.

(In any case, O. can only just have arrived in Greece. Good Lord, it's his sabbatical again. Seven years!)

Mrs N. came oddly near the mark. "You're not close to your brother, then?"

I shrugged it off. We'd grown up apart, 15 years' difference in age, etc. "But you *became* close."

"Yes. Well, only here in Greece. At Dora's."

"So—" throwing up her hands at the devious ways of life—"you *are* Dora's friend after all! Something told me!"

"Dora told you," I said smiling.

"Perhaps you've even taken her side—brothers have been *known* to quarrel over women. Akis, tu écoutes? It's dramatic!"

(With people like the N.s, evidently, I could make light of O. But in my story he must be kept fine & serious. Which means that I must keep sprinkling my sandy heart with that view of him.)

This was our 2nd & last night. The N.'s had booked rooms in a hotel on shore, as being more comfortable than the caïque. I said goodnight on the street, I was going to walk a bit. At 1 end of town a wide white path led round tall cliffs, blue, pulverized in moonlight. L. caught up with me there. Once I'd kissed her she seemed to relax. I led her back to the hotel, my arm around her. Outside her room, kissed her again. I didn't want anything to happen.

Ouf!

I've been writing all morning, my whole body aches. The others are due back from Mycenae. Since I stayed behind, they can tell me what I missed. The plan, as of yesterday, is to sail for Diblos after lunch, pick up some clothes, & move on to other islands for a week or 2 of Pleasure. We are all so congenial, said Mrs N., it was a shame to separate. (Is she really Mme Verdurin?) Lucine is so passive, any suggestion automatically excludes an alternative. She said it sounded lovely. I said I was expecting letters which would have to decide for me. It will be NO.

Diblos. Past midnight. I've seen L. off on the caïque.

Her face in moonlight, gray & mild, as if about to ~~administer~~ receive an anesthetic.

Before that, in the empty street. Her bags packed, the N.'s already aboard. I stepped back from her, trying to reason. She'd given up her room. I couldn't take her to mine.

face in moonlight, grown transparent, a darkness bleeding through lips & eyes. The cricket's gauze-dry

"Yes I see."

I said something.

She: You don't want it to happen. You're writing your book, you don't need anything else.

I said we would meet again. Athens, America . . .

Eaten by light   silver maw

The moon had risen and drunk the water

"I thought the Greek boys weren't human beings, were animals really, thinking just of their bodies. It seemed so selfish—" Whispering.

She was right. The soul's selfishness was worse. The thirst for pattern, whether that of words on a page or stresses in the universe. The hubris that invents tragedy for the glory of undergoing it. As I saw O., Lucine saw me.

In my arms once more. Take me somewhere. I don't care. Please.

She was so young, she thought that to feel love meant that it must be returned. My heart went out to her. My flesh as well.

Neither cold nor hot, the moonlight had the flimsiness of gauze, the intensity of frost. It was a gas inhaled

Holding my hand for comfort
                inhale this gas
            made by the cricket's voice
        acting on ~~dark bl~~   indigo oxygen
                blind I go!

3 a.m. Impossible to sleep.

An opening. Orestes arrives at the Acropolis by full moon, only to have the whistle blow & the gates barred to him.

I could have sailed with them. She thought I would, up to the last.

I had taken her to some rocks above the path to the slaughterhouse.

1.vii.61

At last, the House.

I am sitting on pine-needles overlooking the smaller cove, the one we didn't bathe in. 50 yards away, the House faces across darker water to the mainland. It is, I imagine, "Othonian" in style, with balconies, an empty niche, all pleasantly run down. It has shrunken over the years, or else the surrounding trees—eucalyptus, mimosa, cypress—have grown to disproportionate height.

The "garden" was, is, paved with dirt, one of those that so often adjoins a 19th cent. plastered house. Trees, benches, marble fragments, the table, the geranium urns stand up from the flat ground like pieces of scenery. A plate on a bench. One recognizes it not from life but from productions of Chekhov. One came out of the front door onto a kind of stage apron, a squarish terrace which was in fact the roof of the cistern—can that be right? Beyond it rose the tips of small cypresses planted below; one could reach out and all but touch them. They, too, are higher now, but the flat empty space they protect still catches & holds the eyes. A 10 or 12 foot drop. Across the water: the slopes of the lemon groves, like a modern "textured" hanging done in green & yellow wools.

Most of the action took place, had to, here on the terrace. Lunch, tea. Orson at his typewriter, Dora sewing. I close my eyes to see before me that recurring rubbery dessert of cornstarch & boiled milk & sugar, concocted for me alone by D. who said it would do good. I could get through a few mouthfuls each meal; after 4 days half of it was still left, hardening, a jellyfish in sun. At the meal's end Kosta would come for instructions before taking the boat to town. Maritsa, their soiled child toddling in her wake, would clear the table, dish by dish. One by one we too rose & strolled off. Last of all, the dog Kanella (Cinnamon). An act ending in a theatre where there is no curtain.

Chryssoula had known Kosta & Maritsa; they have moved to Athens.

It is there on the ~~moonlit~~ terrace that (Dora) confronts Orestes on his return from the lemon groves. At dawn. She has sat up all night.

Entering the house: a large square hall, staircase of dark wood. A window on the landing, some clear panes, others of green or amber, making it all the harder to see the old man's paintings. We had to take them outdoors where they showed, I fear, dismally in the live radiance. Dried blues & oranges, villas, vases, women setting tables, windows onto the sea. Blossoms pressed in a History of Impressionism.

Orestes cannot understand why his brother is so touched by them— his own tastes run to Michelangelo, Grunewald, the monumental, the metaphysical. Picasso's Guernica. Have him ask, when they are alone, "Why, (Name), should Tasso's paintings move you so?"

The reply to be carefully phrased, for here we touch an essential point. "Perhaps because they *are* so slight. They will not ~~change ask~~ command anybody to change his life"—O. having quoted Rilke in the Athens museum.

(Dora gives the brother a little harbor scene as they are leaving.)

Also downstairs: the salon—furniture under sheets, a marble mantel; the library—window seats, Morris chairs, a gas heater, a Revue des Deux Mondes of 1936 with a dozen pages cut. Out in back: the well, the oven, the servants' quarters and, further off, Orestes' cottage.

His cottage. *His* rock garden. *His* private cove. How proud & happy it made him! Two whitewashed rooms paved with hexagonal terra-cotta, interspersed with square black, tiles. Rush chairs. A low, wide window. His marble *trouvaille* on the sill. The table strewn with papers, dictionaries. His life-mask, plaster painted dull red, hanging above. Two wooden beds, woven striped coverings. The pillow Mother embroidered for him—neon-pink & yellow flowers on black—which looked so sad, so cheap in Houston but was suddenly at home here

—for although she was by now thoroughly American, (Eleni's) hands still did what they had been taught to do in her childhood.

All this to be recalled in idyllic contrast to the apartment Orestes & Dora take in New York.

A name for O.'s brother: Sandy.

Look! A figure is walking out onto the terrace: no one I have ever seen. He turns round, speaks, is joined by a girl in toreador pants. Why, this will be my "Byron." He has overstayed the weekend.

He is deeply tanned, more gracefully built than the real Byron—than mine, I mean. A libertine?! And his hair is turning gray.

If Sandy ever returns to the House, he can think, "That was my youth, where it bloomed." Will he need to recall his illness?

Once the buds opened, the red blossoms kept their shape for days & days, without perceptibly maturing . . .

I am so sleepy now. Slow bright tears of gum encrust a section of ~~mauve~~ bark, brownish mauve, like

mauve-brown bark, like rouge on a negress.

As they were leaving, (Dora) gave Sandy a little oil sketch of red geraniums.

- 2.vii.61

The Enfant Chic pauses, passing the café, to welcome me back. Mrs N. he pronounces *sarmante*. I smile & nod. But Mazmaselle Lucine, where is she? Gone. Then, like a cat pouncing: And your brother? I reply without hesitation: à New-York.

Seeing the Enfant reminds me, one of his beach friends, Giorgios, practised English on me today. Where are you from? Are you married? How old are you? Why not married? What do you earn a month? What does a car cost in America? A kilo of meat? One egg? It made, I thought, for a delightful conversation. I replied as I thought best, asked my own simple questions, & that was that. Neither knowing more than 50 words of the other's language, we were soon reduced to a friendly goodbye. (Who described talk between friends as the ticking of not quite synchronized clocks on the same shelf?)

Mrs N. shares George's peasant curiosity, but oh the elaborate web she must spin to trap each new fly of fact—while G. can do no better than to thread a single strand across one's path; one sees it from far off, & arranges to trip over it just to please him.

A month after the old painter's death, Orestes revisited (Diblos). He called upon the widow in his soberest aspect, wearing neatly ironed pants & carrying a copy of his book on Euripides which she had asked to see. A preacherly note in his voice made (Dora) smile: it was for her to win *him* back to the world.

She carried the tea tray onto the terrace. They were alone. Byron had stayed a week, was now again in Athens. Orestes knew this. They had drunk a coffee together, by chance, not long before. (Byron: "The estate must be settled, you know what these things are like"—then looked at O. with sudden doubtfulness.) B. drove off in a red sports car. Orestes had thought him quite dashing & friendly.

"Yes," she said without conviction. "We've spoiled him, though. He had the makings of a scholar."

Orestes glowed. She would have liked her son to resemble him!

She has not of course offered him the cottage in a letter. She does so now:

"... come & go as you please ... a place to work ... each other's company if we want it; if not, not. I can tick on alone here quite happily."

Pitched low, her voice proceeded from high in her throat and made her words sound insincere to one who didn't know that she had had an English governess.

Orestes' voice, answering her, shook. His ~~heart~~ pulses beat hard, as after some great physical exertion—a height scaled, blue waters glittering off into haze below. At that moment he had nothing to give her but his whole heart.

He fetches clothes & books from Athens. The cottage needs a new roof. He sleeps the 1st weeks in the big house.

September comes & goes, each week drier, bluer, a season flawlessly expiring toward storms. The question of their becoming lovers never arises; or arises once, later, too late to be answered simply.

He can have asked, concerned for her: Won't the townspeople talk?

She: They'll talk whatever I do.

(A scene in which the Enfant Chic is made to feel unwelcome.)

He would have become her lover, he would have been anything she wanted. Though Orestes, before this, had only loved younger women, he

(Dora), at 56, fulfilled a classic condition. She was "old enough to be his mother." Compared, however, to Eleni—grown puffy & ill-at-ease in unbecoming clothes, dependent on the oven that "thought for her" & the TV that "saw for her"—Dora's person had become refined, stylized, a garment that would always be in style. Age could not wither her? It could, it had; but the process was gentle & dignified, as with an animal, and gave no offense.

Correspondingly:

Orestes' Latinate vocabulary (his emotions) now gave way to authentic, simple forms: sea, sky, vine, house, plate, stone, woman

: rock sea sun wine goat sky.

Each was enchanted by qualities appropriate to the other's age. What energy & imagination Orestes had! From this period dated a round table set up permanently on the terrace, the repainting of the boat (blue & white with a red-fringed awning); also, of course, the cottage itself rejuvenated, beautified, his dream come true. By spring a path that was more like a rock garden connected it with the House. O. gathered the plants on their walks. You would have thought that he had never, that nobody had ever seen a flower before. The anemone. The grape hyacinth. The orchid big as a bee. "Yes, yes," (Dora) had to keep saying, "they are beautiful, you are right!"—laughing because it was true, they were. Still, to be made to say so at every step—! He meanwhile had scrambled up an embankment, waved, recited a stanza, leapt back down into the road. She, thinking of Byron's bored, cool manners, tried to imagine them screening any such blaze of vitality.

Orestes: Do you know that I was 12 when I smelled my first rose? That I'd never been to the country—only to city parks? That's what I would call unnatural: to grow up without nature, without seeing anything else grow. The children I knew never played.

Dora: What did you do?

O.: We fought. I'm playing now, at least.

Her eyes stung. She put her arm through his.

~~He on his side~~ And among the flowers: a nest, a cuttlefish of thorns, the Medusa plant, writhing, 2 red, parted lips at the end of each tentacle. In its involuted, austere sensuality Orestes saw himself.

And she—she looks out for his comfort; it matters to her. She seems not to expect to have her presence felt—a bouquet of basil on the tray with his tea, nothing more. If he thanks or praises her in terms that approach the gratitude in his heart, her eyes widen in a half bewildered, half deprecating look: good manners shouldn't make so much of common thoughtfulness. He is her guest, does he think she means to ignore him? She does nothing well—her cooking can't touch Maritsa's, her darning is grotesque—yet whatever she does

whatever issued from her hands gave pleasure, moved O. beyond all reason. Unlike an American woman who had never outgrown

who demanded

3.vii.61

The shadows on his face, his mouth opening & shutting. The look on Dora's face when, responding to his call from the garden below—O.'s head lifted, the 2 syllables of her name uttered as instinctively as a moo or a whinney; & this instinctiveness a key not just to his joy but to his confidence in hers—she

(shall they have been lovers after all?)

appeared at her window smiling: Here I am.

4.vii.61

A flood of letters yesterday. I wrote no more in the book. One would think *friends* understood the evils of correspondence.

Bit by bit D. & O. hear each other's lives—a page apiece?

(Dora): Memories of St Petersburg. The white nights. A needlecase of green & blue enamel. From there to London. The first Greek lesson. Her great-grandfather's stone house on the waterfront of which town in Crete? The young bluestocking (a photograph at 17, long braids, plump, glowing face bent gravely over her book—Shakespeare? Rostand? She no longer remembered). The wedding trip to Paris & Italy followed by—finding it hard to believe herself—nearly 40 years without leaving Greece. Byron. His nurses. Tasso. His neurasthenia. The war. ~~The lover.~~

Orestes: Parents—the goatherd and the merchant's daughter. The emigration to New York. Old Arthur Orson. The prison of the school-yard. The father's illness. The Christmas he asks for a book & is given an orange. The traffic that night—lights flushing over the blistered ceiling like pages that turn & turn. The prize for an essay on what it means to be an American. Texas. Upstairs, the baby, the half brother, sleeps in the arms of a plush gnome.

Months had to elapse before the evening when O. sat bolt upright from his book, scalp prickling, & stared across at her in her chair, reading or sewing or whatever. He knew that if he were to ask her then & there, "Dora, Dora, what are we doing?" her reply would be promptly, reassuringly forthcoming, in that all but unaccented English of hers—"Why, my dear, we are getting through our lives!"

Save this for N. Y.?

(Or better, what M. & I arrived at, one black afternoon in Turin: "What have you wanted out of this?"

"The experience. What else should one want?")

One day Orestes, returning on foot from town, found the iron gate of (Dora)'s property ajar. He closed it behind him, as he had done on leaving, & started for the house. In the alley of oleanders he met a stranger, a small strong middle-aged man, well enough dressed. They nodded civilly. An artisan, O. sup

On a proprietary impulse Orestes turned and called after him. Had he wanted anything? "Thank you, sir," the man replied. "I've been to the house on business." An artisan, O. supposed. Nevertheless, entering the library, he asked Dora who it had been. "Oh," she said, "are you back? Will you close the door?"

That man was now (she told Orestes) the manager of some olive groves on the mainland. Thirteen years ago, in 1941, when she had taken him as a lover, he had been in the Underground. He brought her the first British fliers to be fed & sheltered. The war over, they continued to meet. Tasso? If he had known, she dared say he would have understood & kept silent. Then he died. The lover did not wait a month before approaching her. He actually came to call! She was not at home to him. He wrote her a letter, two letters. "Ought I to have been touched? Why? It meant that he had learned very little of who *I* was in all those years. When he came today I received him & told him as nicely as I could that he must not come again. It's over. He had no education, but he had a heart and he understood. Tasso old & ill was one thing. Tasso dead is another."

(For something largely surmised, this has the ring of truth. It is how she will treat O. later on.)

There was a further change in Dora's position. Not only was Tasso dead but Orestes was present. He glowed, thinking of this & of her arrogance, reasoning that, as he was not her lover, she would never use it against him.

"ruthless pride"

Today is Independence Day.

5.vii.61

Byron came regularly from Athens to see his mother. Physically vain, he took for granted that a man as plain as he found Orestes could not attract her. He told them about his love affairs & the foreign films they were missing. Once, putting a hand on Orestes' arm, he said, "You really *are* my mother's friend, aren't you?" His tone hovered between ~~wistfulness~~ scorn & a bottomless self-pity. Another time, O. remarked that (Dora) had helped him with a translation he was making. Byron shot him a look of disbelief. "But you know Greek far better than she does. Greek is her third language."

This time Dora was present.

"Yes," she said, pleased, "if I am Greek at all, I am corrupt, late Greek. Or Byzantine like my namesake Theodora."

(But Dora must be called something else.)

"Let's hope the resemblance begins & ends with the name," said Byron, then laughed uproariously.

"Byron is not a true Greek," declared Orestes after that weekend. "Even I, in America, would never dream of directing an off-color remark at my mother."

On the subject of what was & was not authentically "Greek" Orestes fancied himself an expert. A few years later, to be sure, there would be a table of Americans in every taverna of every village, loftily contradicting one another as to what went on in the Greek mind. Few of them had O.'s Greek blood or command of the language to justify their pronouncements. But though he could talk to anyone, and did—often making a dozen new friends in an evening—there was a subtler language at which he could only guess. It was that of Good Society which had no meaning for him outside of books or jokes, yet whose members—like royalty or peasants—resembled each other more than they did "Danes" or "Bostonians" or "Greeks." To the degree that (Dora) had been formed by *class*, Orestes misunderstood her; what was conventional in her manner he found unique. But so was Greece unique, and at this point he surrenders himself lovingly to paradox. Dora, less than Greek by nature, can stand all the more for Greece in his imagination. Hadn't Shakespeare, after all, taken the foreign queen & made "Egypt" out of her— the mysterious, wealthy seasons of the Nile giving substance to the metaphor? It is in landscape, too, that O. finds Dora's correlative. In the clear dry air, in the illusory lightness of islands over water.

(I am right in clinging to my opening page.)

The hot water brought for shaving has cooled as usual. 6.vii.61—a beard begun.

How to keep recent impressions from intruding? I would never have written yesterday's last paragraph, so torturous & smug, had it not been for Mrs N.'s saying that Dora "had a place in society." The phrase clung & tickled; I've had to scratch it compulsively, thus breaking the skin of my story.

On the other hand: Byron having been away in Switzerland throughout my time in Greece, I've gone ahead and sketched in the kind of mother-son thing that leaps to *my* mind. Casual, only mildly neurotic. For all I know, Dora was the revered Mediterranean mother & B. fiercely resented Orson's intrusion (seat at head of table, tone taken with servants). It's a challenge to show something more complex & interesting than either of these banal possibilities. But what?

As Orestes grew older his imagination became an ever stronger magnetic field. New experiences whizzed past his eyes to glue themselves against the cold pull of what he had already felt.

A novel. Not a fantasia.

I should have made some sort of scheme to refer to. This is my 1st *long* piece of work, & the problems it raises are new & different from those of short stories (the single mood or action). Yet I keep imagining, wrongly perhaps, that, once I arrive at the right "tone," the rest will follow. (My plot is of the simplest. The friendship, the marriage, the separation, basta. If the brother would only stop rearing his ugly head—)

In form & tone the book must derive from the conventional International Novel of the last century—full of scenery and scenes illustrating the at times comic failure of American & European manners to adjust to one another. Nothing of *Phèdre* here.

What could I have meant on p. 18? What would my story be concealing? I'd been toying with having Sandy *not* be O.'s brother—was that it? What "horrible action" is implied by the fact of kinship? Well, they have quarreled, Sandy doesn't feel warmly toward Orestes. Splendid! Haven't I only to remember the master's lesson, & dramatize the quarrel, the coldness? Anything rather than let it be glimpsed cutting fishily through the shimmer of a phrase.

Besides, in reading, isn't one most moved by precisely this refreshment of familiar relationships? The word "grandmother," thanks to Proust, will have wind in its sails for the rest of time. Why shrink from doing my best for "brother"?—or half my best for "half-brother"!

Speaking of grandmothers, what irritates me most in what I read (& write) is the whole claptrap of presumed experience. P. C.'s new book, forwarded here, describes itself as "based on his grandmother's early life in Kentucky." It is full of *her* sensations, moral beauty, prowess in the saddle, & I don't believe a word of it. Premise & method both seem false. As if one could still see to write by the dead, pocked moon of *Madame Bovary.*

Always those "he"s and "she"s scattered about like intimate pieces of clothing, when one wants nothing so much as "I"—the anonymous nudity.

Wait—

From the moment of my arrival, I

the world was transfigured for me. The language, the landscape, alike overwhelmed

both of which I had pondered, as it were, in reproduction, now overwhelmed me with their (truth) and (beauty). I was more at home than I could ever have dreamed. Like a statue

As if in a museum some figure streaked & pocked, a "Roman copy of a lost Greek original," and looked at for decades by none but anatomy students, had suddenly been discovered to *be* the original, ~~Orestes I~~

thanks, say, to little more than a ray of sun entering the honey-cells of marble, I felt my whole person cleansed and restored. My skin turned olive brown. The Latinate vocabulary to which I leaned when thinking or speaking in English gave way to authentic, simple forms: rock, sea, sun, wine, goat, sky.

That The land was poor & stony, that the modern language had been, like the wine, thinned and impregnated with resin, made no difference. I myself felt poor & pungent enough to take my place among the marble rubble, the lizards, spiny plants, clouds of dust and sparkle of salt water—all those things on which the Greek sun dotes & which are intolerable without it.

"Artemis is charming," I was able to write a month later. "She is $\frac{1}{3}$ salesgirl, $\frac{1}{3}$ student, $\frac{1}{3}$ Bacchante. Through her I am learning to know this city seen heretofore only in dreams. We walk the night streets, drink in the tavernas. She recites Sophocles, I reply with Keats & Yeats. Her parents were starved to death by the Germans. I am not in love with her, nor she with me, though we have slept together 3 or 4 times out of tenderness. How rarely one encounters this kind of understanding in America! Now I am waiting for her at a café in blinding sunlight. Oh Sandy, if I could send you the pattern cast by sun through my glass of ice water onto this page! A whole world, pure & childlike, awaits your coming . . ."

But the islands were calling me like sirens. I

Not a tone to be kept up for very long. I guess I'm not a "craftsman."

George plays soccer. His team won an island championship last year. (All or any of this may be wrong. Either he cannot spell or my pocket dictionary omits most of the words he uses.) He showed me a photograph: himself very snazzily dressed (check shirt, tight white trousers, pointed shoes) at some awarding of trophies; he is kissing the King's hand with a total fervor that has made the bystanding functionaries break into smiles.

"Kyrios Yannis," I conveyed, pointing to the Enfant Chic's shop, "has—a—photograph—of—me."

George repeated 3 syllables, nodding vigorously.

Blankness on my side.

But it only turned out to mean that he has seen the photograph. Chryssoula happened by in time to clear up that much, then went her way, nose in air—George's monde is not hers. He gazed after her with eyes erotically narrowed, little guessing that her eyes are for me alone.

I am a bad diarist not to have recorded this galloping passion I've inspired. The evening of my arrival I gave C. an immense bag of laundry all unwashed since Venice—shirts, pants, towels, in whose moist depths a half-full can of Nescafé had come open to encrust each item, ineradicably I'd have thought, with foul, sticky blackness. *The very next morning* there it lay, heaped, clean, in a basket hauled upstairs by two of her children. She must have worked all night. I asked what I owed her. A shrug. What you like. I held out 100 drachmas, keeping another 50 ready in my pocket in case she spat at it. Spat! She thrust it back into my hand. It was too much—far too much! I said these were the prices of Athens (where I'm sure double or triple would be charged). Well, she took the 100, & from that day on has stalked me with the love-juice in her eye. She is past 30 but very handsome, profile of a medal, skin white & firm, spit curls, a strong heavy body (those 6 children). She makes 50 dr. a 12-hour day at the hotel. Her husband is hospitalized in Corinth (T.B.) and sends her nothing. She no longer loves him. She loves *me*!

No day begins without its bouquet of basil or bougainvillea or both, picked by her & brought to my bedside, most often by Theodoros the blondish 9 year old. Chryssoula herself follows with tea & biscuits, perhaps a bunch of grapes abstracted from another client's room. If I haven't managed to get up, she will sit on my bed, smile, gaze, stroke my face, her hands scented by another client's perfume. "Bello, come un angelo, come il Cristo." She has teased, pouted, snarled, wept, blasphemed. The whole Mediterranean repertoire. I am training her slowly to respect my privacy. It is half a joke, of course, yet I catch myself, as now, shaking not quite with laughter as I imagine a life of marriage to Chryssoula (Father & Orson have Greek wives, why not I?) or at least the scene in the Houston airport when, stepping from the plane with her & the 6 children & the black cat, I introduce them as the greatest thing since Instant Coffee: My *N*E*W* Immediate Family—just add water & serve!

7.vii.61

Let it be the following spring, the morning after Sandy arrives in Athens. (Artemis, real as you were, hail & farewell.) The brothers will be going to the Acropolis. (O. has taken Sandy there the night before, but too late, whistles were blowing, gates were shutting.) Orestes has come down to breakfast first.

(p. 11) He was a spare, nimble man, etc. . . . at his best when talking

—so long as he didn't smile: it became a grimace, one waited for him to stop. Luckily he would soon be able to resume a conversation with his brother. They were meeting now for the first time in several years.

When O. left the room, Sandy was still in bed. He was taller than his brother, also paler, younger, too young (he was 20) to be plausibly described. ~~He had never been out of America before, and, now that he had obtained permission & a basic allowance from his father to "bum around the world" for a year, he was not to go back there for more than short visits in the 7 years to come. These years would pass as in a dream. A trip would lead to an illness, an illness to a love affair, an affair to a job, a job to another trip. Beyond a certain air of passivity & idealism, there was, that morning in Athens, no trace of the traveler Sandy would become, who avoided whatever countries he knew the language of, or whose art & landscape belonged to his own cultural heritage, preferring rather the relentlessly picturesque, twang of bouzoukia, jabber of fisher-folk~~ His head lay brown-haired & soft-skinned against the pillow. His eyes were almost certainly blue. He had on white & yellow seersucker pyjamas. Orestes had squatted by him, tousling his hair, laughing in delight, "Come on, boy! Wake up! You're in Greece!" Then, guessing that Sandy was too shy to dress in front of him, he had said he would wait at the café below their hotel, and departed, more than ever pleased with his brother.

They were born 15 years apart, of different fathers, & into different worlds. One father was Greek, an immigrant; the other an American ~~oil~~ cattleman.

The older child, born on an island off Asia Minor, christened (Yannis), renamed first (Orson) for a benefactor of his father's, and only later, by himself, Orestes—the older child had been brought as a baby to New York, to the streets, to the prison of the schoolyard, to $2^{1}/_{2}$ rooms so shabby & dark that, even when he revisited them in the glory of adulthood, their belated

(in their glory, too, that single tenement out of the block having escaped demolition) their belated, hard-earned glamor filled him with ~~self-hatred~~ despair.

The younger brother (John), or Sandy to distinguish him from his father, was born in Texas, grew up thoughtlessly in comfort and ~~love~~ love.

O. used to complain that he had no memory, & praise me for remembering so much. He meant that I remembered his life, his versions of things, ideas & tastes ("Did I say that? Really? You amaze me!") which had often ended by impressing me more deeply than they had ever done him. For instance, the theory (Freud's? but first expounded to me by O.) of the Mother- or Father-Substitute struck me like lightning. In New York Orson couldn't remember our ever having talked of it, yet I see it as coloring my entire

(Mrs N.: "The age at which whoever one meets makes an impression.")

I can no more unlearn what O. taught me than I can turn back the clock or regain the body I had 7 years ago. How to describe the change? I use my body less. If I swim at all, it is closer to the shore. Now that I know what liquor does to my liver, I drink ~~less~~ more. I don't take people as seriously. I move from place to place. I no longer think of myself as having a home. (Orson: Home is where the mind is.) I read more (alas) & (alas again) I *write*.

This notebook is one of 30 filled since that morning in Athens when O. made me a present of the 1st one. The stationery store had disappeared last month. But I found a shop very much like it; a girl very much like the 1st girl, pale, dark-eyed, wearing the same black smock, waited on me. The sale went off easily—in Athens one can buy any drug without prescription—& I carried my current notebook out into the sun.

Orestes: What, you don't keep a journal! You amaze me!

Sandy: Oh? Why?

Orestes: Every sensitive young man keeps a record of what he does & feels, writes poems, tears them up, writes others. Didn't you know that?

Sandy: I guess so. But nothing's happened to me yet.

O.: How can you tell, if you don't know what you're like inside?

S.: Anyhow, I wouldn't call myself sensitive. That's a fightin' word in Texas.

O.: It's too early to fight with me. One day you will. I know you better than you think.

S.: You certainly imagine me better than I am.

This last is too true to have been said. If I was bewitched by Orson I see now that he was even more bewitched by me. And say so without vanity. Perhaps we all know our virtues too well to value them, but I see scant evidence, in either past or present, of the marvelous ones he assigned to me (like homework, really).

Perhaps he was in love with me—he said he found me beautiful in every way. For all I know he was (is) queer, but if so, then only on a level at which pederast & pedagogue merge into one dignified eminence. He loved anyone who was willing to learn from him. Instead of making a pass and teaching my body something new (it had mastered little but a few active verbs, all quite regular) he taught me that the mind, that *my* mind, was a holy & frightening thing. Who wouldn't have believed him? I know who. The person I am today.

As soon as he knew when to expect Sandy Orestes accepted an open invitation to lecture in Athens. It mattered hugely that his brother see "what was best" in him. "You mean there's a worst, too?" It had taken some seconds to chortle out this riposte, his first clumsy step in O.'s conversational footprints.

The lecture was delivered at the British Council, a spacious, sallow, turn of the century building, which as I write they are making plans to tear down. Audience: expatriate gentility in beads; young Greek writers & their girlfriends, unsure of their English and ashamed of their un-Bohemian manners; the great poet S——; a movie actress; a sprinkling of Americans, bearded, tongue-tied—premature beatniks. Each after his fashion worshipped O.

Title: "The Tragic Dualism of Man." Today even the speaker would be unable to reproduce this extraordinary piece of rhetoric. As on a stage backed by the unrelieved black velvet of Bertrand Russell's thought & flooded by the rainbow lights of Orestes' own euphoria, his instances leapt forth clad in their classic leotards. Body & Soul, Eros & Death, Time & Eternity, the Mayfly & the Abyss. Beethoven's gaiety, his gloom, his final ambiguous affirmation. Came also Hamlet & Horatio, Dante & Beatrice, Sancho & the Don. Mann, Joyce, Sartre, Dylan

Thomas. Rembrandt & Guernica. Sandy who, for all O.'s view of him as virgin soil, had heard many of these names, had never until that evening seen anyone intoxicated by them. Orestes was. What was more, he communicated his intoxication. By the evening's end—a chorus from *The Bacchae* first in Greek, then in O.'s translation—the young faces in his audience were trembling, flashing masks of insight & purpose. And the old timers, too, had an air of agreeing that, yes, when the smoke cleared, there remained 1 or 2 arguments against total extinction of the species.

Afterwards, breathing heavily like a dancer, Orestes received their homage. He kept Sandy by his side. To those who were personal friends, perhaps ¹/₃ of the crowd, he said merely, "This is Sandy, he arrived yesterday," for them to exclaim with interest &, odd though it seemed, a kind of deference: here was the brother, so long awaited by their hero.

In retrospect, through the flattery, S.'s first sense of constriction.

Orestes' ideas.

If he believed in Earth (the life of sensation & toil) it was as others believed in Heaven or in going to church; it looked well, gave weight & dignity to a person.

Or: O. believed in his body as others did in their souls. His physical movements had the self-conscious grace of a martyr by Botticelli.

~~masochistic grace, inviting harm~~

Or: It was seemly (O. might have said) to taste & praise the joys of the flesh, to be Man at his most sensual. In this spirit he enjoyed both the olive & his idea of it. (From its oil came the light Plato wrote by.) He became surprisingly good at the popular Greek dances, skipping & dipping with zestful diffidence. He did not perspire like those dancers for whom the dance had been, more than play, a meditation, the body itself thinking, choosing, rejoicing.

· · ·

At his worktable he sits & writes. He is in heaven, it is the Platonic table he bends over, the one posited by all the cramped, gouged, unstable surfaces of his growing-up. What is he writing? No epic, not his own work, his *real* work: a mere book-review. When he has called his task "cleaning the stables" he feels better about it.

O. valued the creative act too highly to perform it.

He has told (Dora) & tells Sandy: It is my despair to have grown up without a language.

He had a hollow, radio announcer's voice, no sooner acquired than regretted, no sooner regretted than complicated by a slanginess remembered from the streets, which made his listeners wince. Yet people were swayed by him. This intermittent wrongness of tone heightened their sense of him as mouthpiece for something mysteriously *right*. An oracle.

("Americans are struggling to express themselves in a language they scarcely know."—an English novelist.)

Sandy's ideas:

(Blank minutes follow. I study the wall. Help! Then, God be praised, Chryssoula saves me. Yesterday I was brusque with her, today I gave her a full $1/2$ hour. By its end she was sitting on my lap alternately deploring my rough cheek—Why? Perchè una barba? É brutta!—and passing candies sucked pale from her mouth into mine. My legs are still numb. I have had to invent a fiancée in America, to whom I am being true, lest I wake one day to find C. toute entière beside me.)

What Sandy hasn't known is how much he means to Orestes, & always has meant. O.: "This is what I most regret about being so much older. Missing you, missing your childhood." (S. is discovering that childhood has a peculiar attraction for literary people.) O.: "But who can say? Now may be the right moment after all. Let me look at you. What a guy!"—breaking into the laughter of one puzzled by his luck.

Sandy responds—how can he help it? That they are brothers means they *have* to love each other—what else are brothers meant to do? He overlooked a slight discomfort, a slight constriction of guilt that comes, he feels, from not having prepared a place in his heart worthy of this foreknown companion. Out of good will, in a twinkling, the niche is made and, as it were, predated.

Avoid a "pattern" where S is concerned—his rejecting the love & trust of others. Let him remain gentle, full of sympathy, as if he & his author were quite different people. Aren't they? Would *he* have failed Orestes (or Lucine, or even Chryssoula)? Would he have loved Marianne who for all her charm & experience wanted only

Throughout these days O. and S. are abnormally open to each other. 1st words & gestures of magic figures shaped in darkness, or during a long spell of fasting.

~Eleni~ Houston was the single topic Orestes had resolved they would not discuss. "It is not for me to interfere with your feelings about home."

He let Sandy feel, however, that an inner necessity, quite divorced from whatever had gone on in his stepfather's house, had driven him forth into the world.

(Use table-talk, pp. 29–30.)

On state occasions, when the golden cloud

when dressed in the golden cloth of what he desired to be, Orestes could believe that an inner necessity, quite divorced . . . into the world. True, he & his stepfather were not close. ~Nevertheless~ He reminded his mother of 1000 sorrows & deprivations. And she him. During crucial years she had bent all her energies upon Americanizing herself, a process he came to scorn after it had borne fruits. Both he & Sandy were used to seeing her impulsively kissed, held at arm's length and declared, by a red-, white- or blue-haired neighbor, "just like one of us, Helen, angel, that's what you are, you cute thing!" The point is that Orestes had *not* broken with Houston. He wrote letters, sent gifts, went home a number

of years for Xmas; had been the 1st to speak the names of Homer &
Shakespeare in little Sandy's hearing. Yet it seemed always that some-
body else was doing these things, while he, Orestes,
stayed aloof in self-imposed exile. The larger-than-

Perseus
Oedipus
Odysseus
Joseph (Mann)
Hamlet
Don Q.
Shelley
Houdini

life Orestes acted not from 20 trivial motives, like
press of work or shortage of money, but from one
profound one. Why had he left home, did Sandy
wonder? Why else but that the scripture might
be fulfilled—scripture in O.'s case being the deeds
of a composite literary hero (beginning with Aga-
memnon's son & visiting like a pollen-gathering bee
Perseus, Oedipus, etc.) whose predicament in vary-
ing forms & varying levels of consciousness filled many an avant-garde
volume read by the

Characteristics of cloth-of-gold: Ugly seams. The wearer's skin
suffers.

O. wore myth day & night like an unbecoming color.

"I am Orestes, Perseus, Hamlet, Faust." And, in the piping whisper of
a child, unheard by him: "I am Pinocchio."

Ah, but it made him so happy, made the ills that befell him bearable.
~~Myth~~ Metaphor formed like ice between him & the world. Backwards,
forwards, sideways, he glided, spiraling, curvetting . . . The leaves close
in as we retreat. Their colors—reds, yellows, a mottled purple—are
those of fats & vital organs.

My God, it is sunset—where did the day go?

~~My~~ dear Mrs N.,
~~How can I ever thank you and Mr N. for tell you & Mr N. what a good
a delightful Mr N. what a really enjoyable~~ How can I possibly thank

.   .   .

Dearest Lucine

A few lines to ~~say I am thinking about you. Are you all right? I wish so much~~ wonder if you are still afloat, & where. Part of me wishes very much ~~it~~ I had sailed away with you. ~~Do you think you will ever come back?~~ Will this reach you in Athens? What is it like in summer? (You needn't tell me; I know.) Here nothing changes appreciably. A drizzle of Danes has descended. Giorgios caught an immense frowning Fish which everybody was invited to share. He wants to be remembered. So does the Enfant Sick. I guess I'm at work. ~~Am I remembered?~~ Please send me a card.

Well, those are written, plus one to Houston, sealed in last night's bottles & flung into the foaming tide. A whole day (8.vii.61) frittered away. I still feel quite awful, capable, even, of returning by fall, as promised in my letter home.

Those gallons of wine! George! Those girls—I never want to see *any* of them again. Least of all a voluble Sunflower named Inge who must already have taken 3 of the Enfant's boys into the pine trees when her whim shifted to the New World. And into me as well she sank her golden teeth. There are marks.

In writing the N.'s I felt stupid & awkward, as if I had wronged *them*, her deputy parents, rather than L.

What I want now is to sketch in the scene of the lemon groves, the panegyri, & make it express a number of things. Among them:

1) The community. The abbot. The light. Music & smells.

2) The rapport between Sandy &

3)

But not today.

9.vii.61

Or today.

. . .

This noon, leaving Inge & her friends waiting for the boat to Hydra, I did at least take the 10 minute ferry trip to the mainland & walked the mile or so out to the lemon groves. None of it familiar. Had hoped to find the clearing, the tall (pepper?) trees under which the musicians played, the stones where the fires & spits had been. Not a trace, as after a fairy feast, not even gossamer or the ring of mushrooms. Narrow earthen paths, rows of trees stretching deep on either side. Blink of perspectives—near, far, near, far—in green, dry heat as I passed.

10.vii.61

The morning of the panegyri found them bathing in the cove below Orestes' cottage.

It was in a remoter cove that O., swimming one day, had discovered, wedged among rocks, a water-worn, barnacled fragment of statuary: the upper head (brow, eye, curling locks) of a marble youth. He treasured it above all his belongings. From then on, when he swam, magic upheld him. An element in which anything was possible.

(Dora), O., Sandy, Maritsa and the baby. A palmetto sunshade had been put up. They advise Sandy to use it, but he is plunging in & out of the water, charging here & there with the dog. The brown sand is flecked with tar; soon his feet are back. He sees for the 1st time the beautiful "skeleton" of a sea-urchin, its crust of green- or rose-tinted bisque, stippled, as in formal 18th century stucco, with dotted radii diminishing in size toward a little empty place at the crest.

"Yes, but those are dead stars," said Orestes. "Look out there! Deep in their cool, luminous heaven live the real ones, revising slow, black, threatening constellations."

"What are you saying, Kyrie Oreste?" cried Maritsa, and, when he had translated it for her: "Ah! Imagine!"

"Watch out for them," said (Dora). She removed her bathing slipper

& exhibited a cluster of minute black points sealed beneath the thickened skin of her heel. "Those are from just after the war."

Sandy reached into the shade to touch the place, wonderingly. Their bodies, Dora's and Orestes', fascinated him in ways he hardly knew how to think about.

Seen objectively, Maritsa was shapelier, more sexual, her contours firm & sweet as the melon she now sliced for them. Sandy himself had fine metallic hairs on his arms and legs, he turned a lean white belly to the sun. But what was this? Mere youth. It didn't give out the ~~exotic air~~ sense of alienation between spirit & matter

the romance of accomplished individuality which reached him from (Dora) & his brother.

Orestes' thin body lay, propped on elbows, knees bent; a locust carved out of oiled walnut. His ungoggled eyes gave back the horizon. What must have happened *inside* him to cause that one white hair among the others sprouting round his nipple? The sunken places above his collarbones, the waxlike glimmer of his shins. Dora—the scant fat forming in pearls, thoughtlessly, between arm & breast, the urchin spines in her foot—a constellation in negative; a destiny no longer in the heavens, waiting, but *incorporated,* part of her. Her thighs were shelled with ~~flesh~~ an ivory browned more by age than by sun. These bodies woke no desire in Sandy, yet his imagination ran riot through scenes in which they must have participated—separately of course! —in order to achieve

yet he yearned to a degree that shocked him, to possess their memories of action & delight, so deeply incorporated now in those 2 forms rising from the sea, streaming with brilliant drops that paled to salt in the day's dry blaze.

(The sea of the Past. Lot's wife?)

The baby was still ³/₄ spirit. It flickered fatly, sweetly, a fire in their midst. Orestes would not tire of playing with it, taking it back into the water on his shoulders. A look on (Dora)'s face struck Sandy. Was it possible that, 20 years older than O., she saw in him—whose attempts at play impress S. as so much nostalgic artifice—reserves of innocent animality?

(Sharpen & reinforce this attraction she feels. The showdown is only hours away.)

A revery without end: If X. were young, if I were old. If I were young, if Y. . . .

They had stopped warning Sandy. He lay in the sun & burned.

The Panegyri.

They set out in mid-afternoon. Only Kanella remained behind, tail hopefully wagging even as they glided forth from the dock. A sheer whitish blue rippled on the water like silk. Kosta steered. Maritsa & Orestes, holding a child apiece, sang songs. From the stern, beaming like royalty, Dora & Sandy watched the gold-green shore approach.

When they landed, "We'll start ahead," said (Dora), taking Sandy's arm. They followed a narrow earthen path.

These two were gay & easy together, pleased with each other's (reality) which O.'s advance descriptions had done little to prepare them for. He still knew best, of course, knew them—didn't he? —better than they would ever know themselves or one another. Their friendship was but some slight retrograde expertise in the wider heavens of Orestes' life, from which they were to ~~guide shine down on~~ return his light.

(And time will prove him right. When O. no longer gives it meaning, their intimacy fades.)

At the festival. Continuous music, warm gusts of rosemary & fat, lambs on spits, sun-shafts turning the blue smoke to marble. It would last hours and was paced accordingly. "What we must first do," said Dora when the others had caught up, "is to pay our respects to the abbot."

This person stood black and bearded in the shade of the largest pepper tree. He offered Sandy a strong, white, soiled hand & fixed him with professionally piercing eyes, speaking all the while.

Orestes (translating): He welcomes you to Greece & wants to know your age. He won't believe you're 20, you look 16, kid. I'll tell him 18. They thought I was 25 until I grew a moustache. Ha ha!

(Somewhere else: "Ha ha!" exclaimed O. on a rising inflection, the notes exactly a fourth apart, as at the end of Manon's Gavotte.)

Tiny glasses of ouzo were served, followed by tumblers of cold water & rose-flavored jam on spoons. The entire clearing, trees, glimpses of hills and sea, took on the air of an interior (frescos, mirrors) where, in the absence of the saint whose Day it was, a man in long black robes had agreed to play host.

After further civilities the guests were released.

O. (as they moved away): He wanted to know where you were going after Greece, Sandy. I told him, back to America. He would never have believed a boy your age had money & freedom to travel so extensively.

~~Sandy: Who misrepresented my age to him in the first place?~~ Sandy nodded. At that moment he couldn't imagine leaving (Diblos), let alone arriving in Cairo, Bombay, Yokohama!

A Greek shopkeeper in Houston had given him 5 lbs. of caramels wrapped in colored papers "for the children of Greece." These now, alerted by Orestes, came up in droves to claim them, stopping, however, a courteous meter from the young foreigner.

O.: They're shy. In Greece the stranger is a god. Especially if he's blond & blue-eyed. Hey, fella, (slapping Sandy on the shoulder) you're turning rosy, too!

Each child waited gravely for his sweets &, on receiving them, broke into a slow smile.

O.: That's the smile of the kouros, the archaic smile. Pose a Greek child for a snapshot, his shoulders lift like wings, his arms stiffen at his side, and he smiles. How full of pride that smile is! It's the 1st photograph of Man taken by his new young god—before they've learned how to torment one another.

"What are you saying?" a little boy must have asked. He listened soberly to whatever O. replied. A last phrase sent them all laughing & scrambling away.

Orestes: Greek children love me because I treat them like adults.

Their fathers, meanwhile, had sent many cans of wine to the table cleared for (Dora)'s party. It was the work of the next hour to consume these, toasting the givers or whoever happened by. To eat: a cube of cheese, crust of bread, 2 olives, a segment of grilled octopus. Small plates piled up empty. They could be used later, said O., to throw at Kosta's feet, if he danced well. Kosta blushed.

They had all danced, Sandy included—connected by handkerchiefs to Maritsa & Dora, to numberless others forming a great swaying crescent. Then this simple dance would end, another kind of tune begin, a single young fisherman spin, dip, snap, leap his way through it, eyes always on the earth; or an older dancer, closer to earth in another sense, allude

execute slow allusions to the passion & agility he no longer commanded.

Presently Sandy was able to watch with—and Dora without—astonishment his brother & Kosta alone in the dancing place. ~~Circling one another~~ ~~H~~hissing like serpents, Kosta wriggling his powerful shoulders rapidly, seductively in parody of a belly dancer (fat, clown-white, a dream of beauty to any man present), they circled one another until, suddenly, on an emphatic beat

The very hissing is sexual—ssss! It's of course the consonant missing from a married woman's name (put in the genitive: Mr Pappas, Mrs Pappa, etc.) and so commends itself to the dancer as a tiny linguistic feature related to moustache & phallus, one more fine feather of virility—

beat, Kosta jumped & landed not on the ground but in midair, with legs wrapped about O.'s waist, head fallen back, shoulders still undulating. The two pairs of arms outstretched, the 2 moustached heads oppositely inclined—something was there of Narcissus & his image, something of the Jack of Clubs. Then they sprang apart, to revolve separately, barely smiling, until the piece ended.

"Come now," said Orestes to his brother, later, after a fresh can of wine had been drunk. "You and I this time."

The state of high spirits known as kéfi had descended upon their table. (Dora) at whom Sandy had looked questioningly, merely laughed & said, "Of course!"

Already the instruments were wrangling happily together. Sandy contented himself with repeating, most gracefully, he thought, the basic steps Orestes indicated—forward, sideways, snap your fingers—while the latter went on to dip, whirl, touch earth, strike shoe with palm, resoundingly, rise, dip again, & abruptly, facing Sandy, whisper *Now*.

"I'm too heavy, I'll knock you over."

"Don't worry, come on, boy!"

He places his hands on O.'s shoulders. "Hup!" cries Orestes, and S., with a last desparing look at the world, springs upwards & backwards to lock his thighs around his partner's waist. The rest of him has fallen free, head inches from the ground, arms trailing. Upside down, trees, tables, (Dora), the colored wool embroidery of her bag, everything exuberantly revolves. O.'s face grins down: the look of the initiator. Now Sandy remembers to snap his fingers. O. hisses lightly, provocatively. It ends all too soon. "Up!" cried Orestes & their uncouplement is effected to applause. S. lurches backwards, sustained by the music's beat, by nothing else. His dizziness has hardly passed before O. confronts him—"Ready? Now brace yourself. Hup!"—and in a flash the whole staggering weight of another body has become *his*. But he's mad, S. thinks, I can't hold him up! as they go reeling towards a group of tables and Orestes, blissful & trusting, smiles up at him. I cannot. Sandy has opened his mouth to cry—the blood pounding beneath his sunburn—he cannot—yet within seconds it appears that he can; he can, he can. Power & joy fill him. His eyes fill. He can dance under his brother's weight. Then it is over, & the music, too.

"Bravo," said Dora, welcoming them back. "You're going to make an excellent Greek, Sandy."

It had earned them *lots* more wine.

An hour later (Dora) looked at Sandy more closely. "I think we shall have to take you home."

"Ah, no!" from Orestes. It was a *good* panegyri; Sandy must be allowed to see it all—look, they were carving the lamb at last!

S. (earnestly): I'm not drunk, you know.

Dora: No, but you are bright red. Look at him, Orestes, he's badly burned.

O.: Ah, it's too bad, etc. The upshot (to be written?) is that Kosta takes his family, Dora & Sandy back to the House, then returns to bring Orestes home when the panegyri has run its course.

Sandy feels nothing, notices nothing. The wine has numbed him. He is put to bed.

(Make the dancing less euphoric?)

Just before dawn something woke him. The gray light barely tinged his sheets. Burning all over, head throbbing, Sandy got up to peer into the front room. Orestes' bed had not been slept in. Nor was he to be found lying facedown among the cactuses outside his door. No one was anywhere. Had there been a sound? a voice? It came to S. that if he were to walk down those steps, under those eucalyptuses at every moment more visible, & reach that last tree at its point parallel to the façade of the House, he would see—What? He hardly knows; he would simply *see*.

He walks there. He does see.

First he has met, on his way, Kosta in great good humor, making for his quarters—"Ah, Kyrie Sandy," and touches the sunburn inquiringly, laughing, nodding.

Then the dog Kanella, tail not wagging, puzzled at the edge of the terrace.

20 yards distant stands Orestes. He has been out all night. Sober as stone, he is nonetheless hesitant, blinking, off guard, as if having just gained this level & found it unfamiliar. Between him & the House (Dora) has appeared, in her nightgown and dark blue flannel robe. At the sight of it, Sandy's teeth begin to chatter. Neither sees *him*. Her feet are bare, her hair unkempt. O. breaks the silence, but in Greek.

"The servants," she whispers, warning him.

The air grows a shade paler. It dawns on the audience that she has had no sleep. Her whole body shakes once. She asks where Orestes has been.

He replies. It sounds harmless, plausible. A night of drink, of talk—anything. A few hours sleep at——'s house. *Kosta* hadn't felt like leaving.

"My dear," she said with a light, hysterical laugh. "You're lying to me. Don't."

A very long pause. She turned her clenched face from him, savagely.

"Dora, I never dreamed," said Orestes.

"Nor I," she sobbed. "Help me. Oh my friend. It came too suddenly. I couldn't control. Do you understand. It's not what I."

He goes to her now, draws her hands down from her face, saying her name. She stares: half panic, half outrage. "Go to bed, Orestes."

He will not. She has asked for his help.

~~She throws herself into his arms.~~

~~She gave him a look from which reasonableness had been scrupulously withdrawn and threw herself~~

"Go, go," she sighed. "I'm all right. Go to bed."

Sandy, from behind his tree, obeyed her. Back to the cottage he sped, unseen, bone-cold, with clacking teeth.

In 5 minutes he hears O. come in, say his name &, when he doesn't answer, fall on the bed in the front room.

The day was brighter when Orestes spoke again. "Are you awake, Sandy? Do you feel better? Shall I fetch you a glass of water?"

Now S. lets O. tell what has happened. Orestes is, as usual "amazed," "profoundly disturbed," wonders if he will be able to "cope" with (Dora) —it will be for *him*, naturally, to take charge of the situation.

"Shall I pretend it never happened? Or try to help Dora accept & overcome her feelings?"

Orestes often borrowed this rhetorical device from Greek tragedy. Never "How did you come here?" but "Did you walk today? Or take your bicycle?" So that to answer him (unless one can say *I swam* or *I flew*) one must admit that he has foreseen, in his wisdom, every alternative.

The alternative here—the unforeseen one—would be to return the love.

(Dora's more "Byzantine" device: "I suppose, in this heat, you came by boat . . . ?")

Anyhow, he talks & talks. The prison of words. S. may fall back to sleep in the midst of it—as I am about to do, myself, this hot, hot afternoon.

It *is* a crucial scene. How it was actually resolved I must try to remember. ~~From then on~~

Outdoors, alone.

The setting sun. A clear golden

From the horizon a golden-pink light flows. When I lower my eyes it is to see water breaking on a rock a yard or two below my bare feet. The waves are small, their bravura limitless. One could name

(Sandy, feverish) tried to name their different movements: the ~~swirl~~ pirouette, the recoil, the beat missed on purpose, the upward hurl of white nets, the pounce, the pause for reflection; but no two were ever accomplished with quite the same

Use this to complement description on p. 17

motive or, for that matter, success. Again & again an ornate sequence would inexplicably break down; the sea would shrug, collapse, retire into a slot, a coulisse prudently hollowed out of rock beforehand. For an instant the stage would be empty; one felt a sad kinship with the effaced gesture. Then a new star

a crash of harps! A new, staggeringly assured star, all mist & fretted crystal, had leapt and "frozen"—like only the greatest dancers, a second longer than anyone would have thought possible, in the tense, vivid air.

His feet alone gave scale to the spectacle. He tried to keep them in sight.

The play of water: a fou rire that goes on & on. Successions of rapid, fluid shocks, unending variations, each as simple, each as elaborate, as the last. It bears no message.

It wrote a message in invisible ink, not to be read for 1000's of years, upon the worn, slotted surface of the rock.

12.vii.61

He felt (Dora)'s hand on his forehead. "I came out to see how you were. You looked feverish at lunch."

She sat down beside him. He gazed avidly into her face for signs of ~~unhappiness~~ her own fever. None showed.

"Kosta is bringing some bismuth from town. If you're no better tomorrow we'll have the doctor."

"I'll be all right. I'm all right now," said Sandy. It was what he said & said during the fortnight that followed. There were days, furthermore, when D. & O., occupied by their own dilemma, gave every appearance of believing him. They never told him to stay in bed. He was free to wander about, thinner & weaker daily, as if he were not a child. The doctor materialized. When the bottle of medicine had been emptied, no one suggested that it be refilled. Sandy would rise from lunch, having eaten some soup & 2 spoonfuls of Dora's cornstarch confection which reappeared, larger & sturdier it seemed, from meal to meal. He would totter down to the water's edge with his book & his blanket, there to remain until one of them came for him.

Orestes, he supposed, kept him informed of the unfolding drama. What (Dora) had said, what he in turn had replied. Somehow, by the time Sandy left the hospital—they have stayed on in Athens to be near him—it was all resolved. Her great wave of feeling had spent itself.

Psychologically (O. explains) it was to have been expected. A final sexual upsurge that had little to do with him personally. As he, rather than another, happened to be her guest, he had borne the brunt of it. Patiently, reasonably, he now faced with her all the contributing motives—the delayed shock of widowhood, the sense that this had not brought Byron closer to her. She ended by seeming to accept his interpretations gratefully. She would keep Orestes as her dearest friend.

(In fact she is going to America with him.)

"You see," said O. gravely, "Dora means too much to me now, for me to risk the ambiguities, the tensions of a sexual relationship. She sees it, she agrees with me. We're more than ever in perfect accord, having lived through those anxious weeks together."

Something of the sort, put into talk or not, gets through to Sandy. In his mind Orestes & Dora perform a final somersault: they have chosen imagination, withstood the coarse quicksand of the senses. Platonic love! S. lies back on his pillow, impressed.

(Dora, 5 years later, in her narrow N. Y. flat, studying Chinese. She has aged, seems paler & softer, from spending less time out of doors, perhaps. Her brush, her inkstone. "This is the ideogram of power, this of language, this of island." She & Sandy spend a sweet, elegiac hour together; he is going abroad, who knows if they will meet again? Is he going to Greece? She would like to give him some letters. Speaking of Orestes, as of a character in a novel, she says, "He was Greek, yes, but with the glaze of a Turk.") (It's after hearing—from me—of this visit that O. writes his letter full of hurt withdrawal: Dora's charm had "blinded" me; I was no longer the serious, child-like, brother-loving etc. . . . . It strikes me now that behind these words lay his dismay over my not having sought to bring him & Dora together again. "Love is not merely feeling, but action," he wrote. A dreamer to the last.)

Wait—

One conversation he did remember, from his 1st week in the hospital. The doctors had yet to determine what the matter was. Orestes stuck his daily bouquet in water & seated himself. To cheer S. up, he remarked what a lucky guy he was to be able to afford a private room—all O.'s experiences of hospitals had been wards full of moaning & dying. Well, Sandy was just a gilded youth.

S.: I still don't feel I'm really sick. It doesn't seem possible to *be* sick in Europe.

O.: Oh? Were you often sick at home?

S.: Oh, you know—measles, colds, a sprained ankle. I'd stay in bed and let Mother bring me soup & orangeade.

O.: You enjoyed being sick at home, is that what you mean?

S.: Well, I guess so—compared to *this* place. Did I say something wrong?

O.: Wrong? Of course not. But my dear Sandy, you understand what you *are* saying, don't you?

S. (after thinking): That I'm sick now because I want to go home?

Delighted by his pupil, Orestes develops the theme handsomely. Tuberculosis is the 19th cent. disease—smog of conventions, lungs failing for lack of a purer, fresher air. Asthma. Then comes cancer—20th cent. disease: gnawing of GUILT. Homesickness would naturally express itself by upset tummy & bowels.

Sandy (recapitulating): So I'm not really sick at all?

O.: Of course you are. I never said that.

S.: But only in my mind?

Orestes reassures him; there can be more talk. It is a subtle point, though, & he may never fully grasp it. More & more he ~~is like the oyster who can't feel the grit for the pearl~~ loses faith in phenomena uncolored by the imagination's powerful dyes.

Some days pass. Sandy turns vivid yellow to the very eyeballs, thus facilitating a diagnosis. "What did I say?" joked Orestes, after expressing concern.

"That I wasn't sick."

"No—that you were a gilded youth!"

. . .

July. Sandy leaves the hospital. His father has cabled him to fly home; out of question to proceed, as planned, to Egypt & the Orient. At first S. means to ignore it, to travel by freighter, working his way if need be. As he has known no hardship, the prospect intoxicates. Also, he has gathered from Orestes that sons must *rebel* against their fathers. O., however, is shocked. Learned doctors have prescribed rest & proper food; a diet of amoebas & ghee would be "suicidal." They compromise. Sandy will travel through Italy & France with his brother & (Dora), & sail for New York when they do. This pleases everybody.

Dora's house in Athens. Rents frozen since the war, no income from it. She worries about having money in America. She decides to sell

She decided finally to travel wrapped, as it were, like Cleopatra, in one very fine Oriental rug which, sold, would keep her for the rest of her stay. She wanted not to be a burden to Orestes.

It relieved them both that Sandy was to travel with them. While he was in the hospital, (Dora) & Orestes had begun to miss the company of a 3rd person. By themselves, their talk broke out at strange levels, painfully, as if a device to regulate pressure had been damaged. ("Dora, you went ahead and sold that mirror! Ah, that makes me very cross with you." Or: "I think I'll plan to stay on in Paris with my friends there. *You* go to N. Y.; I'm too old for the New World.")

In saying that their crisis was over, Orestes was mostly correct. Certainly it would never be repeated. But what neither took into account— fancying themselves too civilized, too enlightened—was the sediment of shame & resentment on her side, and on his a blitheness left over from having been found desirable by a woman he ~~idolized~~

a blitheness that emerged as the issues receded. One never minds having been found desirable.

With this one secret of Dora's captured & tamed, O. assumed wrongly that it had no jealous mate. It did, though—a 2nd secret that circled round them both for some time, unperceived. It was that Dora disliked him.

During these last weeks in & out of Athens Orestes met the Holly-wood producer: a Greek American, like himself, sitting at the next table in a café. They fell into

(This will be a strand running throughout the book—O.'s relations with Greek intellectuals, as gleaned here & there over the years. On 1st arriving he naturally seeks them out—men of letters, painters, etc. There is great warmth on both sides. They have felt, what with the war, extremely isolated. O. sets about correcting this state of affairs. He col-lects their books with a view to translating them, placing stories & poems in American magazines. Before leaving Athens he persuades 2 or 3 painters to ship some of their best work to him in N. Y. where he will arrange for it to be shown. And he does what he has promised. In time there is an exhibition, the stories & poems do get published. What goes wrong? Well, the pictures don't sell; the magazines are small, ephemeral, do not pay. Shipping costs actually cause the artists to lose money. Cer-tain British philhellenes, perhaps more out of spite than taste, have things to say about the quality of O.'s translations. None of it, really, is his fault. He has done his best. But several years will have to elapse before Greece is chic, & it will take a more persuasive figure than Orestes to make it so—Mrs Kennedy, for instance, or Melina Mercouri. In any case, he returns to find this chill on the part of men who had once clasped him to their hearts. Those who remain loyal aren't the most distinguished. With one exception. The poet & novelist V— who with his English wife found O. brilliant & charming from the 1st, & never revise their opinion. Voici pourquoi. Along with his immense, mystical odes, at once symbolic and "folkloristic," V. was the author of an historical novel, a picaresque 19th cent. version of the *Agamemnon* in which the hero, back from a campaign against the Turks, is murdered by his wife & her lover, then avenged by his children. In this book, admired by every imaginable reader, Orestes saw the makings of an excellent film. He suggested it over coffee to the Hollywood producer, the latter took fire, read the novel & asked O. to do the screenplay, giving him a contract to sign the day before he & Dora leave Greece. Poor O.! If he had paid his usual attention to myth, he would have known that Hollywood destroys the artist. The process takes years: private planes, costly dinners, conferences leading nowhere. At the end his script is discarded, but the film made. It can still be seen in Greece. O. is left with the taste of ashes in his mouth, and V., left rich & famous, will not hear a word against O.)

Oh dear, I've met Byron.

I broke off & went swimming. Then, from the café, watched the boat from Athens come in & him get off, and thought no more of it until, looking up 20 minutes later, there he was returning along the waterfront, with packages, & talking to of all people the Enfant Chic. The latter smiled venomously at me (George had joined me on the beach, refusing to budge when the E. C. called him) & said something to Byron out of the corner of his mouth. B. looked, stopped, abandoned the Enfant, came over to my table.

"I know who you are. My mother's so fond of you. I'm Byron. Will you let me give you another ouzo? I'm afraid I've been remiss about doing the honors of Diblos."

He is very handsome, very much a man. Slender, well-preserved for over 40 (just Orson's age?). Beautiful hands, knuckles & wrists, tanned, manicured. A flat gold watch, a blood-red seal-ring he removed to show me. "It's a good one, isn't it? Actually it was my mother's engagement gift to my father."

He wanted to know where I was staying, where I ate, whom I knew. An anecdote at the expense of the N.'s. But I *was* comfortable, & *liked* Diblos? Good! His relief just skirted megalomania: the island was his, it had better be run properly.

About Orson:

"How's your brother? He's in Athens, I've heard. Will he be joining you here? I see. Well, it's of no importance. He'd left some books & things on the place, but there couldn't be less rush, he can pick them up any weekend. Tell me, what's he done since that film? Published lots of things? Brilliant chap. The talks we used to have!"

I gather B. & his wife are separated. "I usually bring a girl along. The house is conveniently inconvenient. No, this weekend I'm a bachelor, brought reports to read instead. In fact I'll be off now, I've a putt-putt waiting. Look, come for a drink tomorrow— sixish? Splendid. Cheerio."

Well, Orson doesn't get his cottage, I'm afraid.

B. bubbles over with charm & good will. What a disappointment! My own (Bryon) I'd seen more as the type of heavy, petulant, weak young man so often found in the wake of a powerful mother (Frau Doktor & son in Tangier). *My* Byron would greedily have examined those "books & things" of O.'s, hoping for something to use against him.

(A scene—the Enfant Chic present. The photograph is shaken out of a book. *Yes.*)

Or is the real Byron, in the last analysis, weak? For all his charm, a point keeps recurring when every woman—mistress, wife, mother—rises & tiptoes out of his life, as from the living room of an irksome host, to tear her hair & ask the mirror in the guest john "*How* will I ever get through this evening (or marriage or whatever)?" Doesn't he feel this? And what need has he to be so British in Greece? The vogue nowadays is for Americans & Scandinavians. (This last after 2 more ouzos.)

13.vii.61

A package has come for me but no one can find it, Chryssoula is at home, unwell. The pyjama'd manager says it has gone back to the P. O. which is shut now, as of noon. And tomorrow's Sunday—Bastille Day. Seeing my face, he cries placatingly, "That's all right!"

One last scene in Athens. The Hat on the Acropolis.

(The contract is signed, they sail that evening, Orestes decides he needs a hat.)

Sandy: I thought you didn't like hats.

Dora: We're leaving the worst heat behind us.

Orestes: Won't they be wearing hats in Rome & Paris?

D.: In midsummer! Do they in New York?

O. (laughing): Don't they? They do in all the ads.

S.: Well, you're the one who lives there.

Orestes: Ah, Sandy, I've become so Greek. I think of America as a country known through ~~film~~ movies & magazines, where the sidewalks are made of gold.

They entered the shop. Orestes made his wishes known to the clerk who brought out hat after hat for him to try on. Dora & Sandy exchanged glances. A long time passed before O. said, "I think this one will be suitable."

It was an expensive "young executive" model—gray green felt, snap brim, ribbon, feather, the works. On hearing that it was a Borsalino, imported from Italy, & that while he waited the shop would stamp his initials in gold on the inner leather band, Orestes' joy knew no bounds.

His companions hardly knew where to begin.

Sandy: You look like a businessman.

Dora: It's not a hat for warm weather. You'll have a stroke!

S.: Is that feather real?

Dora: For summer, a straw hat—

S.: We'll be in Italy tomorrow. You can buy a Borsalino there, probably at half the price.

D.: Tasso used to wear a gondolier's hat, it was always cool & becoming. This looks like the Greek-American dream.

But no. Orestes wanted this hat, and at once. He *was* a G. A.; such a hat *was* his dream. "You are sophisticated," he informed them, "but I am more sophisticated than you. I choose this hat precisely because to wear it means that I've arrived."

"Arrived where?" cried his ~~friends~~ tormentors.

O. kept laughing. "It means you're rich, respected, a big shot. Do you want me to go to Hollywood bareheaded? My taste may be bad, but this isn't a question of taste. I could never have *had* this hat a month ago. Now I deserve it."

It was an odd moment. Both sides were, & were not, in agreement. The subject was dropped and never ostensibly

only to be resumed at a higher level.

Orestes wore his hat out onto the street. "Shall we walk up to the Acropolis? Will that tire you, Sandy? We ought to make a ceremony of our last day."

(No one is seeing them off. Dora has been purposely vague about this, well, elopement. From her point of view it's all to the good that Byron has been in Switzerland these past months—let his wife be ~~pregnant difficult~~ in a clinic, something glandular. O. has been more precise. A group of *his* friends, students, very motley, turn up at the sailing, with gifts. Disturbing Dora not at all. These young people will never have entrée to her world.)

"Everything depends," said Orestes cheerfully, "on the spirit in which one enters the arena. It's a game." He was speaking of Hollywood. "I can stop playing when I choose. And I'll be left financially able to do my real work, the work that demands my total dedication."

~~They nodded, swayed by the old refrain.~~

They paused to admire the Tower of the Winds, then climbed a narrow street of pretty houses in disrepair.

"This may have vanished when we return," said (Dora). "The Americans want to dig here."

"How terrible," said Sandy.

D.: When you think that it's Byron's Athens, after all, this district . . .

Orestes: Byron's?

D.: The poet.

O.: Ah. Because I thought you meant *Byron*. Dora's son, whom you haven't met, is named Byron, Sandy.

S. nods.

O.: Well, let them dig. There may be treasures under these old houses.

D.: But the houses are so pretty!

O.: My dear Dora, prettiness can't compare in ultimate value with a head—with an *elbow*—by Phidias. I don't say they'll find one, but more power to them for looking.

(Mention his underwater fragment?)

Dora: Ah, we shall never lack for masterpieces. We take care of them. It's prettiness we're forever sacrificing, sweeping away.

(To be felt in the foregoing: O.'s own past is the issue. A dream of poverty & rubbish swept away to reveal the meaningful plan of temple or market underneath.)

They arrive at the Acropolis, pass through the Propylea onto the blind, bald marble hill. Orestes makes for the Parthenon. Midway he pauses. Runnels of dampness the hot wind would otherwise have dried leak from inside his new purchase.

His eyes also are moist.

He has told them before, he tells them again: his first glimpse of this building, while driving that long straight road from the Piraeus to Athens. Constantly in sight, squat at 1st, more & more elevated as they neared it, stood this Thing, golden

honeycolored, ~~fingered by light~~

a lyre the sun fingered. How dispassionately he had eyed it, not recognizing his oldest dream until, with a cry, just as it vanished from his range of vision, he fell forward onto the taxi's floor. It had been the Parthenon!

They admire it with him.

Sandy (after a bit): And that smaller building over there? I forget its name.

D. (who has draped her whole head in a chiffon scarf, Pernod-yellow, fluttering tightly like a flag): That's the Erectheum. The one *I* love.

O.: I should think that you would love it, Dora. It is a feminine building, all elegance & charm. And of course (laughing) that magnificent balcony—you know what balconies on buildings mean, according to Freud! Even in French, am I right? la balcon has become a euphemism for female charms.

~~Sandy: And what are "female charms" a euphemism for?~~
~~O.: Touché.~~
(Dora): (Something about its original use. A holy place.)
S. (reading the Blue Guide): The Turks used it for a harem.
Orestes: You see!

14.vii..61

What I want, here at what could be an organ point in the book, is this "Dialogue on the Acropolis" in which, starting from a difference in taste (the hat), Orestes' & Dora's two ways of being, their as it were moral differences, are set forth. To keep, if possible, the 2 buildings as symbols.

Dora	Orestes
Erectheum	Parthenon
Monet	Michelangelo
Rameau (Schumann)	Beethoven
Racine	Shakespeare
Herbs	Flowers
The Subtle	The ~~Monumental~~ Sublime

The temples themselves:

The famous one, noble, simple (deceptively so, O. will insist) rises in sunlight, marvelous for its bigness, its openness: a sire, a seer. The father in a novel about a happy childhood.

The other by comparison seems dangerously complex & arbitrary
Japanese   a small-boned woman
a dressing-table at which somebody has assembled the various ele-

ments—powder, eye-shadow, a pleated ~~robe~~ teagown—of a "je ne sais quoi" & vanished, for no more than a moment, surely, into another room.

Orestes: One lives for the sake of one's tragic insights.

(Dora): If that is true, one still has access to them at one's dressing table—more often than at one's prie-dieu.

O. (magnanimous): Let us say that as *symbols* these 2 temples have equal power, but that the states they symbolize do not.

~~Dora (amused): You are more human than I am, is that it?~~

Heavens, am I going to have to *read* Hegel & Marx?

Both buildings are badly flawed. Yet, between them, they represent, with a purity & clarity far from mortal,* the two modes of being. The moon, the sun; the earth, the soul; the wife, the god. What other site in the world so quickens & cleanses the heart? (The *blackness* of Chartres.)

The sun & moon together in the sky.

Still, after a while, prompted by the blurred clamor from below, if not by the voices of those who like oneself have climbed this high & seen fit to describe the experience to one another, it was to the parapet one went, to see what one had left behind. There, below, lay the city, smoking, sparkling. Poverty. Urgency. Cats patrolling the rooftiles, boys playing soccer, women with burdens. Men in pyjamas at 4 p.m. Further off: one's hotel, the house of a friend, the restaurant at which, months earlier, one had become involved in an ugly scene; the bank, the hat shop; the swimming pool; the gardens with peacock & papyrus

---

*far from mortal—here's my mistake. My Dialogue pits 2 dreams against each other, instead of living antagonists. Life, Art—they are words. It's on a lower level that the mongoose closes with the cobra. In a footnote. In the dust.

& the sparse fright-wigs of the papyrus round a pool on whose cement bottom a honeycomb pattern of sun will be trembling; a duck's bamboo bill

A gust of wind lifts Orestes' hat, which has been resting on the parapet, and drops it into ~~the city~~ the cactuses beneath.

He won't reclaim it. To Dora & Sandy: "The gods are on your side."

| They sail that night. | (A hue & cry at customs. The marble half-head found by O. is 1st confiscated then declared ~~a fake~~ worthless, & courteously returned.) |

George keeps sitting with me on the beach. Now that we've shared the fly-by-night Danish beauty, he has decided we are friends. I cannot plumb the mysterious shallows of his nature. Setting out to please, he nevertheless sees no way of doing so except through his mere presence, the offer of 1 initial cigarette & subsequent acceptance of 5. As he rises to leave, a drop of soft soap: "You good man."

I had never asked if he remembered Orson or Dora. He might (aged 12) have received candy from me at the panegyri. Had he? He looked doubtful. I wasn't communicating. Kosta & Maritsa, oh yes, them he had known; they were now in Athens. As for O.—

"The brother you," said George, "no good man."

"Oh? *Why?*" (A word I now use all the time, mimicking G. It is our little joke.)

"Kyrios Yannis (the E. C.) speak no good."

"Kyrios Yannis is wrong." I showed him *wrong* in my dictionary.

George snickered. "Kyrios Yannis is ——. (A word I forget & would not have understood out of context.)

He is a bundle of prejudice. I gathered yesterday that he has no use for Chryssoula. Why? Because she is not a Dibliotissa, but from depraved Rhodes. (C. calls *him* uno teddy-boy, he might care to know.)

We talked a lot about girls. Unmarried Greek girls do not go All The Way. George confessed that Inge was his 2nd *real* experience.

"Only the second?" I looked surprised. *"Why?"*

"Never mind," he grinned. "I am Greek." (!!)

Another hot day. The hollows of the miniature waves were black. They slid onto the beach with the sound of water drops striking a red-hot skillet.

I didn't go to Byron's yesterday. We would have talked about O., I could feel it in my bones—or in my blood which by now is only a bare degree thicker than water. It is not thicker than ouzo; my tongue would have wagged disloyally. Disloyalty partly to Orson (where can he be?); mainly to Orestes, who gasps in these pages.

The modern Greek language can be said to have suffered a stroke. Vowels, the full *oi*'s & *ei*'s of classical days, have been
Dora's   eclipsed to a waning, whining *ee*. Obsessive jumbling of
amnesia   consonants in the dark. Speech of a brilliant, impaired mind. A crime committed in the name of Grimm's Law.

15.vii.61

The boat, white, graceful, is floated not in water but some insubstantial rather in an ultraviolet light against a background of heavy black & gold-green cliffs, ferned ledges for birds to nest on. A real place?

There shall be no more travel, only the Voyage. Is that the message? Voyage (as if derived from *voir*): a Seeing.

The boat at least *is* real. It is the N.'s caïque, a watercolor of it by Lucine which I claimed today at the postoffice. Postmarked illegibly. Am I to guess that she can be found aboard, that stroke of orange against the railing?

It is the voyage not made. The boat missed.

I could *be* a castaway, with my 9-day beard & faded shirt. Shall I be discovered at the water's edge, shirt tied to the oar I brandish, croaking in a half forgotten tongue: I'm here! Rescue me!

Or later, telling the tale: I was seven lean years on that island. With only a ~~notebook~~ parrot for company.

By the time they reach Paris, Sandy is sick again. They take ~~me~~ him to the American Hospital. The doctor assures them that diet & rest will do the trick. No need for alarm, or for O. & D. to stay. They can't afford to, at any rate. O. must resume teaching in September. Sandy promises to follow. If they had waited for him—But life became easy, opened out in strange directions he was too young, too curious not to investigate. He meets (Marianne). The letters from Houston ignored. Now he is through college, if he goes home he will only be taken into the Army. All this 7 years ago next month. It is 1 ½ years before he returns to America & then not for long. Marianne has found him a job as tutor to her little nephews.

As this isn't Sandy's story, I could take out his jaundice altogether when I start to write. Let him vanish into the Orient as planned, while Orestes & Dora proceed from Italy to Paris—making in reverse my final trip with M. (All in that winter's notebooks). The 2 situations much alike—younger man, older woman; monuments, arguments, a love out-lived.

Or did the jaundice mix its yellow with the blue of those far-off
slopes   rustling of new green
Unless that youthful jaundice
indispensable ~~yellow~~ primary color added to the blues of those lost
days, turning them
The savage beak & idiot green wings
Full of my words, the notebook flapped its pages—

24.vii.61
I woke in the small hours, a sharp weight on my chest. It was Chrys-
soula's cat, motors purring, claws kneading me through the sheet. I
guessed rather than saw the dilated shining eyes fixed upon me. Instead
of chasing it away, though, I began mumbling gently in response—
"Good kitty, proud, loyal, generous Cat" —generous!—& other non-
sense words until my eyes filled with tears to think that only then, in the
middle of the night, rinsed by sleep and with only an animal for com-
pany, could I discover words of love. I stroked the strange, cool fur.
Good, proud, loyal, who was I addressing if not this loving self of mine
that had woken, that was digging its claws lightly, voluptuously into
my flesh? It wasn't comfortable, frankly. I had to shift in bed. The cat
jumped to the floor, then to the windowsill, then out. A few feet to the
left is a balcony that gives onto the corridor. I lay back dreaming of day,
of Orson, Lucine, R. in Venice, M. in Tangier, of my mother & father,
of those New York scenes I am trying to compose without opening this
notebook; of the love & sweetness I had woken brimming with, and how
I might nurse it, keep it from draining out of my cupped hands into dust
before it reached its proper objects—O. & L. & the rest, or even (lacking
them) the pages of my novel. But of course I had only to think these
thoughts in order to feel the threat, then the reality, of their withdrawal.
It would seem that love, ἀγάπη, lives by its own laws, like a cat, & will
not be commanded.

PART ~~II~~ III?

They reached New York on an August morning. Arthur Orson had written to Paris, after no little deliberation, offering his guest room for a week or so until they found a flat of their own. Nearly seventy now, a bachelor to boot, his hesitation was natural. Orestes' letter told him worse than nothing regarding This Woman, as Arthur called Dora in a number of dialogues with his better nature. Who was she, and how *much* older than Orestes? Of just what society, please, was she the "cream"? He could hardly trust his godson's judgment in these matters. Arthur was no prude; if they weren't married, it didn't concern him. But, set in his ways, fussy and autocratic from the years spent with nobody to please but himself, he did not exactly look forward to roughing it, high up there in the grand scenery of other people's lives.

The past took over, though. For minutes at a time he was young again, it was thirty-five years earlier, and the letter tucked in his engagement book was not from Orestes but Orestes' father, announcing *his* arrival, with Eleni and the baby, in New York. The annoyance and curiosity felt then as now (who was This Woman? what business had his friend, or godson, involving himself with her, with any woman? She came from a higher class, did she? Hmf! How would *he* know?) gave Arthur the sense that his total personality was smoothly, intelligently functioning. "If I know anything," he told his better nature, "I know the world, its pitfalls and deceptions. They never ask *me* when they make their rash decisions, but you'll see. After one year with this woman, he'll come whining to me, his only friend, just mark my words." Thirty-five years ago, of course, Arthur had done everything in his power to help Orestes' father, found him work, found them lodgings, sent them food, paid for the doctors, the hospital, the funeral of that wonderful, strong, good man. In Arthur's bedroom stood a framed photograph of himself posing with his friend before a whitewashed house. It had been taken on a Sunday in 1915. Both were wearing dark suits and tieless white shirts buttoned at the collar. Orestes' father would have been in his early twenties; he was looking superbly at the camera from behind a thick, curling moustache. Arthur Orson had been, of all things, a spy in the First War. During the Gallipoli Campaign he had met Orestes' father, had in fact been hidden for a month in his house, in his room. "He saved my life," he would say aloud, letting the magic work. "I was ill, he cared for me like a brother. His memory is sacred to me to this day."

"And Eleni?" asked Arthur's better nature, one of whose favorite stories it was.

"Agh. She remarried, miraculously."

"Why so? Wasn't she still very lovely?"

"Yes, perhaps. But a shrew. She drove him to his death."

"Oh? It wasn't cancer, then?"

"Am I expected to remember everything? Whatever it was, he died, Eleni remarried, and my little namesake—he was given Orson as a second name, you recall—went off with her to far-away Texas."

They had kept in touch, but Arthur did not see his godson again until he was thirty and a Professor, with degrees.

To the surprise of both, they became friends. Each probably amused the other by his inexperience. Arthur went so far as to enroll in one of Orestes' night classes for adults. Words like "antithesis" or "metaphysical," or sentences beginning "The poet in his lonely search for belief . . ." made his eyes shift nervously, but he enjoyed the relish with which Orestes could utter them. Afterwards would come a removal to somebody's apartment, wine and cookies, more talk. One night Tennyson was mentioned. "Oh," said Orestes at once, "an extraordinary technician but a minor poet. It is hard for me to feel his greatness." Wasn't "In Memoriam" a great poem? "The poem he wrote for Arthur Hallam," Orestes began, pausing because of the other Arthur in his audience, whom he wanted to savor the pleasant coincidence of names; "Tennyson's friend who died young," he went on, and now met Arthur's eyes, reminded of his similar loss (which was, to be sure, Orestes' own as well)—"Yes, perhaps 'In Memoriam' is a great poem. A sensibility as delicate as Tennyson's could draw from a friend's death insights analogous to those of the saint in contemplation of Christ's passion. These insights are all the more poignant for contemporary readers like ourselves, for whom the Christian myth has fallen to pieces. Only a supreme artist in our day can solder them together. You will understand how I feel about 'In Memoriam' if you compare it with Eliot's magnificent *collage* of faith and faiths—Tennyson on the one hand, content to echo the cadences of Anglican hymns; Eliot on the other, aware in his sophistication that the fragments he has 'shored up' are valid *because* of their flaws, their inefficacy as living doctrine—" Enough. Orestes' talk popped with allusion and paradox. It was like sitting by a fire. At the evening's end Arthur breathed the cool of his own life gratefully.

From him Orestes learned—no, Orestes never learned. He lacked skill and patience to help work the crazy quilt of amenity and obligation that was the older man's daily life. Everything Arthur did related to others. Even in museums he stood longest in front of paintings whose previous owners he had known—Miss A.'s Manet, Lord B.'s Crivelli. On the way out he would stop to say hello to one of the curators. Months later he took Orestes to dinner in this man's apartment. Orestes was the only guest not in evening clothes. He soon found, furthermore, that his discourse curdled the bland flow of talk and gossip. Before long he was listening in appalled fascination, beyond speech as the others were beyond thought—for so he unjustly dismissed them, blind to the intense thought behind the flowers, the china, the menu, and deaf to the truth of any remark clever enough to make him smile. Here Orestes was close, as Arthur pointed out, to contradicting himself. What was this cleverness if not a kind of poetry? Didn't his own lectures sparkle with it? Ah, but no—Orestes' lectures were about serious things. Poetry, for Arthur, might be cleverness, mere icing on the cake; for Orestes it was a way of life. "Believe me," said his friend, "so is cleverness. By the way your manners are improving. You didn't fold your napkin when you got up from table."

It was Aesop's fox and stork all over again. Arthur lapped a bit from the top of the jar; Orestes stabbed guardedly at the shallow dish. Their partings were warm with relief. And when Orestes finally sailed for Greece, Arthur gave him a larger check than he had intended.

At last the doorbell rang. Here they were. As he hastened to admit them, Arthur's numerous misgivings about Dora shrank to one childish prayer: "Let her be able to appreciate me, let her see that I have taste!"

His living room was painted dark red and ivory. It had one antiqued-mirror wall, a piano (Arthur had resumed his lessons, after fifty-five years), velvet chairs, gladiolas in silver vases. There were many Greek objects: amber rosaries, a good ikon, and some large, prominently hung sepia photographs of sculpture—the Charioteer, the Hermes at Olympia, the Ephebe at Constantinople. Indeed, Dora exclaimed with pleasure.

She did feel at home, she had had no idea from Orestes that one could be so comfortable in New York; so that, with no further thought given to the qualms each had felt with respect to the other (for Dora, too, had begun to sprinkle large grains of salt on Orestes' judgments of people), she and Arthur sat down, vastly pleased with their mutual surfaces, to Turkish coffee and a sweet on a spoon. Orestes, overexcited, paced the room. They watched him indulgently, like parents whose child has come home.

Arthur, a little man, sallow and vain, with a mole on his forehead and eyebrows long as antennae, was presently dreaming of taking her over, introducing her as *his* friend and sharing in the invitations she would receive. Orestes wanted her to see *things*; he had been picturing her excitement in zoos, on the top of skyscrapers, in the subway. Dora obliged them both.

Within a few days she had been to Chinatown, Bloomingdale's, the Frick, Staten Island, had watched TV and been given an evening party. Arthur spent most of that day polishing silver candlesticks, washing long-stemmed glasses he hadn't used for months, and arranging flowers. "You've gone to too much trouble," said Orestes, inwardly delighted, on his return with Dora from their apartment hunt. Arthur merely shrugged. He knew no other way to give a party. Certainly the surer thing was to prepare one's background, order things to eat, serve champagne—domestic, if need be—in thin crystal, than to rely on kind words and gestures. What if the heart were not inspired to warmth, the tongue to liveliness? One must provide against that kind of failure. And the party, considering that most of the people Arthur knew were dead or out of town for the summer, went off quite passably. Nothing was broken. The handful of Bohemians invited by Orestes stayed too late but otherwise behaved. Cold cuts and petits fours remained which would do for Arthur's lunch the next day. And he felt that his guests (the museum director, the piano teacher, ten all told) had got the point of Dora. Despite her costume.

Orestes had had her wear an ankle-length black lace dress, old yet in itself becoming. Then, horrors! minutes before the first arrivals, he opened a paper bag and took out a yard of broad crimson moiré ribbon. This he draped Dora with, diagonally, like some ambassadorial decoration fastened by pins at shoulder and hip, and at the breast by a brooch of her own. It cost Arthur an effort to smile and say nothing, as Dora herself did, and wait for the first person to whom Orestes introduced her as the "Greek Ambassadress" to see the joke before he, Arthur, allowed himself to remark that fun was fun but decorations were decorations.

Dora would have agreed with him on a different occasion, but she felt more warmly toward Orestes now than she had in the weeks before they reached New York, and she had resolved to take pleasure in whatever made him happy. Watching him in relation to Arthur, it gratified her to see, as with Orestes and his brother, that two highly dissimilar individuals were drawing closer through her, and was European enough to wonder, where Arthur was concerned—an elderly man, without heirs—if this increased closeness mightn't lead to something rather agreeable for Orestes. For herself, she objected not one bit to dressing up as grander than she was. We all dream of coming back from the Flea Market with a Fragonard. If Orestes wanted to have brought from Europe something more than an old island woman, she would lend herself to his plot, she would impersonate the fabulous souvenir. Meanwhile, her eyes had been open. Beginning with that green, torch-bearing giantess in the harbor, all militant wakefulness compared to her sleeping, natural sister viewed from Diblos, Dora had taken in a type of New York woman—in the street, in the pages of *Vogue*—angular, high-heeled, hatless, being dragged hilarious down the pavement by a huge shaven dog, or squinting heavenwards with a look of utter, harrowed anxiety which must be, in this city at least, as much beauty's indispensable earmark as an enigmatic smile had been in Leonardo's Italy. It was not a type Dora cared to resemble. Yet she already knew, from being dragged down pavements by Orestes, something of what lay in the heart of the woman with the poodle, and beneath Dora's tanned, lined face and fingers placidly, clumsily mending a tear in the black lace dress, had already appeared the psychic counterparts of furrowed brow, strained, painted mouth, knuckles clenched white—all ignored, all nonetheless ready for use at the first proof of her own total folly to have considered (at her age!) making a life among the barbarians.

There, then, she stood among them, the Ambassadress, sipping the Great Western champagne. Compared to her, the others were friendlier, better informed, more intense, or more talkative; her failure in these respects seemed rather to strengthen her position. To have been European *and* immensely charming might have been more than the company could bear. She raised her glass to Orestes across the room.

His eyes had been on her. It had just entered his head to have her talk to his mother on the telephone. In Greek, naturally! "What a good idea," said Dora. Soon she was called into Arthur's bedroom. Eleni, in Texas, was already on the line and Orestes—talking English—had finished what he had to say. Dora found herself uttering a tentative "Hello" into the receiver. "Talk Greek! Talk Greek!" cried Orestes. She did so, found easily a number of cordial phrases, mentioned her fondness for both Eleni's sons, hoped before long to know *her* as well—but then, as Eleni replied, it became plain, with every allowance for fluster, that Greek was no longer a tongue she could speak to any useful degree. It made no difference; Dora slipped back into English, remarked the extent of Eleni's, modified her own to suit it, and so ended the conversation.

"She sounds *very* nice," she told Orestes. "I should love to know her. What an absorbing life that must be!" He, however, dragged her back to the party. "I couldn't believe it!" he told group after group. "My mother can't speak Greek any more! I was amazed! She and I speak English together—*my* Greek was lousy before I went to Greece. But imagine! She's forgotten it! And her English isn't fluent, is it, Dora? Do you see what that means? My mother has no language!"

"There must be more important things in life," said Dora, embarrassed. He had made it sound very dire.

"Than language?"

"Than languages, surely."

"That coming from you who speak four perfectly! Ha ha!" cried Orestes throwing his arms around her and her enhanced value. People did that in America, she had noticed, though he had now gone on to tell some others how physical the Greeks were, how they couldn't talk without touching or hugging each other. "Yes," said Dora, "but you're talking of a certain class. Tasso could never bear to be touched, neither could Byron, even as a child." But anything she said made him like her more. "You see," his smile told the room, "she knows, she's the genuine article."

That evening, for the first time in their friendship, Orestes became "an American" in Dora's eyes. She glimpsed the larger, national mystery behind his manners, that pendulum swinging from childish artlessness to artless maturity and back again. She welcomed the insight gaily, secure in her resiliency. When the museum director, saying goodnight, promised to telephone in the morning to give her the name of "a really dependable rug man" through whom to sell her Bokhara, she begged him not to go out of his way. "Oh well, yes, the rug must be sold eventually, but I won't have my friends feeling responsible for me. I'd be happy on the corner with a cart full of apples!"

Dora and Orestes found an apartment, no floor of a brownstone house, as recommended by Arthur and which was available at great cost (unless in such poor condition as to remind Orestes of the primal tenement he was still running away from); instead, three rooms in a new, mountainous "development" overlooking the East River. It had a uniformed doorman—whom Orestes trained, without letting him in on the joke, to call Dora "Baroness"—and a lobby decorated by Dorothy Draper. There was Musak in the self-operated elevators. The riverfront apartments, it turned out, cost ten dollars per room more each month than those facing other tall buildings. "We'll know the river's there," Dora said.

On the eighteenth floor they had plenty of light. Their living room was too large, the bedroom and kitchen too small. When it came to furniture, Orestes developed a violent phobia of anything secondhand, so that for their first dinner at home they drew two shiny metal and leatherette chairs up to a vinyl-topped cardtable. Dora switched off a three-headed lamp. Candlelight richened the Bokhara and blurred a pattern of orange and green boomerangs on the sofa bed and the wall to wall, ceiling to floor draperies installed that day against the cruel afternoon glare. The friends drank to their new home. It was costing a lot but they had done it, it was theirs, and Orestes, for one, felt that these new, durable, practical possessions would save expense in the long run. Three months passed. The chair seats were cracking to reveal gray cotton wadding, somebody's cigarette had blistered the table. The Bokhara was still on the floor but the curtains did not close, or the bed open, properly, and Dora was working as a governess in New Jersey.

It was better than it sounded. The family was Dutch, the daughters twelve and fourteen. Dora walked them to school, returned to the house, made a bed or two, ate on a tray with the grandfather in his room, read, fetched the girls, took one to her music lesson and did Greek or Italian conversation with the other. The family dined together, Dora with them. Both parents were translators at the United Nations. On weekends Dora was free to join Orestes.

She tried not to feel it as an obligation, those Friday evenings, re-entering the apartment. She was paying her share, true; but more and more it seemed, as she gave him the money each month, that she was buying her own privacy from Orestes. For two nights he would move onto the sofa bed, giving up the bedroom to her. On one night they would go to the theatre; on the other, receive friends. It soon appeared that these sleeping arrangements were unsatisfactory. The weekend found Dora refreshed, ready for the diversions it was thought better to have earned, in America, than mere money; while Orestes, exhausted by work, face green and long as the face in an ikon, might have been happy to slip into his relinquished bedroom somewhat before the last guests had left.

To his regular lectures had been added a weekly TV program, "The World of Poetry." Produced with a minimum of fuss over an educational channel, at the wrong hour of the wrong evening, it nevertheless by spring had gathered a faithful public who wrote letters, telephoned the station, sent Orestes their photographs and sonnets. He took it all very seriously. Wearing a new pale blue shirt, he had arrived for his debut an hour early, ready to put himself in the hands of the cosmeticians. There were none. His disappointment, though concealed, was justified; on the screen he looked unwell and weird. His programs tended to fall into two halves: the classic, the contemporary. After an initial talk on, say, Shelley, with resonant quotation prefaced by sips of water, he would try to wind up with "a Shelley of today"—some odd young man he would have met, who was meant to give the viewers an absolutely authentic image of genius struggling from the chrysalis of society. Orestes relied perhaps too heavily upon his friends to perform, rather than poets whose names were better known. But the public seemed ill-equipped to tell the difference. So much so that, today in New York, these discoveries of Orestes, published by now and with their own disciples, make up a clearly defined battalion in the endless literary wars of our time.

There was the film, too. In these months Orestes was writing the first of six complete scripts. A week in Hollywood, the frequent telephone conferences thereafter, had not helped him form a notion of how to proceed. Each month, when the producer came to town, a big black car would call for Orestes and sweep him, in evening clothes at first rented, eventually his very own, into the countryside for a party with starlets and bigwigs. From one such dinner, near Christmas, he returned with a pair of gold and sapphire cufflinks. It was hard to resist, for Orestes, a little gentle namedropping; and, for others, a little gentle irony at his expense. Certain young poets—infants in Dora's eyes—so devoted to their calling as never to have heard of selling one's talents, dipped into the punchbowl and came up with a hesitant question. Wasn't that what Orestes was doing? Wasn't his time too precious for this kind of drudgery?

He would admit it himself some days. He rose at seven, never retired before midnight.

Only once, one miserable midweek night before Dora had found work, did she and Orestes try a Greek restaurant. A new one had opened near Times Square, and the idea had been to go forth, a company of poets, to taste the richly restorative food and society of Greeks.

The place seemed large and crowded. They were put at a recently vacated table.

"This is strange," said Orestes, moving his face about. "Can you *see*, Dora?"

The lighting was dim but might not have existed, to hear him talk. "I've never seen a Greek restaurant," he went on, "that wasn't a blaze of electric light. The Greeks love light. In Athens, in broad daylight, the butcher stalls are outlined and festooned with lighted bulbs. They are theatres in which brains and hearts have literally been laid bare, all buzzing with flies. And the crowds!" He asked their waiter in Greek, good-naturedly, why it was so dark in the restaurant.

"How's everybody tonight?" said the waiter, removing soiled napkins and glasses. "A cocktail before your meal, folks?"

Dora wanted a Manhattan. Orestes told the young poets to try ouzo, then repeated his question in English.

"You got me," came the answer. "Unless it's the ladies. They often like not too bright a room." He handed round red and gold menus.

"It's true," said Dora, "you see very few women eating out in Athens, except in summer. Here, everyone's brought his wife along."

"Wait," said Orestes to the waiter. "What part of Greece are you from?"

Eager to leave, the waiter admitted Sparta.

"But you don't speak Greek? I'm amazed!"

"Oh, I'm Greek, I speak Greek!" and with a smile of reassurance he escaped.

"That was childish of me," Orestes laughed. "But he should be prouder of his heritage."

As he peered into the dim hubbub, Orestes said goodbye to any hopes of reliving those brilliant evenings in taverns across the water. The crossing itself had wrought a sea change upon the other Greek customers. Young men who, on native ground a few years earlier, would have listened to Orestes with dreaming eyes had already watched dream after dream sinking into a parody of its fulfillment: fortune, family, the wife to dress (or overdress), the child to educate (or worse, since this was America, to be educated *by*)—and all these lives at once insured, reflected, and corroded by conveniences bought on time, in time, *with* time, payments the receipts for which could be examined even here, through smoke, in the form of sallow, untended flesh and the delusive mannerisms of the insider. Dante might have spoken to these diners, gone over the receipts, shown them where they had paid too much; not Orestes. With a shudder of horror and identification he turned back to his party.

"No, but really," Dora remarked when he had said his piece, "you'll see the same class of people in Athens, if you know where to look."

"I give you the light of Greece, then," smiled Orestes, lifting his glass. "Once you have had your vision, no lesser world is altogether tolerable. I used to enjoy places like this. But I've been *there*, I've felt the sun licking at my wings. If I were Icarus, I would set out tomorrow—to melt in that sun, to drown in that sea!"

At least they would have a good meal. Turning to the menu, Orestes ordered portions of souvlakia, moussaka, stuffed vine leaves—ah, and there were calamarákia! Nothing was more delicious (he told the poets) than these little squid, crisp with golden batter. Did they come from

Florida? The waiter couldn't say. "Well, two portions of those," said Orestes. "And of course, wine."

"I'll bring the wine list," said the waiter, by now speaking Greek to oblige him.

"Don't bother. Just two large cans of retsina."

"We have only bottled wine."

"Bottles then," said Orestes with an indifferent wave of his hand.

The bouzoukia orchestra, which had been resting when their party arrived, began to play. Eight men sat in a row, gazing nowhere and deftly worrying their instruments. A soloist advanced to the edge of the platform. Her body, barely contained by a white and silver dress, might have been artificially matured so as to be recognizable as female at immense distances. Black, platinum-streaked curls spilled onto fat shoulders and quivering arms. She held a cloth orchid concealing a microphone. By turns sweet, hoarse, piercing, dripping with ornaments and imperfections, her voice reached them as an aural equivalent of the many-layered, honey-soaked baklava Orestes intended ordering for dessert. This much, surely, was authentic—or was it? One poet thought he recognized an Italian hit of the year before.

Nobody got up to dance. "But nobody's dancing—why?" asked Orestes when the waiter brought their orders.

"It is not permitted."

A plate set before Orestes seemed to contain five or six fingers, swollen purplish pink and trailing oil black roots. What was this? His calamarákia.

"Ah no. I wanted them fried. I've never seen squid served this way. They're not even hot. Take them away, ask the cook to fry them properly."

The waiter removed the two portions.

A second song ended to loud applause. The singer blew one kiss and ambled pouting from the stage. "One likes her," Orestes explained, "because she is the essence of voluptuous femininity." Then he noticed that the vine leaves had come out of a can. He could tell by a certain green dye mixed with the oil. "As a rule I don't let trivial details upset me," he said. "It's not like me to lodge complaints—is it, Dora?"

It was not, and she said so.

"Forgive me, then, if I do this once. It will be for the glory that was Greece."

So the drama moved inexorably to its close. The wine was wrong. The same calamarákia returned, perhaps hotter. Meanwhile, a child-faced poet had been made unwell by a single glass of ouzo. The waiter offered to show Orestes the brine vat in the kitchen, out of which the vine leaves had been taken. Orestes waved him away, calling for the manager.

"Oríste!" cried this person when he appeared.

"He knows you . . . ?" the sick poet moaned, mistaking for Orestes' name the conventional Greek reply to a summons.

"I ordered fresh calamarákia, fried," began Orestes. The manager regretted; there was no fresh squid at this time of year. Then why had it been on the menu? Ah, the menu did not say *fresh* squid. Here as in any Greek restaurant, one basic menu did for all seasons. And some people preferred their squid canned, yes indeed! The two portions in question, however, would not appear on their check.

This concession failed to satisfy Orestes.

"Another thing," he said, shifting to English. "This wine tastes funny, and the ouzo can't have been good. It has made my friend ill."

The manager took a sip of wine, then looked closely at the poet. "He's under age, isn't he? Did he show any identification?"

"I'm surprised you can see him at all in this light!"

"Look, Sir, don't blame me for the New York State Law. I'm just the guy who gets his permit taken away."

"This is ridiculous," said Orestes. "No Greek has ever come within five years of guessing an American's age."

Dream—Venice, a Hospital. O. is to undergo surgery. Reception desk very crowded. Old woman edges in front of him. I make her yield her place & try to tell the nurse O.'s name. We are separated at the elevators. Mine: a moving wooden room like a rustic privy. Hot sun through a knothole burns my wrist (redder & hairier than mine) & I think, Summer at last! Now we move sideways like a train. At the end of a vast streaked palazzo (the Hosp.) I get off. I wear black trousers, black turtleneck, am barefoot. While I wait for O., an attendant—older, heavy accent—talks to me. He cannot believe I'm born in Texas, says there's something "Italian" about the back of my head, I say, conscious of speaking a highly artificial language, "Perhaps I have foreign blood." He: Beg pardon—what? He: Foreign what? "BLOODij!" I shout. And O. comes limping into view.

"I am nineteen," declared the poet haughtily.

"I'm not asking for the gentleman's word," said the manager. "I'm asking to see his driver's license."

"I don't drive."

"It's a matter of principle," said a second poet, beginning to laugh.

Orestes struck the table lightly with his palm. Until now, only his Greek pride had been offended. But the appeal to local ordinances aroused an American dander he hadn't known he had. "Ask the waiter to bring our check."

The manager hesitated. Suppose these were well-connected people? In that brief interval Dora spoke up.

She *didn't* feel like leaving, did they mind? She put her hand on Orestes' and smiled up at the manager. If they could just have some bicarbonate of soda? she said in her plainest, most motherly Greek. It was wet out, the rest of the dinner was so good! "Orestes, you must try my moussaka, they've given me far too much."

It worked. The manager melted away. Orestes let himself be calmed.

The worst, from her point of view, was simply to have lost control in front of the young. Luckily they were poets. Abstractor topics presented themselves, the music continued to please, the baklava was a success. So, perhaps, was the evening as a whole, in every mind but Orestes'. Into him the half averted scene kept biting deeply. What had he expected? Greece in America? He was not used to this grinding confusion of loyalties. Either, it seemed, one was Greek and unfortified against the virus endemic here, or American and a carrier. The two natures absolutely did not mix. To emerge at last, twenty dollars poorer, onto the neon-streaked, puddle-paved streets came as no relief. People of every description jostled them. It was the melting pot with a vengeance. Dora took his arm and led him, the poets following, calmly through the flashing, shrieking labyrinth. She seemed actually to know where they were.

More and more she was coming to baffle a possessiveness he felt for her. From the start it had been of absurd yet paramount importance that she *see* and *feel* New York. After her maiden trip on the subway, he had turned to her, ready for superlatives. But what was Dora to say who had ridden the Métro a month before, who had gone by train under the Alps, for that matter? This was no typically "New York" experience. Orestes looked away in frustration. The contest recurred daily. She had *been* in department stores, she had already tasted doughnuts. She had seen crowds almost as huge crawling at the bottom of chasms less deep, perhaps, than these—but she was no judge of depth. The Louvre allowed her to be critical of the Metropolitan, the Comédie of Broadway. Orestes could teach her nothing. It was as if his very virility were being challenged. Wasn't there something, he asked one day with desperate lightness, something singular about his home-town that had struck her, that she hadn't foreseen? "Ah yes!" she exclaimed, then had to think. "Well, there are many more Negroes than I'd imagined. And many more antique shops."

Reluctantly he evolved the theory that it was too much for her. No woman her age could cope with a world so drastically at odds with all she had known. Her serenity was a defense, a symptom of shock. Neither then nor later when events bore it out did this view of Dora comfort him.

The matter of her finding work arose, horrifying Orestes. He had no claims, could not forbid her (his former hostess, now less than a guest) to look for a job. So he retreated into a childish coldness—let her just try independence, she would see her folly—broken by spells of frenzied rationality, budgets littering the vinyl table, aimed at keeping her by his side.

Dora had taken to going to Arthur Orson's for tea every few days. Here her instinct was applauded. New York without a job could be a living hell—ask him, the idle old man chuckled, he ought to know. They put their heads together over the difficulties. She had come to America on a visitor's, not a worker's, visa—which by the way was due to expire in three months. She could renew it for another six, and would no doubt be quite ready for repatriation at the end of them. "But suppose I'm not," she asked Arthur, "suppose I want never to leave?"

"Then you will simply have to stay."

"It's not that simple. I should have to marry an American." She was joking. "Can you picture it? At my age?"

Arthur looked at his chrysanthemums.

"Why not marry me?" he finally said.

When she told Orestes, he went all to pieces. "You aren't serious," he kept saying.

Dora asked if he could think of a more suitable arrangement.

"I wasn't aware that your fondness for my country had reached such a pitch," he said with the elegance of hurt feelings. "Or should I take it as a personal compliment?"

"If you like, my dear," she replied gently. "Or think of it as self-indulgence." She let her hand rest upon one of that year's anxiety-packed headlines. "I might not care to live through another war in Greece."

"But with Arthur!"

"Really, Orestes. It would be a marriage of convenience. We'd live apart. Nothing's settled in any case. All Arthur did was to bring up the possibility."

"You'd go on living here with me? Would that look proper?"

"Does it look proper now?"

"This once, Dora, don't be witty, I beg you. Marriage is a human sacrament," said he who knew nothing about it. "I'm profoundly shocked to know that you would consider Arthur as a husband."

She saw then and there that it would have to be Orestes whom she married.

Arguments came to support this daring notion. Under scrutiny the margin of years between them changed into an advantage. Arthur, despite his talk of living apart, was old and fragile; age could turn overnight into helplessness. As his wife—for Dora also took marriage seriously, having had thirty-eight years of it with Tasso—she would run the risk of becoming his companion, his nurse. No thank you! Then, Arthur's world. It was too close to Athens society—small, elderly, proper; a little went a long way. She had developed a taste for long bare avenues, glass buildings the light bounced off. With Orestes, now that the dawning on the terrace at Diblos lay behind her and, believe it or not as he pleased, no shred of longing remained, it seemed to Dora that this love overcome—if it had been love, there was no saying now—had earned her certain rights, that he owed her compensation, as if she had hurt herself in his service. And she, why, she owed it to him to marry him! Who had wanted her here? Who had escorted her to this huge, glittering American function? It went against her upbringing to desert him now. No, while the chandeliers blazed, she was under Orestes' protection; while the music played, she would face it at his side.

They exchanged vows and rings in a civil service in January. This time, at the party Arthur gave, the champagne was imported.

That night, a Saturday, Orestes, dressed in red silk pyjamas, knocked on the bedroom door. He was now The Bridegroom; he would have knocked at a cotton-gin's door if he had just been married to one. As it was, his feelings for Dora had deepened and widened under

A miserable moment. Returning unexpectedly after starting for the beach, I found Chryssoula in my room. Cleaning? Something crackled guiltily, she was thrusting her hand into her blouse. I thought of the 500 drachma note hidden in this book. I questioned her. She showed her empty hands. I asked what was hidden in her blouse. Nothing! I knew she was lying. Suddenly she was in a fury. You think I'm a thief, search me! Eyes blazing. She seized my hand & thrust it into her bosom where, along with everything else, was indeed a square of paper. It was my passport photo; there had been several in an envelope in my drawer. C. was in tears. I wanted to comfort her. Her lips compressed, she turned proudly aside. Now she has left. My image lies curled & damp on the table. "Sei bello," she said, "ma non hai cuore." The lagoon shimmers. The torso lies outstretched at its far end. The money was of course safe between these two blank pages. Her scent is on the palm I raise to hide my face. "The only solution is to be very, very intelligent."

the spell of having a sacramental role to perform. He had also drunk wine. Their relationship seemed to him one of infinite possibility.

She was still up and about, in her hairnet and old blue wrapper. "How smart you look," she said, missing the import of his appearance.

"I wanted you to see that I was proud to be your husband," said Orestes, smiling.

"Thank you, my dear. I'm very happy too."

"Let me kiss you good night, Dora."

"Good night, Orestes." She gave him her roughened cheek. He held her a moment, weighing her unreadiness.

"Dora . . . ?"

She drew back. When she raised her eyes it was in a slow look brimming with comfort. She pressed his hand, then let go gently. Speechless, he took his leave.

Man and wife at last, their relationship was virtually at an end. No scenes, no recriminations, only this gradual firm gentleness on Dora's part, and the difficulty of meeting her eyes for long. Who did meet those eyes, or what? The Dutch family's cat. A stand of yellow, shuddering bamboo in a southerly angle of their house. Gray skies. Windows reflected in water.

One morning in March she discovered herself walking along a canal, an embankment anyhow, shining with frost and strewn with rusted fragments of machinery. It would have been quite early. The sun, low and mild, startled her, now in the sky, now glancing off the windows of a warehouse opposite. "But what am I doing here?" she said to herself in Italian. "Tasso will be furious."

She tried to concentrate upon the cryptic litter of metal. A filthy yellow dog squatted in its midst, trembling violently; risen, it sniffed the steaming earth. When it turned to her, she saw a fresh wound on its head. "Cosa vuoi?" she asked it in a sweet, croaking voice, her hand held out appealingly. The air had grown warmer. Smells reached her; it was spring. The dog, grinning like a shark, had not moved. She walked deeper into the scene.

Later she was extremely tired. The police had odd uniforms and spoke English. She answered what she could of their questions. Her name? She gave it calmly. Yes, married; there was the ring on her finger. She told them Tasso's name and where they lived. Was that in New Jersey? Doubt must have crossed her face. Next, they wanted to know what year it was. Really, how stupid! But she couldn't tell from their faces whether her answer was right or wrong. She begged their pardon, adding that she had had little or no sleep. The coffee they gave her was weak but delicious.

In the next room an officer was saying, ". . . Yes, come on down. . . . Legally, you understand, we ought to. . . . Yes . . . all right . . . O. K."

Soon a fair woman who spoke French arrived at the police station, and kissed her. When Dora had not returned last night (the woman said) they had telephoned Orestes to find out if she had missed her train. Whom had they telephoned? Never mind. Hush. The panic was over, they had found her. A doctor was waiting to see her. Hush. Come.

Dora's amnesia disappeared by evening and never recurred. The doctor saw her several times. He asked, had there been any recent shock or upheaval in her life? She told him no.

Orestes said, "Ah, Dora, I understand these things. It's me you're trying to forget. You want to blot out everything that has to do with me."

Arthur said, "If *my* memory went, where would I be? Who would look after me? The very thought sends chills."

On her next weekend in New York, Dora went to a hotel.

Shame was what *she* felt. To be found wandering, a derelict; anything might have happened. To be faced with the frailty of one's reason, there among the rusted parts, the filth, in a glare that assailed one like the dog's gaze, wherever one turned. As she stripped these painful details of a certain prismatic beauty that had overlaid them at the time, she recognized in their poverty, their menace, more and more of her situation with Orestes. Her shame widened to include this, too.

She felt she had had the narrowest of escapes.

"I shall go back to Greece," she said aloud to the hotel wallpaper. But her mistake, if it was one, seemed at once too grave and too recent to acknowledge by such a step.

"If it were not for Byron," she told a tired, sympathetic face in the mirror.

On Sunday she forced herself to visit the apartment.

"Good evening, Baroness," said the doorman.

"Dora!" exclaimed Orestes dramatically. "Are you all right? I've been terribly anxious. We all have. Arthur just phoned. I've had no sleep—"

She pressed his hand, nodding. It was the morning on the terrace, only he had slipped into her role. Well, he was welcome to it.

"We thought it must be another attack of amnesia."

"No."

"Where have you been, then? Arthur was calling the hospitals."

She explained and begged his pardon.

"Give me your coat. Have you eaten?"

"It doesn't matter."

Still, rather than look at her just then, he went to make her a sandwich.

"You are usually so thoughtful," said Orestes, returning, with a smile of awareness. "Believe me, Dora, I understand more than you think."

"Thank you, that looks delicious."

"How you must resent me," he went on. "How guilty you must feel for having used me."

"What do you mean, Orestes?"

"For marrying me," he said carefully as to a child, "so that you could stay in America."

She watched him, wondering how much of the truth it was needful to point out.

Orestes blushed.

"I don't know what I'm saying," he said sadly. "Both of us wanted . . ."

"Go on. Tell me, please."

"The experience. The insight. What else should one want, Dora?"

He had spoken simply. She shut her eyes, touched.

"Your generosity to me," he said, "is something I can never forget— or, it would seem, repay."

"Generosity, I don't know . . ." she echoed vaguely in order not to be silent.

His silence made her look. It was his turn to avoid her eyes. Ah!— "his" cottage on the property at Diblos. She smiled partly with irony— was he afraid she would ask for it back?—partly with pity. How much it must mean to him, if he could think of it now.

The mood changed. Out of habit, Orestes told Dora what he had done and whom he had seen during the week. She listened and commented, then:

"I ought to go now," she said, rising. "I shan't come to town next week. The week after, probably."

What was happening? Orestes looked at her untouched sandwich, at the cracked leatherette seats of his chairs. The phrase, "the mother country," lit on his mind like a flake of soot. He had been waiting for Dora to deny that she was through with him; instead, she stood at the door, an expression of perfect good nature masking her decision and conveying it in all its firmness. Her lover, he thought, the manager of the olive groves, dismissed.

In the days that followed, Orestes tried to reason that Dora was suffering from strain or fatigue or at worst from some passing mental illness; her mind had caught cold; soon she would be cured, they would again be friends. But his fantasies took off from a contrary assumption— she *was* in her right mind, she *had* dismissed him. He woke, weeping, from nightmares he hadn't had since his analysis, dreams of falling in which balconies crumbled from his grasp like birthday cake. What was this? He bent a sharp ear to his motives. The rupture evidently meant more to him than he knew.

All his life, Orestes recognized, he had been oftener at home with disciples than with friends or lovers. The last year was a remarkable exception, having brought him not only Dora but Sandy. After a certain age, however, the heart gives itself, if at all, too easily; the gift can be taken back. Orestes was nearing forty. His prime allegiance remained to his ideals or (if ever they conflicted with it) to his career.

He concluded tough-mindedly that it wasn't Dora alone he would miss, but also the security she had given him and might now withhold. He considered, marveling coldly, how much self-knowledge had brought his cottage to mind at the crucial moment, and how much delicacy had kept him from mentioning it.

He oversimplified. Years later when, back in Greece, Orestes tried to take possession of his cottage pride barely colored his motives, greed not at all. Nor did he expect, with his magic figures absent, to recapture the bliss of that time. But his tiled floor, his rock garden, his cove, the eucalyptus trees veined with leaf-gray and distant azure—a longing for these things, that is, for the sentimental truths they would still bear witness to, had been welling up in him like a madness. He was actually relieved to learn, from Dora's lawyer, that he had no claim on them whatever. It made the spirit purer in which he wrote his last letters to her. Even in America, at the time of their separation, Orestes had principally needed—since he wasn't to have her love—a view of himself as morally finer than Dora.

She had shown him her way of ending an intimacy. He wished her now to sample his. Therefore, on her next coming to town, he arranged an evening. Ceremoniously he called for her at the hotel, pinned a flower to her coat, carried her suitcase—it was Sunday. After dinner in a French restaurant, through which both talked calmly if relentlessly of joint tax returns and not bothering to divorce and a novel Dora had liked and the still unsold Bokhara, he took her to the theatre where they could hold their tongues in peace. The play was *Othello*. "It seemed more fitting to let art have the last word," said Orestes in the taxi, although by then she had seen what he was up to. In due course the beautiful words began to sound, the play to unroll like a great Venetian curtain, first abstracting their life together, then enveloping it. By the last act, Dora was asleep, muffled in gold. Her gentle snores brought it to his attention; as a detail, it seemed ironically right. In the end, screams woke her. The black actor was strangling the white actress. A violence to which all the words had been leading. She turned to Orestes, her eyes opened, inquiringly but with no single inquiry. Would it end in time for her train? came to mind along with, Would it not have helped to strangle *her*?—both frivolous questions, she knew, seeing his face lifted calm into the bluish light of the stage, the shining snail's track of a tear drying along his nose. Soon after that it did end; she was early for her train. On the platform he remembered to give her a letter, addressed to them both, from Sandy in

Colombo. Dora promised to return it, thanked Orestes for the evening, without reflecting offered him her cheek to kiss, did not take in the proud averting of his lips, and entered the coach. He stood watching her framed by her window's lighted oblong. She had made herself comfortable. Her eyes were meeting his with as much gravity as he could have wished until, the train filling up, a Negro sailor took the seat next to her, and she, hoping to make Orestes smile, raised both hands to her throat and pretended to squeeze. Through the glass she felt his sad impatience, dropped her hands, began to glide, before he could think what was happening, out of his sight.

4.viii.61

What has happened is still too strange. I can't

5.viii.61

I've seen Orson. He has come at last, and gone.

Now & then, as I've sat gazing down the lagoon toward the Sleeping Woman, something has taken place within me like the blowing of a fuse when too many lights are turned on for the current to bear. The house of these weeks has gone suddenly, magically dark, & a joy entered me, as my ~~eyes~~ heart adjusted to familiar shapes, & the square of moonlight brightened on the floorboards. What I knew then reached back beyond anything I could see or remember, into a world even my mother has forgotten, though she lives in it, too, joyous, forever young. I have felt tremendously at home in this knowledge. Part of me *does* belong here. There has been no need to use words. But the lights, each time, have had to go on again. I had been looking for something. Soon once more the house has blazed & the voluble search been resumed. That is ended now. I am switching them off one by one. Have I found whatever it was? Probably not. I know chiefly that I am no longer looking.

In fact I'm leaving. Tomorrow, Tuesday, Diblos will lie behind me. America lies ahead, the land of opportunity. I have vowed to find a job before Labor Day. I should be able to make myself very useful in a travel agency.

I reached a standstill after copying out these last pages, plotted & written & rewritten over 3 weeks on separate, unlined sheets. I had hoped to escape the tyranny of the Notebook—all my false starts, contradictions, irruptions of self, bound together, irrevocably. Books ought to consume their sources, not embalm them.

These "finished" pages are the best I can do. They have their own movement, & are often believable. But they have become fiction, which is to say, merely life-*like*. I nearly stopped transcribing them when I came upon that upside down, how-many-weeks-old dream (whose meaning is so ~~plain~~ disturbing today) & again when that most recent entry turned up—I'd have ripped it out but was too tired & indifferent to recopy one side of the page already covered.

Yesterday & today I read the whole notebook through. Actually, this last passage struck me as less artful than the earlier ones, with all their indecisions, pentimenti, glimpses of bare canvas, rips & ripples & cracks which, by stressing the fabric of illusion, required a greater attention to what was being represented. (How telling my never finding a name for Dora—only parentheses as for something private or irrelevant; and my reduction of Orson/Orestes, oftener than not, to his initial: a zero.)

When I reread it, the finished section troubled me. It has Dora & Orestes separating at the end of 8 months in America, instead of the nearly four years it took them to reach this decision. Their visit to Houston is not described, or Sandy's to New York. I leave out dozens of people, notably O.'s student Harriet, & their affair. This telescoping produces a false perspective. The characters, hurried through what was in fact a slow, painful action, become often trivial, like people in a drawing-room comedy. With Sandy absent, his viewpoint gets transferred, and a lot of valuable space given, to *another* 3rd person, Arthur Orson, who is unnecessary to the story, or at least figured in it differently, having refused—but who cares! My point is that I did do my best, but, as the Gorgon's face was mine, never succeeded in getting a full view of it.

Throughout, I observed considerably more interest in D.'s & O.'s estrangement than in their love for one another. Why? Did their love threaten me, or their estrangement comfort me? It was surely no fault of theirs if I were still on this island playing with them in effigy, loving the effigies alone, masks behind which lay all too frequently a mind foreign to them. Dora's amnesia—which comes off as well as anything—is largely my experience at the slaughterhouse (p. 17) transformed. Would I have thought to make her feel shame afterwards, if I hadn't felt it myself vis-à-vis Lucine? *I* was "Dora." *I* was "Orestes." They—whoever "they" were—kept mostly beyond my reach.

"The sun & moon together in the sky."

I wanted to set down these thoughts first, before seeing if I can write what happened on Saturday. Then I will (figuratively) drown my book. Blind I go. Love hasn't worked, not this year, & art isn't the answer.

I hadn't slept well. Around 11:00 I was still half in bed, thinking of nothing, when Chryssoula knocked (she no longer enters my room, except to clean it when I'm out, there are no more bunches of basil, only a reproachful, red-eyed mask; little Theodoros brings me my tea) & deposited George eager on the threshold. Before I could catch her eye, she was gone. My first mistaken thought was that G. had come to repair his behavior of several days earlier, when, having got 200 drachmas from me on a pretext so ridiculous I believed him, he foolishly pressed his winning streak by asking outright for my pale blue slacks. "Never mind," he said—but a *friend* would not have refused him, as had I; this judgment hung in the air of our parting. I'd known all along what kind of person he was. I'd even made out through his complacency & opportunism the milky negative of those traits: loyalty to a code no middle-class foreigner would ever understand. I was sorry that things had come to a head, but relieved. Now, with my initiation into 1 local mystery (George's friendship), it seemed the exorcism of the place could begin. Those last days, I caught myself looking at Diblos as if before long I would never see it again.

"Your friends are here, get up, come quickly!" he announced with words & gestures. Friends? What friends? George groaned, cast about, pounced upon L.'s watercolor which I'd slipped into the framed hotel regulations behind the door. Those friends: the caïque! Yes, and the girl!

He sat on the bed, bouncing with excitement while I washed. I hesitated over a clean shirt; cleverly, with his hands G. shaped Lucine out of thin air—I was dressing up for her? To dampen him, I put on the pale blue slacks. We go caïque Athens, olla mazi, to-geth-er? No, my Giorgios, we do not go Athens.

Another knock—Chryssoula, dead-pan, with a scented note signed "Nicole N." They had been fleeing the heat in Hydra, could stop only an hour at Diblos, wouldn't I join them for an ouzo on the caïque? I asked her to send word back that I would be along fra poco.

Rescued!

I got rid of G., considered shaving my beard, decided to face them with it, & tumbled out of the hotel.

On the waterfront the news greeted me.

As before, Mr N. was striding up & down, and his wife emerging from the Enfant's shop. Waves of excitement. Orson had appeared! Not 15 minutes earlier, he had been rowed across from the mainland. Under the eyes of everyone but the N.'s (who were hearing about it now, at the moment of my joining them) he had sent away the boatman, left his knapsack at the café, set out on foot for the House.

A flurry of speculation & rumor. Was Byron on the island? Yes. No. He had/had not been on yesterday's boat, been seen in town earlier this morning. Was it not rather his old serving woman who had come to buy fish? Ah, but fish was not for old serving women. Byron himself had therefore to be in residence.

We boarded the caïque to escape all this. I asked Mr N. how Dora had responded to the letter from his office.

"*The* letter? We have written 4. Your brother has written, I should think, daily. Dora has never replied."

Had she received the letters, I wondered, or been ill?

She had received them, Mr N. was sure. Other letters sent to the same address had been answered. Byron, too, she had written—without (according to him) one line about Orson or his cottage. As for health, who knew? She was well enough to be spending the summer on Cape, what was it called? Morue in French.

Mrs N.: Cape Cod! Thoreau! Emily Dickinson!

Orson, it seemed, had pretty much grasped the situation, seen that he was making himself a nuisance, wanted to let matters drop. He had telephoned Mr N.'s office some 10 days before to say that he was leaving Athens on a walking tour & might, if he passed nearby, cross over to Diblos to pick up a few belongings he'd left there.

I told the N.'s about seeing Byron, & his hoping that O. would stop by for some books.

Mr N.: Ah well, then, that explains why he's here today.

Mrs N. (busy with ice & ouzo): The Greeks are impossible. Admit it, Akis! My gossipy shopkeeper has invented such a drama you can't imagine. If—how did you call him? If the Enfant Chic is to be believed, your brother has only to set foot on Dora's land to be driven off with a cravache by Byron.

I thought I'd misheard her. "A what?"

Mrs N.: A cravache. A whip.

Mr N.: A riding crop. May I say that your shopkeeper, Nicole, is not one's ideal of the reliable informant?

We sipped our drinks. I was visited by the odd notion that *my* (Dora), too, would have left those letters unanswered, & that *my* Orestes would have set out, on foot, at Orson's side. There had been that much truth, after all, behind those masks.

And *my* Byron? Would he be waiting on the terrace with a whip?

A terrible guilty excitement slowly filled me. I *knew* that the Enfant had spoken the truth, & that I'd done nothing to prevent what was going to happen. A brutal, horrible action (p. 18). How could I have prevented it? In countless ways. By making friends with the E. C.

By having gone to Byron's for a drink that day. By writing O., even, and trying to warn him, since I must have known in my heart that he would come to Diblos sooner or later. By not keeping this notebook! Out of myself, my inertness, as well as a few things Orson had given me (nail parings, his secret name, a drop of his blood) it came over me that I had constructed a magic doll called Orestes, which had drawn him here. ~~I had wanted~~ Awake & asleep, I had dreamed of his punishment.

In French Mrs N. asked her husband how long a walk it was to the house. He answered.

We each calculated silently that O. would be there by now.

I looked up, needing to escape from my thoughts. Where was Lucine? It struck me that we had been sitting here on deck without her.

"Ah, Lucine," said Mrs N. "Let me see, they would be arriving in Paris tomorrow. No, today."

I felt my face change. I thought she was joking. Hadn't George seen L., said she'd come as well as the caïque? As I took it in, I had a rush of silly annoyance with *him*. And who were "they"?

I asked, hadn't L. planned to be in Greece the whole summer?

"In Europe," said Mrs N. "She left Greece, oh, 3 weeks ago. You received the aquarelle from her? It *was* charming, I must say I hoped she had painted it for Akis and me, but she wanted you to have it. I promised to keep it for you, then sent it by mail because how did I know when we'd ever see you again?—what with your deserting us after Epidauros. I mailed it myself, the day after she left. What? Ah, your charming note. Yes, it pleased us so much. No, not alone. With a red-haired girl from Charleston or Galveston & a boy named Rob whose father is a bank president. First to Venice, then Munich, then Paris. So you've missed her!" She was bright & decisive throughout. I am still a fortune hunter in her eyes.

She had forwarded my letter about the watercolor, & will give me an address in London good through August.

"If you were really interested you could have shown it more," said Mrs N. gaily with her eyes on my face. "Girls today don't sit in their parlors waiting for the man to make up his mind."

It was long past twelve. The heat burned through the awnings, melting our ice. The E. C. stood in his doorway. George had found several excuses to pass back & forth. By now I would surely have pointed him out to the N.'s who at any moment were going to invite him on board, offer him a drink, take him to Athens, Paris, New York. It was for our convenience, really, that he kept in sight.

His expectancy was easier than my own to understand.

A deep breath, one might have said, had been indrawn by somebody whose attention was at the same instant so caught & held by 1000 details of the scene—a hot sun-shaft, Mrs N.'s elbow corrugated by the wicker she had leaned upon, a dog on the quai, the dog's reflection in water—so held that he, the breather, simply kept forgetting to exhale. In the harbor a mullet leapt, realized its error, flopped back stunned. The N.'s themselves, who according to her note had been all eagerness to depart, sat becalmed. I cannot think what more we talked about. They did not, I know, suggest my accompanying them to Athens that afternoon. And in the end it was Orson they rescued from this island.

The scene kept brightening & darkening around me. Under his sign ("Tout pour le Sport") the Enfant's pitted moon-face shone—the face of Herodias when she says: My daughter has done well. The Sleeping Woman stirred, at intervals, on her mirror mattress.

~~Orestes~~

Orson appeared at the far end of the waterfront. Mr N. had said, "I believe . . ." The rest of us looked up.

His approach was, or seemed, slow. Something about it had caused a number of little boys to leave the beach & follow him. He couldn't have been walking too slowly; they were having to trot to keep up. From town, a handful of adolescents, as on the green radio beam of the Enfant Chic's gaze, ambled forth to meet him.

"C'est donc lui? Comme il est bronzé," said Mrs N. "Vraiment, on dirait un grec."

Mr N. (God love him): Mais, c'est un grec, idiote. Tu n'as rien compris?

~~He had been whipped He had evidently Byron had~~

We could now see the red weal on Orson's face, & stripes of red on his shirt where he had lifted his shoulder to blot it. He had on walking shorts but carried a jacket over his arm. The visit had been formal.

15 or 20 children and boys completed the procession. The Eumenides—only in this instance they were, without irony, "Kindly Ones." Their faces expressed pity & wonder, they kept pace in silence. Greeks, unlike Americans, are not thrilled by violence. Alone, the Enfant Chic called from his doorway, sarcastically, "Bon zour, Monsieur. Vous voulez quelque chose?"—and somebody did laugh.

"Ftáni, putana!" shouted an angry voice at the foot of our gangplank. It was George. The E. C. (who had been addressed) smirked & looked debonair.

Orson was not looking our way, though close enough to have seen us on the shaded deck. Soon he was abreast of the caïque. His face was calm & exalted.

I rose from my chair. I felt the N.'s glance at me.

I cannot make this sound as if it happened.

He was passing us by, keeping to the water's edge. He was clearly heading nowhere—hadn't he *become* his destination? (But 50 yards more & he would hit the path to the slaughterhouse.)

I felt my eyes sting—L. at Epidauros, surprised by the turn of events. I ran down the gangplank, caught up with him, could not speak, took his arm, & led him onto the caïque.

The dimness under the awning dazed him, otherwise he was in complete possession of himself. Even with my beard he had known me. I turned to him now, arms open. We said each other's names & embraced.

"This is what I meant in my letter," he said, stepping back, hands still on my shoulders. "What I have wanted & never had from you."

I turned away confused.

Part of me is still glowing with pleasure at those words. Part of me is still running away from them.

He was still Orson, in any case. In a moment he too had turned & was replying to the N.'s offers of rest, refreshment, medication in his familiar "teacher's" voice—the voice that says, "I understand these things far better than you. They are useful but irrelevant." Mrs N. made him accept a glass of cognac. He sipped it & set it down. Then Mr N. took him below to bathe his face. Out of sight, Orson could be heard suddenly exclaiming, "But, pardon me, haven't we met before? Long ago, wasn't it you who, etc."—in tones of amazed discovery, & Mr. N.'s replies, too melodious to make out, until a door clicked shut.

Mrs N. went to the rail & said something into the crowd below. Several boys made a dash for the café. Whoever got there 1st, it was George who returned carrying O.'s knapsack. He stood at the top of the gangplank, holding it. Mrs N. thanked him & asked him to put it down. I forget what distracted her; when she looked again he was still there, radiantly waiting, so she thanked him again & he went away.

They were going to take Orson to Athens. Good.

Before she could include me in the assumption, I approached Mrs N. & said I would have to leave them now. I held out my hand. Like an automaton's hers rose, hesitated, came to rest in mine.

I've promised to call on her in Athens this week. She absolutely did not understand. But then, to do justice to the moment, neither did I.

I went up into the hills behind the town. I climbed & climbed, stumbling, not stopping, wanting to think. I felt excited and confused over the way I was acting.

I saw at least how little any of it had been my doing—for better or worse. Orson hadn't known I was on Diblos. No one had drawn him here but himself, his life. Betrayal & rejection are what he has always needed in his dealings with people. When Dora didn't answer his letters, what could he do but seek satisfaction at her son's hands? He hadn't deserved his whipping, rather he had all but made it happen, acting, as he had, in good faith as in bad taste, out of his own ~~blind~~ hopeless allegiance to this country of his dreams. And he had carried it off, made it seem like justice. Even I, in the notebook's blackest depths, would never have dared to construct such a denouement— coincidence, melodrama, every earmark of life's (the rival's) style. Il miglior fabbro!

~~How not to admit admire~~

How not to envy him the total experience? With courage or cunning or luck he had paid

O. had found a currency in which to pay the full price for what he believed. His view of things, his "tragic" view, would never be wholly an illusion, once having interlocked so perfectly with his suffering. I ought to have felt by contrast as I did when the Army rejected me, or like the saints who died painlessly in bed, not complaining really, only whispering the dry fact that they hadn't been found worthy of the martyr's crown.

Instead, I kept breaking into smiles—of pure aesthetic pleasure? Not entirely. I *had* been part of it. I had even paid a little price of my own: that of "missing" Lucine. Missing her, as Mrs N. had implied, by sitting here, doing whatever I was doing. Missing *in* her something I could or should have had, or have wanted at least enough to go after. What I hadn't missed by sitting on Diblos was my moment with Orson. All of it—the running after him, & his words, his hand on my shoulder; *and* the running away, while my heart was still full.

I still feel somewhat as if I had brought off a little raid on life, & escaped with my treasure intact.

I had reached the hilltop with its white chapel, door & window sliced out of unbaked meringue, a baby's confection—yet wholly itself, an innocent, arbitrary shape. I sat in the white shade, sweating, looking back. The wind blew. There below, at different points round the lagoon, were all my landmarks. I felt light & happy, & at rest.

I let the day's events play themselves once more in my head. As they did, I had a sense of other, less personal elements, beauty, joy, truth, splendor—things ideas all whose ebbing over the years had been so gradual that I'd never registered it—flowing back now to their place at the heart of the scene, pure & compelling. In their light, Byron himself seemed not so much a spiteful neurotic as a proud

B. himself, in their light, stood forth in dark, glowing colors, velvet & gold braid, & dagger handle flashing—a costume from the vendetta country of Crete or the Mani. Banked like a coal, his pride had burst into flame at last. He raised

In my head he raised his beautiful clenched hand. The riding crop descended, once, twice, again, upon my

once, twice, again, inscribed its madder penstroke upon my brother's face, at the tempo of a ~~slowly pounding tempo of a giant's drugged pulse—~~

of the dolphin's progress through glittering foam

at the tempo of those 3 blows whereupon the curtain of the Comédie rises to reveal, as foreseen, that universe of classical unity whose suns blaze & seas glitter & whose every action however brutal is nobly, inflexibly ordered & the best of each of us steps forth in his profound dark spotlight with poetry on his lips.

Had anyone discovered me up there, I would have been caught in flagrante with a myth-making apparatus every bit as vigorous as O.'s & probably a trifle more depraved. I come back today to how little I cared for him, how much for the idea of him.

Today I tend, in my better moments, toward chagrin & scruple. *That* orgy must never be repeated!—as with a moistened cloth I dab primly at my mind, where there are telltale stains.

There is evidently *no* excuse for my having left the caïque.

From my vantage I could watch it sail. I walked down the hill & began to pack.

6.viii.61

My last day. Tonight I shall be in Athens. Tomorrow I'll make peace with Orson. I've got to, I want to, before sailing home.

~~It has all been at one remove anyhow. Has the time come to tackle the Houston novel?~~

George looked in this morning. "You no go caïque? Why?"

"I go vapóri. Today."

Again: "Why?" The palm turned out & up as if to catch a grapefruit from above, the face blindly smiling, shaken from side to side—I shall miss the Greek "Why?"

I'd left out the blue slacks he liked, & gave them to him. He printed his name & address for me. "Good my friend," he said, leaving.

I have made peace with Chryssoula, too. We have held each other, foreheads touching sadly, reflectively. My photograph is tucked face-down in her brassiere. A young Englishman has arrived with whom she can laugh tomorrow. She will find a present under my pillow—some money & a little flagon of perfume.

(While in Italy Dora & Orestes & Sandy can stop in Urbino to see the Piero *Flagellation* which O. has greatly admired in black & white.)

Orestes' disappointment was keen to discover that the punishment of the god, for all its monumental aspect in reproduction, was in fact quite small, and ~~unexpectedly~~ subtly, vividly colored.

I must be mad. I've given up this novel.

. . .

"The only solution is to be very, very intelligent." Intelligence, it is implied, will dissimulate itself, will *lose itself* in simplicity. By the same token, any extended show of Mind may be taken as the work of some final naïveté.

On deck. We have sailed past the House. The Sleeping Woman has veered & reshifted into new, nonrepresentational masses. Diblos lies far astern. Here is the open water. A sun preparing to sink. Other islands.

THE PLAYS

THE BIRTHDAY

A PLAY IN VERSE

(1947)

Characters

Charles, *the host*
Mrs. Crane, *the mother*
Max, *the innocent*
Mr. Knight, *the wizard*
Raymond

(*Scene: Charles' living room. Six o'clock in the afternoon.*)

PROLOGUE

(*CHARLES appears before the curtain.*)

■

CHARLES:
   Ladies and gentleman: this is a play about birth.

(*Scene: A pleasant living room whose chief feature is red walls, arranged with a neatness that can mean only a party; it is furnished in no particular period but with good taste. There is a low sofa between the door, R, and window, L, concealed by Venetian blinds. In front of the sofa there is a low table with a bottle of wine and four glasses. There may be flowers in the room, a few books, and a Nativity—preferably Picasso's* Mother and Child—*above the sofa facing the audience.*)

(*As the curtain rises, MRS. CRANE, the first guest, is seated alone on the sofa; she is poised and congenial, on the brink of fifty. She rises, wanders about, inspects her makeup, fingernails, hair, and returns to the sofa at last as CHARLES enters, ushering in two more guests: MAX, the primitive painter, somewhat carelessly dressed, extremely young in appearance, carrying a portfolio; and MR. KNIGHT, slightly past thirty, but also with an unusually young, though tired, expression. CHARLES himself looks uncomfortably like a man of distinction. In his first speech, he speaks as much to the audience as to any of the actors.*)

CHARLES:
   I believe you all know one another. Mrs. Crane,
   Our leading lady for the afternoon,
   Who always makes these gatherings so pleasant.
   My good friend Max, who not only paints *à ravir*
   But to my knowledge has no surname. And Mr. Knight.
   Mr. Knight is a wizard; indeed, we are all wizards—

My dear Mrs. Crane, my good Max, you are wizards also,
And perhaps more fortunate in that you are
Comparatively unaware of your powers.

MAX:

Charles is the most embarrassing person I know.

MRS. C.:

It has been quite a while since I was here last, Charles,
And I shan't say you should entertain more often—
I know you give your parties constantly
And I suppose it's just as well I stay away
Occasionally—but really you might have asked me
Before you changed this room. I scarcely know it.

CHARLES:

You dislike it, of course?

MRS. C.:

Oh, no, except for the walls
Which make me think of . . .

MAX:

                       . . . Of the inside of the mouth!
Exactly! Oh I like them enormously now.
That red is exactly like the inside of the mouth.
You know, Charles, I have just discovered the mouth.
And I spent all of the past week painting Helen
With her mouth open and a background of orange trees.
I brought some sketches with me.

(*He unfastens portfolio.*)
                       Look at this one.

MRS. C.:

Gracious, what splendid teeth! You do have talent.
Don't you agree, he has talent, Mr. Knight?

MAX:

I believe in painting only what I see.

Perhaps in these I have tried to be too precise.

MRS. C.:

But Max, they are lovely.

KNIGHT:

And it is precisely

This precision of yours, this splendid confidence

In your own eye, that makes your paintings good

And in the bargain unbelievable.

A painting is to the face it transforms as a balloon

Is to the hand that holds the string. The worthiness

Of art exists in this tenuous relation.

This will never disturb Max, he is a painter;

But you, Mrs. Crane, and Charles, and I, we are all

Doomed to walk the battlements of the abstract.

MRS. C.:

I'm sure you exaggerate. Who is coming today, Charles?

CHARLES:

He should be here any minute. His name is Raymond.

And allow me to express once more my wishes

As to your attitudes. There must be no argument

Among yourselves; for everything that takes place

Must happen through him, as actors assume credit

For the dazzling lines they speak. You have all attended

Enough of these parties to guess their limitations

That, once imposed, like masks, are not discarded

Till the play ends, sometimes not even then.

Remember also that he is not a wizard.

The single purpose of this celebration

Is that Raymond meet you and opaquely gather

Your more than luminous importance. *You* know—
Give him a cigarette, a glass of wine;
Ask him your riddles: What is your home town?
How old are you? Were you a happy child?
He's not, however, applying for a job.
I'll fetch him now. Let me wish you in advance
A congenial hour. (*Exit.*)

MAX:

It always has such a flavor of excitement.
Charles should have been a seventeenth-century king.

MRS. C.:

The glamour wore off rather suddenly for me.
I don't mind admitting the only reason I come
Is from a sense of obligation to Charles.

KNIGHT:

Obligation, indeed! You deceive yourself, Mrs. Crane.

MRS. C.:

That is why I am here. If anyone is deceiving . . .
I should like just once, however, to be absent.
We might as well, for that matter, be puppets
Or wooden ducks on a lake that might be real.

KNIGHT:

Though you will never stay away, if once you should keep
From coming when Charles needs you, it would be
Impossible to estimate the confusion
And helplessness and anguish of our guest.

MRS. C.:

Are you trying to be clever?

KNIGHT:

No.

MRS. C.:

Thank you.

MAX:

Do you mean to say you don't like these afternoons?
It's funny, but there's nothing I enjoy
As much as being here. As a little boy
I sailed in a glass-bottomed boat. There were circus tunes
Across the water. I always think of them here.

KNIGHT:

This is because you are the spirit of change.
I am Heraclitus barefoot in the streams,
But you are the flattered current. I do not see change,
I create it. I do not see it because,
Like music to a deaf man, it is all
I can believe. Therefore when I come here . . .
When I come here, I come with a single promise.
I swear that in this room I will not explain
Myself, I will not analyze, I will
Not even speak. Once here, I am made to speak,
I am made to reveal.

(*He has risen in agitation.*)

MRS. C.:

But you are the wizard, Charles said.

KNIGHT:

That, like change, is what I cannot bear.
How dare we wear these masks before we accept
What we are masking!

MAX:

I hear them coming. Sit down.

KNIGHT:

I will not speak.

MAX:

So fascinating!

MRS. C.:

I feel
So sorry for them, they could be my own children.

(*Enter CHARLES with RAYMOND, a young man rather ill at ease.*)

CHARLES:

Raymond, I should like you to meet Mrs. Crane,
Max . . .

MAX:

I have no last name.

CHARLES:

. . . And Mr. Knight.

(*MRS. CRANE and MAX shake hands with RAYMOND. There is a pause before KNIGHT rises, crosses, shakes hands and speaks.*)

KNIGHT:

I am very pleased to meet you, Raymond.

CHARLES:

I hope you don't mind if I leave you now.
I will see you later, Raymond, I am sure.

RAYMOND:

    Would you mind before you go telling me what . . . ?

CHARLES:

    You will have to excuse me now. (*Exit.*)

MRS. C.:

    You will have to excuse Charles. He's so often that way.
    I don't suppose you've known him very long;
    Tell me, where did you meet him?

RAYMOND:

                     We shared a taxi.

MAX (*to KNIGHT*):

    I'll never get over being amazed at Charles.

MRS. C.:

    Charles always meets such interesting people.
    I don't know what you do, of course, but Max
    Is a painter and Mr. Knight is a magician.
    I'm nobody in particular, but Charles
    Always invites me because he knows how much
    I like to meet his interesting friends.
    Won't you sit down? How old are you, Raymond?

RAYMOND:

    Nineteen.

MAX:

           Happy Birthday! (*Pause.*)

RAYMOND:

    I don't know what you mean by that. My birthday
    Is not until October twenty-first.

MAX:

No please don't spoil the party; we were told
This was your birthday. We're all here today
To drink your health. Many happy returns!

(*MAX has by this time opened the wine, poured it, and offered glasses to
MRS. CRANE and RAYMOND, at the end of the speech. He now takes a
glass to KNIGHT, who refuses it.*)

RAYMOND:

Who told you it was my birthday? Was it Charles?

MRS. C.:

Yes, but good heavens, we should know his tricks by now.
We can all have a glass of wine at any rate

(*With not altogether forced sentiment.*)

And drink to your birthday on October twenty-first
And to all birthdays in an aging world.
That's all one ever drinks to.

RAYMOND (*who does not drink*):

Who is Charles?

MAX:

Charles is the most wonderful person in the world.
He's simply rather hard to understand.
To your health, Raymond.

(*Drinks.*)

RAYMOND:

But who is he, what does he do?

KNIGHT:

    I am obliged to intervene.

    Now really, Max, you can be dreadfully gauche.

    Today is your birthday in the sense that every day

    Is a birthday, every minute the minute of one's birth.

    You have been asked here, this celebration has been arranged,

    Only that you may begin to realize this.

RAYMOND:

    Thank you for being so explicit.

KNIGHT:

    I cannot speak plainly to you: I cannot speak plainly

    To myself.

MRS. C.:

                    I can speak plainly, Raymond. Today

    Is your birthday. You must accept that to begin with.

    Everything that we may say . . .

RAYMOND:

                            But it's not true.

    My birthday's not today.

MRS. C.:

                        Please let me finish.

    Everything that we may say this afternoon

    Is of the greatest importance. We are here

    Because we are all so deeply involved in you.

    Do you understand, will you take my word for it?

RAYMOND (*indicating them all*):

    Who are you?

MAX:

    We are you. (*Pause.*) I hope you're not disappointed.

(Before RAYMOND can speak, KNIGHT begins.)

KNIGHT:

Raymond, have you ever traveled on the sea?

RAYMOND:

I think we went to Europe when I was nine.

KNIGHT:

The waters are of different colors; the shallows
Pink and green where the reefs are and fish look
Like colored advertisements; where the ocean is grey,
Grey-black, fish lunge like weapons; but far out
In the purple Gulf Stream, blue, it is as though
One were pulling up a cluster of angels seen
Through the reverse end of a telescope.
Sailors, too, with their sense of stylization,
Tattoo blue hips on their arms, rococo veins,
Calling them images of the sea. There are
Innumerable relations, all quite useless.
A drop of human blood, as you will remember,
In chemical proportion is equivalent
To simple seawater.

MAX:

                  That will be my next painting.

RAYMOND:

You were explaining why I should be here.

KNIGHT:

I was explaining nothing, nothing. Communication
Is a peeling leprosy. I was speaking of the sea.

MAX:

Isn't it splendid? I told you it would be.

MRS. C.:

Raymond, listen to me.

RAYMOND:

What is it now?

MRS. C.:

What are your memories? I always feel
A person is what he remembers. We
Must know who you are. Tell us about yourself.

RAYMOND:

There's not too much. I like to go horseback riding.
My father always laughed when I fell off.

(*He is embarrassed.*)

When I was a child I walked between two hedges,
It was late September and there had been a frost,
I remember finding a robin's egg in the grass
And picking it up. But when I turned it over
The bird's foot was sticking through the shell.
It was all frozen, of course. I don't know why
I bother to tell you, except that I've never forgotten it.

MRS. C.:

My poor child.

RAYMOND:

There was one room in our house
I never saw. It was just an empty room.
My cousin went inside and laughed at me
Because I was afraid. I hadn't been afraid,
I simply didn't want to go inside.
But I threw a chestnut once and broke the window.

MRS. C.:

My poor child. Raymond, listen to me.

RAYMOND:

Yes.

MRS. C.:

Raymond, this is the hour of your birth. (*Pause.*)
I am your mother. (*She rises.*)

RAYMOND (*rising angrily*):

This is quite enough.
I've tried to humor you all with a great deal of patience,
And I don't know whether or not you are being amusing
And I may be gullible but really—Good afternoon.

(*He goes to the door; it is locked; he is a little frightened now.*)

This is no longer a joke. Will you please let me out?

MAX:
(*After an exchange of glances, rises, crosses to him.*)

Charles always locks the door. You've scarcely arrived
And you haven't even touched your glass of wine.
Charles will let you go shortly, but not yet.
Resign yourself to that. Now just sit down.
Perhaps you would like to see my watercolors.
This is the best one, Helen with her mouth open.
Are you fond of painting at all? Oh, forgive us,
We must be annoying you dreadfully, but truly
We are sane, normal people, differing from you
Only in point of view. You must talk with us.
If you don't it will be very difficult.

MRS. C.:

How shall we speak to each other if you will not listen?

KNIGHT (*softly to Max*):

Baudelaire's mother, I believe, used those same words.

MAX (*aloud*):

I resent the implication that Mrs. Crane
In any way resembles Baudelaire's mother.

MRS. C.:

Max, please go on.

MAX (*to RAYMOND*):

                No matter how little you speak,
How little you believe, you must listen. Mrs. Crane
Has already told you what she means to you.
Let me tell you about myself: I am a painter,
And Charles thinks you will become a lot like me.
Heaven knows, it's confusing enough to me.
It appears that you will more or less somehow share
My reactions to the world, to people and scenes
And things. Perhaps if I tell you what I'm like
It may grow clearer. I am, people tell me,
Supposed to be very naïve. Actually,
I'm rather proud of that. My paintings show it
And all my teachers have told me I should never
Be afraid of my simplicity. I think
The really brilliant people never think.
I wish I might have been the one to find
That robin's egg of yours. Please have some wine,
Or hold your glass at least; I'm beginning to feel
Somewhat foolish talking to you while you just sit there.

(*RAYMOND rather condescendingly takes his glass and sips.*)

Ah, that's so much better. Tell me, is there a chance
Of your believing anything we say?

RAYMOND:

I'm afraid not. It's rather amusing however.
Since you won't let me go, there's nothing else I can do.
Keep on talking if you like.

(*He rises, while listening to MAX, and wanders with more assurance around the room, glancing unappreciatively at the Nativity on the wall.*)

MAX:

Mrs. Crane is your mother. I am what you shall be.
It's hard to say these things in simple words.
I don't mean, of course, that Mrs. Crane will raise you
From an actual childhood—it's beyond that; or that I
Shall die so that you may become the person I am.

RAYMOND:

Well, that makes it convenient for both of us.

MAX:

You are arrogant; you lose so much by assurance.

MRS. C.:

How shall we speak of goodness or achievement
If you will mock us? The world does not last forever.

(*KNIGHT has risen, and with an effort begins to speak.*)

KNIGHT:

There are as many worlds as cells in the body. They are
Evolving continually: the falling of your hand
Is the birth of a universe, the smile on your face
Is the curtain lowering on one brief world
We might perhaps have shared, or two or three perhaps.

(He stops with a gesture of hopelessness, a kind of anguish.)

RAYMOND:

    Are you ill?

KNIGHT:

               There is a possibility
    That I am very ill.

MRS. C.:

    Raymond, sit down. You must be very careful.
    Sit down with me. What is happening now has nothing
    To do with us. You have no choice. . . . We are here
    Like godmothers in a fairy tale.

MAX *(warningly)*:

               Mrs. Crane . . .

(KNIGHT at last takes up his glass. RAYMOND watches him with interest.)

KNIGHT:

    Allow me to propose a toast to the organs of the body.
    I raise my cup to the hand, the hip and the collarbone.
    To the health of the wrist, breast and ankle who have served us
        so well!
    I salute the mouth and the muddy city in the eye . . .
    They have remained our close friends.
    For you may protest until your eyes are coppered
    That what is behind the face, behind the breast,
    Surpasses nerve and muscle, but you shall never see it
    Except in the mouth's corners and in the wandering eye.
    I would deny profundity and choose to be faithful,
    As long as I shall desire faith, to this unbelievable,
    Most impermanent superficiality.
    The body is the most difficult thing there is

But the world has discovered a means of dealing with it.
If one should wish to suppose the existence of a will,
Of a language—as in the past men supposed God—
We should all grow quickly into monsters and rebuke
The air, the rainwater that separates my house
From your house, and realize that what is spoken
Directly behind these fabulous eyeballs is this:
That we are unhappy, uncertain, unable to perfect
A single moment, word or smile. Something
Is eternally thrust in; eternally not yet—
That is the only serpent in the garden
And the only angel in hell.

RAYMOND:
    Who are you?

KNIGHT:
                    I am the person you will always love.

MRS. C. (*deeply concerned*):
    Good God, it's worse than the Pied Piper! Max,
    Don't laugh. There isn't much time left.
    Oh, it's preposterous.

(*She has risen, moved to the window; she lights a cigarette.*)

MAX:
    Please, Mrs. Crane; everything will be all right.

(*Turning now to RAYMOND.*)

    Let me tell you a story, Raymond, about a child—
    Who was myself, of course—who dreamed of painting
    A world existing only in his heart.
    My father said, "You have never seen this world.

Why should you paint it?" But I had seen that world,
A world of beckoning hands, plants, animals
Parading in the brilliant corridor
Beyond the eye. I think it was a dream.
But I had entered it; I am in it now.
I painted it and that was how I came
To enter it. In it I found my Helen—
You saw her portrait among the orange trees . . .
But what I mean is that I found this world
Because I risked it, as one takes a chance
And throws a chestnut at a secret window
And breaks the window. There's nothing else to say.
You, who have risked nothing, have not yet
Found your proper countryside. It is my hope,
The hope of all of us, that you may find it here
Or privately, where you found your robin's egg.
Perhaps you understand . . . ?

RAYMOND:

And you are?

MAX:

I am the person you will always be.

MRS. C. (*advancing*):
Raymond, my world is not a difficult one.
I mean, not difficult to understand
But a costly world to enter. A world of goodness,
Courage and love, where all activity
Exists like an accommodation of virtue,
Like a mirror that is not vanity. To stand
Watching one's hand in sunlight, the face of one's sweetheart
Laughing in a warm climate; to watch the sea
And the changing colors and bright fish that are
So bright, so beguiling—these become different things,

Of small importance in themselves, except
In the honest structure of a human world.
For a man must be above the things he sees
And snap his fingers at them, and recognize
That they are good only if he is more so.
I sound as if I were preaching, and I'm sorry
That you should have to think of me this way.
I'm not a saintly woman; I am a mother,
And I understand the problems of my sons
Because they are my sons. I don't like pride
But I am proud in some ways of my life.
It is a life I will gladly help you live
With all the blessings and guidance I can give.

RAYMOND:
And you, as you said, are my mother?

MRS. C.:
No.
I am the person you will always remember.

(*Pause. RAYMOND is nearly convinced. Nobody moves. At last MRS. CRANE takes a step towards him. He backs away from her.*)

RAYMOND:
I don't accept it. It's humiliating; it's vulgar—
I doubt if you even know what I mean. I have
A mother; I've already fallen in love.
Listening to these cheap arguments I blushed
And blushed again that I should have to blush.
Where is Charles? I want to go home now.

MRS. C.:
What you mean, my dear, is that it's sudden, isn't it?
It takes only a moment for a life to change
But hours of preparation must come before.

RAYMOND:

    You talk like one who has never lived, as though
    The things you know and the things you believe
    Are somehow different.

MAX:

                       Perhaps you mean
    We've been a trifle blunt? How could we have been
    Less so in the brief time we were allotted?
    There are some others beside you, you understand.

RAYMOND:

    I understand nothing, not even your audacity.

KNIGHT:

    Perhaps you deplore the obvious symbolism
    Of the red walls, that tactless *Madonna and Child*
    Above the sofa, the congratulatory wine?
    They make me shudder too. You feel perhaps
    Our words are in bad taste and I agree.

MRS. C.:

    We may have said things you already know,
    Which is unpardonable; but one forgets
    The importance of things already known.

KNIGHT:

    Or else you have guessed that we are here, in part,
    As elaborate temptations to accept a point of view
    That is, after all, only a point of view.
    Our language crumbles, our makeshift masks betray us.
    It is all an artifice—that is what makes it valid.

MAX:

    Perhaps it's *us* that anger you? You wonder
    Why *we* were chosen. Oh, we're not so bad.

Mrs. Crane is an angel compared with our other mothers,
And you should see who you nearly got instead of me.

MRS. C.:

And so, my boy, goodbye. Good luck. God bless you.

RAYMOND:

You mean it's over?

MRS. C.:

Charles is coming now.

RAYMOND:

I won't go now. I won't go until something at least—
I don't care what—is clear to me. You've told me
Nothing. There's not a thing I've understood.
Why was I brought here? If I am being born,
Into what am I being born, what am I entering?
What world do you belong to? I won't go
Until you tell me something I understand.

(*CHARLES has entered during the last two lines.*)

CHARLES:

Aha! A scene! The birthday's not a success?

KNIGHT (*bitterly*):

Let's speak of it rather as a miscarriage, Charles.

(*CHARLES laughs delightedly.*)

RAYMOND:

How can he laugh?

KNIGHT:

God always laughs, Raymond.
Comedy exists in a distance between two points.

CHARLES:
Well, Raymond, what would you like me to explain?

RAYMOND:
I don't know why you all have to act as though
I understood. You seem to think it's an accomplishment.
I've understood nothing and I'm glad of that;
I'm bewildered and annoyed and want to forget
Whatever has happened. There's nothing you can do
To keep me from that.

CHARLES:
So the child enters the world.
There are so many ways of understanding
Bewilderment and anger and forgetfulness
Are ways of understanding. There's nothing *you* can do,
To keep yourself from that.

RAYMOND:
It's cruel, it's nonsense.

CHARLES:
In spite of all this violence, you shall find—
Walking home tonight, perhaps—against your will
You shall discover something has been shown
Profounder than all your easy barriers.

KNIGHT:
It is only as one scrapes at a frog's skull, scrapes and scrapes,
Till only the thinnest pane of bone remains
Between the small brain and the instrument;
This breaks at last, and wisdom like a bright dye
Makes every part distinct.

CHARLES:
At any rate,
Goodbye. Good luck. I'll take you to the door.

(*He takes RAYMOND's arm to lead him out, but RAYMOND breaks away in a blind violence.*)

RAYMOND:

   Don't ever touch me! (*He runs out.*)

(*CHARLES returns to the center of the room; he is disturbed but not too seriously. There is a pause.*)

CHARLES:

   Sometimes I feel like saying to hell with it.

MRS. C.:

   Then why do you keep on?—Your little party
   Has been, as usual, Charles, about as amusing
   As a crucifixion.

MAX:

                           What an interesting simile.
   What will happen to him, Charles?

CHARLES (*sitting*):

                              I've told you already.
   He will always be the person you are, Max.
   He will always love the wizardry Mr. Knight
   Embodies. He will always remember Mrs. Crane.
   He will die after a certain amount of joy.

MAX:

   Is it always that simple?

CHARLES:

                           It is always that simple.

MRS. C.:

   It's frightful. Charles, you have never been a person,
   Never. I'm sorry I ever came here. You are children

Playing with all the cruelty of children
Who laugh in the face of honor.

CHARLES:

We shan't squabble.
I'll see you next week, Mrs. Crane. Good night.

MRS. C.:
If it weren't so clumsy . . .

CHARLES:

What can you expect?

MAX (*taking his portfolio*):
I think I'll have to be going.
Good night, Charles. I'll see you soon, I hope.
Would anyone care to join me for a cocktail?

KNIGHT:
I'd be delighted if you don't mind. Charles,
As I've said before, you are an incredible artist.
I understand you, envy you, admire you,
And despise you utterly. You are the evil
That we have sought all through our lives. Good night.

CHARLES:
Good night.

MAX:

Good night, Charles.

CHARLES:

Good night.

(*Exit MAX and KNIGHT. MRS. CRANE pauses a moment.*)

MRS. C.:

    Charles, Charles . . .

(*He rises in irritation and pride.*)

CHARLES:

    What is your anguish and your innocence?
    The hall of mirrors that you have not seen
    Expands the grey sky like the sight of Echo.
    The feasting faces, darting or serene,
    Have fallen all to mould and gaze no more.
    But reflections have never ceased. Usurping silver,
    Blood and bone once thrust itself between
    The grey visage of God and This His Glass—
    Groping, endearing. For centuries these have been
    Forever moving delicately through brightest air
    Within my hall, from side to mirrored side.
    Their image is their essence, and except
    For their brief birth and living they have not died.

(*MRS. CRANE can say nothing. She leaves. CHARLES pours himself a glass of wine and, raising it, approaches the audience.*)

CHARLES:

    Ladies and gentleman: this has been a play about birth.

(CURTAIN)

THE BAIT

A PLAY

(1953)

Characters

Julie
John, *her fiancé*
Charles, *her husband*
Gilbert, *her brother*

(The action takes place in Venice and in the Gulf Stream. On one side of the stage, a suggestion of the Piazza; on the other, the stern of a fishing boat.)

(Enter, from Venice, JOHN and JULIE. It is a summer afternoon.)

JOHN:
  You have never told me this before.

JULIE:
  I do not understand what I have told you. That may be why you have not heard it before.

JOHN:
  Go on. After you got back to the dock what happened? What happened that night?

JULIE:
  Evidently I am not able to tell a story. I feel as if I had been talking ever since lunch. And now I'm all talked out and I've missed my siesta.

JOHN:
  I know the sense of imprisonment that comes from being in a very small boat, so far from shore. You can see the land, a ribbon of beach with colorless trees. The ocean calls into play our deepest subjectivity. All this might never have happened under different circumstances.

JULIE:
  What did happen was that in two weeks I left him.

JOHN:
  Left . . . Charles?

JULIE:
  You don't imagine I'd ever leave Gilbert? Well. One would rather not talk about what one has not understood.

JOHN:

Yet it has given you pleasure to do so.

JULIE:

Are we going to sit down? No. I see only one chair. And we have talked enough.

JOHN:

But could anyone have endured? I mean, was it simply Charles not trying to hold out, when he went into the water? Could anyone have held out? Am I of no help to you?

JULIE:

I don't see that *you* need be so solemn, John.

JOHN:

We have talked of solemn things.

JULIE:

It has, you are right, given me pleasure to talk about what I have not understood. Probably I had known that I should fail, but I feel myself virtuous for trying once again to understand it.

JOHN:

You are not a simple person.

JULIE:

I am. Only I have not been able to simplify. One wants a complicated person to do that. Look at those pigeons, how can they bear it?— eating out of people's hands. Yes, you have helped me by letting me talk about it. It is less real now that someone other than myself has failed to understand it.

JOHN:

You are not to blame.

JULIE:

Not to blame for leaving my husband?

JOHN:

Not to blame for the circumstances.

JULIE:

That is the kind of remark that never fails to dazzle me. It makes me feel that my total experience is somehow *here,* within easy reach, like so many rolls of film on a shelf.

JOHN:

I mean simply that the circumstances would seem to narrow down to your brother.

JULIE:

Yes. Gilbert is to blame. I am finer than Gilbert.

JOHN:

I like Gilbert. He makes me laugh.

JULIE:

Gilbert makes everybody laugh. No. He never made Charles laugh. That's conceivably why they were such good friends.

JOHN:

But I laugh more easily with you. When I'm with Gilbert I'm not really laughing.

JULIE:

Neither am I. It must be a power he has over me. Look! There he sits in the *pensione* and here I am giggling . . .

JOHN:

At the risk of irritating you, it does seem curious to me that Gilbert should . . .

JULIE:

Should what?

JOHN:

That Gilbert should be so much in the picture. He goes everywhere you go, he knows everything you do.

JULIE:

You *are* possessive!

JOHN:

Do you mind?

JULIE:

No. I think it's rather sweet. Now what are you saying about Gilbert?

JOHN:

I don't remember.

JULIE:

He is after all one's brother.

JOHN:

There are limits. You say he virtually picked out your husband for you.

JULIE:

Well he didn't pick *you* out darling. I did that.

JOHN:

I don't like to believe that you are as close to him as you seem to be.

JULIE:

But isn't that the delightful thing about relatives? They have to love you, you have to love them! After a certain age one meets few enough people of whom that holds true.

JOHN:

You don't really think in those terms.

JULIE:

Don't I? I sometimes think it's a wonder I think at all.

JOHN:

Did Charles like Gilbert? Afterwards, I mean.

JULIE:

O God in heaven! Did Charles like Gilbert! Does Gilbert like me! Did I like them! Why we positively doted upon one another! We shared an eye and a tooth and woe to the unwary stranger who came our way!

JOHN:

Forgive me.

JULIE:

It's just that I'm so weary! Charles writes, Gilbert talks—

JOHN:

You have had another letter from Charles?

JULIE:

You ask questions!

JOHN:

I feel I have a right to know.

JULIE:

Yes, I have had a letter from Charles. I must really stop going to American Express. Nobody else writes to me there.

JOHN:

You needn't go. You needn't accept his letters.

JULIE:

Gilbert says it makes me feel like a bright young person, the kind who would get such letters from her divorced husband.

JOHN:

"Such" letters? Does Gilbert read them?

JULIE:

Do you suppose *I* do? O what an unkind thing to say! You must not make me talk about Charles. I'll say anything that comes into my head.

JOHN:

I *make* you talk? Gilbert *makes* you laugh? It doesn't seem to me that you are made to do anything.

JULIE:

Now you're angry and you don't love me.

(*Enter GILBERT.*)

GILBERT:

O! Ben trovato! Ah! Flirting at Florian's!
My sweet little sister is beautifully bad!
Come with me, cara, we'll go in a gondola!
Gondoliere!

JULIE:

Gilbert, you're mad!

GILBERT:

I've dawdled all day with impossible people.
John will you join us?

JULIE:

Keep up our morale?

JOHN:

No, I must really—

GILBERT:

Then be a wet blanket,
I'm for a ride down that crazy Canal!

JOHN:

What is this passion of Gilbert's for boating?

JULIE:

See you are laughing! I knew you would be!

JOHN:

Then why are *you* laughing?

JULIE:

I'm not *really* laughing.
But I'm going with Gilbert.

GILBERT:

We'll meet you for tea! (*They go.*)

JOHN:

When Julie and I are married I shall urge her to leave Europe and go back with me. Gilbert is very entertaining but I hope he will not follow us. She has gone about with him for so long that now, even when she wants to, she cannot do justice to the beautiful seriousness I know is in her. Gilbert on the other hand belongs in Italy. For myself I do not enjoy living by the sea. I find a warm climate corrupting.

Here in this sweetness I am not quite at ease.
I should prefer Venice in the winter
All flooded and misted and emptied, fixed in a frown,
To this lax glitter, this warm loose life
Of drifting palaces and uprooted foreigners.
Yet these, for they do not flinch at small misfortunes,
Are what endure

While our cold virtues, once thought durable
But now abstract and frail as snowflakes,
Alter to lazy water in the sun.
Fluidity is proof against major disasters.
The marbles melt and wink at me. "Survive,"
They whisper, dimpling, "be like us, *straniero!*
It won't be Venice or the foreigners
That have gone up in spray, when the end comes.
Survive! We have foreseen a gondola
And in the gondola a German woman
Grandly rejoicing over whatever cornice
Shall have been left standing to elicit
The warm salt water from her eyes." Waiter!
A coffee!

A VOICE:
Yes Mister.

JOHN:
I would not speak *their* language. . . . And yet it may be that the world
is nothing more than an impersonal backdrop, that Venice and the sea
discuss endlessly one another, with never a glance at ourselves. But
no. To place Julie now against that other setting she described to me
this afternoon, can I pretend that I had not somehow foreseen it? It
rang a bell, it had to be. Even before she spoke I saw the fishing-boat,
felt the brightness of the day, the blueness of the Gulf Stream where
they sat trolling for big fish. The things we do not understand are
dangerous. All this had positively worked on her. It calls her still over
and over back into bewilderment. Over and over she enters that scene
to work on *it*, sounding the motives like a sea, wondering . . .

JULIE:
Stop!

(*In the course of JOHN's speech the lights have dimmed on Venice and
brightened on the other side of the stage. GILBERT, CHARLES, and
JULIE have entered the fishing boat.*)

JULIE:

    What did they do when I was with them?

    What did they mean to do?

GILBERT:

    Is he steering us the right way?

    I know we've passed that patch of seaweed once before, today.

JULIE (*sings*):

    Ah gardez-vous de me guérir!

    J'aime mon mal, j'en veux mourir!

GILBERT:

    Was that the last beer, Julie?

    It seems a pity, don't you think,

    That we have nothing more to drink?

    And didn't I tell you to make more sandwiches?

    To be hard of hearing has its advantages.

JULIE:

    Desormais je ne parlerai que français.

    From now on I shall only speak French.

GILBERT:

    And it would serve her right, wouldn't it, Charles?

    It must be by design that nobody speaks to me.

    Have I done something wrong? You see

    I am reduced to the simplest interrogatives.

JULIE:

    We know what happens when we talk to you.

    Nous savons bien ce qui arrive—O what's the use!

    Why is Charles frowning?

GILBERT:

                    Charles isn't frowning.

    That is the way his face looks in repose.

    He is a naturally melancholy person.

JULIE:

                                He knows

That we are looking at him.

GILBERT:

                        Rubbish.

JULIE:

                                He knows

How nervous we become when he ignores us.

GILBERT:

He also knows how nervous you become
When I'm not there to keep you from talking to one another.

JULIE:

Idiot.

GILBERT:

Fishwife.

JULIE:

Cretin.

CHARLES:

Look! Something's at the line! Wait!

GILBERT:

It is only your wife's beer bottle.

CHARLES:

Fish won't strike a damaged bait.

GILBERT:

I think that's rather decent of them.

(*CHARLES reels in his line.*)

JULIE:

O what a beautiful day! What soft air!
See how the light moves through the water
Like strings of a piano. And the water
Is not blue but purple. Look out there!
Think of them threading down, the strings of light,
To where an absolute darkness begins,
How they must sound against a thousand cutting fins
And mouths that would swallow me up in a bite.

CHARLES:

If you're not careful we'll put *you* on the hook.

GILBERT:

The water *is* purple, with the blood of talkative wives.
I do appreciate Charles' point of view. He strives
Overmuch perhaps for integrity. Yet one can but admire
Those moments, admittedly frequent, when like a chestnut from
    the fire
He attains his object. Look at him now. He is perfectly at ease
Baiting his line with a fresh mullet. Deep in the purple seas
How shall mere fish, without a fraction of my high-handedness,
Be able to resist such a display of single-mindedness?

JULIE:

Why is it that we become so interesting
As soon as Charles is listening?

GILBERT:

How shall I, if it comes to that? You are at one with your bait.
And I have swallowed it, Charles, I've got you, it's too late.

CHARLES:

It would seem in that case that I had *you*.

GILBERT:

I suppose it would and I daresay you do.

JULIE:

    It would seem you both had *me*.

GILBERT:

    I hope we always shall. I'm sure Charles will agree.

CHARLES:

    Nobody ever has *her* for very long.

JULIE:

    What a nasty remark! Gilbert, tell him he's wrong.

GILBERT:

    He'd never believe me.

JULIE:

                         A brother ought to defend
    His sister's reputation.

GILBERT:

                         But Charles is my friend!
    I couldn't lie to him!

JULIE:

                      O you're the end!

GILBERT:

    See how we have you?

JULIE:

                      Did you have this in mind
    When you arranged for me to marry Charles?

GILBERT:

    I arranged for you to marry Charles?
    What can you mean? I did nothing of the kind.

JULIE:

> You brought Charles home. You said we should make a perfect
> match.

GILBERT:

> Well haven't you? Of course you have. Charles was a catch.
> And today it is his turn to catch us.
> Tomorrow we shall let you win at cards.
> What could conceivably be more stimulating
> Than for three people to catch one another
> In so many different ways? It keeps us going.

(*JULIE crosses to Venice. GILBERT talks to CHARLES.*)

GILBERT:

> I have had many fascinating fishing experiences . . .

JULIE (*to JOHN*):

> You understand I was talking lightly that day.

GILBERT:

> . . . though I am not a serious sportsman like yourself.

JULIE:

> O I knew what I was saying, but I said it
> More as a spell to keep it from becoming.
> And I am talking lightly now, not laughing
> But lightly talking.

GILBERT:

> Why the first time I ever went deep-sea fishing
> I landed a fifty-pound something-or-other,
> The marvel of all my friends, such a powerful one.

JULIE:

> There is that attribute of speech
> That makes for lightness.

GILBERT:

                               I was only a little shaver.
I had it three-quarters of an hour on the line.

JULIE:

I want to dive down,
Discover, bring back whatever it is, the black
Pearl, the sense of whatever I am,
But my bones are full of air, my words are larks,
The sun is sparkling on the surface of the water
In all directions except from underneath.

GILBERT:

Forty-five minutes is a long time.

CHARLES:

                               A long time for a fish.

GILBERT:

A longer time for anybody who wasn't a fish.

JULIE:

I have not wanted to talk lightly. Do you hate me?
I shall rise above it, such is my lightness.

CHARLES:

I don't know. I'm a fairly good swimmer.

JOHN:

Julie, be near me. This was long ago.

GILBERT:

O my dear Charles, don't consider it!

CHARLES:

I suppose you were only joking.

GILBERT:

Can you for a moment imagine I wasn't only joking?

JULIE:

You hear him? He wasn't only joking.

GILBERT:

Why nobody in his right mind would risk
Dipping his big toe in these waters. Besides—

CHARLES:

You think I couldn't hold out?

GILBERT:

You couldn't possibly hold out for five minutes.

JULIE:

That was how it began. Charles said he could hold out
At the end of a line, like a hooked dolphin.
I shall die remembering all that, die!

JOHN:

Darling, it doesn't *matter*!

CHARLES:

Gilbert, sometimes you annoy the hell out of me.

JULIE:

I tried to reason with them. There had been a man
Whose leg was taken off by a shark in Bermuda.
People on the beach saw the blood streaming out of him
But he kept on swimming, he hadn't felt it.
It was when he looked behind him that he died.

CHARLES:

Would you care to make a little bet?

GILBERT:
A little bet?

JULIE:
A little bet!

GILBERT:
Mercenary Charles! No. Why in ten minutes—

CHARLES:
Hook me up to that line. You'll see.

GILBERT:
I'll do nothing of the sort.

JULIE:
He wanted him to do it. He said five minutes the first time.

CHARLES:
I mean it. Fasten me to the line. Use the harness.

GILBERT:
Can you really be such a good swimmer? No,
I refuse to fall in with this absurd exhibition.

CHARLES:
Stop laughing at me. Hook me to the line.

JOHN:
He wanted it too. Charles was asking for it, Julie.

GILBERT:
You'd positively enjoy it?

CHARLES:
Why not?

GILBERT:

All right. Why not?

JULIE:

It was all at once a question of something terribly funny. They were both wearing those ridiculous harnesses that keep you from being yanked out of your chair when something big hits your line. O the idiots, I kept saying to myself. Gilbert was fastening the line to Charles' harness. The boatman had stopped the motor. One can imagine what he must have thought, which didn't help matters, imagining, I mean, what he must have thought.

GILBERT:

Come, little sister, lend a hand.

JOHN:

In time such incidents grow dim.

JULIE (*reentering the boat*):

I think you're crazy, both of you.

CHARLES:

It's a warm day.

JULIE:

Understand

If they should tear you limb from limb
I'm not to blame.

GILBERT:

I hear a distant band

Strike up in honor of our acrobat.

CHARLES:

I'm just as pleased to have a swim.

JULIE:

    Why am I laughing? What you do
    Is dreadful, Gilbert.

GILBERT:

                To whom?

JULIE:

                        To him.
    To me as well.

GILBERT:

           I don't see that.

CHARLES:

    The sea is calm.

GILBERT:

           The sky is blue.

JULIE:

    The blue's all wrong, the sea's too flat.

GILBERT:

    The monsters are at dalliance far below
    On beds of weed and wantonness.
    It's not on us they will grow fat.

CHARLES:

    I've often wondered where they go.

JULIE:

    I never have.

GILBERT:

          All ready?

CHARLES:

> Yes.

JULIE:

Darling—

CHARLES:

> Julie?

JULIE:

> At least take off your hat!

GILBERT:

Ten minutes, mind you. Nothing less.

(*CHARLES disappears over the side of the boat.*)

GILBERT:

Now we shall let him swim a certain distance from the boat. How quiet it is. One would hope to hear suitable music, some light pre-meditated Impromptu, perhaps the Mad Scene from *The Chocolate Soldier*. Charles *is* a good swimmer. You asked why you were laughing. I daresay you knew no other way of participating in that curious moment.

JULIE:

I have found another way.

GILBERT:

My point is that people simply don't do what they don't want to do. In other words, if there is something they don't want to do, they don't do it. This is amusing.

JULIE:

You are doing what you wanted. You are doing it now.

GILBERT:

Yes.

JULIE:

You have made him and me do what you wanted.

GILBERT:

No. I have made it easy for you to do what you yourselves desired. Here we have the example of Charles doing a thing both absurd and dangerous. He is doing it because he wants to. He is not doing it at my suggestion. Soon he will be out far enough.

JULIE:

You gave him no other choice.

GILBERT:

Is it for me to provide alternatives for Charles when there are, as they say in Shreveport, seventeen different things he might be doing at this very moment? Think, Julie! To pretend, as you have all your life, that other people oblige you to do distasteful things is no more than a failure to admit your own taste for doing them. I admit my taste for doing them. I shall enjoy treating Charles, my old friend, to the experience of nearly drowning. If I admit that, there is no reason why you in turn should not confess that you will enjoy watching your husband nearly drown. Charles himself at this very moment is bound to be thinking of how he will profit—It is strange. Whenever you stop listening to me I begin to feel that I have been talking out of sheer nervousness.

JULIE:

I'm sorry.

GILBERT:

These were things I felt you ought to know. Is there anything on your mind?

JULIE:

It's as though I were a little girl again, after my bath, in a white and yellow dress, all delicate and pure. I can hear Father telling me in that voice of his—you know, you talk very much like him sometimes—"Do one thing and do it well," he used to say. And I would nod with great round eyes . . .

GILBERT:

Nonsense. Your eyes were always small, even as a child.

JULIE:

. . . and my little chin would quiver, and before long it would be as though I had *done* my one thing, and done it well, just by listening to him, you see. And I would feel grave and pure and peaceful, the way I feel now. Isn't it silly?

GILBERT:

Perhaps now you can tell me what it is you have done and done well, for you to feel this way.

JULIE:

I couldn't possibly. That's why I say isn't it silly.

GILBERT:

Ask Charles whether it's silly or not.

JULIE:

I'd nearly forgotten Charles. What's the matter with me?
Did you see the expression on his face? He was very angry.

GILBERT:

I never get angry, why should he?
Charles! Are you ready?

CHARLES (*offstage*):
Ready!

GILBERT:

    Now you will see that for all his struggling
    I need only keep mischievously pulling at the line.
    He will be drawn backwards through the brine.
    He will want to breathe and will breathe water.
    His every gesture will be cut short, he will go
    Counter to his wish and to the motion of the waves.
    In no time at all he will be utterly exhausted.
    If he is angry, the minutes that follow
    Will fit his anger like a glove. Fight, Charles, fight!

(*As GILBERT begins to draw in the line, the stage darkens. Enter CHARLES. He speaks from stage center, beneath a faint green spot.*)

CHARLES:

    I am not one to think much about pain.
    I would not choose to dwell upon myself
    In public, sipping at a tumbler of stale water.
    It has never been my thought to preach to the fish.
    Nevertheless, if I am ever in my life
    To think profitably, to see with clear eyes,

    Let it be now. Although my throat and eyes
    Burn with seawater as with such tears of pain
    No innocent man could shed in his whole life,
    O let me achieve a clearness about myself,
    For it is neither her brother nor big fish
    I fear, nor even the white jaws of water

    That hurt and hold me, but an unkinder water
    Chilling and deepening in Julie's eyes.
    It is there blindly I thrash now, as a fish
    Gasping in air is amazed by the pulse and pain
    Of an element newly thrust upon itself.
    She might have said, "You have made a mess of your life,

But I into whose care you gave that life
Am weeping. Taste, my love, this healing water.
Test me with your hands, your lips, your eyes."
She might have said, "I couldn't care less myself
Whether you sink in pride or swim in pain.
That is for you to decide, you poor fish!"

Instead, neither caring nor careless, she chose to fish,
To fish using as bait my only life,
Waiting in what suspense for the inevitable pain
To swallow me where I hang in her scorn's water.
And indeed, a recognition with phosphorous eyes
Glides slowly upward from the depths of myself.

Innocent visions are those that proceed from self.
Dolphin, medusa, hammerhead shark, starfish
Shall look at me henceforth with Julie's eyes,
Telling me ever and over to give my life
Up to those eyes, sink, as I do through water,
Towards the dark love children would call pain.

Julie! this pain is sweet as a loss of self.
Draw me from water, leave me to the fish—
You cannot save my life. I have seen your eyes.

(*The spot goes out. CHARLES disappears. JOHN and JULIE, on either side of the stage, light cigarettes and hold the burning matches before their faces.*)

JOHN:
   Julie?

JULIE:
   Yes. I'm here.

JOHN:
   Your voice is so strange. Are you all right?

JULIE:

I'm all right.

JOHN:

I love you.

(*JULIE blows out her match. Lights. GILBERT helps CHARLES into the boat. CHARLES collapses, exhausted.*)

GILBERT:

You see, dear Charles, there are things stronger than yourself.
Be still. You are weak and bewildered. Do you feel pain?
You must not think ill of me. I wish you would open your eyes.

CHARLES:

Of you I don't think. Should I?

GILBERT:

Well I should have thought so, yes.
I should have thought that out there in the water
You would be thinking of the line from which your life
Depended, and of who held the line.

CHARLES:

Of Julie?

GILBERT:

It seems to you that Julie——?
Ah Charles, you're a deep one. Can you mean
That at last the scales have fallen from your eyes
To reveal poor Julie as her own vicious self?
Or do you mean, as I fear, that I myself
Simply don't matter?

CHARLES:

Julie . . .

JULIE:

What is it?

CHARLES:

Come here,
Take my hand. I have thought of something.

JULIE:

Charles, you are not on your deathbed. I see no need
For any show of thought.

CHARLES:

But you are angry!

JULIE:

What else can I be? Yes I am angry.
I find what I am thinking disagreeable.

CHARLES:

I suppose that is flattering. I should have thought rather
It was for me to be angry, to be resentful of the pain
Of having endangered what is after all my own life,
And for not only my own amusement. But to my eyes
None of us is amused, least of all yourself.

GILBERT:

Perhaps you should jump back into the water
And take your chances with the fish.
You can always get a laugh out of *them*.

CHARLES:

You ought not to be angry. If you are angry
It cannot be because of what I have done
But because of what I am doing now.
If what I *did* was to have angered you
You would have been angry earlier, I think.

JULIE:

> I am not angry with you.

GILBERT:

> And there is no earthly reason that I can see
> For her to be angry with *me*.

CHARLES:

> And what am I doing now, what am I trying to say
> But that I am incorruptibly yours?

JULIE:

> O pompous! Incorruptibly!
> You talk as if I were a disease.

CHARLES:

> Don't try to misunderstand me, Julie.

JULIE:

> You've lost your bet. You're a bad loser, Charles.

GILBERT:

> No. He has won his bet. He's a bad winner.
> He means we have sought to corrupt him. He is right.

JULIE:

> Speak for yourself.

GILBERT:

>   I do. Speaking for myself
> You are an extremely difficult person, Charles.
> Being, as we are not, simple and good, we suspect you.
> More, we have wanted you idle like ourselves.

JULIE:

> Would anybody object if we started back to the dock?

GILBERT:

Don't pretend you don't know what has happened. You have
    undergone
Trial by water—that trial whereby
The accused was flung, bound, into a ditch.
If he was innocent he stayed afloat.
If guilty, he sank to the bottom like a stone.
I suppose the secret *then* was breath control.
In any event it sounds like a cynical business.

CHARLES:

You meant for me to sink, did you, Julie?

JULIE:

Of course not, darling. How can you allow
Gilbert to talk that way? You'll find me at the prow
Sunning myself. I've had enough for now.

(*Exit JULIE. At the same time JOHN rises and strolls out.*)

GILBERT:

We meant for you to rise up from the waves
Like a revengeful triton, brandishing
Your spear thrice-pronged with wrath,
Embarrassment and pain. We did not want
The meek pearl it appears you offer us now.
We wanted proof that you could, like ourselves,
Fail to profit by an occasion
For much self-knowledge, use it up idly
Thrashing about on the surface of your act.

CHARLES:

Well what did I do instead to anger you?

GILBERT:

Instead, you did the serious human thing,
The earnest painful thing, the thing that we,

Or she particularly—she's very touchy—
Will not forgive. So we condemn you. The code
Is evidently of our own contrivance.

CHARLES:

It is a novel experience, Gilly,
For once to take something less seriously than you.

GILBERT:

You are lighthearted because your conscience is clear.
Wait and see.

CHARLES:

My conscience *is* clear. I am not lighthearted.

GILBERT:

Ah, you're too scrupulous. But you have
Become of permanent value.

CHARLES:

To Julie? To myself?
What are you talking about?

GILBERT:

I have observed
That people do not ask that question
Unless they know the answer. Wait and see.

(*Exit GILBERT. We see the silhouette of CHARLES, alone in the boat, throughout this final scene. Enter, from Venice, JOHN and JULIE. It is night.*)

JULIE:

I think it is a very good suggestion of Gilbert's. We can take the bus at noon tomorrow, and arrive before dark. Gilbert is very fond of Ravenna. He says the mosaics are beyond words glorious.

JOHN:

They must be, if he says so.

JULIE:

They do sound the slightest bit deadly just the same. Asking things of one, you know. Venice is somewhat more my cup of tea. If I am tired of Venice it is because I am tired of myself. Here I see myself wherever I turn, in the exquisite stagestruck façades, in the smell of money and hair, and that green water almost moving. It is very clever of a city to have risen where there was only water, just as I am very clever to be talking about Venice when Venice is the last thing on my mind.

JOHN:

It's late. We must be up early tomorrow.

JULIE:

Do I bore you? What does that pained smile mean?

JOHN:

I was about to ask you that very question.

JULIE:

What does my pained smile mean?

JOHN:

No. Do I bore you?

JULIE:

Forgive me. I'm very tired and very nervous. I *am*.

JOHN:

I believe you. O Julie, can't we just stay here? Can't Gilbert go off by himself? We need these days to ourselves, everything would come right once more between us.

JULIE:

Come right? Are things then so wrong between us?

JOHN:

You know what I mean. We'd have this time, we'd have each other. You're tired. So am I. It's hectic, having to go about together, the three of us, always.

JULIE:

I should hate to miss Ravenna.

JOHN:

We don't care about Ravenna.

JULIE:

Besides, we don't know the language as well as Gilbert. I'm certain, if we were here alone, we should be outrageously cheated on all sides.

JOHN:

That kind of cheating is very innocent, by comparison.

JULIE:

By comparison with what?

JOHN:

All right, we'll go to Ravenna.

JULIE:

By comparison with what?

JOHN:

Julie, I love you. Help me to love you. Be honest with yourself.

JULIE:

Go on. Tell me more about my dishonesty. You asked if I was bored. Far from it, I'm fascinated!

JOHN:

I don't ask you for absolute honesty. There is a need for delicacy between people. I daresay only you know what to tell me and what not to tell me. But when from yourself you disguise things—

JULIE:

For instance?

JOHN:

What you told me today. It's not for myself I want to know, but for *you*. I don't ask for an explanation. What matters is that you be able to explain it to yourself.

JULIE:

Explain what?

JOHN:

Why you left Charles.

JULIE:

There are times when you remind me forcibly of him. I foresaw that we should resume the topic before long.

CHARLES (*to himself*):

Did Gilbert mean that she will leave me? Wait and see, he said.

JULIE:

O John, you are such a reproach to me. I can hear the excuses you are making for me. You are saying "I must bear with her because she is suffering."

JOHN:

Not at all. I don't feel that you *are* suffering.

JULIE:

You're right. I'm not suffering.

CHARLES (*to himself*):

She has arranged it so that there is nothing I can do. I can't talk to her.

JULIE:

Does one like, however, to feel that one has done something arbitrary and ungenerous, and isn't even capable of shedding an honest tear over it?

CHARLES (*to himself*):

But if she leaves me I shall be able to write to her. She will have to understand eventually. She will want to come back.

JULIE:

That's why I can't read his letters. They shame me.

JOHN:

They don't shame Gilbert? No. Gilbert is possessed of a remarkable integrity.

JULIE:

And I am not?

JOHN:

It's all to your credit I guess. But you have tried to blame him.

JULIE:

He *was* to blame. He taunted Charles until it happened.

JOHN:

And what happened made you leave Charles? Isn't that a fantastic pretext, unless—

JULIE:

Yes?

JOHN:

Unless you had been waiting for an excuse to leave him, and ever since have used yourself up pretending it was not your responsibility.

JULIE:

No! You mustn't talk to me this way!

JOHN:

Ah you're selfish, Julie!

JULIE:

I know. I ask everything.

JOHN:

You've talked to me all day of this thing, less, I think, for my enlightenment than your own pleasure. I am not even allowed to comment upon what you have said.

CHARLES (*to himself*):

But if she shouldn't come back, what then? She might fall in love with somebody else.

JULIE:

I'll say no more then.

JOHN:

That's not what I mean!

CHARLES:

How strange! I can already feel sorry for him, the next one to love her.

JULIE:

O why are we quarreling? I have tried only to describe the one inexplicable action of my life. If you love me—

JOHN:

    Julie, Julie . . .

JULIE:

    The one who loves isn't the loser. Charles
    Isn't the loser. By hurting him I have
    Empowered him to unveil within my mind
    As in a public square
    An image tasteless and cheap, which is my own.
    Not even a tourist would stop to look at it
    All thickened as if by dreadful squatting birds.
    But Charles—my dear, I even dream of him.
    I see him continue to act in honest concern
    According to what he feels. I see his face
    Turn beautiful under the pumice of disappointment.
    One could almost pretend I had made him a gift of it.

JOHN:

    And to me what gift do you make?

JULIE:

    I have been happy with you here.
    One is encompassed by things so rich and rare
    They can't be hurt by the conscience one brings to them.
    We stand in the center of this glimmering square
    As we might stand in my own mind, at its most charitable.
    Tomorrow we shall stand in Ravenna, I suppose
    Quite as if standing in the mind of God.
    Much constellated gold, dolphin and seraphim
    Shall blind us with the blessing
    Of something fully expressed, the sense of having
    Ourselves somehow become expressive there.
    The very prospect is unburdening. Kiss me.

JOHN:

    They say it is not the ornament but the architecture
    That is meant to move one most at Ravenna.

JULIE:

> John, you are sublime, so solemn and sweet.
> Isn't it strange how little difference
> It makes, whatever we say or do or are?

CHARLES (*to himself*):

> I have observed
> That people do not ask that question
> Unless they know the answer.

JOHN (*to himself*):

> Now for the first time it is strangely myself I feel
> Endangered. The lover may not be the loser.
> I should not care to win at her expense.

CHARLES (*to himself*):

> No matter what the lines were baited with,
> The prize was that the fishermen could spare
> Themselves the knowledge I am weighted with.

JULIE:

> There is such lightness in the midnight air,
> Do you imagine even an insect capable
> Of resting on your wrist? The orange peel
> Floats by, but on a tide of air. Kiss me.

JOHN:

> What is this beauty that perpetually
> Ignores its consequences, like a flare
> Lighting the field where innocent men hide?

JULIE:

> All that I've said today, let it go by.
> Kiss me. The weightless air
> Has taken my words up into its high gauzes
> Before the first of them could reach your ear.

JOHN (*to himself*):
   No it is not the danger or the hurt I fear
   But vagueness, secrecy, the shapeless sky,
   The iridescent sea, whatever causes
   Us, when all is said and done, to die
   Lightly, not knowing . . .

JULIE:
                              Do not think, my dear,
   That *we* contrive this lightness. No.

JOHN (*to himself*):
   How to endure? O God, must I
   Feel the next kiss I give her disappear
   As music melts into its pauses?

JULIE:
   Something makes light of *us*. Kiss me. Come here.
   I could rise up into the night like a dancer!

JOHN:
   How to endure?

JULIE:
   Kiss me. Kiss me.

(*JOHN turns and kisses her.*)

CHARLES (*to himself*):
   I know the answer.

(CURTAIN)

THE IMMORTAL HUSBAND

A PLAY

(1955)

Characters

Act I:

Mrs. Mallow
Maid
Tithonus
Gardener
Laomedon
Aurora

Act II:

Konstantin
Fanya
Tithonus
Olga
Aurora

Act III:

Mark
Aurora
Enid
Memnon
Tithonus
Nurse

*The play calls for a cast of six. With the ex-
ception of AURORA and TITHONUS, the
remaining roles must be doubled or tripled by the
same actors in each successive act, in this fashion:*

Mrs. Mallow, Olga, Nurse
Maid, Fanya, Enid
Gardener, Konstantin, Mark
Laomedon, Memnon

ACT ONE

(*England, 1854. A parlor in disarray. Beyond shut French doors, a garden. It is a rainy morning in late spring.*)

(*MRS. MALLOW, in black from head to toe, sits mending a dress. The MAID packs a trunk with dresses and other clothes that lie here and there about the room. She hums a little tune. A second trunk stands against the wall. TITHONUS paces up and down, occasionally pausing to watch the two women.*)

MRS. MALLOW:
   You're standing in my light, dear. It's hard enough to see as it is.

(*TITHONUS moves.*)

   Why you should care to watch us at our dismal task, I can't imagine.

(*To the MAID.*)

   Is that trunk full now, Jeannie?

MAID:
   Yes, Mrs. Mallow. I'll call John, shall I?

MRS. MALLOW:
   Wait. This one can go in on top. I'm nearly done.

MAID:
   She's a fortunate young lady who'll be getting these lovely clothes.

TITHONUS:
   Go on, go on! It's the natural thing, to discuss it.

MRS. MALLOW (*handing the dress to the MAID*):
   Here you are, Jeannie dear.

495

TITHONUS:

And it will be natural for Cousin Aggie to feel grateful—

MRS. MALLOW:

What else wants mending?

TITHONUS:

—and natural, she being such a plain young woman, for the clothes to be wasted upon her.

MRS. MALLOW:

Now hush, Tithonus, it was your mother's wish.

MAID (*showing a dress*):

There's a tiny tear right here in the hem.

MRS. MALLOW (*taking it*):

That won't take a minute.

MAID:

Do you know, this is the fifth day of steady rain? John's all upset. He says the rain will wash away the soil from the roots. Rain's not at all good in such quantities, John says.

MRS. MALLOW:

Well, John should know, shouldn't he?

TITHONUS:

Rain is like sorrow. It exposes our roots.

MRS. MALLOW:

And nourishes them.

MAID:

I can't recall the mistress ever wearing that dress.

MRS. MALLOW:

Oh, this was one of her favorite dresses. A wonder it still holds together. She'd wear it on carriage rides, in midsummer—before you came to us, five, six years ago. After that, she grew so thin, poor soul, she said to me, "Mrs. Mallow,"—when I'd already taken in the seams once or twice—"let's put away that dress, and not try to alter it any more." Now is that trunk firmly shut?

MAID:

Yes, Ma'am.

MRS. MALLOW:

Then call John, and I shall lock it. Let's see if we can't squeeze these last things into the other trunk. If we're clever we can get both of them on the afternoon coach.

(*Exit MAID.*)

TITHONUS:

Oh it's wrong, it's wrong! Don't you think it's wrong?

MRS. MALLOW:

Do I think what's wrong, dear?

TITHONUS:

Life . . . the world . . . death. . . .

MRS. MALLOW:

It's not for us to say, Tithonus. Life must go on.

TITHONUS:

That's what I hate, to see everybody humming and sewing and bustling about, Father upstairs in a flowered dressing gown sorting out her jewelry, sending away her clothes, putting everything out of sight, because *she* is out of sight—

MRS. MALLOW:

You're in my light, dear.

TITHONUS (*moving*):

—everything being scrubbed and aired, as if she had done a shameful thing. It's wrong, Mrs. Mallow.

MRS. MALLOW (*biting off a thread*):

It's not for us to say.

TITHONUS:

Who else will say it, if we don't? It's a small thing to ask, that a time be set aside, that we close our eyes and try to see her as she was,

(*Touching a bonnet.*)

dressed to go out, or coming in from a walk. . . .

MRS. MALLOW:

You're right, Tithonus. It is a small thing to ask. But did she ask it? No.

(*Goes to him and strokes his cheek.*)

She asked only that her clothes go to your cousin Agatha. She asked that I keep her thimble. Look now, how it's begun to shine, and it was badly tarnished this morning when I put it on. Think of it that way, dear.

(*Goes to trunk and locks it.*)

Out of sorrow comes beauty. Now where is John?

TITHONUS:

She asked nothing of me.

MRS. MALLOW:

What can a mother ask of her child, but that he grow strong and virtuous? By doing that, a son shows his love. Not by tears, but by living the way she has taught him to live.

TITHONUS (*with irony*):

And by dying the way she has taught him to die?

MRS. MALLOW (*vaguely*):

That's right. Now if only John—

(*TITHONUS starts out.*)

Where are you going, dear?

TITHONUS:

I don't know.

MRS. MALLOW:

Let me give you some tea and muffins. You didn't touch your breakfast.

TITHONUS (*going out*):

I'm not hungry.

MRS. MALLOW (*calling after him*): We must keep up our strength!

(*Enter MAID and GARDENER.*)

Oh John, there you are. Move that trunk over here.

(*He does so.*)

Good. Now Jeannie, I'll let you finish. I'm going up for a word with the master.

MAID:

Why, it's stopped raining, look!

MRS. MALLOW (*darkly*):

I don't like to think what *that* might mean.

GARDENER:

It's good news to me, Mrs. Mallow. Shall I carry the other trunk out to the carriage?

MRS. MALLOW:

Yes, do, John. There's scarcely room to walk about. I'll be down presently. And I'll feel like a cup of tea, Jeannie dear, if the kettle's on. And some muffins and jam. We must keep up our strength.

MAID:

Certainly, Ma'am.

(*Exit MRS. MALLOW. The GARDENER moves behind the MAID and playfully embraces her.*)

Oh John, stop it, do! The poor mistress not cold in her grave!

GARDENER:

Ah Jeannie, don't be taken in by all that talk. One fine day you'll be developing a morbid streak.

MAID:

If I do, that's my own affair.

(*Pause.*)

What kind of streak?

GARDENER:

Morbid. It's when you thrive on tragedy, like a vulture.

(*Pause.*)

That was a joke, Jeannie. Ah, if you could have seen, the day of the funeral, your cheeks glowing through that black veil! I wanted to kiss them then, right in church. You looked so bright and pretty.

(*Pause.*)

That was a compliment, Jeannie.

MAID (*preoccupied*):
You're a proper poet.

GARDENER:
Come now, what is it? Tell John.

MAID:
Has Mrs. Mallow got a morbid streak?

GARDENER:
I hadn't given the matter much thought.

MAID:
I dreamed a dream about her last night.

(*Remembering it.*)

I had a little house with a garden and a lake, and everything I wanted. . . .

GARDENER:
Was I there?

MAID:
I can't recall. . . . No, but all of a sudden, looking up from my knitting, who should I see but Mrs. Mallow, nodding and smiling. "Jean-

nie dear," she said, "you're turning into the best little housekeeper that ever was." And I looked, and all around me were hundreds of little houses, no bigger than—

(*Staring into the open trunk.*)

with somebody in each one. And all the people were dead, and all the houses—I woke up then, I was in such a fright!

GARDENER:
That's so like you, Jeannie, to be frightened of a dream.

MAID:
What does it mean, do you suppose? Is somebody going to die?

GARDENER (*philosophizing*):
We're all of us going to die, so cheer up! It's not so bad!

MAID:
Cheer up, John! What a thing to say!

GARDENER:
What *is* bad's the way the young master takes it. Mooning and moping—as if that changed anything.

MAID:
I think the young master's feeling is beautiful and right.

GARDENER:
It's too beautiful. He keeps standing off and admiring it, like he was painting a picture. No,

(*Looking upward.*)

he's not the one *she* ought to have.

MAID:

And who is the one *she* ought to have? It wouldn't be yourself, would it? And what makes you think Miss Aurora's goddess of the dawn, anyhow? I've never seen her do a single uncommon thing.

GARDENER:

Why should she? Of course she doesn't send off fireworks every quarter of an hour. She's not vulgar. But one day, you wait and see— she'll turn herself into a white peacock, like one of them over to the Manor, and stretch her throat and spread her wings and carry off the lover she fancies, just the way it's done in the mythology book!

MAID:

See that you don't catch it for educating yourself with the master's books.

GARDENER:

I'll catch you first.

(*He does so.*)

MAID (*wriggling*):

Oh John, enough of your foolishness! I hear them!

GARDENER:

I don't.

MRS. MALLOW (*offstage*):

We're doing up the last one now. It will go this afternoon.

MAID:

She's with the master! Hurry! Don't leave the trunk!

(*She goes out. The GARDENER lifts the full trunk. Enter MRS. MAL-LOW and LAOMEDON.*)

LAOMEDON:

Well, Mrs. Mallow, I don't know what we would do without you. Not only at this time, but all during the past year— Oh John, I'll be wanting the carriage later this morning.

GARDENER:

I'll give it a good wash, Sir.

LAOMEDON:

If it clears, we'll inspect that broken pump before I go.

GARDENER:

There's the apple tree too, Sir, I wish you'd have a look at.

LAOMEDON:

Quite so, the apple tree. The whole place has gone to rack and ruin these last weeks. Well, there was a reason for that. . . .

GARDENER:

We'll set it to rights before long, Sir.

LAOMEDON:

Thank you, John.

(*Exit GARDENER with trunk.*)

No, Mrs. Mallow, I think we're all very grateful to you.

MRS. MALLOW:

It's a pleasure to be useful, Sir.

LAOMEDON:

Georgiana said to me, not two weeks ago, "I feel easier, thinking that Mrs. Mallow will be with you." I'll never forget the care you took of her. You seemed to know instinctively whenever she was in pain. The door would open and there you'd be with her medicine, and a kind word, or a little bouquet of spring flowers. . . .

MRS. MALLOW:

Oh Sir, you needn't say these things.

LAOMEDON:

I shan't go on.

(*Offering a brooch.*)

Perhaps this will say what I cannot.

MRS. MALLOW:

Her pearl brooch! Oh, I couldn't, Sir! I'm touched, but—it has too many associations. . . .

LAOMEDON:

That's one reason we wanted you to have it. I spoke to Tithonus. He shares my feeling.

MRS. MALLOW:

Does he now? Well, he's a dear good boy! But it should go to him, for his bride.

LAOMEDON:

Between ourselves, I'm not overly sanguine on the subject of Tithonus's bride.

MRS. MALLOW:

He'll outgrow that, just wait and see. He's young, Sir.

LAOMEDON:

He's no longer a child, but he still acts like one.

(*Closing her hand over the brooch.*)

But please. . . .

MRS. MALLOW:
I'm at a loss for words. I shall never part with it.

(*Looking up, sees that TITHONUS has entered.*)

Tithonus, dear, your father has told me of your share in this beautiful remembrance.

(*Kisses him.*)

TITHONUS:
You've given her the pearl brooch?

LAOMEDON:
With your permission, if you remember.

TITHONUS:
Of course I remember. Keep the brooch, Mrs. Mallow. And the thimble. Why don't you take these clothes, too? Mother's room is empty, move into it. Father, have you ever considered marrying Mrs. Mallow.

MRS. MALLOW:
Tithonus! I've lived in this house ten years, and never yet claimed anything that was not my due.

LAOMEDON:
We know that, Mrs. Mallow.

(*To TITHONUS.*)

The principal use of courtesy is to help others through painful situations. That was not a remark to have made before either Mrs. Mallow or myself.

TITHONUS:

I'm sorry, I believe it's wrong not to show what one feels.

LAOMEDON:

True, but we do not need to make a display of our feelings.

TITHONUS:

It's less of a display than your callousness!

LAOMEDON:

Don't imagine, if I try to hide my sorrow, that I feel it less than you. Life is hard, and suffering the common lot.

TITHONUS:

Oh Father, stop. . . .

LAOMEDON:

As Doctor Johnson said, the hope that we shall meet our loved ones again must support the mind.

TITHONUS:

But I don't have that hope. I believe that we shall *never* see her again! Then what supports the mind? What supports *my* mind, Father?

MRS. MALLOW:

The boy's idle, Sir. What has he had to do these last weeks but sit about a house all hushed and melancholy?

TITHONUS:

I've enjoyed that part of it!

LAOMEDON:

You're right, Mrs. Mallow. An idle mind is the Devil's workshop. Of course, he's missed his term at the University. A new one won't begin—

TITHONUS:

I don't choose to go back to the University.

LAOMEDON:

We'll see about that.

MRS. MALLOW:

Tithonus, why? You'd be with friends your own age.

TITHONUS:

I hate people my own age.

LAOMEDON:

I can't blame you. What is your age? Nineteen?

TITHONUS:

Not yet! Not till August!

LAOMEDON:

Old enough in any event to conduct yourself with dignity. What supports your mind is youth, with all the virtues and vices of youth. Purity and energy on one hand, arrogance and idleness on the other. Times have certainly changed! At your age I had lived through three battles. I was the youngest Englishman to witness the signing of the Treaty of Amiens.

TITHONUS (*slowly and gently*):

Perhaps when I am old I shall no longer feel what I feel now. I hope I shan't. Because I feel that you, both of you, *don't* feel anything. You're dry inside, dry and old, and that's somehow far worse than dying. *You* want even her memory to die. Soon nothing will be left that was hers.

(*Pause.*)

LAOMEDON (*hurt*):
Well, we mustn't stand about all morning. There are a hundred and one things waiting to be done. It's turning into a fine day. I'm going upstairs to dress.

MAID (*entering*):
Cook's just back from the village, Sir, and brought the newspaper.

(*Gives it to him.*)

Oh Mrs. Mallow, I clean forgot your tea!

MRS. MALLOW:
I'll have it in the kitchen, Jeannie, presently.

(*Exit MAID.*)

LAOMEDON (*reading*):
Ha! It seems we are now connected with Ireland, by submarine telegraph.

MRS. MALLOW:
What will they think of next?

LAOMEDON:
A year ago it was France. Well, to work. I slept last night like a child.

(*He goes out.*)

MRS. MALLOW:
Shame on you, Tithonus, for talking so to your father, with all the sorrow in his heart.

(*Opening the trunk.*)

I can't think what's got into you. You used to be such a sweet, considerate boy. You'd come running to show me things you'd found, a caterpillar, an odd stone. . . .

TITHONUS:

I've made a decision, Mrs. Mallow. I can't stay at home any longer. I don't belong here.

MRS. MALLOW (*bustling about, not quite listening*):

Now if you're going to take up my precious time with nonsense— Not belong here, indeed!

TITHONUS:

Everything's changed, yet everything's the same. You heard Father— pompous, callous, as ever before. In a strange way I'm relieved that Mother's dead.

MRS. MALLOW:

I understand that, dear. She suffered greatly, and now she's no longer in pain.

TITHONUS:

No. I'm relieved for *my* sake. I'm not bound by her love. It will be easier to go away.

MRS. MALLOW:

And where had you thought of going, may I ask?

(*Pointedly.*)

And with whom?

TITHONUS:

Anywhere. Italy, Africa, Sweden, Constantinople. If Father were dead, it would be easier yet!

MRS. MALLOW (*shocked*):
Hush now! As if easiness were all we looked for!

TITHONUS:
And if *you* were dead, too, I could walk out that door, through the orchard, whistling a song. Don't mistake me, I mean it tenderly!

MRS. MALLOW:
Enough, Tithonus! Life and death are sacred things. We do not make jokes about them.

TITHONUS:
I don't want anybody dead. But I don't want to die myself—I'm too young! So much is expected of me. I've done nothing yet to make my name endure, to give me immortality. . . .

MRS. MALLOW:
There are other ways to make your name endure. For instance, when you have children of your own—

TITHONUS:
I never want to have children. It's too cruel, that a child should suffer as it does!

(*Pause.*)

MRS. MALLOW:
Tithonus, dear, believe me, this spell of terrible loneliness is at an end. I've been lonely, too, sitting by that bed in silence.

(*Taking a shawl which TITHONUS has picked up, and placing it in the trunk.*)

I may not be a woman of much learning, but I've learned about life. I've sat by many a deathbed.

(*Warmly.*)

Oh, I have such hopes for you, Tithonus! You're turning into such a fine, clever young man!

TITHONUS:
But I don't want to *turn* into anything! Change is what I've always hated—to see people, like leaves on fire, twisted and crumpled by life. . . .

MRS. MALLOW:
No. There is no such violence. At times the eyes remain open, and must be shut.

(*More softly.*)

Dying is part of life, Tithonus. It happens to us from day to day.

TITHONUS:
That's the terrible compromise you make! You let it happen!

MRS. MALLOW:
Yes. We let it happen.

(*Holding out her arms in a motherly gesture.*)

Dear child, dear indignant child, we have no choice!

(*Pause. TITHONUS appears to falter, then slowly draws away from her and goes out. After a moment, MRS. MALLOW resumes her packing. A burst of sunlight on the stage, which has been gradually brightening. Grieg "Morning" music. MRS. MALLOW looks up fatalistically.*)

I might have known, it never rains but it pours.

AURORA (*offstage*):
Tithonus! Lazy one!

(*The French doors part. AURORA stands on the threshold, a young girl of the period, wearing a pale, flowered dress, her hair in a Grecian knot.*)

Oh! He's not here? It's true, he wasn't expecting me this week, but—

(*Laughing, advancing.*)

You weren't expecting me either, judging from your expression. It's been ages since I've seen you. You're always somewhere else when I come. But I daresay you keep up with me through Tithonus.

MRS. MALLOW:
Hardly. He never speaks of you, Aurora.

AURORA:
Perhaps not to you. Oh, look at all the clothes! Whose are they?

(*Holds up a dress, which MRS. MALLOW takes and places in the trunk.*)

Where is Tithonus?

MRS. MALLOW:
I couldn't say. Look for him, why don't you?

AURORA (*starting out*):
Thank you, I shall.

MRS. MALLOW:
Aurora, I have this to say, and then I shall leave you. Take care of what you're doing to the boy. Your influence upon him is a pernicious one. I'm sure you don't mean it so, but the truth is, you stand in his way, in the way of his maturity. You encourage Tithonus to stay a

child. I don't know what else you could do, being so much a child yourself. A lovely child, yes, that's what you are.

(*AURORA begins to giggle.*)

I hadn't hoped to provide entertainment for you.

AURORA:
Have you ever been told that your mouth works in a most killing way when you talk, as though you were eating something? I'm sorry, I'm not really laughing at that. Isn't it a beautiful day? You feel that you want to laugh on a day like this!

(*Inspecting a cloak.*)

What a pretty cloak! I love other people's clothes, don't you?

MRS. MALLOW:
Is it necessary to stand on it in order to admire it?

(*AURORA wanders about.*)

You're beyond your depth with Tithonus. What's right for you isn't right for him.

(*AURORA tries on a bonnet.*)

Kindly put that down!

AURORA:
You're wrong about Tithonus, you know. He has a very special sensibility—more like one of *us*. You don't do justice to him. I do.

MRS. MALLOW:
Call it justice if you like. I don't.

AURORA:

Tell me something—oh, it's no concern of mine—but why do you wear black? Granted it *does* express the real you, still it's not becoming. Besides, Tithonus is very handsome, don't you agree?

MRS. MALLOW:

Goodbye, Aurora. One day you will recognize my usefulness, my good influence, and understand—

AURORA:

I understand enough to know sour grapes when I smell them. We even have *that* up there!

MRS. MALLOW:

You have not only the comprehension but the cruelty of a child. One day *he* will understand that.

(*She goes out.*)

AURORA (*to herself*):
Small wonder the English climate is what it is. What do they ever do to *make* the sun shine?

(*Sees the GARDENER in the garden.*)

You there! Joseph? James?

GARDENER (*starts, then, blushing with pleasure, crosses the threshold*):
Oh, it's you, Miss! Lovely morning, Miss.

AURORA:
Why, thank you!

GARDENER:
I had a feeling you'd be coming, soon as the sky cleared.

AURORA:

Well, here I am. Have you seen Tithonus?

GARDENER:

Yes, Miss. He just now walked out the front door and settled himself by the apple tree. Wrapped in thought.

AURORA:

Tell him I've come, will you please?

GARDENER:

Yes, Miss.

AURORA (*seeing that he does not go*):

What is it?

GARDENER:

Oh, Miss, I—I can't explain. No offense meant.

AURORA:

I shall never be offended by those who find me beautiful, Joseph.

GARDENER:

John, Miss.

AURORA:

John. Now will you call Tithonus?

GARDENER:

Right away, Miss.

(*Exit. AURORA, alone, tries on the cloak and bonnet before a mirror, humming to herself. TITHONUS enters from the garden and stops, unable to choose between laughter and tears.*)

TITHONUS:

Is it you?

AURORA (*turning*):

I couldn't wait. I know you didn't—

TITHONUS:

What are you doing?

AURORA:

Doing? Oh,

(*Laughing.*)

I was seeing if I could look mortal—do I?

TITHONUS:

Yes.

AURORA:

You didn't want to see me today, you're sorry I came—but, my dar-ling, it's been five days!

TITHONUS:

Aurora! You've never looked more beautiful! Your beautiful eyes, your throat. . . . I've missed you, Aurora, I've needed you. . . .

AURORA:

But you told me not to come! You never say what you mean.

TITHONUS:

But you're here! You always do the right thing, whatever I say.

AURORA:

I hope I always shall. Even so, darling, you must *tell* me what you feel and what you need. Don't let's have any confusion. This is love, this is love for the first time, and often I'm on pins and needles. I'm so frightfully unsound—ethically? Is that the word?

(*Starts to take off the bonnet.*)

TITHONUS:

No, stay as you are for a moment! Aurora, I've never loved you so much!

AURORA:

For myself, I know what I need—the sense of its having put forth leaves, our love, like the apple tree out there, where I saw you first, through the blossoms, reading, with a blossom in your mouth. "I want that," I said to myself. *Now* look at our tree—greener and golder and growing stronger. I feel all this has happened because of me, and I am proud of the loveliness around me, for being equal to the love within me. Whose clothes are these?

TITHONUS:

My mother's.

AURORA:

I like her so much, you know. Is she going away?

(*Remembers.*)

Oh, of course, she's— That was why you told me not to come.

(*Instinctively removes bonnet and cloak, placing them in the trunk.*)

I imagine you loved her very dearly. A pity you haven't a really good photograph of her.

(*Embarrassed.*)

Photography—it's rather a new thing I've been learning about. I'd thought of taking it up as a hobby. . . . Oh, will I *ever* know what to say at such moments?

TITHONUS:
Now father's sending away her clothes.

AURORA:
Very sensible of him!

TITHONUS:
That was *not* the thing to say.

AURORA:
You've had a row with him? Another one?

LAOMEDON (*offstage*):
Tithonus!

AURORA:
Here he is!

(*TITHONUS groans.*)

Well, don't let him get the better of you!

LAOMEDON (*enters, fully dressed*):
Tithonus, I was thinking—oh, excuse me, Aurora. Have you succeeded in cheering up your young friend?

AURORA:
Oh, how much you disapprove of me!

LAOMEDON:
You have never heard me say so.

AURORA:

Precisely! If you *had*, I'd have felt some grudging fondness, some weak little seed of liking, for me to warm into flower. It's unnatural of you! I *am* likable!

LAOMEDON:

I'm pleased to have it from your own mouth.

AURORA:

What's more, Laomedon, I don't like to be disliked.

LAOMEDON:

Who does? That must be your human side.

(*To TITHONUS.*)

I came to ask if you cared to go with me to the village in about an hour.

TITHONUS:

I think not, Father, thank you.

LAOMEDON:

My thought was to find some occupation for you, until you return to the University. Mr. Hobbs, for instance, might let you work in his office, if only to oblige me. That would be a most valuable experience.

TITHONUS:

I've told you, Father, that I don't intend to return to the University.

LAOMEDON:

And I replied that we would see about that.

TITHONUS:

And I don't intend to be embalmed in a lawyer's office.

LAOMEDON:

Perhaps you have some alternative of your own.

TITHONUS:

My alternative is to do exactly as I do.

LAOMEDON:

In that case I have something to say to you.

AURORA:

I'll be on my way. . . .

TITHONUS:

Oh stay, please!

AURORA:

Really, I can't bear scenes!

LAOMEDON:

In my opinion, young lady, it might be a good thing for you to hear what I have to say.

AURORA:

Aren't you forgetting as usual who I am?

LAOMEDON:

I know who you are. And I know my place. But since you have condescended to meddle with human affairs, and with my son's life in particular, it wouldn't hurt you to learn how sensible people think down here—whatever the thinking processes may be where you come from.

AURORA (*gaily*):

Oh, we never think!

LAOMEDON:

I thought as much.

AURORA:

And even with people, Laomedon, I never feel the really brilliant ones think at all!

TITHONUS:

Neither do I!

AURORA:

Besides, Tithonus is teaching me about people.

LAOMEDON:

You see me as an old bore, don't you?

TITHONUS:

Of course not, Father.

AURORA:

Or at least, a very distinguished one.

LAOMEDON:

No matter. That is how I saw my father at your age, and how your son will see you. Nature is very economical.

AURORA:

An example to us all!

LAOMEDON:

I am a soldier, a simple man who has worked hard. And what *you* can't believe is that I've enjoyed it. There's nothing finer than to live through every difficulty that comes your way.

TITHONUS:

It may have been so in your own life. But if, as you say, you're a simple person who enjoys the difficulty of living, why can't I be a difficult person who doesn't enjoy it? Because I don't!

AURORA:

Neither do I!

TITHONUS:

I'm wasting my youth, is that what you think? And wilful waste makes woeful want?

LAOMEDON:

You may scoff at your father's maxims, as I once did. That will not make them less true. They are convenient expressions of profound human laws. I have proven them by bitter experience.

AURORA:

Experience isn't always bitter, you know.

LAOMEDON:

I don't speak of *your* experience, Aurora.

(*She giggles. LAOMEDON turns to go.*)

We'll have our talk later. I see I've chosen a bad time.

AURORA (*whispering to TITHONUS*):
Go on! Stand up to him!

TITHONUS:

All right, Father. Tell me plainly what you expect me to do.

LAOMEDON:

Tell me first what you *do* do.

(*A silence.*)

AURORA:

He reads!

TITHONUS:

Yes! I spent much of yesterday reading. Didn't you see me?

LAOMEDON:

I saw you on the sofa with some books.

TITHONUS:

Well, I was reading.

LAOMEDON:

May I know which authors you were reading?

TITHONUS:

Different ones. Ovid. Ossian. Mrs. Browning.

LAOMEDON:

Go on.

TITHONUS:

I'm—ah—about to begin a large painting. The canvas isn't quite pre-
pared, but I have a whole notebook of sketches.

LAOMEDON:

What is to be the subject of your painting?

TITHONUS:

I haven't altogether decided. Possibly a *Massacre of the Innocents*—
or else a pastoral scene of some sort, *Pan Among Nymphs,* you
know. . . .

AURORA:

Oh, do let me pose for you! The way I look on the ceiling at the
Rospigliosi's—well, it's just not *me!*

LAOMEDON (*to TITHONUS*):

What else?

TITHONUS:

At the moment, there's nothing else.

LAOMEDON:

Thank you. You have answered my question.

TITHONUS:

If anything, I'm ashamed there should be so much, at such a time.

LAOMEDON:

I shall now answer yours. I notice that your mother's death does not keep you from agreeable society.

AURORA:

But he's so young! You must make allowances!

LAOMEDON (*cheerfully*):

I do. Since he is unfit to take charge of his own life, I shall have to do it for him. That's the allowance I make for his youth.

(*To TITHONUS.*)

Believe me, I have your interest at heart. I merely expect you to do something serious and responsible, Tithonus. Don't look as if it were the end of the world!

(*Pause.*)

Tell me, have you a genuine distaste for work? Or do you reject as a matter of course whatever *I* recommend?

TITHONUS:

There is one thing I can do, Father, that might satisfy you.

LAOMEDON:

I'm very easy to please, you know. I had a reputation for it through-out my regiment.

TITHONUS:

I told Mrs. Mallow this morning, I've decided to leave home.

AURORA:

Tithonus, how wonderful! You'll come with me!

(*He nods. AURORA turns to LAOMEDON.*)

You can't imagine—I've been asking him for months! He needs to travel, it's so broadening!

LAOMEDON (*after a pause*):

Do as you wish, Tithonus. You may one day regret—no, I have nothing more to say.

TITHONUS:

Father, wait, I want you to understand!

LAOMEDON:

I want to understand. But not now.

(*With faint irony.*)

Will you be leaving before lunch?

TITHONUS:

No, I needn't. . . .

LAOMEDON:

Splendid! Perhaps you can spare a moment or two then, in private.

TITHONUS:

Certainly, Father.

(*Exit LAOMEDON.*)

AURORA:

He is rather pompous, even for one's father. I suppose it's the result of a military career. Ho hum, what shall we do until lunch?

(*Eagerly.*)

We could make love!

TITHONUS:

Really, Aurora! If somebody came in—

AURORA:

All right! It was only an idea!

(*Aside.*)

Modesty, modesty!

(*To TITHONUS.*)

Well, then, on with my education! Last time we took up—let me see, was it pain? Sportsmanship? One's brotherhood to the ape?

TITHONUS:

You remember perfectly well—we talked about religion.

AURORA:

Ah yes, religion! I was fascinated—to see oneself through the eyes of others! Couldn't we go on with that?

TITHONUS:

You're disappointed, aren't you, that I'm not leaving with you until after I've talked to Father?

AURORA:

No, not at all.

TITHONUS:

Well, *I* would be—having to wait even a few hours.

AURORA:

But you see, I have no sense of time. You're giving me what I wanted. A few hours or a few days sooner or later, what difference does it make?

TITHONUS:

It would make a difference to me. I *need* time. Some days I choke on my food. I feel I can't keep up with life.

AURORA:

Really? Why I could sit for days over a meal, even a dull meal.

TITHONUS:

Or else I don't try at all. I lie down. I sleep.

AURORA:

Now this interests me very much. Oh darling, you see why I love you! You show me what people feel. In no time at all I'll be having the same feelings myself! Go on!

TITHONUS:

Aurora, I've tried to put it out of my head, but I can't. You don't *really* understand what I say, do you?

AURORA (*biting her lip*):
No, I don't.

(*He turns away. She giggles.*)

But tell me—darling, I'm serious now—why should I understand?

TITHONUS:

You're forever smiling!

AURORA:

I *am* she who smiles. I am the rosy-fingered one. What do you mean
by understanding?

TITHONUS:

You see!

AURORA:

I *do* see. I see what is shown to me, my dear. When I go into a room
and find, say, a book lying on the table, it is not my way to open it.
I've never held letters to the light in order to read what might be
inside. If the book lies open, if the letter has been dropped, open, to
the floor—why then, I do read it. I feel it has been left for me to read.
I mean, I never see the hidden side of things. That must always be
most unpleasant. If people are unhappy, I don't want to know about
it. I'll do anything—I'll even lie to them!—in order to keep them
smiling. I can't bear to know what people do in the dark.

TITHONUS:

But you do know.

AURORA:

With you, I don't think of it as being in the dark. . . .

TITHONUS (*taking her face in his hands*):

And what do you see now?

AURORA:

I see that you're handsome and full of life. When I get my camera I
shall photograph only you. I see that your ear is translucent. The cap-
illaries fan out like twigs against a sunset—

(*Frightened.*)

You're hurting me! I see what's *there!* I see light and love!

TITHONUS:

You see your own light and your own love!

AURORA:

Darling!

TITHONUS:

I don't mean that. Aurora, I love you. But to see only what is shown to us isn't understanding. Understanding is when we see in the dark, the way a cat does. Some part of me is dark and sad, invisible in your brightness. Understanding will be the day you come to me suffering, or with a capacity for suffering. Understanding has more to do with tears than with smiling. And you've never wept.

AURORA:

No. Would I enjoy that?

(*Pause.*)

Be reasonable! If gloom and murkiness are what you want, there are plenty who'll be delighted to oblige you. Just don't ask—

(*Striking her brow.*)

Oh, silly me! I *have* something that will cheer you up!

TITHONUS:

That's not what I need!

AURORA:

But I have! I'm not the goddess of the dawn for nothing. Ah, now you're interested!

TITHONUS:

Tell me then.

AURORA:

Perhaps now I won't, you've been so horrid.

TITHONUS:

Ah, don't play with me! Tell me or not, as you please, but don't play these games!

AURORA:

I've brought a little gift. Oh, promise you'll like it!

TITHONUS:

What is it?

AURORA:

Nothing at all, really. Something you once said you wanted. . . .

TITHONUS:

Aurora! It isn't—

AURORA (*nodding*):

Are you pleased?

TITHONUS:

Oh my angel! You're sure? There's no mistake?

AURORA:

Mistake! Oh really now!

TITHONUS:

Forgive me. But tell me yourself, then, what it is.

AURORA:

You're such a baby! You *know* what it is!

TITHONUS:

But say it!

AURORA:

One doesn't put these things into words. . . . Must I?

TITHONUS:

You're playing with me again!

AURORA (*annoyed*):

But I love to play! All right. Henceforth you are immortal. There!

TITHONUS:

Say it again!

AURORA:

Henceforth you are immortal.

TITHONUS:

I'll never die?

AURORA:

Never.

TITHONUS:

Can it be that simple? Don't I need to do something?

AURORA:

No. You may kiss me if you like.

TITHONUS:

I can't believe it! And I said you didn't understand! Do you know what it means?

AURORA:

So very much? *I'm* glad, too. To me it means that I shall have you always. Didn't you want to kiss me?

TITHONUS:

Oh, I love you! Aurora—thank you!

AURORA:

You're welcome, I'm sure.

TITHONUS:

But how—I'm sorry, I want to know everything. How did you go about it?

AURORA:

Well, let me see. You expressed the wish—mercy, it must have been a month ago. I didn't think too much about it at first. Then I began to rack my brains. I wanted you to have some little thing from me, something small and useful that you would always have to remember me by. And it came to me! Just the thing, I said to myself.

TITHONUS:

There's nobody like you!

AURORA:

Well, after that I had to wait. Every day I'd ask if he was in a good humor.

TITHONUS:

He?

AURORA (*pointing upward*):

He's fearfully bad-tempered, or can be. It's quite proverbial. And while it was little enough to ask, since everybody's entitled to *one* gift, I didn't want to be refused. Well, to make a long story short, yesterday evening I was given the sign. I slipped right in and spoke my piece, rather prettily, I must say.

TITHONUS:

Just like that!

AURORA:

No. No, you don't understand at all. There's a whole etiquette involved. You have to sort of crouch beside him, with your left hand on his knees and your right hand fiddling with his beard—like Thetis in that Ingres painting. I was the slightest bit nervous, having never done it before. But, you know—it worked!

TITHONUS:

It sounds so easy, how can you be sure?

AURORA:

Don't *worry!* What's the matter with you? You keep complaining about how you hate difficult things, and now that something perfectly simple happens, you're not satisfied!

TITHONUS:

I am, I am! It's all I've ever wanted. I just don't feel any change yet. I guess it takes a certain time.

AURORA:

I wouldn't know. Probably it does. Oh, you *mustn't* frown, I feel responsible for you! Tell me I've made you happy!

TITHONUS:

You've made me infinitely happy. *Now* I think I'm beginning to feel it. Yes. My heart is beating quietly and happily. It will never stop. Look at this hand. It will be mine always.

AURORA (*taking his hand*):
It will be *mine* always.

(*They kiss.*)

TITHONUS:

I'm hungry! Should I be?

AURORA:

Did you have your breakfast?

TITHONUS:

No. But I mean, does one *get* hungry, now that . . . ?

AURORA (*laughing*):

Now that one's immortal? Yes, my darling, one does!

TITHONUS (*ringing a bell*):

How glorious the world is! Look at those flowers glowing, look at the grain of this wood! I feel such excitement, a tingling in me, as if I were never again to be tired or bored, an energy that will never exhaust itself!

(*Enter MAID.*)

Jeannie, bring me some muffins and jam, will you please?

(*To AURORA.*)

Would you care for something?

AURORA:

I couldn't really. I've had my ambrosia.

TITHONUS:

Just the muffins and jam, then. Oh, and a cup of tea might taste good.

MAID:

Right away, Sir. The water's boiling already.

TITHONUS:

And Jeannie, what's my father up to?

MAID:
He's out talking to John, Sir. About the mistletoe. It's killing that beautiful apple tree, Sir.

TITHONUS (*peering into the garden*):
Good. Here they come.

(*Playfully.*)

Now that Jeannie's under the spell of the new gardener, she'll talk of nothing but trees and flowers.

MAID:
La, Sir, you're such a tease!

(*Exit.*)

AURORA:
You're going to tell your father?

TITHONUS:
He'll have to know. Besides, here's the real alternative to Mr. Hobbs!

(*LAOMEDON and GARDENER are seen through the French doors.*)

AURORA:
Oh, I suppose it would be, wouldn't it?

GARDENER:
You mark my words, Sir, that whole fine branch will be dead inside of a year.

TITHONUS:
Father, have you a moment?

LAOMEDON:

My wife loved the mistletoe. . . .

GARDENER:

I don't say it's not pretty to look at, like a little cluster of pearls. But it's a parasite, Sir.

LAOMEDON:

I'm tempted to let it grow, just the same.

AURORA:

I've always heard that mistletoe was something one got kissed under.

GARDENER:

So it is, Miss.

AURORA (*to TITHONUS*):

You see, your father's quite a sentimentalist.

LAOMEDON:

Very well, go ahead with it. And, John, that trunk looks ready. Ask Mrs. Mallow if she will be good enough to lock it. Then you can take it to the carriage.

GARDENER:

Right you are, Sir.

(*Exit.*)

TITHONUS:

It's odd, I felt such a pang a while ago, looking at that trunk. I don't feel it any more.

LAOMEDON (*stepping into the room*):

Well, Son, what is it?

TITHONUS:

   Father—

LAOMEDON:

   You had something to say to me?

TITHONUS:

   Father, I'm sorry. I shouldn't have spoken that way to you.

LAOMEDON:

   Is that all you have to say?

TITHONUS:

   No. . . .

LAOMEDON:

   Then out with it! Time is money.

(*Enter MRS. MALLOW, followed by GARDENER.*)

TITHONUS:

   When I say I'm sorry, I don't mean only for that. I'm sorry for *you*, also.

LAOMEDON:

   Ah. And how have I come to deserve your pity?

TITHONUS:

   I don't mean to be impertinent. I feel so full of warmth and compassion—towards everything and everybody! Mrs. Mallow, I haven't made things easy for you, either.

LAOMEDON (*to AURORA*):

   And what part have *you* played in this worthy transformation?

AURORA:
Oh it's so trivial! I simply—

TITHONUS:
Father, you are going to die!

(*Pause. LAOMEDON and AURORA share a moment of irrepressible gaiety.*)

LAOMEDON (*to TITHONUS*):
Not this morning, I trust, unless someone has prompted you to do away with me.

TITHONUS:
Can't you listen to me? You're going to die and—I'm not!

(*MAID enters with tea things on a tray.*)

LAOMEDON:
Don't talk nonsense! You're wasting my time.

TITHONUS:
Listen to me! I'm never going to die! Aurora has given me immortal life!

AURORA:
It's true. I have given Tithonus immortal life.

MRS. MALLOW:
For shame, Aurora!

MAID:
Immortal life!

GARDENER:
I don't know as how I'd enjoy *that!*

LAOMEDON (*to them*):
That will do, both of you.

(*Takes the tray from the MAID.*)

Not a word of this in the kitchen, you understand.

(*MAID and GARDENER nod dumbly and go out.*)

TITHONUS:
I don't see why you both should act as if something shameful had happened.

MRS. MALLOW:
The less said about it, the better, dear.

LAOMEDON:
Did you mean for me to congratulate you?

TITHONUS (*to MRS. MALLOW*):
I thought he'd be pleased for my sake. For his own sake, too, if it comes to that. He needn't worry about me now.

(*To LAOMEDON.*)

Or are you envious?

LAOMEDON:
No. Here, take this tray from me.

TITHONUS:
You can just hold the tray for a bit! Selfish, pompous old man! Must we learn that suffering is the common lot? When you say that, you mean one thing only—that you want me to suffer!

LAOMEDON:

I have never wanted you to suffer—until perhaps this instant.

TITHONUS:

Stop lying to me! All those warnings, all those homilies! We let it happen, do we, Mrs. Mallow? We have no choice? You'll let it happen, you've made your compromise! Oh Father, even if you live another ten, another twenty years, even if you were my age—you'll dry up and die, each year older and sicker, and your mind gone! And I'll be as I am now, strong, young, a hundred years, a thousand, after you're in your grave!

LAOMEDON (*handing the tray to MRS. MALLOW who puts it down*):

That's enough. Live if you can. I'm glad neither I nor your mother will be here to see what you make of your life. Those are the last words I shall ever speak to you.

(*Turns to go.*)

AURORA:

Oh wait! Please!

LAOMEDON:

I have nothing to say to *you*.

AURORA:

No, it's not that! Oh, please—

(*To TITHONUS.*)

Darling, I'm frightened. You said something just now. . . . Darling, there's nothing in it about not growing old!

TITHONUS (*not understanding*):

What?

AURORA:

Perhaps it doesn't matter. I hope it doesn't matter, but—you know, you won't stay young. You'll never die, but—well, you'll grow old, naturally, the way people *do.*

MRS. MALLOW (*to herself*):

Yes.

TITHONUS (*aghast*):

But that's the whole point!

AURORA:

You didn't ask for that! You never said you wanted to stay young!

TITHONUS:

Then you've *never* understood!

AURORA:

You never bothered to explain!

TITHONUS:

I knew it was too simple! I said so, didn't I? But you smiled and— You can have it changed, you can ask again!

AURORA:

No . . . I'm afraid not. . . .

TITHONUS:

But you must!

AURORA:

I can't. Once only. . . .

TITHONUS:

But what will become of *me?*

AURORA:

Oh my dearest, my only love—what can I say? That it's my fault—does that help? It's a terrible thing, I suppose, but it doesn't change *us!* I don't see that it does! I'm yours, entirely, eternally. . . .

TITHONUS:

Don't say that! Think what I'll be in— Oh God, less than a hundred years! A horrible old man, drooling, deaf!

AURORA:

You needn't be! I've seen some very beautiful old men!

TITHONUS:

But I *will* be! And you won't love me then—wait and see!

AURORA:

I'll love you always, I think.

TITHONUS:

Ah, now you're thinking! It's high time.

AURORA:

My youth, when your own is gone, shall be yours—not yours, but at your disposal. Till the end of time.

TITHONUS (*closing his eyes*):

And there *is* no end. . . .

MRS. MALLOW:

It may be only the threat of dying presses us to live, and he is luckier than he knows.

AURORA:

How?

MRS. MALLOW:

Old age is a kind of death, Aurora. It may be one will do as well as the other.

(*TITHONUS turns to her for comfort, like a child. She strokes his hair.*)

Ah but Tithonus, what you have feared is not death so much as—

AURORA (*wonderingly*):

Life! Fear life? But one's not *meant* to do that!

(*With a new tenderness.*)

Tithonus!

TITHONUS:

Let me be!

AURORA:

I want to come close to you. You asked me to come to you suffering— I'm suffering now. Something hurts, here. . . . Try to imagine how *I* feel, knowing what I've done.

TITHONUS:

You've never felt anything but sunlight and pleasure! I have to be by myself now. Can't you understand even that?

AURORA:

Ah don't!

TITHONUS (*through his teeth*):

I'll be back. Don't forget, we have an eternity ahead of us, all to ourselves!

(*He starts out. But the GARDENER enters with an armful of mistletoe.*)

GARDENER:

Here you are, Sir, look! That tree will live forever now, just like you, Miss, and the young—

(*He falls silent. TITHONUS snatches the mistletoe from him and goes out. A long pause. AURORA is weeping silently. LAOMEDON and MRS. MALLOW turn to go.*)

AURORA (*suddenly looking at her hands, puzzled*):

What is it? My eyes are full of water!

LAOMEDON:

Those are tears, Aurora.

ACT TWO

(Russia, 1894. A grove on the slope of a mountain. A tree stump, scattered leaves. It is a lovely afternoon in early autumn.)

(TITHONUS, nearly sixty, sits at an easel, painting. His clothes suggest the dilettante rather than the bohemian. Laughter offstage. Enter the young lovers, FANYA followed by KONSTANTIN. The latter carries a rug and a large picnic basket. They do not at first see TITHONUS.)

KONSTANTIN:

Laugh all you wish, and run, but I am carrying this basket. Can we Russians go nowhere without a samovar? In ten years I shall have instigated reforms. Tea will be drunk only in the parlor.

FANYA:

But let us stop here then! I'm overheated myself, and here there's a breeze. . . .

(Konstantin puts down his burden and embraces her.)

Kostya, Kostya. Where is Olga Vassilyevna? Can we have left her so far behind?

KONSTANTIN:

Don't think of her. Fanya, my soul, my life!

FANYA:

Sick people have such a power. I'd be afraid not to obey her.

KONSTANTIN:

Come!

FANYA:

She will tell Mamma we ran away together.

KONSTANTIN:

That will be my first reform—the abolition of the chaperon. They'll be herded out in their black dresses and shot like turkeys, if they don't recant.

FANYA:

You're terrible!

KONSTANTIN:

So come with me! We'll leave the basket in this clearing, where she will be sure to stumble on it. She'll decide we've gone only a bit farther, to look at the view.

FANYA:

You know we can't!

KONSTANTIN:

Fanya, she refuses to acknowledge her illness, and you've seen how it vexes her whenever *we* do. Come! She will want to doze off after her climb, like any self-respecting person. While

"Deep in the greenwood who shall spy
Where I and my beloved lie,
Unless the nightingale—"

FANYA:

The wood isn't green. Why aren't you silly more often?

KONSTANTIN:

I? Silly?

FANYA:

The nightingales have gone.

KONSTANTIN:

They have flown into your throat and make their music there.

FANYA (*seeing TITHONUS*):
Oh! We didn't know—

(*As TITHONUS does not respond, she exchanges a look of puzzled amusement with KONSTANTIN, then moves forward gaily into TITHONUS's line of vision.*)

Forgive us, please, for interrupting your work.

TITHONUS:
Not at all, Mademoiselle, I stopped listening almost at once.

FANYA:
You are an artist!

KONSTANTIN:
Fanya Alexandrovna, let us move on. We are intruding upon a rich mind at work.

FANYA:
I am passionately fond of nature. What a satisfaction for you! And what application! Did you climb from the village? Think, Kostya, isn't it inspiring? I must find out from Nurse what became of my sketch-book. I remember doing some rather pretty things, even last year. But now. . . .

KONSTANTIN:
Now you are busy with clothes and carriage rides.

FANYA:
And with you, Kostya, with you! But when we are married I shall do a watercolor every day!

(*To TITHONUS.*)

Imagine, we are to be married next year! Mamma thinks I am too young. I can't agree with her, and yet I don't mind waiting. I am so happy! If you knew him as I do—!

KONSTANTIN:

There are few who would have her patience in that respect. Come, Fanya.

(*In an undertone.*)

Do try to avoid subjects you know nothing about.

(*To TITHONUS.*)

Good day, Sir.

TITHONUS:
Good day.

FANYA:
But we haven't seen his painting!

KONSTANTIN:
Whoever told you that he wanted us to see it?

FANYA:
Ah, you don't understand artists! It used to give me extreme pleasure to have somebody look over my shoulder.

(*To TITHONUS.*)

Mayn't we see it?

(*TITHONUS gestures indifferently that they may, and they do.*)

What exquisite colors! Oh, it's much better than *mine!*

KONSTANTIN:
Have you given it a title?

TITHONUS:

Not really. As you see, it's no more than a view of the village.

KONSTANTIN:

Ah! That's the *village* down in there. . . . ?

FANYA:

Of course that's the village! Kostya, I'm ashamed of you.

KONSTANTIN:

You must understand I know nothing about painting. I should never have thought that was the village, though.

TITHONUS:

The village seen through leaves.

KONSTANTIN:

Interesting. . . .

FANYA:

Well, *I* think it's truly lovely.

TITHONUS:

I don't ask for flattery.

FANYA:

No, it is!

KONSTANTIN:

Can you tell me your purpose in painting such a picture?

TITHONUS:

My purpose? All the young men are talking about purpose nowadays. It may be I did so myself as a young man, but I have forgotten. Yes. And having forgotten, I cannot regret. I am what I am, and it is soothing to know that. The pain that comes from wishing to be what we are not! As for this picture, I'm afraid I had no purpose. Is that old-fashioned of me?

KONSTANTIN:

Far from it, unfortunately. Yet it's curious. Here you have given yourself the bother of a long climb, with your easel on your back—in order to paint the village. And look! The village has vanished! There are only the dimmest traces left on your canvas—a few odd shapes, a few drab colors, like a village destroyed by fire, seen a week later, through a mass of red-gold foliage. . . .

TITHONUS:

Perhaps my purpose was precisely that.

KONSTANTIN:

But why, then?

TITHONUS:

I don't understand you.

FANYA:

Neither do I!

KONSTANTIN:

The village is real! There is an inn and a blacksmith, there are dogs, men, living, dying! All this is hidden away—behind leaves!

TITHONUS:

The leaves are real as well.

KONSTANTIN (*shouting*):

Very good! Paint leaves then!

FANYA:

Kostya!

KONSTANTIN:

Excuse me. I don't like to see a village hidden by leaves, that's all. I didn't mean to offend you.

FANYA:

You see, he does have very good manners. Most of the time you'd never dream he was a Nihilist.

(*KONSTANTIN glares at her.*)

Oh dear, it slipped out! We haven't yet told my parents.

TITHONUS:

Told them?

FANYA (*proudly*):

That Konstantin Stepanovitch is a Nihilist. They would surely be opposed to the match. And yet he's so brilliant! His professors at the Medical School cannot find words to praise him. He has such ideas, so new, so fascinating!

TITHONUS:

Is it possible we have advanced to an age in which men are praised for new ideas? In my day we had our Nihilism. We called it that.

KONSTANTIN:

I believe in mankind. Nihilism is only a name, a negative belief.

(*Pause.*)

Have you ever seen a man's hand cut off at the wrist? The blood leaps out, the man's eyes roll backwards, his cries are—

FANYA (*grasping her wrist*):

Oh stop!

(*TITHONUS listens unmoved.*)

KONSTANTIN:

Even to hear it described is painful. We cannot help thinking of our own mutilation. Isn't this proof of a deep human sympathy that binds all men together? Kuvshenko would agree with me.

TITHONUS (*bored*):

Ah.

KONSTANTIN:

You are objecting, "But does he overlook a man's environment?" I do not. It is the source of every individual mannerism. Take yourself. Already I can tell—what?—that you are a foreigner. How do I know? By observing that you repress your curiosity. Perhaps curiosity isn't the word. One sees that you have traveled much, and reflected. . . .

TITHONUS:

You are right. I have no curiosity.

KONSTANTIN (*taken aback*):

We all have curiosity. No, I mean rather a kind of outward-goingness, a very Russian trait. We are constantly wanting to know about others—their forebears, their professions, their lives. The Germans and the English intellectualize their curiosity. The French restrict it to their private sensations. Our Russian curiosity is human. We are forever inquiring into our own destinies.

TITHONUS:

That is strange. Our destiny is one of the few matters revealed to us.

KONSTANTIN:

But revelation comes to those who seek it!

TITHONUS:

Perhaps.

FANYA:

I know what he means, Kostya. There have been hours when I've seen my whole life ahead of me, like a sunlit valley. I used not to be able to imagine myself living past the age of nineteen. But now that I *am* nineteen—

OLGA (*who has entered unnoticed*):

You can see all the way to thirty-nine?

(*They turn, surprised. She is out of breath and dressed in gray or black with touches of white.*)

And when, dear, you have passed *that* milestone, you will be able to see yourself at a hundred and three, as I do now after this brutal climb!

KONSTANTIN:

Welcome, Olga Vassilyevna!

FANYA:

We've been wondering what became of you.

OLGA:

Have you? I doubt it. Spread out the rug for me, Konstantin. I can't walk another step.

(*She struggles to catch her breath. FANYA touches her arm.*)

It's nothing.

(*Vivaciously.*)

We'll have our tea here, shall we? If this gentleman will pardon us.

TITHONUS:

Please! Don't think of me!

OLGA:

 We come opportunely, perhaps?

TITHONUS:

 You do, after a lonely day.

FANYA:

 He is an artist!

OLGA:

 So I see. Well, I shall not embarrass him by looking at his picture. Artists hate that. Besides, I should have nothing good to say of it, I warn you, Monsieur.

FANYA:

 You should, though! It's very well done.

OLGA:

 No doubt it is. But today I am out for air and exercise. I can look at pictures all winter if I choose. And in a few weeks these colors will be gone, these wonderful dying leaves. . . .

TITHONUS (*to KONSTANTIN*):

 The real leaves.

KONSTANTIN (*with a shrug and a smile*):

 The real leaves.

OLGA (*to TITHONUS, while unpacking the basket*):

 You'll join our little feast, I hope?

TITHONUS:

 Thank you. I should enjoy a glass of tea.

OLGA:

 Ah, you're not the glutton I am! I can do without tea, but not without my smoked meats and preserves.

(*To the others.*)

But my dear friends! Where is the water?

FANYA:
Oh, the water!

OLGA:
Haven't you found the spring yet? What have you been *doing?* Our guest is thirsting for his tea.

(*To TITHONUS.*)

We call this *our* mountainside. We come here every year.

(*To KONSTANTIN, giving him a flask.*)

Don't you remember where it was?

KONSTANTIN (*patiently*):
Yes, of course.

OLGA:
Then find it!

(*To FANYA, who makes to follow him.*)

Stay with us, *chérie*, it will bring him back sooner.

(*KONSTANTIN runs out.*)

Where is your embroidery? A young girl should always be doing something with her hands.

(*To TITHONUS.*)

You're a stranger here. Do you plan to stay long?

TITHONUS:

It's not likely. For years we have had, my wife and I, no fixed home. A *pied-à-terre* in Paris, nothing more. But now we are at the age—or rather *I* am at the age, for my wife is still young—when a home becomes a necessity. I am no longer thrilled by restaurants.

FANYA:

You've never had a home?

TITHONUS:

As a child only. In latter years I have traveled.

FANYA:

And I have lived all my life here—isn't it strange?—a few miles from the village, in my father's big dark house.

OLGA:

Don't boast, dear.

FANYA:

Was I? I'm sorry. Miss Mannering—she teaches me—wrote in my album for my name-day: "Though we travel the world over in search of the beautiful, we must carry it with us, or we find it not."

TITHONUS:

I don't think that saying has any truth in it at all. "Carry it with us"— as if we were turtles! We carry ourselves, that's more than enough.

FANYA:

But I should like to travel, just the same.

OLGA:

I too have never had a home, since early childhood. Schools and convents, positions in genteel families, not altogether a servant, never quite a friend. I married a schoolmaster, an older man, honest, proud of his uniform. He is dead, there were no children. I began to pay long visits, then very long visits—isn't it so, Fanya? As a widow, I had rank of a sort. I knew how to make myself useful. People seemed to appreciate me.

FANYA:

Appreciate! They adore you!

OLGA:

It is a life, in short.

TITHONUS:

Better than some.

OLGA:

Poorer than others.

FANYA:

Have you been to Italy, then?

TITHONUS:

Italy, Africa, Sweden, Constantinople. . . .

FANYA:

How I envy you! Tell us about Constantinople!

TITHONUS:

A fascinating city, but fearful, too. Swarming with life! This ring I wear comes from the Bazaar in Constantinople. A serpent, you see, with its tail in its mouth.

FANYA:

It makes me shiver.

TITHONUS:

It is a symbol of eternity and of wisdom.

OLGA:

Also of evil, I've been told.

KONSTANTIN (*entering with the filled flask*):

Come quickly! The spring's not a hundred steps from here! There's a waterfall—at this season!—and ferns taller than Fanya Alexandrovna!

FANYA:

Oh, let's see it!

OLGA:

Later, perhaps.

KONSTANTIN:

The light's on it now—it won't wait!

OLGA (*laughing*):

And there are a dozen little rainbows, and snails, and gnats. I know. Run along then, drink it all in.

(*KONSTANTIN puts down the flask and goes out with FANYA.*)

And now that *we're* unchaperoned, let us have a quiet tea.

TITHONUS:

How lazy one is, not to have a look at something beautiful, only a few steps away. . . .

OLGA:

How old one is, you mean. *We* should see nothing remarkable, you and I.

TITHONUS:

That young man—

OLGA:

Konstantin? He's my godson.

TITHONUS:

He appears full of ideals.

OLGA:

He picked a quarrel with you, didn't he? Do you enjoy that?

TITHONUS:

Quarreling with people? No. I despise quarrels. Yet I have known others—my own father—who, out of some insane zest for experience, seemed almost to revel in it. Your godson will never permit himself to compromise. I admire that.

OLGA:

Never to compromise? But you pass up a great blessing! Compromise is to our souls what sleep is to our bodies. And who would choose never to sleep? It is the compromise of the body with death, a delicious thing! We don't agree. . . .

(*All at once she stiffens with pain, her hand at her throat. The spasm passes unremarked by TITHONUS.*)

Konstantin Stepanovitch has a good mind, a trifle pedantic still, but clever, resourceful. . . . He is entering into a match with that child whose principal charm is an enormous dowry.

TITHONUS:

Pardon me, isn't the girl very much in love with him?

OLGA:

True. What bearing has that upon her charm?

TITHONUS:

It is charming to he loved.

OLGA (*impatiently*):
Well, of course, if one is a child or an invalid. . . .

(*Laughing.*)

My godson once had me read a pamphlet by a psychologist, proposing love as a cure for all kinds of illnesses.

TITHONUS:
Now that is rubbish!

OLGA:
Ah well, he gave it to me as a joke. I told him, anyhow—"There's nothing comic," I said, "in having grown so old and so poor that nobody who comes along will look twice at you."

TITHONUS:
You're right. There is nothing comic in such a thought.

OLGA (*making the best of an unexpected answer*):
It takes an unusual man to understand that. I'd never met one, till now, who didn't resort to a lot of idiotic compliments. "Why, Olga Vassilyevna, what nonsense! You're hardly out of your cradle!" At least I know better than to believe them.

TITHONUS:
How indelicate of me! You mustn't think I meant—

OLGA:
There, there! I'm teasing you!

TITHONUS:
Teasing me? Why should you want to tease me?

OLGA (*deciding to ignore this*):
As for Fanya, she'll be married, that's the main thing. What if in five years her husband chooses to regret his freedom? He'll never leave

her—unless he *truly* refuses to compromise. And then—well, I ask only that Konstantin not make a silly mistake.

TITHONUS:

You oughtn't to look so much on the dark side! Why, he struck me as caring for her so deeply, so passionately—

OLGA:

Ah, you've forgotten! A young man cares for *everybody* passionately. What's more, you don't know poverty! I should myself care passionately for any pliable person who would not only provide me with absolute material comfort but bring about my advancement in the world.

(*To the samovar.*)

Boil, why don't you?

TITHONUS:

A watched pot. . . .

(*They laugh together.*)

No! What shocking things you say! Material comfort! Advancement in the world! Am I to believe that all that has any hold over a person such as yourself?

OLGA:

Are we talking seriously?

(*In a dramatic whisper.*)

Yes! All that *has* a hold over me! I am the soul of worldliness!

(*The look on his face sends her into a burst of laughter.*)

Come, my friend, I like you! I shall brew you a glass of tea and draw you out.

TITHONUS:
Am I so innocent?

OLGA:
Pristine. Don't frown!

TITHONUS:
Do I frown?

OLGA:
Or are you one of those innocent men who turn out to be the ruin of us all?

(*TITHONUS is embarrassed.*)

Dear friend, forgive me. It's as if we had known each other before, in a different life. Think of me as laughing for joy, to have found you once again.

(*Gives him her hand.*)

TITHONUS:
Yes, it is so. . . . I have no defenses. I feel an extraordinary ease, as though something clogged had been set running again, a stopped watch shaken and set running. . . .

OLGA (*alert to something else*):
Do you hear? The cry of a strange bird. . . .

TITHONUS:
For years something has gone untouched, a spring inside me. . . . What you said just now—reverberates. There is a stirring, as of roots

at the end of winter. Yes. When I turned and saw you standing there, I knew that I . . . had not had a happy life. Forgive me.

OLGA:

One can say anything to a stranger.

TITHONUS (*excited*):

But in all fairness to yourself, you must know—I am not free.

OLGA:

Few of us are!

TITHONUS:

I mean, I told you earlier—I am married.

OLGA (*as if that had anything to do with it*):

Married!

TITHONUS:

Yes. To Au—

OLGA:

Hush, ridiculous man! Married! What do you take me for? On an acquaintance of ten minutes!

TITHONUS:

But you said—! Forgive me, I am a fool. I have never understood the motives of others.

OLGA (*laughing*):

I should say you have not! I feel like La Fontaine's dolphin, who thought to save a man from drowning only to discover it was a monkey—and just in time!

TITHONUS:

I beg you—

OLGA:

Back into the sea he went, poor ape! What a fiasco! "But you said——!"

(*More gently.*)

What did I say? I proposed an orgy of conversation, the only kind permitted to strangers who have reached the age of discretion.

(*TITHONUS smiles with her, unwittingly relieved.*)

Come now! Let us forget this unfortunate passage. It is behind us and casts an amusing light, quite as if we had *had* the miserable liaison, after all. Nothing draws people closer than a misunderstanding.

TITHONUS:

How true that is! In my own life, at perhaps the very moment that determined my life—

(*He is interrupted by renewed laughter.*)

Now why are you laughing?

OLGA:

What an egotist you are! First you imagine that I want you to make love to me, next that I want to hear about your life! Haven't you understood? I *know* your life, I know it without your telling me.

TITHONUS:

What then do you want from me?

OLGA (*with sad intensity*):

Want! Want! Mightn't it be enough to live and breathe? Must one always—?

(*She is overcome by a second spell of illness.*)

TITHONUS (*rising in alarm*):
What is it? You're not well!

OLGA (*choking*):
No! Leave me!

TITHONUS:
Leave you! No! Never!

OLGA (*recovering*):
It is of no importance whatsoever.

(*He helps her to her feet.*)

There, you see, it's over. The laughter brought it on. Last year, it is true, I was ailing. But now I am well, remarkably well. You see, I know my own life, also. . . . Listen, the water's boiling. . . .

(*She brews tea.*)

TITHONUS (*humorously scolding*):
You know, you frightened me!

(*Producing a sheaf of photographs.*)

Ha! These might interest you. My wife is an amateur photographer.

(*Showing them.*)

Here is a remarkable view of her family's home—see how clearly you distinguish the mountaintop. It was taken from the temple below. . . . Here am I, only last year, in the Alps . . . again in Burgos . . . in Amsterdam. A heavenly effect of light there on the canal. She develops all her own photographs. I wonder sometimes if she's ever really happy outside of her little darkroom. . . . Ah! here is

one of her early efforts. That is myself, in the first year of our mar-
riage. Forty years ago.

OLGA (*who by now has given up trying*):
  You were very handsome.

TITHONUS:
  Yes. I was young.

(*A pause.*)

  You spoke just now of wanting. At that age I wanted—oh, scan-
  dalous, impossible things. Since then, I have learned that we can alter
  our wants.

OLGA:
  No. We can uproot them, as I have done. Where I had planted an
  alley of chrysanthemums there is now a little row of herbs.

(*Pouring tea.*)

  Be honest now, haven't you done the same?

TITHONUS:
  I? I have done nothing. And I want nothing.

(*Pause.*)

  But I would accept, if pressed, a glass of tea.

OLGA (*handing it to him*):
  Sugar? Cream? Rum?

TITHONUS:
  Nothing.

OLGA:

No turkey? Not a single tart? They're all for me. . . . I was thinking of an old woman who read tea leaves, old Varya—she's dead, poor soul. . . .

TITHONUS (*after a pause*):

How agreeable this moment is! If only it would not pass away. . . .

OLGA:

Agreeable things *do* pass away. That is how we distinguish them from disagreeable things. They pass away and they reappear, the seasons, the lovers in the landscape. Sometimes the very faces seem to be repeating themselves, faces from long ago.

TITHONUS:

The leaves are falling, but they will return. We read their meaning as in the bottom of a glass of tea. One must be content to sit, to let it run its course.

(*Pause.*)

You look at me with—what is it?—mockery? impatience?

OLGA:

Drink your tea, my friend.

TITHONUS:

Do not fear, I shall not launch into a tedious account of my life, my little daily miseries. Why should one speak of these things? One is never understood. Many of your Russian writers succumb to this— shall we say, gossip of the soul?—and go their way, poor men, without ever achieving that refinement we look for in an enduring life.

(*Pause.*)

An enduring work, I meant to say. At every turning, now, what does one hear but the cries of men whose feelings are too overwhelming to be contained? Feelings indeed! If only they knew what it meant to have a fountain in the breast, flowing, quenching, musical—where I have only a stone! I cannot feel! My heart is dry as dust! You see, I laugh at it, yet . . . I have a wife, I have an unborn child! The deeds we do in the name of love!—not love, for I feel nothing. My wife, do you understand?—dressed in a Chinese robe of the clearest blue! "Husband," she said, "is it I who have failed you? What have I done," she said, "to deserve your reproach?"—I who cannot even feel reproach!—And taking my hand, she laid it below her heart where through the silk and her young flesh I might feel that other heart, the heart of my own child. I felt it, yes, but felt nothing else, not even envy of the child who will never give up the blessing I—I cannot even reproach myself! She rose from the table, upsetting her cup of chocolate. It shattered to the floor, staining us both, a piece of miraculous Sèvres given her by Lady Hamilton. She took my face between her hands, passionately, then pressed her chin against my skull—but not before I had seen her own face wet and bright as a spring dawn.

(*No longer looking at OLGA, but holding before him the photograph of himself as a young man.*)

A dawn, an everlasting dawn!—but for me, no night, no tempest, no cause to rejoice in it. I long for that night in which things lose themselves, the dark negative of my soul, my mild, trivial, terrible soul.

(*Slowly, almost tenderly, TITHONUS begins to tear up the photograph.*)

I have remembered everything and experienced nothing. Sunlight in cities, brilliance of theaters, the phosphorescence of names and places in the mind bent on darkness—nothing but light, light, light! It is not to be borne.

(*He scatters the destroyed photograph.*)

Forgive me. If I talk as I have, senselessly, you must understand that I had glimpsed in your face something, a darkness, a mortality. Olga Vassilyevna, whoever you are, break the spell!

(*Softly.*)

Oh, in my heart I feel you have already done so! Have you already done so? I dare not look. Am I free? Will it end?

(*He turns. OLGA has risen and stands swaying, one hand over her eyes.*)

You *are* ill! Good God!

OLGA:
Yes, I am ill. The doctors say I am dying. I want so much not to.

(*Too late, TITHONUS makes a move towards her.*)

Stay where you are. It will pass.

(*She goes out.*)

TITHONUS (*spent and bewildered, mechanically tastes his tea*):
Cold . . . disgusting . . .

(*He puts down his glass, crosses to the easel and begins to dismount it. Enter FANYA and KONSTANTIN, dreamily oblivious of him.*)

FANYA:
But shan't we perhaps one day go to Sorrento?

KONSTANTIN:
No.

FANYA:
To China? To California?

KONSTANTIN:
   Never.

FANYA (*scattering leaves*):
   Not even if I should wish it?

KONSTANTIN:
   There will be no need to travel. My heart is so full. Fanya! All of life
   will be wherever we are!

FANYA:
   But Italy won't.

KONSTANTIN:
   So much bad painting!

FANYA:
   Not even when we're rich?

KONSTANTIN:
   We shall never be richer than we are now.

FANYA:
   My dearest. . . . Look at the village! How short the days are now. . . .

KONSTANTIN (*suddenly*):
   Fanya, do you see?

FANYA:
   What?

KONSTANTIN (*pointing*):
   A woman—down there! It's not the path we came by. . . . No, right
   below us!

FANYA:

Oh! Isn't she wonderfully pretty! I've never seen such hair—and her clothes! Who could she be?

(*Half-serious.*)

On second thought, Kostya, I don't think it's at all nice of you to look. She's *too* pretty!

(*TITHONUS looks down, rises, waves his hand.*)

KONSTANTIN:

She sees us, look! she's smiling! She's waving her hand!

FANYA:

Do you *know* her?

(*OLGA enters. KONSTANTIN waves to the approaching figure.*)

Kostya!

KONSTANTIN:

It's so silly of you to be jealous. Look, she's out of sight.

FANYA:

Who *is* she? You waved to her!

TITHONUS:

You have just seen my wife, who has charmingly taken it upon herself to join us here.

FANYA (*turning*):

Oh, it's our friend! We keep not seeing you!

KONSTANTIN:

Your wife, truly?

TITHONUS:

Why should you notice an old man? Yes, Sir, my wife.

OLGA:

Children, our excursion is over, come!

KONSTANTIN:

But we mustn't leave now!

OLGA:

Indeed we must. The carriage will be waiting. Put those things in the basket.

FANYA:

Olga Vassilyevna, what is wrong?

OLGA:

Nothing, I assure you.

(*To TITHONUS.*)

What devotion to come this distance on foot, in her condition! One sees that you are a good husband, a happy man. . . . Hurry, Fanya!

(*To KONSTANTIN.*)

Help her, why don't you?

(*To TITHONUS.*)

You're pouting, aren't you?—because I would not receive your confidences. Well, I forgive you.

TITHONUS:

To forgive is to forget.

OLGA:

As you wish. I don't forgive you, then.

TITHONUS:

Nor I you.

(*Offering the serpent ring.*)

But would you accept, as a remembrance, this?

OLGA:

How could I rob you of your only—I meant to say, your most unusual treasure?

TITHONUS:

One likes to offer something with associations.

OLGA:

Then keep it. I don't doubt there's a story behind it.

(*Turning.*)

Are we ready, Fanya?

FANYA:

Nearly.

KONSTANTIN:

I don't see that we have to hurry away.

AURORA (*offstage, calling*):

Where are you, darling?

FANYA (*closing the basket*):

There!

TITHONUS (*calling*):
   This way!

(*To OLGA.*)

   I should be most happy to present you to my wife.

OLGA:
   Pray, make her our excuses.

(*To FANYA.*)

   Lead the way down the mountainside, *chérie*.

FANYA:
   I think we have everything. . . .

(*To TITHONUS, sweetly.*)

   Perhaps we'll meet again. Mamma lets me have *my* friends to tea on
   Tuesdays. If you're staying nearby—

OLGA (*warningly*):
   Fanya!

FANYA (*to OLGA*):
   Oh, shouldn't I have . . . ? I'm sorry.

(*Giving TITHONUS her hand.*)

   Goodbye.

(*To KONSTANTIN.*)

Don't leave the basket, Kostya!

(*She goes out, carrying the rug.*)

KONSTANTIN:
Olga Vassilyevna, I suspect you of a discourtesy!

OLGA:
How they talk, these young people! Take care of your own manners, Konstantin, and offer a sick old woman your arm. I must have the eyes of a cat, I can see nothing in this light.

(*She gives TITHONUS her hand. He kisses it.*)

Au revoir, Monsieur.

(*Turning.*)

Now where is Fanya, gone on ahead? Well, we shall have many things to tell the others, safe in the parlor, tonight. . . .

(*OLGA and KONSTANTIN go, leaving the basket.*)

AURORA (*offstage, closer*):
Tithonus!

TITHONUS:
I'm here! Are you all right?

AURORA:
Of course! I just wanted to see you!

TITHONUS:
I'll pack my paints and join you down there!

AURORA:

Stay where you are! I'm not a bit out of breath!

TITHONUS:

You shouldn't be climbing about!

AURORA:

What?

TITHONUS:

Nothing!

AURORA:

Who are you with?

TITHONUS:

Nobody!

AURORA:

I saw them!

TITHONUS:

I don't know who they were! They've gone, anyhow!

AURORA (*very close*):

Why? They were charming! They waved to me!

KONSTANTIN (*re-entering*):

I left the basket after all. I hope I'm not—

(*He stops. AURORA enters, visibly pregnant and flushed.*)

TITHONUS (*to KONSTANTIN*):

She tries to do too much. It's not right.

KONSTANTIN:
No, it's not right . . .

AURORA (*to TITHONUS*):
Oh, what a climb! But here I am!

TITHONUS (*kissing her hand*):
Yes, here you are, at last.

AURORA:
But what a pretty spot! And you told me your friends had left!

(*To KONSTANTIN.*)

Good afternoon.

(*To TITHONUS.*)

I believe I have not met this gentleman.

TITHONUS:
I must confess, I—

KONSTANTIN:
Konstantin Stepanovitch Tschudin, at your service.

AURORA (*giving him her hand*):
I'm delighted. You'll excuse my appearance. I was ordered—

TITHONUS:
You were ordered to confine yourself to the morning room.

AURORA (*in high spirits*):
Quite so, the morning room, where I belong, if I may have my little joke. But there were too many plants, the air was damp and green with

them, and before I knew it I was out of doors. As I walked through the village, a dozen wise old women with rosy wrinkled cheeks pressed round me, stroking me, kissing me, showing me the way. . . .

(*Her tone changes.*)

I'm all at once extraordinarily tired.

KONSTANTIN (*opening the basket*):
I'm certain we have a drop of cognac here.

TITHONUS:
I trust it's not the sight of me that has tired you.

AURORA:
Darling, you're peevish—why?

(*She picks up one or two bits of the torn photograph, vaguely puzzled.*)

Tell me what you've done today.

TITHONUS:
Oh, nothing, you know. . . .

KONSTANTIN:
A very interesting picture.

AURORA:
I'm so glad! May I see it?

TITHONUS (*coldly*):
I'd rather you didn't. It's unfinished, and I don't know if I care enough to make the necessary changes.

(*Taking up his easel, paintbox, etc.*)

Shall we be on our way?

AURORA (*accepting a glass from KONSTANTIN*):
  Yes, I feel—oh, thank you, you're very kind—quite at the end of my strength. It is a new feeling—

TITHONUS (*petulant*):
  Aurora!

AURORA:
  —and a curiously pleasant one . . .

(*She drinks, returns the glass, and picks up TITHONUS's campstool.*)

  . . . part of the great human adventure. . . .

(*She follows TITHONUS out.*)

ACT THREE

(*America, 1954. A garden adjoining the house of AURORA and TITHONUS. There is a reclining lawn chair among other pieces of garden furniture, a trellis and a neglected plot of geraniums. One feels that no other houses are nearby. It is early morning.*)

(*AURORA sits smoking. She is carelessly and unbecomingly dressed, without make-up. Within reach are gardening tools. After a moment MARK enters. He wears slacks and a white polo shirt.*)

MARK:
Lovely morning, isn't it?

AURORA (*squinting*):
Who's that? Oh. No, it isn't lovely, since you ask.

MARK:
Perhaps you haven't had your coffee.

AURORA:
I have, though. And a filthy egg. And don't expect me to talk about it. My mind is a Black Hole.

(*He touches her neck.*)

And don't make love to me!

MARK:
In that case I'll help you with the flowers.

AURORA:
Flowers! They're a simple scandal. I don't want to weed them, I want to wring their necks. Get away from them, do, they'll smear you from head to foot. I know.

MARK (*laughing*):

All right. What has happened?

AURORA:

Nothing that hasn't happened for the last hundred years. It's like the water-drop torture, it keeps accumulating. I ought at least to be thankful that the boy has come. The boy! He's three times your age. Old enough to give his poor mother some advice. It's clear that *I* can't think any more.

MARK:

But that's wonderful news! I thought I saw a strange car in the drive. When did he come?

AURORA:

At the crack of dawn. For his father's birthday.

MARK:

You should be tremendously relieved.

AURORA:

How so?

MARK:

Why, just that he'll take his share of the responsibility. He's retired, he's come home, hasn't he? You'll have a certain freedom to lead your own life, after these years of strain.

AURORA:

I don't believe he's staying.

MARK:

He's not staying?

AURORA:

I can't blame him. What did Tithonus and I ever do for him? That's what he said to me, his own mother, who cooked his breakfast! But he was right.

MARK:

I don't think I'm going to like Memnon.

AURORA:

He is awfully pompous to be one's son. I suppose it's the result of a military career. His father's father was the same way.

MARK:

It wouldn't hurt him to take over for a little while.

AURORA:

No, it wouldn't. Oh, I never dreamed I'd feel so worn, so old—!

MARK:

You will never be old.

AURORA:

Don't tell me, my sweet. Hand me the shears. No, I meant the trowel. I may *look* the same, but listen to me. I sound like Madeleine Usher.

MARK:

I get angry hearing you make fun of yourself. The beautiful way you bear this situation—

AURORA (*stabbing at the flowers*):

It's not beautiful the way *I* bear it. It's your precious little wife, *she's* the marvel. She sits and holds his hand and changes his linen and at the right interval shouts the right word in his ear, or what he appears to take for the right word. Five days of this! It's too mortifying, meeting you so casually, having you for a month in the country, and letting her do so much. You didn't know us when we still could do things stylishly. But the servants today won't put up with it, and he can't be left alone. I'd hoped that Memnon—ah, well, *speriamo!*

MARK:

Tithonus isn't the one who needs caring for.

AURORA:

It's quite hopeless, you know, trying to care for others. But she appears to enjoy it.

MARK:

She likes to feel helpful. I don't know what she enjoys.

AURORA:

She's really too perfect, an authentic *jeune fille,* the kind that used to read Goldsmith and play the harp, the kind that nowadays—listen to me, please! I talk, I swear, like a vampire at a cotillion. Next, I'll hear myself ask you for a Fig Newton and a cup of Moxie!

MARK:

Aurora, stop this! I know that you're baffled and worried and hurt. You insult me by the tone you take.

AURORA:

Rot. I'm simply indulging myself. Must you take away my last amusement?

MARK:

It's no amusement, either for you or for anyone who has watched you these days.

AURORA:

Have you watched me?

MARK:

You know I have.

AURORA:

It is always amusing to give in to one's baser sentiments.

MARK:

You have no base sentiments, try as you may.

AURORA:

Believe me, I do.

MARK:

Then confess to me the basest of them.

AURORA (*stalling*):

My basest sentiment? How Victorian that sounds! Well, it is a Victorian sentiment.

(*Serious.*)

It is that I find you a very handsome and estimable man. And my most elevated sentiment is my love for Tithonus. You see, I can say anything.

MARK:

Aurora!

AURORA:

And I shall never leave him. And I am not unhappy.

MARK:

You *are* unhappy, you're miserable! You took him as a lover, in all good faith. Well—you loved him, didn't you?

AURORA:

You don't know!

MARK:

Then why be all nervous and guilty because you've changed? What is your change compared to his?

AURORA:

I'm kinder to Tithonus than you are to that poor patient child—who, after all, supports you, doesn't she?

MARK:

If Enid wants to support me, that's her own affair.

AURORA:

Don't be so touchy.

MARK:

I'm ashamed of the whole situation, if you must know. But I'm only human. Shame doesn't become a creature like yourself.

AURORA:

Because I'm *not* human, you mean? You needn't rub it in, Mark.

MARK:

Now who's being touchy?

AURORA:

I know I'm not human. It's not for lack of trying. I've wanted to suffer! I've shed tears, I've borne a child. I've been faithful to Tithonus, not that I've *had* to be by any means. But I wanted to go through what *people* go through. I haven't wanted to snap my fingers and fly off in a glittering machine. I've done my best, but it hasn't really worked. I haven't suffered enough, I suppose.

MARK:

It isn't suffering that makes us human, to begin with. And it certainly isn't living with Tithonus.

AURORA:

It *must* be suffering! If that doesn't make you human, what does?

MARK:

I've always thought it was something you were born with.

AURORA:

Flippancy's not going to help me!

MARK:

Oh Aurora, you're so lovely and young, you can't *not* be all of that, even to please your lover. Of course you talk like an old woman. He wants you old and dim, he wants to drag you down with him into some kind of horrible endless twilight. Don't you see? You're in danger!

AURORA:

Danger . . . ?

MARK:

Think of him. He has hardly a mind and hardly a body, but he has twined himself about you like mistletoe. You're forever draining yourself dry in order to replenish him. How could he die?

AURORA (*bursting into tears*):

Mistletoe!

MARK (*taking her in his arms*):

Oh my lovely. That's it. There.

AURORA:

Do you know, can you imagine, what it means, after so long, to feel that somebody watches you, and knows, and cares, quietly, gently cares and understands? He has never wanted to know what *I* was feeling. He has never known, it has always been *himself*. . . .

MARK:

Leave him. Forget him. You can if you want to. Oh Aurora, come with me. I love you. Tell me you love me. Don't tell me then, I *know*.

AURORA:

Enid loves you.

MARK:

Yes. And what a poor thing it is, to *be* loved! I don't want that. I need to feel it myself, and I do!

AURORA:

Do you mean that you would leave your wife?

MARK:

I would leave her for you.

(*A long pause.*)

AURORA:

There *might* be a way. . . .

(*Controlling herself.*)

You should not have made me weep. Tears are moral. When I've finished weeping, I've finished caring for myself. The sun shines after a little tempest, it's like that. My sense of obligation is revived.

MARK:

But we're both weary to death of obligations!

AURORA:

Are we? Darling, yes, I love you. There it is and there it ends. I am weary of obligations, but not to death. Thank you for these moments. I feel young and strong suddenly, and I love you. And that is all you shall ever have from me. That and this.

(*Kisses him.*)

MARK:

I don't understand. I want only you.

AURORA:

There, enough! I *must* get at those flowers. Is it my turn now to comfort you? You're not cross with me? My voice sounds so fresh and happy, I can't think why. . . . Am I happy? I must be, yes I am, deliciously so, for no good reason. Poor poor dear dear young man!

ENID (*entering from the house*):
Good morning.

AURORA (*blandly*):
And dear lovely good creature that *you* are! We've been talking about you. I was saying, if you *knew* what it does for me, for all of us, to have you here. I may be a goddess, but you are a saint. I'm afraid it's telling on you, though.

ENID:
No, I'm fine, really. I enjoy sitting with him. It's an education, just listening.

AURORA:
I simply meant you look a trifle worn.

ENID:
That's my hay fever. I have it every summer. My eyes swell up.

AURORA:
I want you to rest today, just the same. Read, go down to the lake, do whatever you feel like doing. Memnon will want to be with his father, and I shall want to—

(*Grimacing.*)

be with Memnon. He's only here for the day.

ENID:
I know. He told me.

AURORA:
Oh, you've met then. Doesn't he strike you as rather bourgeois?

ENID:
Oh, I couldn't tell. I met him just now in the hall. Tithonus was awake and had called for you.

AURORA:

And Memnon's with him now?

ENID:

I don't know. I told him he could go in, but he said he thought he would—

AURORA:

Don't tell me what he thought. I don't want to know.

MARK:

Should Tithonus be left alone?

ENID:

Good heavens, I wasn't thinking!

(*Starts off, distressed.*)

AURORA:

No no no no *no*, dear. Let *me* go. Does he know it's his birthday?

ENID:

I don't think so. I had a present for him, but it didn't seem to register.

AURORA:

Aren't you an angel! What did you give him?

ENID:

He complains so of the cold, I've been knitting a little scarf. Rather, it *began* as a little scarf, but if anything, it's too long now.

AURORA:

I'm sure it's perfect. When he gets used to it, he'll love it. It takes a few days, you know, with new things. Well. . . .

(*Starts away.*)

MARK:

Aurora, think about what I've said.

(*AURORA goes out. A pause.*)

ENID:

I think I shall go down to the lake. Will you come? I love to look over the side of a boat. You can see your face in the water if it's calm and you're turned away from the sun. Not a reflection really, a kind of dark transparency, and through it, below, the grasses moving, something white, one or two fish. . . .

(*Covering her eyes.*)

These unbroken shining days! How does she manage them?

(*Pause.*)

I don't want to pry, but tell me—what is Aurora to think about?

MARK:

I suggested we might all go off one of these days, with a picnic. There are some fascinating things not far away, churches, antique shops. You know better than I, after reading the guidebook.

ENID:

I didn't know you enjoyed sightseeing.

MARK:

Whatever made you think I didn't? Once in a while, it's very pleasant. I didn't know you had hay fever.

ENID:

Whatever makes you think I do? And how about Tithonus? You know he can't be moved.

MARK (*lighting a cigarette*):
Strange. I didn't think of that.

ENID:
Didn't she?

MARK:
Didn't she what?

ENID:
See that as an objection to your plan?

MARK:
Yes—so she did.

ENID (*faintly*):
Then why, if the whole thing is impossible, did you ask her to think about it?

MARK:
You'll have to speak louder if you want me to hear you.

ENID (*doing so*):
Or did you intend for me to stay with Tithonus while you and she go off together?

MARK:
No, certainly not. I'm sure she can get someone from the village. We might offer to pay for whoever comes. We can afford it, and it would be a nice gesture.

ENID:
It has to be someone he knows!

(*Pause.*)

Oh dearest, all I mean is that I *don't* take much pleasure in sitting with him the better part of the day and night.

MARK (*losing his temper*):
Then why do it, if you don't enjoy it?

ENID:
Don't be cross.

MARK:
Don't be pathetic.

ENID:
I'm surprised you have any preference in the matter.

MARK:
What matter?

ENID:
The matter of how you want me to be.

MARK (*politely*):
I'm sorry. Be just as you are.

ENID:
Just as I am! With my eyes swollen and my heart sick? If that's how I am—oh Mark, make me stop! I don't want to talk this way, I'm beginning to feel at home in this unhappiness. In another moment I'll start *liking* it!

MARK:
That's so typical of you, Enid, to find the silver lining of an imaginary cloud.

ENID:
What's the matter with us? It's like being in an earthquake. The ground slips from under you, but silently, and in bright sunlight.

(MEMNON enters from the house. He is dressed in a double-breasted business suit, with loud tie and steel-rimmed glasses. He carries a briefcase and before long will light a cigar.)

MEMNON:
Morning!

MARK:
This will be Memnon.

(Turning.)

Good morning.

MEMNON:
Just looking around, thanks. Don't believe you and I have met. I'm the old man's son, retired myself now.

MARK *(shaking hands)*:
How are you? I think you already know my wife.

MEMNON:
Can't say I've had that pleasure—

(Recognizing ENID.)

Why sure! Isn't that the limit? Why, I thought you were the nurse! No offense, I hope?

ENID:
None whatever. I *am* the nurse.

MEMNON *(to MARK)*:
What outfit were you in?

MARK:

Excuse me?

ENID:

What outfit were you in, dear?

MARK:

I was thirteen when the war ended.

ENID (*smoothing it over, to MEMNON*):

How do you think your father looks?

MEMNON:

Oh, pretty much the same, I guess.

ENID:

He *is* remarkable, isn't he?

MEMNON:

Remarkable's the word, all right. Between you and me, though, we never had too much to say to each other, Dad and I.

ENID:

I suppose he always *was* so much older, wasn't he? But you must be very close to your mother.

MEMNON:

Not really. She was always so much younger. They used to look on me like some kind of freak, you know, being human and all. Been sensitive ever since to people making fun of me.

ENID:

I hope you're here for a nice leisurely visit.

MEMNON:

Afraid not. Like to stay but got to get back. Just down to wish Dad many happy returns.

ENID:

What a pity! Really must you? I'd think, now you're retired from active duty, your time would be your own.

MEMNON:

That's what *I* thought till I spoke to my agent last week. He told me I'd have to buckle down hard if I wanted my book to get *published* even, let alone *sell.*

ENID:

Your book?

MEMNON:

My war journal. But like you say, war's over, *has* been for a number of years. Public's beginning to lose interest. My agent said to me, we can't go on living in a fool's paradise.

ENID (*after a pause*):

But that's perfectly thrilling!

MARK:

Does it have a title?

MEMNON:

Not yet. Wanted to call it *Old Soldiers Never Die,* but then I started to wonder how Dad would take it. Seemed a bit inappropriate.

MARK:

How about *From Ranks to Riches?*

(*MEMNON jots it down.*)

ENID:

You must tell your father about it. He has so many wonderful reminiscences of his own. But gracious, if you have work to do, I couldn't imagine a more perfect atmosphere than right here. That west porch, facing the water!

MARK:

Probably the General wants to be within reach of documents and newspaper files.

MEMNON:

Between ourselves, that's the whole point. I could kick myself for not having made some kind of notes at the time. A line a day would have done it. But man! we were in combat! Also, you can't go into seclusion just to write a book. You've got to keep in the public eye! They want your opinions on national affairs. You go after honorary degrees, you lay cornerstones! Show them you're still full of beans!

AURORA (*entering*):

What under the sun are you talking about?

(*She is now beautifully groomed and carries a large straw purse.*)

ENID:

Don't you look lovely!

MEMNON (*whom AURORA kisses on the forehead*):

More like my daughter than my mother.

MARK:

We've had a little talk about literature.

AURORA:

How elevating!

ENID (*to MEMNON*):

Have you a family?

MENMON:

No. Never got around to it. Never regretted it, either.

AURORA (*to MARK*):

I've had such a curious few minutes on the telephone.

MARK:

With whom?

AURORA:

Somebody I'd forgotten all about.

MEMNON (*to ENID*):

You know, the example of Mother and Dad did a lot to discourage me from having a family of my own.

AURORA (*to MARK, hushed but excited*):

I've changed my mind!

MARK (*eagerly*):

What do you mean?

AURORA (*aloud*):

I mean— we might bring Tithonus out into the garden. It's such a beautiful mild day, it would be a little treat for him.

ENID:

I'll get him ready.

AURORA:

He *is* ready. And we have two grown men to work for us, so just sit down with me, my sweet. This is your day of rest.

(*To the others.*)

Will you fetch him, please? One of you can carry him, the other bring his covers.

MEMNON:

Is he much of a load?

AURORA:

Light as a feather. You've lifted him, Mark. It's the same as picking up a baby, you just want to be careful the head doesn't drop off.

(*MEMNON and MARK go out. A pause.*)

Oh living, living. . . . Don't you sometimes feel you'd like to run away, put it all behind you, all the effort, all the pretense?

ENID:

Do you pretend, Aurora?

AURORA:

I never used to. But now I feel I'm constantly pretending, contriving little lies with my face and voice. I try to appear light and calm, to keep something twirling in my hand. . . .

ENID:

Perhaps you simply pretend to be pretending.

AURORA:

Perhaps. What would you say?

ENID:

I would say that you were quite truly happy. I envy you.

AURORA:

Hush! You mustn't, you needn't. . . .

(*Pause.*)

What a child you are!

ENID:
If only I were beautiful!

AURORA:
Appearances aren't everything. Besides, you're lovely!

ENID:
But they *are*, and I'm *not!* It's unfair, the things we were told—by our beautiful mothers, our beautiful sisters, even our beautiful husbands! They made us believe that a sweet disposition meant more than a good figure. They told us that if we were generous and patient and truthful, nobody would care about our not having red-gold hair and gray-gold eyes and wonderful useless hands. I suppose it was sheer human pity on their part, and yet if they *had* told the truth I might have learned to bear it, by now. I try. I sit at the mirror and stare at my face. I say to myself aloud, over and over, "Appearances *are* everything!" It's like dipping my heart in brine!

AURORA:
Are you fond of me, Enid? Sometimes I wonder if you like me at all.

ENID:
Oh, how hard I've tried not to! But I am, I do, so very much! You can't know the thoughts I've had.

AURORA:
Can't I? You have seen me as a young wife tired of her husband. You have imagined me in search of a handsome lover. You have wept all night out of jealousy and helplessness. Isn't it so?

(*ENID bows her head.*)

Well, I have known all of that. And I have had to smile, thinking how little cause for tears I should have if I were in your position.

ENID:

How good you are! Can you guess what a relief—? I'd thought—I hadn't dared think! Then none of it is true?

AURORA (*lying but radiant*):

None of it!

ENID:

There was no reason for me to have—?

AURORA:

No reason!

ENID:

He really and truly—

AURORA:

With all his heart!

ENID:

—loves me?

AURORA (*tears in her eyes*):

Loves you!

(*Squeezing ENID's hand.*)

They'll be coming. Where's your handkerchief?

(*ENID gives it to her. AURORA blows her nose.*)

We must never lose faith in those who love us.

ENID:

Tell me one thing. What was he saying to you, earlier?

AURORA:

You *still* don't believe me!

ENID:

I do, I want to! But please—

AURORA (*glowing*):

It was a secret. He particularly didn't want you to know about it. But you will, I promise, and soon.

(*Voices offstage.*)

Ah, here they are!

(*Enter MEMNON with cushions, covers, and a very long knitted scarf. AURORA and ENID move the lawn chair to the center of the stage. MARK appears carrying TITHONUS, of whom is seen only a withered head emerging from white robes.*)

ENID:

There!

TITHONUS:

It is irritating, irritating beyond words, always to be moved, from the bed to the chair, from the chair to the porch. . . .

AURORA:

Now—gently! So.

(*MARK lowers TITHONUS onto the lawn chair. The women arrange his covers.*)

MARK:
He's heavier than you think.

TITHONUS:
I feel like a migrant, a gypsy, one of those Liszt would describe so amusingly, moving from place to place, from the porch to the bed, bathing, if at all, in the muddy Danube. . . .

AURORA (*to MEMNON*):
Have you spoken to your father?

MEMNON:
Tried to, but couldn't get much of a rise out of him.

TITHONUS:
The little Countess Söderlund, my wife's godchild, she who introduced yoghurt to the Swedish court, also created there the vogue for gypsies.

AURORA:
He's in a good humor today.

(*To TITHONUS.*)

Do you know who has come for your birthday?

MEMNON:
Many happy returns, Dad!

TITHONUS:
They wore earrings, even the men—something that until then had never been seen in Sweden—and played their instruments, what were they called?

AURORA:
Tithonus!

TITHONUS:

No matter. The women told fortunes. . . .

AURORA:

It's Memnon!

MEMNON:

Oh, don't bother. . . .

AURORA:

He's being very naughty.

MARK (*finding ENID's head on his shoulder*):

You're a funny little person.

ENID:

Kiss me.

(*MARK kisses her lightly on the temple.*)

TITHONUS:

They read my palm, the gypsy women, and told me fantastic things.
Her Majesty expressed interest.

AURORA:

I remember. He had only a life line, nothing else.

MARK (*to AURORA*):

Did they read your palm?

AURORA:

Alas, I had only a love line!

TITHONUS:

The sun shone all night. There used to be furs, the Kashmir shawls
were becoming popular, so light, so soft. . . . Now I am always chilly.
If I froze, who would be sorry?

(*ENID, reaching forward, spreads the scarf up to his chin.*)

What is happening? What are they doing? I shall suffocate!

AURORA (*intervening*):
He can't stand anything he hasn't known before. He felt the scarf against his mouth, and was afraid.

MEMNON:
Seems to me you coddle him too much.

TITHONUS:
Aurora! Who are you talking to?

MEMNON:
I didn't realize he could hear.

ENID:
Oh, you'd be surprised!

AURORA:
He hears very well as soon as you begin to talk about *him*.

(*To TITHONUS.*)

It's Memnon, darling! Memnon has come for your birthday! Memnon, *your son!*

TITHONUS:
Memnon? Memnon, my son?

MEMNON:
That's right, Dad. Big as life. Happy birthday!

TITHONUS:
How old are you, my boy?

MEMNON:
> Old enough to know better, ha ha ha!

TITHONUS (*cross*):
> Aruora! How old is the boy?

AURORA:
> I haven't the faintest notion.

(*To MEMNON.*)

> How old *are* you?

MEMNON (*dignified*):
> I'm sixty-one.

TITHONUS:
> How old?

AURORA:
> Memnon says he's sixty-one, darling.

(*To MEMNON.*)

> Are you really? I should have thought younger. . . .

TITHONUS (*cackling with mirth*):
> Sixty-one! Getting along in years, is he not? Not much time left to enjoy life at sixty-one! Tell him, tell him his father says to enjoy it while he can! He can't take it with him!

MEMNON:
> The old buzzard!

AURORA:
> Hush, he's your father, Memnon.

TITHONUS:

Sixty-one!

ENID (*to MEMNON*):

Don't take it that way.

MARK (*to AURORA*):

With children you have to keep changing their pants. When they're old it's their mouths they can't control.

AURORA:

You will be old some day.

MARK:

But I shall have lived. It won't matter.

TITHONUS:

Now, when *I* was sixty-one, or thereabouts—what a difference!

AURORA (*to MARK*):

What can have put it into your head that you are finer than Tithonus? No matter what he may be now, he has had an extraordinary life.

MARK:

I don't believe it!

AURORA:

What you say reflects very prettily on *me*.

MARK:

I can't help that.

TITHONUS:

When I think of all I have seen, people I have known—but intimately, all their lives long!

AURORA:

I don't mean to be snappish. Something's wrong with me today.

MARK:

Come. We have to talk.

(*He leads her to one side. They remain visible and their voices can be heard murmuring in the background.*)

MEMNON:

Must be the old man gets on her nerves. He like this all the time?

TITHONUS:

London! The parties!

ENID (*to MEMNON*):

All the time.

TITHONUS:

None of the postwar gatherings, so artfully informal, could match in brilliance those contrived and permeated by that proud and generous spirit, Mrs. Dickinson Davin, born Lady Milly Rapping. Aurora, do you remember? Aurora!

ENID (*trying to imitate AURORA*):

Yes, darling!

TITHONUS:

Moving idly through the high hushed rooms, pausing, not wholly for effect, beneath an *Emily* Mandible needlepoint, to the informed eye so much more of a piece than the glib if popular designs of her ill-fated niece, only a newcomer—of which but one or two were admitted every season—would have been taken aback at the sight of Field Marshal Pellet in lively banter with Mrs. Mock, the American ambassadress, from whose grandfather I still treasure a handful of mosaic picked up as a very young man in Hagia Sofia. . . . Where am I?

ENID:

Mrs. Mock.

TITHONUS:

The American ambassadress, quite so, from whose grandmother I still treasure a handful of mosaic given her by an urchin, who knew not what it was; or Greta Stempel-Ross, fresh from her native . . . her native . . . oh, how it irritates me! Fresh from her native. . . .

AURORA (*softly to MARK*):

She had splendid references and a very impressive telephone manner.

MARK:

Then it's all settled!

TITHONUS:

Well, no matter—and only the following season to take by storm the small but lofty citadel of Taste—What do I want with Venice? Lady Milly used to ask. I have my own Campanile here! And she would tap her forehead—that even in those uncertain days before the war, no, after the war, before the *other* war, yes, still shone gallantly in our midst, not only by her singing of Krank and Claude Delice, but by her revelation of the folk melodies of her native . . . the folk melodies of her native . . . Aurora!

MEMNON:

I couldn't take *that* for very long.

AURORA (*to MARK*):

It was odd, though—as if she'd been waiting for the call.

TITHONUS:

Aurora! Aurora!

AURORA (*to MARK*):

Excuse me.

ENID (*to MEMNON*):
Aurora's wonderful.

AURORA (*to TITHONUS*):
What is it, my darling?

TITHONUS:
I can't remember, I can't remember! If you knew how it exasperates
me to forget!

AURORA (*tenderly*):
What have you forgotten?

TITHONUS:
Now I've even lost the name. That singer. You've heard the name
hundreds of times. I said it only a moment ago.

AURORA:
Emmy Destinn?

(*To the others.*)

He loved Emmy Destinn.

TITHONUS:
No, no, no! Not Emmy Destinn. Do you suppose I would ever forget
that voice? Now, somebody said of *her*—what was it? We were sit-
ting at supper, there were lanterns. . . . Well, no matter. I have it all
stored away somewhere. Waste not, want not.

(*Whimpering.*)

No, I mean that girl, that girl in London before, *after* the war. Greta!
Greta something-or-other—you know who I mean. Where was she
from?

AURORA:

Greta Stempel-Ross! I'd forgotten all about her.

(*To the others.*)

Really, she did have a heavenly voice, heavenly.

TITHONUS:

But where was she from?

AURORA:

Roumania.

TITHONUS:

Of course. Her native Roumania.

MEMNON:

Well, that's settled!

AURORA:

What time can it be? I must fly to the village, isn't that a bore?

(*MEMNON looks at his watch, then listens, but it has stopped.*)

(*AURORA turns to ENID.*)

Mark said he would go with me—it's what we've been plotting—if you'll let me borrow him?

ENID (*smiling*):

Just bring him back.

AURORA:

Actually I'd go alone, if it were something I could do by myself. But it's a surprise for Tithonus, a rather *big* surprise, which wasn't to have been ready until today.

ENID:
   So many surprises. . . .

AURORA (*beaming, her finger to her lips*):
   My dear, I hate to ask, but for these hours, two at the most, *could*
   you—?

(*She indicates TITHONUS.*)

ENID:
   I'd love to. Are you leaving at once?

AURORA:
   Virtually.

MEMNON:
   Virtuously? Ha ha ha!

ENID:
   Let me just run upstairs and fetch my knitting.

AURORA (*to MARK*):
   You're quite sure you don't mind coming?

MEMNON:
   Where are you going, Mother?

MARK:
   Quite sure.

AURORA (*to MEMNON*):
   I have to run down to the village for something I had forgotten.

TITHONUS:
   I'm chilly. The way they treat me here! Handsome is as handsome
   does, I always say.

MEMNON (*pulling himself together*):
  You know, really think I might be—

AURORA:
  Memnon, be a lamb, run to my room. You'll find an extra blanket in the bottom drawer of the bureau.

MEMNON:
  Was thinking, I might as well be shoving off myself. Long drive ahead of me.

AURORA (*fierily*):
  You will stay here until we return. I've never heard of such utter rudeness, walking out on your father's birthday! It's not as though you had celebrated *all* of them with him! Do I make myself clear? Now kindly fetch that blanket.

(*MEMNON goes out.*)

TITHONUS:
  I'm cold, cold. . . . I could freeze before anyone. . . . Not even in Portugal, that February. . . .

(*AURORA smooths his brow, absently.*)

  Aurora, is the summer over? I shall come begging for grain, like the grasshopper. . . .

MARK:
  It hurts to sever ties. Once we're away—

AURORA:
  Oh my dear, beware of me. Beware of my facility. It's too easy, everything I do.

MARK:

Those years with Tithonus weren't easy.

AURORA:

Oh, they *were,* now that they're over! I feel myself shaking them off, uncontrollably! I couldn't turn back if I wanted to.

MARK:

But think who you are! If you can't easily rid yourself of a problem, who can?

AURORA:

My problem now is you. All too easily I see you as a way out, a little staircase of flesh by which to climb again into the open air. Have I the right? Do I love you that much?

MARK:

Yes. But I don't matter. What matters is that you fulfil your destiny.

AURORA:

I have no destiny, you know.

MARK:

You do, though. You need to live by pleasure and light, anyone who sees you knows. And as long as you love me, I shall help make all that more vivid.

AURORA (*touched*):

Mark, Mark—what can I give you, to show you all the things I feel?

MARK:

Nothing unusual, nothing costly. Just let me keep my own mortality, which you will have made precious.

AURORA:

Your own mortality? Do you mean that you *want* to die?

MARK:

No. Not for a moment. But it won't matter. You can't understand, and why should you?

AURORA (*kissing him*):

You're charming and you're right. Why should I understand?

MARK:

What time are we picking up the nurse?

AURORA:

I told her we'd be leaving almost at once.

MARK:

Then let's go!

MEMNON (*entering with the blanket*):

If *this* doesn't keep him warm enough. . . . Is he asleep?

AURORA:

His eyes are shut. Look, he has thrown his covers off.

(*To MARK, as she begins to arrange them.*)

Help me.

TITHONUS (*shrinking from MARK*):

Aurora, they're hurting me! Their hands are rough!

AURORA (*to MARK*):

I'll do it, then. I thought he knew your touch.

(*She continues to enfold him, like something wrapped away for winter. Enter ENID with her knitting.*)

MEMNON:
Wouldn't have thought he'd care so much.

ENID:
When does one ever finish caring?

TITHONUS:
Aurora, keep me warm. . . . I fear the winter. . . . Soon the winds will be upon us, roaring. . . .

AURORA:
Sleep now, Tithonus.

(*He shuts his eyes.*)

ENID:
There is such a sadness in his face, as though he knew. . . .

AURORA:
Knew what, my dear?

ENID:
That you were leaving, if only for an hour or two.

MARK:
That cover has the look of a cocoon.

AURORA (*her task finished*):
It does. Goodbye. And if by noon we shouldn't have returned, give him some food—a cup of broth, or tea. He needs so little. . . . So.

ENID:
Mark—do you have some money with you?

MARK:
No.

(*To AURORA.*)

Do I need money?

AURORA:
Perhaps she wants something from the village.

(*To ENID.*)

Can we bring you something from the village?

ENID:
No.

AURORA:
Then shall we go?

(*Starts out.*)

Oh wait! Before the light fails, so as not to forget—!

(*She takes a camera from her purse, gets into position, focuses.*)

Smile, everybody! Let's remember this day always!

(*Snaps picture.*)

There! Be good!

(*AURORA and MARK leave. A long pause. MEMNON starts to smooth out a wrinkle in TITHONUS's cover.*)

TITHONUS (*waking refreshed*):
Ah! Have I slept? Yes, I think I have had a nice nap. Aurora! Something is not as it should be. I have an uncanny instinct in such matters.

I once took it upon myself to warn a young friend of mine, the poet Clarence Boiler DeKay, on the eve of his marriage. Forty years later he confessed to me privately that I had been right. A stitch in time saves nine. My mind swarms with interesting observations. I am never bored. I have lived longer than anybody, and acquired a profound experience of the human heart. It is too late to pretend otherwise. You can't teach an old dog new tricks. The pot calls the kettle black.

MEMNON:
He used to tell me *I* talked in clichés!

TITHONUS:
An idle mind is the Devil's workshop.

MEMNON (*hemming and hawing*):
You know, think I'd better be shoving off myself now, if you'll excuse me. Got a long drive ahead of me. Mother wanted me to hang around till they checked in, but if I know her, once she starts whipping out that camera she's gone for the whole day. Guess I don't need to tell you how she appreciates what you're doing. She told me this morning that until you came she hadn't had a holiday for she didn't know how long, years I guess.

(*ENID is silent.*)

You know, it's funny—this place always gave me the creeps. Folks say, home is where you hang your hat. Closer to truth, it's where you hang *yourself*. If you'd like me to stay till they come back, I'd be glad to, really would.

(*ENID shakes her head, forcing a smile.*)

She didn't want me to stay either, if you ask me. Just trying to be polite, being my mother and all.

TITHONUS:

Wilful waste makes woeful want. Nothing succeeds like success. I have learned all this through bitter experience.

MEMNON:

Can't see that it's much fun for you, sitting with him.

ENID (*tonelessly*):

I don't mind. More and more it appears we have interests in common.

MEMNON:

How do you mean?

TITHONUS:

I feel a storm approaching. That is not as it should be.

MEMNON:

Oh, I get it! His wife, your husband, you mean?

(*Laughs weakly.*)

That's pretty good! Well, I guess you don't have anything to worry about *there!*

TITHONUS:

I am still remarkably sensitive to everything around me.

ENID:

I believe a storm *is* coming. You'd best be on your way.

TITHONUS (*dropping off to sleep*):

Though we travel the world over in search of the beautiful, we must carry it with us or we find it not.

MEMNON:

Well, if you're sure there's nothing, I'll say goodbye.

ENID (*giving him her hand*):
  Goodbye.

MEMNON:
  Au revoir, I guess I mean.

ENID:
  Goodbye.

MEMNON:
  Goodbye, Dad.

(*Shouts.*)

  Goodbye, Father!

(*Shrugs.*)

ENID:
  I wish you success with your book.

MEMNON:
  Oh, thank you! I'll send you an autographed copy.

(*Exit, waving his briefcase. A silence.*)

TITHONUS (*dreaming*):
  My love, my love, was it a dream . . . ?

ENID (*stroking his brow*):
  Be still. It *is* a dream.

(*She rests her head on her arm. It is conceivable that she and TITHONUS dream this final scene. AURORA enters upstage with the NURSE. The latter is dressed entirely in white cap, veil, shoes, stockings, etc.*)

AURORA (*whispering*):
There he is. I can't stay, the car's waiting. We must be off at once.

NURSE (*moving about, tidying things up*):
It seems we are hand in glove with one another. You don't want it known that you've sent for me. I have my pride, too. I'm not the sort of woman one sends for.

AURORA:
Oh, I didn't mean—

NURSE:
I am not hired by the hour.

AURORA:
When I needed you I called. I never meant to imply—

NURSE:
Don't try to apologize. You don't know how. You've made your decision, Aurora. Henceforth, if I'm to care for him, I'll do it in my own way. Your way, to judge from the results, has failed.

AURORA:
You will be good to him? You won't try to disillusion him when you talk about me?

NURSE:
We shall never talk about you.

AURORA:
They're both asleep. I think I shall just tiptoe over and kiss him lightly once, on the forehead. . . .

NURSE:
No.

AURORA:
Is it so much to ask?

NURSE:
If you have any fondness left for him, leave him to me. Go. Go now.

AURORA (*after a pause, smiling brilliantly*):
Yes, of course! What *could* I have been thinking of?

NURSE:
Goodbye, Aurora.

AURORA:
Goodbye! Oh, do you *know* what it's like, to feel love, to feel love for the first time? Bless you!

(*She blows a kiss and runs out. An uneasy twilight falls.*)

NURSE (*to ENID*):
You need watch no longer.

ENID (*starting*):
Oh!

NURSE:
I have come to sit with him.

ENID:
Oh, yes of course—no, I don't mean that. I'm sorry, I can't think. Did Aurora send you? Have they been delayed?

NURSE (*as if she had never heard the name*):
Aurora?

ENID:

Well, she's not here. I'm sitting with him. This is Aurora's husband. I'm her guest. . . . I must still be half asleep. . . .

NURSE:

I know.

ENID:

She ought to be back any moment, there are her flowers. They went off, Aurora and—*my* husband, for only an hour or so, to the village. You must have come from there. Perhaps you saw the car? I couldn't describe it, never having kept a journal, but it's Aurora's car, there's no mistaking it.

NURSE:

I have not come from the village. Is there a village here?

ENID:

Well, I don't want to pry. . . . Do sit down, won't you, anyhow?

NURSE:

Yes, I have come to sit with him.

ENID:

Not on my account, I hope. I enjoy sitting with him, really I do. It's an education in itself.

NURSE:

I have not come on your account. He knows why I have come.

ENID:

Oh, you're *his* friend!

NURSE:

He wanted me. I know how to make myself useful.

(*A pause.*)

Thank you.

ENID:
What?

NURSE:
I am here. He will not need you any more.

ENID (*starting out reluctantly, then stopping*):
I—have nowhere else to go.

NURSE:
Are you sure? Isn't it more that you really want to stay?

ENID:
Yes. I want to stay.

NURSE:
Then do. We shan't mind. Yes, by all means, stay. Now that I look at you, I can see that you are very tired.

ENID (*nervously*):
That's my hay fever. Every summer. My eyes swell up.

NURSE:
Do whatever you please. Sit in that chair, why don't you? Knit him a scarf if you enjoy doing things with your hands. You need time, my child, time in which to think about time, to think of it no longer as a packed bright space entered and left behind, to think of it rather as a gray wind, a soft thread wound, endlessly, about you. . . .

ENID (*as it struggling to wake*):
But that isn't true! Time does end!

NURSE (*gently restraining her*):
For some of us perhaps.

ENID:
It does! It must!

NURSE:
Not for him, whom we are here to care for.

ENID:
But we'll be caring for him all our lives!

NURSE (*radiantly*):
Yes!

ENID:
He'll never die!

TITHONUS (*opening his eyes and looking meaningfully from one to the other*):
A watched pot never boils.

NURSE (*sweetly, to ENID*):
You see? You see?

(*TITHONUS chuckles on and on. ENID crumples obediently into her chair and begins to unravel some yarn. The NURSE, with many smiles of encouragement, takes up her position by the lawn chair.*)

APPENDIX

Preface to THE SERAGLIO

When The Seraglio *was reissued in 1987,*
thirty years after it was first published,
Merrill added a preface to the book:

I began *The Seraglio* in the late Spring of 1954, after moving to Stoning-
ton, Connecticut, and finished it by the end of the following year. In
order to escape Manhattan and its pitfalls, David Jackson and I had
rented half of the third floor of a "block"—as several huge wooden gar-
denless constructions were locally known—in the center of the little
dock-fringed peninsula we would call home from then on. Our landlord,
Mr. Hoxie, a former W.P.A. artist who now kept a paint store in Mystic
and a residence down by the railroad tracks, was practically giving away
rooms in this otherwise empty building (the Sanitary Barber Shop and
Marion's Department Store functioned feebly at street level) to members
of the "artistic confraternity" as he called us—painters in need of studio
space, novelists in flight from the telephone and the children. Thus it was
something of a Writer's Block even before our occupancy.

Mr. Hoxie collected books. Rather, he had bought up whole libraries
of travel or medicine or theosophy, topics he might one day wish to
explore, and stored them in the attic above us. His wife made sure that
only Reader's Digest condensations entered their home. When we bought
the old building from him in 1956, Mr. Hoxie promised to "take care of"
all the books we couldn't use ourselves. This meant sending a couple of
high-school boys to the attic where they proceeded to hurl boxful after
boxful down an empty dumb-waiter shaft to the basement, four stories
below. Each book at the thud leapt eagerly out of its binding. It took all
afternoon. Eventually a truck hauled them off to the town dump. David
and I were by then known to be "writers," and this public display of bib-

liophobia required a certain amount of explanation. We hoped, when our turn came, to produce more durable volumes than those by dead-and-gone members of Mr. Hoxie's artistic confraternity.

That first season we patched up our four rooms and furnished them from a nearby warehouse full of now priceless brass bedsteads and wicker armchairs. We knew two people in the village, we had no telephone, we were over a hundred miles from the nearest relative. After some cluttered years out in the great world—Europe, independence, psychotherapy—it was the right vantage for an inward look. Under the dining room's impressive tin cranium David put together a sideboard which doubled as desk for me. He himself was at work, in the kitchen, on his third novel—at least one of us knew the ropes of prose. I secretly counted on beginner's luck, while trying in vain to overlook the one false start I'd already made.

For *The Seraglio* is a hybrid. Its better part is a comedy of manners about the world I was born into and fancied myself to have risen above merely through reading Proust and James, and writing a handful of poems. Its lesser part is the residue of an untitled novel, begun a few years earlier in Europe, which had at no great length refused to take shape. Here, of course, all was to have been symbol and sensibility, fine feelings and writing finer yet. Here also figured Francis and his father, along with clumsy sketches for Xenia and Jane. In both books Jane (or Hermine, as I'm afraid she was named at first) attends the same portentous opera and suffers the same exquisite discriminations. But my early effort came to nothing. Before giving up, I must have retyped its poor beginnings a dozen times, as if a fresh page, rather than the experience it was starved white for lack of, would do the trick.

To my eye, these graftings upon the riper book—completed as its author approached the tremendous age of thirty—stand out glaringly from the rest. A new reader, thirty years later, years during which the novel of manners and that of sensibility have come to seem equally outmoded, may find simple fustiness making for a unity never before attainable.

A borrowing even more shameless was from the transcripts of David's and my initial sessions at the Ouija board. It would take me the two decades between *The Seraglio* and *The Changing Light at Sandover* to arrive at a way of using these to my satisfaction. At the time the best I could do was make them the measure of Francis's "alienation" instead of honestly trying to render their ambiguous and pervasive place in our lives.

Friends who read the book in manuscript begged me to reconsider the episode of Francis's self-mutilation. I was too pleased by its neat "objective correlative" for my quarrel with the prevailing social and sexual assumptions to listen to reason. Freely granting its Grand Guignol aspect, I'll stand by the scene to this day. The victim is after all only a character in a book.

Harder to face were repercussions from the rest of the cast. Before he had met any of them, David Kalstone sent me a postcard of François-Xavier Fabre's *Virgil Reading the* Aeneid *to the Family of Augustus.* The listeners are contorted and drained by their powerful neoclassical emotions. On the back my friend wrote: "The first reading of *The Seraglio* at Southampton?" He had a point.

I like to think that my father's portrait would have entertained him. I sent him the final draft, but he was ill and had never taken to convoluted sentences. Probably he read no more than the opening pages before his death two months later. Others, when the book appeared, dissembled their embarrassment by a kind of domino reaction: "I don't mind for *myself,* but how could you have done what you did to _____?" The book at that level remains a callow act of self-assertion hardly called for in view of the love and tact I had always been shown by my family. I feel the full truth of this observation whenever I encounter—it still happens now and then—some old party connected with the Firm, who tells me with a knowing twinkle that he read *The Seraglio* hot off the press. I twinkle back, biting my tongue not to say, "Indeed? And what business was it of yours?"

The personal rots away, Yeats tells us, unless packed in ice or salt.

What lives on in the brackish puddle is happily not for me to decide. A reader of my poems may linger over certain images, as may the anthropologist of privilege. Few books absolve their authors from the original sin of Class. *If you're so rich, why aren't you smart?*—it was good fun, this turning inside out, as others from Petronius to Proust had done, of the old retort. But the appalling intellectual conditions of Palm Beach or the Hamptons weren't to be stamped out by a foot shod in an evening pump, and there was as yet no other milieu (or only the first inklings of one) that I had more right to call my own.

Afterword to THE (DIBLOS) NOTEBOOK

When The (Diblos) Notebook, *originally published in 1965,*
was reissued in 1994,
Merrill added an afterword to the book:

18.x.93

This little fiction, written to conceal how little of a fiction it is, like the Purloined Letter hides its strategy in plain view.

The book during its composition struck me as perilously drenched with real life. Much of it was written in the field—in the shade of the brilliant midsummer waterfront on Poros, the island where I had visited Kimon Friar and Mina Diamantopoulos on my first trip to Europe, fourteen years earlier. To be sure, Kimon and I were not half brothers. Neither of us had a mother in Texas. "Lucine" is smuggled in from a quite different part of my life, and "Arthur Orson" is based on a fussy old man I knew in Athens, who had no connection whatever with this story. So on second thought, more invention must have come into play than I supposed at the time.

I hadn't, of course, set out to be "experimental"—heaven forbid! Ideally I would have aimed for the readability conferred by a seamless, all-knowing narrative voice. With this voice, however, I kept painting myself into a corner. Surely there were different kinds of readability, texts whose very fragmentation quickened the pulse. If the voice broke in self-revision no harm was done to the quasi-Aristotelian unity of the page. Hadn't I received letters with words scratched out? Seen phrases scored through on the printed page in Buxton Forman's edition of Keats? Worth remembering was how unerringly the eye flew to precisely what the writer had thought better of: there, if anywhere, would be a truth unvarnished, which predated artifice.

Even at the time I glimpsed in my project a wistful, half-conscious critique of the Beat Generation. To Kerouac, Ginsberg, et al., revision was an all but criminal betrayal of the "spontaneity" of their vision. This view I was by temperament unable to share; true spontaneity came for me, as when Rome burned, after hours of Neronian fiddling. Thus the most successful moments in the book may well be those where the device plays with itself, when for instance a notation of the color of night ("~~dark bl~~ indigo") encapsulates the self-dramatizing "Blind I go!"

To lend weight to the device there would ideally have been some justifying narrative twist: a fact thrown into relief by its very suppression, whose discovery leaves a handful of readers wiser than the keeper of the notebook. Possibly some suspicion as to Sandy's and Orestes' "real-life" story might have been made, in more skillful hands than mine, to serve. But I was young and cavalier, and counted on the formal novelty of the book to make up for its not going very deeply into a Theme.

Sitting, then, under an awning on that blazing waterfront, at an hour when the little town nodded off, I cast about for language. When phrases took shape I welcomed them grudgingly, disdainfully, as if "we artists" were entitled to scorn our medium. But entries in a notebook also helped to pass the time, until something better came along. In another hour David Jackson would reappear to show me his afternoon's watercolor, and we could begin to think about wine and company, our reward for time so profitably spent. Those evening pleasures left no trace the next day. But their brevity and recklessness are here between the lines, if anything is.

THE BAIT

REVISED VERSION

(1988)

Characters

Julie
Jan, *her lover*
Charles, *her husband*
Gilbert, *her brother*

(*The action takes place both in Venice and at sea in the Gulf Stream. On one side of the stage, a suggestion of the Piazza; on the other, the stern of a fishing boat. It is a summer afternoon.*)

(*Enter, from Venice, JAN and JULIE.*)

JAN:
   You never told me this before.

JULIE:
   I don't understand what I've told you. That may be one reason. Then, too, aren't we still courting? You can't expect to hear all my stories in a matter of weeks.

JAN:

Go on. After you got back to the dock what happened? What happened that night?

JULIE:

This particular story clearly needs polishing. I feel I've been talking ever since lunch. Now I'm all talked out and I've missed my siesta.

JAN:

There you were in that little boat far from shore. Just a ribbon of beach on the horizon, with colorless trees. The ocean calls our deepest fears into play, our deepest selves. In a city, all this might have happened differently, or not at all.

JULIE:

What did happen was that, back in New York, I left him.

JAN:

Left . . . Charles?

JULIE:

You don't imagine I'd ever leave Gilbert? Well. It's hot. I'd rather not go on. We've talked enough.

JAN:

But could anyone have held out? I mean, was it Charles giving up when he went overboard—giving *in?* Could someone else have held out? I'm no help, am I?

JULIE:

I don't see that *you* need to be so solemn, Jan.

JAN:

I'm still young. Things matter to me.

JULIE:

Touché!

JAN:

Julie! Love! I didn't mean—

JULIE:

You're right. I'm not young, I'm immature.

JAN:

I adore you.

JULIE:

Look at those pigeons, how can they bear it?—eating out of people's hands. Yes, you have helped by letting me talk. It is less real now that someone other than myself has failed to understand it.

JAN:

You are not to blame.

JULIE:

Not to blame for leaving my husband?

JAN:

Not to blame for the circumstances.

JULIE:

That kind of remark simply dazzles me. It makes me feel that my total experience is somehow *here,* within easy reach, like so many reels of film on a shelf.

JAN:

All I mean is that the circumstances seem to narrow down to your brother.

JULIE:

Yes. Gilbert is to blame. I am finer than Gilbert.

JAN:

I like Gilbert. He makes me laugh.

JULIE:

Gilbert makes everybody laugh. No, he never made Charles laugh. That may be why they were such good friends.

JAN:

But I laugh more easily with you. When I'm with Gilbert I'm not really laughing.

JULIE:

Neither am I. It must be a power he has over me. Look! There he sits in the pensione and here I go . . . !

JAN:

At the risk of irritating you, it does seem curious that Gilbert should . . .

JULIE:

Should?

JAN:

That Gilbert should be so much in the picture? He goes everywhere you go, knows everything you do.

JULIE:

You *are* possessive!

JAN:

Can't I be?

JULIE:

Of course. It's rather touching. It brings out the older woman in me. Now what was that about Gilbert?

JAN:

I don't remember.

JULIE:

He is after all one's brother.

JAN:

There are limits. You said he all but picked out your husband for you.

JULIE:

Well, he didn't pick *you* out, darling. I did that.

JAN:

It was Gilbert who came over to my table.

JULIE:

Perhaps. But I'd seen you first.

JAN:

I don't know. If you're that close to one another . . .

JULIE:

But isn't that the great thing about relatives? They have to love you, you have to love them! After a certain age one meets few enough people of whom that holds true.

JAN:

You don't honestly think in those terms.

JULIE:

I don't? It's a wonder I think at all, I sometimes think.

JAN:

Did Charles like Gilbert? Afterwards, I mean.

JULIE:

Oh God in heaven! Did Charles like Gilbert! Does Gilbert like me! Did I like them! Why, we doted upon one another. We shared an eye and a tooth, and woe to the unwary stranger.

JAN:

Forget I said it.

JULIE:

It's just that I'm so weary! Charles writes, Gilbert talks—

JAN:

You've had another letter from Charles?

JULIE:

You ask questions! Yes, I've had a letter from Charles. I must really stop going to American Express. Nobody else writes to me there.

JAN:

You needn't go. You needn't pick up his letters.

JULIE:

Gilbert says it makes me feel modern, to get such letters from my former husband.

JAN:

"Such" letters? Does Gilbert read them?

JULIE:

Do you suppose *I* do? Oh what an unkind thing to say! You must not make me talk about Charles. I'll say anything that comes into my head.

JAN:

I make you talk? Gilbert makes you laugh? It doesn't seem to me that you are made to do anything.

JULIE:

Now you're angry and you don't love me.

(*Enter GILBERT.*)

GILBERT:

Oh! Ben trovato! Ah! Flirting at Florian's!
My sweet little sister is beautifully bad!
Come with me, cara, we'll go in a gondola!
—Gondoliere!

JULIE:

Gilbert, you're mad!

GILBERT:

I've dawdled all day with impossible people.
Jan, will you join us?

JULIE:

Keep up our morale?

JAN:

No, I must really—

GILBERT:

Then be a wet blanket.
I'm for a ride down that crazy canal!

JAN:

What is this passion of Gilbert's for boating?

JULIE:

    See, you are laughing! I knew you would be.

JAN:

    Then why are you laughing?

JULIE:

                            I'm not *really* laughing,
    But I'm going with Gilbert.

GILBERT:

                            We'll meet you for tea!

(*GILBERT and JULIE go.*)

JAN:

    When Julie and I settle down, it will have to be
    back home. I'll need to work. On my own I could
    have held out until next year—not now. My parents
    are already up in arms, and sharing expenses with
    Julie and Gilbert isn't the answer. I hope Gilbert
    stays on in Europe. He belongs here.
    If we return to Venice, let it be winter,
    The mirror whitewashed, empty and aloof.
    Drifting with this warm glitter, this loose life,
    I'm out of my depth—oh, not very far as yet,
    And learning, thanks to Julie; being changed;
    Loving, loved in return; no end to either
    The changing or the loving. And Julie's changing,
    Or says she is, at least—some days it's more
    Like changing back to what she was before.
    The self I was, at any rate, that day
    Three months ago in Rome, at the café,
    When Gilbert asked was I American,
    Lies sanded over, deep in sparkling water.
    Fifty years from now, what will I be—

A drowned blue-green theater of memory?
A Bridge of Sighs? Well, Venice and reflections . . .

And that other setting? Even before Julie spoke I could feel the shudder of the engine, the heat and brightness of the day, the blue of the Gulf Stream pitching. There they sat in the white boat, the men with their bait and their tackle. That whole endless afternoon trembles and brightens around her still. Over and over she enters the scene, trying to read it like a compass, sounding its depths, wondering—

(In the course of JAN's speech the lights have dimmed on Venice and brightened on the fishing boat now occupied by JULIE, GILBERT, and CHARLES.)

JULIE *(sings the Barcarolle from* Les Contes d'Hoffmann):
   Nuit plus douce que le jour,
   O belle nuit d'amour!

GILBERT:
   Is he steering us the right way?
   I know we've passed that patch of seaweed once before, today.

JULIE:
   Le temps fuit et sans retour
   Emporte nos tendresses!

GILBERT:
   Was that the last beer, Julie?
   It seems a pity, don't you think,
   That we have nothing more to drink?
   And didn't I tell you to make more sandwiches?
   To be hard of hearing has its advantages.

JULIE:
   Desormais je ne parlerais que français.
   From now on I shall speak only French.

GILBERT:

And it would serve her right, wouldn't it, Charles?
It must be by design that nobody talks to me.
Shall we call it a day? Have I done something wrong? You see,
I am reduced to these childish interrogatives.

JULIE:

We know what happens when we talk to you.
Nous savons bien ce qui arrive—oh what's the use!
Why is Charles frowning?

GILBERT:

He is a naturally thoughtful person.

JULIE:

He knows

That we are looking at him.

GILBERT:

Rubbish.

JULIE:

He knows

How boring we become when he ignores us.

GILBERT:

He also knows how boring *you* become
When I'm not there to keep you from baiting him.

JULIE:

Crumb.

GILBERT:

Fishwife.

JULIE:
Cretin.

GILBERT (*sings*):
Loin de cet heureux séjour
Le temps fuit sans retour!

CHARLES:
Look! Something's at the line! Wait!

GILBERT:
It's only your wife's beer bottle.

CHARLES:
Fish won't strike a damaged bait.

(*CHARLES reels in his line.*)

JULIE:
Oh what a beautiful day! What soft air!
See how the light moves through the water
Like harp strings. And the water
Isn't blue but purple. Look out there!
Think of them shimmering down, the strings of light,
To where an absolute darkness begins,
How they must sound against a thousand cutting fins
And mouths that would swallow me up in a bite.

CHARLES:
If you're not careful we'll put *you* on the hook.

GILBERT:
But, back to Charles. I think the world of him. He strives
Overmuch, perhaps, for integrity. Yet one can only admire
Those moments, thrillingly frequent, when like a chestnut from the fire

He attains his object. Look at him now. He's wholly at ease,
Baiting his line with a fresh mullet. Deep in the purple seas
How shall mere fish, without a fraction of my high-handedness,
Be able to resist such a display of single-mindedness?
How shall I, if it comes to that? You are at one with your bait,
And I have swallowed it, Charles. I've got you, it's too late.

CHARLES:
It would seem in that case that I had *you*.

GILBERT:
I suppose it would and I daresay you do.

JULIE:
It would seem you both had *me*.

GILBERT:
I hope we always shall. I'm sure Charles will agree.

CHARLES:
Nobody ever has *her* for very long.

JULIE:
What a nasty remark! Gilbert, tell him he's wrong.

GILBERT:
He'd never believe me.

JULIE:
                          A brother ought to defend
His sister's reputation.

GILBERT:
                          But Charles is my friend,
I couldn't lie to him!

JULIE:

Oh you're the end!

GILBERT:

See how we have you?

JULIE:

Did you have this in mind
When you arranged for me to marry Charles?

GILBERT:

I arranged for you to marry Charles?
What can you mean? I did nothing of the kind.

JULIE:

You brought Charles home. You said we'd make a perfect match.

GILBERT:

Well, haven't you? Of course you have. Charles was a catch,
And today it is his turn to catch us.
Tomorrow we shall let you win at cards.
What could conceivably be more stimulating
Than for three people to catch one another
In so many different ways? It keeps us going.

(*JULIE returns to Venice. GILBERT talks to CHARLES.*)

GILBERT:

I have had many fascinating fishing experiences . . .

JULIE (*to JAN*):

You understand I was talking lightly that day.

GILBERT:

. . . though I am not a serious sportsman like yourself.

JULIE:

    Oh, we knew what we were saying, I suppose,
    But doesn't one talk lightly of a thing
    With fingers crossed to keep it from becoming?

GILBERT:

    Why, the first time I ever went deep-sea fishing
    I landed a fifty-pound something-or-other,
    The marvel of all my friends, such a powerful one.

JULIE:

    Words lend themselves to lightness, then too late
    The veils float off, leaving the naked threat.

GILBERT:

    I was only a little shaver then.
    I had it three-quarters of an hour on the line.

JULIE:

    I want to dive down,
    Discover, bring back whatever it is, the black
    Pearl, the sense of whatever I am,
    But my bones are full of air, my words are larks,
    The sun is sparkling on the surface of the water
    In all directions except from underneath.

GILBERT:

    Forty-five minutes can be a long time.

CHARLES:

                             A long time for a fish.

GILBERT:

    A longer time for anybody who isn't a fish.

JULIE:
I hadn't wanted to talk lightly. What's worse,
Such is my lightness, I shall rise above it.

CHARLES:
I don't know. I'm a fairly good swimmer.

JULIE:
You hear him? He wasn't only joking!

GILBERT:
Why, nobody in his right mind would risk
Dipping his big toe in these waters. Besides—

CHARLES:
You think I couldn't hold out?

GILBERT:
You couldn't hold out for five minutes.

JULIE:
That was how it began. Charles said he could hold out
At the end of a line, like a hooked dolphin.

JAN:
Love, it's *over!*

CHARLES:
Gilbert, sometimes you annoy the hell out of me.

JULIE:
I tried to reason with them. There had been a man
Whose leg was taken off by a shark in Bermuda.
People on shore saw the blood streaming out of him
But he kept on swimming, he hadn't felt it.
It was when he looked behind him that he died.

CHARLES:
Would you care to make a little bet?

GILBERT:
A little bet?

JULIE:
A little bet?

GILBERT:
Mercenary Charles! No. Why in ten minutes—

CHARLES:
Hook me up to that line. You'll see.

GILBERT:
I'll do nothing of the sort.

JULIE:
Gilbert wanted it. He said five minutes the first time.

CHARLES:
I'm serious. Fasten me to the line. Use the harness.

GILBERT:
Can you really be such a good swimmer? No,
I refuse to fall in with this absurd exhibition.

CHARLES:
Will you stop laughing! Hook me to the line.

JAN:
He wanted it, too. Charles was asking for it, Julie.

GILBERT:
You'd positively enjoy it?

CHARLES:
Why not?

GILBERT:
If you put it that way—why not!

JULIE:
It was all at once a question of something terribly funny. Charles had rigged himself into one of those little harnesses that hold you in your chair when something big hits your line. Oh, I kept saying to myself. Gilbert was fastening the line to the back of Charles's harness. The captain had stopped the motor. He could have stopped *them* while he was at it. What could he have been thinking? Was he deaf and dumb?

GILBERT:
Come, little sister, lend a hand.

JAN:
In time such incidents grow dim.

JULIE (*reentering the boat*):
I think you're crazy, both of you.

CHARLES:
It's a warm day.

JULIE:
But understand
If they should tear you limb from limb
I'm not to blame.

GILBERT:
I hear a distant band
Strike up in honor of our acrobat.

CHARLES:
I'm just as pleased to have a swim.

JULIE:
Why am I laughing? What you do
Is dreadful, Gilbert.

GILBERT:
To whom?

JULIE:
To him.
To me as well.

GILBERT:
I don't see that.

CHARLES:
The sea is calm.

GILBERT:
The sky is blue.

JULIE:
The blue's all wrong, the sea's too flat.

GILBERT:
The sharks are playing hooky far below.

JULIE:
I never have.

GILBERT:
All ready?

CHARLES:

        Yes.

JULIE:

  Darling—

CHARLES:

      Honey?

JULIE:

           At least take off your hat!

GILBERT:

Ten minutes, mind you. Nothing less.

(*CHARLES disappears over the side of the boat.*)

GILBERT:

Now we shall let him swim a certain distance from the boat. How quiet it is. This is the moment for your Barcarolle. You don't feel like singing? Shall I try the Mad Scene from *The Chocolate Soldier?* I haven't done that for ages. Charles *is* a good swimmer. You asked why you were laughing. Perhaps you had no other way to participate in that curious moment.

JULIE:

I have found another way.

GILBERT:

My point is that people simply don't do what they don't want to do. In other words, if there is something they don't want to do, they don't do it. This is amusing.

JULIE:

You are doing what you wanted. You are doing it now.

GILBERT:

Yes.

JULIE:

You have made him and me do what you wanted.

GILBERT:

No. I have made it easy for you to do what you yourselves desired. Here we have the example of Charles doing a thing both absurd and dangerous. He is doing it because he wants to. He is not doing it at my suggestion. Soon he will be out far enough.

JULIE:

You gave him no other choice.

GILBERT:

Is it for me to provide alternatives for Charles when there are, as we used to say on the plantation, seventeen different things he might be doing at this very moment? Think, Julie! To pretend, as you have done all your life, that other people oblige you to do distasteful things is no more than a failure to admit your own taste for doing them. I shall enjoy treating Charles, my old friend, to the experience of nearly drowning. If I admit that, why shouldn't you in turn admit that you'll enjoy watching your husband nearly drown. Charles himself at this very moment is bound to be thinking— It's strange. Whenever you stop listening I begin to feel that I've been talking out of sheer perversity.

JULIE:

I'm sorry.

GILBERT:

These were things I felt you ought to know. Is there anything on your mind?

JULIE:

We must have been almost babies, you and I, taking our bath together one afternoon. We had toys in the bathtub—a little boat, a floating goldfish that could roll its eyes, a little deep-sea diver. He was attached to a bulb, bubbles came out of him when you squeezed. We were fighting, or I got soap in my eyes. Father must have heard us, he came storming in, pulled out the plug, yanked us out of the water and dried us off. I remember to this day how it hurt, being put into my pajamas. That must have been our last bath together. I can see the drained tub, with its green stain where the faucet joined the enamel, like a beard of seaweed hanging down. Our toys were lying every which way on the bottom. Isn't it silly to remember all that?

GILBERT:

Ask Charles whether it's silly or not.

JULIE:

I'd nearly forgotten Charles. What's the matter with me? Did you see the look on his face? He was very angry.

GILBERT:

I never get angry, why should he?
Charles! Are you ready?

CHARLES (*far off*):
Ready!

GILBERT:

Now you will see that for all his struggling
I need only keep playfully pulling at the line.
He will be drawn backwards through the brine.
He will want to breathe and will breathe water.
His every gesture will be cut short, he will go
Counter to his wish and to the waves.
In no time at all he will be utterly exhausted.

If he is angry, the minutes that follow
Will fit his anger like a glove. Fight, Charles, fight!

(*As GILBERT begins the struggle, everything goes dark. CHARLES now appears, eerily lit.*)

CHARLES:
I am not one to think much about pain.
I would not choose to dwell upon myself
In public, sipping at a tumbler of stale water.
It has never been my thought to preach to the fish.
Nevertheless, if I am ever in my life
To think usefully, to see with clear eyes,

Let it be now. Although my throat and eyes
Burn with seawater—or such tears of pain
No innocent man could shed in his whole life—
Let me attain a clearness about myself.
For it is neither her brother nor big fish
I fear, nor even the white jaws of water

That hurt and hold me, but an unkinder water
Chilling and deepening in Julie's eyes.
It's there blindly I thrash now, like a fish
Gasping in air, shocked by the pulse and pain
Of an element newly thrust upon itself.
She might have said, "You've made a mess of your life,

But I into whose care you gave that life
Am weeping. Taste, my love, this healing water.
Test me with your hands, your lips, your eyes."
She might have said, "I couldn't care less myself
Whether you sink in pride or swim in pain.
That is for you to decide, you poor fish!"

Instead, neither caring nor careless, she chose to fish,
To fish using as bait my only life,
Keen at line's end for weariness and pain
To swallow me, spun giddily in water.
And sure enough, insight with phosphorous eyes
Glides upward, a slow law unto itself.

Inborn vortex, pressures of unself,
First love, deep-water spell, before the fish
Grew legs and clambered up with narrowing eyes
Onto the rocks. Who wouldn't give his life
For that lost paradise of the first water—
Rapture of depths, no turning back, no pain!

Julie, pain sweeter than a loss of self,
Draw me from water, leave me to the fish—
You cannot save my life. I see your eyes.

(*CHARLES disappears. JAN and JULIE, on either side of the dark stage, light cigarettes, holding the burning matches before their faces.*)

JAN:
  Julie?

JULIE:
  Yes. I'm here.

JAN:
  Your voice—are you all right?

JULIE:
  I'm all right.

JAN:
  I love you.

(*JULIE blows out her match. Lights. GILBERT helps CHARLES into the boat. CHARLES collapses, exhausted.*)

GILBERT:
You see, dear Charles, there are things stronger than yourself. Be still. You are weak and bewildered. Do you feel pain? You must not think ill of me. I wish you'd open your eyes.

CHARLES:
Think? Of you?

GILBERT:
Well, I should have thought so, yes.
I should have thought that out there in the water
You would be thinking of the line your life
Depended from, and of who held the line.

CHARLES:
Of Julie.

GILBERT:
It seems to you that Julie—?
Ah, Charles, you're a deep one. Drink this water.
Do you mean that the scales have fallen from your eyes,
Revealing Julie as wretchedly herself?
Or do you mean—perish the thought—that I myself
Simply don't matter?

CHARLES:
Julie . . .

JULIE:
Here I am.

CHARLES:
We were together there—
It was a honeymoon—

JULIE:
Be still. Don't speak.

CHARLES:
A honeymoon, salty and sweet—deeply together—
I thought, I had to think. Come closer. Listen.

JULIE:
Darling, you're not on your deathbed. I see no need
For any show of thought.

CHARLES:
But you are angry?

JULIE:
When have you ever seen me angry? I confess
My own thoughts, these past minutes, leave me less than—

CHARLES:
Well, that's flattering! I should have thought
It was for me to be resentful of the pain,
The risk I ran with my one and only life—
And not for my own amusement. But to my eyes
Nobody's amused, least of all yourself.

GILBERT:
Perhaps you should jump back into the water
And take your chances with the fish.

CHARLES:
You ought not to be angry. If you are angry
It cannot be because of what I've done
But what I'm doing now—because of what I am.
If what I did was to have angered you
You would have been angry earlier, I think.

JULIE:

    I am not angry with you.

GILBERT:

    And there is no earthly reason I can see
    For her to be angry with me.

CHARLES:

    And what am I doing now, what am I trying to say
    But that I'm yours in spite of all—in spite—

JULIE:

    In spite of all my what? My ways? My wiles?
    Pompous! Ponderous! The Prince of Whales!

CHARLES:

    Don't try to misunderstand me, Julie.

JULIE:

    You've lost your bet. You're a bad loser, Charles.

GILBERT:

    No. He has won his bet. He's a bad winner.
    He means we've sought to corrupt him, and he's right.

JULIE:

    Speak for yourself.

GILBERT:

                    I do. Speaking for myself,
    You are an extremely difficult person, Charles,
    In your simple goodness. We suspect that. More,
    We've wanted you a trifler like ourselves.

JULIE:

    Would anyone mind if we started back to shore?

GILBERT:
Don't pretend you don't know. You have undergone
Trial by water—that trial whereby
The accused was flung, bound, into a ditch.
If he was innocent he stayed afloat;
If guilty, he sank to the bottom like a stone.
I suppose the secret then was breath control.
In any event it sounds like a cynical business.

CHARLES:
You meant for me to sink, was that it, Julie?

JULIE:
Of course not, darling. How can you allow
Gilbert to talk that way? You'll find me at the prow
Like a figurehead. I've had enough for now.

(*Exit JULIE. JAN leaves the stage at the same time.*)

GILBERT:
We meant for you to rise up from the waves
Like a revengeful triton, brandishing
Your spear thrice-pronged with wrath,
Embarrassment and pain. We did not want
Meekness on the half-shell. We wanted proof
That you as well could turn down an occasion
For much self-knowledge, use it up idly
Thrashing about on the surface of your act.

CHARLES:
What did I do instead?

GILBERT:
Instead you did the serious human thing,
The earnest painful thing, the thing that we,

Or she particularly—she's very touchy—
Cannot forgive. So we condemn you. The code
Is evidently of our own contrivance.

CHARLES:

It's a brand-new experience, Gilly,
For once to take something less seriously than you.

GILBERT:

You're lighthearted because your conscience is clear.
Wait and see.

CHARLES:

My conscience *is* clear. I am not lighthearted.

GILBERT:

Always so scrupulous. But you have a higher
Specific gravity than you did this morning.
You know what happens to carbons under pressure—
They become gems. Keep at it, you're turning precious.

CHARLES:

Precious to Julie? To myself?
What on earth are you talking about?

GILBERT:

I have observed
That is a question people do not ask
Unless they know the answer. Wait and see.

(*Exit GILBERT. We see CHARLES silhouetted in the boat during this final scene. Enter, in Venice, JAN and JULIE. It is night.*)

JULIE:

That was a very good suggestion of Gilbert's. We'll take the bus tomorrow at noon, and arrive before dark. Gilbert is very fond of Ravenna. He says the mosaics are beyond words glorious.

JAN:

They must be, if he says so.

JULIE:

They do sound the slightest bit deadly, just the same. Asking things of one, you know. Venice is more my cup of tea. If I am tired of Venice it's because I'm tired of myself. My exquisite stagestruck façades, my smell of money and hair, my watery reflections. It is clever of a city to have risen where there was only water, just as I am clever to be talking of Venice when Venice is the last thing on my mind.

JAN:

We must be up early tomorrow.

JULIE:

Do I bore you? What does that pained smile mean?

JAN:

I was about to ask you the same question.

JULIE:

What does my pained smile mean?

JAN:

No. Do I bore you?

JULIE:

Forgive me. It's been a long day and I'm tired. I *am*.

JAN:

I believe you. Julie, couldn't we just stay here? Let Gilbert go off by himself? We'd have these days to ourselves. Everything would come right between us.

JULIE:

Come right? Are things so wrong between us?

JAN:

You know what I mean. We'd have this time, we'd have each other. You're tired? So am I. I'm still a little girl, I need my naps.

JULIE:

I should hate to miss Ravenna.

JAN:

We don't care about Ravenna.

JULIE:

Besides, we don't know the language as well as Gilbert. If we were here alone we should be outrageously cheated on all sides.

JAN:

That kind of cheating is fairly innocent.

JULIE:

By comparison with . . . ?

JAN:

All right, we'll go to Ravenna.

JULIE:

By comparison with what, dearest?

JAN:

Julie, help me to love you!

JULIE:

Go on. Tell me more about my dishonesty. You asked if I was bored. Far from it, I'm fascinated!

JAN:

I don't ask for absolute honesty. You alone know what to tell me and what not to. But when—

JULIE:

Yes?

JAN:

What you told me today. It's not for myself I want to know, but for you. I'm not asking for an explanation. What matters is that you begin explaining it to yourself.

JULIE:

"It?"

JAN:

That episode with Charles, your leaving him.

JULIE:

There are times when you remind me forcibly of him. I foresaw that we'd be returning to the topic.

CHARLES (*to himself*):

Julie's leaving me? Is that what Gilbert meant? Wait and see, he said.

JULIE:

Oh Jan, you are such a reproach. I can hear the excuses you're making for me. "I must bear with her because she's suffering."

JAN:

Not at all. I don't feel that you *are* suffering.

JULIE:

You're right. I'm not suffering.

CHARLES (*to himself*):

Whatever I do, it's the wrong thing. And talking to her leads nowhere.

JULIE:

I've been arbitrary, I've been heartless. Is that what you want to hear? I was brought up to have the proper feelings.

CHARLES (*to himself*):
But if she leaves me I'll be able to write to her. Letters will say what I can't say to her face. She'll understand, she'll want to come back.

JULIE:
That's why I can't read his letters. They shame me.

JAN:
They don't shame Gilbert? No, Gilbert has his own funny integrity.

JULIE:
And now you're trying to shame me. You mustn't.

JAN:
Ah Julie, you're selfish.

JULIE:
I know. I ask everything.

JAN:
You've talked all day—less for my enlightenment than for your own pleasure. I'm not even allowed to comment upon what you say.

CHARLES (*to himself*):
And if she doesn't come back, what then? She can fall in love with somebody else.

JULIE:
I'll say no more then.

JAN:
That's not what I mean!

CHARLES:
Strange. I can already feel sorry for him, the one who loves her next.

JULIE:

Oh why are we putting ourselves through this? If you love me—

JAN:

Julie, Julie . . .

JULIE:

The one who loves isn't the loser. Charles
Isn't the loser. To have hurt him unveils
In me, as in a public square,
An image tasteless and cheap, I mean my own.
The tourist wouldn't even stop for it,
Whitewashed at day's end by dreadful birds.
But Charles—my dear, I even dream of him.
I see him continue to act in honest concern
According to what he feels. I see his face
Turn beautiful under the pumice of rebuff.
One could almost pretend I'd made him a gift of it.

JAN:

And to me what gift do you make?

JULIE:

I have been happy with you here.
Encompassed by things so fabulous and rare
They can't be hurt by the conscience we bring to them.
We stand in the center of this glimmering square
As we might stand within a human mind
At its most charitable. By tomorrow
We shall be standing in Ravenna,
Quite as if standing in the mind of God.
Much constellated gold, dolphin and seraphim
Shall blind us with the blessing
Of something fully expressed, the sense of having
Ourselves become expressive there. Kiss me.

JAN:

    My book says it's not the ornament but the architecture

    That is meant to be most moving at Ravenna.

JULIE:

    Jan, you are sublime, my student princess.

    Isn't it strange how little difference

    It makes, whatever we say or do or are?

CHARLES (*to himself*):

    I have observed

    That is a question people do not ask

    Unless they know the answer.

JAN (*to herself*):

    Now it is not just myself I feel

    Endangered. The lover may not be the loser.

    I've no desire to win at her expense.

CHARLES (*to himself*):

    No matter what the lines were baited with,

    The fishermen concluded their affair,

    Reached land without a certain sinking sense

    I am still weighted with.

JULIE:

    There is such lightness in the midnight air.

    The undulating dome, the orange peel,

    The very stars drift outward on its tide.

JAN:

    Beautiful. Ignorant, too, of any real

    Human consequences, like a flare

    Lighting the field where innocent men hide.

JULIE:

    The story's finished now. Kiss it goodbye.

    No, kiss me. The cool night air

Has taken my words up into its high gauzes
Before the first of them could reach your ear.

CHARLES:
I have observed . . .

JAN:
It's not the danger or the hurt I fear
But vagueness, secrecy, the shapeless sky,
The iridescent sea, whatever causes
Thousands every day to live and die
Not knowing.

JULIE:
Never think, my dear,
That we contrive this lightness. No.

JAN:
Each little wave, before it crests it pauses,
Gathering its nerve to disappear?

CHARLES:
. . . that is a question people do not ask . . .

JULIE:
Something makes light of *us,* that much is clear.
Hold me down, I'm rising like a dancer!

JAN:
Wait, come back here!

(*She does. They kiss.*)

CHARLES:
. . . unless they know the answer.

NOTES

page 355   When the narrator of *The (Diblos) Notebook* refers back to previous pages in the notebook, as he here refers to "pp 29–30," the passage can be found, in this volume, on pages 331–332. On pages 366 and 410, when he refers back to his own "p. 17," the corresponding page is now 322; on page 412, he refers to his "p. 18," also corresponding to page 322 in this volume.

page 425   *The Birthday* was first presented at Kirby Theater, Amherst College, Amherst, Massachusetts, on May 22, 1947, as part of an evening of three one-act plays produced by the Dramatic Arts Class. The play was directed by Robert Brown; the designer was Perry Minton; the technician was Perley Boone.

Cast

Charles *Thomas Howkins*
Mrs. Crane *Thelma White*
Max *James Maxwell*
Mr. Knight *William Burford*
Raymond *Chauncey Williams*

page 453   *The Bait* was first presented by The Artists' Theatre at the Comedy Club in New York City on May 18, 1953. The production was directed by Herbert Machiz; setting and costumes were designed by Al Kresch; lighting was by Mildred Jackson; incidental music was by Ben Westbrook; and Jack Harpman was the stage manager.

Cast

Julie *Gaby Rodgers*
John *Alan Shayne*
Charles *John Hallo*
Gilbert *Jack Cannon*

The Bait was later presented by the BBC on its Third Programme, November 28 and December 1, 1955. Mary Hope Allen was the producer.

Cast

Narrator *Rolf Lefebvre*
John *Richard Hurndall*
Julie *Pamela Alan*
Gilbert *Phil Brown*
Charles *Simon Lack*

The text of *The Bait* first appeared in *The Quarterly Review of Literature* (vol. VII, no. X, 1955), and later in *Artists' Theatre: Four Plays*, ed. Herbert Machiz (New York: Grove Press, 1960).

page 493   *The Immortal Husband* was first produced by John Bernard Myers in association with The Artists' Theatre at the Theater de Lys in New York City on February 14, 1955. The production was directed by Herbert Machiz; settings and costumes were designed by Richard V. Hare; lighting was by Peggy Clark; and Gene Perlowin was stage manager.

Cast

Mrs. Mallow, Olga, Nurse *Jean Ellyn*
Maid, Fanya, Enid *Mary Grace Canfield*
Tithonus *William Sheidy*
Gardener, Konstantin, Mark *Scott Merrill*
Laomedon, Memnon *Frederick Rolf*
Aurora *Anne Meacham*

The Immortal Husband was next presented on September 29, 1969, at the Dublin Gate Theatre as part of the Dublin Theatre Festival. This production, mounted in association with The Artists' Theatre, was directed by Herbert Machiz, with settings by Brian Collins from designs by Jane Eakin; the stage managers were Douglas Wallace and Alan Coleridge.

Cast

Mrs. Mallow, Olga, Nurse *Jacqueline Brookes*
Maid, Fanya, Enid *Garn Stephens*
Tithonus *Bruce Kornbluth*
Gardener, Konstantin, Mark *Jack Ryland*
Laomedon, Memnon *Edward Fuller*
Aurora *Elizabeth Franz*

The text of *The Immortal Husband* first appeared in *Playbook: Five Plays for a New Theater* (New York: New Directions, 1956).

page 635   *The Bait* was extensively revised for a new production of the play, paired with *The Image Maker*, which was first presented at the National Arts Club in New York City on November 19, 1988. The production was directed by James Sheldon, with sets by Paul Merrill and lighting by Amy Whitman.

Cast

Julie *Mary Bomba*
Jan *Diane Dreux*
Charles *Martin Donovan*
Gilbert *Peter Hooten*

BIOGRAPHICAL NOTE

James Merrill was born in New York City on March 3, 1926, the son of the financier and philanthropist Charles E. Merrill, one of the founders of the brokerage firm Merrill Lynch & Co., and his second wife, Hellen Ingram. Merrill, who attended St. Bernard's School, was raised in Manhattan and Southampton, Long Island, where his family had a country house that was designed by Stanford White, and in Palm Beach, Florida. His parents divorced in 1939, and the reverberations of the "broken home" can be heard throughout his poetry. After attending the Lawrenceville School, Merrill enrolled at Amherst College, his father's alma mater, took a year off to serve in the army, and graduated summa cum laude with the class of 1947. He taught at Bard College in 1948–1949 and although he fought shy of academe in the following years he did accept short appointments at Amherst, the University of Wisconsin, Washington University, and Yale University. In 1954 he moved with his companion, David Jackson, a writer and painter, to a house in Stonington, Connecticut, which is still maintained by Stonington Village and houses an artist-in-residence every year.

In 1957 Merrill and Jackson undertook a trip around the world, and for two decades beginning in 1964 they spent a part of each year in Greece. They owned a house in Athens at the foot of Mt. Lycabettus and were famous among the local literati for the terrace parties they threw. Beginning in 1979 Merrill spent winters in Key West, Florida, where he and Jackson acquired another house. Key West was a place he had an affinity for partly because it had previously attracted two of his favorite poets, Wallace Stevens and Elizabeth Bishop, the latter his close friend for decades. Merrill, a gifted linguist and a lover of different cultures, always traveled widely, and the displacements and discoveries of his travels, along with the routines of his life in his different homes, are the stuff of many of his poems. He died away from home, in Tucson, Arizona, on February 6, 1995.

A selection of Merrill's earliest writings, taken from his contributions to the *Lawrenceville Literary Magazine,* was privately printed by his father as a sixteenth-birthday gift in 1942, under the title *Jim's Book.* The young writer proudly distributed most of the one hundred copies as soon as possible—and before long began to retrieve as many of those copies as he could. A group of his poems appeared in *Poetry* in March 1946, the same year that saw the publication in Athens, Greece, of a limited edition of poems entitled *The Black Swan*. He published his first full-fledged book, *First Poems*, when he was twenty-five, in 1951. He next tried his hand at playwriting: *The Bait* was produced at the Comedy Club in 1953 (and published in a journal in 1955 and in a book in 1960), and *The Immortal Husband* was performed at the Theater de Lys in 1955 (and published in 1956). Meanwhile, his first novel, *The Seraglio*, a Jamesian roman à clef, appeared in 1957 (it was reissued in 1987), and his second commercial volume of poems, *The Country of a Thousand Years of Peace*, in 1959 (revised edition, 1970). His third volume of poems, *Water Street*—its title refers to the street Merrill lived on in Stonington—came out in 1962, and his second, experimental novel, *The (Diblos) Notebook*, based in part on his first experiences in Greece, in 1965 (reissued in 1994).

In 1966 his collection *Nights and Days* received the National Book Award. The judges for that year, W. H. Auden, James Dickey, and Howard Nemerov, cited the book for its author's "scrupulous and uncompromising cultivation of the poetic art, evidenced in his refusal to settle for an easy and profitable stance; for his insistence on taking the kind of tough, poetic chances which make the difference between esthetic success or failure." *The Fire Screen* appeared in 1969, followed in 1972 by *Braving the Elements*, which was awarded the Bollingen Prize for Poetry, and in 1974 by a selection of previously uncollected poems, *The Yellow Pages*. When *Divine Comedies* came out in 1976, it won the Pulitzer Prize.

The narrative poem "The Book of Ephraim," which was originally included in *Divine Comedies*, later served as the first installment of an epic visionary poem based in large part on Merrill and Jackson's communications with the Other World by way of the Ouija board. The subsequent two parts were *Mirabell: Books of Number*, which received the National Book Award for Poetry in 1978, and *Scripts for the Pageant*, published in 1980. In 1982 Merrill brought together these three long poems and "Coda: The Higher Keys" in a comprehensive edition of the work he now called *The Changing Light at Sandover*. That landmark volume won the National Book Critics Circle Award in 1982, the same year in which Merrill published his first selected poems, *From the First Nine: Poems 1946–1976*. His book of poems *Late Settings* was published in 1985, and a collection of essays, interviews, and reviews entitled *Recitative* appeared in 1986. In 1988 *The Inner Room* was honored with the first Bobbitt National Prize for Poetry, awarded by the Library of Congress. Merrill's memoir, *A Different Person*, came out in 1993. *A Scattering of Salts*, the last book of poems that he saw through production, was published posthumously in 1995. His *Collected Poems* appeared in 2001.

A NOTE ON THE TYPE

Pierre Simon Fournier le jeune, who designed the type used in this book, was both an originator and a collector of types. His services to the art of printing were his design of letters, his creation of ornaments and initials, and his standardization of type sizes. His types are old style in character and sharply cut. In 1764 and 1766 he published his Manuel typographique, a treatise on the history of French types and printing, on typefounding in all its details, and on what many consider his most important contribution to typography—the measurement of type by the point system.

Composed by NK Graphics, Keene, New Hampshire
Printed and bound by R. R. Donnelley & Sons, Crawfordsville, Indiana
Designed by Chip Kidd